Verbal Behavior
and General
Behavior Theory

Verbal Behavior
and General
Behavior Theory

EDITED BY

THEODORE R. DIXON
Texas Christian University

DAVID L. HORTON
University of Kentucky

PRENTICE-HALL, INC., Englewood Cliffs, New Jersey

Prentice-Hall Psychology Series

James J. Jenkins, *Editor*

Prentice-Hall International, Inc., *London*
Prentice-Hall of Australia, Pty. Ltd., *Sydney*
Prentice-Hall of Canada, Ltd., *Toronto*
Prentice-Hall of India Private Ltd., *New Delhi*
Prentice-Hall of Japan, Inc., *Tokyo*

Library of Congress Catalog Card No.: 68-11705

PRINTED IN THE UNITED STATES OF AMERICA

Current printing (last digit):

10 9 8 7 6 5 4 3 2 1

Preface

Approximately three years ago it was our observation that the general area of verbal behavior was characterized by a great diversity of content and theoretical language. We suspected that much of this diversity was due less to content requirements than to a lack of representative communication across specialties within verbal behavior. Probing the matter further, we also began to suspect that much of this diverse theoretical language, though frequently under the rubric of "S-R" theory, was really quite independent of any common or formal reference that might be regarded as general S-R behavior theory. It appeared that the category of "S-R behavior theory" itself was nearly as heterogeneous as the diverse specialties which used various S-R references.

We would have left well enough alone at that point were it not for our conviction that a general area as active and as central to psychology as verbal behavior should have some semblance of theoretical formality and that individuals representing the various specialties—in collaboration—could formalize the S-R constructs they used. Moreover, we anticipated that the experimentally oriented theoretical developments in one specialty might well be of value to other specialties if there were occasion for adequate communication. The manner in which to provide such an occasion was, however, not so apparent. For one thing, it was not at all clear that the time was right, in terms of development within the area or in terms of sufficient interest in such a theory-oriented project. Nonetheless, we devised a tentative plan for a large-scale conference at which established psychologists, from a representative sample of the specialties within verbal behavior, would address themselves to the topic of verbal behavior theory and its relation to general S-R behavior theory.

As we now see it, the goals were, to say the least, quite ambitious. Were it not for the assistance of many people along the way, the project would never have been completed. At the outset, Dr. A. D. Albright, Executive Vice President of the University of Kentucky, both encouraged and arranged for University sponsorship of a summer workshop. The workshop participants, Drs. William Battig, Charles Cofer, Don Dulany, Paul Kjeldergaard, and Carl Sherrick, helped us to evaluate the timeliness and potential contributions of such a conference and also helped us to select representative areas and potential contributors. Next, a rather heterogeneous group of well-qualified psychologists put forth the considerable effort necessary to prepare papers to be presented at the conference. The conference was held in the spring of 1966 under the sponsorship of the National Science Foundation. Graduate students Arthur Blaiwes, David Grover, Richard Weist, and Ronald Wiley assisted in the large number of chores associated with the conference and preparation of the manuscript. We are deeply indebted to all of these individuals and organizations.

The proceedings which follow are divided into five parts. Within Parts I, II, III, and IV, the first three papers listed deal with theory in specific areas. These papers were prepared in advance of the conference and were precirculated. The remaining papers in these sections are discussion papers which were read at the conference. Part V contains the three general discussion papers which were also read at the conference and a paper especially prepared by us for inclusion in this volume. Finally, a special paper —included as an appendix—was prepared by Drs. Bever, Fodor, and Garrett. Portions of this paper were also presented at the conference.

The results of these efforts may not be what the reader expects. A single, formalized statement of either verbal behavior theory or general S-R behavior theory is not contained here. Nor will one find a straightforward presentation of competing theoretical positions, as we would all probably like to think is actually the case. Instead, we think we have given a fair representation of the current status of theory in much of verbal behavior and—to the extent that this area is not unlike most others—implications for the status of theory in most of psychology. It may, of course, be argued that as a "new" science we need not encumber ourselves with the demands of formal theory; or it may be argued that, as an experimentally oriented discipline, adequate theory will ultimately be developed. However, it is our conviction that the issues and problems brought forth in the present volume, from many different perspectives, must be acknowledged, clarified, and resolved if appropriate and productive theory is to serve psychology. Such statements demand considerable support to be justified. We leave it to the reader to judge whether or not the present work offers such support.

T.R.D. and D.L.H.

Contents

Associative Processes

PART I

Theoretical Issues in Free Recall[1]

1 ENDEL TULVING

The task of the psychologist interested in memory, like that of any other scientist, is the description and explanation of phenomena subsumable under the general heading of his chosen subject matter. Although his ultimate concern lies in the understanding of these phenomena as they occur in the natural environment, the descriptive and explanatory statements he makes are based on the evidence gained from laboratory experiments. Experimental paradigms used in the study of memory represent miniature analogues of various kinds of "real life" situations.

When we ask a person to tell us the names of all the people he met the day before, or the names of all the books he read in 1965, or the names of the cities he has visited at least once in his lifetime, we are asking the person to utilize stored mnemonic information in the same manner as he does in free-recall experiments. In these experiments the subject is presented with a collection or series of stimulus items, and at some later time he is asked to reproduce from memory the names of

as many of these items as he can, in any order he wishes. The analysis of the respondent's performance in both tasks begins with the assumptions that he has had a number of separate and temporally successive experiences and that his ability to recall these experiences depends on a multitude of factors. In laboratory experiments these factors can be identified, isolated, and controlled, and their effect on performance evaluated, but there are no compelling reasons to believe that the relevant variables determining the subject's mnemonic performance and the underlying processes involved in remembering past experiences in the laboratory are different from what they are outside the laboratory.

Human memory, of course, encompasses a great deal more than storage and retrieval of information about occurrences of certain events in a smaller or larger segment of a person's life. We may ask the person only to list the names of people he has met, or of books he has read, or of cities he has visited, but he undoubtedly remembers a great deal more about each event than just its general identifying label. In a free-recall experiment the subject likewise remembers more about the items he saw in the window of the memory

[1] The preparation of this chapter has been supported by the National Research Council of Canada (Grant No. APT-39) and the National Science Foundation (Grant No. GB-3710).

drum than just their names. But since the ability to reproduce aspects of individual experiences *qua* individual experiences is one of the fundamental properties of the human mind, and since more complex mnemonic skills of an articulate person both inside and outside the laboratory include this ability, the study of free recall constitutes a logical starting point in our quest for the understanding of human memory.

In this chapter we will review the present status of conceptual developments in free recall by focusing on those theoretical issues that seem to have generated more than passing interest. Because of the relative novelty of the subject matter of free recall, the chapter begins with a short excursion into the history of this phenomenon. The subsequent five main sections of the chapter are concerned with (a) some orienting attitudes and pretheoretical assumptions, (b) single-trial free-recall phenomena, (c) secondary organization in free recall, (d) repetition effects in multitrial free recall, and (e) storage versus retrieval processes. A summary will present a résumé of theoretical issues and an evaluation of the present state of our understanding of free recall.

Some Historical Antecedents

The method of retained members

Free recall as an experimental method of studying memory is the descendant of the method of retained members. The latter method was first used by several investigators before the turn of the century (e. g., Bolton, 1892; Kirkpatrick, 1894; T. L. Smith, 1896; W. G. Smith, 1896). It received

its name from Ebbinghaus (1902), although the great master himself had no use for it. It involved either simultaneous or successive presentation to the subject of a collection of items—objects, pictures of objects, words, syllables, geometric figures, letters, digits, and the like—either once or more, and the recall by the subject of as many of the responses corresponding to the presented items as possible, usually immediately or a few seconds after the completion of the presentation. The order of recall in which the subject recalled the items was not specified by the experimenter.

The method of retained members proved to be quite popular with early students of memory and was adopted for the study of a variety of problems. In 1906, for instance, Pohlmann listed almost thirty publications reporting on the work done with this approach. These early experiments were concerned with recall of individual items as a function of variables such as characteristics of items, amount of material presented, sensory modality in which material was presented, number of repetitions or amount of study time, grouping of items, constant versus variable order of presentation, serial position, length of retention interval, nature of activities interpolated between presentation and recall, age and sex of subjects, and the like. This list of independent variables must look quite familiar to experimenters of the present generation, although many of the early experiments would not quite measure up to the more exacting standards of today's research.

The initial popularity of the method of retained members, however, was relatively short-lived. The orienting attitudes of investigators using it did not fit into the contemporary *Zeitgeist* that had emerged under the powerful impact of Ebbinghaus' and his followers' work. The method of retained members was geared to the study of retention and forgetting of individual items, whereas for Ebbinghaus the study of memory was synonymous with the study of acquisition and retention of associations among items. Theoretical concepts that had been derived from experiments in the Ebbinghaus tradition—such as Ebbinghaus' own general law of associations, Jost's law, Müller and Pilzecker's law of retroactive inhibition, and others—seemed to have no immediate relevance to the processes assumed to be involved in retention of individual items *qua* individual items. Since no alternate theoretical generalizations emerged from work done with the method of retained members, the method gradually lost its power to excite the imagination of psychologists interested in memory and was overshadowed by other experimental paradigms. Its sinking into oblivion was undoubtedly aided by Ebbinghaus' dogmatic verdict that it had only a limited usefulness and that it did not provide as sensitive a measure of retention as did his own method of savings, sentiments that were faithfully echoed by the next generation of writers (e.g., Busemann, 1911; Messer, 1922; Woodworth, 1938).

The method of free recall

Although scattered reports of experiments using the method of retained members appeared from time to time, the method was not an important part of the armamentarium of verbal learning laboratories between the First and Second World Wars. McGeoch's (1942) influential book and its successor (McGeoch and Irion, 1952) did not even mention the method by name. But McGeoch seems to have been the first writer to use the term "free recall" in discussing the experiments by Welch and Burnett (1924) and Raffel (1936). Thereafter, free recall came into more general use (e.g., Postman, Egan, and Davis, 1948; Postman and Jenkins, 1948), being regarded as "a test sensitive to intermediate degrees of associative strength" by Postman, Adams, and Phillips (1955, p. 10).

Under its new name, the method of retained members has gradually become respectable again. This newly found respectability, however, has little historical connection with the more remote past. Rather, it seems to be a consequence of the general broadening of outlook and interests of students of memory as well as of certain methodological and theoretical developments both within and outside the field of verbal learning.

In the first place, several mathematical psychologists found in multitrial free recall what they believed to be a relatively simple learning process whose various behavioral manifestations could be well described by mathematical models (Bush and Mosteller, 1955; Miller and McGill, 1952; Waugh and Smith, 1962). Secondly, other psychologists interested in mental organization (Bousfield, 1953; Bousfield and Cohen, 1953) or associative habits (Jenkins and Russell, 1952) started to use free recall as a vehicle for demonstrating the orderliness of the effects of past verbal experience. This line of work quickly underwent a reversal of its direction of orientation and came to be focused on free recall as influenced by mental organization and pre-existing associations (Bousfield and Cohen, 1956; Bousfield, Cohen, and Whitmarsh, 1958; Cohen and Bousfield, 1956; Gonzalez and Cofer, 1959; Jenkins, Mink, and Russell, 1958; Rothkopf and Coke, 1961). The third impetus to the development of the interest in free recall was provided by the conceptual separation of paired-associate learning into two stages, the response learning stage and the associative stage (Underwood, Runquist, and Schulz, 1959; Underwood and Schulz, 1960). Since response learning was thought—and by some still is thought —to occur independently of specific inter-item associations, free recall naturally suggested itself as a means for probing the response learning stage. Finally, with the general growth of the field of verbal learning and memory, many other experimenters began to employ the free-recall paradigm to study a variety of problems. Their findings have posed challenging problems for the theorists and have pointed to the potential usefulness of the free-recall paradigm in studying processes of memory, Ebbinghaus' peremptory protestations notwithstanding (e.g., Bruner, Miller and Zimmerman, 1955; Dallett, 1963, 1964; Deese, 1957, 1959a, 1960; Ekstrand and Underwood, 1963; Meyer and Miles, 1953; Miller and Selfridge, 1950; Murdock, 1960; Tulving and Thornton, 1959; Waugh, 1961, 1962).

Some Orienting Attitudes and Pretheoretical Assumptions

Free recall and other paradigms

Thus it is that we now find ourselves in possession of a number of reasonably reliable empirical facts gleaned from free-recall experiments and can afford to examine their theoretical implications. Many theoretical problems implicit in free-recall phenomena have their counterparts in the work done with other paradigms. The question therefore arises as to the advisability of breaking the domain of memory into

compartments defined in terms of different experimental paradigms. Would it not be more profitable or strategically more advantageous to gloss over the mere methodological differences in data-collection procedures, and instead attempt to delineate the significant empirical facts and search for the comprehensive laws of memory as they apply to all paradigms?

Several closely related reasons argue against such an approach. The conceptual framework of serial and paired-associate learning has become quite formalized. Such a state of affairs readily provides analogies that the theorist can draw upon in his own efforts to speculate about the processes involved in free recall, but quite frequently the fitting of free-recall findings into the existing conceptual framework built around other situations could be achieved only by using Procrustean methods. Given even the remote possibility—and there are some who would argue that the possibility is indeed remote—that the traditional conceptual framework built around other paradigms has only limited generality, the shotgun wedding of free recall to the paradigms that have hitherto dominated the field may hinder rather than advance the progress of our thinking about free-recall phenomena. There are several rather clear-cut cases on record where the findings of free-recall experiments do not readily fit into existing theoretical molds. For instance, Waugh's (1961) finding, antedated to a limited extent by Abbott (1909), that multitrial free-recall performance is identical for constant and variable order input lists, could not be accommodated easily by existing theories that emphasize the importance of repeated contiguity of items for the development of associations between items. Similarly, Battig, Allen, and Jensen's (1965) demonstration that subjects in multitrial free-recall experiments tend to recall newly learned items prior to those items that have been recalled correctly on previous trials seems not to be easily reconcilable with principles according to which the order of recall is a direct function of "strength" of items (e.g., Underwood and Schulz, 1960). Finally, evidence provided by Garner and Whitman (1965) that learning of a part of the list following the learning of the whole list, and by Tulving (1966a) that learning of the whole list following the learning of a part of the list shows no positive transfer, also seems to lie outside the scope of the extant theoretical formulations based on traditional rote-learning paradigms.

For these reasons then, consideration of theoretical implications of free-recall phenomena is better initiated in relative isolation from the traditional conceptual formulations. The risks involved in divorcing ourselves from the dominant *Zeitgeist* are not as great today as they were fifty years ago. Some rapprochement between free-recall theories and, say, serial and paired-associate learning theories is undoubtedly possible even now and hopefully will be extended in the future. But such an alliance will probably require a certain modification (perhaps "liberalization" is the word) of the orienting attitudes that lie at the root of traditional formulations. Battig's assessment of paired-associate learning elsewhere in the present volume may become an important milestone on the road to such liberalization.

Learning in free recall

The minimal free-recall experiment consists of presentation of a series of items to the subject for study in the "input phase" and the measurement of the subject's recall in terms of the number of items he can reproduce in the "output phase" of a single trial. The minimal experiment of this kind will be referred to as a single-trial free-recall experiment. When two or more trials are given, each consisting of a single input phase and a single output phase, and the material presented in input phases is the same over trials, the experiment will be referred to as a multitrial free recall, or a free-recall learning experiment.

Other arrangements of sequences of input and output phases are also possible. A single input phase, for instance, may be followed by two or more output phases, in each of which the subject attempts to recall all presented items (Estes, 1960), or several input phases may be followed by a single output phase (Bousfield and Cohen, 1953; Raffel, 1934). Repeated "cycles," consisting of single input phases followed by two or more output phases, or of several input phases followed by a single output phase, have also been used (Tulving, 1966b).

Typical multitrial free-recall experiments have sometimes been referred to as free learning experiments (Underwood, 1964; Ekstrand and Underwood, 1963). Although this label has the merit of brevity, it implies that in multitrial free-recall experiments "learning" is free. Regardless of the meaning of the term "learning," it is difficult to argue that "learning" is any more "free" in this experimental paradigm than in any other paradigm. What is "free" in both single-trial and multitrial free-recall tasks is the order in which the subject may recall the remembered items. For this reason, the name "multitrial free recall," or perhaps "free-recall learning," seems to be preferable to the name "free learning."

The basic unit of analysis of the subject's performance in free-recall experiments is a single item. Exactly what constitutes a single item is not always easy to determine (Deese, 1961); some of the problems arising in this connection will be considered in a subsequent section. For the time being, we define a single item as an item that can be identified by the subject in terms of a highly integrated and invariant response, a response that could be readily elicited by stimuli other than the specific experimental stimulus (Mandler, 1966b), or a response that can be readily completed if a substantial part of it is given. Thus, common words with which the subject is familiar before entering the experiment are single items. A sequence of letters such as *PRAJ*, however, does not constitute a single item, even if the experimenter defines it so (Garner and Whitman, 1965). Memorization of sets of such verbal units involves both response integration and response selection. As a consequence, theoretical analyses of the processes underlying successful performance in free recall of such units are more complicated than those concerned with free recall of single items. In this paper we will limit our discussion primarily to free recall of lists of single items.

A single item is always "learned" when it is first presented, regardless of whether it occurs alone or in a series of other items, in the sense that the probability of its recall increases from a value near zero immediately prior to the presentation to unity immediately after the presentation (Tulving, 1964). "Learning" of individual items is equivalent to their perception, since the operations involved in testing learning and perception in this case are identical.

Thus, to talk about learning or degrees of learning of single items is meaningless, since at least at the present time learning cannot be measured

independently of recall. Measures of recall, however, depend on many factors other than the hypothesized degree of learning, regardless of the temporal point at which recall is tested. For this reason, the question sometimes raised whether *learning* of a single item is all-or-none or incremental can never be answered. Single-trial free-recall experiments are experiments concerned with *remembering of perceived items* and not with learning of items.

The term "learning," however, does serve as a useful and nonredundant descriptive term in multitrial free-recall experiments. In this case it refers to the more-or-less systematic increase in the number of items recalled over successive trials or, more specifically, to the slope of the function relating number of items recalled to the ordinal number of the trial (Murdock, 1960). Whenever this slope is positive, learning can be said to have occurred over trials. The rate of increase in trial-by-trial recall can be specified quantitatively, and rates obtained under different experimental conditions can be directly compared. Since this rate, or the slope of the "learning curve," is a measure *derived* from measures of recall, it need not be identical with these measures. Degree of learning can be the same in different experiments or under different experimental conditions, even if recall scores on corresponding trials are not the same.

Thus, when "learning" is used as a descriptive term in multitrial experiments, it serves as a shorthand expression for the fact that recall increases over trials. To ask why learning occurs, or to ask what processes are involved in learning (Tulving, 1962, 1964), means to ask why recall scores increase from trial to trial, or what processes are involved in such an increase. Learning, defined in terms of increments in the number of items recalled as a function of trials, is always "incremental" by definition.

Measurement of free recall : Units of analysis

While specification of independent variables in free-recall experiments poses no problems different from those that arise in connection with many other verbal learning and memory tasks, definition and measurement of response variables do. What does "amount of material recalled" mean and how is it to be measured?

The long-standing tradition has been to count the number of experimentally defined single items. For the purpose of initial descriptions of relations between independent and dependent variables, specification of both input and output material in terms of units such as trigrams, two-digit numbers, or words may do quite well. But when we begin to speculate about underlying processes, the procedure becomes questionable, its usefulness depending on the nature of the independent variables whose effects are being investigated. The difficulty arises because of a possible discrepancy between single items defined as such by the experimenter and those that are handled as single items by the memory system. Let us designate these two kinds of units as nominal and functional units, or as E-units and S-units.

Ebbinghaus pointed out that individual elements may be perceived either as a collection of unrelated elements or as parts of a whole. When the elements belong to a whole, associations between them can be formed very rapidly. Ebbinghaus also noted that it is not the number of letters or the number of syllables that determines the ease of learning, but rather the number or kind of ideas these elements represent: a

series of monosyllabic words is learned as readily as a series of dissyllabic words. Similar observations have been made by Holmes (1934).

As we noted earlier, experimenters who used the method of retained members or the method of free recall usually took pains to select "unrelated" items for inclusion in their lists. But such attempts were seldom successful. Smith (1896), for instance, whose subjects had to recall nonsense syllables, reported that most subjects showed a tendency to associate "foreign" ideas with the syllables or "to make the syllables into intelligible phrases." This tendency was "a very troublesome feature from beginning to end" with one individual. Pohlmann (1906) found that subjects recalling randomly ordered series of consonants or sets of two-digit numbers tended to output the consonants in the order in which they occurred in the alphabet or as groups of items of similar pronunciation. One group might consist of consonants S, N, M, and F, another of D, G, and B, still another of H and K, for which the German pronunciation is similar. Numbers were also frequently recalled in pairs such as 26 and 27, 42 and 84, 23 and 46.

Other early investigators even objected to the name of the method of retained members, since it conveys the impression that the observer is called upon to remember isolated items, while "in fact he much more frequently endeavors to remember the total impression and to retain the items only as component parts of the total impression" (Meumann, 1913). Meumann also suggested that "learning is not a mere matter of the number of elements but of the number of independent memorial units. . . . The only things which we remember are wholes; and particular things are remembered only as parts of unitary wholes" (p. 291).

Bowers, whose subjects recalled a list of 135 words, could also "not help being impressed by the frequency with which certain words were found paired together in the reproduction list. It would appear that the phrase 'words isolated from context' requires modification, for there is evidently a striving after artificial context when a natural one is not provided" (Bowers, 1931, p. 276). To eliminate the effect of "common associations" and to study the retention of words isolated from the context, Bowers constructed a matrix similar to the one named by Tulving "intersubject recall matrix," tabulated the frequencies with which a given word was followed by another word in recall protocols, and excluded such word-pairs from the subjects' recall scores. He noted that this method of "purifying" the data, however, did not tap "private associations" peculiar to the individual, which, he said, cannot be detected objectively. "Even introspection will frequently be at fault in uncovering the most subtle private associations" (Bowers, 1931, p. 277).

Such observations, repeated by many later investigators as well, strongly suggest that S-units do not always correspond to E-units, that E-units are frequently perceived and remembered as parts of larger wholes or higher-order units, and that it is difficult to discover what the S-units are.

The possible discrepancy between nominal and functional units does not affect the interpretation of data from certain types of experiments as much as it does in others. For instance, if the independent variable of interest is the length of the retention interval, and other conditions are held constant, it is reasonable enough to assume that differences in recall measured in terms of E-units also reflect differences in recall of S-units. It would be interest-

ing, of course, to know whether the loss in recall scores over a retention interval is attributable to the loss of some intact units or to the disintegration of larger S-units, but such information would not affect the conclusion that less material can be recalled following a long retention interval than after a short interval.

The difficulty of interpretation is much greater in experiments where the independent variable is a task variable such as length of the list or the nature of the material. If one compares the recall of n meaningful words with the recall of n meaningless trigrams, one does not know how many S-units were presented in each case and how many were recalled. If subjects recall more words than trigrams, the conclusion that words are remembered better than trigrams ignores the possibility that recall might be identical if it were measured in terms of the number of S-units.

Miller and Selfridge (1950), in a well known experiment, showed that subjects can recall more words from long lists of higher order statistical approximations than from lists of lower order approximations. Higher order lists presumably contain fewer but larger S-units than lower order lists. Even if subjects recalled the same number of S-units from both kinds of lists, the number of correct word-responses would vary directly with the order of approximation.

In an experiment patterned after the Miller and Selfridge study, Tulving and Patkau (1962) examined subjects' recall in terms of "adopted chunks." An adopted chunk was defined as an uninterrupted sequence of words in the recall protocols corresponding to a similar sequence in the input list. Thus, given an input list of words A, B, C, D . . . Z, in this order, and a recall protocol of words K, L, M, A, G, H, in this order, the subject was said to have recalled six words and three adopted chunks—*KLM*, *A*, and *GH*. The results of the analyses showed that neither the Thorndike-Lorge word frequency nor the interaction between word frequency and order of approximation were significant sources of variance in the recall of adopted chunks, although both were highly significant when the response measure was the number of words recalled. McNulty (1966) also found that the number of "words" recalled at the first, third, and text order of approximation, as defined by Miller, Bruner, and Postman (1954), varied enormously with the order of approximation but that the number of adopted chunks remained invariant over the three orders.

The "adopted chunk," incidentally, corresponds to what Rozov (1964) has called an "original cluster." Original clusters represent the retention of the contiguity relations among items under conditions where no such retention is experimentally required—that is, in free recall. Such "contiguity transfer," according to Rozov, is not accidental, but due to the fact that the items presented together form some larger unit in recall. Rozov presented 30 words in six topic categories in a scrambled order in a single input phase and tested the subjects' recall in two successive output phases. An interesting finding was the fact that in all cases where original clusters found in the first output phase were broken up in the second phase, their component items were transferred into their proper topic clusters.

The invariance in the number of recalled S-units observed by Tulving and Patkau (1962) and McNulty (1966) is also apparent in the data reported by Jenkins, Mink, and Russell (1958). They used four lists of 12 associatively related pairs of words, lists varying in the strength of intrapair associations.

Number of recalled words varied directly with the strength of associations over a range of 14.5 to 19.1. However, counting a related pair of words recalled in immediately adjacent output positions as one rather than two units, we find that the number of units recalled for the four lists, ordered in terms of increasing associative strength, becomes 13.4, 14.5, 13.2, 14.0, indicating no systematic differences among lists.

All these experiments suggest that the kinds of results we get and have to interpret depend very much on the kinds of units of analysis we use. Variation in the number of E-units recalled as a function of order of approximation or of inter-item associative strength would require an explanation different from that required by the finding of invariance in the number of S-units. The S-unit invariance illustrates limited recall capacity of human subjects which is independent of the number of presented units, provided that the total time of presentation is held constant (cf. Murdock, 1960).

One of the important problems facing experimenters and theorists interested in free-recall—as well as those concerned with other memory tasks—lies in the specification of the functional units of material that are remembered and recalled. We may be ignorant as to the exact S-units in any given situation, and we may have to temporize by counting such easily identifiable units as trigrams or words, but sooner or later we have to come to grips with the S-units in an objective fashion. In the long run, nothing will be gained by pretending that gaps between sequences of printed letters or between sequences of spoken phonemes define the units of information processed by the human memory system.

Stevens (1951) has suggested that there is only one problem in psychophysics, or indeed in all psychology—

that of the definition of the stimulus. In free recall, the problem of the definition of the response is equally vital.

Single-Trial Free-Recall Phenomena

Apart from the evidence on the relation between various characteristics of the material and the amount recalled, there are two major facts that have emerged from single-trial free-recall experiments in which single items are used as units of analysis. The first has to do with the relation between the ordinal position of an item in the input list and its probability of recall, while the second is defined by the relation between the amount of presentation time and the amount of material recalled. We will consider these two phenomena in turn and examine their theoretical implications.

The serial position curve: Evidence for two retrieval systems

If the input material consists of randomly ordered familiar items, if the presentation rate is not greater than two seconds per item, and if subjects have had some prior practice in the task, the function relating probability of recall of an item to its position in the input list, the serial position curve, is usually characterized "by a steep . . . primacy effect extending over the first three or four words in the list, an S shaped recency effect extending over the last eight words in the list, and a horizontal asymptote spanning the primacy and recency effects" (Murdock, 1962, p. 488). Murdock's experiment represents the most extensive investigation of the serial position curve under the conditions stated, but data similar

to his have been reported by others as well (e.g., Deese, 1957; Deese and Kaufman, 1957; Postman and Phillips, 1965).

The primacy effect has so far eluded explanation. Two main lines of argument have been advanced to account for it, but neither has much unequivocal support. The first postulates that items from early input positions are recalled more readily than items from the middle input positions because the former are subject to smaller amounts of intraserial proactive inhibition. The second states that subjects tend to rehearse earlier input items while being exposed to middle items, with the consequence that earlier items are strengthened at the expense of middle items. Both hypotheses share the assumption that earlier items are in some sense "stronger" at the beginning of the output phase than are the middle items; this is a simple restatement of the fact that there is a primacy effect. No incisive experimental data to elucidate the processes involved have been reported so far.

The recency effect is much better understood. Most explanations that have been advanced constitute elaborations of the suggestion made by Robinson and Brown (1926) who, in discussing the pronounced recency effect reported by Welch and Burnett (1924), proposed that it was attributable to the shorter time between learning and recall of last items. Several investigators have demonstrated sizable negative correlations between probability of recall and output positions of individual items (Bousfield, Cohen, and Silva, 1956; Deese, 1957; Deese and Kaufman, 1957; Waugh and Norman, 1965). There are exceptions to this general rule in special cases (e.g., Green and Harding, 1962), but under the typical conditions of free recall of series of homogeneous items, the correlation between output order and probability of recall does imply that recall of terminal input items is high because they are recalled earlier than other items. Murdock's (1962) finding that the recency effect is independent of the rate of presentation further clarifies the picture by suggesting that it is not the length of the intratrial retention interval, but rather the number of items presented and recalled between the presentation and attempted recall of a given item, that is of critical importance in determining the probability of recall of the item.

The results of important experiments by Murdock (1962), Postman and Phillips (1965), Glanzer and Cunitz (1966), and Glanzer and Meinzer (1967) provide strong support for the hypothesis that at least two different recall mechanisms are involved in free recall. Murdock, as we have noted, found that the recency effect was independent of rate of presentation of items. He also found that it was independent of list length. Both of these variables, however, did affect recall of items from input positions preceding the range of the recency effect. Postman and Phillips demonstrated that the typical pronounced recency effects for lists of 10, 20, and 30 words were washed out when recall was delayed for 30 seconds, the interpolated interval being filled with activity assumed to prevent rehearsal. The rest of each serial position curve, however, was only little affected. Very similar data were obtained by Glanzer and Cunitz, who used lists of 15 words and delays of 10 and 30 seconds. The loss of recall over the interval of 30 seconds in the Postman and Phillips' experiment was approximately constant at two words for all list lengths. This finding is in good agreement with the hypotheses that the loss of recall involves primarily items from the terminal input positions

and that the recency effect is independent of list length. Finally, the experiment by Glanzer and Meinzer demonstrated that overt repetition of words during the intervals between successive words in the input phase reduced the recall of words from the prerecency range of the serial position curve but did not affect the recall of terminal items.

All these findings, in showing that certain experimental variables affect one part of the serial position curve while leaving another part invariant, strongly suggest that the curve reflects the operation of at least two types of recall mechanisms. Waugh and Norman (1965) refer to these two mechanisms as primary and secondary memory, following James' (1890) distinction, and identify them with different storage systems. Glanzer and Cunitz also discuss their data in terms of two kinds of storage mechanisms, the short-term and the long-term storage. We will briefly consider the Waugh and Norman model as representative of the two-factor theories of memory having something to say about single-trial free recall.

According to the Waugh and Norman model, as an item is perceived by the subject, it enters into primary memory, which has a very limited capacity. Items in primary memory are displaced by other incoming items unless they are rehearsed. As long as they are rehearsed, they remain in primary memory and may be transferred into secondary memory, which has a much larger capacity. The two storage systems are independent, in the sense that the contents of one at a given time have no bearing on the contents of the other at the same time, and yet not mutually exclusive, in the sense that any given item can be in either or both of the two systems at a given time.

An important assumption Waugh

and Norman make is that any item in either system can always be recalled by the subject. They thus equate retention with recall, or storage with retrieval. The recency effect is determined by the contents of both the primary and secondary memory, while the asymptotic level of the serial position curve reflects the amount of material stored in secondary memory. The contents of primary memory can be estimated from the observed values of probability of recall of late input items and of the asymptote of the serial position curve, while the contents of the secondary memory can be inferred from the pre-recency range of the serial position curve.

The easy retrieval of recently perceived items has been referred to by Waugh and Norman as the "echo box" phenomenon, "echo box" representing the primary memory storage. The existence of the "echo box" was known to early students of memory. Pohlmann (1906), for instance, pointed out that under the method of retained members recall of last items in the series may occur by virtue of their *"flüchtiges Nachklingen"*—fleeting reverberation —and recommended that an interval of a few seconds always be interpolated between presentation and recall to reduce the contamination of true memory effects by such *Nachklingen*.

Although the distinction between primary and secondary memory is heuristically useful, the identification of the two types of memory with different storage systems may not constitute the most promising stepping stone to further theoretical analyses. The very term "storage" or "store" implies a location of some sort in the nervous system in which information is held for future use. Do the two types of storage then imply two different locations where the engrams Lashley (1950) never found are tucked away?

To be sure, all models of memory represent only "as if" pictures of the human mind or the human nervous system, and the terms we use are just figures of speech that help us to relate something we know to something we do not quite understand. But, as Wechsler (1963) has recently reminded us again, the metaphors and analogies of which students of memory are so fond are frequently accepted as literal explanations. When this happens, the analogies may well stifle further inquiry. McGeoch's remark, made more than 35 years ago, that experimentalists have generally preferred to content themselves with analogies, such as that of the phonograph record, rather than to confront the real problem is probably applicable today, if we substitute "conditioning paradigm" or "electronic computer" for "phonograph record." Where shall we go next, once we have accepted the notion of two storage systems whose capacity and contents determine how much the subject can recall?

I prefer the view that all input information is stored in the same unitary storage system, whatever its nature, and that differences in recall of early, middle, and late input items reflect primarily differences in the accessibility of these items (cf. Miller, Galanter, and Pribram, 1960). Late input items may be retrieved more easily because certain kinds of additional auxiliary information, stored with each item at the time of presentation, are available for these items and not available for items perceived earlier. The acoustic trace of an item the subject hears—or the acoustic trace of an item the subject sees and recodes acoustically (Sperling, 1963)—may be one kind of such auxiliary information that might serve as a retrieval cue for the item. Such an acoustic trace may rapidly decay or be blotted out by other traces, even if its loss does not affect the rest of the information stored at the time of input. The item for which the acoustic trace is lost may still be potentially retrievable through other, less powerful but more permanent retrieval cues. Serial position or temporal dating of items in the input phase may constitute another kind of auxiliary information which can serve as a retrieval cue. Such information may be greater for early and late input items than for the middle ones and may be initially more powerful and yet decay more rapidly than other retrieval cues.

Regardless of the nature of retrieval cues affecting the recall of individual items, such cues must be postulated, since the alternative formulation of the organism or his homunculus "searching" for lost objects in memory (James, 1890) will lead us down the path of infinite regress. Until we know more about the retrieval mechanisms and retrieval cues, it is at best unnecessary and at worst misleading to identify primary and secondary memory with different storage systems. All we need to say is that at least two different types of retrieval systems must at this time be postulated. Eventually we may have not only primary and secondary memory, but as many different "types" of memory as we have found different types of retrieval cues.

Total presentation time

One of the most easily demonstrated facts about single-trial free recall is the direct dependence of the amount of material recalled on the amount presented. "Immediate" memory is limited in free recall as it is in many other tasks, but the limit, at least when measured in E-units, depends on the amount of material presented.

When items are presented successively at a fixed rate, the amount of material presented covaries directly with the total presentation time. Murdock (1960), on the basis of a series of experiments, suggested that this total presentation time is the critical variable responsible for the covariation between the amount of material presented and recalled. This general hypothesis was supplemented by a more specific one according to which the number of items recalled is a linear function of the total presentation time, with the intercept constant in the linear equation $R = kt + m$ representing the value of the memory span and the slope constant representing the number of items per unit of time that can be recalled over and above the span.

The boundary conditions of Murdock's two hypotheses have not yet been determined. Although a number of experimental reports exist in the literature providing data on the relation between amount of material presented and amount recalled, few experiments, apart from that of Murdock, have explored the relation over a sufficiently wide range of list lengths or presentation times to permit a fair check on the tenability of the linearity hypothesis. One of the experiments that comes closest to the necessary standards was done by Deese (1960). Deese used lists of 12, 25, 50, and 100 words and combined list length orthogonally with six different frequency-of-occurrence levels of words. For the two highest levels of word frequency, the relation between number of words recalled and list length was approximately linear, but for the lower four levels of frequency linearity did not hold. Cohen (1963b) also reported nonlinearity for lists of 20 words presented at the rate of 3 seconds and 10.5 seconds per word.

In some other experiments both the presentation-time and the linearity hypotheses run into difficulty. In one of Murdock's own experiments (1962), for instance, recall was no greater for 20-word and 40-word lists presented for 40 seconds than for 15-word and 30-word lists presented for a total time of 30 seconds.

The presentation-time hypothesis also breaks down when subjects have to recall names of objects shown in a simultaneous display. Michel (1923) reported a series of experiments in which immediate recall was studied as a function of number of objects presented—the number varying from 5 to 30—and the total presentation time, varying over a range from 5 to 150 seconds. Number of objects recalled was a direct function of the duration of display, but when the presentation time was held constant, the number of items recalled still increased systematically with the number of objects presented. One of the interesting findings reported by Michel was that even with very short exposure times recall was substantial. Thus, for instance, mean recall of 10 objects presented for a total duration of 2 seconds was 5.6, and mean recall of 25 objects presented for 5 seconds was 8.6. Hence Michel's method of a simultaneous display of a set of small objects recommends itself for the study of memory under conditions where reading-in time is to be minimized.

Despite the uncertainty as to the exact boundary conditions of the two hypotheses, "immediate" recall of a list of words does seem to be generally a positive function of the total amount of presentation time. Nothing much can be said about this phenomenon by way of theoretical speculation. Deese's (1960) suggestion, however, that the proportionality between recall over and above recall from the primary memory on the one hand, and the total presentation time on the other, can be explained in terms of interword associations

constitutes a promising starting point for the search of underlying processes, provided that we define "interword associations" very broadly. The probability that two or more E-units are stored by the subject as a single S-unit is likely to increase with list length and with the total time the subject has available for the discovery or fabrication of relevant interitem relations. If groups of related items can be handled by the memory system as single S-units, longer lists and longer presentation times would be expected to yield larger recall scores if recall is measured in terms of E-units.

Secondary Organization in Free Recall

We have already noted that subjects usually produce their responses in recall in an order different from the presentation order. Discrepancies between input and output orders cannot occur in serial learning tasks, and when they occur in paired-associate tasks, they are of no theoretical significance since the output order is determined by the experimenter. In free recall, however, the output order is free to vary, and discrepancies between input and output orders, under conditions where output orders show systematic consistencies, provide evidence for organizational processes in remembering.

Organization defined in the weak sense refers to consistent discrepancies between input and output orders that are independent of the subjects' prior familiarity with a set of input items. We will label this type of organization "primary organization." The recency effect, for instance, being related to the subjects' tendency to recall terminal input items from a homogeneous list before recall of other items, regardless of the characteristics of these items, is one of the manifestations of primary organization.

In this section we will discuss some of the issues that emerge from observations of organization defined in the strong sense. Such organization occurs when the output order of items is governed by semantic or phonetic relations among items or by the subjects' prior, extra-experimental or intra-experimental acquaintance with the items constituting a list. We will label this type of organization "secondary organization." It can be measured in a variety of ways and can be related to both independent variables and other dependent variables, thus illuminating some of the underlying processes in free recall.

Clustering

Two types of measures of secondary organization as a response variable have so far been developed. The first type of measures can be obtained in situations where the total set of L items is constructed and conceived by the experimenter to consist of two or more mutually exclusive subsets of items. Each item within a given subset is assumed to be more "similar" to other items within the same subset than it is to any other item in other subsets. Subsets have been defined in terms of belongingness of items to a conceptual category, associative relations among items, parts of speech, etc. The items in the total list are presented in a random or quasi-random order, and organization is said to have occurred when items from a subset are recalled in immediately adjacent output positions more frequently than one would expect by chance.

Secondary organization measured in this manner has been referred to as clustering. A long line of studies by

Bousfield and his associates, beginning with the experiments by Bousfield (1953) and Bousfield and Cohen (1953), as well as those by many other investigators (e.g., Cofer, 1959; Cofer, 1965; Dallett, 1964; Gonzalez and Cofer, 1959; Jenkins, Mink, and Russell, 1958; Jenkins and Russell, 1952; Postman, Adams and Bohm, 1956; Wicklund, Palermo and Jenkins, 1965) have been concerned with the phenomenon of clustering. Clustering has been shown to be a function of many variables, such as number of repetitions of the material, strength of associative relations among words, number of subsets, prior practice, instructions, and developmental level of subjects. In many cases, although not invariably, it has been shown to be directly related to the number of words recalled.

An obvious advantage of clustering measures is that they can be calculated for recall obtained in a single output phase, although Rozov (1964) has suggested that the practice of giving subjects only single recall trials may have prevented investigators from obtaining greater insight into the processes underlying clustering. Furthermore, if the single output phase follows a single input phase in immediate succession, subjects tend to recall the late input items first, regardless of the specific meaning of these items or their semantic relations to other items in the list. This primary organization probably interferes with, or at least attenuates, secondary organization. Bousfield (1953) and Bousfield and Cohen (1953) have shown that the function relating the degree of clustering to successive deciles of words produced in the output phase has the shape of an inverted U, clustering being strongest in the middle of the output period. Bousfield and Cohen (1953) have proposed a rather elaborate explanation for the low degree of clustering obtained at the beginning of the output phase, but the phenomenon may be at least partly attributable to the priority of retrieval of terminal input items, i.e., to primary organization. The fact that the degree of clustering is maximum in the first few deciles when recall is tested following five immediately successive input phases (Bousfield and Cohen, 1953) is consonant with this interpretation, since the recency effect is probably less pronounced under these conditions.

The main disadvantage of the clustering measures is related to the fact that they only tap organization of the kind that the experimenter is looking for and hence tend to underestimate the extent to which organization has occurred in a given situation. To take an extreme case, the failure to find clustering of words according to their form classes (Cofer and Bruce, 1965) does not mean that recall is unorganized; it only means that form class normally does not provide a basis of organization. Even when input material consists of words of different conceptual categories and there are good reasons to expect that secondary organization should be governed by the belongingness of words to such categories, S-units consisting of words from disparate categories may be formed. These units are not detected in a typical clustering analysis.

Subjective organization

The second type of measure of secondary organization, referred to as subjective organization, requires data from more than a single output phase, but it does not require that the experimenter know in advance of the experiment what items are to be grouped together. It is, therefore, applicable to any set of items.

Measures of subjective organization are defined in terms of the consistency of output orders, either for a single subject recalling the same material in two or more output phases or for a group of subjects recalling the same material in at least one output phase. When two or more items occur in close temporal contiguity in different output phases, they can be thought to represent elements of a larger S-unit which is being processed as a unit.

I have described a method for the measurement of subjective organization based on certain notions derived from information theory (Tulving, 1962). The measure of subjective organization (SO) is positively correlated with the number of words recalled, both across subjects with trials held constant and across trials with subjects held constant (Tulving, 1962, 1964).

A measure closely related to that of SO, labelled ITR (intertrial repetitions) has been used by Bousfield, Puff, and Cowan (1964). The subjects in their experiment had to memorize a list of ten words having zero interitem associative strength according to the Russell and Jenkins (1954) norms. Bousfield, Puff, and Cowan's main findings were that ITR increased over trials and that there was a significant agreement among subjects in the final order in which they recalled the words, this order being unrelated to the frequency of usage of the words.

Other methods of quantifying subjective organization have been described by Seibel (1965) and Ehrlich (1965). Seibel has used what he calls "the study sheet paradigm" for objectively defining the subjective clusters in recall. He has found that the degree of subjective clustering increases with learning and that it is highly correlated with the number of words recalled. Ehrlich has measured the development of organization over trials in terms of interitem distances (number of items intervening between any two items) in successive output phases, with the interitem distances in the final output period constituting the reference level. He has obtained high positive correlations between his "coefficient of structure" and the number of items recalled by individual subjects, the correlation increasing with the length of the list, and has found that, over successive trials, the number of correct responses is a linear function of the amount of structure, which in turn is a logarithmic function of the learning time.

Nature of secondary organization

Ordering of recalled items in terms of their associative relations, membership in obvious superordinate categories, phonetic or letter-structure similarity, degree of familiarity, and other such characteristics (Ehrlich, 1965; Tulving, 1962, 1965), a phenomenon that we have referred to by the generic term of secondary organization, is a ubiquitous phenomenon in free recall. It can always be found in any experiment when one looks for it. From the earliest days of experimental study of memory, it has intruded into experiments designed to examine the recall of individual items *qua* individual items, and it has been noted in many more recent free-recall experiments that were not directly concerned with the problem of organization (e.g., Kintsch and Morris, 1965; Miller and McGill, 1952; Waugh, 1961). How is this secondary organization to be explained or interpreted?

Bousfield, Steward, and Cowan (1964) have posed the question with respect to clustering, but it applies equally well to subjective organization: "There is the question of whether organization of verbal responses can be explained in terms of relatively simple associative connections between words, or whether it is necessary to invoke an additional principle such as superordination" (Bousfield, Steward, and Cowan, 1964, p. 206). The principle of superordination as an explanation of clustering had been put forth earlier by Bousfield and his associates (Bousfield, 1953; Bousfield and Cohen, 1953, 1955). The results of the Bousfield, Steward, and Cowan (1964) experiment again supported the principle of superordination—as did the results of the study of Bousfield and Puff (1964)—permitting the authors to conclude that response-produced cues function mediationally to promote clustering of words. They were careful to point out, however, that their findings did not in any way negate the "potency of direct associative connections for determining clustering."

Postman, in a brief review of studies of clustering, also has distinguished between associative and categorical clustering and has pointed out:

The relationship between the two types of clustering remains uncertain. Associative clustering appears to reflect directly the associative structure of the words in the list, and no recourse to a mediational process is compelled by the data. On the other hand, at least some forms of category clustering strongly suggest mediation by cue-producing responses. The question now is whether it is necessary to assume two distinct types of clustering, and if it is, what their relative priorities are in determining sequential order in recall (Postman, 1964, p. 180).

A rather detailed discussion of associative and categorical bases for clustering has been presented by Cofer in two papers (1965, 1966). After considering a great deal of evidence relevant to the problem of mechanisms underlying clustering, Cofer concluded,

"It now seems to me, and this represents a change of heart, that such a contrast is neither useful nor heuristic. In free-recall . . . subjects will use either or both of these bases to accomplish their recalls and will find ways to organize recalls even though the experimenter has not provided means in the list he presents" (Cofer, 1965, p. 271). In a subsequent paper, however, Cofer apparently found the distinction between associative and mediational clustering useful again and concluded that in some situations, such as Bousfield's four-category lists, associations are the dominant factor in clustering, while in some others the operation of a coding factor (in addition to association) seems highly plausible (Cofer, 1966).

In my opinion, the attempts to distinguish between associative and mediational mechanisms of clustering, even if only to assess their relative effects in various learning processes (Bousfield and Puff, 1964), are futile in the present state of the art. The first difficulty lies in the concept of association itself. It is a descriptive concept, not an explanatory one. Association is a name for the fact that one event leads to another, and as such it carries no theoretical implications (McGeoch, 1942). If the association between two items, A and B, is strong, the probability of A given B, or vice versa, is high. If the probability of A given B, or vice versa, is high, the association between A and B can be said to be strong. Thus, the demonstration that word B is given frequently as a free-association response to word A, and that the two words are recalled together when they are both members of a list, is a demonstration that similar events occur in different situations. It suggests that similar processes may be involved in both cases, but associations observed in free-association tests do not *explain* associations in free-recall tasks any

more than the latter associations explain the former. Association between words A and B, whether observed in a free-association test or in a free-recall task, is a fact that remains to be explained.

The second difficulty in seeking the explanation of clustering in the distinction between associative and mediational mechanisms is related to the simple fact that any two words that can be shown to be associatively related— or any other two words, for that matter—are always members of some superordinate category that subsumes both. Thus, two or more words may function as a more or less intact unit either because of the direct associative relations among them, even if we do not know what the underlying mechanism is, or because of some indirect association (cf. Marshall and Cofer, 1963) indicating membership in a common category. To measure the strength of the direct association between two words, to compare it with the strength of the indirect association between the same words, and then to conclude that recall of the words as a unit is determined by direct associations or indirect associations in degrees reflected in the two strength measures would not serve any useful purpose. The conclusion one would draw from such a comparison would be no better than are the measures of strength of associations, and even if the measures were "perfect," we would still have only information about the correlation between events in two situations—free or restricted association tests and free-recall tasks. Such a correlation requires explanation; it does not constitute one.

The third difficulty in current attempts to explain the mechanisms of clustering is related to a large variety of apparent bases of organization observed in free-recall experiments. At Toronto, we have been experimenting with the application of a modified method of McQuitty's (1963) rank order typal analysis to the data from various free-recall experiments, with a view to extracting higher order S-units (Tulving, 1964, 1966a) from these data. An S-unit, most rigidly defined (although we have sometimes relaxed the criterion somewhat) is a subset consisting of two or more list items each of which is recalled more frequently in an output position immediately adjacent to other items constituting the S-unit than it is recalled in output positions immediately adjacent to items from other S-units. Some of the S-units gleaned from the data make good sense, while others do not. S-units such as *WAR-SHIP, MASSACRE,* and *SHRAP-NEL; RUBBER, IRON,* and *SAND; AGREEMENT* and *SETTLE; NAME* and *CLIFF; JEWEL* and *JELLY; BALAP, VOLVAP,* and *ZUMAP,* all obtained from experiments using "unrelated" words, can be "explained" on various obvious grounds, as can S-units from a Bousfield type categorized list used in an unpublished study by Dronsejko (1963), units such as *BUGLE, HORN,* and *TRUMPET; BASS* and *VIOLA; BEE, HORNET,* and *WASP; CAVE* and *CAVERN; MOUNTAIN* and *VOLCANO; GUN, SPEAR* and *STICK.* But what are we to do with S-units such as *PEACE* and *SURVEY; CONQUEST, ORNA-MENT,* and *DEMAND; SPOON* and *CHIMNEY; LATUK* and *TAROP,* that have also emerged from the data? Are these "determined" by direct or indirect associations?

Attempts to classify bases of organization are reminiscent of attempts to classify free associations into different types. After reviewing some of the early efforts at such classification, Ebbinghaus concluded that the results had been disappointing, partly because the classifying schemes that had been proposed were based on grammatical and logical rather than psychological considerations, and partly because the classification of many associations into disparate categories in most cases would not be possible anyway. If "coffee" and "tea" are associated, Ebbinghaus asked, is it because of the similarity of the circumstances under which coffee and tea are consumed, because of similarity of their effects, because of their belongingness to a class of potable things, or because of the frequency with which the two words have been seen or heard together in shop windows, on menus in restaurants, and in price lists? He concluded that all of these factors probably play some role in determining the association and that the assignment of an association between the two words to a single exclusive category would be misleading.

More recently, Deese (1962) has also rejected attempts to classify associations. Instead he defines the associative meaning of a word in terms of the total distribution of associative responses to that word. It would seem to be reasonable to suggest that secondary organization in free recall is at least partly governed by associative meanings of words constituting a list, but this statement again would only explicate a correlation between free-association and free-recall phenomena. Besides, it is conceivable that some of the "unrelated" words that are organized into an S-unit may never show any associative overlap in free-association norms, unitization being determined by the total intralist verbal context and accidental contiguity relations among words in input and output phases. To the extent that verbal contexts differ in free-association tests and in free-recall tasks, the correlation between the strengths of associations in these two situations will probably always fall far short of unity and the extent of the involvement of the associative meaning of words in determining secondary organization will remain uncertain. Bousfield, Puff, and Cowan's (1964) finding of subjective organization of words having zero interitem associative strength is a case in point.

Instead of attempting to explain the nature of the mechanism of secondary organization in terms of extra-experimental correlations, it seems more profitable at this time to start with the fact that certain words are more likely to be formed into clusters or S-units than others and to ask what *intra-experimental* conditions determine the ease with which such S-units are formed. For instance, would it be necessary for two prospective members of an S-unit to be presented in close temporal contiguity in the input list for unitization to occur? Does the probability that two words such as "man" and "woman" become members of an S-unit vary directly with the intraserial distance between them in input and output phases? If so, what is the effective range of distances over which possible unitization of the two words remains effective? If intraserial distance is an important variable, is it to be specified in terms of E-units or S-units? Would the subject have to be able to remember that "man" occurred earlier in the list to bring it into the S-unit with "woman" shown later in the list, or does the presentation of "woman" later in the list somehow resuscitate the trace of "man" even if the latter would not be recallable by itself?

Very little work relevant to these problems has been done, although experiments comparing the effectiveness of blocked and random presentation of word lists categorized on the basis of restricted word-association norms (Bourne and Parker, 1964; Cofer, Bruce, and Reicher, 1966; Dallett, 1964) or on the basis of free-recall data (Tulving, 1965) probably constitute steps in the right direction.

Repetition Effects in Multitrial Free Recall

The limited capacity of immediate memory is one of the basic puzzles confronting the student of mental processes; the increase in recall as a function of practice is another. How should learning—increments in recall over successive trials—be conceptualized?

Serial and paired-associate learning usually has been explained to be a consequence of strengthening of associations between the members of the series or individual pairs. As we have already noted, however, a statement that the strength of association increases over trials does not explain learning. Strength of associations cannot be measured independently of the frequency with which a response follows another response, and thus learning and strengthening of associations are inferred from the same data. The statement that associations in serial and paired-associate lists are strengthened is synonymous with the statement that learning occurs—it does not explain learning.

The situation is different in multitrial free-recall experiments. Learning is inferred from the positive slope of the function relating the number of items recalled to the ordinal number of the trial. Strengthening of associations among specific items, on the other hand, can be inferred from the increased probability that one item follows another item in recall. These two events, learning and strengthening of associations, are logically independent in free-recall tasks. Strengthening of associations can occur even if there is no learning, and learning can occur in the absence of strengthening of interitem associations. "Statistical" subjects in free-recall experiments can recall more and more items over trials independently of strengthening of interitem associations, a feat they cannot accomplish in serial and paired-associate learning experiments. If it is observed, therefore, that free-recall learning in human subjects is accompanied by strengthening of specific interitem associations, the fact has psychological implications of considerable importance.

Relation between secondary organization and learning

To the extent that measures of secondary organization reflect the strength of interitem associations, the findings of increased secondary organization over trials in free-recall experiments (Bousfield, Berkowitz, and Whitmarsh, 1959; Bousfield, Puff, and Cowan, 1964; Ehrlich, 1965; Tulving, 1962, 1964) can be interpreted to mean that interitem associations are strengthened as a consequence of repeated presentations and recall of the material. What are the implications of this fact for the problem of why learning occurs?

On intuitive grounds, if nothing else, the obvious answer seems to be that learning is a consequence of the strengthening of interitem associations. Such an interpretation has been put forth explicitly elsewhere (Tulving, 1962, 1964, 1966a). It was argued, by way of an extension of a position proposed earlier with respect to immediate memory by Miller (1956a, 1956b), that the subject can recall a limited number of S-units on each of the successive trials and that the learning curve expressed in E-units reflects only the increasing size of S-units.

This hypothesis is not unlike Deese's (1961) conjecture that the number of words remembered on a single trial is the same under a variety of experimental conditions and that observed variations in the number of words recalled can be accounted for by associations evoked by the remembered "core" words as well as by subject's constructions of additional words on the basis of his knowledge of the language. The S-unit invariance hypothesis, however, holds that all items recalled are those *actually remembered* from previous input and output phases. Extralist intrusions, sometimes highly predictable from the nature of the material (Deese, 1959b), probably represent remembered associative responses made to list-words in the input phase rather than associative constructions at the time of recall. They are intrusions only in the sense that they do not correspond to the experimenter's tally sheet, and not necessarily in the sense that the ideas they represent are not *remembered* from earlier parts of the same or similar experiments.

Although it seems reasonable to assume that the correlation between measures of subjective organization and number of items recalled over trials indicates the dependence of increments in recall on the strengthening of specific interitem associations, alternative interpretations are possible. The first such interpretation holds that increments in organization depend on increments in recall. This position was implicit in Carterette and Coleman's (1963) suggestion that increments in subjective organization *follow* increments in recall. The second alternative is that both increments in recall and increments in organization are parallel but otherwise unrelated manifestations of a common underlying process and that one has no more effect on the other than the second has on the first. So far no champion of this point of view seems to have stepped forth.

Availability of items and contextual associations

If free-recall learning occurs independently of increments in organization, what other mechanisms can be postulated to account for learning? Asch and Ebenholtz (1962) have suggested that free recall is not a function of interitem associations and that it depends solely on "availability" of items. They have even claimed, on the basis of the results of several experiments involving memorization of lists of eight nonsense syllables, that no interitem associations are established in the course of repeated free recall of items, but such a claim is not logically necessary for the integrity of their main assertions. Availability, according to Asch and Ebenholtz, "refers to the accessibility of an item to recall; the index of availability is the ease with which a datum of past experience can be produced. Central to our conception is the definition of availability as a phenomenon of recall, distinct from associations between items; availability refers to a property of memory traces" (p. 21). Availability as a fundamental condition of recall, and presumably of increments in recall, is said to be determined by factors such as frequency, primacy, recency, and isolation of individual items in a series. Thus, an item that has been perceived frequently and recently is more available for recall than another item perceived less frequently and less recently.

Asch and Ebenholtz's (1962) concept of availability seems to be another descriptive label for recall probability, and as such it does not take us beyond the immediate empirical data. More-over, as we shall see presently, some experimental data clearly contradict the assumption that probability of recall unconditionally depends on frequency and recency.

The assumption that free-recall learning occurs in the absence of inter-item associations also has been made by all authors of stochastic models of free-recall learning (Bush and Mosteller, 1955; Miller and McGill, 1952; Kintsch and Morris, 1965; Waugh and Smith, 1962), but this assumption is made only for the sake of mathematical convenience. All these writers have pointed out that clustering is one of the most persistent characteristics of free-recall data. Phenomena of secondary organization, or, for that matter, primary organization, as they occur in free recall have not yet been incorporated into mathematical models. Miller and McGill (1952) did deduce the prediction from their model that associative clustering should affect only the variability and not the rate of learning, but this deduction seems to be at variance with the data that have since been accumulated by many experimenters.

A different approach to the problem of learning in free recall is implicit in the writings of those psychologists who have postulated associations between list-items and the general experimental context to account for the response-learning stage in paired-associate learning (Keppel, 1964; McGovern, 1964; Underwood, 1964; Underwood, Runquist, and Schulz, 1959; Underwood and Schulz, 1960). According to these formulations, increments in recall of individual items *qua* individual items over trials reflect the strengthening of such contextual associations, the context being defined in terms of "all stimuli, other than the specific items, which contribute to the recall of the response terms under the conditions of free recall" (Keppel, 1964,

p. 92). Postman (1964) also has stated, "Rehearsal will strengthen the connection between each item and the situational context, but it will serve other functions as well, depending on the characteristics of the items in the list" (p. 176). Unlike Asch and Ebenholtz, and like the authors of stochastic models, these writers do not deny the possible role of interitem associations in determining free recall. Underwood and Schulz (1960) and Postman (1964) have stated explicitly that associations among items in the list may facilitate recall.

Evidence for organizational factors in learning

Is it necessary to postulate the strengthening of both contextual and specific interitem associations to account for learning in free recall, or can the whole burden be carried by organizational processes alone? This is not an easy question to answer, and it may be that the issue will not be satisfactorily settled for a long time. But I will argue that at least at the present time there is no compelling need to postulate the strengthening of contextual associations to account for trial-by-trial increments in free recall and that the available evidence points only to secondary organization or strengthening of interitem associations as the critical ingredient of free-recall learning. This is not to say that contextual associations—which I would like to define as associations between different aspects of the subject's total experience in an experimental situation and the to-be-remembered items—play no role at all in free recall. It is logically necessary that at least one item—and psychologically plausible that a small but fixed number of items—be initially associated with the context to make

later recall of the list possible. What seems to be unnecessary is the assumption of the *strengthening* of direct contextual associations; it is at least unnecessary to assume that they play anything more than a minor role in memorization of a list.

The first reason for this view is that while it is exceedingly simple to demonstrate the development and strengthening of interitem associations in the course of trial-by-trial practice—or in the course of a prolonged study period—and only a little more difficult to show that these associations facilitate recall, it is quite difficult, if not impossible, to prove that associations between items and the general context are strengthened *independently* of specific interitem associations, as long as items are presented in the context of other items, as they are in free-recall experiments.

The second and a more germane reason for the suggestion that strengthening of contextual associations plays only a minor role in free-recall learning lies in some experimental evidence reported by several investigators. We will consider this evidence briefly.

Murdock and Babick (1961) measured probability of free recall of a single critical word presented on a number of successive trials, but always in the context of new sets of words. In this situation the association between the critical word and the general nonverbal context can become stronger over trials, since the context remains stable; but interitem associations cannot be strengthened, because the verbal context changes from trial to trial. The results were quite clear in showing that the recall of the critical word remained constant over trials. This finding is directly contrary to the hypothesis that repetition strengthens associations between the general nonverbal context and individual words within the verbal context. It provides indirect support to the notion that repetition effects are mediated through interitem associations.

The next source of relevant evidence is a series of experiments we have done at Toronto (Tulving, 1966a). In one type of experiment, subjects read aloud a list of 22 words, all words being presented six times in a quasi-random order. Immediately after the completion of this task the subjects were presented the same set of 22 words for learning on 12 trials under the typical free-recall conditions. The resulting learning curve was identical with that obtained from another group of subjects who learned the identical list after reading a different set of words. This finding demonstrates that frequency and recency alone are not sufficient to increase the availability of responses, although it does not negate the possibility that general background associations could be strengthened under conditions where subjects are instructed to memorize the material. However, evidence is available from at least two other experiments on single-trial free recall that does cast considerable doubt on this possibility.

Mechanic (1964, Exp. III) had two groups of subjects learn a list of 24 pronounceable trigrams under typical learning instructions. Trigrams were presented at the rate of 11 sec. each. One group had to pronounce each trigram over and over again until the next one was shown in the input series, while the second group was left free to do whatever they wished in the intervals between items. The mean number of trigrams recalled was significantly higher in the second group, despite the fact that the first group made many more overt responses corresponding to list items. Similar findings have been reported by Glanzer and Meinzer (in press) in an experiment already cited.

One group of their subjects also was asked to repeat words overtly during interword intervals in the input phase of a single-trial free-recall experiment, while the other group was left to their own devices in trying to remember the material. Again, subjects who did not have to repeat the words showed higher recall than those who were instructed to do so. Thus, whatever else overt repetition does, it does not seem to contribute very much to recall. It probably only prevents subjects from organizing the material, thus producing lower recall than that of subjects who are free to organize the material.

Coming back to multitrial experiments, we note the second type of experiment reported by Tulving (1966a). Experimental groups learned a list of words under typical free-recall conditions and then learned another list, twice as long as the first one, which contained all the words learned previously. The control groups learned the same second lists as the experimental groups but different first lists. The learning curve of the experimental group was only initially higher than that of control groups. Following four to six trials the curves crossed, the control subjects recalling more words than the experimental subjects. This finding again is contrary to the hypothesis that strengthening of associations between individual list words and the stable nonverbal context takes place and is an important determinant of learning in free recall.

The next line of evidence relevant to the issue comes from a series of experiments by Mandler (1966a). Subjects were first asked to sort sets of words into a number of categories of their own choice. After they had arrived at a consistent set of categories, indicated by their ability to produce two identical sorts in succession, they were asked to recall as many words as they remembered. The number of words recalled was a linear function of the number of categories used by subjects but independent of the number of trials required for reaching the sorting criterion. Again it seems that it is not the frequency with which each word had been responded to by the subject in the presence of the general experimental stimuli that determined recall, but rather the number of higher-order units into which words were organized.

The final bit of relevant evidence, though somewhat less direct, can be gleaned from data published by Bousfield and Cohen (1953). In their experiment, different groups of subjects were presented with a categorized list of 40 words from one to five times. The number of words recalled increased directly as a function of the number of presentations, but the increase was attributable solely to the formation of larger clusters with repeated presentations. As shown in their Table 5, the number of nonclustered items, as well as the number of small clusters, showed no systematic trend over the range of one to five repetitions, although such a trend was very pronounced for "statistical" subjects. The effect of repetition lay in the production of larger S-units and not in the strengthening of background associations of individual items.

While all this evidence is still rather fragmentary, these findings are difficult, if not impossible, to reconcile with the hypothesis that repetition strengthens associative connections between individual items and the general nonverbal contextual stimuli. They make good sense, however, if we assume that repetition is effective to the extent to which it permits the subjects to organize E-units into larger S-units. I have been unable to think of any evidence that would unequivocally support the hypothesis

that repetition strengthens contextual associations of individual items independently of interitem associations. Until such evidence becomes available, theoretical conceptions of the free-recall process and of the effect of repetition on free recall, which attribute increments in availability of individual items to frequency and recency stimulation, or to strengthening of associative bonds between individual items and their nonverbal context, must be rejected in favor of the view that repeated presentation of the material over trials, or increasing study time, produces increments in recall because individual items can be organized into larger cohesive units and are processed as parts of these units.

Storage versus Retrieval Processes

Melton (1963) has defined the domain of the theory of memory in terms of two broad classes of problems, one having to do with storage of traces and the other with utilization or retrieval of traces. Some of the more specific issues Melton lists under the general rubric of problems of retrieval seem to be as relevant to storage as to retrieval. But at least one of them, namely the dependence of retrieval on the reinstatement of original stimulating conditions, illustrates the feasibility of analytical separation of storage and retrieval processes (or retention and recall) and implies that retrieval depends not only on the contents of the storage at any given time, but on some other factors as well.

Theories of free recall have had little to say about retrieval processes. We have already seen that some theoretical formulations (e.g., Asch 1964; Asch and Ebenholtz, 1962; Waugh and Norman, 1965) sidestep the issue completely by assuming that recall is determined by the availability of items in the storage or by the availability of traces of items. Others suggest that recall of individual items is primarily dependent on the development of higher-order S-units (Tulving, 1962, 1964) or on the total number of categories into which material has been organized (Mandler, 1966a, 1966b), but they have not been explicitly concerned with retrieval processes, independently of storage processes.

The heuristic usefulness of the distinction between storage and retrieval or, more specifically, between potential availability of information in the storage and accessibility of this information is indicated by certain experimental data. First, it is a well-known fact that many items a subject cannot recall can nevertheless be readily recognized as members of a previously seen experimental set. Michel (1923), for instance, found in one of his experiments that subjects could correctly recognize all items they had failed to recall. Such demonstrations, however, do not prove that information sufficient for the *reproduction* of items is sometimes potentially available in the storage even though it is not accessible. Scores on a recognition test are determined by different retained information from that measured by recall tests.

The second and more relevant fact is provided by demonstrations that subjects can recall more items at a later time than at an earlier time without the benefit of interpolated presentation. In an early experiment (Nicolai, 1922) subjects were shown a simultaneous display of ten small objects. Free recall tests were given twice, once immediately after the presentation and the second time following various intervals up to 96 hours. The number of objects recalled was invariably greater in the second test than in the first. The

largest difference occurred in the 96-hour group, in which the mean immediate recall score was 7.5 and the second test score was 9.4.

It might be argued that the first test responses provide additional practice or that subjects rehearse the material during the retention interval and that such practice is responsible for increased recall from the first to the second test, but unless certain additional assumptions are made about the retrieval process, these arguments are beside the mark. How would practice or rehearsal of items the subject could recall on the first test lead to subsequent recall of items the subject could not recall on the first test? In a recent experiment at Toronto (Tulving, 1966b) subjects were shown 36 words and asked to recall as many words as they could remember in each of three successive output phases. A total of six such "cycles" were given with the same list. One interesting finding was that only approximately 50 per cent of all the words a typical subject could recall at least once in any of the three intracycle output phases were recalled consistently in all three phases, even though the total number of words recalled in each output phase within a cycle was relatively constant. These findings were interpreted in support of the view of memory as a limited capacity retrieval system in which the limit is set by the number but not by the nature of the contents of accessible memory units. It is as if retrieval of one unit makes access to another unit impossible even though the latter is available in storage.

All these findings indicate that in free-recall situations the retrieval mechanism does not have access to all of the relevant information available in the storage. This indeed was one of the reasons why Ebbinghaus rejected the method of retained members as not particularly suitable for the study of memory. He failed to recognize that subjects' inability to recall all the material they have retained poses one of the truly challenging problems for the theory of memory. Why can the subject not recall everything he has "learned" and retained?

There is nothing in the free-recall literature that would provide a very meaningful answer to this question. About all we can say at the present time is that accessibility of individual items seems to depend on the degree of organization of items into higher-order units. Miller and McGill's (1952) casual observation that "many pairs of words are recalled together or omitted together on successive trials" (p. 389) suggests that one member of a higher-order S-unit serves as a retrieval cue for other members. One higher-order unit may similarly serve as a retrieval cue for another unit, in keeping with the hierarchical nature of organization described by Miller (1956a) and elaborated by Mandler (1966a). Exactly which of the available items within S-units are recalled would then depend on the order in which retrieval proceeds.

The role of experimentally manipulated retrieval cues in recall of words from a categorized list was examined in an experiment by Tulving and Pearlstone (1966). Lists consisted of words belonging to explicitly designated conceptual categories. Three levels of list length (12, 24, and 48 words) were combined with three levels of number of words per category (1, 2, and 4 words) to yield nine input conditions. Both category names and words belonging to categories were presented in the input phase, but subjects were told that only their recall for words would be tested. For half the subjects in each of the nine input conditions, recall of words was tested in the presence of category names as retrieval cues, for the other half recall was not cued. Since all subjects in a given input condition were treated identically until the end of the input phase, availability of information at the beginning of the output phase was equated for subjects in the cued and non-cued recall groups. Any differences in recall between these groups could thus be attributed to differences in accessibility.

Cued recall was greater than noncued recall for all nine input conditions, the difference varying directly with list length and inversely with the number of words per category. The word-recall scores in all groups were further analyzed in terms of two components of such scores—number of accessible categories, i.e., categories for which at least one word was recalled (Cohen, 1963a, 1963b) and number of words within accessible categories. This analysis yielded two important findings. First, the presentation of category names as retrieval cues affected only the number of accessible categories but not the number of words within accessible categories. Thus, given that the subject could recall at least one word from a category, the number of additional words recalled for that category was the same regardless of whether he remembered the category on his own or was reminded of it by the experimenter. Second, the number of accessible categories was considerably greater for 48-word lists than for 24-word lists, but again the number of words within accessible categories was identical for both list lengths. Similar results have been reported by Cohen (1966). Cohen also found recall of words within accessible categories to be independent of the length of the lists varying from 35 to 70 words, although the total number recalled varied directly with the length.

These findings demonstrate the independence of word-recall within higher-order units from the recall of higher-order units. The proportion of words accessible within higher-order units is not influenced by the number of accessible higher-order units or by the availability of names of higher-order units as retrieval cues. Although these data were gleaned from experiments in which organization of the material was suggested to subjects by the experimenter, there is no reason to believe that the basic processes are different in situations in which individual E-units are organized into higher-order units subjectively. In either case the functional significance of organization lies in its facilitating effect on retrieval— organization makes individual list items more accessible to recall. Whether or not it also affects the amount of mnemonic information available in the storage, and whether or not it helps to conserve storage capacity, must for the time being remain open questions.

Summary

The free-recall paradigm is the descendant of the method of retained members which was widely used in the experimental study of memory around the turn of the century. The early work on free recall yielded a fair amount of evidence on first-order relations between a variety of experimental variables and recall performance, but at the theoretical level it remained quite sterile. As a consequence, the method was overshadowed by other paradigms, notably serial-anticipation and paired-associate learning, and for a while almost disappeared from the scene. In the past decade and a half, prompted by several parallel developments in the field of verbal learning, it has been revived, and it is now gradually evolving as an area of investigation in its own right.

While the more recent work has produced a number of relatively stable facts, and while initial attempts at theoretical analysis of some of the phenomena have been made, research in free recall still seems to lack a firm sense of purpose. This state of affairs is perhaps to be expected in any new area of research, but in the case of free recall it probably also stems from the heterogeneity of orienting attitudes of investigators and from the ambivalence of the logical status of free recall. Is it just another "method" of measuring retention? Is it an alternate proving ground of empirical relations and phenomena established in the context of other paradigms? Or does it constitute a somewhat different and in some sense a unique memory task whose analysis opens up new theoretical vistas and dictates the introduction of new concepts? The orienting attitudes reflected in these questions can all be discerned in the recent literature. Their very existence tends to retard the crystallization of important theoretical issues and to militate against the emergence of unifying focal points of experimental inquiry.

Typical free-recall experiments have little to do with learning of individual items. Rather, they are concerned with retention and recall, or with storage and retrieval, of mnemonic information of the sort that permits later reproduction of desired aspects of earlier experiences. The subject may be said to retain and recall individual list items only insofar as the experimenter adopts as a measure of the subject's performance the number of correct responses; that is, responses corresponding to experimentally designated discrete units of material.

Evidence shows that individual list items are not always processed independently of one another, thus hinting at the discrepancy between nominal and functional units of material, or between E-units and S-units. If biological memory systems, such as that of a human being, have limited capacity for processing information, and if the limitation depends on the number of units of information that can be processed within a given period of time—two fundamental assumptions which for good reasons seem to be widely accepted—it would also seem to be reasonable to assume that the limit of free recall is set by the number of functional units rather than nominal units. Some experimental findings suggest that this is indeed the case. An important theoretical problem in free recall lies in the identification of functional S-units.

The discrepancy between E-units and S-units is most difficult to detect under conditions where the associative relations among individual list items are minimized, where the amount of time available to the subject for thinking about the items is very limited, and where recall of a set of items by a given subject is tested only once. If, under these conditions, frequency of recall is plotted against the position of items in the input list, characteristic serial position effects are found. Evidence shows that different parts of the serial position curve are affected by different independent variables. These findings support the hypothesis that at least two different kinds of underlying process, referred to as primary and secondary memory, are involved in recall. Some theorists have identified primary and secondary memory with separate storage systems. This formulation is contrasted with an alternative view that storage is unitary and that differential recall of items from different serial positions and the differential effects of various independent variables on such recall are to be attributed to different kinds of retrieval mechanism. Whether the two approaches will generate testable hypotheses, and how

these will fare in the laboratory, remains a problem for future research.

The liveliest theoretical activity in the context of free-recall experiments has been focused on organizational processes. Organization as a response variable refers to sequential constraints in output sequences that can be shown to be independent of the order of items in input sequences. Two types of organization may be distinguished. Primary organization is relatively independent of both the associative meaning of input items and the subject's prior familiarity with a given list as a list. Primary organization lies at the root of the recency effect and may also be related to the primacy effect. Secondary organization is largely determined by the pre-experimental and intraexperimental (intertrial) experiences the subject has had with individual input items.

Measures of secondary organization can be divided into two broad classes—clustering and subjective organization. The two classes of measures are predicated on somewhat different assumptions and are not equally applicable in all situations. Clustering can be assessed only for lists consisting of items belonging to specifiable subsets, while measures of subjective organization can be obtained for any set of items that are recalled by subjects more than once. Nevertheless, both types of measures presumably reflect the effects of common underlying processes. In keeping with the tradition of "two-factor" theories of psychology, explanations of clustering—and by implication, of subjective organization—have also postulated two different kinds of mechanism: organization based on direct associative relations among items, and organization based on indirect associations or on mediation through response-produced cues. This conceptual distinction reflects the empirical distinction between associative and category clustering, which in turn is determined by the relations of list items to normative data collected in free and restricted word-association tests.

While the importance of the subject's prior verbal habits in determining what specific list items are organized into which S-units is beyond dispute, attempts to distinguish between mechanisms of secondary clustering on the basis of extra-experimental word-association data seem to be rather pointless. At the stage of our present ignorance as to the mechanisms underlying associative relations between verbal units in any situation, it appears more fruitful to begin with the observation that some items are more likely to be organized into a given higher-order unit than are others, and then to seek the explanation of such organization in intra-experimental conditions, such as the contiguity relations, both in input and output sequences, between potential members of a functional S-unit.

The fact that recall increases systematically over trials in multitrial experiments constitutes a theoretical puzzle of long standing, not only in free recall, but in other paradigms as well. Some writers have suggested that individual list items are processed independently of one another and that repeated presentation or recall, or both, increases the availability of items for subsequent recall. Others have conceptualized trial-to-trial learning in terms of strengthening of traces. And still others have implied that such learning reflects the strengthening of associative bonds between individual items and the general experimental context in which rehearsal occurs. None of these formulations have been stated explicitly enough to make it possible to derive critical testable hypotheses from them. More often than not they simply represent restatement of the fact that trial-

to-trial learning occurs and that it is influenced by those variables that influence them.

A more promising approach consists in the postulation of processes underlying secondary organization as the mechanism of learning. According to this view, the retrieval system can have access to only a limited number of functional S-units in a given output phase, and any increase in the recall of nominal E-units reflects the increase in the size of the accessible S-units as a consequence of secondary organization. Evidence supporting this type of formulation is provided by findings that secondary organization increases over trials and that it shows sizable correlations with the number of recalled E-units. Other evidence contradicts the hypothesis that repeated presentation of items in presence of stable nonverbal contextual stimuli alone is sufficient for the strengthening of traces or general background associations of items or for the enhancement of their availability for recall.

The conceptual distinction between retention and recall, or between storage and retrieval, has only recently been translated into operations that allow for experimental separation of these two stages of remembering as they occur in free recall. The results from a number of studies suggest that the amount of relevant information available in the memory storage and thus potentially usable for reproduction of list items is greater than the amount of information accessible to the retrieval system. Accessibility of relevant information, and hence the amount of recall, depends not only on the contents of the storage, but also on retrieval cues. For a long time, identification of retrieval cues was the Achilles' heel of theoretical formulations of free recall, but now some progress has been made in remedying this weakness. Initial experimental results suggest that the retrieval system operates independently at different levels of organization of the material to be remembered.

In general, at the present time we are nowhere near a cohesive theory of memory which would explain free-recall phenomena in all their complexity. Theoretical speculation about these phenomena is mostly restricted to restatements of known empirical facts. The major concepts of General Behavior Theory have been conspicuously absent in such restatements. It looks as if conceptual analyses of free recall have been developed not just in isolation, but almost in defiance of the traditional S-R models of behavior. Whether this isolation is only semantic, and hence temporary, or whether it represents a substantive and more permanent break with the past is a question which can be answered only by future research.

References

Abbott, E. A., "On the Analysis of the Factor of Recall in the Learning Process," *Psychological Monographs*, **11** (1909), 159–177.

Asch, S. E., "The Process of Free Recall," in C. Scheerer, ed., *Cognition: Theory, Research, Promise.* New York: Harper and Row, 1964, pp. 79–88.

——, and S. M. Ebenholtz, "The Principle of Associative Symmetry," *Proceedings of the American Philosophical Society*, **106** (1962) 135–163.

Battig, W. F., M. Allen, and A. R. Jensen, "Priority of Free Recall of Newly Learned Items," *Journal of Verbal Learning and Verbal Behavior*, **4** (1965), 175–179.

Bolton T. L., "The Growth of Memory in School Children," *American Journal of Psychology*, **4** (1892), 362–380.

Bourne, L. E., and B. K. Parker, "Interitem Relationships, List Structure, and Verbal Learning," *Canadian Journal of Psychology*, **18** (1964), 52–61.

Bousfield, W. A., "The Occurrence of Clustering in the Recall of Randomly Arranged Associates," *Journal of General Psychology*, **49** (1953), 229–240.

——, H. Berkowitz, and G. A. Whitmarsh, "Associative Clustering in the Recall of Minimally Meaningful Geometric Designs," *Canadian Journal of Psychology*, **13** (1959), 281–287.

——, and B. H. Cohen, "The Effects of Reinforcement on the Occurrence of Clustering in the Recall of Randomly Arranged Associates," *Journal of Psychology*, **36** (1953), 67–81.

——, and ——, "The Occurrence of Clustering in the Recall of Randomly Arranged Words of Different Frequencies-of-Usage," *Journal of General Psychology*, **52** (1955), 83–95.

——, and ——, "Clustering in Recall as a Function of the Number of Word-Categories in Stimulus-Word Lists," *Journal of General Psychology*, **54** (1956), 95–106.

——, ——, and J. G. Silva, "The Extension of Marbe's Law to the Recall of Stimulus Words," *American Journal of Psychology*, **69** (1956), 429–433.

——, ——, and G. A. Whitmarsh, "Associative Clustering in the Recall of Words of Different Taxonomic Frequencies of Occurrence," *Psychology Reports*, **4** (1958), 39–44.

——, and C. R. Puff, "Clustering as a Function of Response Dominance," *Journal of Experimental Psychology*, **67** (1964), 76–79.

——, ——, and T. M. Cowan, "The Development of Constancies in Sequential Organization during Repeated Free Recall," *Journal of Verbal Learning and Verbal Behavior*, **3** (1964), 449–459.

——, J. R. Steward, and T. M. Cowan, "The Use of Free Associational Norms for the Prediction of Clustering," *Journal of General Psychology*, **70** (1964), 205–214.

Bowers, H., "Memory and Mental Imagery," *British Journal of Psychology*, **21** (1931), 271–282.

Brown, W., "To What Extent Is Memory Measured by a Single Recall?" *Journal of Experimental Psychology*, **6** (1923), 377–382.

Bruner, J. S., G. A. Miller, and C. Zimmerman, "Discriminative Skill and Discriminative Matching in Perceptual Recognition," *Journal of Experimental Psychology*, **49** (1955) 187–192.

Buseman, A., "Lernen und Behalten: Beiträge zur Psychologie des Gedächtnisses," *Z. angew. Psychol.*, **5** (1911), 211–271.

Bush, R. R., and F. Mosteller, *Stochastic Models for Learning*. New York: John Wiley and Sons, Inc., 1955.

Carterette, E. C., and E. A. Coleman, "Organization in Free Recall." Paper presented at the meeting of the Psychonomic Society, Bryn Mawr, Pa., August, 1963.

Cofer, C. N., "A Study of Clustering in Free Recall Based on Synonyms," *Journal of General Psychology*, **60** (1959), 3–10.

———, "On Some Factors in the Organizational Characteristics of Free Recall," *American Psychology*, **20** (1965), 261–272.

———, "Some Evidence for Coding Processes Derived from Clustering in Free Recall," *Journal of Verbal Learning and Verbal Behavior*, **5** (1966), 188–192.

———, and D. R. Bruce, "Form-Class as the Basis for Clustering in the Recall of Nonassociated Words," *Journal of Verbal Learning and Verbal Behavior*, **4** (1965), 386–389.

———, ———, and G. M. Reicher, "Clustering in Free Recall as a Function of Certain Methodological Variations," *Journal of Experimental Psychology*, **71** (1966), 858–866.

Cohen, B. H., "An Investigation of Recoding in Free Recall," *Journal of Experimental Psychology*, **65** (1963), 368–376.

———, "Recall of Categorized Word Lists," *Journal of Experimental Psychology*, **66** (1963), 227–234.

———, "Some-or-None Characteristics of Coding," *Journal of Verbal Learning and Verbal Behavior*, **5** (1966), 182–187.

———, and W. A. Bousfield, "The Effects of a Dual-Level Stimulus-Word List on the Occurrence of Clustering in Recall," *Journal of General Psychology*, **55** (1956), 51–58.

Dallett, K. M., "Practice Effects in Free and Ordered Recall," *Journal of Experimental Psychology*, **66** (1963), 65–71.

———, "Number of Categories and Category Information in Free Recall," *Journal of Experimental Psychology*, **68** (1964), 1–12.

Deese, J., "Serial Organization in the Recall of Disconnected Items," *Psychology Reports*, **3** (1957), 577–582.

———, "Influence of Interitem Associative Strength upon Immediate Free Recall," *Psychology Reports*, **5** (1959), 305–312. (a)

———, "On the Prediction of Occurrence of Particular Verbal Intrusions in Immediate recall," *Journal of Experimental Psychology*, **58** (1959), 17–22. (b)

———, "Frequency of Usage and Number of Words in Free Recall: The Role of Association," *Psychology Reports*, **7** (1960), 337–344.

———, "From the Isolated Verbal Unit to Connected Discourse," in C. N. Cofer, ed., *Verbal Learning and Verbal Behavior*. New York: McGraw-Hill Book Company, 1961, 11–31.

———, "On the Structure of Associative Meaning," *Psychology Review*, **69** (1962), 161–175.

———, and R. A. Kaufman, "Serial Effects in Recall of Unorganized and Sequentially Organized Verbal Material," *Journal of Experimental Psychology*, **54** (1957), 180–187.

Dronsejko, K., "The Role of Organization in Verbal Learning." Unpublished M. A. thesis, University of Toronto, 1963.

Ebbinghaus, H., *Grundzüge der Psychologie*. Leipzig: Von Veit, 1902.

Ehrlich, S., "Le rôle de la structuration dans l'apprentissage verbal," *Psychologie Française*, **10** (1965), 119–146.

Ekstrand, B., and B. J. Underwood, "Paced versus Unpaced Recall in Free Learning," *Journal of Verbal Learning and Verbal Behavior*, **2** (1963), 288–290.

Estes, W. K., "Learning Theory and the

New 'Mental Chemistry,'" *Psychology Review*, **67** (1960), 207–223.

Garner, W. T., and J. R. Whitman, "Form and Amount of Internal Structure as Factors in Free-Recall Learning of Nonsense Words," *Journal of Verbal Learning and Verbal Behavior*, **4** (1965), 257–266.

Gonzalez, R. C., and C. N. Cofer, "Exploratory Studies of Verbal Context by Means of Clustering in Free Recall," *Journal of Genetic Psychology*, **95** (1959), 293–320.

Glanzer, M., and A. R. Cunitz, "Two Storage Mechanisms in Free Recall," *Journal of Verbal Learning and Verbal Behavior*, **5** (1966), 351–360.

———, and A. Meinzer, "The Effects of Intralist Activity on Free Recall," *Journal of Verbal Learning and Verbal Behavior* (1967).

Green, R. T., and G. Harding, "Sequential Recall of a Mixed List," *British Journal of Psychology*, **53** (1962), 389–396.

Holmes, F.L.D., "Syllabic Length, Recognition and Immediate Recall," *Journal of Applied Psychology*, **18** (1934), 831–841.

James, W., *The Principles of Psychology*. Vol. 1. New York: Holt, Rinehart and Winston, Inc., 1890. Reprinted by Dover Publications, Inc., 1950.

Jenkins, J. J., W. D. Mink, and W. A. Russell, "Associative Clustering as a Function of Verbal Association Strength," *Psychology Reports*, **4** (1958), 127–136.

———, and W. A. Russell, "Associative Clustering during Recall," *Journal of Abnormal and Social Psychology*, **47** (1952), 818–821.

Keppel, G., "Facilitation in Short- and Long-term Retention of Paired Associates Following Distributed Practice in Learning," *Journal of Verbal Learning and Verbal Behavior*, **3** (1964), 91–111.

Kintsch, W., and C. J. Morris, "Application of a Markov Model to Free Recall and Recognition," *Journal of Experimental Psychology*, **69** (1965), 200–206.

Kirkpatrick, E. A., "An Experimental Study of Memory," *Psychology Review*, **1** (1894), 602–609.

Lashley, K. S., "In Search of the Engram," in *Symp. Soc. Exp. Biol.*, No. 4 (1950), pp. 454–482.

Mandler, G., "Organization and Memory," in K. W. Spence and Janet T. Spence, eds., *The Psychology of Learning and Motivation*. New York: Academic Press, 1966. (a)

———, "Verbal Learning," in *New Directions of Psychology*, III. New York: Holt, Rinehart & Winston, Inc., 1966. (b)

Marshall, G. R., and C. N. Cofer, "Associative Indices as Measures of Word Relatedness: A Summary and Comparison of Ten Methods," *Journal of Verbal Learning and Verbal Behavior*, **1** (1963), 408–421.

McGeoch, J. A., "Memory," *Psychology Bulletin*, **27** (1930), 514–563.

———, *The Psychology of Human Learning*. New York: Longmans, Green & Co, Inc., 1942.

———, and A. L. Irion, *The Psychology of Human Learning*. New York: Longmans, Green & Co., Inc., 1952.

McGovern, J. B., "Extinction of Associations in Four Transfer Paradigms," *Psychological Monographs*, Vol. **78**, No. 16 (1964).

McNulty, J. A., "The Measurement of 'Adopted Chunks' in Free-Recall Learning," *Psychonomic Science*, **4** (1966), 71–72.

McQuitty, L. L., "Rank Order Typal Analysis," *Educational Psychology Measurement*, **23** (1963), 55–61.

Mechanic, A., "The Responses Involved in the Rote Learning of Verbal Materials," *Journal of Verbal Learning and Verbal Behavior*, **3** (1964), 30–36.

Melton, A. W., "Implications of Short-term Memory for a General Theory of Memory," *Journal of Verbal Learning and Verbal Behavior*, **2** (1963), 1–21.

Messer, A., *Psychologie*. Stuttgart: Deutsche Verlagsanstalt, 1922.

Meuer, H., "Experimentelle Beiträge zur Lehre vom Wortgedächtnis nach der Methode der Polyeidoskopie," *Arch. ges. Psychol.*, **47** (1924), 14–44.

Meumann, E., *The Psychology of Learning*, trans. J. W. Baird. New York: Appleton-Century, 1913.

Meyer, D. R., and R. C. Miles, "Intralist-Interlist Relations in Verbal Learning," *Journal of Experimental Psychology*, **45** (1953), 109–115.

Michel, O., "Experimentelle Untersuchungen über das Gedächtnis. Reproduktion und Wiedererkennen von optischen Eindrucken," *Arch. ges. Psychol.*, **44** (1923), 244–271.

Miller, G. A., "Human Memory and the Storage of Information," *IRE Transactions on Information Theory*, **2** (1956), 129–137.

———, "The Magical Number Seven Plus or Minus Two: Some Limits on Our Capacity for Processing Information," *Psychology Review*, **63** (1956), 81–96.

———, J. S. Bruner, and L. Postman, "Familiarity of Letter Sequences and Tachistoscopic Indentification," *Journal of General Psychology*, **50** (1954), 129–139.

———, E. Galanter, and K. H. Pribram, *Plans and the Structure of Behavior.* New York: Holt, Rinehert & Winston, Inc., 1960.

———, and W. J. McGill, "A Statistical Description of Verbal Learning," *Psychometrika*, **17** (1952), 369–396.

———, and J. A. Selfridge, "Verbal Context and the Recall of Meaningful Material," *American Journal of Psychology*, **63** (1950), 176–185.

Murdock, B. B., Jr., "The Immediate Retention of Unrelated Words," *Journal of Experimental Psychology*, **60** (1960), 222–234.

———, "The Serial Position Effect in Free Recall," *Journal of Experimental Psychology*, **64** (1962), 482–488.

———, and A. J. Babick, "The Effect of Repetition on the Retention of Individual Words," *American Journal of Psychology*, **74** (1961), 596–601.

Nicolai, F., "Experimentelle Untersuchungen über das Haften von Gesichtseindrucken und dessen zeitlichen Verlauf," *Arch. ges. Psychol.*, **42** (1922), 132–149.

Pohlmann, A., "Experimentelle Beiträge zur Lehre von Gedächtnis." Berlin: Göttinger Diss., 1906.

Postman, L., "Short-term Memory and Incidental Learning," in A. W. Melton ed., *Categories of Human Learning.* New York: Academic Press, 1964, 145–201.

———, P. A. Adams, and A. M. Bohm, "Studies in Incidental Learning: V. Recall for Order and Associative Clustering," *Journal of Experimental Psychology*, (1956), 334–342.

———, ———, and L. W. Phillips, "Studies in Incidental Learning: II. The Effects of Association Value and of the Method of Testing," *Journal of Experimental Psychology*, **49** (1955), 1–10.

———, J. P. Egan, J. Davis, "Rate of Recall as a Measure of Learning: I. The Effects of Retroactive Inhibition," *Journal of Experimental Psychology*, **38** (1948), 535–546.

———, and W. O. Jenkins, "An Experimental Analysis of Set in Rote Learning: The Interaction of Learning Instruction and Retention Performance," *Journal of Experimental Psychology*, **38** (1948), 683–689.

———, and L. W. Phillips, "Short-term Temporal Changes in Free Recall," *Quarterly Journal of Experimental Psychology*, **17** (1965), 132–138.

Raffel, G., "The Effect of Recall on Forgetting," *Journal of Experimental Psychology*, **17** (1934), 828–838.

———, "Two Determinants of the Effect of Primacy," *American Journal of Psychology*, **48** (1936), 654–657.

Robinson, E. S., and M. A. Brown, "Effect of Serial Position upon Memorization," *American Journal of Psychology*, **37** (1926), 538–552.

Rothkopf, E. Z., and E. H. Coke, "The Prediction of Free Recall from Word Association Measures," *Journal of Experimental Psychology*, **62** (1961), 433–438.

Rozov, A. I., "Formation and Dynamics of Topic Clusters in Free Recall," *Soviet Psychology and Psychiatry*, **2** (1964), 19–26 (transl. from *Voprosy Psikhologii*, 1961).

Russell, W. A., and J. J. Jenkins, "The Complete Minnesota Norms for Responses to 100 Words from the Kent-

Rosanoff Word Association Test," *Technical Report No. 11, Contract N8-ONR-66216,* Office of Naval Research and University of Minnesota.

Seibel, R., "Organization in Human Learning: The Study Sheet Paradigm and Experiments One and Two," paper presented at the meeting of the Psychonomic Society, Chicago, Oct., 1965.

Smith, T. L., "On Muscular Memory," *American Journal of Psychology,* **7** (1896), 453–490.

Smith, W. G., "The Place of Repetition in Memory," *Psychology Review,* **3** (1896), 21–31.

Sperling, G., "A Model for Visual Memory Tasks," *Human Factors,* (1963), 519–531.

Stevens, S. S., "Mathematics, Measurement and Psychophysics," in S. S. Stevens ed., *Handbook of Experimental Psychology.* New York: John Wiley & Sons, Inc., 1951, pp. 1–49.

Tulving, E., "Subjective Organization in Free Recall of 'Unrelated' Words," *Psychology Review,* **69** (1962), 344–354.

———, "Intratrial and Intertrial Retention: Notes towards a Theory of Free Recall Verbal Learning," *Psychology Review,* **71** (1964), 219–237.

———, "The Effect of Order of Presentation on Learning of 'Unrelated' Words," *Psychonomic Science,* **3** (1965), 337–338.

———, "Subjective Organization and Effects of Repetition in Multi-Trial Free-Recall Learning," *Journal of Verbal Learning and Verbal Behavior,* **5** (1966), 193–197

———, "The Effects of Presentation and Recall of Material in Free-Recall Learning, "*Journal of Verbal Learning and Verbal Behavior,* **6** (1967), 175–184.

———, and J. E. Patkau, "Concurrent Effects of Contextual Constraint and Word Frequency on Immediate Recall and Learning of Verbal Material," *Canadian Journal of Psychology,* **16** (1962), 83–95.

———, and Z. Pearlstone, "Availability versus Accessibility of Information in Memory for Words," *Journal of Verbal Learning and Verbal Behavior,* **5** (1966), 381–391

———, and G. B. Thornton, "Interaction between Proaction and Retroaction in Short-term Retention," *Canadian Journal of Psychology,* **13** (1959), 255–265.

Underwood, B. J., "The Representativeness of Rote Verbal Learning," in A. W. Melton ed., *Categories of Human Learning.* New York: Academic Press, 1964, 47–87.

———, and R. W. Schulz, *Meaningfulness and Verbal Learning.* Chicago: J. B. Lippincott Co., 1960.

———, ———, W. R. Runquist, "Response Learning in Paired-Associate Lists as a Function of Intralist Similarity," *Journal of Experimental Psychology,* **58** (1959), 70–78.

Waugh, N. C., "Free versus Serial Recall," *Journal of Experimental Psychology,* **62** (1961), 496–502.

———, "The Effect of Intralist Repetition on Free Recall," *Journal of Verbal Learning and Verbal Behavior,* **1** (1962), 95–99.

———, and D. A. Norman, "Primary Memory," *Psychology Review,* **72** (1965), 89–104.

———, and J. E. K. Smith, "A Stochastic Model for Free Recall," *Psychometrika,* **27** (1962), 141–154.

Wechsler, D., "Engrams, Memory Storage, and Mnemonic Coding," *American Psychologist,* **18** (1963), 149–153.

Welch, G. B. and C. T. Burnett, "Is Primacy a Factor in Association Formation?" *American Journal of Psychology,* **35** (1924), 396–401.

Wicklund, D. A., D. S. Palermo, and J. J. Jenkins, "Associative Clustering in the Recall of Children as a Function of Verbal Association Strength," *Journal of Experimental Child Psychology,* **2** (1965), 58–66.

Woodworth, R. S., *Experimental Psychology.* New York: Holt, Rinehart & Winston, Inc., 1938.

Associative Structure and Verbal Behavior

2

HOWARD R. POLLIO

For the past thirty years or so, the concept of structure has occupied a position somewhat beyond the pale of psychological respectability. Part of the reason for this attitude relates to structure's early flirtation with Mind, Introspection, and the like, a flirtation that brought little satisfaction and much subsequent grief. After a vigorous and youthful Behaviorism exorcised Mind from the psychological scene, structure seemed to have little future, and few respectable psychologists would have anything to do with her. Currently, in a style appropriate to a determined lady of literature (Cleland, 1749), the concept of structure has been able to rise above her past and to demonstrate once more her usefulness to psychology in general and to verbal behavior in particular. Unfortunately, however, snide remarks still persist. The lady has not entirely lived down her past.

In what regard does psychology currently hold the concept of structure? Probably the best way for a proper associationist to answer this question is to ask a group of psychologists for their associates to the stimulus phrase *PSYCHOLOGICAL STRUCTURE*. This procedure has the joint advantage of restricting his verbose colleagues to

short responses and of demonstrating fidelity to the methods of word-association.

Table 1 presents a categorized listing of responses produced by seven members of the Department of Psychology at the University of Tennessee who were asked to give ten associates to the stimulus phrase *PSYCHOLOGICAL STRUCTURE*. The interests of these men cover many different areas of psychology and may be considered as representative of psychologists in general.

The first remarkable thing about these norms is their lack of agreement. Out of a total of 70 different possible responses, the data show 58 different associates, with 6 others being given twice each. Qualitative examination indicates that these responses can be grouped into a number of subcategories. These are presented in the table where each grouping has been assigned a descriptive phrase. A few random comments about these clusters seem inevitable. Cluster I includes responses which interpret the stimulus in a nonpsychological sense, one response demonstrating laudable fidelity to a professional organization and another to the University of California. Cluster II seems appropriate enough, but

Table 1

TENTATIVE CATEGORIZATION OF ASSOCIATIVE
RESPONSES TO THE STIMULUS PHRASE:
PSYCHOLOGICAL STRUCTURE *

Cluster I *" Very free associates "*

APA—2
building
house
Tolman Hall

Cluster II *General terms*

Psychology
stimulus
theory—2
concept
predict
analysis
basic
behavior
interaction
neuron

Cluster III *Descriptive adjectives*

" poetry "
wrong-way
pretentions
irrelevant
crap

Cluster IV *Rationale for*
history
structuralist
inside
reality
affect
mind
idea
"cognitive"
figure-ground
autochthonous
configuration
form
depth
contour

organization
habit family hierarchy
habits
hierarchy
learned
memory trace
reflex

Clusters V *Areas of Use and Misuse*

personality—2
id
traits
development
linguistics
verbal
words

Cluster VI *Properties of :*

relationships—2
psychological space
construct
hypothesis
multidimensional—2
dimensions
attributes
scaling
measurement

Cluster VII *Tenants of :*

Deese
associative strength
Osgood
semantic differential
Pollio—2
associates

Cluster VIII *Inexplicable*

man
one

*The number following each word denotes the number of times a given response was produced.

Cluster III begins with "poetry" and ends on "crap." Cluster IV reiterates in part the opening paragraph of the present discussion, while Cluster V presents some contemporary usages.

Clusters VI and VII include much of the vocabulary to be used in this chapter, and VIII inexplicably extends to the cosmos.

What these responses demonstrate

clearly is that there is little consistency in contemporary usages of the term "structure," although there is some agreement on certain areas in which "structure" is met. These areas relate to human Ss, where these Ss bring fully developed and complexly patterned response tendencies to the observational situation. We will attempt to show that such response tendencies provide precisely the requisite materials for a structural analysis.

The Structure of Structure

A very general statement of the concept of structure defines it as a relatively enduring abstract system of relationships found to exist among a number of identifiable elements. Although some structural theories such as the one proposed by Hebb (1949) have a potentially denotable referent, a structural hypothesis need not have any explicit or implicit physical locus. Psychological structure can be, and often is, a purely hypothetical arrangement inferred on the basis of prior behavioral observations. Such is the case with most models of cognitive functioning (e.g., Peak, 1958; Osgood and Tannenbaum, 1955; etc.) where the elements of the theoretical structure are abstractions derived from specified assessment procedures. The utility (or lack of it) of these structures depends not on their potential denotability but on their ability to summarize pre-existing data and to predict hitherto unobserved phenomena.

Conceptually, psychological structure is inferred from overt behavior by explicit sets of operationally meaningful assumptions about the particular structural arrangement and the observed specific relationship between structure and behavior. One such fairly frequent assumption is that the probability of two unitary behavioral events occurring together (given the stimulation of one of these events) is an inverse monotonic function of their structural distance (Peak, 1958; Shepard, 1962). Thus, when S in the course of learning a code substitution task incorrectly intrudes the letter B as a response for the letter A, such substitution defines and provides a measure of the structural proximity between these responses.

Given such an approach to associative structure, a number of considerations need to be explicitly explored:

1. What are the most empirically useful units for dealing with the phenomenon of verbal behavior?
2. What are the procedures by which relationships among such units may be determined?
3. What kinds of relationships emerge from this assessment?
4. What are the operational principles relating structure to behavior? What kinds of behavioral effects are to be expected in accordance with the system of relations established?

Given these orienting considerations, the search for associative structure appropriately begins with a search for its constituient units, elements, or parts.

Units of associative structure

Although the problem of defining what is meant by a unit of behavior has been with psychology at least as long as psychological data have been gathered, most workers take an extremely pragmatic approach. The unit chosen is defined most often in terms of the apparatus employed or more generally in terms of the procedures followed in the investigation. When, however, the purpose of an investigation is to examine behavior in a setting that may be considered as naturalistic (and this must be the case with such aspects of verbal behavior as the production of speech), the investigator must consider his choice among possible units most carefully.

Two recent articles have treated the problems involved in selecting a unit for the description of how speech is generated and understood. Osgood, for example, has argued that such a unit must be the largest meaningful segment of language that is highly redundant, frequent in occurrence, and of relatively short duration (Osgood, 1963a, p. 744). Johnson (1965a) cites a number of essentially similar criteria and summarizes as follows: "The behavior psychologists have defined as response units seems to maintain a certain internal integrity and interdependence among response elements." For the analysis of speech, he calls attention to the probability that different units may be required for different speech functions. Although suggesting that "language might be encoded in units larger than the morpheme or the word," he does indicate that the development and organization of the vocabulary pool pose significant psychological problems.

In both these analyses, the sought-after unit is conceptualized in terms of its function in the articulation and comprehension of speech. However, speech alone does not exhaust the domain of verbal behavior, let alone the more extensive domain of symbolic activity. Whole sets of problems, e.g., the free flight of ideas, the nature of thinking (both creative and prosaic), the formation of concepts, etc., pose questions for symbolic behavior at least as significant as those set by language. The list of symbolic activities provided by Langer (1951) in her *Philosophy in a New Key* indicates the possible breadth of such a larger domain.

One unit that seems to some degree at least to appear in all aspects of verbal behavior is the word. In discourse, slight pauses in speech often signify the boundaries of words, while spaces usually occur between words in the orthography of a language. Traditional linguists found it convenient to define verbal response classes on the basis of their occurrence in probabilistic relation to other words (Fries, 1952). Correlated with this latter type of analysis, Maclay and Osgood (1959) have found that different types of hesitation phenomena (i.e., False Start vs. Repeats) are more likely to occur following "Lexical" as opposed to "Function" word classes. Goldman-Eisler (1958a; 1958b) similarly has been able to show that discontinuities in the flow of speech most often occur at the boundary of a word and that these pauses are correlated with the predictability of the next word within the sequence. When words are randomly deleted from positions within smoothly flowing discourse, they are quickly guessed by other speakers making a judgment as to the missing word.

In laboratory studies using verbal materials, the word has a number of practical advantages that are not shared by such more rigorously defined units as the morpheme or phoneme. For one, words are easily and understandably utilized by naive subjects in an experimental situation. No specific training is required to insure that Ss will be able to discriminate the boundaries of a word and subsequently utilize it as a response in an experimental situation. Similarly, words, considered as responses, are easily and reliably discriminated by relatively untrained observers. Perhaps the major practical advantage of considering words as a basic unit of verbal behavior is that much is known about their quantitative and qualitative properties. Sources exist which provide the investigator with normative estimates of word frequency (Thorndike-Lorge, 1944); word-association characteristics (Kent and Rosanoff, 1910; Russell and Jenkins, 1954); semantic differential ratings (Jenkins, Russell, and Suci, 1958); a combination of these three (Gerow and Pollio, 1965); as well as many other significant properties (e.g., Noble, 1952; Underwood and Schulz, 1960, etc.).

The original papers by Cofer and Foley (1942) and their associates (Foley and Cofer, 1943; Foley and MacMillan, 1943; Foley and Mathews, 1943) as well as the more recent work of the Staats' (Staats and Staats, 1957, 1959, 1962) indicate the significant role played by the word as an element in thinking. Similarly, Mednick (1962) has demonstrated, both conceptually and empirically, that individuals judged to be highly creative in their particular vocation are extremely facile in combining originally disparate words into meaningful groupings on the basis of associates common to the constituent words. Verplanck and Krueger (1964, 1965) have also shown that a simple variation of the standard word association procedure may be quite effectively utilized as an assessment instrument in evaluating students' performances in an academic course in place of the standard multiple-choice or other usual testing procedures. Underwood and his group (e.g., Underwood, 1952; Underwood and Richardson, 1956) have studied concept formation using word-association data.

From theoretical, empirical, and practical vantage points, the word presents a serviceable unit for the analysis of a wide variety of verbal and symbolic behaviors. If we so accept the word as an important component of such behavior, the problem is then to determine the ways in which words may be related to one another. This is the second step in a structural analysis.

The assessment of associative structure

The nature of associative structure depends upon the methods used to evaluate it. Characteristically, two different assessment procedures have been used: one employs some variety of the classical word-association procedure, and the second, some variety of rating scale exemplified best by the Semantic Differential. Both methods assume that semantic structure can be demonstrated, even though the hypothetical processes giving rise to an associative response or to a specific semantic placement differ considerably.

INTERVERBAL RELATIONS. For the word-association approach, the evocation of a particular associative response is taken to reflect a pre-established habit or link between the stimulus and response word(s). The fact that every word evokes a recurring associative response hierarchy and that associative reaction time (RT) is inverse to hierarchy order (Thumb and Marbe, 1901) further strengthens this assumption. One class of causal variables commonly used to describe the conditions under which such habits are formed has to do with frequency; both the frequency of occurrence of the units themselves and the frequency with which units have been paired. Thus, Underwood and Schulz (1960) develop the empirical postulate of a "spew principle" whereby associative responses are emitted in order of their frequency of occurrence. Support for this assumption is found in the word-association literature (Howes, 1957; Johnson, 1958) where a strong correlation is found between hierarchy order and word frequency. Frequency shares in determining how large the associative hierarchy will be; e.g., Noble's m is found to correlate with unit frequency. Osgood and Anderson (1957) similarly have demonstrated that frequency of co-occurrence significantly affects the composition of an associative response hierarchy.

Important in all of these analyses is the implicit or explicit assumption that a particular associative response reflects a single-step habit or link between two words; no additional principles are required to explain how one word evokes another. In this discussion such a connection will be called an *interverbal relation*.

Psychological analyses of associative structure have distinguished among a number of different types of interverbal relations. In the recent history of this problem, Noble (1952) was concerned exclusively with the number of associates given in response to a particular stimulus word. Given the proposition that words evoke stable response hierarchies, more recent analyses have been concerned with assessing the degree of overlap in specific responses among the hierarchies of a number of different stimulus words. Once the problem is stated in this way, it is no longer appropriate to talk of stimulus and response words in the usual sense; every word functions jointly as a "stimulus" for any other word connected to it and as a "response" for any word to which it is connected. Deese (1959a; 1959b) was among the first to point this out and was the first to suggest that the number of interconnections common to a group of words should be a significant factor affecting such verbal behavior as free recall. Deese (1962; 1964) and others (Rothkoff and Coke, 1961; Pollio, 1963b) have since gone on to demonstrate empirically the fertility of this initial observation.

Once the realization is made that it is fruitful to conceptualize associative structure in terms of networks of words, a subsequent problem is to devise metrics yielding quantitative indices of such structural concepts as interitem associative strength (IIAS), associative similarity, and the like. The first of these problems has been handled by making explicit or implicit use of matrices. Deese (1962), for example, sets up an $n \times n$ matrix in which the same words considered as row headings serve as stimuli and considered as column headings serve as responses. The entry in any cell is the proportion of time a column word is evoked as an associate of the row word; diagonal entries are assumed to be unity. A slight variation of this procedure simply denotes each associative relation, regardless of relative magnitude, by a unit entry (e.g., Rothkoff and Coke, 1961; Pollio, 1963b). As we will see, certain advantages accrue to this simpler assumption. Interitem associative strength, which gives an indication of the number of words that produce each other as associates, is defined either as the sum of the matrix or more generally, as the sum divided by the size of the matrix.

The possibility of assessing the degree of similarity among two or more words follows directly from this type of matrix analysis. If we consider each row as a response vector, the degree of similarity between two words is given by some measure of the overlap in vector elements. Thus, Garskof and Houston (1963) view the degree of similarity between two words as the ordered vector product of two words, where each vector is defined as above. Other mathematically simpler metrics have been proposed (Deese, 1962; Marshall and Cofer, 1963; etc.); all assume that two words are similar to the degree that they share common response elements.

Almost all of the metrics developed to assess interverbal relations have been concerned only with a one-step link or habit between two words. An examination of word-association data makes it quite clear that two words may be interrelated by their common connection with a third word. In the simplest case, let us assume word A produces word B as an associate; B produces C as an associate, and C produces D as an associate. It is then possible to consider that A has a two-step connection with C and a three-step connection with D. The series of studies concerned with mediation processes carried out in the Minnesota Laboratories (see Jenkins, 1963; 1965 for a partial review) and in its subsequent Diaspora (e.g., Horton and Kjeldergaard, 1961) provide an empirical basis for multistep associative connections.

Given the finding that such connections have significant empirical consequences, any account of interverbal associative structure that considers only single step connections must necessarily provide a somewhat inadequate metric. In an attempt to quantify such interconnections, Pollio (1964) raised associative matrices of the 1–0 variety (i.e., where one indicates the presence of an associative connection and zero the absence of any connection) to their nth power (the rank of the initial matrix) in order to assess multistep associative pathways. The specific matrices used were constructed from the associative pattern present in six different sets of 22 words each. Two metrics found to be of particular value were the power at which the IIAS value derived from this analysis reached asymptote and the particular asymptotic level reached. For example, one of these six sets contained 22 associates evoked by the word MUSIC, while a second set contained 22 associates evoked by WHIS-TLE. The number of one-step connec-

tions present in the $MUSIC$ set is 82, while the comparable figure for the $WHISTLE$ set is 56. The asymptotic number of potential interconnections for $MUSIC$ is 274, and for $WHISTLE$, 262. The MUSIC set reaches this level in four steps, while the $WHISTLE$ set takes ten steps.

The growth of IIAS over successive powers denotes the rate at which potential interword pathways or connections are being established among members of the original set. Since all possible interconnections must by definition be attained by the nth power, the power at which asymptote is reached indicates how rapidly the words of a given set are capable of "recruiting" associative connections among their constituent words. Thus, the MUSIC set may be considered as a collection of words having a great many single-step connections whose rate of associative recruitment is extremely rapid, while the WHISTLE set may be considered as having relatively fewer single-step connections, and a considerably slower rate of associative recruitment. Both sets, however, reach roughly comparable asymptotic levels.

Still another type of interverbal structure involves word sets in which the constituent words have a clearly sequential pattern, such as $FRESH$-MAN, $SOPHOMORE$, $JUNIOR$, $SENIOR$; ONE, TWO, $THREE$, $FOUR$, $FIVE$; etc. The properties of such sequential word collections were first described by DeSoto (DeSoto, 1959; DeSoto and Bosley, 1962) who termed them serial structures. To determine how serial orders are reflected in verbal behavior, DeSoto made use of such sets in various verbal learning tasks. Perhaps the most frequent of these techniques employed the members of the serial structure as either stimulus or response terms in a paired-associates task, in which a number of different responses or stimuli were paired with the same term (DeSoto and Bosley, 1962; Pollio and Deitchman, 1964; Pollio and Draper, 1966; Ebenholtz, 1966). Regardless of the serial structure used, the results were extremely similar: measures of learning yielded the usual bowed curve when plotted against serial position of the word in its sequence. This was true despite the fact that words were never presented in other than random order; the only "seriality" present in the experiment was in S's structure incorporating the words themselves. This was true whether long-established or newly learned serial orders were used.

DIMENSIONAL RELATIONS. A second way in which meaningful words may be related is in terms of their location on some dimension(s). Although precisely what in psychology is implied by the use of the term dimension is often unstated, what is clear is that a dimension is inferrable only on the basis of discriminative responding in a circumscribed assessment situation. It is possible to infer the existence of a dimension if S responds differentially to a class of stimuli where these stimuli may be arranged in some conceptually meaningful order. Once a dimension is exhibited in this way, it can be represented by an ordered metric such as a line in the unidimensional case, or by a space in the multidimensional case. After selecting a metric, however, a more important problem is to determine the nature and number of dimensions required to locate the elements of a given domain. From here, it is necessary to explicate the psychological process by which stimuli are positioned on the dimension(s) selected.

In verbal behavior, operations used to define relevant dimensions have developed from a rating-scale procedure known as the semantic differential. The question of how many and what kinds of scales are needed to define a space of sufficient breadth to encompass the words of a language has been undertaken empirically by Osgood and his collaborators (Osgood and Suci, 1952; Osgood, Suci and Tannenbaum, 1957; Osgood, 1963). They demonstrated that a heterogeneous group of polar adjective rating scales tend to be segregated into three stable major groupings and into a number of highly variable minor groupings. Subsequent work has demonstrated that these groupings are relatively invariant both over changing subject and language populations.

The psychological process serving to locate words in this tri-dimensional space is based on a theoretical rationale derived from the fractional mediation hypothesis described initially by Hull (1930) and subsequently developed by Osgood (1953). In verbal behavior, this view assumes that stimulus words serve to evoke implicit fractional components of the response associated with the physical or linguistic environment in which the word was initially encountered. These responses are indexed by the semantic differential; their qualitative characteristics serving to select relevant dimensions (and direction on these dimensions); their quantitative properties, the degree of polarization on these dimensions.

In the preceding discussions a distinction has been drawn between interverbal and dimensional relations. Bousfield (1961) and others (Johnson, Miller, and Wall, 1965) have attempted to consider the process of semantic differentiation as a special class of highly circumscribed word-associations. A given semantic placement is taken, not to reflect the operation of implicit mediational responses, but rather to indicate that contained within the associative response hierarchy evoked by the stimulus word is the polar adjective used to define the semantic scale. Actual empirical analysis (Johnson, Miller, and Wall, 1965) does indeed show that the more extreme the location of a word on a semantic differential scale, the more likely it is that one of the polar adjectives defining that dimension will be included in its associative response hierarchy. Semantic placement reflects associative strengths, not mediational response evocation. Judging by the tenor of remarks made at a previous conference on verbal behavior (Cofer, 1961, pp. 106–109), a preference for this more parsimonious hypothesis was clearly in evidence.

In responding to this confrontation, Osgood (1961) cited the phenomena of *semantic satiation* (Lambert and Jakobavitz, 1961) and *semantic generalization* as primary evidence for the existence of an independent nonverbal mediation response. He argues that no single verbal event is capable of accounting for these phenomena. Perhaps the best single line of evidence supporting Osgood's contention that nonverbal mediators are capable of affecting verbal behavior appears in the series of studies conducted by Staats and Staats and their associates (Staats and Staats, 1957, 1958, 1959; Staats, 1961; etc.). In these studies, *S*s are presented with a nonsense syllable which is paired, once each, with a series of meaningful English words. At the conclusion of these paired presentations, *S*s are required to rate the originally neutral nonsense syllable on the evaluative dimension of the semantic differential. The results show that syllables so conditioned come to produce the evaluative rating of the words paired with them.

This evidence can be interpreted in terms of word-associations as suggested by Bousfield for the process of semantic differentiation. Here the argument runs something as follows: Each of the meaningful words used as a UCS word may be thought to evoke an implicit associative response hierarchy. Undoubtedly, there is some overlap in associates among these words, with the word *GOOD* (or some variation thereof) being the most likely common associate largely because UCS words were chosen on the basis of their evaluative "goodness." Under these conditions, the argument runs, "*GOOD*" would be the response most strongly conditioned to the syllable and consequently would serve to bring about a good evaluative rating.

To evaluate this interpretation of the Staats and Staats' conditioned meaning experiment, it is necessary to select meaningful words with known response hierarchies, and thereby control for their pattern of interitem associative structure. Pollio (1963a) reports a study in which the UCS words were selected so as to produce an equal number of "good" and "bad" associates, by using words in the "good" list such as *SMOOTH, BEAUTIFUL*, etc., and words such as *ROUGH, UGLY*, etc. in the "bad" list. Both lists had a great many obvious cross-list associates. On the assumption that fractional mediation is a significant determiner of word-association, *S*s were asked after the conditioning procedure, not to rate the nonsense syllable, but to produce an associate to it, thereby providing a direct test of the assumption that *S*s learn the UCS words as responses. The results showed that the evaluative semantic differential ratings of the associates produced were similar to those of their paired UCS group, whether or not the associate given was contained originally in the UCS group or was an extra-UCS group response.

Although the preceding study decreases the plausibility of a word-association interpretation of semantic conditioning and rating, it fails to demonstrate that conditioned affective responses are indexed by the semantic differential technique. Pertinent to this point, Staats, Staats, and Crawford (1962) demonstrated a concommittant variation of the GSR to an aversively conditioned stimulus with the semantic rating of that stimulus, as well as a moderate correlation between the magnitude of the GSR and the degree of polarization of the obtained semantic rating. Such data seem to provide evidence for an implicit fractional response not accountable on the basis of word association responses.

A tentative hypothesis about associative structure

The preceding discussion indicates that any word evokes at least two different classes of events: word-associations and conditioned meaning responses. Associations serve to relate a particular word to a network of other words, while conditioned meaning responses serve to locate it in some position in semantic space. Considered as stimuli, the members of an associative response hierarchy must also evoke both word-association and conditioned meaning responses. As Deese (1962, 1964) and others (e.g. Pollio, 1963b) have demonstrated, the associates to these associates tend to overlap with other words contained in the hierarchy aroused by the same initial word. The conditioned meaning responses evoked by other words of the hierarchy must also be similar, and this too has been found to be the case for associates evoked in both child and adult populations (Staats and Staats, 1959; Pollio, 1964b; DiVesta, 1965). For individual Ss, associatively linked words occurring in extended samples of speech are separated by smaller semantic distances than is true for nonlinked words (Johnson, Miller, and Wall, 1965).

On the basis of this and other evidence, Pollio (1962, 1965) has argued that verbal clusters of the type so usefully described by Bousfield (Bousfield and Sedgewick, 1944; Bousfield, 1953) are composed of words that are both highly interconnected in terms of word-association measures and share highly similar semantic locations. On the assumption that shared interverbal and dimensional structure are related to the speed of overt association, response bursts occurring during the course of continuous word-association (such as were described initially by Bousfield and Sedgewick, 1944) should be composed of words that are more highly connected in terms of associative overlap measures and more highly similar in terms of SD ratings, than should be true for words produced more slowly. This prediction has been verified empirically (Pollio, 1964a).

If clusters of this sort represent a significant aspect of verbal organization, it should be possible to demonstrate their role in such processes as free recall. To this end, Pollio and Kasschau (1965) presented Ss with 22 words contained in the associative hierarchies evoked by the words *MUSIC* and *COMMAND*. These word sets have known semantic and interverbal characteristics. For one group of Ss these words were presented for a single exposure, for a second group the words were presented for three exposures, while for a third group, for five exposures. The specific order of presentation was randomly determined for each S in the one presentation group, as well as randomized over successive exposures for Ss in the three- and five-exposure groups. After viewing these words for the predesignated number of exposures, Ss were asked to record their free recall on a tape recorder. The temporal characteristics of individual recall were determined from these recordings.

The first result of interest was that almost all *S*s showed variations in their rates of recall. For *S*s in the five-exposure group, the number of alternations between high and low rates for individual *S*s was correlated with the number of different items appearing in free recall by correlations of .77 ($N = 10$) for the *MUSIC* list and of .78 ($N = 15$) for the *COMMAND* list. Correlations for the one- and three-exposure groups were positive but considerably smaller in magnitude.

Specific examination of words contained in rapidly produced recall sequences indicated a tendency to show overlapping associative connections and similar semantic ratings. Differences between fast and slow recall sequences in terms of both dimensional proximity and associative overlap were significant for bursts produced during the recall of the *MUSIC* list, although only differences in associative overlap reached an acceptable level of significance for the *COMMAND* list.

The implication of these results is that both dimensional and interverbal relations affect the composition of associative clusters, with response bursting denoting the momentary limits of such clusters. In terms of recall it is possible to argue that where structured materials are involved, the structure facilitates recall. On the basis of available evidence, the effectiveness of such structures seems to be facilitated by repeated presentation, with recall not so much a matter of establishing new bonds among words but rather of strengthening the associative structure of the list itself. Such strengthening seems to take more than a single exposure to develop sufficiently to be exhibited in recall. Parenthetically, it should be noted that when nonstructured materials are used (Tulving, 1962), *S*s still show organization of the list. In this case, organization is provided by the sequential characteristics of initial list presentation and recitation.

From Structure to Behavior

The description of a particular psychological structure is valuable only to the degree that predictions are possible relating that structure to behavior. For dimensional relations, predictions must specify the effect dimensional location has on verbal behavior. For interverbal relations, predictions must specify how associative connections affect verbal behavior. In both cases, predictions can be made only on the basis of principles that relate structure to behavior.

Dimensional principles

Psychological dimensions represent an act of creation by an investigator attempting to provide an abstract representational system for his observations. Dimensions are, in principle, no different from other concepts except that they provide a continuous ordering for behavioral events rather than a simple categorization. In the case of semantic dimensions almost all predictive principles depend upon an empirical or theoretical understanding of the response dispositions associated with a particular dimensional location. For dimensions based on the semantic differential technique, prediction from structure to behavior must be predicated on the reactive properties of the mediational response associated with a particular location in that space.

Although such an approach seems obvious, only Carroll (1959, 1964) has attempted to state the behavioral consequences of a given semantic placement. Thus, he has argued that the *evaluative dimension* may represent the evocation of either approach or avoidance tendencies, the *activity dimension* the necessity or nonnecessity of making movements, and the *potency dimension* the amount of effort required in completing these movements. These conceptual principles make possible an unambigious prediction of the types of responses that may be associated with given semantic placements.

Although any or all the major semantic dimensions described by Osgood may be taken as a starting point in relating semantic location to overt verbal behavior, most experimental effort has been expended on the evaluative dimension. This is largely the result of historical factors, the most notable of these being the so-called "judgmental theory of emotion" (McGeoch and Irion, 1952) and the Freudian concept of repression of the unpleasant. The basic hypothesis involved in these studies is similar to that proposed by Carroll; it assumes that a pleasant placement reflects implicit approach tendencies, while an unpleasant placement reflects avoidance tendencies. From such an assumption, it is reasonable to predict that associative responses that are either pleasant or evoked by pleasant stimuli will be produced with shorter associative RT's than associative responses that are unpleasant or are evoked by unpleasant stimuli. In the earliest study concerned with this hypothesis, Tolman and Johnson (1918) demonstrated that the associative reaction latency to a pleasant stimulus was shorter than to an unpleasant stimulus. Subsequent studies (White and Powell, 1936; Pollio and Lore, 1965), employing a wide variety of control conditions for stimulus frequency, length, etc., have found essentially similar results.

The most analytic and perhaps the most direct test of the hypothesis that implicit approach and avoidance tendencies are associated with the evalua-

tive location of a word is provided by Solars (1960) who demonstrated a differential reaction time for responses to pleasant and unpleasant stimulus words. His results showed that "compatible" word-movement responses (pleasant words—toward; unpleasant words—away) were initiated with significantly shorter latencies than "incompatible" word-movement responses. Probably more than any other, these data indicate the approach-avoidance nature of the mediational response associated with a pleasant or unpleasant evaluative location.

All of the preceding studies have been concerned with the reactive properties associated with locations on the evaluative dimension of the semantic differential. Stimuli also vary along dimensions not necessarily derived from the semantic differential. Two studies (Buss, 1961; Geer and Buss, 1962) involved an attempt to determine whether or not generalization would occur along the dimension of "aggression." In one experiment, two different groups of Ss were required to learn either to whisper or to shout their response to stimulus words differing in their location on such a dimension. The result of particular interest for the present discussion was that regardless of the conditions of training, Ss tended to shout very aggressive words and to whisper mildly aggressive words. Further work by Geer and Buss (1962) essentially substantiated this conclusion, even when a nonverbal reaction, such as pulling on the handle of an automobile brake, was employed as the indicator response.

What all of these studies suggest is that dimensional location (whether operationalized through the semantic differential or some other measurement procedure) predicts the characteristics of overt responding. An evaluatively pleasant location can be construed as indicating a potential for approach responses, while an aggressively located stimulus implies a potential for vigorous responding.

MULTIPLE INPUT. It is a truism that stimuli always occur in some context, and this is particularily true for verbal material. In terms of dimensional properties, contextual elements can be conceptualized as providing input to a number of different dimensional locations. Predictions to behavior must be made on the basis of principles that deal with the interaction of multiple inputs in semantic space. The basic conceptual notions involved all deal in one way or another with the dimensional distance between temporally contiguous or near-contiguous inputs.

Peak (1958) has noted that the magnitude of the distance between two events may have different effects on behavior. In terms of perceptual and judgmental tasks, small distances generally give rise to assimilation effects; that is, the evoked reaction has properties characteristic of a response associated with a position intermediate to both input events. Large distances characteristically give rise to contrast effects; that is, the evoked response represents an exaggeration of the response to one or both of the input events. Unfortunately, the dimensions along which verbal materials are related are nowhere near as fine-grained as those involved in perceptual or judgmental tasks. Consequently, multiple inputs have been considered as providing input either to the "same" or to a "different" location. Considerations of magnitude, other than these crude extremes, cannot be assessed reliably.

When successive inputs are to the same location, they have been termed "*congruent*"; when they are to disparate locations, they are termed "*incongruent*." Two different classes of predictions to behavior have been made on the basis of congruent and incongruent inputs: one deals with the location of the response evoked by the compound; the second deals with the speed with which the response is evoked. Since Osgood and his associates (Osgood and Tannenbaum, 1955; Osgood, Suci, and Tannenbaum, 1957) have been most concerned with the role of congruence and incongruence in determining the dimensional location of the evoked response, it is appropriate to examine this work first.

Their basic assumption can be stated quite simply: "When two events are simultaneously elicited, each exerts a modifying effect on the other in proportion to its degree of polarization and in the direction of the other's position of perfect congruence (Osgood, Suci, and Tannenbaum, 1957; p. 277)." Expressed in terms of deviations from the neutral origin, the polarization of the compound, d_{12}, is described in terms of the deviation of word 1, d_1, and the deviation of word 2, d_2, by the following expression:

$$d_{12} = \frac{d_1}{|d_1| + |d_2|} d_1 + \frac{d_2}{|d_1| + |d_2|} d_2$$

In terms of the data cited by Osgood, the available results support the general prediction (i.e., the location of the response to the compound is intermediate between those of the constituent words) although imprecise quantification makes it impossible to evaluate the model unequivocally. In a general way, the congruity principle does hold true for verbal combinations.

For Osgood's analysis, adverbs represent an anomolous word class in that although they are capable of modifying the location of adjectives and nouns, they themselves have relatively neutral semantic locations. Their function is to polarize the location of other word classes. In three different analyses, (Mosier, 1941; Cliff, 1959; Howe, 1963) the ability of adverbs to modify the position of stimulus words on an evaluative dimension has been demonstrated. In the Cliff study the combinatorial rule by which adverbs served to polarize the location of adjectives was multiplicative, i.e., the polarization of a given combination could be predicted as the product of the numbers associated with each of the words. The results involving adverbs should be taken as a limitation on the general hypothesis proposed by Osgood, although adjective-noun, and noun-noun pairings have been shown to follow the principles of congruent combination.

A second aspect of overt behavior potentially predictable from the location of a word on the evaluative dimension is the speed with which an associative response may be produced. In terms of the hypothesis proposed earlier (words judged as evaluatively pleasant induce fractional approach tendencies while words judged as evaluatively unpleasant induce fractional avoidance tendencies), a context composed of unpleasant words preceding an unpleasant target word should serve to augment the strength of avoidance tendencies aroused by the target word and consequently to increase associative RT. Further, this delay should increase over more extended prior contexts. In the case of pleasant words in pleasant contexts, decreases in associative RT's are expected over increasingly lengthy contexts. If in this case the zero-context condition represents a lower limit for RT, the only prediction possible is that associative RT's to pleasant target words embedded in pleasant contexts will show no increase.

These predictions have been put to empirical test by Pollio and Lore (1965) who found that associative RT's to pleasant stimulus words were significantly faster than to unpleasant

stimulus words at all context lengths and that only the associative RT for unpleasant stimuli increased over increases in context. Their results further indicated that the mean semantic distance between a pleasant target word and its associative responses was significantly smaller than comparable distances evaluated from the associates to unpleasant target words. This result was taken to mean that *S*s, in responding appropriately to the fractional avoidance responses evoked by unpleasant stimuli, produced associates evoking weaker avoidance responses, hence tended to give more evaluatively neutral responses. This analysis seems to explain why in normative data the average semantic distances between unpleasant stimuli and their associated response words is larger than comparable distances calculated from responses to evaluatively pleasant stimuli (Pollio, 1964b).

Another possible situation involves multiple inputs in evaluatively incongruent contexts. In terms of a mediational analysis, unpleasant contexts should serve to increase RT to a pleasant stimulus word, and pleasant contexts should serve to decrease RT to an unpleasant stimulus. These effects should increase as the length of the prior context increases. The results of a study by Pollio and Gerow (1966) are presented in Figure 1, where complete confirmation for these suppositions is provided. As can be seen, associative RT's for pleasant stimuli embedded in unpleasant contexts increase, while those produced in response to unpleasant stimuli in pleasant contexts decrease. The data for two groups of *S*s who responded to congruent context-stimulus word combinations are presented for purposes of comparison. As can be seen, the RT's evoked by incongruent combinations fit snugly between those evoked by congruent

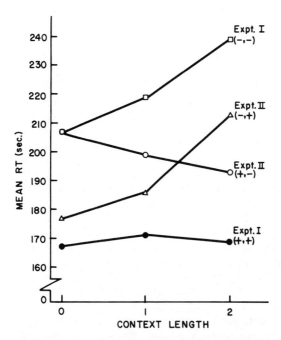

Figure 1. The effect of congruent and incongruent contexts on associative RT (From Pollio and Gerow, 1966)

Note: The first symbol (+ or —) in any pair refers to the evaluative characteristics of the context while the second symbol refers to the evaluative characteristics of the target word.

combinations, exactly as required by the mediation response hypothesis.

Almost all of the available studies concerned with the role of dimensional location in verbal behavior have made use of stimuli positioned on the evaluative dimension. In principle there is no reason why these investigations should not and could not be extended to the potency and activity dimensions as well. While an RT measure might be expected to show differences as a consequence of location on the activity dimension, Buss's results seem to suggest that the amplitude of an indicator response might well provide a better dependent variable for other dimensions such as potency. In any

event, meaningful predictions do seem possible on an *a priori* basis.

Interverbal principles

While predictions from dimensional location to overt behavior are strongly dependent on theoretical principles, predictions for the interverbal case are relatively atheoretical in nature. As Gough and Jenkins (1963) have noted, verbal associations do not provide a unitary theory. Predictions of behavior depend strongly on individual experimenter bias, although almost all employ the empirical axiom that words given as associative responses function as habits. For this group of investigators, predictions are made informally on the basis of *E*'s sometimes idiosyncratic expectation as to how a given pattern or magnitude of interconnections may be expected to affect such behaviors as free recall or serial and paired associates learning. Nowhere is the operation of a general theory in evidence.

PATTERN AS AN INTERVERBAL PRINCIPLE. The role of interverbal pattern in verbal behavior has been most ingeniously handled by DeSoto (DeSoto and Bosley, 1962) who has been concerned primarily with serially ordered word sets such as 1, 2, 3, 4, and 5; *FRESHMAN, SOPHOMORE, JUNIOR, SENIOR;* etc. The value of using serial structures such as these is that their relational properties may be assumed to be similar to the properties of a list of items learned through a rote learning procedure and accordingly may be expected to show many of the empirical phenomena that characterize the learning and recall of lists serially ordered in presentation.

In the first experiment on this topic, DeSoto and Bosley (1962) had their *S*s learn a series of many-into-one paired associates involving 16 monosyllabic men's names as stimuli and the four words: *FRESHMAN, SOPHOMORE, JUNIOR,* and *SENIOR* as the response terms. What this means is that each of four different names had the same response term paired with it. The specific pairs were randomized on each trial (so that no serial order was present in the learning task *per se*) until *S*s were able to anticipate the correct response for all 16 pairs. An examination of the number of trials taken to learn each of the response terms showed that it required 13.3 trials to learn pairs involving *FRESHMAN*, 17.5 trials to learn *SOPHOMORE*, 16.4 trials to learn *JUNIOR*, and 14.6 trials to learn *SENIOR*. In other words, the usual relationship of ease of learning to serial

position appeared *despite* the fact that no serial order was present except for the definitional serial structure inherent in the words.

In an attempt to extend the generality of these results and to relate the data more specifically to classical rote learning, Pollio and Draper (1966) report two studies involving three different nonsense syllables as stimulus terms and the serial structure 1, 2, 3, 4, and 5 as responses. In terms of the number of trials taken to learn each of these five items as responses Experiment I showed that 10.2, 13.4, 14.0, 14.7, and 13.4 trials were required to learn pairs involving the responses 1, 2, 3, 4, and 5, respectively; while comparable values for Experiment II were 13.7, 15.9, 18.9, 16.6, and 15.4. All differences between the rate of learning pairs involving each of these response terms were significant at considerably beyond the .01 level in exhibiting the usual serial position effect.

Since in both the DeSoto and Bosley (1962) and Pollio and Draper (1966) experiments an already established serial order was used, we have tried to duplicate these results where *S*s actually learn a new serial structure in the laboratory. In a preliminary study already completed, in which 24 *S*s were required first to learn a serial order of four nonsense syllables to the criterion of five overlearning trials, and then to use these syllables as response terms in a De Soto paired-associates procedure, we have failed to find any of the serial effects associated with the learning of longstanding serial structures. In this experiment, *S*s were asked to "say in serial order as fast as they could" the serial order of the four nonsense syllables both at the conclusion of the serial learning portion of the experiment and at the conclusion of paired-associates learning. The results indicated that over all 24 Ss the mean response time for producing the serial order after rote learning was 5.0 seconds, while after paired-associates learning the value was 31.0 seconds. Only 8 of 24 Ss were able to produce their correct serial order after paired-associates learning. Of all 24 Ss run, only one was able to produce a shorter post- than pre-paired-associates latency for recalling the serial order. An examination of this S's data showed the effects reported earlier as characterizing paired-associates learning of the DeSoto type. For most Ss, retroactive interference seems to have eliminated it.

In the experimental procedure described above, Ss were required to use the newly learned serial order as responses in a paired-associates task. Ebenholtz (1966), whose research has been concerned with the role of perceptual factors in serial learning, has been able to demonstrate that when nonsense syllables, previously learned in a new serial order, served as stimuli in a paired-associates task comparable to the one used by DeSoto, the usual relationship of ease of learning to serial position is found. Perhaps under these conditions dissolution of the newly learned serial order does not take place as Ss do not have to produce newly learned items but only to recognize them. As is well known, item production is considerably more difficult then item recognition.

There is one type of serial order that is of particular importance to an analysis of associative structure; one in which the termini of the series are high probability, opposite word associates. Sets such as *BEAUTIFUL, PRETTY, FAIR, HOMELY, UGLY; COLD, COOL, MILD, WARM, HOT* exemplify serial orders with end items having such properties. The usual assumption applied to word-association data is that words which produce each other as high probability associates occupy proximal locations in some conceptual measurement space.

If a serial structure of items such as the *COLD-HOT* set mentioned above produces effects similar to other serial structures, it would be possible to infer that the opposite-meaning, but associatively related, end items are semantically the most distant member of the set. Under this condition, logically opposite word-associates must be considered as comprising a special class of associates not exhibiting the usual semantic congruity between stimulus and response words. If, on the other hand, serial structures of this type produce unique learning and error characteristics, then some doubt would be cast on the validity of rating procedures such as the semantic differential which operate on the assumption that logical opposites define the most distant points of a meaningful semantic dimension.

In an attempt to answer these questions, Pollio and Deitchman (1964) had 15 female Ss learn the words *BEAUTIFUL, PRETTY, FAIR, HOMELY*, and *UGLY* as response terms in the DeSoto paradigm. The results showed that Ss took 8.9 trials to learn pairs involving *BEAUTIFUL* as the response term; 15.0 for *PRETTY;* 16.1 for *FAIR;* 15.8 for *HOMELY;* and 13.1 for *UGLY*. Thus, the usual serial position effect was found to apply for these response terms.

In what probably should be regarded as an extremely fortunate accident, Pollio and Deitchman (1964) also had three groups of subjects run through the DeSoto procedure when the *HOT-COLD* set was used. The experiment fortuitously was run at three separate times throughout the year. The first run took place entirely in the winter quarter (January-March), the second run during the spring quarter (March-

June), and the third run during the summar quarter. All *S*s were run in a comfortable laboratory room (heated in winter; air-conditioned in the late spring and summer), and all were exposed to the same procedure involving the five *COLD-HOT* words mentioned above and 15 moderately high-association value nonsense syllables as stimuli.

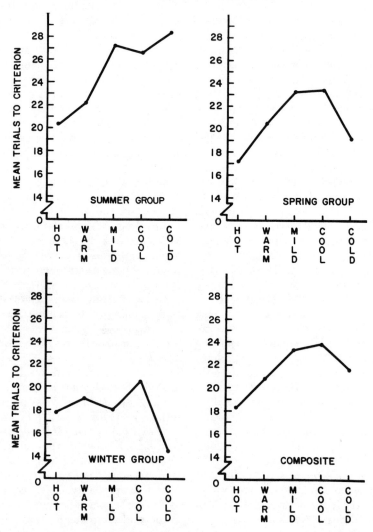

Figure 2. Serial position effects for the 3 testing periods (From Pollio and Deitchman, 1964)

Figure 2 shows the number of trials taken to reach criterion for each of the five response words for the three different groups; as well as a composite graph involving the data for all *S*s. The overall trend presented in the composite graph is consistent with all previous findings and exhibits the usual position effects characteristic of serial structures. Of the separate results for each of the three seasons, only the spring group yielded the expected relationship of ease of learning to serial position. The winter group showed a very strong anchor at $COLD$, while the summer group showed its strongest anchor at HOT. These data provide us with an extremely good demonstration of the sensitivity of this procedure to gross changes in input to particular points on the structure as a function of extra-experimental events and clearly reveal the effects of such input on the operational characteristics of relevant items in associative structure.

Another way in which associative pattern may be related to overt verbal behavior depends upon the matrix analysis of associative structure described by Pollio (1964c). As may be recalled, the pattern of associative interconnection in any given word set is described by three different values: the initial degree of interconnection (i.e., the number of single-step connections), the total number of interconnections over all powers, and the power at which asymptote is reached. Table 2

Table 2

MATRIX CHARACTERISTICS OF 5 DIFFERENT WORD SETS *

Set	IIAS	Steps to Asymptote	Terminal IIAS Value
SLOW	54	6	273
BUTTERFLY	67	7	307
CHAIR	67	7	277
MUSIC	82	4	274
WHISTLE	56	10	262
COMMAND	45	8	263

*Data from Pollio, 1964c.

presents these values for five different word sets; each set containing the associates evoked by the word appearing in the first column. Thus far, only one study has been completed based on these indices. In that study, four groups of 38 Ss each were asked for the free recall of words contained in either the $MUSIC$ or $WHISTLE$ set. For 19 of the 38 Ss in the $MUSIC$ Group the words were presented at a 0.7 interword rate while the remaining Ss had these words presented at a 3.0-second rate. A similar split was made for Ss in the $WHISTLE$ Group. Since the $MUSIC$ set reaches its limiting value in a very few steps (i.e., by the 4th power), the expectation was that presentation rate would have little effect on the number of words recalled from this set. On the other hand, recall of the $WHISTLE$ set, which requires ten steps to reach its asymptotic value, should be facilitated significantly by an increase in presentation rate. The results conform exactly to these expectations and are presented in Figure 3. An analysis of variance applied to these data showed a significant presentation rate effect $[F(1,148) = 25.82; \ p < .001]$ and a significant interaction of presentation rate by word set, $[F(1,148) = 5.65; \ p < .025]$. From partial data such as these it is reasonable to conclude that at least one of the values derived from a matrix analysis of associative interconnections does have predictable empirical consequences for verbal behavior.

MULTIPLE INPUT. For interverbal relations, multiple inputs may arise from one of two sources: (*a*) from associative connections in a series of items serving as prior context for a target word, and (*b*) from interitem associative connections present in a set of words. Although it seems obvious that an associatively related context will have a profound effect on the associate evoked by a particular stimulus word, few empirical studies have been concerned specifically with this problem.

(*a*) Context Effects: The earliest

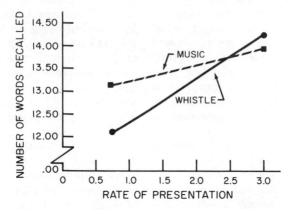

Figure 3. Mean number of words recalled for the *MUSIC* and *WHISTLE* sets as a function of presentation rate, (Pollio, 1964c)

study concerned with examining the effect of multiple input on word-association was done by Howes and Osgood (1954), who varied three aspects of prior context: (1) the number of items interposed between a critical context word and the stimulus word; (2) the density of critical context words; and (3) the frequency of occurrence of critical context words. Results showed that the effect of context on subsequent associative behavior was a decreasing function of the number of interposed words; an increasing function of the density of context items; and an increasing function of the frequency of the context element. These data may be taken to imply that when a number of different words supply input to a particular set of associative responses, the probability of occurrence of an item from that set is increased.

In an attempt to examine the conditions under which multiple inputs (i.e., contexts) facilitate and interfere with the magnitude and clustering characteristics of free recall, Gonzalez and Cofer (1959) made use of adjective-noun pairs. Some of these pairs were composed of clustering adjectives and clustering nouns in which the clustering tendencies of the adjectives and nouns were similar. Under these conditions, facilitation appeared in both the number of items appearing in recall and in the tendency of these items to cluster. When pairs were set up in which the clustering tendencies of the adjectives were in conflict with the clustering tendencies of the noun, both recall and clustering were depressed. A further result indicated that when unmodified nouns which characteristically yielded clustering effects were modified by appropriately chosen adjectives, the noun-members of these pairs became extremely specific and failed to show their usual clustering effects.

In both of these studies it is possible to argue that when multiple inputs serve to evoke the same response dispositions (in the Howes and Osgood case, an associate from a particular set; in the Gonzalez and Cofer case, a tendency to cluster), an increase in these dispositions occurs. When multiple inputs arouse different dispositions, a decrease in one or the other results. There are other cases, however, in which single items are members of two different classes of responses; e.g., words such as *POUND, SOCK, TRIP,* etc., which have both hostile and non-hostile connotations. With those items, context should serve to clarify the response class appropriate to the situation.

In an attempt to examine the role of prior context in interpreting words of this type, Pollio, Wilcox, and Sundland (1966) had six groups of 50 Ss each produce associative responses to a set of 12 hostilely ambiguous words, where these stimuli were preceded either by 1, 2, or 3 word contexts. For half of these groups the context items were clearly identifiable as hostile words, while for the remaining three groups, nonhostile, neutral context items were used. The results showed almost no overlap in the distribution of responses produced by these stimuli; hostile contexts served to augment the number of hostile responses, while neutral contexts depressed the number of such responses relative to a normative baseline. These results are in agreement with those described earlier and tend to reveal that context renders stimuli unambiguous by selectively providing input to one of the associative clusters potentially evocable by the ambiguous stimuli.

All of these studies deal with the role of multiple input on verbal behavior *per se.* It is appropriate to note that perceptual recognition thresholds have been found to vary as a function of the relevance of the associative or grammatical context preceding the to-be-recognized word (O'Neill, 1954; Cofer and Shepp, 1957; Rouse and Verinis, 1962; Tulving and Gold, 1963). In the last of these experiments, Ss were provided with different length sentence fragments (consisting of from 0–8 items, e.g., "Three people were killed in a terrible highway") which were either relevant to the to-be-recognized word ("Collision") or irrelevant to it ("Inflation"). The results were as expected; detection thresholds decreased over more lengthy relevant contexts and increased over more lengthy irrelevant contexts.

The results of these investigations give rise to an obvious yet powerful empirical generalization: where stimulus events provide multiple input to the same interverbal structure, both the speed and probability of occurrence of an item within that structure are facilitated; where such input is to different interverbal structures, the speed of evocation and the probability of occurrence of an item from one or the other of these structures are decreased.

(*b*) Interitem associative strength (IIAS): The principle that seems to describe the operation of associatively interconnected word sets provides further confirmation for the empirical generalization just described. For example, where IIAS is high, recall is extremely good; where IIAS is low, recall is at a proportionally lower level. This is true for total lists (Deese, 1959a; Pollio and Christy, 1964), for individual words within a list (Rothkoff and Coke, 1961), and even for particular intrusions in recall (Deese, 1959b).

The free-recall task provides an "uncomplicated" test of how IIAS operates in verbal behavior. In serial learning, on the other hand, it is not enough for the learner to have items available on a free recall basis; the task requires that these items be emitted in a specific order. Given the fact that serial learning has both a response availability and a response placement phase, IIAS should have mutually compensatory facilitative and interfering consequences for serial learning: (1) it should make responses more available on the basis of the multiple input mechanism described; and (2) it should, on the basis of the associative structure of the items interfere with the arbitrary serial order required by the task. If this analysis is correct, then IIAS level should have minimal effects on the speed of serial learning. This conclusion is supported by experimental evidence (Postman, 1963; Pollio and Cave, 1965) where no differences have been found in the rate of learning serial lists of high and low IIAS levels. In terms of the second property of the present analysis, Weingartner (1963) has been able to show that if the to-be-learned serial order is in agreement with the associative structure of items in the series, serial learning proceeds considerably more rapidly than if the arbitrary serial order is in conflict with associative structure.

These results indicate that the greater the number of interconnections in a particular word set the more likely it is that items from that set will be available to *S*. Wh n no constraints are imposed on *S*'s performance, such availability is maximum, with decreases in availability occurring as a function of the degree of agreement between the nature of the associative structure present, and of the requirements of the task.

The problem of response habituation

One special class of multiple input in both the dimensional and interverbal case concerns repeated evocation of an individual word. In terms of the logic of the semantic differential, such evocation serves to habituate the correlated mediational response and thereby to decrease the polarity of the semantic rating obtained. In terms of interverbal relations, such repeated evocation should serve to disrupt the usual associative response(s) to the target word and lead to the evocation of uncommon associates.

In both the dimensional and interverbal case, initial results conformed quite well to these expectations. Thus, Lambert and Jakobovitz (1960) found that words that had been repeatedly pronounced showed a marked loss of polarization in their semantic differential ratings i.e., they revealed "semantic satiation." Further confirming evidence was provided shortly thereafter when these same authors (Jakobovitz and Lambert, 1962) showed that the speed with which a number was used in an addition task depended on whether or not it had been repeatedly evoked prior to the addition task. In the interverbal case, Smith and Raygor (1956) were able to demonstrate an increased tendency to produce more uncommon (i.e., low commonality) associates following repeated viewing of a target word than under standard word-association conditions.

Further evidence, however, in both the dimensional and interverbal case, indicates that a general principle of response habituation is not to be found quite so easily. Early indications that simple repetition did not affect all words equally was provided by Wertheimer and Gillis (1958), and even Jakobovitz and Lambert (1961) failed to find clear-cut satiation effects for coordinate bilinguals. Their results showed that under a cross-language repetition condition (i.e., where *S* repeatedly says *MAISON* aloud for 15 seconds and then rates the word *HOUSE*) there was a significant tendency for the word rated to increase its degree of polarization; or, as they put it, "to exhibit a 'generation' of meaning." Although the reasons for this generative effect were not clear, Yelen and Schulz (1963) were able to pinpoint particular semantic scales that showed satiation effects and other scales that showed generation effects. Their results, involving four different studies, containing from 30–60 *S*s in each, failed to yield either generation or satiation effects convincingly. Whatever effects were obtained seemed to be highly dependent on the specific scales examined.

The effects of repeated evocation on word association behavior have also failed to stand up under further experimentation. Fillenbaum (1963) had *S*s repeatedly speak or write a given target word, a highly related synonym, or a completely unrelated word for either 4, 30, 60, or 180 seconds and then asked *S*s for an associate to that word. Under a fifth condition *S*s were required to repeat the target word aloud until a "loss of meaning occurred" and then to produce an associate. The surprising result was that under all conditions repetition of synonyms served to produce a more uncommon response than repetition of the word itself. Under the 4-second and 180-second conditions, repetition of the word served to produce a more common associate than if an unrelated word had been repeated. Only under the 30-second and repetition-until-loss-of-meaning conditions did associative responses become more uncommon after self-repetition.

In a follow-up to the Fillenbaum study, Gumenik and Spencer (1965) had *S*s repeatedly write either the target word, a high-related synonym, a low-related synonym, or an unrelated word, before asking for associates to the target word. Results showed that repetition of the low-related synonym produced the most uncommon associative response, while repetitions of the high-related synonym and of the target word produced the most common responses. They interpreted their results as indicating "repetition of a synonym . . . sets *S* to respond to the test word in terms of the meaning which the synonym shares with the test word" and therefore serves to produce uncommon associates.

The analysis offered by Gumenik and Spencer provides an avenue of approach toward explaining why the repetition of a close synonym produces a more common response than the repetition of either a far synonym or of an unrelated word. These three conditions (repeat close synonym—associate target; repeat distant synonym—associate target; and repeat unrelated word—associate target) all provide a condition of multiple input different from the one used to produce satiation effects (i.e., repeat target—associate target). Since associative responses are profoundly affected by the context within which they are embedded, it is not surprising to find that repetition of anything but the target word itself serves to produce uncommon associates. Far from being an appropriate base line against which to evaluate the effects of repeated evocation, these operations only serve to becloud the effects of repeated evocation. The appropriate control condition is the one used by Smith and Raygor; namely, nonrepetition vs. many repetitions. The conditions used by Fillenbaum and by Gumenik and Spencer actually deal with a different problem and are not directly relevant for the topic of semantic satiation *per se*. With respect to inververbal relations then, the initial intepretations still seem valid; repeated evocation results in a loss of meaning and in consequent uncommon associates.

The contradictions involved in the case of dimensional relations do not lend themselves to so easy an explanation. It is possible to argue, however, that semantic satiation does occur (as indexed by a decrease in polarization) although only for specific scales. In the Yelen and Schulz studies, two of the three dimensions (Good-Bad, Beautiful-Ugly) yielding satiation effects are clearly Evaluative Dimensions while the third (Active-Passive) loads most highly on the Activity Factor. Two of the three scales (Large-Small, Wide-

Narrow) yielding "generation" effects (i.e., an increase in polarization after 15 seconds of repetition) were potency scales while the third generation scale (Fast-Slow) was found to have factor loadings of .35 and .25 on the Activity and Potency Factors respectively. The particular words repeated had greater initial polarization on the satiation scales than on the generation scales, a condition that led Yelen and Schulz to hypothesize that satiation effects might be due to statistical regression. In this regard, it is also possible to argue that more polarized ratings denote more vigorous evocation of the representational response and consequently lead to faster habituation. At present, which alternative is correct is unknown.

Theoretically it is also possible to argue that the response properties associated with certain dimensions are more easily evocable than response properties associated with other dimensions. It would seem likely that responses associated with either positive or negative evaluation would be more easily aroused (and satiated?) than those associated with the Potency Dimension. If such is the case, 15 seconds might be sufficient time to satiate an Evaluative placement while seeming only to arouse more vigorously the "sluggish" response associated with a Potency placement. The study that is obviously required by these considerations has not as yet been done, although the results seem obvious enough: With a sufficiently short repetition period, so-called satiation scales may be expected to show generation; while with a sufficiently long repetition period, so-called generation scales may be expected to show satiation.

In all, these experiments show that repeated input can alter the probability of occurrence of one or another of the responses characteristically evoked by a word. A few repetitions may serve to prime the response evoked. In the dimensional case, a "generation of meaning" may be expected while in the interverbal case, a few repetitions of the stimulus word (Fillenbaum's 4-second repetition case) may augment the occurrence of the most common associates. If repetition is continued over a more extended time period, some dimensional locations become less polarized (Lambert and Jakobovitz, 1960) and the usual interverbal connections deteriorate (Smith and Raygor, 1956). More complicated effects occur as a consequence of systematic variations in the relationship of the word repeated to the word rated, as well as in terms of the particular dimension evoked. The most useful generalization that can be gleaned from these studies is that in making predictions from structure to behavior, the preceding reactive state of the structural element under consideration is a critical factor. The obvious is often overlooked.

Reprise: Verbal Behavior and Associative Structure

If associative structure presents a particularly apt approach to the problems of verbal behavior, it is because verbal behavior seems itself to demand such an approach. The phenomena of language, of speech, of thinking, of association, and of concept formation are all highly organized behavior; and organization is the *sine qua non* for a structural analysis. As we have noted, the first steps in such an analysis deal with the search for a usable structural unit. Although a number of different disciplines eagerly provide a variety of verbal *tessera*, the most appropriate one (from a number of practical and empirical viewpoints) seems to be the word.

Once we identify the word as a unit of interest, the next step is to discover the kinds of relationships that exist among words. In the case of verbal behavior, relations based on word association and semantic rating procedures have proven of prime experimental interest and importance. Relations based on these procedures have been termed interverbal and dimensional relations, respectively.

Predictions from structure to behavior are made on the basis of a series of empirical or theoretical statements that attempt to describe what will happen given the presentation of a certain word. In this final section, an attempt will be made to provide a tentative set of the more useful and well established of these relationships between structure and behavior. In the paragraphs that follow, each statement will be phrased in the form of a general proposition. Since the empirical data on which these propositions are based have already been presented, no attempt will be made to review them at this time.

Dimensional principles

1. Evaluative semantic dimensions reflect the operation of approach and avoidance response tendencies. Stimuli located at one or the other extreme may be expected to affect behavior on the basis of these tendencies.
2. Congruent dimensional input serves to augment the response tendencies associated with a given placement.
3. Incongruent dimensional input serves to produce a response having properties associated with a location somewhere between the incongruent inputs. The resulting location is predictable on the basis of the following equation:

$$d_{12} = \frac{d_1}{|d_1| + |d_2|} d_1 + \frac{d_2}{|d_1| + |d_2|} d_2$$

4. Continued input to the same dimensional location serves to decrease the strength of the response potential associated with that location.

Interverbal principles

1. Word-associations reflect the operation of a previously learned connection or habit between two words.
2. When stimulus words provide multiple input to the same interverbal structure, both the speed and probability of occurrence of that structure (or components thereof) are facilitated:

(*a*) In the case of two context stimuli (*A* and *B*) having an associative connection with a third or target stimulus (*C*), Peak (1958) has suggested that the probability of occurrence of *C* may be described by the following equation:

$$P_{(c)} = 1 - (P_{\overline{ca}} \cdot P_{\overline{cb}})$$

where $P_{\overline{ca}}$ is "the probability that A alone will not evoke *C* and $P_{\overline{cb}}$ is the probability that *B* alone will not evoke *C*."

(*b*) In the case of associatively connected word sets, the greater the number of interconnections across a particular set of words, the more probable it is that these words will appear in free recall.
3. When stimulus words provide multiple input to different interverbal structures, the speed of evocation and probability of occurrence of one or both of these structures (or components thereof) are decreased.
4 Continued evocation of the same stimulus word brings about a deterioration of the usual associative connections involving that word.

In both the dimensional and interverbal case, the initial propositions describe theoretical mechanisms whereby a structural representation is related to behavior. Both hypothesize specific response dispositions. The second and third propositions in both cases describe the effects of congruent and incongruent multiple inputs, while the fourth propositions concern the reactive state of the stimulated organism.

Although all of these propositions have been stated in the declarative mode, they should be evaluated for what they are: tentative generalizations about extremely complicated behaviors. Only future research can guarantee them any degree of greater certainty.

References

Bousfield, W. A., "The Occurrence of Clustering in the Recall of Randomly Arranged Associates," *Journal of General Psychology*, **49** (1953), 229–240.

———, "The Problem of Meaning in Verbal Learning," in C. N. Cofer, ed., *Verbal Learning and Verbal Behavior*. New York: McGraw-Hill Book Company, 1961.

———, B. H. Cohen, and G. A. Whitmarsh, "Verbal Generalization: A Theoretical Rationale and an Experimental Technique," *Technical Report: Contract Nonr—631*, 1958.

———, and C. H. W. Sedgewick, "An Analysis of the Sequences of Restricted Associative Responses," *Journal of General Psychology*, **30** (1944), 149–165.

———, C. H. W. Sedgewick, and B. H. Cohen, "Certain Temporal Characteristics of the Recall of Verbal Associates," *American Journal of Psychology*, **57** (1954), 111–118.

Buss, A. H., "Stimulus Generalization and Aggressive Verbal Stimuli," *Journal of Experimental Psychology*, **61** (1961), 469–473.

Carroll, J. B., "Review of *The Measurement of Meaning*," in *Language*, **39** (1959), 58–77.

———, *Language and Thought*. Englewood Cliffs, N. J.: Prentice-Hall, Inc., 1964.

Cleland, J., *Fanny Hill*. London: Privately printed; 1749.

Cliff, N., "Adverbs as Multipliers," *Psychological Review*, **66** (1959), 27–44.

Cofer, C. N., ed., *Verbal Learning and Verbal Behavior*. New York: McGraw-Hill Book Company, 1961.

———, and J. P. Foley, "Mediated Generalization and the Interpretation of Verbal Behavior: I. Prolegomena," *Psychological Review*, **49** (1942), 513–540.

———, and B. E. Shepp, "Verbal Context and Perceptual Recognition Time," *Perception and Motor Skills*, **7** (1957), 215–218.

Deese, J., "The Influence of Interitem Associative Strength upon Immediate Free Recall," *Psychological Reports*, **5** (1959), 305–312.

———, "On the Prediction of Occurrence of Particular Verbal Intrusions in Immediate Recall," *Journal of Experimental Psychology*, **58** (1959), 17–22.

———, "On the Structure of Associative Meaning," *Psychological Review*, **69** (1962), 131–175.

———, "The Associative Structure of Some Common English Adjectives," *Journal of Verbal Learning and Verbal Behavior*, **3** (1964), 347–357.

DeSoto, C. B., "Learning a Social Structure," *Journal of Abnormal and Social Psychology*, **60** (1959), 417–421.

———, and J. J. Bosley, "The Cognitive Structure of a Social Structure," *Journal of Abnormal and Social Psychology*, **64** (1962), 303–307.

DiVesta, F. J., "Semantic Differential Ratings of 200 Concepts," *Technical Report No. 11, Research Grant No. HD-00872*, National Institute of Child Health and Human Development, 1965.

Ebenholtz, S. M. "The Serial Position Effect of Ordered Stimulus Dimensions in Paired Associate Learning," *Journal of Experimental Psychology*, **71** (1966), 132–137.

Fillenbaum, S., "Verbal Satiation and Change in Meaning of Related Items," *Journal of Verbal Learning and Verbal Behavior*, **2** (1963), 263, 271.

Foley, J. P., and C. N. Cofer, "Mediated Generalization and the Interpretation of Verbal Behavior: II. Experimental Study of Certain Homophone and Synonym Gradients," *Journal of Experimental Psychology*, **32** (1943), 169–175.

————, and Z. L. MacMillan, "Mediated Generalization and the Interpretation of Verbal Behavior: V. Free Association as Related to Differences in Professional Training," *Journal of Experimental Psychology*, **33** (1943), 299–310.

————, and M. Mathews, "Mediated Generalization and the Interpretation of Verbal Behavior: IV. Experimental Study of the Development of Interlinguistic Synonym Gradients," *Journal of Experimental Psychology*, **33** (1943), 188–200.

Fries, C. C., *The Structure of English.* New York: Harcourt, Brace and World, Inc., 1952.

Garskof, B. E., and J. P. Houston, "Measurement of Verbal Relatedness: An Idiographic Approach," *Psychology Review*, **70** (1963), 277–288.

Geer, J. H., and A. H. Buss, "Generalization of a Nonverbal Response to Aggressive Verbal Stimuli" *Journal of Experimental Psychology*, **63** (1962), 413–414.

Gerow, J. G., and H. R. Pollio, "Word Association, Frequency of Occurrence, and Semantic Differential Norms for 360 Stimulus Words," University of Tennessee, *Technical Report No. 1, Contract MH08903*, 1965.

Goldman-Eisler, F., "Speech Analysis and Mental Processes," *Language and Speech*, **1** (1958), 59–75.

————, "The Predictability of Words in Context and the Length of Pauses in Speech," *Language and Speech*, **1** (1958), 226–232.

Gonzalez, R. C., and C. N. Cofer, "Exploratory Studies of Verbal Context by Means of Clustering in Free Recall," *Journal of Genetic Psychology*, **95** (1959), 293–320.

Gough, P. B., and J. J. Jenkins, "Verbal Learning and Psycholinguistics," in M. H. Marx, *Theories in Contemporary Psychology*. New York: The MacMillan Company, 1963.

Gumenik, W. E., and T. Spencer, "Verbal Repetition and Changes in Meaning of Synonyms: Satiation or Set?" *Journal*

of Verbal Learning and Verbal Behavior, **4** (1965), 286–290.

Hebb, D. O., *The Organization of Behavior.* New York: John Wiley & Sons, Inc., 1949.

Horton, D. L., and P. M. Kjeldergaard, "An Experimental Analysis of Associative Factors in Mediated Generalization," *Psychological Monographs*, **75** (1961), 1–26.

Howe, E. S., "Probabilistic Adverbial Qualification of Adjectives," *Journal of Verbal Learning and Verbal Behavior*, **1** (1963), 225–242.

Howes, D. H., "On the Relation between the Probability of a Word as an Associate and in General Linguistic Contexts," *Journal of Abnormal and Social Psychology*, **54** (1957), 75–85.

————, and C. E. Osgood, "On the Combination of Associative Probabilities in Linguistic Contexts," *American Journal of Psychology*, **67** (1954), 241–258.

Hull, C. L., "Knowledge and Purpose as Habit Mechanisms," *Psychological Review*, **37** (1930), 511–525.

Jakobovitz, L. A., and W. E. Lambert, "Semantic Satiation among Bilinguals," *Journal of Experimental Psychology*, **62** (1961), 576–582.

Jenkins, J. J., "Mediated Associations: Paradigms and Situations," in C. N. Cofer and B. S. Musgrave, eds., *Verbal Behavior and Learning.* New York: McGraw-Hill Book Company, 1963, pp. 210–245.

————, "Mediation Theory and Grammatical Behavior," in S. Rosenberg, ed., *New Directions in Psycholinguistics.* New York: The MacMillan Company, 1965.

————, W. A. Russell, and G. Suci, "An Atlas of Semantic Profiles for 360 Words," *American Journal Psychology*, **71** (1958), 688–699.

Johnson, D., "Word Association and Word Frequency," *American Journal of Psychology*, **69** (1958), 125–126.

Johnson, N. "Linguistic Models of Functional Units of Language Behavior," in S. Rosenberg, ed., *New Directions in Psycholinguistics*. New York: The MacMillan Company, 1965.

Johnson, R. L., M. D. Miller, and D. D. Wall, "Content Analysis and Semantic Classification," mimeo, (1965), Contract No. DA 49-193-MD2490.

Kent, G. H., and A. J. Rosanoff, "A Study of Association in Insanity," *American Journal of Insanity*, **67** (1910), 37–96.

Koen, F. "Polarization, *m* and Emotionality in Words," *Journal of Verbal Learning and Verbal Behavior*, **1** (1962), 183–187.

Lambert, W., and L. Jakobovitz, "Verbal Satiation and Changes in the Intensity of Meaning," *Journal of Experimental Psychology*, **60** (1960), 376–383.

Langer, S. K., *Philosophy in a New Key*. New York: Mentor Books, 1951.

Maclay, H., and C. E. Osgood, "Hesitation Phenomenon in Spontaneous English Speech," *Word*, **15** (1959), 19–44.

Marshall, G. R., and C. N. Cofer, "Associative Indices as Measures of Word Relatedness: A Summary and Comparison of Ten Methods," *Journal of Verbal Learning and Verbal Behavior*, **1** (1963), 408–421.

McGeoch, J. A., and A. L. Irion, *The Psychology of Human Learning*. New York: Longmans, Green and Co., Inc., 1952.

Mednick, S. A., "The Associative Basis of the Creative Process," *Psychological Review*, **69** (1962), 220–232.

Mosier, C. I., "A Psychometric Study of Meaning," *Journal of Social Psychology*, **13** (1941), 123–140.

Noble, C. E., "An Analysis of Meaning," *Psychological Review*, **59** (1952), 421–430.

O'Neil, W., "The Effects of Verbal Association on Tachistoscopic Recognition," *Technical Report No. 4., Contract N8 onr-66216*, University of Minnesota, 1965.

Osgood, C. E., *Method and Theory in Experimental Psychology*. New York: Oxford University Press, Inc., 1953.

———, "Comments on Professor Bous-

field's Paper," in C. N. Cofer, ed., *Verbal Learning and Verbal Behavior*. New York: McGraw-Hill Book Company, 1961.

———, "On Understanding and Creating Sentences," *American Psychology*, **18** (1963) 735, 751.

———, "Psycholinguistics," in *Psychology: A Study of a Science*, S. Koch, ed. New York: McGraw-Hill Book Company, 1963.

———, and L. Anderson, "Certain Relations among Experienced Contingencies, Associative Structure, and Contingencies in Encoded Messages," *American Journal of Psychology*, **70** (1957), 411–420.

———, and G. J. Suci, "Factor Analysis of Meaning," *Journal of Experimental Psychology*, **50** (1952), 325–338.

———, ———, and P. H. Tannenbaum, *The Measurement of Meaning*. Urbana, Illinois: University of Illinois Press, 1957.

———, and P. H. Tannenbaum, "The Principle of Congruity in the Prediction of Attitude Change," *Psychological Review*, **62** (1955), 42–55.

Peak, H., "Psychological Structure and Psychological Activity," *Psychological Review*, **65** (1958), 325–347.

Pollio, H. R., *Word Association as a Function of Semantic Structure*. Unpublished doctoral dissertation, University of Michigan, 1962.

———, "Word Association as a Function of Conditioned Meaning," *Journal of Experimental Psychology*, **66** (1963), 454–460.

———, "A Simple Matrix Analysis of Associative Structure," *Journal of Verbal Learning and Verbal Behavior*, **2** (1963), 166–169.

———, "Composition of Associative Clusters," *Journal of Experimental Psychology*, **67** (1964), 199–208.

———, "Some Semantic Relations among Word-Associates," *American Journal of Psychology*, **77** (1964), 249–256.

———, "Some Characteristics of Associative Structure Matrices," Mimeo, University of Tennessee, 1964.

————, *The Structural Basis of Word Association Behavior.* The Hague: Mouton & Co., 1966.

————, and R. L. Cave, "The Effects of Interitem Associative Strength and Presentation Rate on Serial Learning," Paper read for the Southeastern Psychological Association. March, 1965.

————, and E. G. Christy, "Variation and Interitem Associative Strength and Some Measures of Free Recall," *Psychology Reports,* 15 (1964), 527–534.

————, and R. Deitchman, "The Activational Characteristics of a Serial Cognitive Structure Having Oppositional End Points," Mimeo, University of Tennessee, 1964.

————, and D. O. Draper, "The Effect of a Serial Cognitive Structure on Paired-Associates Learning," *Journal of Verbal Learning and Verbal Behavior,* 5 (1966), 301–308.

————, and J. G. Gerow, "Incongruent Evaluative Context and Associative Behavior," Mimeo, University of Tennessee, 1966.

————, and R. Kasschau, "Associative Structures and the Temporal Characteristics of Free Recall," Paper presented, Psychonomics Society, October, 1965.

————, and R. K. Lore, "The Effect of a Semantically Congruent Context on Word Association Behavior," *Journal of Psychology,* 61 (1965), 17–26.

————, R. W. Wilcox, and D. M. Sundland, "The Effect of Context on the Production of Hostile Associates to Ambigious Verbal Stimuli," *Language and Speech,* 9 (1966), 103–113.

Postman, L. J. "Does Interference Theory Predict Too Much Forgetting?" *Journal of Verbal Learning and Verbal Behavior,* 2 (1963), 40–48.

Rothkoff, E. Z., and E. U. Coke, "The Prediction of Free Recall from Word Association Measures," *Journal of Experimental Psychology,* 62 (1961), 433–438.

Rouse, R. O., and J. S. Verinis, "The Effect of Associative Connections on the Recognition of Flashed Words," *Journal of Verbal Learning and Verbal Behavior,* 1 (1962), 300–303.

Russell, W. A., and J. J. Jenkins, "The Complete Minnesota Norms for Responses to 100 Words from the Kent-Rosenoff Word Association Test," *Technical Report No. 11, Contract N8-onr-66216.* University of Minnesota, 1954.

Shepard, R. N., "The Analysis of Proximities: Multidimensional Scaling with an Unknown Distance Function, I," *Psychometrika,* 27 (1962), 125–140.

Smith, D., and A. Raygor, "Verbal Satiation and Personality," *Journal of Abnormal and Social Psychology,* 52 (1956), 323–326.

Solars, A. K., "Latency of Instrumental Responses as a Function of Compatability with the Meaning of Eliciting Verbal Signs," *Journal of Experimental Psychology,* 59 (1960), 239–245.

Staats, A. W. "Verbal Habit Families, Concepts, and the Operant Conditioning of Word Classes," *Psychological Review,* 68 (1961), 190–204.

————, and C. K. Staats, "Meaning Established by Classical Conditioning," *Journal of Experimental Psychology,* 54 (1957), 74–80.

————, and ————, "Attitudes Established by Classical Conditioning," *Journal of Abnormal Social Psychology,* 57 (1958), 37–40.

————, and ————, "Meaning and *m:* Correlated but Separate," *Psychological Review,* 66 (1959), 136–144.

————, ————, and H. L. Crawford, "First-Order Conditioning of Meaning and the Paralleled Conditioning of a GSR," *Journal of General Psychology,* 67 (1962), 159–167.

————, J. R. Finley, and W. G. Heard, "Independent Manipulation of Meaning and *m,*" *Journal of General Psychology,* 69 (1963), 253–260.

————, and W. G. Heard, "Language Conditioning of Meaning to Meaning Using a Semantic Generalization Paradigm," *Journal of Experimental Psychology,* 57 (1959), 187–192.

Thorndike, E. L., and I. Lorge, *The*

Teacher's Word Book of 30,000 Words.
New York: Teachers College, Columbia
University Press, 1944.

Thumb, A., and K. Marbe, *Experimentelle
Untersuchungen über die psychologischen
Grundlagen der sprachlichen Analogie-
bildung.* Leipzig: W. Engelmann, 1901.

Tolman, E. C., and I. Johnson, "A Note
on Association Time and Feeling,"
American Journal of Psychology, **29**
(1918), 187–195.

Tulving, E., "Subjective Organization in
Free Recall of Unrelated Words,"
Psychological Review, **69** (1962), 344–
354.

————, and C. Gold, "Stimulus Information and Contextual Information as
Determinants of Tachistoscopic Recognition of Words," *Journal of Experimental Psychology,* **66** (1963) 319–
327.

Underwood, B. J., "An Orientation to
Research on Thinking," *Psychological
Review,* **59** (1952), 209–220.

————, and J. Richardson, "Some Verbal
Materials for the Study of Concept
Formation," *Psychology Bibliography,*
53 (1956), 84–95.

————, and R. W. Schulz, *Meaningfulness
and Verbal Learning.* New York: J. B.
Lippincott, Co., 1960.

Verplanck, W. S., and R. L. Krueger,
"The Associative Character of Human
'Knowledge,'" Paper presented, Psychonomic Society Meeting. October,
1964.

————, "Associations, Connected Discourse, and 'Knowledge,'" Paper presented, Psychonomic Society Meeting,
October, 1965.

Weingartner, H., "Associative Structure
and Serial Learning," *Journal of Verbal
Learning and Verbal Behavior,* **2** (1963)
476–479.

Wertheimer, M., and W. M. Gillis, "Satiation and the Rate of Lapse of Verbal
Meaning," *Journal of General Psychology,* **59** (1958), 79–85.

White, M. M., and M. Powell, "The
Differential Reaction Time for Pleasant
and Unpleasant Words," *American
Journal of Psychology,* **48** (1936),
126–133.

Woodworth, R. S., *Experimental Psychology.* New York: Holt, Rinehart &
Winston, Inc., 1938.

Yelen, D. R., and R. W. Schulz, "Verbal
Satiation?" *Journal of Verbal Learning
and Verbal Behavior,* **1** (1963), 372–377.

The present paper, as well as much of the
research on which it is based, was supported
by research grant MH-08903 from the United
States Public Health Service.

Transfer
and Mediation
in Verbal Learning[1]

3 PAUL M. KJELDERGAARD

The history of the study of transfer phenomena, an area which was among the first to attract the attention of experimental psychologists in this country, may be found in many sources (McGeoch and Irion, 1952; Osgood, 1949; Woodworth and Schlosberg, 1954). Among the most important writings in terms of verbal learning were the studies of Poffenberger (1915), Yum (1931), Bruce (1933), and Gibson (1941), and the theorizing of Wylie (1919), Robinson (1920), Gibson (1940), and Osgood (1949). No attempt will be made to cover this early literature systematically.

Goss (1961) has made an exhaustive analysis of the history of the mediation hypothesis and has cited the work of Birge (1941), Miller and Dollard (1941), and Cofer and Foley (1942) as representing the starting point of the modern developments in verbal mediation. To this list must be added, I think, the work of Hull (1939), who made the distinction between types of generalization and who postulated the basic

constructs that were refined and extended by others who have speculated about the nature of mediation (cf. Bousfield, 1961; Cofer and Foley, 1942; Jenkins, 1963; Mowrer, 1960; and Osgood, 1952). Except for recent years, a review of most of the major empirical studies dealing with mediation may be found in the Horton and Kjeldergaard (1961) monograph. Thus, the emphasis of this paper will be on the studies and theorizing subsequent to 1960.

An analysis of the transfer and mediation literature soon indicates that the terms "transfer" and "mediation" are often used interchangeably. An investigation of A-B, A-B' where B and B' are assumed to be related semantically (e.g., Postman and Stark, 1965) is identical to the B-C, A-B, A-C mediation paradigm if the first stage is inferred from word association norms (e.g., Mink, 1963). Similarly, the A-B, B-C, A-C mediation paradigm is, technically, the same as the A-B, A-B' transfer paradigm as studied by Schwenn and Underwood (1965), since these investigators linked B with B' experimentally. Since the two areas are related but have tended to be treated relatively independently, benefits may result from the simultaneous considera-

[1] The research reported in this paper was supported primarily by a grant from the National Service Foundation. The author also gratefully acknowledges computer time made available by the Massachusetts Institute of Technology and the University of Pittsburgh Computations Centers.

tion of the respective literatures. Beyond the obvious advantage of consistent labels, the treatment of transfer as mediation or mediation as transfer may offer insights, or at least parsimony, which may not be otherwise accomplished.

The purpose of this paper, then, is to relate systematically the areas of transfer and mediation emphasizing verbal learning and verbal learning phenomena. The fundamental assumption in the presentation which follows is that all transfer, or at least all verbal transfer[2], can be accounted for on the basis of the mediation hypothesis.[3] This paper

manner consonant with the general S–R literature. For example, the definitions as stated by Mandler (1954), Newman (1960), and Horton and Kjeldergaard (1961) would all be considered basically compatible with the assumptions that follow and the subsequent discussion.

Assumptions[4]

1. The presentation of any verbal stimulus (which in paired-associate learning may be a response term) elicits one or more implicit or explicit responses. Thus:

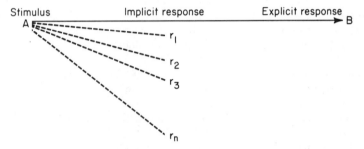

attempts to explore the relationship between mediation and transfer, to review the major factors which are known or presumed to affect each, and to elaborate the postulated mediation mechanism in order to account for known phenomena.

Definitions and Assumptions

No attempt will be made to define the "critical terms" used throughout the paper insofar as they are used in a

The free association literature (Jenkins and Russell, 1964), work on attention (Maltzman, 1966), semantic conditioning studies (Razran, 1949), and studies utilizing the semantic differential (Osgood, Suci, and Tannenbaum, 1957) basically supports this assumption with respect to verbal material. The number and nature of the responses to a particular stimulus depend upon the properties of the stimulus and the conditioning history of the organism involved. Familiar

[2] The scope of this paper will be limited to an examination of verbal phenomena or "primarily verbal phenomena," i.e., where verbal behavior can be assumed to play a dominant role. Occasionally, nonverbal experiments are cited either to demonstrate the generality of the findings or because evidence in the verbal domain is lacking.

[3] A similar suggestion was made by Osgood 1953.

[4] The following are recognized as being neither completely necessary in that all of them are not directly invoked as explanations in the discussion of empirical studies, nor are they sufficient in that certain areas, e.g., intralist similarity, are not systematically accounted for. Further, these assumptions represent a mixture of empirical "laws" and theoretical formulations which seem tenable in terms of the verbal learning literature.

stimuli tend to be responded to as a whole; unfamiliar stimuli tend to evoke responses associated with one or more components of the stimulus.

2. Implicit responses are composed of two classes: "covert" responses (subvocal) and "representational" responses.

3. "Covert" responses are available to the respondent as discriminative stimuli; "representational" responses are not.

The above distinction seems to be necessary to account for such phenomena as mediation with awareness versus mediation without awareness, e.g., micro muscular responses of which the subject is unaware (Simon, 1962), instances of self-editing, etc.

4. Each implicit response, whether covert or "representational," tends to elicit the overt response with which it has been associated.

5. Learning an *A-B* pair consists of three functionally separate processes: the integration of the stimuli, the integration of the responses, and the associaciation of the appropriate stimulus elements with the appropriate response elements. These processes need not occur sequentially but may overlap in time.

The division of paired-associate learning into response integration and associative aspects, an analysis first suggested by Underwood, Runquist, and Schulz (1959), has received support in numerous empirical investigations and has been used widely as an explanatory principle in the literature. This assumption extends the integration concept to the stimuli.

6. Stimulus elements are integrated only to the extent that it is necessary to discriminate one stimulus from another or to the extent that they have been previously integrated.

Support for the above assumption is found in the literature reviewed and examined by Underwood (1963) and in

subsequent experiments designed specifically to test Underwood's view (e.g., Musgrave and Cohen, 1966).

7. Response elements tend to be integrated only to the extent demanded by the experimental response requirements. If the response is to be produced or differentiated, then the response unit must be completely integrated. If recognition or a related general response, such as semantic differential ratings, is required, a less well integrated response may be adequate.

8. Subelements of a stimulus or response may form integrated subunits even though the whole stimulus or response is not familiar or has not been integrated in the past.

Assumption eight accounts for generalization based on formal overlap and probably accounts for the typical response to relatively low meaningful material. For example, $|EX|$ in $|GEX|$ is responded to as an integrated subunit due to frequent prior exposure of the *EX* bigram in print. In free association, $|GEX|$ tends to elicit $\langle SEX \rangle$, or in Pennsylvania, $\langle HEX \rangle$, whereas $|MAB|$ tends to elicit $\langle MAD \rangle$ or $\langle MAP \rangle$ due to the prior exposure frequency of the $|MA|$ configuration.

Similarly, an inspection of Table 1, taken from Kjeldergaard (1960) shows that 22 of 28 primary associative responses to the low frequency stimuli used by Horton and Kjeldergaard are dependent upon the formal overlap between the stimulus word and the associative response which it elicits. The response *MILTON* to *MERLE* seems to represent a two stage mediational process, $MERLE \rightarrow BERLE \rightarrow MILTON$. Data reported by Dallett (1964) shows that the free association responses to nonsense syllables follow the same pattern; namely, that the stimuli tend to evoke responses based upon formal overlap with the stimulus, but they may evoke, presumably through mediation, responses that are

Table 1

THE HORTON-KJELDERGAARD STIMULUS
WORDS AND THE PRIMARY RESPONSE
ELICITED IN A FREE ASSOCIATION TEST.
N = 100.

Experimental Word	Primary Response	Per Cent
ARRAS	HARASS	12
BANAL	CANAL	20
BEDEW	WET	18
BLEAR	SMEAR	11
CAIRN	CORN	3
DAVIT	AFFIDAVIT	9
DELFT	DEFT	16
DRAFF	DRAFT	25
ETUDE	MUSIC	34
FAGOT	MAGGOT	12
GNOME	ELF	14
KRAAL	CRAWL	17
KRONE	PRONE	10
LIMBO	LIMBER	11
LIANO	LLAMA	27
MERLE	MILTON	9
NADIR	GEORGE	6
NILUM	NOTHING	6
NONCE	ANNOUNCE	8
PRAWN	PAWN	33
REAVE	WEAVE	22
RENAL	RENEWAL	5
SWALE	SWALLOW	15
TAUPE	TAPE	11
TRIPE	TRIP	7
TRYST	TAPE	11
UMBER	SLUMBER	12
WINCH	WENCH	10

associated with stimuli that are physically similar to the stimulus in question.

9. The probability that elements of a stimulus or response will form an integrated subunit is a joint function of the absolute frequency with which these elements have occurred contiguously in an organism's past and the relative frequency of the stimulus pattern to which the stimulus belongs.

Although Baddeley (1961) and DiMascio (1959) have shown that sequential probabilities of letters can account for much of the meaningfulness and familiarity effects obtained with

trigrams, sequential probabilities alone are not sufficient to account for all of the effects even with low meaningfulness material, and such an explanation appears grossly inadequate with material high in meaningfulness. It is suggested that even though $|CK|$ has a higher frequency count than $|AG|$, $|AG|$ is more apt to be responded to as an integrated unit than $|CK|$ due to the fact that the former belongs to a more frequently occurring stimulus pattern, the vowel-consonant pattern. The work of Esper (1925) and Miller (1958) supports the notion that Ss respond to the stimulus pattern as well as to the specific elements in the pattern.

10. Response integration is presumed to be established temporally prior to stimulus-response associative learning. Response integration need not be complete, however, for associative learning to take place. The work of Peterson and Peterson (1959) is taken as support for this assumption.

11. Due to stimulus generalization, stimulus A, when presented, elicits one or more responses which have been conditioned to stimuli which are similar to A (to be called A primes).

Assumption 11 is simply the extension of the principle of generalization, well established with physical continua, to the verbal domain. The material cited above in Table 1, as well as transfer studies of Yum (1931) and of Bruce (1933), demonstrate this in terms of formal properties. Numerous studies, some of which will be cited later, demonstrate the effect based upon semantic properties. It is maintained that the distinction between formal and semantic similarity is arbitrary[5] and that those terms represent ends of a continuum. As in the case of semantic generalization, generalization based

[5] This refers to interlist similarity; intralist similarity is assumed to sometimes function on the basis of physical similarity alone.

upon formal properties is assumed to be based upon common (meaningful?) responses.

12. Due to response generalization, when A-B habit exists, the presentation of stimulus A tends to elicit one or more habits which are similar to B.

Meaningful intrusions, etc., would fall into this category. It is also presumed that this could account for such effects as priming (Storms, 1958), context (Martin, 1964), the effects of order of stimulus presentation (Wynne, *et al.*, 1965), or what is generally referred to as "set."

13. During the establishment of a new response B to stimulus A, prior habits tend to become extinguished. The net loss in habit strength to the prior connection is a direct function of the number of A-B trials and an inverse function of the similarity between B and the previous response to A.

Assumption 13 is based upon the work of Barnes and Underwood (1959), Postman (1962), Briggs (1954), McGovern (1964), and Postman and Stark (1965), and seems empirically sound.

14. The gradient of extinction is less steep than the gradient of acquisition so that several responses may be associated simultaneously to a given stimulus A.

Assumption 14 is supported by all the studies of retroactive inhibition which show savings in terms of first list learning when the second list has achieved strength equal to the terminal strength of the first list.

15. The probability that a given response in a response hierarchy will be emitted to a given stimulus on a given trial is a joint function of the specific stimulus response habit strength, the generalized response habit strength, and the response list differentiation. This is supported by Morgan and Underwood (1950) and others.

16. The strength of a habit A-B is a negatively accelerated asymptotic function of the number of reinforced pairings of A and B and of the tendency of A to elicit responses which are similar to B, i.e., the A-B' generalization gradient.

17. The response list differentiation is a direct function of the number of trials on a given list and an inverse function of the interlist stimulus-response similarity.

18. The occurrence of the response element B, either explicitly or implicitly, raises the probability of all the members of response classes to which B belongs.

This is the mechanism assumed to account for the findings of Mink (1963), Martin (1961), Storms (1958), and Maltzman and Belloni (1964), as well as for meaningful intrusions and for free-learning effects such as associative clustering (Bousfield, Whitmarsh, and Berkowitz, 1960; Jenkins, Mink, and Russell, 1959).

19. The establishment of a habit A-B simultaneously establishes a habit B-A.

Assumption 19 seems to be well established in the literature, (e.g., Jantz and Underwood, 1958; Murdock, 1956, 1958). The postulated mechanism is that each element elicits a mediated implicit response, e.g., A elicits r_a, which persists for a period of time. This implicit response tends to elicit the overt response with which it is associated and any other responses, implicit or overt, which are contiguous with it. Thus:

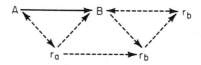

20. The strength of the habit B-A covaries linearly and positively with both the strength of the A-B habit and with the degree to which the A functions as an integrated unit.

21. The strength of the habit A-B is

always greater than the associated habit *B-A*.

This assumption is supported by the research listed under assumption 19 cited above.

22. Responses which have been associated with *B* also tend to become associated with *A* upon the establishment of an *A-B* habit; thus an *A-B-C* chain is formed.

23. The tendency of *A* to elicit *C* through the common associate *B* is a multiplicative function of the momentary strength of the *B-C* connection and the momentary strength of the *A-B* connection. This assumption is based upon the work of Jarrett and Scheibe (1963) and the subsequent study by Palermo and Jenkins (1964).

24. All transfer is mediated via common implicit responses.

25. When implicit responses tend to evoke the appropriate explicit response term, positive transfer is obtained.

26. When the implicit responses tend to evoke an explicit response other than the appropriate response term, negative transfer is obtained.

The Transfer Paradigms

Since the terminology within the transfer literature is not consistent, since transfer and mediation terminology are often used interchangeably, and since it is the task of this paper to relate the two, the first-list-second-list relationships shown in Figure 1 are offered as a representation of the possible stimulus and response conditions which may exist in transfer studies. The middle boxes, 2, 4, 5, 6, and 8, may be thought of as representing continua where the prime condition(s) extend from the terminal condition of the box to the left (or above) to the initial condition of the adjacent box to the right (or below). Briefly, this may be

thought of as representing nine segments of Osgood's transfer surface (Osgood, 1949) from stimulus and response identity to stimulus and response neutrality.

Paradigms three, seven, and nine, representing facilitation, interference, and control (or neutral) paradigms respectively, are those which have received the most attention in the literature. One additional paradigm, originally suggested by Gagné, Baker, and Foster (1950), and usually referred to as *A-B*, *A-Br*, has received much attention. Although this paradigm is generally treated as a special one, it will be argued that it represents an instance of paradigm seven, i.e., identical stimuli and different responses. The element *C* (a new response) in the *A-B*, *A-Br* paradigm represents a subset of *C* responses which are particularly interfering due to the competition of habits established during first-list learning, the lack of list differentiation, and mediated interference from the first list reverse associations.

It is assumed in Figure 1 that those terms followed by a prime in the second list learning represent some degree of similarity greater than zero, i.e., $A' \neq D$ and $B' \neq C$. Further, it is assumed that like terms represent the same degree of similarity; that is, A' in paradigm 2 is the same as the A' in paradigm 5. Given these assumptions, it is possible to predict the relative transfer effects of the nine paradigms in Figure 1. As implied above, if the similarity between elements were very low, i.e., if *A* and *A'*, or *B* and *B'* were relatively dissimilar, though related, it is possible that the difference between certain paradigms in terms of transfer effects might be negligible or absent. The $\geqslant$ symbol in certain relationships is used to indicate that the effect might, as a limit, be equal. The ? symbol is used to indicate that the relative

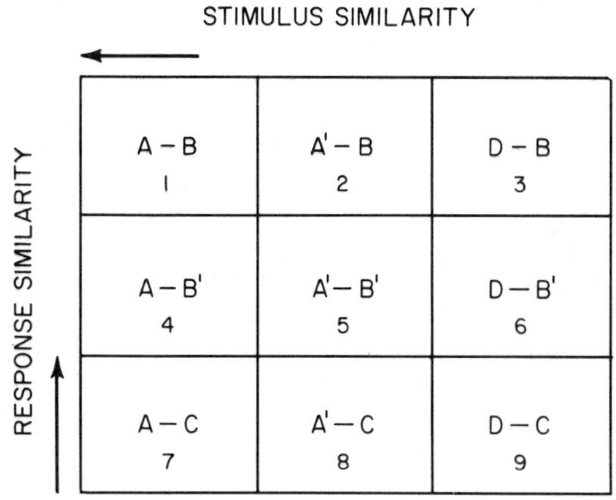

STIMULUS SIMILARITY

Figure 1. Transfer paradigms in terms of stimulus and response similarity

transfer effects could favor either paradigm depending specifically upon the degree of stimulus or response similarity involved.

Table 2 shows the relative effects of

Table 2

TRANSFER RELATIONSHIPS AMONG
THE NINE PARADIGMS.

	2	3	4	5	6	9	8	7
1	>	>	>	>	>	>	>	>
2		≥	?	>	>	>	>	>
3			?	?	>	>	>	>
4				>	>	?	?	≥
5					≥	≥	≥	>
6						≥	≥	>
9							≥	>
8								>

each paradigm with respect to the other eight.[6] Paradigm 1, a continuation of first list learning is by definition the strongest; paradigm 7, the classic interference paradigm, is the weakest.

In addition to the above nine basic transfer paradigms, verbal material, which has the property of being able to function both as a stimulus and as a response, yields additional paradigms. By reversing the elements of the second stage, eight paradigms, amenable to test with verbal materials, are generated.[7] The latter paradigms will be labeled with the basic transfer paradigm numbers followed by a prime, e.g., 1′ represents *A-B*, *B-A* or S–R followed by R–S learning. Similarly, 8′ would represent *A-B*, *C-A′*, the second list consisting of new stimuli and responses which are similar (or related) to the stimuli of the *A-B* list.

In evaluating the transfer effects of the derived transfer paradigms, two sets of possible comparisons evolve either from the standpoint of empirical laws or based upon the principles stated above. It is possible to compare the basic paradigm with its derivative or to make comparisons among the derived paradigms. Again, it should be noted that a question mark indicates that the effect depends upon the similarity relationship represented by the prime term (or terms) rather than an unspecifiable effect. For example, in comparing 4 with 4′, if *B* and *B′* were

[6] Relative effects are measured in terms of distance from perfect positive transfer. The table does not show which paradigms, or under what circumstances, transfer effects would be negative.

[7] Paradigm 9, since it involves new elements on both the stimulus and response side, has no meaningful reversal.

"highly similar," then 4 should show greater facilitation than 4′. If B and B' were relatively dissimilar, then 4′ should show some positive effects due to "response integration" and 4 should show interference effects as it becomes more like the interference paradigm, paradigm 7. Table 3 shows the predicted comparison of each paradigm with its derivative. The predicted relative effects of the derived paradigms compared to each other are shown in Table 4. According to the assumptions stated above, paradigm 1′ should show the greatest amount of facilitation and paradigm 3′ due to the B term being familiar, integrated, and tending to elicit a competing response A, should show the greatest amount of interference.

Table 3

THE RELATIVE TRANSFER EFFECTS OF THE EIGHT BASIC TRANSFER PARADIGMS AND THEIR COUNTERPARTS DERIVED BY REVERSING THE TRANSFER STAGE ELEMENTS.

		A–B		
(1)	A–B	>	B–A	(1′)
(2)	A′–B	>	B–A′	(2′)
(3)	D–B	>	B–C	(3′)
(4)	A–B′	?	B′–A	(4′)
(5)	A′–B′	?	B′–A′	(5′)
(6)	D–B′	>	B′–C	(6′)
(7)	A–C	<	C–A	(7′)
(8)	A′–C	<	C–A′	(8′)

Table 4

THE RELATIVE EFFECTS OF THE DERIVED TRANSFER PARADIGMS.

1	≥	≥	≥	>	>	>	>
2		?	≥	?	?	≥	≥
4			≥	≥	≥	>	>
5				?	≥	≥	≥
7					>	>	>
8						>	≥
6							≥

The transfer surface

Osgood's transfer surface (Osgood, 1949) was favorably received in general, but the portion of the curve dealing with response opposition and antagonisms has been either implicitly or explicitly rejected by most investigators. This is not surprising since Osgood's own research (Osgood, 1946, 1948) provided relatively weak empirical evidence to support the extension of the curve. Conversely, it is easy to demonstrate facilitation with verbal opposites, and, though no distinction was made, opposites comprised a high portion of the associates in the Bastian (1961), Mink (1963), and Ryan (1960) studies, all of which showed positive transfer. Further, numerous Japanese studies have successfully demonstrated that opposites are facilitative rather than interfering (cf. Umemoto, 1959). In addition, when dealing with verbal material, logically one would have to extend the stimulus dimension to include opposition, an extension not provided by Osgood. A reasonable solution to these problems has been suggested by E. Martin (1965). He proposes that the similarity dimensions be treated in terms of associative similarity; opposites, therefore, are conceptualized as similar and lie somewhere between identity and neutrality on each of the dimensions. Furthermore, if one treats "oppositeness" behaviorally (cf., Carroll, Kjeldergaard, and Carton, 1962) rather than logically, the knotty problems of definition are avoided and it becomes possible to speak of degrees of oppositeness. Thus, associative similarity in terms of opposites may occupy an interval rather than a point on each of the dimensions.

Accepting Martin's suggestion, the following discussion will deal only with the truncated transfer surface. There have been three attempts to investigate systematically the remaining portion of the curves, the first by Bugelski and Cadwallader (1956). Their results were reported in terms of the retroactive effects on the recall and relearning of the first list. The transfer data are difficult to interpret since the second-list learning scores are based upon different lists and the adjustments necessary to compensate for the significant group differences in first-list learning have not been made. Judging from the magnitude of the adjustments on the first-list recall scores, it appears that such modifications would not alter appreciably the conclusions concerning the stimulus-response similarity relationships. Basically their results support Osgood's predictions with respect to the stimulus dimension, but contrary to his analysis, they found interference or negative transfer which exceeded that of the neutral responses for all levels of response similarity. Since their results conflict both with the transfer surface predictions and with the findings of several other investigations, the discrepant findings must be attributed to differential second-list difficulty (cf., Underwood, 1961) or to other factors which make the results idiosyncratic.

Dallett (1962) using the same materials, Gibson's figures and Osgood's adjectives, found effects which resemble the truncated transfer surface more closely. Dallett's design was more appropriate in terms of evaluating transfer effects in that the transfer list was constant across all paradigms, the manipulations being made in terms of the first-list relationships. Although the findings parallel the hypothesized transfer surface, only two effects were statistically significant, the two levels of stimulus similarity with identical responses. It is interesting to note that large differences emerged with respect

to first-list difficulty, thus lending credence to the notion that list difficulty may have been a confounding factor in the Bugelski and Cadwallader findings.

Wimer (1964), using pairs of adjectives selected from Osgood's original lists (Osgood, 1946), tested stimulus and response opposition and antagonism as well as the points under consideration here. Wimer's findings lacked statistical significance for all points and showed little in the way of apparent effects except for similar stimuli and responses varying from identity to neutrality (paradigms 2, 5, and 8). In these instances the relative effects are directly opposed to those found by Dallett.

The three studies viewed jointly show little in the way of common results except for the previously well established finding of negative transfer for paradigm 7. The responses were drawn from the same pool and two of the studies had the same basic design, so one must look elsewhere for an explanation of the lack of correspondence. Several factors are suggested as a possible means of making a more adequate test of the transfer surface. Since all of the studies show the general effect of similarity to result in few significant contrasts, the problem may be the imprecision of point estimates. Although this cannot reasonably account for the total lack of correspondence, precision could be improved through selection of homogeneous subjects, blocking on the basis of paired-associate learning speed, pretraining on paired-associate tasks, etc. Second, an increase in the number of points sampled on each dimension would increase the probability of detecting a chance deviation from a general trend or relationship. Morgan and Underwood (1950), who found one disparate mean along an otherwise smooth gradient, may be cited as an example of the utility of this approach. Third, there is need for greater precision in the specification of the similarity relationships. It may be that the common pool of adjectives from which the above investigations sampled have sufficient "noise" so that when the adjectives are redistributed and repaired, different effects emerge.

In addition to the above tests of nine or more points from the transfer surface, there have been numerous tests of the corners of the truncated surface, frequently including the *A-Br* paradigm. Since the findings in terms of effects, both relative and absolute, are quite mixed and since these studies were generally concerned with the influence of some other variable on the transfer paradigms, these studies will be discussed in terms of the various factors.

Transfer

MEANINGFULNESS AND FIRST LIST LEARNING. Several writers (Mandler, 1954; Postman, 1962; E. Martin, 1965) have discussed the theoretical mechanisms responsible for the magnitude and direction of transfer effects as a function of the amount of first list training, the meaningfulness of the response terms, and the interlist stimulus-response similarity. Where responses are identical (paradigms 1, 2, 3, 4', 7'), all concur in attributing facilitative effects to response integration. With low meaningfulness material, the magnitude of the effect increases up to the point where other factors become dominant. With high meaningfulness material, there is little to be gained through response integration so that the facilitative effects are present only with the first few trials of the first-list.

A second effect attributable to the amount of first-list learning is the amount of forward associative inter-

ference when identical stimuli are used (paradigms 4, 7). This is a direct function of the number of first-list trials and should produce negative transfer, other things being equal.

Backward associative interference was not formally part of Mandler's model, but presumably it is implicit. He said "whenever a stimulus [such as an S-R pair] evokes two separate integrated responses, the two symbolic analogues may also be activated and associated so that, on future presentations of a stimulus which evokes only one of the responses, both symbolic responses will be activated" (Mandler, 1954, p. 237). Coupled with the assumption that the symbolic response tends to evoke the overt response, R-S learning as well as S-R learning is derivable. Backward associative interference leads to negative transfer whenever responses are the same and stimuli are different, e.g., paradigms 2, 3, 4', 7'. Again the amount of negative transfer is an increasing function of the strength of first-list learning and is related to meaningfulness since partial response integration is assumed to be a necessary prerequisite to associative learning.

Finally, Mandler and Postman emphasize the effects of list differentiation. In fact, Mandler argues that extensive first-list practice, by combining the positive effects of response integration and list differentiation (achieved through an implicit editor), should lead to positive transfer in the *A-Br* paradigm. Two studies, one with a motor response (Mandler, 1954) and the other involving *CCC* trigrams (Mandler and Heinemann, 1956) as responses, both showed positive transfer with the *A-Br* paradigm. The motor response showed a shift to positive transfer at 100 overlearning trials; the *CCC* responses showed facilitation as a consistent increasing function of the first-list learning. Since the *A-Br* paradigm showed consistently more positive transfer than paradigm 3 in the latter study, an effect not predictable from Mandler's model, perhaps, as suggested by Postman (1962b), the results may be attributable to sampling errors associated with the small number of pairs used (two) for each paradigm.

THE *A-B, A-Br* PARADIGM. As stated earlier, the *A-Br* paradigm can be considered as an instance of paradigm 7 (identical stimuli, different responses). It is a special case of this paradigm only in that the different responses happen to be a selected subset of possible different responses, a subset that leads to added interference effects due to prior connection with other stimuli that comprise the stimulus side of the list. The analysis offered by Postman and by Martin that the *A-Br* paradigm is affected by three factors, forward and backward associative interference and lack of list differentiation, seems adequate to account for the observed effects. The exact nature of backward associative interference is usually not specified, but Martin attributes the effect to competition with backward associations being formed in the second stage. Since backward association appears to be a form of incidental learning (Jantz and Underwood, 1958), it would seem that such competition would not produce much of a decrement. The analysis described above postulates mediated interference; the response elicits a mediator which in turn tends to become associated with the new stimulus. The mediated response competes with the response to be learned. It should be noted that mediated interference is not limited to *A-Br* paradigm nor to paradigms with new responses; the work of McCullers (1965) demonstrates the same phenomenon with intralist similarity, on both the stimulus and the response sides.

If the above analysis of the *A-Br* paradigm is correct, then it need not be given special consideration such as the extension of the transfer surface proposed by Dallett (1965) to handle variation in S-R similarities with repaired elements, e.g., A'-Br'. Furthermore, Dallett's data fails to justify the need for such an extension.

To summarize the effects of first-list learning and meaningfulness on the paradigms represented in Figure 1, it can be said that when the responses of the two lists are identical and the stimuli are new, (paradigms 3 and 7'), first-list exposure facilitates via list differentiation and response learning for low meaningfulness material; with high meaningfulness responses, only list differentiation facilitates. With all levels of meaningfulness, competitions from reverse associations contribute negatively. Further, when response meaningfulness is low, the effects of increasing first-list trials should change the relative effects from positive to negative as facilitation due to response integration gives way to increasing backward associative interference; when response meaningfulness is high, increasing trials should lead to greater negative transfer due to mediated interference.

When the stimuli are the same and the responses are different (paradigms 7 and 3'), only list differentiation is operative on the positive side, whereas associative interference contributes negatively. Negative transfer should tend to increase as a function of trials for all levels of meaningfulness. When the responses are different but selected from those in the first list, (*A-Br*), list differentiation is very difficult and competition from the response associations must be added so that the transfer should be strongly negative except for some slight positive effects resulting from response integration in the early list-one trials for low meaningfulness responses. The effects of list differentiation should have a positive effect on all paradigms, but the relative effects should be consistent with the initial predictions, positive transfer decreasing for paradigms 3, 7, and *A-Br* in that order.

Martin (1965) proposed that the three factors—forward and backward associations and response learning—be considered as three transfer surfaces: the forward associations being represented by Osgood's surface, the backward association surface by a complex surface influenced most by response similarity, and response learning by a surface showing facilitation as a function only of response similarity. He has also reviewed and summarized the literature related to the transfer of verbal habits and finds agreement between the above analysis and the results from various investigators.

The Three-Stage Mediation Paradigms

It is possible to recast the three-stage mediation paradigms, discussed originally by Jenkins (1959) and subsequently investigated by Horton and Kjeldergaard (1961), Cramer and Cofer (1960), and Peterson, et al., (1964) in terms of the basic transfer paradigms. The first stage of the mediation paradigm can be thought of as establishing the stimulus or response similarity. The second and third stages can then be conceptually treated as basic transfer paradigms. Figure 2 presents the eight three-stage mediation paradigms, the corresponding transfer paradigms (with the transfer paradigm number in parenthesis) and the parallel transfer-control paradigms (with appropriate designation in parenthesis).

When the eight possible three-stage mediation paradigms are considered to be transfer paradigms, the prediction of paradigm difference in terms of the

MEDIATION PARADIGMS: STANDARD

	I	II	III	IV
1st Stage	C–A	B–C	B–C	C–A
2nd Stage	A–B	A–B	A–B	A–B
Test Stage	C–B	A–C	C–A	B–C

	V	VI	VII	VIII
1st Stage	C–B	C–B	A–C	A–C
2nd Stage	A–B	A–B	A–B	A–B
Test Stage	C–A	A–C	C–B	B–C

MEDIATION PARADIGMS: TRANSFER

	I	II	III	IV
1st Stage	A'–A	B–B'	B–B'	A'–A
2nd Stage	A–B	A–B	A–B	A–B
Test Stage	A'–B	A–B'	B'–A	B–A
	(2)	(4)	(4')	(2')

	V	VI	VII	VIII
1st Stage	B'–B	B'–B	A–A'	A–A'
2nd Stage	A–B	A–B	A–B	A–B
Test Stage	B'–A	A–B'	A'–B	B–A'
	(4')	(4)	(2)	(2)

MEDIATION PARADIGMS: TRANSFER CONTROL

	I	II	III	IV
1st Stage	D–C	D–C	C–D	C–D
2nd Stage	A–B	A–B	A–B	A–B
Test Stage	D–B	A–C	C–A	B–D
	(3)	(7)	(7')	(3')

	V	VI	VII	VIII
1st Stage	C–D	C–D	D–C	D–C
2nd Stage	A–B	A–B	A–B	A–B
Test Stage	C–A	A–C	D–B	B–D
	(7')	(7)	(3)	(3')

Figure 2. The three-stage mediation paradigms in terms of standard symbols, transfer symbols, and transfer-control symbols with transfer paradigm numbers in parentheses.

third stage effects turns out to be identical to the predictions made on the basis of a mediational analysis by

Horton and Kjeldergaard. In terms of the controls, however, it now becomes possible to make differential predictions. The control paradigms according to a transfer analysis should order themselves as follows: I–VII (3), III–V (7′), IV–VIII (3′), II–VI (7). The means for the control pairs for these sets of paradigms from the Horton and Kjeldergaard (H-K) and Peterson (P), *et al.*, studies are reported below:

	I–VII	*III–V*	*IV–VIII*	*II–VI*
H-K Words	7.22	6.83	6.52	6.00
P-CCC	2.37	1.84	1.79	1.80
P-CVC	2.88	2.77	2.50	2.48

It must be acknowledged that there is a certain amount of confusion in terms of the I–VII paradigm combination. Since they are predicted to be the most facilitative for both the mediation pairs and the control pairs, more rapid learning in one may enhance the other by making the list functionally easier. With the II–VI combination, however, the mixed effect should work against the hypothesis since they were predicted to be second strongest in terms of facilitation but weakest in terms of control.[8] The remaining sets of paradigms are intermediately affected.[9] Within the limitations of the data, the predictions based upon a transfer analysis appear to be supported. The important point is that this analysis leads to conceptual differences among treatments that were previously thought equivalent and those differences are supported empirically through several independent investigations which span part of the range of meaningfulness.

The mechanisms

The mechanisms postulated by Horton and Kjeldergaard (1961) were included and extended above. Briefly, they postulated bidirectionality of associations, a contiguity factor stating that nonadjacent elements in an associative chain are weaker than adjacent elements, and that the directionality factor is more potent than the contiguity factor. The results tended to support the directionality factor but gave little support for the contiguity factor. Interestingly, an analysis of the Cramer and Cofer (1960) results in terms of the Horton and Kjeldergaard hypotheses[10] strongly supports the contiguity factor ($\bar{X}_c = 1.29$ vs. $\bar{X}_{nc} = 1.01$)[11] and gives little or no support for the directionality factor ($\bar{X}_f = 1.17$ vs. $\bar{X}_b = 1.13$). Cramer and Cofer, however, used an assumed first stage, drawing pairs of words from word-association norms. A reasonable assumption is that such word-lists yield pairs that are highly bidirectional (in spite of norms), very strong, and resistant to extinction. Similarly, in one of the Peterson experiments involving low association value CVC's significant differences emerged among the paradigms in terms of contiguity but not in terms of directionality. Since the study also included the mediator as an incidental stimulus presented to the S in the second stage, it might be hypothesized that the presence of the mediator in the second-stage lessened the effects of the directionality factor. Thus when the effects of directionality are minimized either by using highly bidirectional associates,

---

[8] This may account for the lack of differences in the IV–VIII vs. II–VII contrasts in the Peterson, *et al.*, study.

[9] The question of III–V vs. IV–VIII which, according to this analysis is 4′ vs. 2′, is not clear-cut.

[10] Directionality was used by Cramer and Cofer to mean directions of associate strength (A-B). Horton and Kjeldergaard speak of the direction of the mediation with respect to the test stage (A-C).

[11] No statistical test was possible from results available in the publication.

as did Cramer and Cofer, or by explicitly providing the mediator, as did Peterson, the effects of the contiguity factor become apparent.

Habit strength

GENERAL EFFECTS. An important factor in determining the outcome of mediation experiments, a factor touched upon by Horton and Kjeldergaard in a post hoc analysis of mediation failures, but not part of their formal analysis, is the effect of habit strength. Their results show that the greatest generalization effects were exhibited by those Ss who were neither very fast nor very slow in the first learning stage, but who took an intermediate number of trials. It is proposed here that it is not the number of first-list exposures *per se*, but rather it is the relationship between first-list and second-list learning that is crucial in determining the outcome of mediation. If the number of trials on the second-list is "excessive" with respect to the strength of the associative bond established during the first stage (or pre-experimentally), the mediators tend to become extinguished. The optimal condition for mediation is where there is sufficient exposure to the mediator to form an associative link without extinguishing or weakening the mediator. As a first approximation to testing this hypothesis, the Horton-Kjeldergaard data were reanalyzed by classifying all Ss into generalizers and nongeneralizers and by classifying the stage 1—stage 2 learning trial relationship into favorable and unfavorable with respect to producing mediation. The former classification is the one used previously by Horton and Kjeldergaard (generalizers were those whose correct responses on experimental pairs exceeded their correct responses on the control pairs in the test trials). A favorable learning trial relationship was defined as one in which the number

of first-stage trials equaled or exceeded the number of second-stage trials; more second-stage trials than first-stage trials was considered unfavorable. This 2×2 classification yielded a $x^2 = 4.07$ ($p < .05$), thus supporting the hypothesis.

To explore further the relationship between the learning stages and mediation effects, mediation scores were converted into scores which took into account the magnitude of the mediation effect relative to the speed of acquisition of the test-stage. On the assumption that a difference between experimental and control pairs $(E\text{-}C)$ of 5 points should be weighted more heavily if the difference was $5 - 0$ than if it was $25 - 20$, scores for each S were computed by the formula $(E - C)/(E + C)$, a formula paralleling that used to evaluate transfer effects. Correlating the number of trials in each of the learning stages with the transformed mediation scores yielded no effects for the chaining paradigms but an interesting pattern of correlations for the stimulus and response equivalence paradigms. The latter are shown below:

	V	VI	VII	VIII
1st stage & mediation	.41*	.10	.03	.76*
2nd stage & mediation	.07	.59*	.50*	−.08
p value of r*	.09	.0004	.008	<.0001

Since the effects for at least three of the paradigms exceed even the most conservative standard of significance, it seems worthwhile to speculate about the difference in correlational patterns which emerged. Directionality appears to be the key factor; for those paradigms in which the mediator forms a forward link, paradigms VI and VII, the amount of second-stage practice is linearly related to the generalization effects. In the remaining paradigms, where the mediator forms a backward link, it is the amount of first-stage practice which is crucial. Since the results with the chaining paradigms were not comparable, even though the analysis in terms of mediators runs parallel, these data suggest that other factors, as yet unspecified, influence the chaining paradigms. Subtle indications in the literature, such as the paradigm differences reported by Mink (1963) and by Martin (1961) and the seemingly stronger mediation effects in the equivalence paradigms contrasted with the chaining paradigms in the studies cited above which tested all eight paradigms, support the notion of basic differences between the two sets of paradigms.

An experiment which attempted to assess the hypothesis that the list 1—list 2 relationship is the critical variable in producing mediation effects utilized the Horton-Kjeldergaard material in paradigm I. The lists were arranged so that mediation was to be expected for all pairs in the test-list. Two groups of 15 Ss each learned the three lists, group I having 15, 10, and 10 trials and group II having 10, 15, and 10 trials on stages one, two, and three, respectively. Equal prior exposure of the test-list words was accomplished by differential familiarization trials in the learning stages. It was predicted that group I would show greater mediation effects than group II since group I would have stronger habits and would present less opportunity for the mediators to be extinguished in stage 2. The hypothesis was confirmed. The mean correct responses on the first two anticipation trials were: group I = 3.6, group II = 2.6, which yielded a $t = 3.80$ ($p < .001$). Learning was very rapid and the differences beyond the second trial lacked significance. The above experiment was replicated on two additional groups (15 Ss each) using the same materials and procedures and varying only the word pairings. This experiment showed differences favoring group I in the early trials, but the effect lacked statistical significance for any one trial or for the sum over the test trials. Again learning was very rapid for both groups and tended to mask the effect.

It should be noted that the above results, to the extent that they are stable, bear directly on the recent controversy between Mandler and Earhard (Earhard and Mandler, 1965; Mandler and Earhard, 1964), and Jenkins (Jenkins, 1965; Jenkins and Foss, 1965). These results are directly opposite to those which would be predicted from the "pseudo-mediation" hypothesis. The above analysis assumes, as suggested by Mandler and Earhard, that the first-list associations are weakened during second-stage learning. Contrary to their conclusion, however, it is also assumed that during the early trials, or up to the point where the first-stage associations have been extinguished, these responses are available to act as mediators. Further, as pointed out by Jenkins, the Mandler and Earhard results appear to be qualitatively different from mediation effects; the effects are small and detectable only over a relatively long learning span. Mediation effects, like transfer effects, tend to emerge early and to be overshadowed by other factors and later trials. This position is also amply supported in the study by Schulz, Weaver, and Ginsberg (1965).

Another experiment to be taken into account with respect to this controversy is a recent study by Horton and Wiley (1967). Using several groups, they tested paradigm I against the appropriate control, delaying third stage learning over several time periods. In addition to the usual procedures, Horton and Wiley had the Ss relearn the first stage. As pointed out by the authors, the "pseudo-mediation" hypothesis would predict either no differences in relearning between the first-stage experimental and control pairs due to the third-stage acquisitions or it would predict differences in favor of the control pairs due to the greater opportunity for the unlearning of the experimental associations in the second stage. For each of the time-delay periods, large differences favoring the experimental pairs emerged. Horton and Wiley view this as a negation of the

in terms of habit strength and mediation trials, mediation takes place; where mediators are extinguished or are not given an opportunity to occur, no differences, or other phenonema such as "pseudo-mediation," appear.

LEARNED SIMILARITY. There are relatively few studies in which the strength of experimentally acquired associations have been manipulated in a three-stage

PARADIGM I

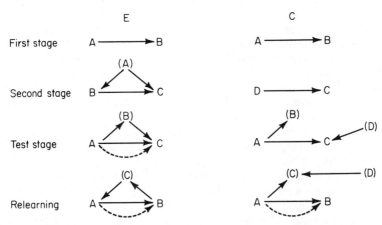

hypothesis concerning the weakening of the first-list associations. An alternative explanation which can plausibly account for three sets of findings, the Mandler and Earhard results, the effects of differential first-list and second-list practice, and the first-stage relearning differences, is to consider the latter experiment as a four-stage paradigm (above).

The mechanisms have been simplified with respect to the control paradigm for some mediation presumably could occur in the relearning stage due to association of implicit responses in the test-stage. Nevertheless, differences should favor the experimental paradigm under most circumstances. It seems reasonable to conclude that mediation, competition, and extinction take place at all except the initial learning stage. Where the conditions are appropriate

mediation paradigm. Only the studies by Barclay (1961, 1963) and by Martin (1961, 1964) manipulated one of the stages independently of the other. In both of Barclay's studies, CVC's were associated with random shapes, the mediator being a variable-frequency incidental stimulus in the first study and a variable ratio reinforcer in the second study, i.e., it occurred randomly a fixed percentage of the time, contingent upon a correct response. Negative results coupled with the unique design make the results difficult to evaluate. Martin paired a Kent-Rosanoff (K-R) word with a motor response and tested for generalization effects to the associate of the K-R word. Two-versus six-exposure trials in the second stage were found to have no effect on the third-stage generalization. Peterson (1963) reports an experiment, involving low m CCC's, in which Ss read aloud A-B, B-C, and were tested immediately with A-CDE, i.e., a multiple choice test where the S was told to pick the response which went best with the stimulus. The presentation of both of the first stages was varied, simultaneously, one, three, or six presentations. Although mediation effects, evaluated against controls, were significant, there was no effect attributable to the frequency of presentation. Horton and Hartman (1963) tested paradigm I against paradigm IV and presented both first and second stages either 10 or 15 times. Again mediation was found favoring the paradigm with an implicit forward link, paradigm I, but there was no effect due to stage-one and stage-two exposure. Morning and Voss (1964) tested a modified form of paradigm VII in which the A-B and A-C learning was collapsed into one stage. Each of the two responses was correct 50 per cent of the time on a random basis. The test-stage was split into mediated facilitation, mediated interference, and control pairs. Relative to the control, both facilitation and interference increased for the appropriate paradigm as a function of the learning trials. The latter two experiments both used the Horton-Kjeldergaard words as learning materials.

With the exception of the studies by Barclay, the above studies offer general support for the analysis of mediation presented earlier. With standard paired-associate procedures, with the modified design tested by Peterson, or with the very strong associates used by Martin, there is no reason to expect joint variation in list exposure to affect mediation. The Morning and Voss design, however, is in essence a series of repetitions of the first two learning stages involving both acquisition and extinction. Since acquisition is presumed to take place at a higher rate than extinction, the end product should be two relatively strong

responses elicited by the common stimulus and capable of eliciting each other. Furthermore, this tendency should be an increasing function of the number of trials.

INFERRED SIMILARITY. Studies of mediation or transfer which have assured a relatedness among verbal items have drawn these items from three basic types of pools: judged similarity of adjectives, measures derived from word-association norms, and semantic differential profiles. The first of these, synonymity, tends to be used only in broad general classes such as high, moderate, or low. With a few exceptions, such as the study by Morgan and Underwood (1950), little has been done to specify quantitative relationships between the ratings and the dependent variables of learning.

Similarly, with associative strength, the emphasis has been upon demonstrating an effect rather than upon relating habit-strength, as judged from the normative material, to learning effects (e.g., Bastian, 1961; Cramer and Cofer, 1960; Martin, 1961; Mink, 1963; Russell and Storms, 1955; and Ryan, 1960). One study which did investigate the effects of associative strength on transfer was that of Carlin (1958). Although transfer effects were readily found with transfer paradigms 2 and 4 measured against control paradigms 3 and 7, respectively, there were no consistent effects which could be attributed to list differences when the lists varied from strong associates to very weak ones. Using a split-plot design to gain sensitivity to differences among lists and to control for intersubject differences, Kjeldergaard (1964a) performed a partial replication of Carlin's experiment testing only paradigm 2 vs. 3. By using only a subset from each of Carlin's lists, it was possible to control for extraneous sources of similarity, such as semantic similarity, which Carlin had ignored. In spite of additional controls, Carlin's findings were confirmed; there were no list differences except between the experimental and the control pairs. Two recent studies, one by Kurcz (1964) and one by Brown, Jenkins, and Lavik (1966), have reported moderate relationships between inferred associative strength and transfer. The studies are similar in that they both used generalization measures rather than learning tests in the transfer stage. Kurcz measured muscle potentials to the associates of stimuli which had been paired with a motor response; Brown, Jenkins and Lavik had the *S*s guess the response to a new stimulus where the appropriate response, in terms of transfer, had been paired with the associate of the new stimulus in the original learning. Both studies report correlations in the .40–.60 range.

Several experiments have demonstrated that when children are asked to learn pairs of associates, where the associative strengths are judged from the norms, differences in effects can be found if the pairs are selected from widely separate segments of the associative frequency distribution (Castenada, Fahel, and Odom, 1961; McCullers, 1961; Wicklund, Palermo, and Jenkins, 1964).

Testing the associative model presented by Jarrett and Scheibe (1963), Palermo and Jenkins (1964) showed that when children are used as *S*s, children's associative norms would predict not only the learning of pairs directly associated, but also the learning of pairs that were associated indirectly via a mediate response, e.g., *WORKING (HARD) SOFT*. Such results have not been found with adults (Haun, 1960).

A third way in which verbal associations are used as a measure of verbal habits and habit strength is to relate words through their common responses (cf. Bousfield, Whitmarsh, and Danick,

1958; and Deese, 1962. A measure based upon the frequency of common associations, including an implicit repetition of the stimulus, has been shown to relate to clustering (Bousfield, Whitmarsh, and Berkowitz, 1960), intrusions in recall (Deese, 1959), and semantic conditioning (Whitmarsh and Bousfield, 1961). Higa (1963), using material high in associative overlap but relatively free from direct association of one word to the other, found no effect in terms of intralist associative interference, whereas synonymity and standard associative measures did produce interference effects. Since standard associative measures and overlap statistics tend to be correlated, it is difficult to assess the effect of the selective process. The materials from the Higa study were used by Kjeldergaard (1964b) in a test of paradigm 2. Although all measures of similarity yielded transfer relative to the controls, the effect of the response overlap was the weakest.

It is suggested that the difficulty in establishing a relationship between associative strength and learning and the weakness of such a relationship, if one is found, are related in part to the inherent problems of the norms and the techniques used to obtain them. The standard instructions call for a single response to each stimulus word. The end product, particularly where the strongest response is very strong, represents the relative position of the responses in the hierarchy rather than some measure of absolute strength. That is to say, the responses must compete, and if the primary response is very strong, one has no way of judging the absolute strength of the weaker associates. To support this proposition, the data presented in Table 5 are offered as documentation. Table 5 shows the distribution of responses to one stimulus from a word-association experiment which deviated from the standard procedures in that only one stimulus word was printed per page and Ss were instructed to give four responses rather than one. Ss were cautioned to respond repeatedly to the stimulus word and not to their previous associations.

Table 5

RESPONSES AND POSITION OF RESPONSES TO MULTIPLE ASSOCIATION TEST N = 30.

STIMULUS WORD

Black

Response Word	1st %	2nd %	3rd %	4th %	Total* %
white	63	7		7	77
dark	3	10	3	10	26
cat	3				3
light					0
color	3	3		3	10
dress		3	3		7
gloomy			7		7
Negro		10		3	13
night	3	13	26	7	49
red	7	3	3		13
room			3	3	6
sky			3	3	6
Idiosyncratic Responses	18	51	52	64	185
Total	100%	100%	100%	100%	400%

*Total Number of Different Words = 65

The table shows the percentage of Ss who gave each common response (i.e., a response that occured more than once for the group) as well as the position in which the response was given. The first four responses listed represent the four most frequent responses in the Minnesota Norms (Russell and Jenkins, 1954). It is apparent that the distribution of the first response in this study tends to parallel the response distribution in the Minnesota Norms. Looking at only the first responses, the response *NIGHT* would be judged to be at low strength, both here and in the Minnesota Norms, however, it occurs at some time or other for approximately half of the Ss. Even if one assumes that the Ss were chaining through the word *DARK*, the only obvious chain, more than one third of the Ss would have had to have given *NIGHT* independently of the word *DARK*. Although one example is not conclusive and all stimuli did not result in the same discrepancy between single-association and multiple-association patterns of strength, all stimuli whose primary response is an opposite, as well as many others, did exhibit this tendency. Obtaining multiple responses is probably not the answer to the problem, since in spite of the instructions, there are instances of responses being affected by prior responses either by chaining or by response generalization, e.g., *MOTHER, FATHER, BABY, BROTHER, SISTER*, etc.

A fourth measure of verbal similarity which has been shown to produce facilitative effects among "similar" pairs is semantic distance taken from the semantic differential developed by Osgood and his associates (Osgood, Suci, and Tannenbaum, 1957). Several studies, all concerned with demonstrating an effect rather than establishing quantitative relations, have shown that semantically similar pairs produce positive transfer effects (Brown and Jenkins, 1965; Dicken, 1961; Ryan, 1960). Ryan, and the replication by Brown and Jenkins, found that semantically related pairs produced significantly less facilitation than associated pairs which were otherwise comparable. Higa, in the study cited above, divided semantically related words into two classes, synonyms and non-synonyms, and found interference effects only with the former. In the correlational study by Kjeldergaard (1964a) which compared various indices of similarity and transfer effects across 40 pairs, the distance function correlated +.28 with effects, about the same magnitude as all of the other indices. Although the semantic differential has intuitive appeal due to its sensitivity in other areas and due to the precise mathematics associated with a special conceptualization, the disappointing results, coupled with the cogent criticism of the technique put forth by Carroll (1959), have removed some of the luster.

The Four-Stage Mediation Paradigms

The four-stage mediation paradigms, as discussed by Jenkins (1963), may also be translated into transfer terminology. Figure 3 presents examples from each of the three types of paradigms, chaining, stimulus equivalence,

and response equivalence, subjected to such a translation.

Insofar as the four-stage paradigms are generated by combining sets of the first two stages of the three-stage paradigms, examples rather than a complete listing of all possible paradigms are shown. Figure 3 shows combinations of each of the three types of learning-stages with each of the three types of transfer-stages. It can be seen that the test-stages of the four-stage paradigms fall into three classes, transfer types 1', 2, and 4 for the mediation paradigms subscripted 1, 2, and 3, respectively. The corresponding transfer control paradigms are 9, 3, and 7.

Prediction among the four-stage paradigms is difficult. Even if one considers only the third and fourth

FOUR-STAGE MEDIATION PARADIGMS

	Chaining			Stimulus Equivalence			Response Equivalence		
	α_1	α_2	α_3	β_1	β_2	β_3	Δ_1	Δ_2	Δ_3
Stage 1	D–C	D–C	D–C	C–D	C–D	C–D	D–C	D–C	D–C
Stage 2	A–D	A–D	B–D	A–D	A–D	B–D	D–A	D–A	D–B
Stage 3	A–B	A–B	A–B	A–B	A–B	A–B	A–B	A–B	A–B
Test	B–C	C–B	A–C	B–C	C–B	A–C	B–C	C–B	A–C

TRANSFER EQUIVALENTS OF FOUR-STAGE MEDIATION PARADIGMS

	α_1	α_2	α_3	β_1	β_2	β_3	Δ_1	Δ_2	Δ_3
Stage 1	D–A'	D–A'	D–B'	A'–D	A'–D	B'–D	D–A'	D–A'	D–B'
Stage 2	A–D	A–D	B–D	A–D	A'–D	B–D	D–A	D–A	D–B
Stage 3	A–B	A–B	A–B	A–B	A–B	A–B	A–B	A–B	A–B
Test	B–A'	A'–B	A–B'	B–A'	A'–B	A–B'	B–A'	A'–B	A–B'
	(1)	(2)	(4)	(1)	(2)	(4)	(1)	(2)	(4)

TRANSFER-CONTROL EQUIVALENTS OF FOUR-STAGE MEDIATION PARADIGMS

	α_1	α_2	α_3	β_1	β_2	β_3	Δ_1	Δ_2	Δ_3
Stage 1	X–C	X–C	X–C	C–X	C–X	C–X	X–C	X–C	X–C
Stage 2	A–D	A–D	B–D	A–D	A–D	B–D	D–A	D–A	D–B
Stage 3	A–B	A–B	A–B	A–B	A–B	A–B	A–B	A–B	A–B
Test	B–C	C–B	A–C	B–C	C–B	A–C	B–C	C–B	A–C
	(9)	(3)	(7)	(9)	(3)	(7)	(9)	(3)	(7)

Figure 3. Examples of four-stage mediation paradigms and corresponding control paradigms translated into transfer terminology (transfer paradigms in parenthesis)

stages, it will be recalled that no specific predictions were made concerning the relative effects of paradigm 2 versus 4 as the outcome depends upon the degree of similarity of the prime terms. Further, little is known about the transfer effects when the stimulus and response terms are interchanged so that there is no empirical basis for comparing paradigms 2 and 4 with 7'. Since the only comparative study met with failure (Jenkins, 1963), there are no empirical findings upon which to base speculation. Jenkins' failure, along with the findings reviewed with respect to the three-stage paradigms, leads one to expect a complex structure in terms of mediation outcome.

Habit strength

LEARNED. Paralleling the famous Shipley-Lumsdaine paradigm, paradigm B_2, Simon (1962) demonstrated that it was possible to get mediation effects using strictly motor responses and that the effects seemed to be a function of the number of pairings of the response terms during the training stages. It should be noted that Simon was able to demonstrate such effects due to the sensitivity of his measuring device; he mechanically amplified visibly imperceptible muscular movements. Thus, his techniques as well as his findings parallel those of Kurcz (1964), discussed previously.

Martin, *et al.*, (1963) also used a motor response to test for mediation strength. In a test of a_2, the first two stages were inferred from word association norms and the initial element of an association chain was paired with a lever-press. The third stage consisted of either two or six pairings. The test-stage consisted of a recognition task in which the S was told to press the lever only if he had seen the stimulus during the third stage presentation. Mediation was judged by comparing

the number of presses to the associates of stage three stimuli. Mediation effects decreased with increased stage three exposure. Since the task is basically one of discrimination rather than learning, the effects of the two processes may be quite different. List differentiation should increase with practice and if sufficient trials were given with stage three stimuli, no generalization effects should appear in a discrimination task.

James and Hakes (1965), although they did not systematically vary learning strength, were able to demonstrate mediation effects in one of the paradigms where Jenkins (1963) had failed, by having the Ss relearn the prior stages after each new stage was acquired. Thus there are complex opportunities for mediators to be acquired and extinguished, but basically such a procedure should favor the acquisition of strong mediational chains.[12] In this case, it must be acknowledged that the James and Hakes materials were much higher in meaningfulness than those used by Jenkins and this may have some effect on the results. A second procedural difference which is a potential source of the differences in effects is that James and Hakes used a matching task in the test stage. Since only subjects who were aware gave evidence of mediation, it may be that the instructions to "find the one that fits best" tends to make the subject aware of mediational relations that he would not attend to in a learning task. That these latter variables are not crucial is indicated by the positive findings of Grover, Horton, and Cunningham (1967), who used the same paradigm but the more typical learning procedures in the test stage. The common term in learning stages was a high frequency noun or verb, but the test

---

[12] It should be noted that the explanation being offered parallels that given for the Morning and Voss results for the three-stage paradigm.

was made to CVC's (70%–80%). Since the procedure here involved the relearning of the first two stages after the second stage had been learned for the first time, the two experiments viewed jointly, and contrasted with the findings of Jenkins, offer strong evidence as to the importance of habit strength and the subtle mediation-extinction relationship.

INFERRED. The only attempt to investigate associative habit strength in a four-stage paradigm is an unpublished study by Kjeldergaard, a study involving paradigm Δ_3; 40 $CVCCVC$'s were paired with 10 stimuli from the Minnesota Norms. The $CVCCVC$'s were divided into four lists and the 10 K-R words were paired with the stimuli in each list. Ss learned the four separate lists and then relearned the pairs as the four lists were merged. On the following day, Ss relearned the materials of the first day, by the same procedure, separate lists followed by the merged list, and then learned a list consisting of 40 new pairs constructed so that the response term was an associate of the first-list response or was a control word. The example at the top of the next column will serve to illustrate the procedure.

The particular K-R pairs were selected in order to investigate two aspects of associative strength simul-

First List (40 pairs)		Second List (40 pairs)	
ZAMBIC	FOOT	ZAMBIC	SHOE
BEMRIL	FOOT	BEMRIL	HAND
CAKSUL	FOOT	CAKSUL	TOE
FOLNOM	FOOT	FOLNOM	STAGNANT

taneously: the relative response strength as measured by the position of the response in the hierarchy and the absolute response strength as measured by the normative frequency of an S-R pair. Pilot work and logical considerations based upon the presumed difficulties with association norms discussed above lead to the hypothesis that relative strength might show a better quantitative relationship with transfer effects than absolute strength. Pairs were selected to span the range of associative frequency for each of the relative positions, primaries 16–84%, secondaries 20–30%, tertiaries 2–19%.

Table 6 shows the mean correct anticipations over ten learning trials for each of the K-R hierarchies. Successive rows represent the primaries, two responses successively lower in the hierarchy and the control or unrelated word. It can be seen, and the effect is supported statistically, that there are consistent differences between related and unrelated pairs, but there is no consistent relationship between transfer

Table 6

MEAN CORRECT ANTICIPATIONS OVER TEN TRIALS FOR TEN SETS OF K-R RELATED PAIRS USED IN AN A-B, A-B' PARADIGM.*

Stimulus	Foot	Tobacco	Red	Spider	Bitter	Table	Needle	Baby	King	Thirsty	Total
Primary R	14.74	13.33	15.54	18.54	19.30	13.98	11.94	18.74	20.21	7.39	15.38
Associate 2	15.61	8.65	16.99	13.67	7.77	11.37	10.60	12.04	11.32	9.23	11.73
Associate 3	15.78	15.39	19.66	10.53	11.08	12.14	12.86	14.59	12.88	7.54	13.25
Control	7.44	7.49	8.27	12.89	7.72	6.60	10.48	9.73	9.27	7.58	8.75
									Grand Mean =		13.45

*$F_1, 36 = 8.32, p < .01$

and position in the response hierarchy. The correlation between associative frequency and transfer effects is $+.35$. By using $\log_{10}$ in place of frequency, the correlation becomes $+.28$. It should be noted that in terms of effect, there have been several studies to show that four-stage mediation could be produced with an a_2 paradigm where the first two stages are inferred from associative norms. The study by Russell and Storms (1955) has been replicated with several procedural modifications (cf., Cieutat, 1962; Cofer and Yarczower, 1957; Martin and Dean, 1964; McGhee and Schulz, 1961) and all studies have confirmed the original findings.

Meaningfulness

Again due to the fact that there are relatively few studies in the literature involving verbal material in the four-stage paradigms, it is difficult to reach any conclusions concerning the role of meaningfulness beyond its influence on learning in general as discussed in the earlier portions of the paper. Other than the study by Jenkins cited above, research has been confined to four paradigms, a_2, a_3, b_2 and Δ_3. All of those involving a_3 (Russell-Storms design), the one test of a_2 (Martin, et al., 1963), and the Δ_3 experiment (Kjeldergaard, 1964) used word chains inferred from the free association norms for the first two stages. Two of the three tests of paradigm b_2, the study by James and Hakes (1965) as well as the one by Grover, Horton, and Cunningham (1966), had as response elements in the first two stages, high frequency words. If it were not for the study by Murdock (1952) using the same paradigm but with low association value CVC's (27%) as the response terms in the learning stages, one would be tempted to suspect that mediation was dependent upon meaningful mediators. Mur-

dock, however, found mediation effects under two treatments of deceptive instructions, success or failure, using a combination of nonsense materials, both figures and syllables, paired with a motor response.

Mediation: General Factors

MEANINGFULNESS. When one considers the variable of meaningfulness, the literature presents a uniform picture not often found in a learning area: mediation effects increase with meaningfulness. Peterson, *et al.*, (1964) tested the eight three-stage paradigms with both low association CCC's (40–55%) and high association CVC's (100%) and found more of the paradigms showing mediation effects with the more meaningful material. Later Peterson (1965) used the same materials together with an assumed stage made up of Kent-Rosanoff pairs in a test of the effects of meaningfulness and of time delays between paradigm stages. She found mediated facilitation for all levels of meaningfulness, but only the high meaningfulness pairs, K-R pairs, showed positive effects at the longest delay interval, eight seconds. Horton (1964) compared paradigms I and VII and the two extremes of Noble's (1952) scale and found no interaction of the variables but sizable differences in mediation favoring the high meaningfulness material.

It should also be pointed out that where researchers have failed to find mediation effects, the learning materials are relatively low in meaningfulness (d.g., Barclay, 1961, 1963; Crawford and Vanderplas, 1959). The same dichotomy seems to hold with respect to the admittedly more complex four-stage paradigms. The findings of Jenkins (1963) using the Horton-Kjeldergaard materials are to be contrasted with the positive results of Martin, *et al.*, (1963); James and Hakes (1965); Grover, Horton and Cunningham (1966); and Kjeldergaard (reported above), all of whom found mediation effects with high frequency materials. In addition, the Russell and Storms (1955) experiment and its subsequent replication, cited earlier, all produced positive effects with the high frequency Kent-Rosanoff materials.

AWARENESS. That subjects are sometimes aware of mediational processes seems irrefutable (cf., Barnes and Underwood, 1959; Horton and Hartman, 1963). It also seems well established that awareness is often related to the magnitude or the presence or absence of mediation effects (Earhard and Mandler, 1965; Horton, 1964; Yarmey, 1965). Some have interpreted the interrelations between mediation and awareness in particular experiments as an indication that awareness is a necessary condition for mediation (e.g., James and Hakes, 1965; Runquist and Farley, 1964). It seems equally well established, however, that mediation can occur without awareness (cf., Bulgelski and Sharlock, 1952; Horton and Kjeldergaard, 1961).

EXPERIMENTAL SENSITIVITY. In contrasting studies where mediation effects have been found with those studies in which they do not occur and by examining the magnitude of mediational and transfer effects, the literature suggests that the outcomes in the area may be related to the sensitivity of the learning measures that are used. Matching techniques, such as those used by James and Hakes (1965) and by Schulz, Weaver, and Ginsberg (1965); multiple choice responses, such as used by Peterson (1963), by Brown and Jenkins (1965), and by Brown, Jenkins, and Lavik (1966); and tests of generalization by measuring micro-muscular

responses, such as by Simon (1962) and by Kurcz (1964) all seem to be more sensitive to effects than the traditional dependent variables. In some of these instances, effects have been demonstrated with materials or paradigms that previously had failed. In other instances, quantitative relations between variables have been established where previously only gross effects were detectable.

Similarly, although less easy to document, transfer and mediational effects may be limited to the early trials of the transfer list, differences between some of the transfer paradigms may show effects where magnitude is less than expected on theoretical grounds, paradigms may sometimes show facilitation when interference is expected and vice versa, because all of these effects are related to the lack of sensitivity of the traditional learning measures. Noise and intersubject variability mask and distort the true effects.

Verbal Learning and General S-R Theories

To reflect upon the relationship between verbal learning theory and general S-R theory is a very difficult task. As I see it, interest in the current conceptualizations of mediation and transfer in terms of S-R psychology had a common starting point in the work of Hull and his associates. With a few exceptions, such as the work on semantic conditioning, the subsequent developments in verbal learning theory as opposed to general S-R theory have followed divergent paths. General S-R theory has led to investigations which emphasize motivation, reinforcement, and variables influencing classical conditioning; whereas verbal learning theory has led to investigations which place emphasis upon stimulus and response properties and their influence upon transfer and mediated transfer.

Independent development and lack of mutual interests has meant that each has contributed relatively little to the other. Both appear to be about equally sophisticated in terms of developing an exact theory of sufficient scope that is capable of mathematical expression.

References

Baddeley, A. D., "Stimulus-Response Compatability in Paired-Associate Learning of Nonsense Syllables," *Nature*, **191** (1961), 1327–1328.

Barclay, A., "Objective Mediators in Paired-Associate Learning," *American Journal of Psychology*, **74** (1961), 373–383.

———, "Mediated Transfer in Verbal Learning," *Psychological Reports*, **12** (1963), 751–756.

Barnes, J. M., and B. J. Underwood, " 'Fate' of First-List Associations in Transfer Theory," *Journal of Experimental Psychology*, **58** (1959), 95–105.

Bastian, J., "Associative Factors in Verbal Transfer," *Journal of Experimental Psychology*, **62** (1961), 70–79.

Birge, J. S., "The Role of Verbal Responses in Transfer," Ph.D. thesis, Yale University, 1941.

Bousfield, W. A., "The Problem of Meaning in Verbal Learning," in C. N. Cofer, ed., *Verbal Learning and Verbal Behavior*. New York: McGraw Hill Book Company, 1961, 81–91.

———, G. A. Whitmarsh, and H. Berkowitz, "Partial Response Identities in Associative Clustering," *Journal of General Psychology*, **63** (1960), 233–238.

———, ———, and J. J. Danick, "Partial Response Identities in Verbal Generalization," *Psychological Reports*, **4** (1958), 703–718.

Briggs, G. E., "Acquisition, Extinction, and Recovery Functions in Retroactive Inhibition," *Journal of Experimental Psychology*, **47** (1954), 285–293.

Brown, L. K., and J. J. Jenkins, "The Use of Interspersed Test Items in Measuring Mediated Response Transfer," *Journal of Verbal Learning and Verbal Behavior*, **4** (1965), 425–429.

———, ———, and J. Lavik, "Response Transfer as a Function of Verbal Association Strength," *Journal of Experimental Psychology*, **71** (1966), 138–142.

Bruce, R. W., "Conditions of Transfer of Training." *Journal of Experimental Psychology*, **16** (1933), 343–61.

Bugelski, B. R., and R. C. Cadwallader, "A Reappraisal of the Transfer and Retroaction Surface," *Journal of Experimental Psychology*, **52** (1956), 360–366.

———, and D. P. Sharlock, "An Experimental Demonstration of Unconscious Mediated Association," *Journal of Experimental Psychology*, **44** (1952), 334–338.

Carlin, J. E., "Word-Association Strength as a Variable in Verbal Paired-Associate Learning," Ph.D. thesis, University of Minnesota, 1958.

Carroll, J. B., "A Review of: Osgood, C. E., G. J. Suci, and P. H. Tannenbaum, *The Measurement of Meaning*," *Language*, **35** (1959), 58–77.

———, P. M. Kjeldergaard, and A. A. Carton, "Number of Opposites vs. the Number of Primaries as a Response Measure in Free-Association Tests," *Journal of Verbal Learning and Verbal Behavior*, **1** (1962), 22–30.

Casteneda, A., L. S. Fahel, and R. Odom, "Associative Characteristics of Sixty-Three Adjectives and Their Relation to Verbal Paired-Associate Learning in Children," *Child Development*, **32** (1961), 297–304.

Cieutat, V. J., "Replication Report: Implicit Verbal Chaining in Paired-Associate Learning," *Perception and Motor Skills*, **14** (1962), 45–46.

Cofer, C. N., and J. P. Foley, "Mediated Generalization and the Interpretation of Verbal Behavior: I. Prolegomena,"

Psychological Review, **49** (1942), 513–540.

————, and M. Yarczower, "Further Study of Implicit Verbal Chaining in Paired-Associate Learning," *Psychological Reports*, **3** (1957), 453–456.

Cramer, P., and C. N. Cofer, "The Role of Forward and Reverse Associations in Transfer of Training," *American Psychologist*, **15** (1960), 463.

Crawford, J. L., and J. M. Vanderplas, "An Experiment on the Mediation of Transfer in Paired-Associate Learning," *Journal of Psychology*, **47** (1959), 87–98.

Dallett, K. M., "The Transfer Surface Re-examined," *Journal of Verbal Learning and Verbal Behavior*, **1** (1962), 91–94.

————, "Implicit Mediators in Paired-Associate Learning," *Journal of Verbal Learning and Verbal Behavior*, **3** (1964), 209–214.

————, "A Transfer Surface for Paradigms in which Second-List S-R Pairings Do Not Correspond to First-List Pairings," *Journal of Verbal Learning and Verbal Behavior*, **4** (1965), 528–534.

Deese, J., "Influence of Interitem Associative Strength upon Immediate Free Recall," *Psychological Reports*, **5** (1959), 305–312.

————, "On the Structure of Associative Meaning," *Psychological Review*, **69** (1962), 161–175.

Dicken, C. F., "Connotative Meaning as a Determinant of Stimulus Generalization," *Psychological Monographs*, **75** (1961), 1 (whole 505).

DiMascio, A., "Learning Characteristics of Nonsense Syllables: A Function of Letter Frequency," *Psychological Reports*, **5** (1959), 585–591.

Earhard, B., and G. Mandler, "Pseudomediation: A Reply and More Data," *Psychonomic Science*, **3** (1965), 137–138.

Esper, E. A., "A Technique for the Experimental Investigation of Associative Interference in Artificial Linguistic Material," *Language Monographs*, **1** (1925), 1–46.

Gagné, R. M., K. E. Baker, and H. Foster,

"On the Relation between Similarity and Transfer of Training in the Learning of a Discriminative Motor Task," *Psychological Review*, **57** (1950), 67–79.

Gibson, E. J., "A Systematic Application of the Concepts of Generalization and Differentiation to Verbal Learning," *Psychological Review*, **47** (1940), 196–229.

————, "Retroactive Inhibition as a Function of Degree of Generalization between Tasks," *Journal of Experimental Psychology*, **28** (1941), 93–115.

Goss, A. E., "Early Behaviorism and Verbal Mediating Responses," *American Psychologist*, **16** (1961), 285–298.

Grover, D. E., D. L. Horton, and M. Cunningham, "Mediated Facilitation and Interference in a Four-Stage Paradigm." *Journal of Verbal Learning and Verbal Behavior*, **6** (1967), 42–46.

Haun, K. W., "Measures of Association and Verbal Learning," *Psychological Reports*, **7** (1960), 451–460.

Higa, M., "Interference Effects of Intralist Work Relationships in Verbal Learning," *Journal of Verbal Learning and Verbal Behavior*, **2** (1963), 170–175.

Horton, D. L., "The Effects of Meaningfulness, Awareness, and Type of Design in Verbal Mediation," *Journal of Verbal Learning and Verbal Behavior*, **3** (1964), 187–194.

————, and R. R. Hartman, "Verbal Mediation as a Function of Associative Directionality and Exposure Frequency," *Journal of Verbal Learning and Verbal Behavior*, **1**, 5 (1963), 361–364.

————, and P. M. Kjeldergaard, "An Experimental Analysis of Associative Factors in Mediated Generalization," *Psychological Monographs*, **75** (1961), 11, (whole 515).

————, and R. E. Wiley, "The Effect of Mediation on the Retention and Strength of Previously Formed Association," *Journal of Verbal Learning and Verbal Behavior*, **6** (1967), 36–41.

Hull, C. L., "The Problem of Stimulus Equivalence in Behavior Theory," *Psychological Review*, **46** (1939), 9–30.

James, C. T., and D. T. Hakes, "Mediated Transfer in a Four-Stage, Stimulus-Equivalence Paradigm," *Journal of Verbal Learning and Verbal Behavior*, **4** (1965), 89–93.

Jantz, E. M., and B. J. Underwood, "R-S Learning as a Function of Meaningfulness and Degree of S-R Learning," *Journal of Experimental Psychology*, **56** (1958), 174–179.

Jarrett, R. F., and K. E. Scheibe, "Association Chains and Paired-Associate Learning," *Journal of Verbal Learning and Verbal Behavior*, **1**, 4 (1963), 264–268.

Jenkins, J. J., "A Study of Mediated Association," *Studies in Verbal Behavior. Report No. 2*, 1959, University of Minnesota.

———, "Mediated Associations: Paradigms and Situations," in C. N. Cofer and B. S. Musgrave, eds., *Verbal Behavior and Learning: Problems and Processes*, New York: McGraw-Hill Book Company, 1963, 210–245.

———, "Comments on Pseudomediation," *Psychonomic Science*, **2** (1965), 97–98.

———, and D. J. Foss, "An Experimental Analysis of Pseudomediation," *Psychonomic Science*, **2** (1965), 99–100.

———, W. D. Mink, and W. A. Russell, "Associative Clustering as a Function of Verbal Association Strength," *Psychological Reports*, **4** (1958), 127–136.

———, and W. A. Russell, "Word Association and Behavior: The Minnesota Studies," Unpublished mimeo, 1964.

Kjeldergaard, P. M., "Verbal Transfer Processes in Acquired Stimulus Equivalence and Acquired Response Equivalence Paradigms," Unpublished Ph. D. thesis, University of Minnesota, 1960.

———, "Stimulus and Response Relationships and the Hypothetical Transfer Surface," *Annual report*, 1964a.

———, "Interlist Transfer of Related Word Pairs as a Function of First-List Learning," *American Psychologist*, **19** (1964b), 722 (abstract).

Kurcz, I., "Semantic and Phonetographic Generalization of a Voluntary Response," *Journal of Verbal Learning and Verbal Behavior*, **3** (1964), 261–268.

Maltzman, I., "Individual Differences in 'Attention': The Orienting Reflex," in R. M. Gagné, ed., *Learning and Individual Differences*. Columbus, Ohio: Charles E. Merrill Books Inc., 1966.

———, and M. Belloni, "Three Studies of Semantic Generalization," *Journal of Verbal Learning and Verbal Behavior*, **3** (1964), 231–236.

Mandler, G., "Response Factors in Human Learning," *Psychological Review*, **61** (1954a), 235–244.

———, "Transfer of Training as a Function of Degree of Response Overlearning," *Journal of Experimental Psychology*, **47** (1954b), 411–417.

———, and B. Earhard, "Pseudomediation: Is Chaining an Artifact?" *Psychonomic Science*, **1** (1964), 247–248.

———, and S. Heinemann, "Effects of Overlearning of a Verbal Response on Transfer of Training," *Journal of Experimental Psychology*, **52** (1956), 39–46.

Martin, E., "Transfer of Verbal Paired-Associates," *Psychological Review*, **72** (1965), 327–343.

Martin, J. G., "Mediated Transfer in Two Verbal Learning Paradigms," *Studies in Verbal Behavior. Report No. 5*, (1961), University of Minnesota.

———, "Word-Association Frequency and the Proximity Effect," *Journal of Verbal Learning and Verbal Behavior*, **3** (1964), 344–345.

———, M. Oliver, G. Hom, and G. Heaslet, "Repetition and Task in Verbal Mediating Response-Acquisition," *Journal of Experimental Psychology*, **66** (1963), 12–16.

Martin, R. B., and S. J. Dean, "Implicit and Explicit Mediation in Paired-Associate Learning," *Journal of Experimental Psychology*, **68** (1964), 21–27.

McCullers, J. C., "Effects of Associative Strength, Grade Level, and Interpair

Interval in Verbal Paired-Associate Learning," *Child Development*, **32** (1961), 773–778.

———, "Type of Associative Interference as a Factor in Verbal Paired-Associative Learning," *Journal of Verbal Learning and Verbal Behavior*, **4**, 1, (1965), 12–16.

McGehee, N., and R. Schulz, "Mediation and Paired-Associate Learning," *Journal of Experiment Psychology*, **62** (1961), 568–570.

McGeoch, J. A., and A. L. Irion, *The Psychology of Human Learning*. New York: Longmans, Green, & Co., Inc., 1962.

McGovern, J. B., "Extinction of Association in Four Transfer Paradigms," *Psychological Monographs*, **73**, 16 (1964),

Miller, G. A., "Free Recall of Redundant Strings of Letters," *Journal of Experimental Psychology*, **56** (1958), 484–491.

Miller, N. E., and J. Dollard, *"Social Learning and Imitation*. New Haven: Yale University Press, 1941.

Mink, W. D., "Semantic Generalization as Related to Word Association," *Psychological Reports*, **12** (1963), 59–67.

Morgan, R. L., and B. J. Underwood, "Proactive Inhibition as a Function of Response Similarity," *Journal of Experimental Psychology*, **40** (1950), 592–603.

Morning, N., and J. F. Voss, "Mediation of R_1-R_2 in the Acquisition of S-R_1, S-R_2 Associations," *Journal of Experimental Psychology*, **67** (1964), 67–71.

Mowrer, O. H., *Learning Theory and Behavior*. New York: John Wiley & Sons, Inc., 1960.

Murdock, B. B., "The Effects of Failure and Retroactive Inhibition on Mediated Generalization," *Journal of Experimental Psychology*, **44** (1952), 156–164.

Murdock, B. B., Jr., " 'Backward' Learning in Paired-Associates," *Journal of Experimental Psychology*, **51** (1956), 213–215.

———, " 'Backward' Association in Transfer and Learning," *Journal of Experimental Psychology*, **55** (1958), 111–114.

Musgrave, B. S., and J. C. Cohen, "Abstraction in Verbal Paired-Associate Learning," *Journal of Experimental Psychology*, **71** (1966), 1–8.

Newman, S. E., "A Selective Mediation Model of Paired-Associate Learning," Paper presented at the meeting of the Psychonomic Society. Chicago, 1960.

Noble, C. E., "An Analysis of Meaning," *Psychological Review*, **59** (1952), 421–430.

Osgood, C. E., "Meaningful Similarity and Interference in Learning," *Journal of Experimental Psychology*, **36** (1946), 277–301.

———, "An Investigation into the Causes of Retroactive Interference," *Journal of Experimental Psychology*, **38** (1948), 132–154.

———, "The Similarity Paradox in Human Learning: A Resolution," *Psychological Review*, **56** (1949), 132–143.

———, "The Nature and Measurement of Meaning," *Psychological Bulletin*, **49** (1952), 197–237.

———, *Method and Theory in Experimental Psychology*. New York: Oxford University Press, Inc., 1953.

———, G. J. Suci, and P. H. Tannenbaum, *The Measurement of Meaning*. Urbana, Illinois: University of Illinois Press, 1957.

Palermo, D. S., and J. J. Jenkins, "Paired-Associate Learning as a Function of the Strength of Links in the Associative Chain," *Journal of Verbal Learning and Verbal Behavior*, **3**, 5 (1964), 406–412.

Peterson, L. R., and M. J. Peterson, "Short-term Retention of Individual Verbal Items," *Journal of Experimental Psychology*, **58** (1959), 193–198.

Peterson, M. J. "Effects of Knowledge of Results on a Verbal Mediating Response," *Journal of Experimental Psychology*, **66** (1963), 394–398.

———, "Effects of Delay Interval and Meaningfulness on Verbal Mediating Responses," *Journal of Experimental Psychology*, **69** (1965), 60–66.

———, F. J. Colavita, D. B. Sheanan, III, and K. C. Blattner, "Verbal Mediating Chains and Response Availability as a Function of the Acquisition Paradigm," *Journal of Verbal Learning and Verbal Behavior*, **3** (1964), 11–18.

Poffenberger, A. T., "The Influence of Improvement in one Simple Mental Process upon Other Related Processes," *Journal of Educational Psychology*, **6** (1915), 459–474.

Postman, L., "Retention of First-List Associations as a Function of the Conditions of Transfer," *Journal of Experimental Psychology*, **64** (1962a), 380–387.

———, "Transfer of Training as a Function of Experimental Paradigm and Degree of First-List Learning," *Journal of Verbal Learning and Verbal Behavior*, **1** (1962b), 109–118.

———, and K. Stark, "The Role of Response Set in Tests of Unlearning," *Journal of Verbal Learning and Verbal Behavior*, **4** (1965), 315–322.

Razran, G., "Semantic and Phonetographic Generalizations of Salivary Conditioning to Verbal Stimuli," *Journal of Experimental Psychology*, **39** (1949), 642–652.

Robinson, E. S., "Some Factors Determining the Degree of Retroactive Inhibition," *Psychological Monographs*, **128** (1920).

Runquist, W. N., and F. H. Farley, "The Use of Mediators in the Learning of Paired-Associates," *Journal of Verbal Learning and Verbal Behavior*, **3** (1964), 280–285.

Russell, W. A., and J. J. Jenkins, "The Complete Minnesota Norms for Responses to 100 Words from the Kent-Rosanoff Word Association Test," *Technical Report No. 11*, University of Minnesota, 1954.

Russell, W. A., and L. H. Storms, "Implicit Verbal Chaining in Paired-Associate Learning," *Journal of Experimental Psychology*, **49** (1955), 287–293.

Ryan, J. J., III, "Comparison of Verbal Response Transfer Mediated by Mean-ingfully Similar and Associate Stimuli," *Journal of Experimental Psychology*, **60** (1960), 408–415.

Schulz, R. W., G. E. Weaver, and S. Ginsberg, "Mediation with Pseudomediation Controlled: Chaining Is not an Artifact!" *Psychonomic Science*, 2, (1965), 169–170.

Schwenn, E., and B. J. Underwood, "Simulated Similarity and Mediation Time in Transfer," *Journal of Verbal Learning and Verbal Behavior*, **4**, 6 (1965), 476–483.

Simon, S. H., "Response-Mediated Generalization with Simple Skeletal-Motor Responses," *Journal of Experimental Psychology*, **63** (1962), 458–463.

Storms, L. W., "Apparent Backward Association: A Situational Effect," *Journal of Experimental Psychology*, **55** (1958), 390–395.

Umemoto, T., "Japanese Studies in Verbal Learning and Memory," *Psychologia*, **2** (1959), 1–19.

Underwood, B. J., "An evaluation of the Gibson Theory of Verbal Learning," in C. N. Cofer, ed., *Verbal Learning and Verbal Behavior*. New York: McGraw-Hill Book Company, 1961, 197–217.

———, "Stimulus Selection in Verbal Learning," in C. N. Cofer and B. S. Musgrave, eds., *Verbal Behavior and Learning: Problems and Processes*. New York: McGraw-Hill Book Company, 1963, 33–47.

———, and R. W. Schulz, *Meaningfulness and Verbal Learning*. Philadelphia: J. B. Lippincott Co., 1960.

———, ———, and W. N. Runquist, "Response Learning in Paired-Associate Lists as a Function of Intralist Similarity," *Journal of Experimental Psychology*, **58** (1959), 70–78.

Whitmarsh, G. A., and W. A. Bousfield, "Use of Free Associational Norms for the Prediction of Generalization of Salivary Conditioning to Verbal Stimuli," *Psychological Reports*, **8** (1961), 91–95.

Wicklund, D. A., D. S. Palermo, and J. J. Jenkins, "The Effects of Associative

Strength and Response Heirarchy on Paired-Associate Learning," *Journal of Verbal Learning and Verbal Behavior*, **3** (1964), 413–420.

Wimer, R., "Osgood's Transfer Surface: Extension and Test," *Journal of Verbal Learning and Verbal Behavior*, **3** (1964), 274–279.

Woodworth, R. S., and H. Schlosberg, *Experimental Psychology*. New York: Holt, Rinehart & Winston, Inc., 1954.

Wylie, H. H., "An Experimental Study of Transfer of Response in the White Rat," *Behavioral Monographs*, **16** (1919).

Wynne, R. D., H. Gerjuoy, H. Schiffman, and N. Wexler, "Word-Association: Variables Affecting Popular Response Frequency," Unpublished mimeo., 1965.

Yarmey, A. D., "Word Abstractness, Awareness, and Type of Design in Verbal Mediation," Unpublished Ph. D. thesis., University of Western Ontario, 1965.

Yum, K. S., "An Experimental Test of the Law of Assimilation," *Journal of Experimental Psychology*, **14** (1931), 68–82.

Association
and Memory

4 JAMES DEESE

More than most experimental psychologists generally realize, I think, the substance of the experimental investigation of associative processes has been influenced by the philosophic views which occasioned associationism in the first place. The general view of the process of association held by most experimental psychologists, more or less evident in the nature of the experimental arrangements of materials in the laboratory and in the variables chosen for investigation, is at least implied in the *Phaedo* and rather concretely stated by Aristotle. In their modern form, the essential ideas behind the experimental study of associations are clearly exposited by Hobbes and elaborated (though not significantly altered) by the English empiricists, the Scottish associationists, and the German experimentalists, including Ebbinghaus. All of this history is fairly well known to students of learning and verbal behavior. Nevertheless, I think we need to remind ourselves that the whole course of the experimental investigation of association, including nearly all of its most recent manifestations, has been determined in a fundamental way by the oldest of philosophic—i.e., arm-chair—doctrine. In fact, the fundamental assumptions of the

study of associative processes have been untouched by nearly an entire century of empirical investigation. It is hard to think of another discipline in which so long a period of investigation has not been accompanied by a fundamental change of assumptions. It is by no means obvious to many students of verbal behavior that radically different assumptions about the nature of associations are even possible.

I take this way of introducing my comments on the study of association because the two papers by Pollio and Tulving reveal significant attempts in different ways to escape the limitations imposed by the so-called laws of contiguity, frequency, and all the other age-incrusted legacies from psychology's past in philosophic empiricism. Kjeldergaard's paper remains more firmly in the tradition. Pollio tries to escape the history we have recapitulated through the study of the interrelations among naturally occurring associations and Tulving through the exploitation of the potentially information-rich technique of free recall.

The classical view of the associative process is determined, I think it is fairly obvious to see, by the most evident and superficial property of the flow of ideas, their temporal succession.

One idea seems to succeed another in thought. Subjectively, a succeeding idea seems to be occasioned by the one that preceded it. Clearly, the most elementary and obvious hypothesis to account for this phenomenological impression of one idea growing out of another is to suppose that it is the result of some previous experience of the same succession. One idea succeeds another because it has always done so. That bit of folk-reasoning can be made explicit and scientifically respectable by saying that the experience is determined by the principle of temporal contiguity. Frequency and all the other associative laws (except similarity) become clearly secondary to contiguity (and, of course, similarity can become secondary to contiguity through the doctrine of mediation).

The law of contiguity, so far as I know, has never been doubted as the cornerstone of the associative process, at least until quite recently. Locke, in his analytic approach to the structure of knowledge, complicates the notion of contiguity by introducing the concept of simultaneous associations as *analytic* elements, and modern experimental investigations of derived associations, mediating processes, and the like complicate the matter in a quite different way. The idea that one thing is recalled on occasion of another because those two experiences have occurred in that way before, however, is the essential heart of classical associationsim. This idea has an appeal for the experimental psychologist, because it suggests stimulus control, and it leads to devices like the memory drum, etc., for controlling the input conditions. One can "manipulate," as the common metaphor goes, the behavior of subjects in the learning experiment by alterations in the stimuli and methods of presentation. Furthermore, the general arrangement of the verbal-learning experiment, together with the secondary principles of frequency, etc., lend themselves to statement in the form of differential equations and other variable by variable process analyses. Finally, the essential notions of associationism found congenial, familial company with the various forms of behavioristic analysis and the peripheralism often so entailed.

I should like to explore the implications, suggested by the two papers we are considering, of abandoning the limitations of that history and leaving behind our philosophical heritage exemplified in the law of contiguity and the secondary principles. Certainly, traditional experimental studies of verbal associative processes do not, in the richness of their empirical findings, command us to be cautious in this respect. We have discovered remarkably little that is stable or of general significance, given a century of investigation and thousands upon thousands of experiments. The comparison with the remarkable progress in the past few years that has been made in linguistic theory—in part concerned with much the same subject matter—is especially revealing.

Linguistic theory, as we now know, has gone into a revolutionary phase in which many of the assumptions standing behind earlier investigations have been abandoned in favor of far richer assumptions leading to broader investigations that much more reasonably permit the characterization of the phenomena under study. The assumptions that are being abandoned in linguistic theory, by the way, bear a suspiciously familiar resemblance to the concepts of classical associationism. It is not just radical empiricism that is in common between older structural linguistic theories and associationism, but substantive matters as well. Current linguistic theorists exaggerate their success, I think, and treat too lightly the formidable obstacles to further progress. However, it is impossible to deny that a genuine revolution has taken place. Given the similarity—perhaps underlying identity—in the subject matter of the two disciplines, and the difference in rate of progress, I think we have something that should give the experimental student of verbal behavior cause for reflection.

Modern linguistic theorists, of course, have abandoned the notion that language or its representation in speech is produced by a kind of left-to-right generation process of the sort implied by classical associationism. They have abandoned it (if, in fact, they ever seriously considered it) because such an analysis is too poverty-stricken to handle the manifest and obvious facts about language. Furthermore, as has often been pointed out by linguists—and a few psychologists—the learning of the general properties of language, such as the vocabulary and the grammar, would be literally impossible in a lifetime, given the best possible conditions for the operation of the variables of classical associationism, including the auxiliary apparatus provided by mediation.

Within experimental psychology itself, there have always been hesitant and tentative doubts that the really interesting aspects of associations, their curious patterns of interrelations, should be determined by the notions implied in so simple a theory as the classical one. These doubts are made stronger by the inherently interesting data presented by Pollio and Tulving. What I shall have to say in comment on the two papers by these authors is by way of some tentative suggestions for abandoning the law of contiguity and replacing it with some analyses which do not assume it and which are, in Charlotte Bühler's apt phrase, less

geradezu naiv in describing how sequences in thought, language, or, for that matter, in learning strings of nonsense syllables actually arise. The data referred to above, as well as broader linguistic and psychological considerations, suggest that the fundamental problem in the study of associations does not consist of individual contiguities but of patterns of organization and structures which can generate those arrangements. The fundamental analytic fact is not that *A* leads to *B*, but that the interrelations of *A*, *B* and other verbal elements related to both imply a structure, an organization which cannot be in any sense described by the elements which enter into the manifest sequence (see Fodor and Katz, 1964). Those same structures that seem to be revealed by manifest associations are also revealed in the patterns of organization in free recall and the like, as is suggested by the close relation between manifest associations and patterns of organization in recall. The left-to-right or read-out feature of memory and related phenomena is not one of the essential structural characteristics but is determined by the human limitations in information processing. What an individual *knows* is not constrained by what apparently leads to what in a particular verbal sequence or what he can put into a single association. Thus, the important fact in the manifest organization of associations is not that *mother* leads to *father*, *hot* to *cold*, and *sleep* to *dream*, not that these superficially similar pairs are contiguous or derived in any form from the law of contiguity, but that they in their *obvious* differences—obvious to the most obtuse speaker of the English language—reflect different organizational processes at work. In this respect, much of the current experimental literature cited by Pollio and Tulving is the most interesting aspect of the current work on memory, because it faces us with the fact that such must be the case. However, the works does not go far enough. It is not enough to show that the output in recall protocols is correlated with associative relatedness or various patterns of organization in association, as the experiments in interword associative strength, category clustering and subjective clustering show, but in the interests of arriving at a general characterization of these and other facts about human linguistic ability, it is necessary to show that both kinds of processes are determined by some more basic structures.

Associations, then, are only indices of underlying patterns of relation. They cannot be, in themselves, the deepest level of organization (using "deepest" in something like the sense employed by generative linguists). They are certainly not the *cause* of organization in recall, as I think I implied in an earlier series of papers (Deese, 1959a, 1959b, 1960, 1961) or as Bousfield implied in his later papers (e.g. Bousfield, 1961) though not, interestingly enough, in his earlier ones (Bousfield, 1953). Bousfield was closer to a more general analysis in 1953 than most of us were a decade later. Unfortunately, we seem to have persuaded Bousfield instead of the other way around. The nature of this deeper pattern of organization is, of course, a matter of theory. Here, I think, the early Bousfield was clearly wrong. The supraordinate-subordinate structure he proposed—and apparently got from Hebb—is simply too elementary to describe the obvious complexities in the interrelations of associations, and Bousfield did not even pursue the notion as relentlessly as he should have in the experimental analysis of category clustering. Where he was right was on a matter of principle. He abandoned the doctrine of contiguous associations.

I do not think it is my function in this paper to push for any particular theoretical analysis of the nature of the deeper structures of association, though in the course of commenting upon the Tulving and Pollio papers it will be convenient to take some general point of view as a point of reference. The one that I prefer at the moment is a distinctive feature analysis of the problem of accounting for or describing the organization in associations and in memory retrieval. There are certainly difficulties with this idea, but it may be used even so, to illustrate how utterly inadequate are any of the ideas arising out of classical associationism. By this view, we are not to regard retrieval in memory of a morphophonemic element in the manifest language as the retrieval of a single source item but as the intersection of some set of distinctive source features which, in turn, enables the production of a single item. These features may be regarded as independent (i.e., uncorrelated) and binary (Deese, 1966). All scalable or intensive aspects of the manifest strings in memory are, by this view, added as the result of a special operation.

I do not intend to expand upon or to justify this view here, but what I have just said will enable me to comment on the literature cited by Tulving and Pollio (as well as suggest some additions to it) in a concrete way. Take, for example, the implication (which stems indirectly from classical associationism, I think) that the basic unit of analysis of the subjects' performance in a free-recall experiment is the single item, as Tulving seems to assert. In the first place, there are difficulties in determining exactly what a single item is, as I have pointed out before (Deese, 1961). In fact, the difficulties are insurmountable. I cannot refer to a general proof here; however, a demonstration of the limitations is possible. The nonsense syllable, as the work by Underwood and his students on response integration testifies, is not a single item. We might suppose—at least for Underwood's late adolescent subjects—that a single letter would constitute a single item. Therefore, each nonsense syllable, before response integration, is defined as a chain of three items having some contingent probability between them. The recognition of individual letters, phonemes, syllables or any unit at any level of analysis requires a knowledge of the deeper linguistic structures (see Chomsky, 1964). Some indication of the difficulties may be achieved by considering Wickelgren's (1966) recent work on the recall of the morphemic labels for individual letters (Ay, Bee, Cee, etc.) which shows letter names are not, for adult users, single items in the old-fashioned associationistic sense which stems back at least to James Mill's metaphor about the molecules or bricks of the mind. Wickelgren shows that mistakes in memory, intrusions and the like, are determined by at least the phonemic distinctive features underlying the components of the letter-name morphemes (compare Dee, Eee, Tee, etc., with Eff, Ess, Ell, etc.). The strong implication is that the letter names themselves are retrieved by combination of the distinctive features composing them, not as units in themselves. Recognition of the phonemes (hence their features) is dependent upon syntax.

Furthermore, the implication of Garner's (1962) analysis needs to be considered here. Garner has been insisting that it is not the individual item in perception and learning that is important, but the set—inferred set in some cases—to which that item belongs which determines the various behavioral characteristics associated with the perception, cognition, and recall of that item. The experimental program which he has embarked upon as the result of that analysis makes, from a totally nonlinguistic approach, an eloquent case for the abandonment of the item-in-isolation notion. The notion of distinctive features provides one—though not the only—way for describing the organization of the underlying sets proposed by Garner as being, at least in some crucial cases, an absolute necessity for describing what subjects *can actually do* in a laboratory task.

Therefore, I think Tulving makes a mistake in emphasis by insisting on the assumption that the theoretical analysis of the processes underlying successful performance in free recall of single units is inherently simpler than the free recall of units which are obviously more than one. Wickelgren's demonstration, referred to above, should lead us to expect that some distinctive feature analysis of ordinary English words—for example, a dimensional analysis that can be recovered from their correlated patterns of associative relations, clustering in recall experiments, and use in ordinary English sentences—should lead us to a more powerful treatment of the relations between words that occur in the recall process.

As an empirical process, the generalization of the very useful and significant method for determining size of S-units pioneered by Tulving and Patkau (1962) has some potential utility. However, even this method is limited by the implicit assumption behind it, which is that there is a one-to-one correspondence between the manifest verbal elements emitted in recall and the form of storage in the head. I can illustrate the difficulties imposed by this extremely limiting assumption by reference to a problem which has so plagued students of verbal learning that, for the most part, its study has been put off for the indefinite future. I refer to the recall of ordinary English prose.

Cofer (1941) courageously tackled the problem in his Ph.D. dissertation. Others have tried to solve the problem of scaling down memory for ordinary prose to the analytic techniques of the verbal-learning laboratory by mutilating English in various ways and resorting to rote-practice devices. Cofer, however, was closer to the real solution that will be required before we can sensibly attack this problem in the laboratory (closer, incidentally, than his student King some years later). Cofer applied intuition and judgment, though he never offered any analysis of the nature of his intuition or judgment; which, of course, is the difficult problem.

Intuition and judgment are required because the really important aspect of the recall of ordinary prose completely escapes our usual methods of analysis in laboratory-memory studies. It is obvious that it is not the reproduction of the exact sequence of words that is important (or any mechanically characterizable deviation from that sequence) but is instead something we can describe as "paraphrase of the essential ideas." Even the most devoted memory-drum users among us realize this fact in examinations. No one lets his Ph.D. candidates pass their examinations by scoring them on the number of words they get right on the memory drum. All pretense to rigor is abandoned and judgments are based upon subjective assessment of the student's performance. Such an assessment requires that we have an implicit concept of the important linguistic fact of paraphrase. It is an astounding fact, when considered in an objective light, that experimental students of memory have so long neglected serious theoretical treatment of this essential concept of paraphrase.

There is, in the words of the linguists, an underlying competence in memory (the content of memory) that we are looking for. We are not really looking for the manifest string of words, and the fact that we are not is responsible for the failure of nearly a century of experimental work on memory to apply to the recall of ideas in ordinary language in anything except a vague and unsatisfactory way. It is *always* the case, in ordinary language, that a very different string (in theory totally different in surface constitutent structure and lexicon) would do about as well as the one actually recalled. Our traditional methods of analysis in the study of memory are as restrictive for the more revealing and important problems of memory as the obsession with performance was for the earlier structural linguists. The study of the more important problems need not be amorphous and vague. It is again worth reminding ourselves that the recent advances in linguistics show us that the characterization of intuitions and judgments about language can be done with far greater rigor and depth of mathematical analysis than has ever been applied in the field of verbal learning. I do not wish to imply that the linguists have solved all of their problems, much less ours. They too readily dismiss problems of reliability of data. They have at least shown us the magnitude of the problem we face and how hopeless it is to expect general solutions to important questions in memory thus far from the methods we have favored.

It is significant in this respect that Tulving had occasion to refer to the engrams which Lashley never found. Lashley's (1951) paper revealed that he had begun to abandon the search for those engrams in favor of the search for an underlying structure that could describe and perhaps explain the ability of people to remember the things they do. Tulving shows us we can begin to consider these problems, given the potential richness of the techniques which enable us to characterize subjective organization and the like. We are getting closer to a concern with the genuine problems of human performance and abilities and further away from our philosophic heritage, as Tulving's paper reveals.

Among the problems that are well put and well answered in Tulving's discussion is the question of how we should characterize the increment in recall over successive trials or the improvement of performance with practice. He points out the advantage of free recall in providing independent estimates of strength (or probability of occurrence) and organization. It might be argued that the various methods suggested by Underwood and his associates and by Horowitz for the separation of strength and association in paired-associate learning do so also. If so, however, it is only for a highly restricted set of circumstances (paired-associate practice) and with the unnecessarily confining assumption that strength (response learning) and organization (associative learning) must go on successively. I am surprised, however, that Tulving does not relate his view to the equally important distinction between storage and retrieval or between the potential availability of information for the human being and the accessibility of this information.

I cannot resist one further comment on Tulving's paper, though I think it concerns a less essential aspect of the matters we have discussed, and perhaps it is more of a matter of taste and scientific strategy than anything else. It concerns the question of primary and secondary systems of storage, immediate memory (memory span), and per-

manent or quasi-permanent memory. I doubt very much that we can make much sense of the issues here until we solve the question about what it is that is stored when "an item" is stored. If, in fact, a bundle of distinctive features is brought together to produce the recall of an item in memory, the nature of the distinction between a short-term and long-term memory—if one is to be made—would be very different from such a distinction if in fact an item is stored as such.

Now I should like to turn briefly to Pollio's paper before summarizing my views on the matters under discussion. First of all, I am delighted by his little empirical venture into the associative meaning of the concept of *structure* for psychologists, or, in any event, for Tennessee psychologists. I am certainly not surprised to see lurking in the background of the meaning of this word for hard-headed experimental psychologists a system represented by the words "poetry," "pretentious," and "crap." I submit that these three words are part of a well-defined and very nearly homogeneous system in the associative structures of experimental psychologists. Nor am I surprised to find some for whom the word *structure* has no psychologically determinable meaning at all—significantly, perhaps, at least one such person must have been for a time a denizen of Tolman Hall.

One thing that I liked very much about Pollio's paper represents, I think, my fundamental allegiance as an experimental psychologist. He insists upon tying underlying competence to manifest data in a clear and unambiguous way, something linguists do not always do. He says, "Conceptually, psychological structure is inferred from overt behavior by explicit sets of operationally meaningful assumptions about the particular structural arrangement and the observed specific relationship between structure and behavior." Also, I like Pollio's insistence, as a psychologist, that we are not constrained in the study of verbal learning to restrict data to overt speech or "well-formed" sentences or some other linguistically determined reduction of the raw data. He wants us to bring in, as fundamental matters for the determination of theories about cognition, memory and the like, such things as the free flight of ideas, the nature of thinking (both creative and prosaic), and the formation of concepts.

Pollio, like Tulving, makes a mistake in assuming the fundamental unit of analysis to be manifest—to be the word, the morpheme, or something similar. It is again the search for the molecule of James Mill's mental chemistry. Lamentably I tried to argue for the same view in the original ONR verbal learning conference (Deese, 1961), and now I think that it is thoroughly wrong. I am unalterably opposed to the making of analogies between psychology and physics, particularly when formally adequate arguments are available. However, the scientific nature of the atom and molecule constructs is a useful reminder that fundamental structures do not come in manifest data. The basic structures of chemistry and physics are not observable; they are theoretical. The word (and the morpheme) are really observable (however difficult we find it to characterize them). But our understanding of wordiness or morphemity is based upon some more fundamental understanding. The fundamental units of memory are, I think, also theoretical, and yet we do not know how to characterize them after so much experimental work.

Pollio puts mistaken emphasis upon interassociative networks. This emphasis is partly the outcome of too heavy a reliance upon classical associationism, but superficially it seems to stem from other sources as well. It seems to be the direct outcome of the mathematical method he has chosen by which to analyze associative relations. Nevertheless, his choice of the mathematics is an outcome of classical theory. There are, if not an infinitude, at least a very large number of other methods available. It is possible that the underlying structures of associations are in the form of abstract networks of some sort rather than, say, associative types. In this case, Pollio would be right and I would be wrong. However, if associations were cast in the form of some abstract networks, it would be very difficult to see how associations could be related to the phenomena of ordinary language. They would be a unique linguistic phenomenon, in fact. I have a strong suspicion (in fact, I have been told so on occasion) that at least some theoretical linguists think that associations have nothing much to do with anything, much less ordinary language. However, my intuition and some empirical data (some of which is summarized in Deese, 1966) tell me that manifest associations and aspects of ordinary language are so closely related as certainly to arise, in part at least, from the same source devices. Furthermore, it is almost impossible to characterize certain peculiar kinds of language (poetry, fanciful metaphor, schizophrenic speech, and the like) without recourse to associative data, explicit or implicit.

Pollio's network analysis enables him to consider generalized chained mediation-relations of any particular order by raising stimulus-response associative networks to the nth power. That he must reduce his matrices to zero-one form in order to do so places one restriction on such analyses. However, I think that the difficulties with mediation as a generalized concept (which I do not really wish to comment on here) place an even greater restriction on the potential interest that is to come out of such operations upon associative networks. Pollio can summarize certain data of interest with his operations upon matrices, but other operations would probably do as well. For example, the rate at which relations are specified in such a treatment gives some measure of insight into the "tightness" or "homogeneity" of the arbitrary word-sets forming the matrix. In one case, Pollio shows that a set of words centering around the concept of *music* achieves an asymptotic number of potential interrelations more rapidly in taking successive powers of the matrix than an equal-sized matrix having the same total interrelations and centering around the concept *whistle*. Pollio shows that the comparative tightness is correlated with other behavioral features of these two matrices. However, it would be possible to show much the same thing through other analyses which are related but not identical. For example, an ordinary factor analysis in which the usual communality estimates are entered in the diagonal will show *music* to have a simpler factor structure than *whistle*. Both of these analyses are, strictly speaking, empirical and unmotivated by any theoretical considerations. The factor analysis (or, perhaps, more appropriately, multidimensional scaling analysis) makes it possible to establish relations with these same words in ordinary linguistic and cognitive use, which I think would be difficult to do with Pollio's network analysis.

I am in fairly general agreement with the plan of investigation revealed by Pollio. Where I disagree, I think, it is primarily because I sense that he is going in the wrong direction in trying to establish the validity of his analyses. Validity in the sense I am using it here refers to examination of the relations between the various abstract characterizations of associations and other ways of finding out how people think about and use some of the aspects of language. He uses as his main source of validity (or criteria, if you prefer) rather traditional experiments in verbal learning, usually paired-associate experiments. I would have preferred studies which came closer to usage in natural language, which examined reasoning processes and concept formation, and, perhaps, which looked at anthropological data, such as the various accounts of kinship systems. I think that Pollio has constrained himself too much to look at the traditional laboratory problems rather than the more general questions to which his and similar methods of associative analysis can properly be addressed. To be sure, DeSoto who is interested in how people think, has used the paired-associate task by way of validation in the analysis of his ordering relations (DeSoto and Bosley, 1962), but I think he has done this more as a kind of *tour de force* than anything else.

I think that Pollio and I share the view that the various specific techniques we have for examining "verbal behavior" are designed to get at that which is not directly enumerable in the manifest chain of behavior. Whether one wishes to characterize what is searched for as underlying competence, cognitive structures or intervening variables seems to me to make little difference at the level of analysis discussed here (though there will be a level at which it will be important). The point is that most of us seem to be searching for something hidden beneath the surface of the manifest stream of behavior. Perhaps that is what provides the contrast between most students of verbal behavior—psychologists as well as linguists—and the radical positivists who find their inspiration in the views of Skinner. Despite fairly broad agreement on this matter, some of the consequences in the study of verbal behavior need to be brought to our attention.

If people could describe their own processes with complete accuracy so that, for example, they could tell us just how they generate sentences or how they reason through a syllogism, there would be no need for the elaborate paraphernalia of association tests and the like (nor for theories of a psychological nature, for that matter; all theories, I think, would then be properly addressed to explanations of the relation between these manifest processes and the physically characterizable processes of the individual). However, introspection has nowhere been more thoroughly discredited as unreliable and subject to constant error than in the study of verbal behavior (a matter, by the way, which linguists should consider a bit more carefully than they are accustomed to). The result of introspection's failure is that we are forced to apply a number of more or less indirect devices in order to understand how people think about and use the elements of language. Often, however, the form that our speculations take about underlying structures is determined by some nonessential feature of the data we take.

At the beginning of this discussion I argued that such was the case in the formation of classical-association theory out of the introspectively justified interpretation of manifest associations. Before long it happened that the theory, with its emphasis upon an accidental property, began to determine the nature of the data we use to find out more about the underlying conditions we seek to characterize. The result is that we now find ourselves in a kind of intellectual *cul-de-sac* because we have

ignored what is before our noses. I am fond of quoting George Mandler's (1965) *bon mot*, the essence of which says, "People really do think—even in a paired-associate experiment." Our failure to appreciate that fact renders many of our experiments rather strange and pointless to the disinterested outsider. For example, in the typical paired-associate experiment we carefully control temporal relations, order of presentation, etc. Yet we leave totally unspecified and uncontrolled the nature of the relation the subject is to attribute to the stimulus and response terms. Even to characterize the range of possibilities open to the subject in this respect is difficult. We can point, by way of examples, to such relations as "A is B," "A implies B," or "A dominates B." How much more adequately controlled in the traditional sense would be the paired-associate experiment in which subjects learned the subject and predicate of simple sentences as the stimulus and response terms respectively. It would not solve all the problems of the limitations of the paired-associate paradigm, but I would rather think that it would, among other things, reduce intersubject variability both in the intellectual operations applied to the task and the outcome in the form of traditional data protocols.

In summary, while I have some specific disagreements with the programs suggested by Tulving and Pollio, my main concern is that they shall go further in the directions they have indicated. Formal theorists (and, for the most part, formal theorists seem to be among linguists rather than psychologists in this field) will undoubtedly be dismayed by the sketchiness of the views presented by Tulving, Pollio, myself and others who examine matters of structure in memory and association. But I think we are working toward the content that will have to be considered by any general, formal theory, and we are certainly beginning to free ourselves from the constraint of S-R associationism.

It is not my function here to present my own views of the nature of the associative processes. I have made suggestions in this direction elsewhere (Deese, 1966) however, and I think I would be remiss if I did not point out that these suggestions differ substantially from those presented by Pollio and Tulving despite a common concern in the abstract description of associative relations. In general, my account of associations would place less emphasis upon the procedures of learning, since, by my view, the main features of the course of learning are determined by conditions *intrinsic* to the individual doing the learning rather than to the external conditions which determine the choice of various procedures. In this sense, my views are closer to the nativistic theories sketched by McNeill in a later paper in this conference than to the empirical, S-R theories also sketched by him. At this point, I suspect, Pollio and Tulving would prefer to part company with me.

In general, the description of the conditions intrinsic to the individual would describe the operations the human mind performs upon the informational input. First of all, the mind must discriminate between noise and signal, whether the signal is linguistic or not. There is every reason to believe that such discrimination, in part, is determined by structures which, though they may be aroused by experience, are independent of the content of experience. Linguistic signals are quantized in some various ways and then assimilated to underlying paradigms by the application of rule-forming devices of various sorts. For associative data, I think that these paradigms would include at least two basic types: (1) antonymy, which demands a single attribute matched to the structure and which is independent of (uncorrelated with) any other attribute and is contrasted, in a binary way; and (2) analogy or a principle of exclusion-inclusion in which the relations between associative concepts are determined by many attributes (probably best conceived of as independent) in primarily two states. Any concept is assimilated to these structure types and is revealed in how people think about the name of that concept (including the specific associates yielded by that name). It is possible, with these two types, to summarize a great deal of associative data and to reveal striking relations between the associative data and how people scale, make judgments about, and use in ordinary sentences the words that occur in associations. Among the weaknesses of the point of view summarized here is the fact that there does not seem to be very much relation between the two structural types (and others) that I have proposed and the structures proposed by theoretical grammarians, though, interestingly enough, the structure types do describe very well how people think about grammatical paradigms so labeled, such as, for example, the class of prepositions in English.

I mention this brief sketch of my views primarily to illustrate the point that however adventurous some experimental students of verbal behavior may find the notions suggested by Pollio and Tulving, there is a context in which they can be regarded as highly conservative.

References

Bousfield, W. A., "The Occurrence of Clustering in the Recall of Randomly Arranged Associates," *Journal of General Psychology*, **49** (1953), 229–240.

————, "The Problem of Meaning in Verbal Learning," in C. N. Cofer, ed., *Verbal Learning and Verbal Behavior.* New York: McGraw-Hill Book, Company, 1961.

Chomsky, N., *Aspects of the Theory of Syntax.* Cambridge: MIT Press, 1964.

Cofer, C. N., "A Comparison of Logical and Verbatim Learning of Prose Passages of Different Lengths," *American Journal of Psychology,* **54** (1941), 1–20.

Deese, J., "Influence of Interitem Associative Strength upon Immediate Free Recall," *Psychological Reports,* **5** (1959a), 305–312.

————, "On the Prediction of Occurrence of Particular Verbal Intrusions in Immediate Recall," *Journal of Experimental Psychology,* **58** (1959b), 17–22.

————, "Frequency of Usage and Number of Words in Free Recall: The Role of Associations," *Psychological Reports,* **7** (1960), 337–344.

————, "From the Isolated Unit to Connected Discourse," in C. N. Cofer, ed., *Verbal Learning and Verbal Behavior.* New York: McGraw-Hill Book, Company, 1961.

————, *The Structure of Associations in Language and Thought.* Baltimore: The Johns Hopkins University Press, 1966.

DeSoto, C. B., and J. J. Bosley, "The Cognitive Structure of a Social Structure," *Journal of Abnormal and Social Psychology,* **64** (1962), 303–307.

Fodor, J. A., and J. J. Katz, eds., *The Structure of Language.* Englewood Cliffs, N. J.: Prentice-Hall Inc., 1964.

Garner, W. R., *Uncertainty and Structure as Psychological Concepts.* New York: John Wiley & Sons, Inc., 1962.

King, D. J., "On the Accuracy of Written Recall: A Scaling and Factor Analytic Study," *Psychological Record,* **10** (1960), 113–122.

Lashley, K. S., "The Problem of Serial Order in Behavior," in L. A. Jeffress, ed., *Cerebral Mechanism in Behavior.* New York: John Wiley & Sons, Inc., 1951.

Mandler, G., "Subjects Do Think: A Reply to Jung's Comments," *Psychological Review,* **72** (1965), 323–326.

Tulving, E., and J. E. Patkau, "Concurrent Effects of Contextual Constraint and Word Frequency on Immediate Recall and Learning of Verbal Material," *Canadian Journal of Psychology,* **16** (1962) 83–95.

Wickelgren, W. A., "Phonemic Similarity and Interference in Short-term Memory for Single Letters," *Journal of Experimental Psychology,* **71** (1966), 396–404.

Association
and Organization :
Facts, Fancies,
and Theories

5 GEORGE MANDLER

Students of verbal behavior, and of associative phenomena in particular, are currently wrestling with major theoretical and empirical problems. The search for a viable theory that will account for the data of functional associationism concerns all of us and has presented psychology with new insights and new problems. I plan to discuss some of these problems and to present an argument for a theoretical underpinning for the literature on verbal associations. This argument will be based on a general discussion of the concept of association and will be expanded into one particular model of verbal organization.

It is patently impossible to discuss adequately even a selective sample of the assertions and facts that Kjeldergaard, Pollio, and Tulving have presented. However, their material offers an excellent starting point for a general discussion of theory in the study of associative behavior. In addition, I expect to apply the model to be described to some specific problems raised by these three papers.

First, I would like to dispose of two central problems: an empirical solution to the first will be assumed, and the puzzle of the second applies to many of my comments. The first one concerns the question of the unit of response that psychologists wish to employ in their study of association in general and verbal behavior in particular. I agree with Pollio that simple pragmatics and past experience suggest that the "word" is probably the best empirical (as opposed to theoretical) unit we can use at the present time. Linguists have told us that psychologists are unsophisticated in choosing this particular definition of the verbal unit. However, it has certain advantages in that we can appeal to a consensus as to its definition, a consensus which is really not much more than common sense enumeration. Sooner or later psychology must come to grips with the response unit problem, not only in verbal behavior but generally. The direction that this kind of definition must take is fairly clear. The unit of empirical analysis will be the integrated or organized response sequence. The integrated sequence is a sequence of behavior that runs off automatically once it is initiated; it is defined by a very low degree of variability from time to time; it has a "unitary" aspect (Mandler, 1954, 1962). It should be noted that the emphasis here is on the word as the "empirical" unit of analysis. As such it is used as an index, but not the equivalent, of the underlying theoretical unit. I shall return later to the question of the appropriate theoretical unit of verbal organization.

The other problem that concerns me is the implication of a term which most psychologists have imbued with a meaning far above its status. I am referring to the use of the concept of "similarity." All three gentlemen to be discussed here assume that there is a theoretical dimension of similarity. Even brief reflection makes it quite clear that "similarity" is not a dimension but must always refer to some other dimension as well. For example, any two words are "similar" to each other in their printed form, in terms of simple light-dark discriminations. Certainly, the word "table" and the word "propinquity" are more similar to each other, as physical stimuli, than either one of them is to a horse. However, most of us would say that "table" and "propinquity" are not similar; that they are not similar in respect to some particular dimension, which usually remains unspecified. Typically, statements about similarity should add the statement "similar in respect to. . . ." It is what similarity is *about* that is important in discussing the problem of similarity.

What Is Association?

I fully agree with Tulving that association is primarily a descriptive concept. It tells us that when A occurs there is a certain likelihood that B will also occur. At that level, no theoretical statements are implied that lead any further, and most of our discussions are confined to simple empirical statements or, at best, empirical generalizations. Pollio similarly deplores the fact that no general associative theory is available and that when theory is invoked it tends to be "idiosyncratic."

One of the difficulties and confusions that have plagued the field of associative behavior is that the descriptive concept is often confused with statements from some associative theorists, particularly Pavlov and Hull. When "associations" are assumed to imply some of these theoretical statements, the theory is frequently used in an invocatory fashion. Both Pollio and Kjeldergaard invoke the term "habit." I assume that they are referring to Hull's concepts of habit and habit strength. But is their use more than an invocation? If it is, then one must assume that all the things we know about habits in Hull's theory apply to the verbal habits discussed. This involves the antecedent conditions that determine habit strength, such as frequency, the multiplicative interaction of habit strength and drive, and the conditions for the extinction of habits. Is anybody really willing to assume that the general laws of habits, as developed in simple behavior in lower animals, apply to verbal behavior in man? Sometimes, and to my consternation, it appears that the answer is yes! For example, Pollio seems to be convinced that simple frequency and contiguity determine clustering; he even suggests that Tulving's data on subjective organization in free recall are a function of contiguity in the input lists. We know that this is not the case. Pollio also talks about a "single-step habit" and assumes that no additional principle is needed to "explain" its occurrence. Again, this is descriptive rather than explanatory. The single-step habit apparently refers to the observation that A and B are associated in some context, that B occurs if A is presented. This observation is invoked in some sense to "explain" the fact that A and B occur together in some other context. None of the theoretical richness of Hull's habits is invoked; as a matter of fact, the theoretical implications are frequently denied, and the consumer of such terms as "habits" is willing to discard all theoretical pretense, even of an associative nature, and to use "habit" as a shorthand way of saying "If A then B"; but that "explains" nothing.

Another instance of invocation is Pollio's use of the concept of "retroactive inhibition." It simply will not do to say "retroactive inhibition!" whenever subjects learn material A, then learn material B, and then show some decrement in remembering or relearning material A. In that sense, "retroactive inhibition" again has no theoretical status but only describes a very general phenomenon.

The most extreme case of invocation and evocation is demonstrated in Kjeldergaard's paper. We are presented with 26 assumptions which are supposed to generate transfer and mediation phenomena. To some extent these assumptions are empirical generalizations; on the other hand, they represent invocations of quasi-Hullian theory. Such problems as the definition of similarity are not discussed but simply assumed. What really disturbs me is the increasing complexity and involuted character of this kind of theoretical endeavor. The image it evokes is one of Ptolemaic epicycles, a multiplication of assumptions and conjectures designed to buttress an existing and vague theoretical system. As a theoretical endeavor, it cannot be gainsaid; what is more important is that this complex superstructure fails to account for important aspects of transfer and mediation behavior. I do not see how these 26 assumptions can generate predictions about response choice, response suppression, clustering involving more than response triplets and, most important, the effect of instructions. If these are important phenomena, then obviously some other kind of theoretical enterprise is necessary.

I share Tulving's puzzlement with the distinction between associative and categorical clustering, which has been advocated by Postman and others. I will argue that all clustering involves categorical behavior of some sort. To say that some clusters are purely associative is to restate that these clusters occur but does not tell us how or why they occur. It may be the case that in categorical clustering we know, or can infer, the basis for the cluster, while in "associative" clustering the experimenter is unaware of its categorical basis.

The problem of "association" then becomes a search for a theory which will generate observations and empirical findings which show that certain verbal items occur in pairs, triplets, and clusters, that previously "unrelated" items may come to occur contiguously in the production of our subjects; in short, a theoretical model that does justice to the rich variety and complexity of associative behavior. Items are associated in behavior and such behavior may be used as an index or symptom of an underlying structure. The paramount problem is: What is that structure?

An Organizational Model

In presenting an outline for one possible model for the structure of mental organization, I would like to begin with two assumptions and two disclaimers. At the behavioral level, I assume that such a system will deal with integrated verbal units, i.e., words, and that the burden of dealing with word acquisition or response learning does not fall on a structure dealing with storage and retrieval. The second assumption follows from the above, namely that verbal "learning" and memory deal not with learning in any classical sense but rather with the restructuring and reorganization of units already organized in a permanent storage system.

My disclaimers concern ultimate utility and generality. I have no ax to grind for the essential rightness or utility of this model. It is the best that I can construct on the basis of some of our own and other people's data, and it does account for some of the phenomena discussed at this conference. Second, the model does not deal with the problem of sequential structure; in particular, it does not pretend to address itself to syntactic structures. The task at hand concerns the organization of single verbal units, a semantic model independent of syntactic considerations. The categorical model has been discussed at length elsewhere (Mandler, 1966b), and I will present here only some of its very general characteristics.

First, a word about the constituent units of such a structural model; I have already suggested that the interpreted unit—the empirical referent—is likely to be the word. I assume that the theoretical units in the system are word-equivalents, or what Morton (1964) has called *logogens*. Such a dictionary of logogens suggests a very different storage model than one which insists on distinctive features as the storage units. I believe that the number of units to be stored by the latter mechanism would not be substantially smaller than a storage system of word-equivalents. In any case, the problem as I see it is not to find a suitably small set of units to be stored but an acceptably efficient and fast retrieval system. I am also sympathetic to the view expressed by Morton (1964) and Morton and Broadbent (1964) that higher order "thought units" or *idiogens* are needed in such a system, though I believe that the higher order categories

used in the model below represent the same general notion.

Figure 1 shows the general outline of a categorical system of organization for verbal units. We assume that the basic limit of the organized system is about five units per set. For any single chunk (cf. Miller, 1956), the organism can only handle that many units. At the lowest level of organization, each set contains about five words. These basic sets are organized in categories so that each category subsumes five of these words. At the second level of the hierarchy there is again a set of five categories which belong to a single set. This organization continues upward in the hierarchy, but any five categories belonging to a category set are subsumed under a superordinate category. A single organizational hierarchy has five such levels. This limitation is imposed because we assume that the system must "know" or remember at which level a particular search starts. Given such a single organizational hierarchy, we can start from the top with a single superordinate category, which names that particular hierarchy, and proceed downwards until at the fifth level the system can accommodate 3,125 units.

Let me add two general points: First, there is nothing about any single organizational hierarchy that implies that the units subsumed under it may not participate in another organizational hierarchy. For example, it is quite clear that words can function in two different semantic contexts. The word "table" may be organized in one organizational hierarchy, or in one category, which lists it as "furniture," as well as in another one which categorizes it as a "written system of organization." In addition, it is highly likely that all words are independently categorized in systems that organize some of their distinctive features. I have also suggested that the limit of the organiza-

AN ORGANIZATIONAL HIERARCHY

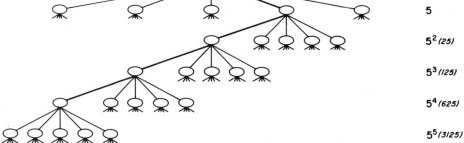

I

5

5^2 (25)

5^3 (125)

5^4 (625)

5^5 (3125)

AN IDIOSYNCRATIC EXAMPLE

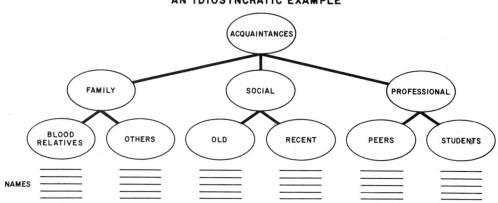

Figure 1. Schematic model of a single organizational hierarchy with five units per category, five categories per level, and five levels. The lower diagram shows an idiosyncratic example of a subsection of such a hierarchy.

tional system may be reached by an additional hierarchical organization of simple schema, which provides for a total of 5^5 possible units of memory. However, this number is reassuringly large; it accommodates about 10^{17} units.

We assume that the organization of words in permanent storage follows such a hierarchical schema. For example, Figure 1 shows a personal example of how one might organize an organizational hierarchy of "acquaintances." This particular model accommodates 30 names in a hierarchy, and retrieval from permanent storage would follow the hierarchical system shown here.

Data obtained by Bousfield and Sedgewick (1944) and Pollio (1964) suggest that retrieval does take the form of chunks representative of the categories of this model. Tulving has alluded to some characteristics of this model and has agreed that retrieval from categories produces a constant number of words from a category of a given size. Our model goes one step further and says that the number of categories recalled from a set of categories of a given size also is constant. Data supporting this particular contention have been discussed elsewhere (Mandler, 1966b).

In a typical free-recall experiment, it can be assumed that a subject will, first of all, use the existing categories and sets of permanent storage for retrieval. However, to the extent that the existing organizational system cannot accommodate the words in the input list, it is quite possible that new sets will be organized for retrieval or that a re-formation of sets will be instituted. It is quite clear that in such a process time becomes an extremely important variable; the more time available, the easier it will be to form retrievable new sets. I also would suggest that these experimentally formed sets are transient. They probably do not survive the experimental situation more than a few minutes or hours. In this connection, I am for once in agreement with some frequency notion; the permanent sets in storage are those that are most frequently formed and used. In other words, the established categories of any organizational hierarchy are those that have been most frequently used, while categories that are used only once or twice probably decay when the members of the set are redistributed to more permanent organizations.

Following Garner (1962), I maintain that such a theoretical view eliminates the need for independent definitions of the common notions of synonymy, meaning, or concept. Two terms are synonymous or mean the "same" when they occupy contiguous or even identical positions in the theoretical structure. We can thus define structural distances within the model and may frequently arrive at a notion that will be adequately close to common sense terms. Similarly, the meaning of a word is defined by its position in the hierarchy, though let it be noted that such a procedure does not necessarily exhaust the common uses of the term "meaning."

As I indicated earlier, the model represents a preliminary statement.

Much is still to be learned and added. Of primary importance is the development of unequivocal rules that permit us to make statements about category formation and about search patterns and paths within the organization. In addition, psychologists are still faced with one truly associative problem, the initial location within the system. Given a certain set of physical characteristics, the human organism will, with surprising speed, give a verbal label for it. The mechanism whereby we may proceed from physical stimulus to location and production of the verbal response is at present unknown. We know what it is not, namely a one-to-one correspondence between retinal stimulation and organizational location of the stored verbal response. It is disheartening and surprising that we know more about how to move within storage than how to get into it.

As far as associative processes are concerned, the organizational theory is relevant to the identification or mapping of the location of an item and the establishment of paths that lead from one item to another. Interitem associations and their empirical strength are indices of existing organizations. For example, the high probability of unit A eliciting unit B implies that A and B are located close together in an organizational hierarchy. The farther apart two units are, the lower will be the probability of their association, but more important, the longer will be the reaction time for B given A. If, for example, A is located in one of the clusters at the bottom of the hierarchy, and B is located several clusters over, search time is necessary in order to retrieve B by going from A to its superordinate category, or to an even higher category before descending the hierarchy again to the appropriate place where B is stored. In other words, this kind of organization explains the frequency-reaction time relationship found by Marbe (1908) and similar relations discussed by Pollio. We assume that the strengthening of an associative structure means that the organism learns more efficient search paths among the members of that structure. But in any case, the structure or the organization is essential for recall since the search for and location of the items are necessary before production can occur.

Let me comment on some aspects of Pollio's discussion relevant to this model. For example, the fact that reaction times to unpleasant words are longer than for pleasant words may be due to the fact that unpleasant items are less frequent and need longer location times, or that unpleasant items are not tightly organized, i.e., that different unpleasant items can be found in various parts of the hierarchy, in which case a long path time would be necessary to find associates. Either one or both of these mechanisms would account for the longer reaction times. The data of Howes and Osgood (1954) show that locating a particular word may be facilitated by the context; in other words, the locator mechanism is already in the general area of the word when the word is in fact being retrieved. Context directs the search program, and ambiguity can best be reduced by telling subjects what they are supposed to do. Too many of our experiments in the area of verbal learning are designed to give the subject minimal information about the required task, and many context experiments do not take into account that the subject may not use the context as a search mechanism. Certainly, the easiest way to get somebody to say "table" is to ask him to say it. Another way of doing it is by asking him to find common associates for words like "chair" and "wood," but then he has to guess what you are trying

to get him to do. The discovery of the particular task or rule involved must precede its use (Mandler, 1966a); otherwise we are fooling the subject into simply not doing what we expect him to do.

One more word on the problem of meaning. An organizational or categorical hierarchy like the one outlined here describes the semantic space discussed by Pollio and others. As a matter of fact, Pollio's evidence for the emission of categories is very similar to our model; members of a category come from the same semantic location, and items that are admitted as members of a category come from locations which have very short interitem distances in the hierarchy.

I do not think it is necessary to divide the concept of structure into word-association structures versus conditioned meaning structures. In the first instance, there is no good evidence that the conditioning model explains the transfer of meaning. I will not attempt to discuss this problem in detail, but some recent experiments by Hare (1964) suggest that data generated by the kind of experiments performed by Staats and others can best be accounted for by a "cognitive" model. Second, word-association clusters and meaning clusters are all parts of a categorical system. To say that two words come from the same area in the categorical hierarchy is equivalent to saying that they are categorized according to some criterion, known or unknown to the experimenter.

Clustering

Clustering in the protocols of either free-emission or free-recall experiments provides us with some clues to the underlying organizational hierarchies. The subjective units that Tulving talks about are the units derived from the subject's organization of integrated verbal units. Interitem associative hierarchies such as Deese's provide us with maps of subsets of the total organization of these units. It should be clear that any two words can be organized under this schema. Some words are preorganized; they already have locations in the same low level category in the hierarchy. However, the organization may be rearranged by a subject so that he can generate a subjective unit of any two words. The model says that the limiting factors in such novel organization are the distance between the two words in the organizational hierarchies and the time to find and to learn the path between those two words. If, for example, the list is preorganized, as in some of Bousfield's experiments, then we are providing the subject with sets of words that are highly likely to be preorganized for *him*, and, therefore, learning will proceed rapidly, and the clusters will often represent those in the preorganized lists. It is assumed that some consensual organizations arise out of common use of the language. For example, items in the furniture category tend to be the same items for different individuals, though there will be some idiosyncratic organizations in practically all cases. In general, organization will be most effective when the subordinate units are limited to five members to each set. The emphasis that Tulving places on couplets cannot be justified, since all evidence we have indicates that organizational sets contain, in most cases, more than two units.

Measures of clustering and of associative probabilities provide us with some index of the underlying organizational hierarchy. For example, Pollio's measure of associative recruitment may estimate the density of a category. Thus, sets of words that reach asymp-

tote for the "interitem associative strength" very rapidly are sets of words that are located close together in the hierarchy. Similarly, the experiments on presentation rate suggest that a tightly organized set of words needs less time to produce recall because the word-to-word distances are relatively short.

Finally, to follow up on the problem of rate, I agree with Tulving that time or repetition "permits the subject to organize . . . larger subjective units." Repetition, or rather time, permits the subject to lay down initial categories and to fit items into them or to reorganize the categories. With time pressure, such reorganization or path learning becomes more difficult; and, conversely, adequate time permits more rapid development of stable organizations. However, the time needed to develop a stable organization of a particular list of items will vary from subject to subject, depending on his pre-established organizations, i.e., past experience, as well as pre-established, possibly innate, organizational factors.

Serial Effects and Sequential Organization

I have previously disclaimed any intention to subsume sequential or syntactic organizations under the categorical schema. However, one must be careful not to confuse quasi-serial effects with true sequential organization. We can learn much from Lashley's 1951 article on the problem of sequential organization in this respect. Sequential organization lays down a particular schema or template relevant to highly specific units such as meaningful chains and syntactic organizations. It is only when we can specify what this organization is and does, independent of the units involved, that we can talk reasonably about sequential organization. For example, Pollio assumes that "rote learned" lists are organized in the same way as structured serial patterns. However, there is no independent criterion for the serial organization of a list such as "glub-flim-krel-larm," while there is a temporal structure implied in a series that reads: "freshmen - sophomore - junior - senior." Pollio's data indicate that a serial list without such an underlying rule does not follow the same pattern as an organized list based on some sequential rule.

I believe that Tulving makes the same error in discussing serial sets. He seems to assume that a serial list is necessarily organized in terms of a numerical serial pattern. The latter would, of course, be one of the true sequential organizations, but I am not sure that subjects necessarily impose this organization on an otherwise unorganized list. In contrast, I do believe that a subject learning a serial list does utilize two different systems, at least in the early trials. These two systems, corresponding to the early and late part of the list, cannot be differentiated in terms of pure "rehearsal." I reject the rehearsal notion, if for no other reason than that rehearsal does not produce recall; only organization does. Rehearsal is a descriptive term. Rather, serial recall initially involves two components, an organized component for the early items and a primary memory component (cf. Waugh and Norman, 1965) for the items presented just prior to recall. The first three to five items are organized in the sense that some categorical or sequential (e.g., syntactic) organization is applied to them, and they are stored accordingly. It appears that the subject uses the time of presentation of the series to organize some such three to five items, and Murdock's (1962) data

suggest that the number of items organized from the early part of a list is independent of the length of the list. In other words, we are dealing with two systems, one a primary memory system which is transient; another one, an organizational system which is generally not different from that operating in the recall of an unstructured list.

Mediation

Before entering the arena of the mediation-pseudomediation argument, it seems essential that I restate one important point. I have no quarrel with a mediation theory that applies its operations to the occurrence of mediating links in natural language units or chains. What Earhard and Mandler (1965) stressed was that under conditions where the mediating links are not the result of natural language habits or overlearning, so-called mediational effects are more reasonably accounted for by interference and unlearning effects, i.e., the pseudomediation mechanism. What remains to be done is to define the boundaries between pseudomediation and mediation effects, where one mechanism leaves off and the other one takes over. We may have set that boundary line too high, but the pseudomediation effect is now well established in our and other laboratories (cf. Earhard and Earhard, 1966, for a further extension). The establishment of the boundary lines for true mediation will also give us some further information about organizational effects, of which mediation is an example. In the meantime, there is no doubt that some studies will show mediation, others will show pseudomediation, and still others will produce mixed effects.

I have suggested that the likelihood that two items will be associated depends on their distance in the organizational hierarchy or, if they are not members of the same subset, the degree to which subjects can learn or have learned the search path from one item to the other. Search paths that are learned in an experimental situation are transient or, more precisely, these paths are easily wiped out, or unlearned, when new paths from a particular item have to be learned to a new item. This essentially restates the position taken by Earhard and Mandler (1965) in respect to the mediation problem. Mediation, as commonly conceived, takes place only if the mediating link is well established, i.e., if the search path or the location process from one item to another has been overlearned. When these search patterns have been established over relatively few trials, then they have the transient character described above and are likely to be wiped out or lost in successive stages of the mediation paradigm.

As far as the pseudomediation effect is concerned, I am pleased that Kjeldergaard seeks a resolution of the current controversy by attempting a model which will subsume both true mediation and pseudomediation effects. Any model about experimentally established mediation links which takes into account, as Kjeldergaard's model does, the availability of mediators and the unlearning of experimentally established associations, is not only welcome but will converge on a theoretical position that accounts for both mediation and pseudomediation effects and may also handle some of the phenomena that have been embarrassing to a classical mediation position, such as the absence of interference effects in an interference paradigm.

Whatever the direction of the theoretical resolution of these various findings will be, I see no reason to diverge from the basic position taken in the Earhard and Mandler paper—

that mediation effects can easily be found whenever conditions of prior learning or instruction are such that the mediators will be accessible. When the conditions do not favor the continued availability of mediating items as, for example, in the case of uninformed subjects or rapid presentation rates, then the pseudomediation effect is likely to be found.

In reference to the Horton and Wiley (1966) study, I think it should be noted that this report not only found increasing mediation as a function of time since original learning, but also decreasing availability of the $A–B$ association as measured by relearning. If B really mediates and is also less available as time goes on, I do not see how a mediation effect can increase. If, however, we are dealing with a pseudomediation effect, then the decreasing availability of B should produce a pseudomediation effect.

In closing, let me again question a position, such as Kjeldergaard's, which is supposed to account for data which lead him to invoke such phrases as "subjects aware of mediational relations," or "awareness can have a significant effect on the magnitude or the presence or absence of mediation." "Awareness" does not appear as a variable in his assumptions, but it may be a measure of the ready availability of cognitive rules that subjects impose on the input material. Awareness or report of a rule is just another index of rule use and must be employed as carefully as all other behavioral indices. We are only beginning to understand how transformation rules are programed for an organism; prior tasks and instructions are two such possibilities. But giving a subject a rule, for example by instructions, does not necessarily mean that he will use it, nor is the report of a rule any guarantee that it has been used.

We are only at the beginning of a rather imposing task. We must specify the nature of mental organization, the rules for storage and retrieval, and the initiation and operation of transformation rules. The literature on associative behavior is the beginning; it tells us what must be explained. And we have a lot of explaining to do.

References

Bousfield, W. A., and O. H. W. Sedgewick, "An Analysis of Sequences of Restricted Associative Responses," *Journal of General Psychology*, **30** (1944), 149–165.

Earhard, B., and Marcia Earhard, "The Role of Interference Factors in Three-Stage Mediation Paradigms," Unpublished manuscript, 1966.

————, and G. Mandler, "Mediated Associations: Paradigms, Controls, and Mechanisms," *Canadian Journal of Psychology*, **19** (1965), 346–378.

Garner, W. R., *Uncertainty and Structure as Psychological Concepts*. New York: John Wiley & Sons, Inc., 1962.

Hare, R. D., "Cognitive Factors in Transfer of Meaning," *Psychological Reports*, **15** (1964), 199–206.

Horton, D. L. and R. E. Wiley, "The Effect of Mediation on the Retention and Strength of Previously Formed Associations," *Journal of Verbal Learning and Verbal Behavior*, **6** (1967), 36–41.

Howes, D., and C. E. Osgood, "On the Combination of Associative Probabilities in Linguistic Contexts," *American Journal of Psychology*, **67** (1954), 241–258.

Mandler, G., "Response Factors in Human Learning," *Psychological Review*, **61** (1954), 235–244.

————, "From Association to Structure," *Psychological Review*, **69** (1962), 415–427.

————, "Verbal Learning," in *New Directions in Psychology III*. New York: Holt, Rinehart and Winston Inc., 1966.

————, "Organization and Memory," in K. W. Spence and Janet T. Spence, eds., *The Psychology of Learning and Motivation: Advances in Research and Theory*. New York: Academic Press, 1966.

Miller, G. A., "The Magical Number Seven, Plus or Minus Two: Some Limits on Our Capacity for Processing Information," *Psychological Review*, **63** (1956), 81–97.

Morton, J., "A Model for Continuous Language Behavior," *Language and Speech*, **7** (1964), 40–70.

————, and D. E. Broadbent, "Passive vs. Active Recognition Models, or Is Your Homunculus Really Necessary?" Paper delivered at AFCRL Symposium on models for the perception of speech and visual forms. Boston, November, 1964.

Murdock, B. B., Jr., "The Serial Position Effect of Free Recall," *Journal of Experimental Psychology*, **64** (1962), 482–488.

Pollio, H. R., "Composition of Associative Clusters," *Journal of Experimental Psychology*, **67** (1964), 199–208.

Waugh, Nancy C., and D. A. Norman, "Primary Memory," *Psycholical Review*, **72** (1965), 89–104.

Learning and Retention

PART II

Serial Learning[1]

6

ROBERT K. YOUNG

Within the last few years a great deal of interest has centered on the question of the effective or functional stimulus in serial learning. Interestingly enough, the theory of the effective stimulus and, more generally, the theory of the mechanisms which underlie serial learning phenomena are perhaps among the oldest in psychology. In the 1880's Ebbinghaus did extensive work using serial learning procedures, formulating hypotheses to explain his results; these have lasted until the present day in a state of rather robust health.

For this reason, any discussion of serial learning, the mechanisms which underlie it, and its functional stimulus should first take an unhurried look at the work of Ebbinghaus. Initially, it is well to ask why his conception of serial learning, in an area in which no theory seems to last very long without considerable modification, should have stood for nearly three quarters of a century without serious attack.

Three major reasons are apparently responsible for this state of affairs. The

first is simply that his results were in agreement with what might be expected from a common sense point of view. They were obvious, and his explanation of them conformed to a position which had considerable intuitive appeal. In addition, results such as the serial position curve, found by later workers, were easily assimilated into his system. Finally, the third reason for the extended success of the Ebbinghaus viewpoint is that his methods were exact, his procedures clear, and his data overwhelming. Upon reading *Uber das Gedachtnis*, even in translation, it is easy to understand why his work remained seriously unchallenged for so long. Subsequent research workers sought, perhaps, to supplement his work, but little effort was made to examine his system and the procedures he used.

The topics Ebbinghaus covered include the areas of massed *vs.* distributed practice, learning as a function of length of list, retention as a function of degree of learning, meaningfulness, retention as a function of length of retention interval, retention as a function of the number of repeated relearnings, and serial associations. In the latter area he investigated serial transfer as a function of degree of remoteness in the

[1] This chapter was prepared under National Science Foundation grant GB 3629 to David T. Hakes and the author. The conclusions reached in the paper represent the product of many conversations between these two individuals.

122

forward direction and in the backward direction. Each of these topics is still current, and the work done by Ebbinghaus in 1880 would be of interest today, especially if he changed his experimental designs to conform to presently accepted methodology.

It would be well to take an extended look at his procedures, at least before concluding, as Slamecka (1965) did, that his Haus is Ebbing. Ebbinghaus placed a series of items, German nonsense syllables, before him and went through the list at a .4-second per item pace, timed by the clicking of a clock. When he thought he had learned the list, he went through again to recite it. If he had to hesitate over a syllable, he went back to studying the list. His procedure obviously is not the serial anticipation method which is today commonly used to investigate serial learning; rather, it is much more akin to a serial recall technique.

In general, Ebbinghaus tried to avoid knowing which condition a list was in by learning lists from several different conditions simultaneously. Since he was interested in the outcome of the experiment, he wanted to protect his results against bias. And by protecting his data from bias he eliminated, he hoped, the effects of self-instruction. (One of the more generally neglected variables in the area of serial learning is the influence of instructions. Instructional variables, as will be seen later, have been attracting some attention recently and are becoming recognized as being of great importance in this area.) The Ebbinghaus technique for learning and recall in the derived-list studies (and in many others) was to learn a list one day and then learn the derived list the next day in the same time period. Again, to protect himself against bias, on Day 1 he would learn lists from conditions of several different degrees of remoteness and then would learn the derived lists

at the proper time on Day 2. The success of his procedure rests on the assumption that he did not recognize the relationship between successive lists. That this would hold true even after several trials on List 2 seems a little doubtful.

The studies of Ebbinghaus which have attracted the most interest are his derived-list studies, for it is these which form the historical basis for the present day "chaining" hypothesis—the hypothesis that assumes that associations are formed between adjacent items in a serial list.

In these studies, he would learn one list, symbolized 1, 2, 3, 4, 5, 6, 7, 8, etc., and then, if the derived-list condition was one of one degree remoteness, he would learn a list composed of alternate first-list items. Thus his second list would be 1, 3, 5, . . ., 2, 4, 6, . . ., etc. If the degree of remoteness desired was of the order of two, then the second list would be constructed by skipping 2 first-list items: 1, 4, 7, . . ., 2, 5, 8, . . ., 3, 6.. Similarly, lists of three and seven degrees remoteness were derived, as well as lists which were randomly ordered.

The method Ebbinghaus used to measure the transfer from the first to the second list was the savings method in which the time saved in learning the second list when compared to the first was the response measure. During the second-list learning, the greatest saving was obtained in the list of one degree of remoteness, the next greatest in the list composed of items of two degrees of remoteness, and so on until the least saving was obtained in the random list. Ebbinghaus used the latter condition as his base-line or control condition and concluded that the results represented the effects of differential associative strengths between items. It is, of course, unfortunate that Ebbinghaus used this latter condition as a control condition since it was shown, some 60 years later (Irion, 1946) that a random condition was a negative transfer condition. But it is difficult to fault him for failing to anticipate methodological changes which took place more than half a century later. It is also interesting to note that Ebbinghaus came too early for proper statistical evaluation of his data. (If the fact that all measures were taken on the same person is ignored, in the derived-list study, $F(4,80) = 5.26$, $p < .01$.)

Ebbinghaus also conducted a backward learning study which measured the effects of relearning lists which were derived in the backward direction. In this case, he did not fare so well; he was able to find savings only for the one degree remoteness condition.

Largely on the basis of the results of the derived-list studies, Ebbinghaus (1913) favored the theory advanced by Herbart. His statement of the theory is sufficiently clear to warrant rereading:

> The ideas which are conceived in one act of consciousness are, it is true, all bound together, but not in the same way. The strength of the union is, rather, a decreasing function of the time or of the number of intervening members. It is therefore smaller in proportion as the interval which separates the individual members is greater. Let a, b, c, d be a series which has been presented in a single conscious act, then the connection of a with b is stronger than that of a with the later c; and the latter again is stronger than that with d. If a is in any way reproduced, it brings with it b and c and d, but b, which is bound to it more closely, must arise more easily and quickly than c, which is closely bound to b, etc. The series must therefore reappear in consciousness in its original form, although all the members of it are connected with each other.
>
> Such a view as this has been logically worked out by Herbart (p. 92):

According to this conception, therefore, the associative threads, which hold together a remembered series, are spun not merely between each member and its immediate successor, but beyond intervening members to every member which stands to it in any close temporal relation. The strength of the threads varies with the distance of the members, but even the weaker of them must be considered as relatively of considerable significance (p. 94).[2]

As was noted before, this is the chaining hypothesis with the addition of a remote-associations assumption. Coupled with the data which support it, the theory has the advantage of being intuitively appealing, obvious, unequivocal, and straightforward—so much so that even today many people hold the theory in high esteem (e.g., Bugelski, 1965).

In addition to the impetus provided by the derived-list studies of Ebbinghaus, the theory of remote associations was used over the years to account for various phenomena observed in serial learning. The development of this theory was accepted so readily that Slamecka (1964) referred to it as the "Doctrine of Remote Associations." The theory says, for example, that the more remote an association, the weaker it is. Both Lepley (1934) and Bugelski (1950) have used this assumption to predict the commonly observed, bowed serial-position curve. Both assume that every item in a serial list is associated with every other item in the list. Thus there is a network of associations which occur during serial learning, and all but the correct association interfere with learning. Unfortunately, the Lepley

[2] From Uber das Gedächtnis: Untersuchungen zur Experimentellen Psychologie. Leipzig: Dunker & Humblot, 1885 (translated as Memory: a Contribution to Experimental Psychology by H. A. Ruger and C. E. Bussenius, New York: Teachers College, Columbia University, 1913) by H. Ebbinghaus.

hypothesis predicts a symmetrical serial position curve and the commonly-observed curve has its most difficult items not in the middle of the list but somewhat beyond the middle. Bugelski (1950) attempted to overcome this objection by assuming differential associative strengths for associations of the same degree of remoteness with the stronger associations being placed toward the back of the list. Under these assumptions, a closer approximation can be made to the bowed serial-position curve.

Similarly, the commonly-observed error gradient in serial recall has also been used to argue for the formation of remote associations which decrease in strength with an increase in degree of remoteness. McGeoch (1936) noted that in the recall of serial lists the items closest to the one the subject is attempting to call out will be more likely to be selected and elicited incorrectly. Thus a gradient of incorrect responses is formed. Raskin and Cook (1937) pointed out, however, that errors vary in probability of being elicited. That is, in a 10-item list, the subject on eight occasions during a trial can make an error of one degree remoteness but has only one opportunity per trial to make an error of 8 degrees remoteness—when the first item is presented, he can call out the last one. Thus even if only chance were operating, the subject would be expected to provide a gradient of remote associations. Raskin and Cook suggest as a solution that a correction be so made as to equalize the probabilities of obtaining errors of varying degrees of remoteness. When this is done, the gradient becomes much less striking and appears to provide much less evidence for remote association.

In any event, it is apparent that overt errors and gradients of overt errors exist. The only difficulty is in interpreting them. Alternative explana-tions for such gradients exist, and the remote-association data can be taken as favorable evidence for any one of them. Hence, such data cannot be considered damaging to any theory. Confirmation or disproof of Ebbinghaus' theory will have to rest on other data.

The position taken by Ebbinghaus stimulated considerable research on serial learning. In nearly every case the results have been taken as favorable to Ebbinghaus' theory. Those few studies which did not support his position have been in large part ignored. For example, the study by Trowbridge (1938) failed to find predicted facilitation from prior serial learning when subjects relearned the list in reverse order or as a derived list of one degree remoteness. In this case, the verbal materials used were consonant series which were practiced on a typewriter.

In the half century after Ebbinghaus, considerable research on serial learning was conducted. While it is grossly unfair to summarize these fifty years of research in a few sentences, it would seem that the studies conducted during this period were not as well designed or executed as were those done by Ebbinghaus himself. The reason for this might be that the theory seemed so obviously "true" that little needed to be done in the way of testing; the need was seen, rather, as extending the basic findings. Thus, whenever a few studies were found which disagreed with the theory, they tended to be ignored in the face of apparently overwhelming evidence favorable to the theory.

Within recent years this approach to research in serial learning has changed somewhat, and experimenters are looking more closely at the theory and the predictions which can be made from it. Studies have been conducted which have essentially repeated some of the classical experiments conducted by Ebbinghaus.

Modern Derived-List Studies

The Hakes, James, and Young (1964) derived-list study was designed to test the generality of the Ebbinghaus data and was not, for obvious reasons, designed to be an exact replication of the study itself. Thus the serial anticipation method was used rather than the serial method which Ebbinghaus employed. The Hakes, *et al.*, study employed three degrees of list derivation—one, two, and three degrees of remoteness. The learning of these groups was compared to a control group which learned two unrelated serial lists. The results of this study indicated that the derived-list paradigms were paradigms of negative rather than positive transfer. For example, the list derived with one degree of remoteness—the list which Ebbinghaus found to yield the greatest amount of positive transfer of any of the derived list paradigms—yielded the greatest amount of negative transfer. While all the paradigms yielded negative transfer, however, only the first degree list showed significant negative transfer. Thus in this case, the results of Ebbinghaus were not found.

A study by Young, Hakes, and Hicks (1965) investigated transfer in the one-degree remoteness paradigm of serial learning as a function of the length of the list. When lists of 12 and 16 adjectives were learned, negative transfer was obtained. When, however, lists of eight adjectives were learned, the negative transfer disappeared and slight positive transfer was obtained. Young, Patterson, and Benson (1963) studied another Ebbinghaus derived-list paradigm. In this case, backward serial learning was studied simply by having the subject learn a serial list of adjectives and then relearn it in reverse

order. Again, in contrast to the results obtained by Ebbinghaus, positive transfer was not obtained. Instead, the subjects who relearned the serial list in reverse order learned their lists no faster than control subjects who had learned, as their first list, a completely unrelated list.

With the failure of the Ebbinghaus theory to predict results presently obtained in The University of Texas laboratory and elsewhere, it is a good idea to look at the theory itself. Upon close examination, it is apparent that the Ebbinghaus theory does *not* predict positive transfer in the derived-list studies (Hakes and Young, 1966). Rather, a strict interpretation of the Ebbinghaus theory would lead to a prediction of negative transfer when, say, transfer from one serial list to a second of one degree remoteness is being studied. The reason for this is that after the first list is learned the strongest associations in the list *must* be those associations which are correct. Although these associations may not at first be the strongest, if the subject is going to learn the list, at some point the correct responses must become the strongest. Under these conditions, when transferring to the second (derived) list, the previously correct associations become incorrect and should be a source of interference. Thus what has been generally overlooked in predicting positive transfer from serial list to derived serial list has been the disposition of the correct associations from the first list. They do not disappear; rather, according to the theory, they would be a strong source of interference. Thus the Hakes, James, and Young (1964) and Young, Hakes, and Hicks (1965) negative transfer data are consistent with theory as developed by Ebbinghaus, while his own data do not appear to support his hypothesis. It should be recalled, however, that the control condition used by Ebbinghaus was in fact a negative transfer paradigm consisting of a serial list and a second list randomly derived from the first. Thus the direction of transfer in the Ebbinghaus experiments cannot be evaluated.

Turning now to the apparent disagreement between the positive transfer apparently predicted by the theory and the zero transfer found in the Young, Patterson, and Benson experiment, we find that this also is not a crucial attack on the theory. That is, even in backward serial learning the absence of positive transfer is not crucial to the Ebbinghaus position. For example, interference is observed when the analogous situation is encountered in paired-associate learning (Young and Jennings, 1964). But serial learning differs from paired-associate learning in that a constant order of item presentation is used. Not enough is known about the conditions present in the serial learning procedure which might enable the subject to differentiate between forward and backward associations. Hence predictions about the direction of transfer in backward serial learning cannot be readily made from the theory.

The difference between procedures used by Ebbinghaus and those employed by present-day experimenters should be more closely examined in an attempt to resolve the apparent disagreement in results obtained in what seems to be the same transfer paradigm. Two major procedural differences between Ebbinghaus and the present-day derived-list studies have been noted previously. The first involves different methods for presentation of the verbal material—Ebbinghaus used a serial-recall procedure, while the studies cited above used an anticipation procedure. The second difference includes all those differences which would

surround the continued use of the same person as a subject as compared to the use of naive subjects who have never previously served in a verbal learning experiment. The experienced subject is well practiced, knows the procedures employed, and can be expected to have considerable interference from previously learned lists (Underwood, 1957).

Some data concerning the differences in method of presentation are available. Battig and Lawrence (unpublished manuscript) had subjects learn a serial list and then relearn it in reverse order. Some of the subjects learned the lists by the serial-anticipation method, while others learned it by the serial-recall method. Their results supported both the results obtained by Ebbinghaus and those obtained by Young, Patterson, and Benson (1963). That is, Battig and Lawrence found positive transfer to the backward list when the serial-recall method was used, but when the serial-anticipation method was used, no transfer, positive or negative, was found. The first result, of course, supports that obtained by Ebbinghaus, while the second replicates the result found by Young, Patterson, and Benson. It is well to remember, however, that Ebbinghaus used a negative transfer paradigm as a control condition, and the resolution of the two sets of conflicting results may be more apparent than real.

The serial-recall method should be used to determine the relationship between the several types of derived serial lists. It may well be that when the serial-recall procedure is used, different results will be obtained than when the serial-anticipation method was used in the same experiment. If the results obtained by Ebbinghaus are found when the serial-recall procedure is employed—and the results of Battig and Lawrence suggest that this may be the case—then a more critical comparison of the serial-anticipation and serial-recall procedures is warranted. But it should be noted that even if the results of Ebbinghaus are replicated exactly, this would not save his theory as it stands. Instead, it would appear that replication of his results would only make a theory such as the one outlined by Ebbinghaus even less tenable. That is, his theory of serial learning would need to be modified so that it could predict zero or negative transfer in derived-list studies when the serial-anticipation procedure is used.

Transfer from Serial to Paired-Associate Learning

Within the past few years Ebbinghaus' conception of the nature of serial learning has come under serious attack. Studies which were designed to test the validity of the chaining hypothesis have often not supported the Ebbinghaus position (Underwood, 1963). There were, of course, several studies conducted earlier which indicated the direction research would be taking and it is well to look at these first.

Primoff (1938), for example, studied transfer from paired-associate to serial learning and found considerable positive transfer when the serial list was compared with an appropriate control. He also compared serial learning (Symbolized A-B-C-D-E-F, etc.) with the learning of the same items in a double-function paired-associate list in which the chaining aspect of the serial list was kept intact but in which the successive pairs constructed from the serial items were presented in random order (symbolized A-B, D-E, B-C, E-F, C-D, etc.). In this case, the paired-associate list was considerably more difficult than the same items when learned in the

serial list. Irion (1946) has been mentioned previously as demonstrating that the condition which Ebbinghaus used as a control condition actually is a condition of negative transfer.

Finally, we should mention the Schulz (1955) study in which meaningfulness and degree of learning were manipulated. Following the learning of his serial lists, Schulz provided the subject with the serial items, in random order, and asked that the subject identify the position which the item held in the list. The items at either end of the list were relatively easy to identify as to position, while those in the middle were relatively difficult to name. Subsequent research (Hicks, Hakes, and Young, 1966) has shown a similar difficulty when the subject is provided with the position the item holds in the list and is asked to give the response which was in that position. That is, given the position the item held in the list, the subject can provide the item with relative ease when the items come from either end of the list but has difficulty providing the item when the position named is in the middle of the list.

The experiments which have provided the bulk of the basis for the attack on the chaining conception of serial learning are those which have investigated transfer from serial to paired-associate learning. Young (1959, 1961) argued that if the effective stimulus in serial learning is the preceding item, then the preceding item and the item itself when paired in a subsequent paired-associate list should be learned faster than appropriate control pairs. For example, if a serial list (A-B-C-D-E-F etc.) is first learned and then the pairs formed from successive items are learned in a subsequent double-function paired-associate list (A-B, B-C, C-D, D-E, E-F, etc.), then this paired-associate list should be learned faster than some control paired-associate list.

The typical finding is that a considerable amount of transfer is observed early in learning. This transfer gradually decreases until a criterion of one perfect recitation is reached, at which time no transfer is evident. Thus where the chaining hypothesis predicts position transfer, no positive transfer is observed.

One explanation of these data is that in the learning of a double-function list, wherein each item serves both as a stimulus in one pair and as a response in another, considerable interference is generated during the learning of the list. To test this hypothesis (Young, 1961), a random rearrangement between the serial list and the subsequent paired-associate list was employed. Thus, if the serial list is as symbolized above, the paired-associate list might be symbolized *A-D*, *D-F*, *F-B*, *B-E*, *E-C*, etc. Under these conditions, the negative-transfer paradigm along with the interference present in the double-function list should yield negative transfer. Contrary to these expectations, no transfer was obtained.

Finally, to avoid the possibility of interlist interference, single-function lists were used (Young, 1962, Exp. I). In this type of paired-associate task, each item serves as a stimulus or as a response, but not both. In this experiment, the subject learned a serial list of adjectives and then learned a paired-associate list composed of half experimental pairs—constructed from items in sequence in the preceding serial list—and half control pairs which the subjects had never seen before. As in the two previous experiments (Young, 1959, 1961), no positive transfer was observed. Instead, the experimental and control lists took the same number of trials to learn. And again, considerable positive transfer was observed early in the paired-associate learning.

The validity of the conclusions based on the research cited above rests, as Postman and Stark (in press) have pointed out, upon the demonstration of the truth of the null hypothesis. That is, while the chaining hypothesis predicts that the experimental lists will be learned faster than the control lists, failure to obtain these results does not necessarily demonstrate the falsity of the hypothesis. Other variables may confound the expected results and simply yield no difference between the groups. For example, Jensen and Rowher (1965) suggest that the use of mixed-list design may be inappropriate to test the hypothesis assumed to be tested in Young (1962, Exp. I). However, in an unpublished experiment by Dr. David T. Hakes, significant transfer was not obtained when an unmixed list design was used. While the differences were in the direction predicted by the chaining hypothesis, significant positive transfer was not obtained in the positive transfer group.

Similarly, it can be argued that the criterion of one perfect recitation during serial learning is too low a criterion of learning to form associations which would transfer effectively to a subsequent paired-associate list. Thus a similar experiment, measuring transfer from a serial list to a single-function mixed paired-associate list (Young, 1962, Exp. Ia) was conducted. The only difference between this experiment and the one conducted previously is that the criterion of serial learning was increased to a criterion of one perfect recitation plus ten trials. Items which were subsequently paired in the paired-associate task were given correctly as often as 36 times in the serial list and yet no positive transfer was observed from the serial to the paired-associate list, at least in terms of trials to one perfect recitation.

In any event, the validity of the negative finding rests upon the assumption that no other variables were involved which would confound the results of the experiment.

The absence of positive transfer from serial to paired-associate learning has been demonstrated in a large number of experiments by several different experimenters. Erickson, Ingram, and Young (1963), for example, conducted an experiment and based their predictions upon remarks made by subjects who had indicated that rate of PA presentation was too fast to make use of associations formed in previous serial learning. To test this hypothesis, Erickson, et al., increased the rate of presentation in their serial list to 1.5 seconds per item and decreased the rate of presentation in the paired-associate list to as low as 4 seconds for the stimulus alone and 4 seconds for the stimulus and response together. Again, the results were the same as before—the experimental and control sublists were learned at the same rate. The chaining hypothesis was not supported, and no evidence was found to support the subjects' conception of what was going on in the serial to paired-associate transfer task.

Similar negative results were obtained by Jensen and Rohwer (1965) in an experiment in which the verbal materials consisted of high-frequency three-letter words. In their *sequential learning* experiment the subjects initially learned a serial list, which was followed by the learning of a double-function list derived from the preceding list. The arrangement of the items in the paired-associate list was consistent with their arrangement in the serial list. Compared to the appropriate control, this group showed an insignificant amount of negative transfer.

Not all studies measuring transfer from serial to paired-associate learning find negative evidence for the chaining hypothesis. Postman and Stark (in press)

have obtained results in such an experiment which support the chaining hypothesis. Postman and Stark argue that use of a one-perfect-recitation criterion is not an adequate measure of transfer from serial to paired-associate learning because this measure depends upon the learning of the most difficult item in the list, and "since serial associations vary widely in strength. . ., weakly associated pairs from the center of the serial list may be expected to have a disproportionate influence on the speed with which criterion is reached (in press)." For this reason, a fixed-trials design was used in which ten paired-associate trials were given each subject. Each subject first learned a serial list and then learned a double-function paired-associate list in which each item served as a stimulus in one pair and as a response in another. For Group E, the arrangement of the items in the paired-associate list was consistent with the arrangement in the serial list; for Group E_R, the arrangement of the items in the paired-associate list was inconsistent with the arrangement of the serial list; and for Group C, the items of the paired-associate and serial lists were unrelated. Another dimension was added by dividing each group in half and instructing one half as to the relationship between serial and paired-associate learning and not instructing the other half. A within-subjects variable was added by studying transfer as a function of cycle of learning. The data reported here are taken from the first cycle of transfer.

The results differed from previous research, e.g., Young (1959), in that significant positive transfer was not obtained for the uninstructed groups, either on the first trial of paired-associate learning or on the ten trials taken as a whole. On the other hand, the instructed groups showed differences favoring the chaining hypothesis in that Group E was found to give more correct responses than either Group C or E_R on the first trial and all three groups differed on the ten-trial total. Furthermore, the instructed Groups C and E_R differed on both the first and ten-trial total. These results are taken as strong evidence by Postman and Stark supporting the chaining hypothesis of serial learning.

The failure of the uninstructed Groups E and C to differ is puzzling both because previous research found positive transfer early in learning and also because of the fact that if some items in the serial list are learned by chaining and others by different mechanisms, Group E should be favored. Furthermore, if there are individual differences in serial learning such that some subjects learn by chaining while others learn by different mechanisms, this, too, should favor a difference between Groups E and C. Such a difference was not observed, however.

Thus it would appear that when subjects are not instructed, there is relatively little evidence which supports the chaining hypothesis in the studies measuring transfer from serial to paired-associate learning. It should, however, be noted that these studies tended to use highly meaningful and unrelated materials. Other studies have sought to examine the effects of transfer from a serial to a paired-associate list under other conditions.

Horowitz and Izawa (1963) investigated transfer from serial to paired-associate learning under conditions of varying associative strength between the items within their lists. They selected a list of words for which the interitem associative strength had been determined. The words were selected so that each item tended to elicit another item from the list more strongly than any other item. From these materials Horowitz and Izawa

constructed three lists: List F (forward), where the dominant words were arranged in a progressive forward order; List B (backward), where the items of List F were arranged in reverse order and List R (remote), where the items were arranged randomly within the list. A fourth list, List I (independent) was constructed from a list of words which were not associates of one another. Although lack of an appropriate control group does not permit us to determine the amount of transfer from serial to paired-associate learning, the results of the experiment indicate that interitem association strength did have some effect on the learning of the lists. Further research is needed to clarify the relationship.

Horowitz and Izawa suggested a modification in the chaining hypothesis be made so that more than one item could be considered to be the stimulus in a serial list. That is, it may be that several preceding items serve as the stimulus in serial learning. They also suggested that a previous test of the Compound-Stimulus hypothesis (Young, 1962, Exp. II) had not been adequate because the members of the compund stimulus has been presented simultaneously rather than in serial order as is typically done in serial-anticipation learning. Young and Clark (1964) conducted an experiment to test the hypothesis in the manner suggested by Horowitz and Izawa. Each subject learned a serial list and then learned a list composed of three-item "clusters" which were presented in random order. The sets of three items from the preceding serial list were arranged and presented in the same order as they were in the serial list. For the three items in each set, items $n-2$, $n-1$, and n, the subject was presented $n-2$ and required to call out $n-1$, and when $n-1$ was presented, the subject was required to call out n. A set of three-item clusters never before seen by the subject served as the control sublist. Both the n item and the $n-1$ item sublists were learned faster than their control sublists. Young and Clark found it difficult, however, to interpret the results of this experiment as unambiguously supporting either a compound-stimulus hypothesis or a simple chaining hypothesis, because the individual experimental items which were learned faster than their control items were taken from the ends of the previously learned serial list. This latter finding supports previous research which suggested that associations are formed between the items at the ends of the serial list but not in the middle (Young, 1963, Exp. I).

Thus the major portion of the results of the research involving transfer from a serial list to a paired-associate list constructed from the serial list has yielded relatively little support for the hypothesis that associations are formed between the items of a serial list. In addition, beyond the apparent continued demonstrations of the null hypothesis, the previously cited research has given us little insight into what might be the stimulus in serial learning.

The Ordinal-Position Hypothesis

There are several alternative hypotheses concerning the functional stimulus in serial learning. One is the ordinal-position hypothesis which states that the functional stimulus is the position the item holds in the list. This hypothesis was tested in an experiment by Young (1962, Exp. III). In this study, the experimental group learned two serial lists in which alternate items held the same ordinal position in both the first and second lists. The second half of the items were randomly rearranged from the first to the second list. Thus half the items held the same position in both lists (S items) and half the items held different positions in both lists (D items). The ordinal-position hypothesis would predict that the learning of the S-item sublist would be facilitated because the transfer paradigm conforms to an A-B, A-B paradigm of positive transfer with A referring to the same serial positions in both lists and the B referring to the same item in the two serial lists. On the other hand, the D-item sublist should show interference because different first-list responses are paired with the same (position) stimuli in the second list forming an A-B, A-B_r (repaired) paradigm of negative transfer.

When the chaining hypothesis is considered, all of the second-list items conform to an A-B, A-B_r (repaired) paradigm of negative transfer. Thus the chaining hypothesis is able to predict no difference between the S and D sublists, while the ordinal-position hypothesis would predict positive transfer for the S items and negative transfer for the D items.

As predicted by the ordinal-position hypothesis, the S-item sublist was learned faster than the D-item sublist. The lists containing the S and D items were, however, learned more slowly than a control list which contained a new set of items.

Ebenholtz (1963b) conducted a study which was similar to Young's. In this experiment, one group learned a serial list followed by a second in which alternate items from the first were employed in the second in the same position as they held in the first list. New items were substituted for the remaining items so that the following represents the learning of the two lists:

List 1: A B C D E F etc.
List 2: K_1 B K_2 D K_3 F etc.

The learning of the second list for this *coordinate* position group was compared to the second list learning of a *disparate* position group in which the items retained from the first list were arranged in the second list with the restriction that no items common to the first and second list occupy positions within four positions of each other. Finally, the learning of these two groups was compared to the second-list learning of a control group which had previously learned an unrelated serial list. The *coordinate* position, the *disparate* position, and the control group learned the *B, D, E,* etc., item second-list sublist in about 10, 16, and 18 trials, respectively. These results also support the hypothesis that position is an important aspect of the serial-learning situation.

The Young and Ebenholtz experiments differ in that both the *S* and *D* lists of the Young experiment were learned more slowly than the control, while the two experimental lists in the Ebenholtz experiment were learned more rapidly. One possible explanation of these results is that Ebenholtz used low meaningful nonsense syllables, while adjectives were used in the Young experiment. That is, while the effects of item learning were somewhat reduced in the Young experiment by use of highly familiar two-syllable adjectives, this was not the case in the Ebenholtz experiment; thus it is difficult to evaluate the comparison between the experimental and control lists. This, of course, does not fault the basic finding that items holding the same position are likely to be learned faster in the second list than items which change positions from one list to another.

In both the Ebenholtz and Young experiments alternate items retained the same position in both lists and as such the superior learning of the items holding constant serial positions in both

lists may simply reflect mediation via the associations learned to the missing items of List 1.

This possibility was investigated by Keppel and Saufley (1964). Using essentially the same materials as Young (1962, Exp. III), Keppel and Saufley included in their experiment a group which shifted positions of items from List 1 to List 2 but which allowed for the mediation mechanism to work. That is, the items of this list were shifted systematically, thus apparently allowing mediation to occur but not allowing transfer between comparable serial positions. A second group was included which allowed for transfer due to comparable serial positions but which avoided the possibility of mediation via missing first-list items. The results of the experiment gave little support to the mediation hypothesis but gave considerable support to the ordinal-position hypothesis. It is also interesting to note that over-all negative transfer (experimental vs. control group comparison) was obtained in this experiment as was the case in the Young (1962, Exp. III) experiment.

It would appear on the basis of these experiments that the weight of the evidence supports the hypothesis that the position an item holds in a serial list operates as the functional stimulus in serial learning.

Other Tests of the Ordinal-Position Hypothesis

There is also another class of experiments which tend to emphasize the importance of ordinal position as a stimulus in serial learning. For example, if associations are formed between the items of a serial list, then it would appear to make little difference if the serial list started at the same point on every trial, varied randomly from trial to trial, or had no starting point at all. On the other hand, a strict interpretation of the ordinal-position hypothesis would say that it is very important that the serial list start on the same item from trial to trial, for if this does not occur, then the position an item holds in a list would vary from trial to trial, and hence position learning would be difficult.

Variations on this experiment have been conducted by several experimenters. Bowman and Thurlow (1963), Ebenholtz (1963b), and Winnick and Dornbush (1963) have all demonstrated that the difficulty of learning a serial list is increased considerably by starting the list at a different position from trial to trial. Thus these data support the contention that ordinal position plays an important role in serial learning.

Other experiments by Lippman and Denny (1964) and Breckenridge, Hakes, and Young (1965) have also demonstrated that learning a serial list which has no starting point at all (i.e., a list which runs continuously and which has no starting symbol) is also much more difficult to learn than a list which is learned in the usual fashion with a constant starting point. In these experiments, serial-position effects are obtained but they appear to be subject defined. That is, if the item given correctly most often by each subject is called Item 0, then Items 1, 2, . . . n which follow Item 0 in that order conform to the usual serial position curve. These results suggest that despite the fact that subjects are given no explicit starting position, they may provide their own starting point and make use of ordinal position from that point. This procedure may, of course, be less efficient than learning by a chaining procedure, but it would explain the bowed serial-position effects obtained.

Keppel (1964) has assumed that it is possible to eliminate positional cues in a serial list by varying the starting point from trial to trial. To test this hypothesis, he investigated retroactive inhibition with lists learned with a constant starting point and with lists learned with varying starting points. If ordinal position is the stimulus when serial lists are presented in constant order, then the learning of two unrelated lists should conform to an A-B, A-C paradigm of negative transfer in which the A terms are the constant serial positions and the B and C terms are the items of the serial lists. On the other hand, if the position cues are eliminated by varying starting positions from one trial to the next, then chaining occurs during serial learning, and the learning of two successive serial lists would conform to the A-B, C-D paradigm of no transfer in which the A and C terms are items from the serial list which preceded the B and D terms. In investigating these two transfer paradigms, Keppel found that the first lists differed in difficulty with the variable-starting point list being much more difficult than the constant-starting-point list. No differences were observed, however, between the learning of the constant and varied lists during second-list learning, and recall of the first list learned indicated poorer recall of the items from the constant list than from the variable list. These data support the ordinal-position hypothesis inasmuch as the recall data conform to what would be expected in a comparison of A-B, A-C (for the constant groups) and A-B, C-D (for the variable groups) transfer paradigms. In addition, the absence of a difference during second-list learning would seem to indicate a relative transfer which is greater for the variable groups than for the constant groups. This conclusion must, however, be accepted with reservations, since the variable and constant groups had differential amounts of first-list practice. In any event, these results would argue for a conception of serial learning in which associations are formed between positions and items when the list is presented in constant order and between successive items of the serial list when the list is so presented that the starting point will vary from trial to trial.

Unfortunately, there is no general agreement about Keppel's assumption that serial position cues are eliminated when a serial list is presented with a different starting point on every trial. This is especially true since serial position curves, which argue for position learning, have been found in experiments in which the starting point has either been eliminated or omitted, as in Breckenridge, Hakes, and Young (1965).

Keppel's assumption may be tested directly by measuring transfer from a variable-starting-point serial list to a paired-associate list in which the items and their arrangement are the same as that used in the preceding serial list. Shuell and Keppel (in press) measured transfer from this type of serial list to a double-function paired-associate list using a fixed-trials design in which ten trials were given on the paired-associate list. Under these conditions, positive transfer was found, thus supporting Keppel's notion. In contrast, an unpublished experiment conducted in the Texas laboratory found no difference in amount of transfer between groups learning either variable-starting-point or constant-starting-point serial tests. In this experiment transfer to single-function paired-associate lists was measured by comparison of the variable and constant groups to their own controls. A one-perfect-recitation criterion was used. The variable-starting-point group should have shown more transfer

than the constant-starting-point group if the Ss in the variable group were forced to abandon use of position cues and start learning by a chaining type of learning as suggested by Keppel.

There is, however, no general disagreement between the Shuell and Keppel results and the Texas results, because in the latter experiments positive transfer was obtained early in learning; these results may be taken as supporting the findings, if not the interpretation, of Shuell and Keppel. The question of the choice of appropriate learning criteria is critical, however, in this type of research when use of one learning criterion will support a hypothesis and use of another fails to support the same hypothesis. (The Postman and Stark experiment points up this same problem.) It would appear that development of other experimental designs is needed to resolve this problem.

Effect of Instructions

The procedures used in the Shuell and Keppel study and those used in the experiments conducted in the Texas laboratory differ in another important manner. Shuell and Keppel told their subjects about the relationships existing between successive lists. Subjects used in the Texas experiments were not informed about the relationships. The instruction variable is one which has been ignored for the most part in studies in this area; yet the differences obtained between the studies just mentioned point up the potential importance of this variable.

The influence of instructions, the effects of which Ebbinghaus attempted to eliminate, is illustrated in a series of derived-list studies by Slamecka (1964). In his first experiment, Slamecka had his subjects recite the alphabet in order and then had them learn the same items in a derived list of one degree remoteness. Positive transfer was observed when list learning was compared to the learning of a control list constructed in the same manner as Ebbinghaus constructed his control lists. When Slamecka had his subjects learn nonsense-syllable lists with the same experimental design as he used in his first experiment, no positive transfer was observed. Slamecka concluded that the difference in results between Experiments I and II was due to the fact that the subjects recognized the derived-list pattern in Experiment I but not in Experiment II. The reason for this is that the alphabet is highly overlearned, and a patterned arrangement might be readily perceived. To test this hypothesis, Slamecka repeated Experiment II, but he told the subjects of the relationships between the first and second lists. When this happened, results similar to those obtained in Experiment I were found—the derived list was learned faster than the control. Thus in this experiment, while the direction of transfer cannot be determined because of the control paradigm used, it can be seen that the instructions had the effect of reducing the number of trials to learn the list.

Similarly, the results of the Young, Hakes, and Hicks (1965) study which investigated transfer in a derived-list paradigm as a function of length of list found negative transfer with 12- and 16-item lists but found slight positive transfer with an 8-item list. These results were interpreted in terms similar to those of Slamecka—the subjects were able to recognize the patterned construction of the short list and this recognition facilitated learning. Thus it is apparent that instruction, whether subject- or experimenter-provided, is an important variable and seems to make for positive transfer in the derived-list experiments.

The Postman and Stark (in press) study which investigated transfer from a serial to a paired-associate list failed to obtain differences between the uninstructed groups but found large differences between the instructed groups in the direction predicted by the chaining hypothesis. That is, the positive transfer groups learned faster than the control, and the negative transfer groups learned more slowly than the control. Thus in this case the result of instruction was to heighten the effect either toward greater positive or greater negative transfer. Similar effects were also noted in the comparison of the instructed Shuell and Keppel (in press) groups and the uninstructed Texas groups.

The serial list, following learning, is a highly organized group of items which are related to one another through a chain of associations, through associations between ordinal positions and items or through something else entirely. Instructions would tend to encourage the subject to make use of his knowledge of the structure of the list when learning a subsequent list derived from the first. It is conceivable that the instructed subject making use of his knowledge of the organization of the serial list might learn in a manner which could provide evidence favoring a chaining or an ordinal-position hypothesis and yet simply reflect the strategy employed by the subject rather than the manner in which a serial list is learned. For this reason, conclusions about the functional stimulus in serial learning when subjects have been instructed should be made with considerable caution. In any event, instructions have been shown to have great influence both on the learning of a single serial list (e.g., Winnick and Dornbush, 1963) and on the learning of subsequent lists following serial learning.

Further Investigations of the Ordinal-Position Hypothesis

It seems reasonable to conclude that subjects can learn a serial list using position cues. This conclusion seems to be even more justified in view of the results of an unpublished experiment conducted by Dennis Cogan and Charles C. Erickson in The University of Texas laboratory. In this experiment, the effects of percentage of ORM (Occurrence of Response Members) were studied in serial learning. That is, groups of subjects would learn a serial list in which either 100 per cent, 66 per cent or 33 per cent of the items would be presented on each trial. To preserve a constant position for the items in the list, a 000 symbol would be presented whenever the item was not presented. Thus in the 33 per cent condition, a trial might look like this: 000, 000, *MORBID*, 000, *SUDDEN*, 000, 000, *WESTERN*, 000. And *MORBID*, the item in the third position, would occur only once on the average of every three trials and would be replaced on the other trials with a 000. In contrast to paired-adjective experiments in which variation in %ORM tends to produce relatively little effect, variation in %ORM in serial learning tended to produce considerable differences, the magnitude of the difference being something larger than 2 to 1 when the trials to criterion of the 33 per cent and 100 per cent groups are considered. Serial position curves are, however, obtained which are very nearly like those obtained in the usual constant order serial learning. These curves are presented in Figure 1.

The most noticeable aspect of these curves is that they become more and more asymmetrical as %ORM de-

creases. That is, the difference between the beginning and end items becomes larger as %ORM decreases. This is reflected in a significant interaction between the quadratic trends for the three groups. In addition, in response to questions as to how they learned the list, the percentage of subjects reporting that they used position cues rose from 45 under 100 per cent ORM to 68 under 66 per cent ORM to 91 under 33 per cent ORM. Thus, under these conditions it seems apparent that subjects can use position cues almost exclusively in the learning of a serial list. Whether they use position cues as extensively under 100 per cent ORM remains to be determined.

Not all the evidence gathered about the ordinal-position hypothesis is in support of it. In the Jensen and Rohwer (1965) study, it was argued that if the position an item holds in the serial list is the stimulus, then positive transfer should be obtained from a serial list to a paired-associate list in which the responses are the previously learned serial items and the stimuli are the serial positions the responses previously held in the serial list. In the *position learning* group, each subject learned a serial list and then learned a paired-associate list in which the responses were the items from the serial list and in which the stimuli consisted of rows of 12 boxes. For each stimulus a red dot appeared in a different box. The position of the dot in the boxes coincided with the position the response held in the previous serial list. For example, when a red dot appeared in the box on the extreme left, this served as the stimulus for the response item which held the initial position in the previous serial list. The relationship between the position of the red dot in the box and the position the response held in the serial list was pointed out to the subject. No significant transfer was found when

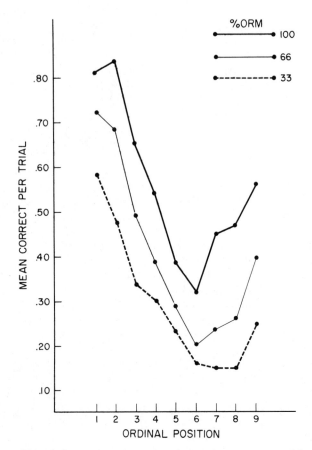

Figure 1. Mean Correct Per Trial as a Function of %ORM

the learning of the position group was compared to an appropriate control group. If ordinal position and spatial position are thought to be equivalent, these results are contrary to what would be expected from an ordinal position hypothesis.

Other Hypotheses

Several investigators have suggested that both chaining and position learning may take place in serial learning. These multiple-cue theories, called dual-process hypotheses by Jensen and Rohwer (1965), hold that chaining occurs in one part of the list and that position learning occurs in another. Thus Young (1962) and Young, Patterson, and Benson (1963) suggested that position learning takes place in the middle of the list, while chaining takes place at the ends of the list. Ebenholtz (1963a) took exactly the opposite position, concluding that position learning takes place at the end of the list and that chaining occurs in the middle. (Keppel and Saufley, in their 1964 analysis of S vs. D items, report results which favor the Ebenholtz interpretation.) Battig, Brown, and Nelson (1963), in a somewhat different context, suggest a multiple cueing type of learning in which chaining and position learning supplement each other so that each subject may "come up with some combination possibly quite unique and individualistic. . . ." to help him learn the list.

Other conceptions of the nature of the stimulus in serial learning would include Jensen's (1962) position that serial learning involves a process of response integration. By this is meant that the items in the list can be given by the subject in some particular sequence without their being "individually dependent upon specific eliciting stimuli or cues." This conception of the nature of the stimulus in serial learning would appear to be similar to that of Slamecka (1964), who states that serial items are fixed in "their relative positions in the list, through associating them, not with each other but with a self-generated sequential or spatial symbol (such as first, second, etc.)." Both of these hypotheses may in turn be distinguished from the ordinal-position hypothesis by noting that *relative* ordinal position is stressed in Jensen and Slamecka's positions.

The inability of an *absolute* ordinal-position hypothesis to provide adequate predictions in a wide variety of experimental contexts is illustrated by an unpublished dissertation by Shiryon (1965). He reports a study in which each subject (second grade students) learned three 8-item serial lists which consisted of common pictures. For the two experimental groups, E_1 first learned a list symbolized $A–B–C–D–1–2–3–4$, then a list symbolized $5–6–7–8–E–F–G–H$ and then learned a list symbolized $A–B–C–D–E–F–G–H$; E_2 first learned a list symbolized $1–2–3–4–A–B–C–D$ and then a list $E–F–G–H–5–6–7–8$ and then a list $A–B–C–D–E–F–G–H$. A control group learned two unrelated serial lists and then the common third list. It will be noticed that the position of the items in the first two lists in Group E_1 was consistent with their position in the subsequent test list. On the other hand, the position of the items in E_2 was not consistent. A strict interpretation of the ordinal-position hypothesis would predict that the E_1 list would be easier to learn than the E_2 list. The reason for this would be that the E_1 items retain the same serial positions in lists where they appear and because of this positive transfer should occur. On the other hand, the E_2 items change serial positions from the first or second lists to the test list and thus should yield negative transfer.

In contrast, the chaining hypothesis would predict no difference between the learning of the E_1 and E_2 lists, because the same number of appropriate associations is formed between the items of the first and second lists which may be used in the learning of the third list. Both of these lists should, however, be learned faster than the control list, which has not contained any relevant items.

The results were exactly as would be predicted by the chaining hypothesis. The two groups E_1 and E_2 learned their test lists in the same number of trials, while the control group took longer to learn their test list.

While little is known about the generalizability of the results because of the subject population involved, the results do indicate that a strict interpretation of the ordinal-position hypothesis does not appear to be tenable and that new formulations of this hypothesis will have to take Shiryon's data into consideration. For example, the position hypothesis could handle the results of Shiryon's experiment if it were to assume, as suggested by Jensen (1962) and Slamecka (1964) that the relative rather than the absolute position of the item in the serial list were of importance. Under these circumstances, both the ordinal-position and chaining hypotheses would make the same predictions.

The *relative* ordinal-position hypothesis does not fare as well in a study by Ebenholtz (1963a), in which transfer was investigated from a serial to a paired-associate task. The paired-associate task had a "window location as the stimulus and nonsense syllable as response" to emphasize spatial location. Similarly, the sequence of presentation of the nonsense syllables in the serial-learning task was from the top window of the apparatus to the bottom window. Three transfer conditions were used: Condition *C* (coordinate), in which the positions of the syllables in both serial and paired-associate tasks were the same; Condition *R* (relative), in which the relative but not absolute positions of the syllables in both tasks were the same; and Condition *D* (disparate), in which the syllable positions varied randomly from serial to paired-associate learning. In contrast to what would be expected from the relative ordinal-position hypothesis, Condition *C* was learned faster than Conditions *D* and *R*, which did not differ from each other. Thus with reference to experiments testing the effects of ordinal position, neither the absolute- nor the relative-position hypothesis can account for all the data.

Transfer as a Function of the Position the Item Holds in the List

Previous research has consistently shown differences between the transfer found in the middle of the list and that found at the end. For example, Jensen and Rohwer (1965) found evidence for positive transfer at the ends of the list for their position-learning experiment and no transfer in the middle. Furthermore, they found positive transfer at the beginning of the list in their sequential learning and negative transfer in the middle of the list. Similarly, Erickson, Ingram, and Young (1963) found negative in the middle of the list and positive transfer at the end, when measuring transfer from a serial to a paired-associate list. Young (1962) found positive transfer at the ends of the list when measuring transfer from serial to paired-associate learning and positive transfer in the middle of the list while measuring transfer from serial to serial list (Young, Patterson and Benson, 1963). These results would tend to indicate that associations are formed between the items at the end of the list and that associations between items and their positions are formed in the middle of the list. On the other hand, Keppel and Saufley (1964) found exactly the opposite result; hence, while there is no general agreement about which portions of the serial list are learned in what fashion, there does seem to be general agreement that both positive and negative transfer seem to occur within the same list during testing.

Young, Hakes, and Hicks (1965) conducted an experiment to determine the differential effects of transfer as a function of position in the serial list. This experiment came about as a result of two studies investigating transfer from a serial list to a paired-associate list in which the responses consisted of the items learned in the serial list and the stimuli consisted of numbers. In Experiment Ia, the stimuli of the paired-associate list consisted of numbers which corresponded to the ordinal position the responses held in the previously learned serial list. This experiment, it will be seen, is almost identical to the position learning experiment of Jensen and Rohwer (1965). The results of this experiment were also the same as those of Jensen and Rohwer—no over-all transfer, but positive transfer was obtained when those pairs taken from the ends of the previously learned serial list were compared to the control pairs. Next, in Experiment Ib, following serial learning, the responses of the paired-associate list were randomly paired with the numbers representing the ordinal position of the items in the serial list. Thus a response which was first in the serial list might have as a stimulus the number 6. The relationship between the first and second list was such, if position were the stimulus in serial learning, as to expect negative transfer. The results obtained were much the same as those found previously—no difference in trials to learn between the experimental and control groups. In this case, however, negative transfer was obtained with those pairs containing items which previously had been at the ends of the serial list.

Thus it would appear that while evidence for position learning at the ends of the serial list had been found, no measure in terms of trials to learn confirmed this result. In Experiment II, reported in Young, Hakes and Hicks, a 16-adjective serial list was first learned. Next, each subject learned an 8-pair paired-associate list employ-ing adjectives as responses and numbers as stimuli. In Group E (end), the responses consisted of the four first and four last items of the previous list; in Group M (middle), the responses consisted of the eight middle items and for each group the stimuli consisted of the numbers corresponding to the ordinal position each of these items held during serial learning. Each of these groups was broken down into two subgroups; the first was given instructions which indicated the method of construction of the paired-associate list. The second subgroup was simply given standard paired-associate learning instructions.

The results of this experiment are presented in Table 1. It can be seen that positive transfer occurred when subjects were transferred from the serial list to the pairs constructed from the ends of the serial list and that negative transfer occurred when sub-

Table 1

MEAN TRIALS TO LEARN THE PAIRED-ASSOCIATE LIST AS A FUNCTION OF THE ORDINAL POSITION OF THE ITEMS IN THE SERIAL LIST AND INSTRUCTIONS

| | | GROUP | | |
		Uninstructed	Instructed	Control
Position	End	7.06	5.31	7.88
	Middle	9.81	16.06	8.50

jects were transferred from the serial list to the pairs constructed from the items in the middle of the serial list. Furthermore, the transfer effects, both positive and negative, were increased by instructions. Thus it would appear that use of ordinal position, as a cue in the learning of paired-associate lists based on items taken from the middle of a serial list, is inappropriate and results in negative transfer. On the other hand, use of position as a cue in learning when items taken from the ends of the serial list are being learned is appropriate. Thus these data appear to support the position of Ebenholtz (1963a) and disagree with that of Young (1962) in that no evidence is available which would indicate that ordinal position is an appropriate cue in the learning of the middle of a serial list. This, of course, does not indicate that subjects do not use the ordinal position cue in the middle of the list. Rather, it indicates that use of the position cue in the middle of the list under these conditions is inappropriate and retards learning.

The data of the above experiment, together with those of the Erickson, Ingram, and Young (1963) study, suggest that neither chaining nor ordinal-position learning occurs in the middle of the serial list. That is, in the Erickson, *et al.*, experiment, negative transfer was found when transfer was measured from a serial to a paired-associate list in which the "links" of the serial chain were left intact, indicating that chaining is inappropriate in the middle of the list. Taken with the above result, which suggests that ordinal position is also inappropriate in the middle of the serial list, the combination of results suggests that neither a "pure" chaining nor a "pure" position hypothesis is an adequate explanation for the stimulus in the middle of a serial list.

On the other hand, Young (1962, Exp. I) and the results of Erickson, *et al.*, when considered with the Ebenholtz (1963) and Keppel (1964) data, suggest that subjects can use either position or chaining cues at the ends of the list. That is, if the learning situation is structured properly, the subject will learn by use of ordinal-position cues; or if it is structured in a different way, the subject may find that it is more convenient to use chaining cues. Thus the learning at the ends of the list appears to be done through use of chaining cues, position cues, or both, while the learning in the middle of the list appears to be done by neither.

This conception of serial learning is supported in a study by Battig, Brown, and Schild (1964). In this study, subjects learned two successive 12-item serial lists of bigrams. For some subjects, three adjacent items from the first list were in the same ordinal position or held a different ordinal position in the second list. Another group learned lists containing items which held the same separate nonadjacent positions in both lists. In addition, the three adjacent items in the first list were either at the beginning for some subjects or in the middle of the list for others and the three adjacent items in the first list were learned either to a one-correct or a three-successive-correct criterion. If chaining were to occur in the learning of serial lists, it would be expected that adjacent items would be learned faster than nonadjacent items. And if position learning would occur in serial learning, it would be expected that both adjacent and nonadjacent items holding the same positions in both lists would be learned faster than items changing serial position. Although nonadjacent items held the same serial position in both lists, performance was poorer on these items than was the case for the other groups. In addition second-list performance for those clusters taken from the middle of the first list was superior to clusters taken from the beginning of the first list. This was true whether the clusters changed or retained positions from the first to the second list.

Since neither a chaining nor a position hypothesis could account for these results, Battig, *et al.*, concluded that different learning processes were "involved at the beginning and middle of a serial list" and that these processes changed systematically with practice. That is, the beginning of the serial list can be learned by a simple chaining or position learning process while the middle of the first requires "more complex multiple-item associative units."

All of this suggests that serial learning involves a relatively idiosyncratic situation in which the subject may learn by chaining, by position, or both, in which case the results could be explained by the position hypothesis when the design of the experiment is such as to expect learning through the use of position cues and conversely, by the chaining hypothesis when the design of the experiment is such as to expect serial learning to occur through the use of sequential associations. Finally, certain experiments may be designed so that evidence for both the chaining and position hypotheses may be found.

There seems little reason to doubt, however, that subjects can learn a serial list using only ordinal-position cues, as was demonstrated in the Cogan and Erickson experiment in which %ORM in serial learning was studied; and alternately there appears little reason to doubt that subjects can also learn a serial list employing only associations between successive items, as was suggested by Young, Milaukas, and Bryan (1963). Use of one or the other of these cues exclusively may retard the learning of the serial list, but it appears that it can eventually be accomplished.

The Ordinal-Position Curve

It has been noted previously that the asymmetry of the serial-position curve does not lend itself to easy analysis in the Ebbinghaus tradition and that attempts have been made to develop subsidiary hypotheses which could be used to predict the curve. Bugelski (1950) has already been mentioned as one of these theorists. Ribback and Underwood (1950) assumed that serial chaining occurred forward from the first item and backward from the last. In demonstrating that learning in the forward direction was more rapid than in the backward direction, they provided an empirical explanation of the asymmetry of the serial-position curve.

More recent studies by Murdock (1960) Jensen (1962), and Ebenholtz (1965, 1966) indicate that the bowed serial-position curve may be more general than has usually been assumed. That is, this phenomenon can be observed under a variety of conditions other than serial learning.

Murdock (1960), in a theoretical article concerned with the distinctiveness of stimuli, discussed a study in which subjects had to learn the correct color name for each of eight weights varying from 1 to 16 pounds in approximate 2-pound steps. Although a typical paired-associate anticipation method was used, the weight-color pairs differed in difficulty. When the pairs were arranged according to weight, an ordinal-position curve was obtained with the middle pairs—the pairs of intermediate weight—being more difficult to learn than the end pairs.

Jensen (1962) reports a series of experiments in which ordinal-position curves were also obtained in the absence of any temporal sequence of presentation of items. For example, in his first experiment, he showed a group of randomly arranged geometric forms to his subjects and told them that the forms would be arranged in a row in front of them. The subjects were then allowed to study the properly arranged items for a 10-second interval and then were asked to put them in proper order. The observation-test trial sequence was continued until the subject got all the items arranged in proper order. The task was quite easy, but even so the usual bowed curve was obtained.

In Jensen's second experiment, nine geometric figures were presented, one at a time, again in random order, and the subject had to learn to match the geometric forms with one of nine buttons on the apparatus. The only serial aspect of the task was the spatial arrangement of the buttons associated with the geometric forms. Again, when the percentage of incorrect responses was computed for each button, a serial-position curve was found. When the position curve is obtained under conditions of this sort, it would appear that observation of the phenomenon is not restricted to serial learning.

Similar curves were found by Ebenholtz (1966) in another series of experiments. In Experiment I, Ebenholtz had his subjects learn a paired-associate list which employed common nouns as responses and the numbers 1 through 10 as stimuli. An ordinal-position curve was obtained with the pairs which had stimuli at the ends of the number series (1, 2, 9, and 10) being easier to learn than the other pairs. Similar results were obtained in Experiment II, when nonsense-syllables were used as responses and the numbers 1 through 8 were used as stimuli. When this list was reversed to make the responses numbers and the stimuli nonsense syllables, however, no position curve was obtained.

Experiment III used the same design as Experiment I, but instead of numbers, the items from a previously learned serial list were used as stimuli. Again, serial position curves were obtained so that pairs which employed stimuli taken from the ends of the previously learned serial list were easier to learn than the other pairs. These results suggest that in the serial to paired-associate transfer situation when the arrangement of the items is such as to expect positive transfer (e.g., Young, 1962, Exp. I), responding according to position would give the same pattern of results—positive transfer at the ends of the paired-associate list. Unfortunately, this cannot be determined because Ebenholtz' major interest was in the shape of the position curve, and for this reason a control condition in which an irrelevant prior serial list was learned was not included.

In another experiment (Ebenholtz, 1965) each subject learned two paired-associate lists. One list contained stimuli which varied in reflectance from black to white in eight steps, one for each of the pairs. The second-list stimuli consisted of black lines varying in length in eight steps from 1/2 to 4–5/8 in. Transfer was measured from one list to the other. The S (same) group learned successive lists which had responses paired with stimuli holding equivalent rank in the two series. Thus, if position in the series were the stimulus, the transfer task would constitute an $A–B$, $A–B$ paradigm of positive transfer. The R (random) group learned lists with the responses randomly repaired from one list to the next and thus, if position were the stimulus, this should constitute an $A–B$, $A–B_r$ paradigm of negative transfer. On the other hand, if the stimulus is not assumed to be the position it holds in the series, then both transfer conditions are $A–B$, $C–B$ transfer paradigms.

The second-list pairs of the S group were learned faster than were the pairs of the R group in which the responses were randomly repaired from one list to the others. In addition, bowed position curves were obtained in the learning of both the first and second lists in both the S and R groups.

It would appear from the Murdock (1960), Jensen (1962), and Ebenholtz (1965, 1966) studies that the serial-position curve is produced if the subject responds to the ordinal character of a set of items which are perceived as varying along a continuum such as time, position, color, line, length, etc. Thus explanation of the serial-position curve appears to resolve itself into the more general question of why an ordinal-position curve is obtained when subjects respond to the ordinal characteristics of a group of items. It would appear that use of generalization of ordinal position (Schulz, 1955) or the Distinctness of Stimuli (Murdock, 1960) as explanatory concepts will prove fruitful in future explanations of this phenomenon.

Summary and Conclusions

It becomes clear that the serial-learning task presents considerable problems for the verbal learning researcher who wishes to investigate problems other than those associated with learning of material in some sequence. Not only are the stimulus and response functions of the items in a serial list confounded, but there remains considerable question as to what constitutes the functional stimulus in serial learning. Thus it would seem that the serial-learning task by itself does not constitute a good vehicle to investigate processes which are assumed to underlie verbal behavior and learning. This point has, of course, been made several times, but the usual criticism of the use of serial learning as a technique for the analysis of processes in verbal learning has been that stimulus and response functions are confounded, since the same items serve both as stimulus and response and thus make analysis of response processes independent of stimulus processes impossible. While this is undoubtedly true, especially if a form of the chaining hypothesis is ultimately shown to be correct, it is also true simply because the stimulus in serial learning has not been identified.

While the evidence would seem to support some form of relative-position interpretation, the data are far from consistent. Postman and Stark (in press) and Shuell and Keppel (in press) find results which they interpret as supportive of a chaining hypothesis. On the other hand, it would appear the bulk of the research, including Ebenholtz (1963a, 1963b, 1965, 1966), Jensen and Rohwer (1965), Young (1961, 1962), and Young, Hakes, and Hicks (1965) would tend to support a position which emphasizes the effect of position as a stimulus in serial learning. If position is shown to be the stimulus in either all or part of the serial list, then manipulation of the characteristics of the stimuli in serial learning with respect to such variables as intralist similarity, meaningfulness, etc., becomes impossible. The reason for this, of course, is that the stimuli would remain the same—the position the item holds on the list—despite whatever variations in the characteristics of the response might be employed. Thus it would appear that whatever stimulus ultimately emerges as the one employed by the subject in serial learning experiments, whether sequential learning, position learning, a combination of the two—or something else entirely—analysis of the verbal processes underlying serial learning will be all but impossible. Whether the stimuli and responses are confounded, as would be the case in a chaining hypothesis, or if the stimuli remain constant through the manipulation of other variables such as similarity and meaningfulness, as would be the case with a position hypothesis, serial learning emerges as a relatively poor method to use for the analysis of the processes which are assumed to underlie verbal behavior. This is not to say that serial learning should not be investigated; rather, other techniques such as paired-associate learning are more appropriate because the experimenter has greater control over the stimulus characteristics (and response characteristics possibly) than would be the case in serial learning where the question of what constitutes the functional stimulus remains unresolved.

While, no doubt, serial learning

studies will continue to be conducted, it would appear that other techniques, such as paired-associate learning, may supply the forthcoming data which aid us in the understanding of the processes involved in verbal behavior. That is, no advantage to the use of serial learning techniques can be seen other than when one is interested in studying those processes specifically involved in serial learning. If an investigator is interested in studying verbal learning processes independent of the learning technique, he would do well to choose some method other than serial learning. Meanwhile, such problems as the question of the functional stimulus in serial learning and the explanation of the bowed serial position curve remain interesting and fruitful areas of research.

References

Battig, W. F., S. C. Brown, and D. Nelson, "Constant vs. Varied Serial Order in Paired-Associate Learning," *Psychological Reports*, **12** (1963), 695–721.

————, ————, and M. E. Schild, "Serial Position and Sequential Associations in Serial Learning," *Journal of Experimental Psychology*, **67** (1964), 449–457.

————, and P. S. Lawrence, "Serial Anticipation and Recall Learning with Constant and Varied Starting Points, and Transfer to Reversal or Scrambled Lists," *Journal of Experimental Psychology*, **73** (1967), 257–262.

Bowman, R. E., and W. R. Thurlow, "Determinants of the Effect of Position in Serial Learning," *American Journal of Psychology*, **76** (1963), 436–445.

Breckenridge, K., D. T. Hakes, and R. K. Young, "Serial Learning in a Continuous Serial List," *Psychonomic Science*, **3** (1965), 139–140.

Bugelski, B. R., "A Remote Association Explanation of the Relative Difficulty of Learning Nonsense Syllables in a Serial List," *Journal of Experimental Psychology*, **40** (1950), 336–348.

————, "In Defense of Remote Associations," *Psychological Review*, **72** (1965), 169–174.

Ebbinghaus, H., *Memory: A Contribution to Experimental Psychology*. trans. by H. A. Ruger and C. E. Bussenius. New York: Teachers College, Columbia University Press, 1913.

Ebenholtz, S. M., "Position Mediated Transfer between Serial Learning and a Spatial Discrimination Task," *Journal of Experimental Psychology*, **65** (1963), 603–608.

————, "Serial Learning: Position Learning and Sequential Associations," *Journal of Experimental Psychology*, **66** (1963), 353–362.

————, "Positional Cues as Mediators in Discrimination Learning," *Journal of Experimental Psychology*, **70** (1965), 176–181.

————, "The Serial Position Effect of Ordered Stimulus Dimensions in Paired-Associate Learning," *Journal of Experimental Psychology*, **71** (1966), 132–137.

Erickson, C. C., R. D. Ingram, and R. K. Young, "Paired-Associate Learning as a Function of Rate of Presentation and Prior Serial Learning," *American Journal of Psychology*, **76** (1963), 458–463.

Hakes, D. T., C. T. James, and R. K. Young, "A Re-examination of the Ebbinghaus Derived-List Paradigm," *Journal of Experimental Psychology*, **68** (1964), 508–514.

————, and R. K. Young, "Theoretical Note: On Remote Associations and the Interpretation of Derived-List Experiments," *Psychological Review*, **73** (1966), 248–251.

Hicks, R. Y., D. T. Hakes, and R. K. Young, "Generalization of Serial Positions in Rote Serial Learning," *Journal of Experimental Psychology*, in press.

Horowitz, L. W., and C. Izawa, "Comparison of Serial and Paired-Associate Learning," *Journal of Experimental Psychology*, **65** (1963), 352–361.

Irion, A. L., "Retroactive Inhibition as a Function of the Relative Serial

Positions of the Original and Interpolated Items," *Journal of Experimental Psychology*, **36**, (1946), 262–270.

Jensen, A. R., "Temporal and Spatial Effects of Serial Position," *American Journal of Psychology*, **75** (1962), 390–400.

———, and W. D. Rohwer, Jr. "What is Learned in Serial Learning," *Journal of Verbal Learning and Verbal Behavior*, **4** (1965), 62–72.

Keppel, G., "Retroactive Inhibition of Serial Lists as a Function of the Presence or Absence of Positional Cues," *Journal of Verbal Learning and Verbal Behavior*, **3** (1964), 511–517.

———, and W. A. Saufley, Jr. "Serial Position as a Stimulus in Serial Learning," *Journal of Verbal Learning and Verbal Behavior*, **3** (1964), 335–343.

Lepley, W. M., "Serial Reactions Considered as Conditioned Reactions," *Psychological Monographs*, **46** (1934), 1.

Lippman, L. G., and M. R. Denny, "Serial Position Effect as a Function of Intertrial Interval," *Journal of Verbal Learning and Verbal Behavior*, **3** (1964), 496–501.

McGeoch, J. A., "The Duration and Extent of Intra-Serial Associations and Recall," *American Journal of Psychology*, **48** (1936), 221–245.

Murdock, B. B., Jr., "The Distinctiveness of Stimuli," *Psychological Review*, **67** (1960), 16–31.

Postman, L., and Karen Stark, "Studies of Learning to Learn, IV. Transfer from Serial to Paired-Associate Learning," *Journal of Verbal Learning and Verbal Behavior*, in press.

Primoff, E., "Backward and Forward Association as an Organizing Act in Serial and in Paired-Associate Learning," *Journal of Psychology*, **5** (1938), 375–395.

Raskin, E., and S. W. Cook, "The Strength and Direction of Associations Found in the Learning of Nonsense Syllables," *Journal of Experimental Psychology*, **5** (1937), 375–395.

Ribback, A., and B. J. Underwood, "An Empirical Explanation of the Skewness of the Bowed Serial Position Curve," *Journal of Experimental Psychology*, **40** (1950), 329–335.

Schulz, R. W., "Generalization of Serial Position in Rote Serial Learning," *Journal of Experimental Psychology*, **49** (1955), 267–272.

Shiryon, M., "A Test of the Serial-Position Interpretation of Verbal Serial Rote Learning," Unpublished doctoral dissertation. Berkeley: University of California, 1965.

Shuell, T. J., and G. Keppel, "A Further Test of the Chaining Hypothesis of Serial Learning," *Journal of Verbal Learning and Verbal Behavior*, in press.

Slamecka, N. J., "In Inquiry into the Doctrine of Remote Associations," *Psychological Review*, **71** (1964), 61–76.

———, "In Defense of a New Approach to Old Phenomena," *Psychological Review*, **72** (1965), 242–246.

Trowbridge, M. H., "A Study of Backward and Forward Remote Associations," *Journal of Experimental Psychology* **22** (1938), 319–337.

Underwood, B. J., "Interference and Forgetting," *Psychological Review*, **64** (1957), 49–60.

———, "Stimulus Selection in Verbal Learning," in C. N. Cofer and B. S. Musgrave, eds., *Verbal Behavior and Learning: Problems and Processes*. New York: McGraw-Hill Book Company, 1963, pp. 33–48.

Winnick, W. A., and R. L. Dornbush, "Role of Positional Cues in Serial Rote Learning," *Journal of Experimental Psychology*, **66** (1963), 419–421.

Young, R. K., "A Comparison of Two Methods of Learning Serial Associations," *American Journal of Psychology*, **72** (1959), 554–559.

———, "The Stimulus in Serial Verbal Learning," *American Journal of Psychology*, **74** (1961), 517–528.

———, "Tests of Three Hypotheses about the Effective Stimulus in Serial Learning," *Journal of Experimental Psychology*, **63** (1962), 307–313.

———, and J. Clark, "Compound-Stimulus Hypothesis in Serial Learning," *Journal of Experimental Psychology*, **67** (1964), 301–302.

——, D. T. Hakes, and R. Y. Hicks, "Effects of List Length in the Ebbinghaus Derived-List Paradigm," *Journal of Experimental Psychology*, **70** (1965), 338–341.

——, ——, and ——, "Ordinal Position Number as a Cue in Serial Learning," Unpublished manuscript.

——, and P. C. Jennings, "Backward Learning When the Same Items Serve as Stimuli and Responses," *Journal of Experimental Psychology*, **68** (1964), 64–70.

——, E. W. Milauckas, and J. D. Bryan, "Serial Learning as a Function of Prior Paired-Associate Training," *American Journal of Psychology*, **76** (1963), 82–88.

——, Judith Patterson, and W. M. Benson, "Backward Serial Learning," *Journal of Verbal Learning and Verbal Behavior*, **1** (1963), 335–338.

Paired-Associate Learning[1]

7

WILLIAM F. BATTIG

At the outset, it must be noted that any attempt to assess the relevance of research in paired-associate (PA) learning to general theoretical issues must suffer from the unpredictability so inextricably associated with the state of uncertainty that currently characterizes the PA research area itself. Less than a decade ago, the answer would have been very simple. This is because until very recently, the only significant general theoretical relevance of PA learning research derived from the use of the PA task as the favorite complex learning task for attempted extension of stimulus-response (S-R) learning principles developed within simpler types of conditioning or learning situations (e.g., Gibson, 1940). Thus rather than representing a source of new theoretical formulations with relevance for general behavior theory, the theoretical role of PA learning has been as the type of complex learning task to which concepts already developed within S-R behavior theory appear to be most directly applicable. This nontheoretical character of PA research

has been enhanced further by its close association with the functionalist tradition (McGeoch and Irion, 1952), so that the specification and description of quantitative relationships involving manipulated independent variables has been the primary research aim, rather than the development or testing of underlying theoretical assumptions or principles.

It is not difficult to understand or to justify the rationale underlying the still prevalent view that PA learning represents a straightforward extension of simpler S-R conditioning principles. As in conditioning situations, the essential elements of the PA task can be described as stimuli and responses, with the associations or connections of each stimulus with its paired response being what is learned in the PA situation, so that the presentation of any stimulus leads to the occurrence of its paired response. The apparent correspondence to conditioning situations is extended further by designating as "reinforcement" the presentation of the correct response that characteristically follows the subject's attempted anticipation of that response under the typical PA anticipation procedure. Thus theoretical interpretations of PA learning have relied heavily upon the

[1] Preparation of this chapter was greatly facilitated by work accomplished under Public Health Research Grant HD-01062 from the National Institute of Child Health and Human Development.

strengthening of correct S-R associations resulting from the reinforcement of these correct associations combined with the nonreinforcement of all incorrect associations, thereby opening the door also to a host of other simpler S-R learning concepts such as generalization, discrimination, extinction, spontaneous recovery, and the like.

But although PA "theory" has thus consisted primarily of the extension with minimal modifications of theoretical concepts and principles originally developed within simpler learning situations, this unfortunately has *not* been accompanied by the actual use of the PA learning task as a means of testing empirically the adequacy of these general theoretical formulations. To the extent that such empirical tests have been made using the PA task, they have often indicated the inadequacy of the underlying simpler S-R theoretical principles to account for observed PA phenomena. As a consequence, one of the most interesting features of recent theoretical developments associated with PA research has been the remarkable "resistance to extinction" demonstrated by these simpler S-R theoretical concepts. As a prime example, the presentation of the correct response immediately following the subject's attempted production or anticipation of that response has been demonstrated to be not only nonessential to PA learning, but under many conditions actually inhibitory (e.g., Battig and Brackett, 1961; Jones and Bourne, 1964). This anomalous result, however, has thus far had little inhibitory effect upon the use of the term "reinforcement" to refer to the presentation of the correct response or stimulus-response pair (e.g., Estes, 1960). Likewise, the failure of learned associations to diminish in strength with repeated "nonreinforced" presentations following "reinforced" acquisition (e.g., Goss, 1965) has not served to

extinguish the use of the term "extinction" as a descriptive and explanatory concept in PA tasks.

This is not to say that PA theory has remained impervious to any effects of these failures of observable stimulus or response events to produce or manifest effects in PA situations comparable to those demonstrated in simpler learning situations, wherein such concepts as reinforcement and extinction were operationally defined behavioral phenomena for which theoretical explanations were being sought.[2] But what now appears to have happened to these concepts when used in PA tasks, as a consequence of their nonproducibility in terms of the presence or absence of the appropriate specified classes of stimulus events, is that they have attained the status of inferred unobservable processes. Even more surprisingly, they commonly are used to explain or account for other behavioral phenomena which have been observed directly (e.g., Postman, 1961; Underwood, 1961). In other words, there has been a subtle but drastic shift in the theoretical status of concepts like reinforcement and extinction when these are applied to PA learning situations, one that is conveniently obscured by their terminological communality with simpler behavioral situations. Thus concepts which originally were defined operationally in terms of specified observable behavioral phenomena, the theoretical status of which was primarily descriptive rather than explanatory, have failed to attain such operational specification in PA learning situations. Rather than being rejected or supplanted by more adequate descriptive concepts, however, these nonobserved phenomena have been inferred to be operative at an underlying process level and have been

---

[2] The author is indebted to Gregory A. Kimble for a comment which initially set him to thinking along these lines.

used to explain and account for other behavioral phenomena that can be observed directly.

This surreptitious means of preservation of simpler S-R concepts in theoretical formulations of PA learning has served primarily to obscure the need for and prevent the development of alternative theoretical interpretations adequate to the complexities of the PA learning situation. In an attempt to demonstrate this point, the present discussion will begin with a brief summary and evaluation of three of the recent and controversial issues developed primarily within a PA learning framework (one-trial learning, stimulus learning, and backward associations). All of these, it will be argued, have forced PA researchers to recognize the multiprocess nature and complexity of PA learning and thus have shown the inadequacy of any theoretical account predicated primarily or exclusively upon the establishment of S-R associative connections within each individual pair. This will be followed by a brief presentation and discussion of what little currently exists in the way of multiprocess theoretical accounts, with emphasis upon the need to take into account interpair relationships and learning processes whereby subjects overcome intratask interference as a prerequisite to any satisfactory theory of PA learning. Finally, we shall address ourselves to some important implications deriving from some of these newer and as yet relatively undeveloped theoretical formulations of PA learning, which call for substantial modifications in several prevalent assumptions underlying present-day versions of general behavior theory.

One-Trial Learning

Probably the most active and controversial of the theoretical developments associated with PA research has been the one-trial or all-or-none learning issue initially instigated by Rock's (1957) demonstration that presentation of exactly the same PA pairs from trial to trial produced no better PA learning than a "drop-out" procedure whereby after each trial all incorrect pairs are removed from the list and replaced by new pairs which the subject has never seen before. Rock interpreted this apparent equivalence of new pairs to previously seen incorrect pairs as indicating that nothing had been learned about the latter, and he concluded that PA learning is complete within a single trial, as is required under his drop-out procedure.

Rock's experiment immediately evoked a host of other investigations involving the drop-out procedure and various modifications, most of which were concerned with replicability of the phenomenon under modified conditions and/or the investigation of uncontrolled variables in Rock's procedure that might provide alternative explanations for his results. An early trend toward a predominance of successful replications (e.g., Clark, Lansford, and Dallenbach, 1960; Rock and Heimer, 1959; Wogan and Waters, 1959) subsequently was more than counteracted by demonstrations of poorer PA performance under the drop-out than standard PA recall procedure (e.g., Battig, 1962a; Battig and Nelson, 1962; Brackett and Battig, 1963; Gregg, Chenzoff, and Laughery, 1963; Lockhead, 1961; Postman, 1962; Underwood, Rehula, and Keppel, 1962; Williams, 1961). But the variety of results from these comparisons has been far less impressive than the number of contaminating variables demonstrated to contribute thereto, notably (a) the differential selection of easier pairs permitted by the drop-out procedure (e.g., Underwood, *et al.*, 1962; Williams, 1961); (b) differential effectiveness of a part-learning strategy under the drop-out procedure, whereby the subject learns only a few pairs within any given trial and ignores the remainder (Brackett and Battig, 1963); (c) failure of the technique either to control for or to take into account the effects of response (and possibly also stimulus) learning as distinguished from the critical S-R associative stage (Postman, 1963a); and (d) interpair interference, of which there is less from the new pairs involved in the drop-out procedure than from the repeated previously-incorrect pairs under the standard PA procedure (Brown, 1964).

These sources of contamination and the inability of investigators to devise adequate techniques to eliminate their influence within the Rock paradigm have resulted in the virtual extinction of the paradigm itself in current one-trial-learning research. That the drop-out technique itself, or modifications thereof (Battig, 1965), may be quite useful for the investigation of such other PA learning phenomena as interpair interference (Brown, 1964) has been largely overlooked. Moreover, future research may well show some of the contaminations inherent in Rock's drop-out procedure to be of greater interest and theoretical significance than the one-trial-learning issue to which it was originally addressed. Whatever the deficiencies associated with Rock's drop-out paradigm, PA research and theory most certainly would be the poorer had it never been introduced.

Other ingenious and less violently criticized new procedures and techniques also have been developed as a result of one-trial-learning research (e.g., Bower, 1961; Estes, 1960; Williams, 1962). Curiously, it has been the least satisfactory of these (the miniature single-cycle RTT paradigm introduced by Estes) that in retrospect appears to have been the most important single

influence in the attainment of scientific respectability and theoretical tenacity by the one-trial-learning issue. As pointed out by Underwood and Keppel (1962), among others, the Estes RTT paradigm is subject to each of the contaminations described above for Rock's drop-out paradigm and adds to them at least the differential selection of fast- and slow-learning subjects as well as of easy and difficult items.

Mainly due to the mathematical tractability of the "one-element" model emanating from an all-or-none conception of PA learning, a new class of psychologists commonly referred to as "mathematical modelers" has recently become interested in and been largely responsible for the perpetuation of the one-trial-learning position. As a consequence, there has been a significant shift in the character of PA research related to one-trial learning. Whereas bona-fide PA researchers have become increasingly disenchanted with the issue, they have been more than supplanted by the "modelers" whose concern has been less with the analysis and understanding of PA learning *per se* than with the use of the PA task as a means for formulating and testing various types of mathematical learning models (Estes, 1959). Also contributing to the popularity of all-or-none theorizing has been the compatibility of all-or-none processes with the characteristics of computer programs constructed to simulate the behavior of human subjects in verbal learning tasks (e.g., Feigenbaum and Simon, 1963; Miller, Galanter, and Pribram, 1960). Thus the perseverance of all-or-none conceptualizations of PA learning reflects less the efforts and interest of researchers primarily concerned with PA learning *per se* than it does the attraction of the PA task to the theoretical ventures of those who previously had shown no concern whatever with PA learning.

It is therefore both interesting and reassuring to note the remarkable extent to which recent developments in mathematical models, as applied to PA data, have led to conclusions like those that somewhat earlier had caused nonmathematically oriented PA researchers to lose interest in one-trial learning. These conclusions result from the recognition that the processes involved even in greatly simplified versions of the PA task are so complex that a simple one-element model is inadequate to account for the data. Modelers reaching such a conclusion have included Atkinson and Crothers (1964) and Restle (1965), and even Estes explicitly recognized the complexity and multiprocess nature of the PA task at a recent public discussion on PA learning held at the 1965 APA meetings. Restle's (1965) discussion emphasizes the inappropriate "all-or-none" statement of the all-or-none theoretical position in terms indicating its general applicability to all PA learning situations and its failure to pay adequate attention to variations in materials and procedures as determinants of whether PA learning represents an all-or-none, multiprocess, or incremental affair.

Atkinson and Crothers (1964) reject outright the one-element model even as applied to experimental situations where all response alternatives are previously learned and readily available or where each of a few (three or four) response alternatives is correct for more than one pair, even though these had been the simplified PA conditions under which support for the all-or-none conceptualization previously had been forthcoming (e.g., Bower, 1961). The discrepancy derives from the authors' recognition that certain minor deviations of a one-element model from the observed PA data, notably the non-stationality of errors on trials prior to

the last error, are indicative that at least two distinguishable learning processes must be invoked. They consider a number of closely related alternatives to the one-element model, most of which rest upon the assumed distinction between a temporary short-term memory storage or "buffer," (Atkinson and Shiffrin, 1965) from which a learned item can be "forgotten," and a permanent long-term storage state. Also considered as important factors involved in PA learning are the retrieval of learned items from this long-term storage state and interference produced by other lists or by unlearned items within the same list that are interpolated between presentation and testing for recall of a given item.

Some of the alternatives accepted as reasonable possibilities by Atkinson and his associates actually involve processes which represent continuous variations in strength as a function of number of presentations or time that a given item occupies a place in the limited short-term storage. Also considered is an information-theoretic conception whereby each item consists of several elements or bits of information, each of which may be represented independently in memory storage. Such multiprocess accounts are in substantial agreement with, and in some respects even extend beyond, those that have evolved from non-mathematical approaches to PA learning to be discussed in subsequent sections. The major difference reflects the general preference among modelers to consider each separable process as all-or-none in nature. Unfortunately, available analytic techniques are insufficient to distinguish between such multiprocess all-or-none and continuous or incremental models of PA learning.

Although the extent of its contribution remains to be determined, the mathematical-model approach clearly offers a promising means of formulating theoretical accounts of PA learning and of identifying the type and nature of the different underlying processes involved. Unfortunately, problems associated with the high order of complexity of mathematical models, even as applied to oversimplified PA learning situations, have produced an understandable reluctance among modelers to extend their formulations and analyses to the types of situations characteristically employed elsewhere in PA research. At the very least, however, the mathematical-model approach has pointed to several insufficiencies in the single-association S-R-reinforcement conceptualization that previously had prevailed as accepted PA learning theory and has supported other research within the one-trial-learning framework in pointing to the involvement of several complex variables and processes associated with PA learning tasks which prevent the meaningful resolution of such oversimplified questions as whether or not PA learning is all-or-none or gradual in nature.

Stimulus Learning

Historically, the first influential theory to be explicitly applied to PA learning (also representing the dominant PA theory for well over a decade) was Gibson's (1940) postulation of stimulus generalization and discrimination as important verbal learning processes. Subsequently, these and other PA processes involving stimulus learning had been relegated to no better than a secondary role as a result of the recent development and widespread acceptance of the two-stage (response learning and associative) analysis of PA learning (e.g., Underwood and Schulz, 1960). However, more recently there has been a substantial renewal of interest in PA

stimulus-learning processes, as demonstrated by the vigorous competition with stimulus and nonstimulus oriented theories alike provided by such modern successors to Gibson's theory as Saltz's (1961) differentiation theory.

Probably most influential among these stimulus-learning theories, however, has been the stimulus-selection interpretation presented by Underwood (1963), predicated upon the frequent noncorrespondence between the nominal stimulus as defined by the experimenter and the functional stimulus actually used by the subject. One impetus for this view had come from studies ostensibly concerned with context effects in PA learning and retention in which it has been found that the verbal nominal stimulus often was replaced by the background color upon which it was presented as the functional stimulus for PA learning (Weiss and Margolius, 1954; Sundland and Wickens, 1962; Underwood, Ham and Ekstrand, 1962). However, Underwood's (1963) own recognition of the significance of the selection of a component part of the total stimulus situation to serve as the functional PA stimulus derived mainly from Mattock's unpublished finding that, after learning a PA list with trigram stimuli, the majority of postexperimental reports indicated that the subject had used only the first letter of the trigram as the functional stimulus. In any event, there has been widespread acceptance of the joint implication of both types of experiments that subjects tend to select certain component parts of the total available set of stimulus cues to serve as the functional stimulus for PA learning.

This stimulus-selection conceptualization has already served to stimulate selectively a number of recent experiments involving the use of various multiple-element and compound stimuli in PA tasks, with the purpose of determining the extent to which each of these multiple components was represented in the functional stimulus with which the response ultimately became associated (e.g., Cohen and Musgrave, 1964; Horowitz, Lippman, Norman, and McConkie, 1964; Jenkins and Bailey, 1964; Leicht and Kausler, 1965; Newman, 1963; Saufley and Underwood, 1964; Spear, Ekstrand, and Underwood, 1964). While these studies have identified a number of variables associated with the likelihood of stimulus selection (e.g., meaningfulness, similarity, spatial or serial position), they have as yet accomplished relatively little toward the specification of conditions determining such selection or the extent to which stimulus-selection processes are operative in PA learning tasks. Moreover, it has been argued (Saltz, 1963) that the data offered in support of stimulus selection are more amenable to an interpretation based on stimulus differentiation, which allegedly involves the selective learning of stimulus cues whereby items or pairs constituting the PA list can be discriminated from one another.

Besides its historical priority, a differentiation interpretation of stimulus learning in PA tasks has been fostered also by a recent attempt to develop a two-stage mathematical model of PA learning, including stimulus discrimination or differentiation as one of the two component stages (Polson, Restle, and Polson, 1965). This theory, together with Saltz's (1961, 1963) emphasis on differentiation of both stimuli and responses as the most important processes involved in PA learning, has been sufficient to maintain a stimulus-differentiation process as a viable alternative interpretation to stimulus selection.

Our own analyses of stimulus-learning processes in PA tasks are quite compatible either with stimulus selection or differentiation interpretations but place primary emphasis upon stimulus learning as an increasing function of the amount of interference present within the PA task. According to this view, stimulus selection of a small component part of the nominal stimulus would most likely occur under conditions where intralist interference was minimal and the stimuli were readily differentiated. Within the typical PA list, however, our research has indicated intralist or interpair interference to be sufficient in magnitude to require considerably more than the selection of a single minimally adequate stimulus cue to serve as the functional stimulus. Thus when a constant serial order provides serial position as an additional stimulus cue, we have found no evidence that this cue is "selected" in place of the nominal PA stimulus term as a functional stimulus to be associated with the paired response term (Battig, Brown, and Nelson, 1963). Instead, it appears that subjects make use of this added serial-position cue primarily during intermediate or later stages of learning, to be employed along with the cues provided by the nominal stimulus as a means of combating interpair interference, which is then at its maximum (Brown, 1964). Further evidence supportive of this view comes from a recent study (Brown, Battig, and Pearlstein, 1965) in which opportunity for selection of a single letter as the functional stimulus was maximized through a successive-addition procedure, whereby a one-letter stimulus was used on initial trials with second and third letters being added at intermediate and later stages of learning. Under these conditions, which also involved considerable intratask interference induced by the use of highly similar response terms, the subjects showed considerable evidence of having learned these successively added stimulus letters in order to overcome this intratask interference.

The above results, in conjunction with other evidence showing systematic and consistent increases in accuracy of recognition of nonsense-shape stimuli with increasing intratask interference within a PA pretraining task (Johnson, 1964; see also Battig, 1966a), seem to indicate that the type and amount of stimulus learning will vary considerably depending on the amount of intratask interference produced by other factors and conditions.

Like the one-trial-learning controversy, the major impact of PA research directed toward the specification and analysis of stimulus-learning processes in PA tasks has been to demonstrate their complexity and multifaceted nature, as well as their relevance to the involvement of other component processes in PA learning.

Backward Associations

The existence in PA learning tasks of backward associations, where presentation of the response term as a stimulus elicits the stimulus term as a response, is far from a newly demonstrated phenomenon. As a matter of theoretical interest, however, backward associations have only recently attained central status. Less than a decade ago, such backward associations were being dismissed as a form of "incidental learning" to be understood and interpreted in the same manner as other incidental-learning phenomena (Feldman and Underwood, 1957).

The attainment of current theoretical prominence by backward associations is due largely to the "associative symmetry" principle proposed by Asch and Ebenholtz (1962) although actually preceded by other theoretical interpretations attributing a more fundamental role to backward associations

(e.g., Newman, 1961). According to this principle, all associations are completely bidirectional and "there are no conditions that will produce an association between *a* and *b* without producing an association of equal strength between *b* and *a*" (Asch and Ebenholtz, 1962; p. 136). The influence of this principle has been sufficient to produce a sharp increase in PA research concerned with backward associations and a surprisingly widespread acceptance of the associative-symmetry principle by a variety of investigators (e.g., Horowitz, Brown, and Weissbluth, 1964; Houston, 1964; Murdock, 1962, 1965), despite what appear to be obvious deficiencies in the data offered in its support. Since a thorough review and critique of the literature on backward associations and the principle of associative symmetry has recently become available (Ekstrand, 1966), we shall not attempt here to cover all of the complex artifacts that have thus far precluded a clearcut resolution to the controversy surrounding associative symmetry. For present purposes, it will be sufficient to note that most of these complications have revolved around the fundamentally different learning processes involved with stimulus and response terms within the PA task. Consequently, attempts to demonstrate associative symmetry of forward and backward associations have concentrated upon increasing the "availability" of the stimulus term to a level comparable with that of the response term. Unfortunately, those efforts along this line which apparently have demonstrated associative symmetry have either involved making the stimulus term *more* available than the response term (e.g., Asch and Ebenholtz, 1962, Experiment V; Asch and Lindner, 1963; Horowitz and White, 1965) or have increased the availability of both items constituting a few critical pairs to the point where they probably become insensitive to any differences in strength between forward and backward associations (e.g., Horowitz, *et al.*, 1964; Horowitz, Norman, and Day, 1966). In addition, the procedures used to produce increased stimulus availability typically introduce learning processes foreign to the usual type of PA task, thereby rendering the results and conclusions of questionable relevance to the evaluation of forward and backward associations as these are characteristically involved in PA learning.

The equivalence of stimulus and response terms in availability can be established with certainty only when exactly the same items serve both stimulus and response functions, as is uniquely characteristic of double-function PA lists where each item appears once as a stimulus term and again as a response term but is paired with two different other items in these two pairs. As noted by Ekstrand (1966), the very fact that subjects are capable of learning double-function PA lists at all appears incompatible with the Asch-Ebenholtz principle of associative symmetry, since each backward association in such a list is incorrect and in direct competition with a different correct forward association (e.g., if A-B and B-C are two pairs in the double-function list, the B-A backward association is incompatible with the correct B-C forward association). At the very least, the Asch-Ebenholtz principle requires substantial modification to account for the fact that double-function PA lists can be learned, which presumably would be accomplished by assuming that the subject additionally learns to discriminate incorrect backward from correct forward associations in terms of whether or not an item appears as a stimulus or as a response term. Research employing a double-function list further demonstrates the identification of items as stimulus or response terms to play an important role in PA learning (Young and Bickerstaff, 1966), a process which is further complicated by the considerably greater difficulty of learning double-function than single-function lists (e.g., Young, 1961).

Empirically, however, Battig and Koppenaal (1965) have shown that in double-function lists where identical sets of items are used both as stimulus and response terms, backward associations are systematically weaker than forward associations both in actual and rated strength. Thus it is clear that backward and forward associations can be separated and made to differ in strength through the use of double-function lists. Further evidence indicative of a distinction between forward and backward associations derives from recent demonstrations of the inferiority of bidirectional (each pair presented in both A-B and B-A orders on various PA trials) to the usual unidirectional PA conditions (Schild and Battig, 1966; Underwood and Keppel, 1963; Voss, 1965). This bidirectional inferiority demonstrates that the requirement of actually producing both forward and backward associations during PA learning involves substantially more than do forward associations alone under unidirectional conditions. Whether or not this "something more" represents the addition of new backward associations or can be attributed to increased stimulus availability and/or a loss of the distinction between classes of items serving stimulus and response functions is indeterminate from presently available data. It should be noted, however, that all three of the aforementioned investigators of bidirectional PA learning present evidence indicating the formation of associations in one direction unaccompanied by associations of equal strength in the opposite direction. Nonetheless, since both the double-function and bidirectional PA tasks involve substantial differences from the typical single-function unidirectional PA task, the results therefrom do not preclude the possibility that associative symmetry may occur within certain types of PA tasks and conditions.

One interesting consequence of the use of lesser stimulus-term availability as the explanation for the lesser strength of backward than of forward associations has been the introduction of the stimulus-selection interpretation discussed in the preceding section. Thus Houston (1964) concluded that backward recall of the background colors, shown by Underwood, *et al.* (1962) to represent the functional stimuli when presented along with nonsense-trigram stimuli, was equivalent to forward-association strength after PA learning of single-digit numbers paired with the compound trigram-color stimuli. The legitimacy of Houston's conclusion and the comparison leading thereto unfortunately suffers from his failure to demonstrate the equal availability of color names and single-digit numbers, as would be necessary in order to conclude that backward recall of functional stimuli was indistinguishable from forward recall of response terms. Moreover, the common occurrence in postexperimental recall tests of correct forward recall unaccompanied by *any* backward recall whatever is difficult to reconcile with any associative-symmetry interpretation predicated upon the equivalence of forward associations to backward associations with the functional stimulus.

While it is too early to assess the outcome of research comparing the relative strength and separability of forward and backward associations in PA learning, the development of the controversy has closely paralleled the one-trial-learning and stimulus-learning controversies in a number of important respects. Beginning with the Asch-Ebenholtz attempt to demonstrate the identity and indistinguishability of forward and backward associations and thus to simplify any theoretical account of PA learning, subsequent developments have instead pointed increasingly toward the complexity and multiprocess nature of PA learning and the close relationship of backward associations not only to various stimulus-learning processes, but also to the differentiation and identification of stimulus and response sets or classes in PA tasks. The results of studies on backward associations have also demonstrated substantial differences between the processes involved in stimulus and response learning in the typical single-function unidirectional PA task. As a consequence, efforts to distinguish between and relate backward and forward associations within PA tasks have served instead to point to the extensive involvement of other stimulus and response learning processes, thereby adding further evidence pointing to the complex multiprocess nature of PA learning.

Multi-Process Theories of PA Learning

The preceding discussion of current theoretical controversies in PA learning has made frequent reference to two-process theories, particularly the distinction between response-learning and S-R associative processes or stages (e.g., Underwood and Schulz, 1960). Other two-process theories, applied primarily to situations where all responses have previously been well learned or are made readily available to the subject, have replaced response learning by a stimulus coding (Atkinson and Crothers, 1964) or stimulus differentiation phase (Polson, *et al.*, 1965). While PA theorists have shown a notable reluctance to consider more than two processes or stages within a single theoretical formulation, the results described in the preceding sections agree in indicating that a complete account of PA learning is probably going to involve many more than two processes. Thus the present section will be devoted (and also dedicated) to those few hardy PA theorists who have developed multiprocess accounts encompassing three or more distinguishable PA processes.

The first such multiprocess account appears to have been that offered in a 1954 Ph.D. dissertation by McGuire, which has had little impact on PA research due to its long delayed publication (McGuire, 1961). McGuire's fundamental distinction was between three types of PA learning processes, involving respectively the stimulus, the response, and the S-R association between them. The stimulus-learning process was further specified to consist of "associating with each stimulus a mediating stimulus-producing response," which constituted a partial representation of the stimulus sufficient to distinguish it from other stimuli in the list. Moreover, McGuire considered the S-R association to develop between the stimulus properties of this mediating response to the stimulus term and the correct paired response term itself. The third process in this theory represented the response learning or integration process involved with new or unfamiliar responses, as was postulated also by Mandler (1954) and later by Underwood and his associates (Underwood, Runquist, and Schulz, 1959; Underwood and Schulz, 1960).

Another type of multiprocess theory of PA learning, differing from McGuire's primarily in its greater reliance upon mediating responses to both stimulus and response terms and consequent distinction of one or more additional learning processes, is represented by Newman's (1961) selective-mediation model. This model is a more detailed and formal version of one originally proposed by Cook and Kendler (1956) and has proved to be quite influential not only for the extensive PA research program carried out recently by Newman and his associates, but also for several other PA investigators, despite the fact that a formal statement of the theory has never been readily available in published form (see, however, Newman, 1964).

In addition to the three processes constituting McGuire's theory, Newman also incorporates a mediating response to the response term of the PA list and thus distinguishes between a response-learning process whereby the response is learned so that it can be produced by the subject and a response-discrimination process whereby a mediating response is developed to the response term that permits its differentiation from other response terms (as well as stimulus terms) included in the list. Under certain conditions (e.g., required overt pronunciation of the stimulus term) Newman proposes also a distinction between stimulus-learning and stimulus-discrimination processes, thus increasing the total number of processes to five (stimulus-term discrimination, stimulus learning, response-term discrimination, response learning, and S-R associations). Newman's model also makes use of a Hullian response-hierarchy concept (see also Goss and Nodine, 1965) whereby a hierarchical arrangement of several alternative responses is considered to exist for each of the following: (a) the stimulus term; (b) the stimulus properties of the mediating response to the stimulus term; (c) the response term; and (d) the stimulus properties of the mediating response to the response term. Thus while the final associative stage is considered to be between the mediating responses to the stimulus and the response terms, PA learning is conceptualized by Newman as involving systematic changes in each of these four response hierarchies.

This selective-mediation model has been applied by Newman to a wide variety of PA variables and phenomena. One of its most significant features is its specification of the mediating response to the stimulus term as being less likely to be sufficient to elicit the overt production of that stimulus term than is the case for the mediating response to the response term. Through this derivation, Newman successfully predicts or accounts for both the typical inferiority of stimulus- to response-term recall and the apparent inferiority of backward to forward associations, as well as the heavy dependence of both of these effects upon meaningfulness and pronunciability of the stimulus terms.

All of these multiprocess theories to date have concentrated exclusively upon the learning of individual stimulus and response terms and S-R associations between them and have ignored the extensive involvement in PA tasks of interpair relationships or grouping processes (Battig, 1966b). Moreover, except for the implication that either stimulus or response discrimination processes are dependent upon a high level of interitem similarity, the overcoming of intratask interference has also played little if any role in these theoretical accounts, which tend to treat such intratask interference merely as a source of increasing difficulty in PA learning rather than as producing systematic changes in the nature of learning processes involved in PA tasks.

The effects of intralist similarity on PA learning and the sources of inter-ference associated with it have recently led Underwood, Ekstrand, and Keppel (1965) to extend Underwood's previous two-process (response-learning and associative stages) account of PA learning to encompass additional subprocesses designated as "stimulus versus response differentiation" (distinction between classes of stimulus and response terms), "interstimulus interference" (produced by associative connections among similar stimulus terms), and "associative interference" (produced by incorrect associative connections between stimulus and response terms). The application of the term "interference" to the latter two subprocesses seems unfortunate, inasmuch as it appears to designate effects of intralist similarity which lead to the invocation of stimulus and associative learning processes, rather than the actual learning processes themselves. Nonetheless, this recent Underwood, *et al.*, formulation clearly involves the addition of a stimulus-learning process much like that proposed by McGuire and Newman, as well as an additional subprocess apparently involving identification of and differentiation between stimulus and response classes. This latter contribution, along with the Underwood, *et al.*, application of the multiprocess model directly to the analysis of various types of intralist similarity (formal, meaningful, and conceptual), thus represents an important advance in the direction of incorporating interpair grouping processes into PA multiprocess theories.

Although the role of such intratask grouping and interference processes has not been elaborated therein, Feigenbaum and Simon's (1963) EPAM information-processing theory of verbal learning, prepared in the form of a computer program to simulate subjects' performance on verbal-learning tasks, contains the mechanisms whereby such processes could be readily invoked. The most recent version of this theory, and the first to be applied explicitly to PA learning, identifies three distinct component processes (Simon and Feigenbaum, 1964). Two of these processes, identified by the theory as learning processes, involve the construction and elaboration of internal images of stimulus terms, response terms, or pairs thereof (image building), and the elaboration of the complex network built up from these individual images by adding new nodes or branches thereto (discrimination learning). These two processes are considered to be closely interrelated, with the first serving to guide the second, and both are closely associated with a third "performance system" involving the noticing of some characteristic of the stimulus and following the branch associated therewith through the discrimination network in a search for and attempted retrieval of the correct paired response. The authors claim considerable success in simulating the results of PA experiments varying intralist and interlist similarity, meaningfulness, and familiarity, through the application of this theory.

The importance of interitem relationships and organizational processes has also been central to Mandler's (1967) tentative application of a general information-processing account of verbal learning to PA tasks. While similar in many respects to the Feigenbaum-Simon formulation, Mandler's approach places particular emphasis on the learning and application of "rules" whereby the subject can accomplish the selection, transformation, and retrieval of information about the stimuli, responses, and associations between them in a PA task. Mandler's interpretation clearly implies that the typical PA task involves several learning processes in addition to the establishment of direct S-R associations. Except for the maintenance of his earlier (Mandler, 1954) emphasis upon a distinct response integration process, however, Mandler's approach is not yet developed to the point where individual component processes are explicitly identified. Rather the very legitimacy of such a theoretical endeavor is seriously questioned by Mandler's emphasis upon the idiosyncratic nature and dependence of both number and type of PA learning processes upon such factors as the extent to which individual items have been learned previously and associated with other items appearing in the PA list.

The most notable exception to the general failure to incorporate interpair relationships into PA learning theory is a recent as yet unpublished formulation by Voss. In addition to the required S-R associations within each individual pair, Voss argues that each individual item also becomes associated to some extent with every other item in the list. Thus the strength of a given S-R association is not solely a function of the absolute strength of that association but depends upon the difference of the strength of that correct association from the associative strength of each of its two component terms with all other items in the list. Furthermore, the extent to which a given item is associated with items from other pairs in the list is considered to be maximal immediately upon initial learning or "absorption" of that item and before the correct intrapair association can be given.

While many details of Voss' formulation remain to be worked out and subjected to empirical test, its explicit recognition of the significance for PA learning of associations between items belonging to different PA pairs represents a necessary advance bringing us closer to a complete theory of PA learning. Probably the major limitation of Voss' theory is its assumption of an undifferentiated associative strength of each item with all other items in the list rather than a selective development of interpair associations primarily within partial subsets of the complete PA list. Moreover, while the very existence of PA learning implies a relative decline in the strength of these interpair associations with practice on the PA task, even Voss' own data offer little evidence that such associations reach an absolute maximum upon initial learning of the individual item and decline in absolute strength as the correct intrapair associations become learned.

Unfortunately, the recognition of the complex multiprocess nature of PA learning is far too recent and speculative to justify a formal statement of such a theory here, and such will continue to be the case as long as PA theorists and researchers alike persist in ignoring a major portion of the key processes and variable manipulations essential to an adequate PA theory. Primarily to point up the extent to which even the most complex current multi-process theories still fall short of this goal, we shall list here merely those processes which our research has indicated to be involved in PA tasks, in approximate order of their development from the beginning to the completion of PA learning. Most of these processes, it should be noted, have already been implied by our discussions of one-trial learning, stimulus learning, and backward associations, and several also have been explicitly proposed as important PA processes by one or more previous researchers or theorists.

(1) LIST DIFFERENTIATION. A necessary prerequisite to the learning of any PA list is the identification of the class(es) of items constituting the list and of which particular members or subsets thereof are and are not included in the list.

(2) CLASSIFICATION OF ITEMS AS STIMULUS AND RESPONSE TERMS. Another necessary early stage of PA learning, often overlapping with the list-differentiation stage, consists of the identification of the stimulus or response function served by each individual item. The importance of this stage is obviously maximal when both stimulus and response terms represent the same class of items and is minimized under conditions where items do not uniquely serve as stimulus or response terms, as in bidirectional or free-recall PA tasks.

(3) DISCRIMINATION OF STIMULUS AND RESPONSE TERMS. Once the subject has identified the classes of stimulus and response terms, he must then learn to discriminate among the individual members within each class, especially if these members are highly similar to one another. Although available evidence is not entirely clear on this point, it may be that discrimination among stimulus terms is more important and/or involves different processes than discrimination among response terms.

(4) RESPONSE LEARNING OR INTEGRATION. In addition to the identification of and discrimination between response terms, the typical PA task also requires that the subject learn the response well enough to be able to produce or recall it in the absence of the response term. It is this response-learning stage that was first and most widely accepted as a process of PA learning distinct from an S-R associative process.

(5) STIMULUS SELECTION AND CODING. In addition to the identification of and discrimination between stimulus terms, the subject must learn to encode or select part(s) of the total set of stimulus cues as a functional stimulus to be associated with the response term.

(6) S-R Associations. Having learned to discriminate, select, and encode an appropriate functional stimulus and to produce and discriminate between response terms, the defining S-R associative process of PA learning can effectively be developed by the subject. Whether or not this S-R associative process can be meaningfully separated into forward and backward associations probably depends upon the requirements and conditions of the PA task, as well as one's theoretical position concerning associative symmetry (my preference here is to consider forward and backward associations as distinct processes unless it is conclusively proved otherwise).

(7) Classification of Pairs as Learned and Unlearned. Especially during intermediate stages of PA learning when some pairs have been given correctly and others have not, the subject's identification and differential attention to pairs belonging to learned and unlearned categories becomes an important process involved in PA learning. Even after all pairs have been given correctly, a distinction between difficult and easy or poorly and well learned pairs may continue to play a significant role in later stages of PA performance (Battig, 1966b).

(8) Additional Stimulus Learning. During and following the intermediate stages of PA learning where intratask interference is at its maximum, there may be substantial learning of and S-R associations involving stimulus cues over and above those initially selected or encoded as the functional stimulus.

(9) Mediated and Extralist Associations. As an additional means of overcoming intratask interference, the individual S-R associations may be buttressed by extralist mediated linkages between the stimulus and response

terms, particularly under conditions where such processes were not extensively involved in the initial development of these S-R associations.

(10) Interpair Grouping. In addition to the intermediate grouping of pairs as learned-unlearned or easy-difficult, the advanced stages of PA learning typically involve the development of a hierarchical organizational structure, whereby the overall list is subcategorized into subsets or groups of pairs with some common property or interrelationship among them. Such interpair grouping becomes particularly important where subsets of the PA pairs can be clustered together on some formal basis or in classification-learning tasks where each response is paired with more than one stimulus term.

I am not suggesting that all of these listed stages or processes of PA learning operate independently of one another, nor that every one of them is importantly involved in any and all PA learning tasks. Not only does there appear to be considerable variation in relative involvement of these processes across various PA tasks and conditions, but further complications are introduced by the marked differences between individual subjects as to which processes are employed and to what extent. As a result of these individual differences, there has been an increasing reliance upon "strategies" or "hypotheses" as critical determinants of the way in which a PA task is learned. Thus a completely adequate PA theory must not only incorporate each of the several distinguishable learning processes involved in PA tasks but also must account for individual and task differences with respect to selection and relative significance of these various component processes. Besides demonstrating the inadequacy of current PA theories, even those of the multiprocess variety, these latter requirements also point to the need for a great deal of empirical data concerning relatively uninvestigated determinants of PA performance under a variety of conditions before any theoretical attempt can be more than an exercise in futility.

One final comment appears appropriate before concluding the present discussion of multiprocess theories of PA learning, to clarify why I have taken the position that PA learning theory requires much more than can be provided by principles and concepts derived from general S-R behavior theory. Many of the proposed PA learning processes display extensive overlap with simpler S-R concepts or principles, and some of them may even be ultimately reducible to some combination of these S-R theoretical concepts. The sum total of all PA learning processes, however, clearly cannot be accounted for on the basis of presently available S-R principles. The latter offer little that is relevant to the specification of how or why these various PA processes combine or interact with one another to determine the complicated multiprocess nature of what ultimately gets learned within the PA task. And since such a complete account must be provided even by a minimally satisfactory theory of PA learning, it also follows that this cannot be accomplished by any theory limited to S-R principles that are derived from simpler behavioral situations.

The Critical Role of Intratask Interference in PA Learning

Since the requirements and instructions of the typical PA task involve learning only of intrapair S-R associations, along with sufficient learning of individual stimulus and response terms to permit these learned S-R associations to be manifested in actual PA performance, why should PA learning take on such a complex multiprocess character as we have indicated here? The answer, we suspect, lies in the fact that PA learning tasks almost universally include considerably more than a single S-R pair, thus requiring that a major portion of PA learning be directed toward overcoming the sizable amounts of intratask interference produced by the context of other pairs within which each required individual S-R association must be learned. As a necessary consequence of these multiple sources of intratask interference, the magnitude of involvement of the variety of PA learning processes becomes markedly increased, inasmuch as these represent the means whereby subjects endeavor to overcome the decremental effects of intratask interference upon PA performance. It is in this sense that intratask interference must represent an especially critical concept to any satisfactory theoretical account of PA learning.

It has long been tacitly assumed that intratask interference is an important factor in PA learning only under conditions of appreciable similarity between individual stimulus and response components of the PA task and that such interference plays a negligible role under the low intratask similarity conditions characterizing the bulk of PA research. As a consequence, PA learning theorists have virtually ignored intratask interference and the learning processes associated with it. It appears somewhat paradoxical that the same cannot be said with regard to extratask sources of interference, as convincingly demonstrated by the extensive role attributed to extratask interference in accounting for proactive and retroactive phenomena in the chapter by Keppel immediately following this one. Nonetheless, we shall attempt to show here the importance of PA intratask interference as a key but largely neglected explanatory concept in accounting for intertask transfer and retention phenomena, thereby providing what we regard as an especially convincing argument for the critical significance of intratask interference in any successful theory of PA learning.

As discussed in Keppel's chapter, current interference theories of retention and intertask transfer are currently encountering serious difficulties due to the almost total insensitivity of the usual measures of retention, forgetting, and transfer to the predicted effects thereupon of systematic variations in amount and type of extratask interference that interference theories specify to be important determinants of retention and transfer (e.g., Postman, 1961; Underwood and Postman, 1960). Such difficulties are not unexpected, inasmuch as these extralist interference theories have overlooked the fact that the techniques used for varying extralist interference also produce concomitant variations in intratask interference.

We have presented in detail elsewhere (Battig, 1966a) the evidence leading us to the conclusion that, unlike the effects of extratask (and also intertask) interference, increasing amounts of interference *within* a PA task serve primarily to *facilitate* subsequent retention and intertask transfer for items constituting this PA task. Formulated as a theoretical principle, *intratask interference represents an important source of intertask facilitation.* Thus when both extratask and intratask interference increase or decrease together, as is virtually inevitable according to the techniques by which the latter manipulation has been carried out in the retention experiments discussed in Keppel's chapter, we actually have counteracting sources producing facilitation as well as interference. Consequently, any factor producing greater extratask interference and poorer retention, according to extralist interference theories of retention, also produces greater intratask interference and thus facilitates subsequent retention performance, according to the present principle. With counteracting sources of facilitation and interference cancelling one another out, the characteristically observed insensitivity of retention performance to the effects of systematic variations in extratask interference is precisely what would be predicted by a combination of previous versions of interference theory with the present formulation based on intratask interference.

The meaningfulness and significance of the present invocation of PA intratask interference may be more compelling, both at a theoretical and pragmatic level, by an oversimplified common sense statement of the essentials of this position. To the extent that a given PA task involves intratask interference, successful PA learning must inevitably include the development of processes (such as those listed in the previous section) whereby this intratask interference can be overcome. Thus the total amount of PA learning is increased as a consequence of this intratask interference. Moreover, to the extent that these sources of intratask interference are comparable or overlap with those extratask sources of interference that are responsible for forgetting, they can hardly fail to increase the resistance of PA learning to the decremental effects produced by subsequent interference from extratask sources. Thus we have not one but two plausible mechanisms whereby facilitation of subsequent retention or intertask transfer can result from increased intratask interference, involving (a) greater total amounts of PA learning, and (b) greater resistance to the negative effects produced by normally operating extratask sources of interference. This latter explanation, it should be noted, is similar to Postman's (1963b) recent attempt to account for the excessive amount of forgetting predicted by interference theories of retention, although he fails to tie his suggested mechanisms explicitly to the level of intratask interference present within a PA learning task.

Implications for General Behavior Theory

To summarize the foregoing, I have argued that general S-R behavior theory has provided researchers in PA learning with an oversimplified set of concepts grossly inadequate to handle the complexities of the learning processes involved therein, and that the development of a satisfactory theoretical account of PA learning has been significantly retarded by excessive dependence upon these inadequate concepts borrowed from S-R behavior theory. I have further attempted to list some of the manifold processes and factors that must be incorporated into even a minimally adequate theory of PA learning, most of which bear little resemblance to their precursors as defined by general S-R behavior theory. So now we turn to the question of what significance, if any, these developments and conclusions concerning PA learning theory may have for general behavior theory.

To begin with, we must reiterate once again that the popularity of PA research derives largely from the fact that the PA task represents the verbal multiple-response task which is the simplest and closest counterpart to the simpler conditioning and animal learning situations wherein S-R behavior

theory was originally formulated. As a consequence, any inadequacies of S-R behavior theory as applied to PA learning are indicative of even greater inadequacies for the multitude of learning situations that are more complex than the PA task. At the very least, this indicates that so-called general behavior theory suffers from a considerable lack of generality.

Perhaps more importantly, PA research provides the further implication that a behavior theory of any generality cannot be developed exclusively out of research on the simplest possible type of learning or behavioral situation. Contrary to the implicit view held by many behavior theorists, simplicity is *not* tantamount to generality. Instead, the simpler the empirical underpinnings of a theory of behavior, the less likely that theory is to apply generally to more complex behavioral situations. Certainly a PA theory of the complexity envisioned by the present discussion would be far more generally applicable to other behavioral situations, simple and complex alike, than is the case for current oversimplified versions of general S-R behavior theory. A general behavior theory of this high order of complexity would clearly run counter to the scientific preference for maximal simplicity, as commonly given scientific respectability by the pseudonym of parsimony (Battig, 1962b). But when simplicity becomes a substitute for adequacy, as has frequently seemed to be true of attempts at the development of general behavior theories, it is clearly the simplicity that must give. Whatever its deficiencies, PA learning research convincingly demonstrates the processes and phenomena involved to be exceedingly complex and therefore subsumable only under a general behavior theory which itself is of a high order of complexity.

Yet another significant implication for general behavior theory derives from the common finding that in the course of learning a PA task, subjects often employ complicated symbolic, problem-solving, or conceptual processes beyond what is actually required by the PA task and instructions. In fact, the notion that only the lowest order processes minimally necessary for learning need be considered in a theoretical account may well be one that is unique to behavior theorists; certainly there is precious little evidence that adult human subjects restrict themselves solely to simple lower order learning processes in the course of learning a PA task. And if problem-solving and conceptual processes are involved in PA learning, it is not entirely unreasonable to expect that they may also be involved in simpler conditioning situations, as is becoming increasingly recognized by classical and operant conditioning researchers alike (e.g., Prokasy, 1965; Spielberger, 1965).

Inasmuch as adequate experimental designs and methodologies represent essential prerequisites to the development and empirical verification of an adequate theory, some additional implications primarily of a methodological nature emanating from PA reasearch also should be mentioned explicitly here. With but a few notable exceptions (e.g., Goss and Nodine, 1965), the typical experimental approach to the study of PA learning has involved the manipulation of only a single experimental variable at a time over a restricted range or number of values. More recently, extensive efforts have been made to reduce the complexity of PA learning through the use of tasks involving minimal stimulus and response learning. This approach overlooks the fact that simple experiments are appropriate only to simple theories and that what little is currently known about PA learning is sufficient to indicate that however satisfactory a theoretical account may be for some particular oversimplified version of a PA task, it is unlikely to be similarly applicable, without extensive modifications, even to other equally oversimplified PA tasks. The complexity of even a minimally satisfactory theory of PA learning is sufficient to demonstrate the greater appropriateness to the experimental task at hand of complex multifactor experimental designs applied to PA tasks of sufficient complexity to require the entire gamut of component processes that become involved in such tasks. In fact, the most efficient possible experimental approach (although an impractical one without the cooperation of a large number of PA researchers) would probably represent a single mammoth investigation involving the simultaneous orthogonal manipulation of all PA task and procedural variables known or suspected to have any effect whatever within any kind of PA learning task.

Another methodological implication of PA learning research for general behavior theory relates to the multiple sources of confounding and contamination inherent in the anticipation method that still continues to be employed in the bulk of PA research, despite a variety of unrebutted criticisms of this procedure and the ready availability of alternative methods not subject to these serious shortcomings (Battig, 1965). The long-delayed recognition of the inadequacy of simpler general S-R theoretical conceptualizations as applied to PA tasks can in large measure be attributed to this predominant usage of the PA anticipation procedure and its joint inappropriateness to either of the twin goals of unconfounded investigation of component learning processes or the attainment of performance measures that represent sensitive and accurate indices of what has been learned within and at the conclusion of any given individual trial on the PA task. Moreover, procedural modifications offer one of the best available means for investigation of specific processes or variable effects in PA learning tasks, which represents another argument against the continued limitation of PA research either to the anticipation or to any other single method.

In conclusion, it appears that research in PA learning is much richer in implications for general S-R behavior theory than the latter has been with respect to implications for theories of PA learning and that this would be no less true even if the direction of implications from general S-R behavior theory had not been largely negative. While it is unlikely that general behavior theorists will pay any heed to this plea, they could do far worse than to use recent developments in PA learning research and theory as guidelines pointing toward the direction that an adequate general behavior theory must inevitably take.

References

Asch, S., and S. M. Ebenholtz, "The Principle of Associative Symmetry," *Proceedings of the American Philosophical Society*, **106** (1962), 135–163.

——, and M. Lindner, "A Note on 'Strength of Association.'" *Journal of Psychology*, **55** (1963), 199–209.

Atkinson, R. C., and E. J. Crothers, "A Comparison of Paired-Associate Learning Models Having Different Acquisition and Retention Axioms," *Journal of Mathematical Psychology*, 1964, 1, 285–315.

——, and R. M. Shiffrin, "Mathematical Models for Memory and Learning," *Technical Report No. 79*, Institute for Mathematical Studies in the Social Sciences, Stanford University, 1965.

Battig, W. F., "Paired-Associate Learning under Simultaneous Repetition and Nonrepetition Conditions," *Journal of Experimental Psychology*, **64** (1962), 87–93. (a)

——, "Parsimony in Psychology," *Psychological Reports*, **11** (1962), 555–572. (b)

——, "Procedural Problems in Paired-Associate Learning Research," *Psychonomic Monographs Supplements*, **1** (1965), No. 1.

——, "Facilitation and Interference," in E. A. Bilodeau, ed., *Acquisition of Skill*. New York: Academic Press, 1966. (a)

——, "Evidence for Coding Processes in 'Rote' Paired-Associate Learning," *Journal of Verbal Learning and Verbal Behavior*, **5** (1966), 177–181. (b)

——, and H. R. Brackett, "Comparison of Anticipation and Recall Methods in Paired-Associate Learning," *Psychological Reports*, **9** (1961), 59–65.

——, S. C. Brown, and D. Nelson, "Constant vs. Varied Serial Order in Paired-Associate Learning," *Psychological Reports*, **12** (1963), 695–721.

——, and R. J. Koppenaal, "Associative Asymmetry in S-R vs. R-S Recall of Double-Function Lists," *Psychological Reports*, **16** (1965), 287–293.

——, and D. Nelson, "Effect of Kind of Material and Previous Experience on Paired-Associate Learning under Repetition and Nonrepetition Conditions," *Canadian Journal of Psychology*, **16** (1962), 106–111.

Bower, G. H., "Application of a Model to Paired-Associate Learning," *Psychometrika*, **26** (1961), 255–280.

Brackett, H. R., and W. F. Battig, "Method of Pretraining and Knowledge of Results in Paired-Associate Learning under Repetition and Nonrepetition Conditions," *American Journal of Psychology*, **76** (1963), 66–73.

Brown, S. C., "Interpair Interference as a Function of Level of Practice in Paired-Associate Learning," *Journal of Experimental Psychology*, **67** (1964), 316–323.

——, W. F. Battig, and R. Pearlstein,

"Effect of Successive Addition of Stimulus Elements on Paired-Associate Learning," *Journal of Experimental Psychology*, **70** (1965), 87–93.

Clark, L. L., T. G. Lansford, and K. M. Dallenbach, "Repetition and Associative Learning," *American Journal of Psychology*, **73** (1960), 22–40.

Cohen, J. C., and B. S. Musgrave, "Effect of Meaningfulness on Cue Selection in Verbal Paired-Associate Learning," *Journal of Experimental Psychology*, **68** (1964), 284–291.

Cook, J. O., and T. S. Kendler, "A Theoretical Model to Explain Some Paired-Associate Learning Data," in G. Finch and F. Cameron, eds., *Symposium on Air Force Human Engineering, Personnel, and Training Research*. Washington, D. C., National Academy of Science, National Research Council Publication 455, 1956. Pp. 90–98.

Ekstrand, B., "Backward (R-S) Associations," *Psychology Bulletin*, **65** (1966), 50–64.

Estes, W. K., "The Statistical Approach to Learning Theory," in S. Koch, ed., *Psychology: A Study of a Science*. Vol. 2. New York: McGraw-Hill Book Company, 1959. Pp. 380–491.

———, "Learning Theory and the New 'Mental Chemistry,' " *Psychological Review*, **67** (1960), 207–223.

Feigenbaum, E. A., and H. A. Simon, "Brief Notes on the EPAM Theory of Verbal Learning," in C. N. Cofer and B. S. Musgrave, eds., *Verbal Behavior and Learning: Problems and Processes*. New York: McGraw-Hill Book Company, 1963. Pp. 333–335.

Feldman, S., and B. J. Underwood, "Stimulus Recall Following Paired-Associate Learning," *Journal of Experimental Psychology*, **53** (1957), 11–15.

Gibson, E. J., "A Systematic Application of the Concepts of Generalization and Differentiation to Verbal Learning," *Psychological Review*, **47** (1940), 196–229.

Goss, A. E., "Manifest Strengthening of Correct Responses of Paired-Associates under Postcriterion Zero Percent Occurrence of Response Members," *Journal of General Psychology*, **72** (1965), 135–144.

———, and C. F. Nodine, *Paired-Associates Learning: The Role of Meaningfulness, Similarity, and Familiarization*. New York: Academic Press, 1965.

Gregg, L. W., A. P. Chenzoff, and K. R. Laughery, "The Effect of Rate of Presentation, Substitution, and Mode of Response in Paired-Associate Learning," *American Journal of Psychology*, **76** (1963), 110–115.

Horowitz, L. M., Z. M. Brown, and S. Weissbluth, "Availability and the Direction of Associations," *Journal of Experimental Psychology*, **68** (1964), 541–549.

———, L. G. Lippman, S. A. Norman, and G. W. McConkie, "Compound Stimuli in Paired-Associate Learning," *Journal of Experimental Psychology*, **67** (1964), 132–141.

———, S. A. Norman, and R. S. Day, "Availability and Associative Symmetry," *Psychological Review*, **73** (1966), 1–15.

———, and M. A. White, "Producing Symmetrical Associations," *Proceedings of the American Psychological Association* **1** (1965), 31–32.

Houston, J. P., "S-R Stimulus Selection and Strength of R-S Association," *Journal of Experimental Psychology*, **68** (1964), 563–566.

Jenkins, J. J., and V. B. Bailey, "Cue Selection and Mediated Transfer in Paired-Associate Learning," *Journal of Experimental Psychology*, **67** (1964), 101–102.

Johnson, R. B., "Recognition of Nonsense Shapes as a Function of Degree of Congruence among Components of Pretraining Task," Unpublished doctoral dissertation, University of Virginia, 1964.

Jones, R. E., and L. E. Bourne, Jr., "Delay of Informative Feedback in Verbal Learning," *Canadian Journal of Psychology*, **18** (1964), 266–280.

Leicht, K. L., and D. H. Kausler, "Functional Stimulus Learning as Related to

Degree of Practice and Meaningfulness," *Journal of Experimental Psychology,* **69** (1965), 100–101.

Lockhead, G. R., "A Re-evaluation of Evidence of One-Trial Associative Learning," *American Journal of Psychology,* **74** (1961), 590–595.

Mandler, G., "Response Factors in Human Learning," *Psychological Review,* **61** (1954), 235–244.

———, "Verbal Learning," in *New Directions of Psychology III.* New York: Holt, Rinehart, & Winston, Inc., 1967.

McGeoch, J. A., and A. L. Irion, *The Psychology of Human Learning.* New York: Longmans, Green & Co., 1952.

McGuire, W. J., "A Multiprocess Model for Paired-Associate Learning," *Journal of Experimental Psychology,* **62** (1961), 335–347.

Miller, G. A., E. Galanter, and K. H. Pribram, *Plans and the Structure of Behavior.* New York: Holt, Rinehart & Winston Inc., 1960.

Murdock, B. B., Jr., "Direction of Recall in Short-Term Memory," *Journal of Verbal Learning and Verbal Behavior,* **1** (1962), 119–124.

———, "Associative Symmetry and Dichotic Presentation," *Journal of Verbal Learning and Verbal Behavior,* **4** (1965), 222–226.

Newman, S. E., "A Mediation Model for Paired-Associate Learning," Technical Report No. 1, 1961, North Carolina State College, Contract Nonr 486(08), Office of Naval Research.

———, "Performance during Paired-Associate Training as a Function of Number of Elements Comprising the Stimulus Term," Technical Report No. 4, 1963, North Carolina State University, Contract Nonr 486(08), Office of Naval Research.

———, "A Mediation Model for Paired-Associate Learning," in J. P. DeCecco, ed., *Educational Technology.* New York: Holt, Rinehart & Wiston Inc., 1964.

Polson, M. C., F. Restle, and P. G. Polson, "Association and Discrimination in Paired-Associates Learning," *Journal*

of Experimental Psychology, **69** (1965), 47–55.

Postman, L., "The Present Status of Interference Theory," in C. N. Cofer, ed., *Verbal Learning and Verbal Behavior.* New York: McGraw-Hill Book Company, 1961. Pp. 152–179.

———, "Repetition and Paired-Associate Learning," *American Journal of Psychology,* **75** (1962), 372–389.

———, "One-Trial Learning," in C. N. Cofer and B. S. Musgrave, eds., *Verbal Behavior and Learning: Problems and Processes.* New York: McGraw-Hill Book Company, 1963. Pp. 295–321. (a)

———, "Does Interference Theory Predict Too Much Forgetting?" *Journal of Verbal Learning and Verbal Behavior,* **2** (1963), 40–48. (b)

Prokasy, W. F., ed., *Classical Conditioning.* New York: Appleton-Century-Crofts, 1965.

Restle, F., "Significance of All-or-None Learning," *Psychological Bulletin,* **64** (1965), 313–325.

Rock, I., "The Role of Repetition in Associative Learning," *American Journal of Psychology,* **70** (1957), 186–193.

———, and W. Heimer, "Further Evidence of One-Trial Associative Learning," *American Journal of Psychology,* **72** (1959), 1–16.

Saltz, E., "Response Pretraining: Differentiation or Availability?" *Journal of Experimental Psychology,* **62** (1961), 583–587.

———, "Compound Stimuli in Verbal Learning: Cognitive and Sensory Differentiation versus Stimulus Selection," *Journal of Experimental Psychology,* **66** (1963), 1–5.

Saufley, W. H., Jr., and B. J. Underwood "Cue-Selection Interference in Paired-Associate Learning," *Journal of Verbal Learning and Verbal Behavior,* **3** (1964), 474–479.

Schild, M. E., and W. F. Battig, "Directionality in Paired-Associate Learning," *Journal of Verbal Learning and Verbal Behavior,* **5** (1966), 42–49.

Simon, H. A., and E. A. Feigenbaum, "An Information-Processing Theory of Some Effects of Similarity, Familiarization, and Meaningfulness in Verbal Learning," *Journal of Verbal Learning and Verbal Behavior*, **3** (1964), 385–396.

Spear, N. E., B. R. Ekstrand, and B. J. Underwood, "Association by Contiguity," *Journal of Experimental Psychology*, **67** (1964), 151–161.

Spielberger, C. D., "Theoretical and Epistemological Issues in Verbal Conditioning," in S. Rosenberg, ed., *Directions in Psycholinguistics*. New York: The Macmillan Company, 1965.

Sundland, D. M., and D. D. Wickens, "Context Factors in Paired-Associate Learning and Recall," *Journal of Experimental Psychology*, **63** (1962), 302–306.

Underwood, B. J., "Ten Years of Massed Practice on Distributed Practice," *Psychological Review*, **68** (1961), 229–247.

———, "Stimulus Selection in Verbal Learning," in C. N. Cofer and B. S. Musgrave, eds., *Verbal Behavior and Learning: Problems and Processes*. New York: McGraw-Hill Book Company, 1963. Pp. 33–48.

———, B. R. Ekstrand, and G. Keppel, "An Analysis of Intralist Similarity in Verbal Learning with Experiments on· Conceptual Similarity," *Journal of Verbal Learning and Verbal Behavior*, **4** (1965), 447–462.

———, M. Ham, and B. R. Ekstrand, "Cue Selection in Paired-Associate Learning," *Journal of Experimental Psychology*, **64** (1962), 405–409.

———, and G. Keppel, "One-Trial Learning?" *Journal of Verbal Learning and Verbal Behavior*, **1** (1962), 1–13.

———, and ———, "Bidirectional Paired-Associate Learning," *American Journal of Psychology*, **76** (1963), 470–474.

———, and L. Postman, "Extraexperimental Sources of Interference in Forgetting," *Psychological Review*, **67** (1960), 73–95.

———, W. N. Runquist, and R. W. Schulz, "Response Learning in Paired-Associate Lists as a Function of Intralist Similarity," *Journal of Experimental Psychology*, **58** (1959), 70–78.

———, and R. W. Schulz, *Meaningfulness and Verbal Learning*. Philadelphia: J. B. Lippincott Co., 1960.

———, R. Rehula, and G. Keppel, "Item Selection in Paired-Associate Learning," *American Journal of Psychology*, **75** (1962), 353–371.

Voss, J. F., "Effect of Pairing Directionality and Anticipatory Cue in Paired-Associate Learning," *Journal of Experimental Psychology*, **69** (1965), 490–495.

Weiss, W., and G. Margolius, "The Effect of Context Stimuli on Learning and Retention," *Journal of Experimental Psychology*, **48** (1954), 318–322.

Williams, J. P., "Supplementary Report: A Selection Artifact in Rock's Study of the Role of Repetition," *Journal of Experimental Psychology*, **62** (1961), 627–628.

———, "A Test of the All-or-None Hypothesis of Verbal Learning," *Journal of Experimental Psychology*, **64** (1962), 158–165.

Wogan, M., and R. H. Waters, "The Role of Repetition in Learning," *American Journal of Psychology*, **72** (1959), 612–613.

Young, R. K., "Paired-Associate Learning When the Same Items Occur as Stimuli and Responses," *Journal of Experimental Psychology*, **61** (1961), 315–318.

———, and T. R. Bickerstaff, "Change of Item Function in Paired-Associate Learning," *Journal of Experimental Psychology*, **72** (1966), 514–518.

Retroactive
and Proactive
Inhibition [1]

8

GEOFFREY KEPPEL

Two general types of experimental paradigms have been employed in the study of the forgetting process. The first is concerned with the measurement of forgetting following the introduction of unfilled retention intervals of various lengths. The purpose of these studies is the determination of the effect upon rate of forgetting of variables which have been manipulated during learning, and it is the goal of theory to account for the functional relationships established between conditions of learning and retention loss. The second type of study usually involves two sets of learning materials and concentrates upon a determination of rate of forgetting as a function of variables introduced during the acquisition of the learning materials. The single-list paradigm describes the typical retention study, while the multiple-list design refers to the familiar retroactive and proactive designs. In the retroactive design, recall of the first list is taken following second-list interpola-

tion, whereas in the proactive design, the second list is recalled following a retention interval filled with an unrelated rest activity. Recall under both conditions is referred to a control group which recalls a single list following an appropriate length of rest activity; poorer performance under the multiple-list conditions is termed retroactive inhibition (RI) and proactive inhibition (PI) and better performance is called retroactive and proactive facilitation.

Since an interference theory of forgetting generally attempts to specify interference stemming from extra-experimental sources, both proactive and retroactive, it seems quite natural for the forgetting process to be studied in the laboratory by means of the RI and PI designs. Not only do these paradigms allow for an acceleration of the rate of forgetting but, more importantly, provide for a relatively precise control over the amount and characteristics of the interfering materials. As a consequence, this paper will be divided into two main sections, the first consisting of a consideration of factors presumed to be involved in the RI and PI paradigms and the second presenting a discussion of the success with which these factors have been applied to a specification of the proc-

[1] The preparation of this paper was facilitated by a grant (MH-10249) from the National Institutes of Health. The paper was written at the Institute of Human Learning, which is supported by grants from the National Science Foundation and the National Institutes of Health.

esses involved in the retention of a single list of verbal materials.

Retroactive and Proactive Inhibition

Several excellent summaries of the RI and PI literature have appeared relatively recently. In the introduction to their monograph, Postman and Riley (1959, pp. 271–311) provided a comprehensive review of the area up to 1958, while Slamecka and Ceraso (1960) focused upon the period from 1941 through 1959. Finally, Postman (1961b) offered a useful statement of current interference theory which was based upon the data of RI and PI designs. In view of the availability of these various summaries, the present discussion will center upon research reported after the appearance of these reviews. Moreover, since the most comprehensive and ambitious account of RI and PI is offered by the two-factor theory, emphasis will be given the further development of this theory as required by the recent data. In addition to a description of the theory, there will be a detailed consideration of the two factors—unlearning and response competition. Finally, the interference theory will be evaluated and alternative proposals will be considered.

Two-factor theory of forgetting

The two-factor theory, originally proposed by Melton and Irwin (1940) and tentatively accepted during the 20 years which followed, received its clearest statement in a chapter by Postman (1961b) in the report of the first Gould House Conference. Briefly, the theory identifies two factors which are responsible for the occurrence of RI: unlearning of originally learned

responses (OL) as a consequence of interpolated learning (IL) and competition between OL and IL responses at the time of OL recall.[2] Since the interfering list occurs before OL in the PI paradigm, the occurrence of interference in this design is attributed only to response competition factors. In the years following Melton and Irwin, the basic argument leading to the postulation of the unlearning factor was questioned (e.g., Thune and Underwood, 1943) and was assigned a minor role in the later statements of the theory, e.g., Underwood (1945). In fact, Postman and Riley (1959) were able to account for the RI and PI of serial lists solely on the basis of competition factors. Perhaps the one single finding which changed this situation was the demonstration by Barnes and Underwood (1959) that large amounts of RI were primarily the result of nonavailability of OL (unlearning) at the time of recall, in a testing situation which minimized the influence of competition factors.

The two-factor theory is summarized in Table 1. The upper half of the table lists the factors presumed to be involved in the RI paradigm and the lower half the factors in the PI paradigm. In the first column are listed the various components assumed to be responsible for the production of RI and PI. The variables which either have been demonstrated or postulated to be effective contributors to the particular component in question are enumerated in the second column. Several comments are necessary to elaborate the terminology employed. The first two factors listed under "Unlearning," response similarity and IL strength, were the

---

[2] As a matter of convenience, the first and second lists in the RI paradigm will be referred to as OL (original learning) and IL (interpolated learning), while in the PI paradigm they will be indicated as PL (prior learning) and OL (original learning).

two variables manipulated by Barnes and Underwood (1959) and discussed by Postman (1961b) in his statement of interference theory. The remaining variables listed in this section have been shown to be effective in recent research (e.g., McGovern, 1964; Postman, 1962d, 1965). Variations in stimulus and response similarity are indicated by a prime, with the first two letters referring to first-list pairs and the second two letters to second-list pairs. Listed as variables affecting competition are similarity, number of competitors, and ratios of OL/IL and OL/PL (prior learning) for RI and PI respectively. While the early statements of the relationship between competition and similarity were in terms of formal similarity and similarity of serial position (e.g., Irion, 1946; Melton and von Lackum, 1941), the similarity variable, as it affects competition, has not received the elaboration which the unlearning factor has. The OL/IL and OL/PL ratios refer to contrasts between first-list and second-list strengths, a large ratio indicating OL strength which is much greater than either IL or PL strength and a small ratio indicating the opposite relationship. A final point of clarification involves a consideration of generalized and specific competition. The former type of competition refers to S's tendency to give the last-learned list at the time of recall, while the latter type refers to competition between specific responses associated with identical or similar stimuli. It should be noted that generalized response competition will tend to increase RI, whereas the presence of this type of competition should act to reduce PI. Consequently, this competition factor must be added to the total specific competition in the RI paradigm and subtracted in the PI paradigm.

The third column specifies the relationship between the variables listed and the type of interference by indicating the direction of manipulation required to produce increases in the amount of unlearning and competition factors. While most of these relationships are self-explanatory, it might be useful to examine more closely the functions involving generalized competition. For the RI paradigm, decreases in the OL/IL ratio (IL becoming stronger relative to OL) produces an increase in generalized competition; on the other hand, since this factor is positive for PI, an increase in the strength of PL relative to OL will tend to *increase* the net competition effects by reducing the positive influence of generalized competition. This relationship is indicated in the Table as a decrease in the OL/PL ratio producing an increase in effective competition. The final column in Table 1 describes the effect of a delayed retention test upon the magnitude of the various factors. The main temporal changes assumed to occur are the recovery of OL (or PL) and a decrease in generalized competition. While statements have been made concerning a loss of list differentiation over the retention interval, it is not clear whether this loss will affect the magnitude of RI or PI or merely the occurrence of interlist intrusions. This question will be discussed at a later time. Again considering generalized competition, a decrease in this component will have opposite effects for RI and PI, producing a decrease in the former and an increase in the latter.

Inspection of Table 1 reveals two expectations which have figured importantly in the research on the two-factor theory. The first is that on the immediate test there are two components which tend to increase the magnitude of RI relative to PI. These components are the unlearning factor, which adversely affects the list to be

Table 1

SUMMARY OF THE TWO-FACTOR THEORY

		Immediate Test	Delayed Test
Components	*Variables*	Component Increases as Variable :	Effect on Component as Interval Increases
RI			
Unlearning			
	Resp. Sim. (*AB, AB'*)	Decreases	n/c
	IL Strength	Increases	n/c
	OL Strength	Decreases	Decreases
	Stim. Sim. (*AB, A'B*)	Decreases	n/c
	Resp. Sim. (*AB, CB'*)	Increases	n/c
	Stim. Sim. (*AB, A'C*)	Increases	n/c
	No. of IL Lists	Increases	n/c
Competition			
Generalized	Ratio of OL/IL	Decreases	Decreases
Specific	Similarity	Increases	n/c
	Ratio of OL/IL	Decreases	Decreases
	No. of Competitors	Increases	n/c
PI			
Competition			
Generalized	Ratio of OL/PL	Decreases	Increases
Specific	Similarity	Increases	n/c
	Ratio of OL/PL	Decreases	Increases
	No. of competitors	Increases	n/c

recalled in the RI paradigm and reduces in strength the interfering list in the PI paradigm, and generalized competition, which acts to increase RI and to decrease PI. On the delayed test, however, with the unlearned material (OL and PL) recovering and generalized competition decreasing, RI will tend to decrease and PI will tend to increase. These predictions are indicated in the last column of the Table.

In summary, Table 1 and the discussion above represent a relatively current statement of the two-factor theory. In the next sections, the unlearning and competition factors will be analyzed separately, with attention being given to the recent research on these factors and to the various methodological and theoretical problems which have been unearthed by this research.

Unlearning

As indicated earlier, the first unequivocal evidence for the unlearning factor came from the Barnes-Underwood study. Following various numbers of IL trials, recall of both lists was taken by means of the modified free recall test (MMFR).[3] Since the MMFR test was unpaced, minimizing the influence of response competition, and allowed S to give responses from both lists, essentially eliminating failures of list discrimination which might be

---

[3] Actually, the MMFR test refers to a modification of the modified free recall test (MFR) utilized earlier, e.g., Underwood (1948b), in which S was asked to give only a single response from either list on the recall test.

present when S is asked to recall a single list, any loss of OL was attributed to the unlearning factor. Thus, the finding of a progressive decline in OL responses as a function of increasing numbers of IL trials was taken as conclusive proof that the interpolation of a second set of paired associates corresponding to the $A-C$ paradigm[4] results in an impressive loss of first-list availability.

MEASUREMENT. It is interesting to note that the vast majority of studies reported since 1961 have employed some variation of the MMFR test. Perhaps this reflects a desire on the part of the investigator to utilize an experimental technique which involves, theoretically at least, the measurement of the unlearning factor, uncontaminated by the presence of response competition. While in practice most investigators have assumed the "purity" of the MMFR test, there have been several studies, all employing the $A-C$ paradigm, which were designed to examine this assumption directly. For example, Houston, Garskof, Noyd, and Erskine (1965) contrasted MMFR, in which responses from both lists are requested, with MFR, in which either first- or second-list responses are required; they found no difference in the recall of either list. On the other

hand, while Postman, Stark, and Fraser (in press) repeated this finding, they also found that a third condition in which S recalled OL, but was provided with appropriately paired second-list responses, produced significantly inferior recall. Thus, there is some question concerning the equivalency of the various estimates of response availability which have been reported.

One final comment concerns the means by which the MMFR test is actually administered. Although the original MMFR test (Barnes and Underwood) consisted of a sheet of paper on which Ss listed first- and second-list responses, other investigators have conducted the MMFR test directly on the memory drum. While there are no data directly contrasting these two methods, it is possible to speculate upon the virtues and vices of each. Presumably, the former method allows stimulus cues which are provided by the presence of the other stimuli and the previously recalled responses. These effects, if present, would tend to increase recall on the paper test. The drum-recall method, however, attempts to duplicate the context under which the lists were originally learned. Obviously these two methods can be brought under experimental investigation, although a comparison across different experiments suggests that differences between drum and paper recall will be small. Perhaps a difference will be observed under conditions of high interlist interference, such as provided by the $A-Br$ paradigm. Under these circumstances, S should be able to recall all response terms but will have difficulty in sorting out the correct pairings. In this case, a test which gives S complete freedom to arrange first and second-list pairings may produce higher recall than the drum test in which S is exposed to each stimulus singly. Such a problem would

---

[4] In the remainder of the paper, transfer paradigms will be referred to in terms of second-list designation, with the first-list designation, $A-B$, being assumed. As in Table 1, a repetition of a letter in both lists indicates the occurrence of the same stimulus or response term in both lists, while the use of different letters in the two lists indicates the presence of different stimulus or response terms. Thus, the $A-C$ paradigm specifies the arrangement of identical stimuli, different responses in the two lists, the $C-B$ paradigm indicates different stimuli identical responses in the two lists, and the $C-D$ paradigm different stimuli and responses. Finally, the $A-Br$ paradigm refers to a re-pairing of first-list stimuli and responses in the second list.

not arise with the $A-C$ paradigm since most responses which are recalled on either the paper or drum MMFR test are correctly paired.

TYPES OF ASSOCIATION. The most comprehensive analysis of the phenomenon of unlearning was reported by Barnes (1960) in her doctoral dissertation and later published in the *Psychological Monographs* (McGovern, 1964). Briefly, McGovern separated unlearning effects into specific and contextual components, the former consisting of forward $(A-B)$ and backward $(B-A)$ associations and the latter referring to an association between the response term, B, and the experimental context. Specifically, it was assumed that an association would be unlearned whenever an $A-B$, $A-C$ relationship exists between two lists. Her analysis of the unlearning components involved in four common transfer paradigms, when OL response recall is taken, is presented in the left side of Table 2. A similar analysis, which was applied to the same paradigms by Keppel and Underwood (1962) for OL *stimulus* recall, is presented in the right side of the table. In both cases, the potential unlearning of a specific or contextual association is indicated by a "yes," with a dash signifying the nonimplication of a particular factor. Considering first McGovern's breakdown, it can be seen that the contextual association is assumed to be unlearned in the $C-D$ and $A-C$ paradigms, since new responses (D and C, respectively) must be learned to the same general experimental context. That is, unlearning occurs because of the $A-B$, $A-C$ relationship between successive response terms in the two lists and the contextual stimuli. In addition to the specification of the contextual association in the $A-C$ paradigm, there is the obvious involvement of the OL forward $(A-B)$ association. While neither the

forward nor the contextual associations form an $A-B$, $A-C$ relationship between lists in the $C-B$ paradigm, the OL backward $(B-A)$ association may be unlearned. This may be seen by considering the relationship between the two backward associations in the $C-B$ paradigm, *viz.*, $B-A$, $B-C$, a relationship which should result in the unlearning of $B-A$. Finally, the $A-Br$ paradigm involves the potential unlearning of both forward and backward associations, since in both cases an $A-B$, $A-C$ relationship is formed between lists. Turning next to an analysis of the unlearning components presumed to be involved in OL stimulus recall, a similar breakdown is possible. For each of the paradigms listed in the left side of Table 2, there is a listing of the same paradigms in terms of the assumed backward associations in the right side of the table. Thus, the $C-D$ paradigm becomes the $D-C$ paradigm (assuming $B-A$ as the OL backward association) and the $A-C$ paradigm becomes the $C-A$ paradigm, and so forth. Under "Types of Association," the "forward" and "backward" directions are with reference to stimulus $(B-A)$ recall. As in the McGovern analysis, a "yes" refers to an association which is presumedly unlearned and a dash refers to an association which is not affected by the interpolation.

The major evidence for the unlearning of specific and contextual associations will now be presented. Since these results are most conveniently based upon the McGovern (1964) and Keppel-Underwood (1962) studies, the essential details of the two experiments will be mentioned. McGovern employed a total of eight experimental groups, four of which were given an MFR test and four an associative-matching test following 15 IL trials. On the MFR test, Ss were provided with the stimulus terms and asked to recall the first-list

Table 2

UNLEARNING OF SPECIFIC AND CONTEXTUAL FACTORS IN FOUR PARADIGMS

	Response Recall *Type of Association*				*Stimulus Recall* *Type of Association*		
Forward				Backward			
	Forward	Backward	Contextual		Forward	Backward	Contextual
Paradigm	(A–B)	(B–A)	(X–B)	Paradigm	(B–A)	(A–B)	(X–A)
Control	—	—	—	Control	—	—	—
C–D	—	—	Yes	D–C	—	—	Yes
A–C	Yes	—	Yes	C–A	—	Yes	—
C–B	—	Yes	—	B–C	Yes	—	Yes
A–Br	Yes	Yes	—	B–Ar	Yes	Yes	—

responses.[5] The matching test required *S*s to pair correctly the first-list stimuli and responses which were provided at the beginning of the test. The analytical advantage of the matching test is that it effectively neutralizes the contextual factor so that recall is primarily influenced by the integrity of specific forward and backward associations. The four transfer paradigms indicated in Table 2, *C–D, A–C, C–B,* and *A–Br,* were represented in each of the two testing conditions. The Keppel-Underwood study duplicated the McGovern experiment with the exception that only the MFR test was employed and backward (i.e., stimulus) recall was taken. In both studies an RI control was given either a forward or backward test following an appropriate retention interval. Evidence for the unlearning of the forward association was obtained by comparing the recall for the *A–C* and *C–D* paradigms (4.79 and 6.54 correct pairings, respectively) and the

[5] While it is possible that the MFR test is affected by failures of list differentiation, it is unlikely that unlearning measures are greatly influenced, since the test was administered immediately following IL and *S*s were able to provide, covertly, correctly designated second-list responses.

A–Br and *C–B* paradigms (4.75 and 6.42 correct pairings), since in both comparisons the forward component is the only nonoverlapping factor. Similar findings were reported for the matching test, *A–C* vs. *C–D* (6.54 and 7.83 correct matchings) and *A–Br* vs. *C–B* (5.58 and 6.87 correct matchings). Direct evidence for the unlearning of the *B–A* association comes from the MFR test of the Keppel-Underwood study and can be found by comparing *B–A* recall for the *C–B* and *C–D* paradigms (1.85 and 4.60 correct pairings) and for the *A–Br* and *A–C* paradigms (3.40 and 5.05 correct pairings).

One question raised by these data involves the symmetry of the unlearning effect. For example, does the unlearning of a forward association in the *A–C* paradigm also produce unlearning of the corresponding backward association? While Asch and Ebenholtz (1962a) were not specific on this topic in their proposal of associative symmetry, it would seem consistent with their position to predict symmetry of unlearning. In addition, Mandler and Earhard (1964), in their discussion of the various mechanisms involved in the demonstration of mediation, have assumed associative unlearning in both directions.

In the context of the present discussion the basic question being asked is whether or not there is any evidence for the presence of *backward* unlearning in the *A–C* paradigm and *forward* unlearning in the *C–B* paradigm, associations which are not theoretically involved in the model presented in Table 2. Unfortunately, the data of the present experiments cannot be utilized because of the problem of differential stimulus and response exposures in the two paradigms (Keppel and Underwood, 1962). Birnbaum (1966) attempted to eliminate this problem through the use of highly available stimulus and response terms. However, since bidirectional OL training was employed in which each pair is practiced an equal number of times in both directions, this experiment does not provide a test of the state of affairs obtained with the typical paired-associate study. Also using available stimuli, Houston (1964) was able to demonstrate *B–A* unlearning in the *A–C* paradigm. Unfortunately, no comparison of the magnitude of *B–A* unlearning with *A–B* unlearning was available in this study.

Evidence for the unlearning of the contextual association is obtained through the comparison of the *C–D* paradigm with the RI control in the McGovern and Keppel-Underwood studies. In both experiments significant RI was obtained for response and stimulus recall, respectively. Additional evidence is provided by a comparison of lenient and stringent recalls reported by McGovern for the various paradigms. For the two paradigms in which the contextual association is presumed to be unlearned, *C–D* and *A–C*, there was relatively little difference in the two methods of scoring (.08 and .21 responses, respectively), while for the two paradigms in which the contextual association is assumed to be unaffected by IL, *C–B* and *A–Br*, there was a large

difference between the measures (1.29 and 2.21 responses, respectively). Finally, it will be remembered that the matching test was employed as a means by which the operation of the contextual association could be neutralized. If the contextual association is unlearned in the *C–D* and *A–C* paradigms, there should be a greater increase in the number of correct pairings obtained for these paradigms with the matching test than with the MFR test as compared to the *C–B* and *A–Br* paradigms. Differences between the two tests were in line with these expectations, 1.29 and 1.75 being obtained for the *C–D* and *A–C* paradigms, and .45 and .83 being reported for the *C–B* and *A–Br* paradigms.

While McGovern's strongest evidence for the unlearning of the contextual association is the loss of response availability in the *C–D* paradigm, where specific forward and backward associations are presumed to be unaffected by IL, this conclusion might be questioned since there must have been some degree of stimulus overlap between her two lists of paired associates —i.e., letters were duplicated between lists. Whether unlearning in the *C–D* paradigm is due to this overlap, which forms an *A–B*, *A'–C* paradigm, can be tested easily through the use of two sets of nonoverlapping stimuli, e.g., single letters. Perhaps the purest case of contextual unlearning is the RI observed in free learning (Asch and Ebenholtz, 1962b; Tulving and Thornton, 1959; Postman and Keppel, in press). However, the amount of unlearning found in free learning is considerably greater than that produced with the *C–D* paradigm. This should not be expected since the unlearning in both tasks is assumed to be due to the unlearning of the contextual association. There are several possible explanations of this finding. (*a*) Much lower degrees of OL and IL are normally employed in free learning. (*b*) The unlearning of specific responses in free learning may occur because of an overlap of specific stimulus cues between the two lists, e.g., serial position, similar organizational rules (see Tulving, 1962), or formal interlist similarity.

While the contextual association is useful in explaining various data, e.g., response recall, unlearning in the *C–D* paradigm and the free-learning task, and a reduction in RI as a function of contextual change, little is known about its theoretical properties. For instance, what elements constitute the contextual stimulus? Which elements are most critical? Can the strength of the contextual association be manipulated? In answer to the last question, perhaps an important parameter is the length of time spent during the response-learning stage and not the number of trials *per se*. A final conceptual problem which must be noted is the implication that specific associations may be intact, while the contextual association is not, i.e., the response is not known. This implies the existence of stimuli with "latent" associations attached to them. Perhaps one solution is a combinatory one, that recall on MMFR is jointly determined by the strength of specific and contextual associations. This is the intent of the McGovern analysis and has been suggested by others, such as Asch and Ebenholtz, 1962b; Rock and Ceraso, 1964. With this notion, it is clear that the occurrence of most responses is overdetermined. However, it is the response for which only one member of the combination is present that is of critical interest. On this latter point, certain relevant findings can be noted. (*a*) Keppel, Postman, and Zavortink (in press) suggested that there are some responses which are available only in the presence of the specific stimulus

term. (*b*) The data from the *C–D* paradigm imply an intact specific association but without a recallable response. (*c*) The findings for the *A–Br* paradigm suggest unlearned specific associations but intact contextual associations. (*d*) The presence of "latent" forward associations is implied by McGovern's matching data, where there was an increase in the number of correct pairings when the response terms were supplied, and the data of Taylor and Irion (1964) which showed transfer effects being produced by unrecallable *A–B* associations.

Now that the presence of three unlearning factors has been verified, there remains the as yet unsolved problem of working out the relationship between specific and contextual unlearning. An obvious way to distinguish between specific and contextual factors is to contrast MMFR and matching tasks. A major difficulty with this comparison, however, lies in the differential sensitivity of the two retention tests, the former being a recall test and the latter representing what amounts to a recognition test. Since it has been suggested that the primary difference between recall and recognition is sensitivity (e.g., Bahrick, 1964), it is inappropriate to utilize unpaced recall scores to estimate the magnitude of the response-availability loss and the matching scores to estimate the magnitude of specific associative loss. Functional relationships established for the two tests will undoubtedly prove to be useful in assessing the relative contributions of specific and contextual factors, but just what weights to assign these factors remains an exceedingly difficult problem. Another means by which specific and contextual associations have been estimated is through the comparison of stringently scored and leniently scored MMFR. Clearly, the presence of any responses which are incorrectly paired indicates some degree of associative loss. However, this procedure fails to consider the fact that there may be responses which are unavailable on MMFR and have also been associatively unlearned.

UNLEARNING IN OTHER EXPERIMENTAL DESIGNS. While unlearning has been studied almost exclusively with lists of paired associates, there have been some attempts to extend the phenomenon to other learning paradigms. In two experiments, Keppel (1964, 1966) has demonstrated unlearning in serial learning. In one study (1966), Ss in the experimental conditions received two serial lists (OL = 9/12 correct responses; IL = 20 trials), followed by either an MFR test in which Ss recalled OL, being supplied with the IL responses, or a re-ordering test in which they attempted to reconstruct (or match) the serial order of OL. Under both conditions of testing, significant RI was observed. The particular analysis of this finding depends upon which aspect of the serial list is chosen as the stimulus (see Young, 1962). If it is assumed that Ss utilize item-to-item associations, the transfer relationship formed between successive lists becomes an *A–B, C–D* paradigm. Since unlearning of the OL responses has been demonstrated with this paradigm, it is possible to explain the deficit observed on the MFR test. On the other hand, there is no mechanism by which the unlearning of first-list serial order may be explained, because of the minimal similarity between the words in the two lists. In contrast, if it is assumed that Ss employ serial position associations, an *A–B, A–C* paradigm is formed in which contextual as well as specific unlearning can occur, accounting for both the RI found with MFR and the re-ordering task.

The free learning task, in which Ss are allowed to recall responses in any order, presents an interesting problem for the analysis offered in the preceding section. Three experiments are available in which unlearning was observed with this task. In one of these studies, Asch and Ebenholtz (1962b) had Ss learn two sets of eight nonsense syllables to a criterion of one perfect recitation; 20 minutes following the end of OL, Ss were asked to recall both sets of responses, either by MFR (list order dictated) or MMFR. Under both methods, which did not differ reliably, significant RI was found. Asch and Ebenholtz argued that the RI could not be attributed to the unlearning of specific associations, but reflects a loss of general response availability. One source of *specific* interference which was overlooked in their analysis, however, involves the duplication of letters between the two lists. While the authors attempted to minimize intralist and interlist similarity in the construction of the two lists of nonsense syllables, it is impossible to eliminate interlist similarity in the arrangements as reported. Thus, RI may have been due, in part, to specific letter interference. On the other hand, unlearning has been demonstrated with dissimilar materials. For example, Postman and Keppel (in press) presented OL for 4 trials and IL for either 2, 4, or 6 trials, followed by an MMFR test; the learning materials consisted of two sets of twenty low-frequency nouns. A progressive decline in first-list availability was found with increases in IL. Tulving and Thornton (1959) also reported reliable RI with various numbers of word lists. Since these two studies minimized specific stimulus overlap, an explanation of the unlearning effect may have to include a consideration of the contextual association. This point was discussed in the preceding section.

It should be mentioned that unlearning has been demonstrated in the area of short-term retention. Although a great deal of work has involved determinations of recall following various short periods of unrelated rest activity, e.g., backward number counting, there have been several demonstrations of RI and PI where there has been a formal interpolation (e.g., Murdock, 1961; Neimark, Greenhouse, Law, and Weinheimer, 1965; Peterson and Peterson, 1962; Wicklegren, 1965). Perhaps the most useful demonstration for this discussion is an experiment by Goggin (1966), in which Ss were presented just once, two lists of two pairs each, forming either an $A–C$ or $A–B'$ paradigm. (B and B' were associatively related.) An MMFR test was administered after 6, 22, or 40 seconds in which S recalled both responses associated with the two stimuli in the two lists. Results showed no RI for the $A–B'$ paradigm and significant RI for the $A–C$ paradigm, essentially replicating the findings of Barnes and Underwood.

MECHANISMS OF UNLEARNING. Many writers have noted a similarity between the phenomenon of unlearning and the phenomenon of extinction in classical conditioning. One example of this equation is the assumption that unlearning occurs as the result of the nonreinforced evocation of a first-list response during second-list learning. Melton (1961) stated this point quite explicitly when he asked for " . . . evidence that there is some correlation between the specific responses that were unavailable in specific subjects and the specific nonreinforced intrusions of these same responses during IL" (p. 184). Unfortunately, this expectation is difficult to test since the number of interlist intrusions which occur during IL is extremely small. Furthermore, it now appears that the specific occurrence of an OL response during IL is not critical for the demonstration of the unlearning effect. For instance,

a great many such intrusions are known to occur in the $A–B'$ paradigm, but there is only a slight indication that the OL responses are unlearned (Barnes and Underwood). Although it might be argued that the intrusions in this paradigm reflect the operation of other processes, e.g., mediation, it is clear that intrusion rate and degree of unlearning are not necessarily correlated. Another type of evidence which argues against the critical nature of the overt intrusion during IL is found in an experiment by Keppel and Rauch (1966). In this study, IL error rate was varied through the use of instructions asking Ss to maximize or minimize guessing. Although second-list error rate was greatly affected by guessing instruction, the obtained increase or decrease in specific interlist intrusions was still quite small. Moreover, the magnitude of the unlearning effect was not related to the variations in second-list error rate. Similar results have been reported by Houston (in press). Thus, it seems likely that the actual occurrence or nonoccurrence of an interlist intrusion during learning is not a necessary condition for unlearning to occur.

Consonant with the results of Keppel and Rauch, however, is the notion that the critical elicitation is *covert* rather than overt. It is known that Ss tend to restrict response attempts to items which are included on the list being learned. It seems perfectly reasonable, then, that Ss are able to identify interlist intrusions as incorrect and reject them as a response. Admittedly, the conception of the elicitation of an implicit response during IL removes the process from direct observation. On the other hand, the notion of the implicit intrusion, as an intervening concept, is easily tested and has received considerable support in the literature. In the discussion which follows, it is assumed that conditions which tend to reduce the elicitation of first-list responses during second-list learning will also reduce the magnitude of the unlearning effect. Evidence for this notion comes from various sources: (*a*) Postman and Stark (1965) reported a positive relationship between degree of IL and OL availability, holding degree of OL constant. Under the assumption that the lower the IL rate the greater the opportunity of first-list elicitation, these data are in line with the mechanism under discussion. Moreover, it should be pointed out that this finding is directly opposite the prediction based on a suppression-like hypothesis of unlearning in which increases in IL rate would be expected to produce increases in unlearning. (*b*) Goggin (in press) reported a relatively direct test of the elicitation hypothesis. Specifically, she measured OL following the presentation of IL under either the anticipation or prompting methods of presentation. The prompting method, in contrast to the usual anticipation procedure in which *S* first attempts to give the correct response and is then shown the correct answer, exactly reverses this operation with the correct answer being shown first and then "anticipated" immediately following its presentation. Since *S*s were never formally asked to anticipate the second-list response in the prompting method, first-list elicitation was assumed to be at a minimum. The results showed a significantly greater deficit in OL recall when the second list was presented under the anticipation method. (*c*) The fact that unlearning appears to reach an asymptote which is considerably less than complete (see Barnes and Underwood) may be interpreted to mean that unlearning ceases once second-list responses have become dominant. Of course, such an asymptote could occur for other reasons, e.g., mediation of

some *A–C* pairs or the successful rehearsal of some *A–B* pairs during *A–C* learning. (*d*) Unlearning is reduced when the successive responses come from different form classes (Postman, Keppel, and Stark, 1965), it being assumed that a change of form class provides *S* with a means by which he can avoid the implicit elicitation of OL responses. Theoretically, the manipulation of experimental context (e.g., Bilodeau and Schlosberg, 1951; Greenspoon and Ranyard, 1957) provides an important test of the elicitation hypothesis. By changing the contextual stimuli, it should be possible to change the transfer relationships for paradigms involving the contextual association from *A–B*, *A–C* to an *A–B*, *D–C* relationship. The implication of this transformation is that change of context should reduce RI for the *C–D* and *A–C* paradigms, which involve contextual unlearning, and produce no change for the *C–B* and *A–Br* paradigms, in which contextual unlearning is not involved. (*e*) Another way to manipulate the rate of IL and thus to manipulate the number of opportunities for OL elicitation is to vary the number of IL lists presented, holding the number of IL trials constant. In line with expectations, Postman (1965) found that unlearning increased with the number of IL lists. Although intrusions were few in number, their occurrence did add some support to the elicitation hypothesis. (*f*) In an unpublished study, Postman compared the unlearning of number-trigram pairs, when the IL responses consisted of either high or low meaningful trigrams. While the overall effect was not large, the condition in which the second list was acquired most quickly (high) produced a smaller amount of unlearning. In summary, all of these results can be interpreted in terms of the elicitation hypothesis. As now stated, the hypothesis predicts a direct relationship between the amount of unlearning and the degree of first-list elicitation, and any variable which can be shown to affect rate of elicitation should reflect this relationship.

While there is no question that unlearning is a basic process in the production of RI in the $A-C$ paradigm, it is almost equally true that unlearning is not an important process in the $A-B'$ paradigm, although Barnes and Underwood did report a progressive loss of OL as a function of increasing IL trials (7.75 to 7.08 responses), which they attributed to the dropping out of the $A-B-B'$ mediator. To date there has been no adequate theoretical explanation of the relationship between unlearning and mediation. Postman (1961b) has discussed this relationship and suggested that mediation is the primary mechanism, with the S's attempts to mediate from B to C in the $A-C$ paradigm resulting in the production of incorrect B' responses which are unlearned together with the useless B responses. While there are no definitive studies on this problem, two different experimental approaches can be mentioned which at least provide the beginnings of an answer. One such approach involved instructions asking Ss either to attempt to mediate or to unlearn in the $A-C$ paradigm (Dallett and D'Andrea, 1965). (A similar technique has been employed by Martin and Dean, 1964.) Although there was higher recall of OL with the mediation group, it is not possible to determine whether mediation instructions were effective in reducing RI, since no normal condition was employed. Moreover, while the number of reports of mediation were greater for the mediation condition, the overall number of such reports was small relative to the number of reports of $A-C$ associations which were independent of $A-B$ associations.

Assuming that the reports of mediation are an accurate indication of successful attempts to mediate in the $A-C$ paradigm, it is clear that such a procedure is enormously unsuccessful when compared to the reports of mediation in the actual $A-B'$ paradigm (Barnes and Underwood).

A second approach, reported by Postman and Stark (1963), allowed S to generate his own response during $A-C$ learning. Presumably, if S's first tendency is to mediate, as Postman (1961b) has speculated, this tendency should be reflected in the second-list responses produced by these Ss. Contrary to these expectations, Ss selected associates to the stimulus term rather than the response term an average of 87% of the time. In fact, even under optimal conditions for mediation, where Ss were told to expect a recall of OL following IL, this selection was greater than for Ss not so instructed. While it is admitted that these results are not necessarily damaging to the mediation hypothesis, response selection perhaps representing a different process than that involved when a response is prescribed, it is still surprising, however, that there was no evidence for this presumed basic mechanism. It is conceivable that the mediation process will be observed under circumstances where there are no strong associates to the stimulus term, e.g., nonsense syllables. On the other hand, these findings may indicate that unlearning is the basic process and that mediation is discovered during the initial presentation of $A-B'$ (the study trial) when B should tend to be elicited reliably in the presence of $A-B'$. Thus, first-list associations are preserved because they are instrumental in the acquisition of the $A-B'$ list. By way of contrast, the OL response tends not to be used during $A-C$ learning, is elicited either covertly or overtly in the presence of $A-C$, and is unlearned. Also arguing against the notion that response mediation is an initially strong tendency in unpracticed *S*s is the fact that the magnitude of the mediation effect in the *A–B′* paradigm largely depends upon *S*'s stage of practice (Keppel and Postman, 1966; Postman, 1964). At any rate, it is clear that the relationship between the mechanisms of response mediation and unlearning is far from obvious and that additional research is necessary to clarify the issue.

SPONTANEOUS RECOVERY. As another example of the extinction analogy, it has been assumed that responses which have been unlearned during IL will recover in strength as the IL-recall interval is lengthened. Such an assumption was necessary, in part, to account for the convergence of RI and PI on a delayed test (see Table 1). While evidence for recovery has been reported (e.g., Briggs, 1954; Underwood, 1948b), the most useful demonstration, for analytical purposes, is with the MMFR test. At the outset, it must be emphasized that the appropriate experimental design consists of pairs of RI experimental and control groups which are tested for recall following retention intervals of various lengths. Absolute recovery is defined by an actual *increase* in OL recall with time, while relative recovery is defined by a smaller decrease in OL for the experimental group than for the control group. The demonstration of absolute recovery, however, still requires an interaction of the control and experimental functions, in addition to the absolute rise for the experimental groups. Such an interaction is demanded by the operational definition of spontaneous recovery. Moreover, two studies (Koppenaal, 1963; Slamecka, 1966) have shown increases in the control function which corresponded to the increases in the experimental function.

The nine studies testing for recovery with the MMFR test, which were available to the writer, are listed in Table 3. As indicated, only three of the nine experiments showed absolute recovery. Of the experiments which demonstrated absolute recovery, one found sizable increases over 20 minutes (Postman, Stark, and Fraser, in press), while the other two found increases over 24 hours (Ceraso and Henderson, 1965) and 48 hours (Adams, 1962). In the latter study, almost complete recovery was found with high degrees of OL (OL = 19 trials; IL = 10 trials). Specifically, recall for the control groups was 5.6 and 5.0 on the immediate and delayed tests, respectively, and 2.8 and 4.5 for the experimental groups. Other than Postman's study, there have been no systematic investigations of recovery over intervals less than 20 minutes. In this regard, Koppenaal (1963) reported a small amount of recovery between 1 and 20 minutes. In addition, both he and Slamecka (1966) reported increases between the immediate and 24-hour intervals, but, as noted earlier, these trends were not reliably different from those obtained by the control groups. Finally, Goggin (1966) found no temporal changes from 6 to 40 seconds with short paired-associate lists (two pairs) presented only once. Failure to find recovery in Goggin's study is not necessarily contradictory to Postman's demonstration, considering the many differences between the two studies, e.g., number of pairs, degree of OL and IL, and length of retention interval. Just why some investigators have not found absolute recovery, while others have, is not immediately apparent.

As indicated in Table 3, relative recovery has been more successfully demonstrated than has absolute recovery. While the original explanation of this convergence was given by

Underwood (1948a, 1948b) and consisted of the assumption that the absence of a temporal change in the recall of OL was the result of spontaneous recovery balancing out the "usual forgetting" which occurs over time, other explanations of the phenomenon have been offered. Koppenaal (1963; Koppenaal and O'Hara, 1962), for example, has suggested that unlearning is a negatively accelerated function of IL. Under the further assumption that unlearning can occur during the retention interval, a greater loss will be predicted for the control condition (no previous IL) than for the experimental condition. A second explanation, while closely related to Koppenaal's, has been given by Birnbaum (1965). In this explanation, it is assumed that the distribution of OL strengths represented by the experimental and control Ss on the immediate recall test are different, the weak OL items having been unlearned during IL, but are still present for the control Ss on the immediate test. Since degree of OL and forgetting are inversely related (cf, Underwood and Keppel, 1963), a greater item loss will be observed for the control than for the experimental Ss. One implication of this notion is that the relatively faster rate of forgetting for the control

Ss will be due largely to the loss of the weak items. Attempts to demonstrate this implication by selecting strong-weak items on the basis of first-list learning (Birnbaum, 1965; Grayson, 1966), however, have failed. These failures are not particularly damaging to these explanations since OL strength, as measured by first-list learning rate, is not perfectly correlated with availability following IL. That is, whether or not an investigator is successful in identifying the specific OL items which will be unlearned, the fact remains that certain items have survived IL and are probably less susceptible to uncontrolled IL occurring during the retention interval than are some of the essentially unselected items available to the control Ss on the immediate test. Until a way is found to determine the probability with which items will be affected by formal and uncontrolled IL, these two explanations remain an interesting and reasonable alternative to Underwood's explanation of relative recovery.

SUMMARY. As noted earlier, a great deal of research effort has gone into the study of unlearning as a factor in the production of RI. This has been accomplished through the use of the unpaced MMFR test. With this tech-

Table 3

EXPERIMENTS TESTING FOR ABSOLUTE AND RELATIVE RECOVERY

Experiments	Absolute Recovery	Relative Recovery
Adams (1962)	Yes	Yes
Birnbaum (1965)	No	Yes
Ceraso and Henderson (1965)	Yes	Yes
Goggin (1966)	No	No
Grayson (1966)	No	Yes
Houston (1966)	No	Yes[a]
Koppenaal (1963)	No	Yes[a]
Postman, Stark, and Fraser (in press)	Yes	Yes
Slamecka (1966)	No	Yes[a]

[a] not significant

nique it has been possible to show the unlearning of specific and contextual associations in various types of verbal-learning tasks. Although the mechanism by which unlearning is produced is by no means clear, an explanation which assumes that unlearning is the result of the unreinforced evocation of a first-list response during IL has received some support in the literature.

Competition

MEASUREMENT. Research on response competition has lagged far behind that reported on unlearning. This is true in spite of the fact that response competition is assumed to be the sole contributor to PI (Table 1). The term "competition" implies that there is more than one response which is vying for expression at the point of recall. This competition may take two forms, interlist intrusion and failure to respond (blocking). It should be clear, however, that the occurrence of either an intrusion or a failure to respond does not necessarily mean that response competition was the factor producing it. Specifically, it is conceivable that some of the interlist intrusions are the result of S's filling in with a "reasonable" response when unable to think of the correct response and that some of the failures to respond are due to S's reluctance to give an IL response and his inability to produce the unavailable OL response. Alternatively, it is possible to hold to a conception of competition in which the IL response is so strong that the OL response is effectively unavailable. As Barnes and Underwood pointed out, this conception of competition becomes isomorphic with the concept of unlearning. It has been convenient to decide between competition and unlearning in terms of the ultimate availability of

the response in question. Thus, if S fails on a test of recall, this failure will be credited to response competition if it can be shown that the correct response was in fact available or to unlearning if this response is unavailable. In short, unlearning refers to the loss of response recallability, while response competition refers to a struggle between two available responses elicited by the same stimulus.

An experimental operation which satisfies the definition of competition given above was suggested by Postman (1962a) and involves a comparison between a conventional paced-recall test and an unpaced MMFR test. It is assumed that the MMFR test minimizes the influence of competition factors so that if a response is not recalled on MMFR, it is said to be unavailable. The paced test, on the other hand, is presumably sensitive to loss of availability as well as to the effects of response competition. Consequently, competition is defined as the degree to which RI under paced conditions exceeds the RI produced with MMFR. As far as is known, this type of comparison has been employed exclusively with the RI paradigm.

There is one difficulty with this comparison that should be mentioned. This is the problem of distinguishing between a long latency response and a response which has been affected by competition at recall. That is, there may be "partial" unlearning in which IL affects OL response latency but not its ultimate recallability. Such an occurrence would be mistaken for an instance of response competition. Thus, to the extent that partial unlearning occurs and produces response latencies which are greater than the length of the anticipation interval, the paced-unpaced measure will overestimate the amount of response competition.

Two different estimates of competition have been used. The measure introduced by Postman involved the comparison of RI produced on the paced and MMFR tests with analyses performed on absolute control-experimental differences rather than percentage measures. Grayson (1966), on the other hand, suggested that a "pacing decrement" provides a more useful measure. With this method, scores are transformed into ratios which reflect the deficit to be attributed to the paced test relative to the responses available on the MMFR test, i.e., (MMFR—Paced Recall)/MMFR. These percentages then become the basis for comparison of the control and the experimental conditions. A contrast of these two methods involves two questions: (*a*) absolute versus relative measures, and (*b*) RI comparisons (Postman) versus comparisons of pacing decrements (Grayson).

The merits of absolute and relative measures have been widely discussed in the measurement of retention. The argument for absolute measures was clearly stated by Postman and Riley (1959, p. 369) when they pointed out that absolute measures focus upon the specific items lost and that it is an experimental goal to determine the conditions which produced these losses. In the context of the present discussion, this would involve asking how many responses are available but not given on the paced test. The experimenter could then attempt to explain why these particular responses were not given. On the other hand, there is reason to prefer a relative measure. Consider, for example, the occurrence of complete forgetting for one group, e.g., an experimental group dropping from 3 to 0 correct responses, and less than complete forgetting for another group, e.g., a control group dropping from 8 to 4 responses. A relative measure reflects this point by indicating greater forgetting in the experimental group

(100%) than in the control (50%). The absolute measure indicates that the control group showed more forgetting. Such a difference in conclusions can occur whenever groups are not equivalent on an immediate retention test. Obviously, both types of measures can be defended and the ultimate choice of a measure will depend upon the purposes of the investigator and the nature of the theory.

The second question concerning a measure of competition is a choice between RI comparisons and a comparison of pacing decrement. Postman's measure is in terms of RI and provides for a direct comparison of RI on the paced and MMFR tests. Grayson's measure, on the other hand, first obtains the relative effect of pacing upon the total number of responses which are available and then determines the influence of interpolation on this ratio. Again, the choice of measure is somewhat arbitrary, except in this case Grayson's method comes closer to satisfying the verbalized definition of competition, i.e., a condition which affects *available* responses. Of the two questions, probably the distinction between absolute and relative is most important, because, as was shown, it is possible to reach different conclusions from the two methods, while the RI comparison and the comparison of pacing decrements do not produce drastic changes in the overall picture of the results. From a practical point of view, a report of obtained means for experimental and control groups on the paced and MMFR tests allows the computation of all possible combinations of measures. In the discussion to follow, the method suggested by Grayson will be used.

GENERALIZED RESPONSE COMPETITION. Generalized competition refers to a tendency for *S* to continue responding with the most recently presented list. This form of competition would tend to increase the total competition (generalized + specific) in the RI paradigm and to decrease the total in the PI paradigm. This concept was originally suggested by Newton and Wickens (1956) to account for the fact that RI increased as the OL–IL interval increased for the C–D paradigm but not for the A–C paradigm. Since no specific interlist similarity was assumed to be present in the C–D paradigm, the effect was attributed to a nonspecific, generalized response competition. Postman and Riley (1959) employed the concept to explain the form and nature of RI produced with serial lists. Specifically, serial-position curves at recall were considerably flatter for the RI conditions than for the PI or control conditions, with the flattening being most pronounced in the initial portions of the list. On the second relearning trial, however, the RI conditions produced bowed curves. Postman and Riley interpreted these findings to mean that generalized competition adversely affects the RI conditions, is at its maximum at the start of the recall trial, and is dissipated once the OL responses have been re-introduced into the immediate experimental context. As final evidence for the operation of generalized competition, Postman (1961b) cited the change-of-context studies in which RI was shown to be decreased when OL and IL were acquired under different experimental environments or different instructional sets.

There have been no published attempts to determine whether or not the above mentioned phenomena, which are ascribed to generalized competition, are in part the result of unlearning. Such a re-interpretation is possible, however. For instance, the effect of variations in the OL–IL interval with the C–D paradigm may be interpreted in terms of unlearning and spontaneous recovery. That is, if IL occurs immediately following OL, and if the OL-recall interval is constant, spontaneous recovery of the unlearned contextual association can account for the results of Newton and Wickens. Admittedly the evidence for recovery is not strong, but an unlearning mechanism is at least possible and its presence is testable by means of the MMFR test. If the Newton-Wickens' effect is due to generalized competition, it should not be produced under MMFR, while if some portion of the effect is due to unlearning and recovery of the OL contextual association, it should be found with MMFR. Similarly, the change-of-context studies may be explained in terms of unlearning. Specifically, the elicitation hypothesis would predict reduced interlist responding under changed contextual conditions.

Finally, it is possible to interpret the findings of Postman and Riley (1959) in terms of unlearning mechanisms. For instance, Keppel and Zavortnik (in press) found a large loss of the initial responses in the serial list with an MMFR test. These findings suggest that the flattened position curve reported by Postman and Riley is primarily due to unlearning than to generalized response competition.

SPECIFIC COMPETITION. In contrast to generalized competition, this type of competition refers to the competition between two or more responses which are associated with the same stimulus (Postman and Riley, 1959). Studies which have employed a comparison between paced and MMFR tests are listed in Table 4. The first two columns in Table 4 indicate the degrees of OL and IL administered in the various experiments. The results of these determinations, expressed in terms of percentage pacing decrement (MMFR minus Paced

Recall / MMFR), are given for the control and experimental conditions. For comparison purposes all percentages were based upon averages taken from tables or estimated from figures. For all experimental groups, IL consisted of a single A–C list presented immediately following OL criterion with the exception of Grayson's "E_4" which received four different A–C lists (A–C, A–D, A–E, A–F) for five trials each. Inspection of Table 4 reveals a consistently higher pacing decrement for the experimental conditions, indicating the reliability of the competition effect. For the single IL conditions, there appears to be a consistent increase in competition as the retention interval is lengthened, perhaps decreasing again after one week (Houston, 1966). This would suggest that response competition increases in importance with time, a finding which is directly in line with the expectations of the two-factor theory. A comparison of the effect of single and multiple IL (Grayson) is also of interest. It will be noted that the increase in competition associated with the single IL conditions is

not found with the multiple IL condition, competition being at a maximum on the immediate test and decreasing over the retention interval. This reverse in temporal trend may be interpreted in terms of the number of effective competitors present at the time of recall. Specifically, it is quite likely that OL/IL strengths are roughly equivalent for E_4 immediately following IL, while IL is much stronger than OL for E_1. This has come about through the greater unlearning of OL and the reduced learning of individual IL responses in E_4. Consequently, at the time of recall several poorly differentiated responses will be competing in E_4 while only one well-differentiated response will be a potential competitor in E_1. Assuming that competition increases with the number of effective competitors (Underwood, 1945), the difference between E_1 and E_4 on the immediate test may be understood. Over a time period, though, as OL recovers or as IL is forgotten, the initially strong IL responses in E_1 will become more equivalent in strength to OL while the relatively weaker IL responses in E_4

Table 4

RESPONSE COMPETITION IN TERMS OF
PERCENTAGE PACING DECREMENT

Experiments	OL	IL		Immediate	Recall One week	Two weeks
Postman (1962a)	8/8	20 Tr.	C	16.8	—	—
			E	26.4	—	—
Houston (1966)	8/8	15 Tr.	C	8.9	18.3	28.2
			E	13.0	44.1	44.0
Houston (1967)	8/8	15 Tr.	C	—	39.0	—
			E	—	52.3	—
Grayson (1966)	9/12	20 Tr.	C	24.4	−2.2[a]	—
			E_1	39.6	57.2[a]	—
			E_4	52.4	18.1[a]	—
Keppel, Postman, and Zavortink (in press)	7/8	15 Tr.	C	8.3	—	—
			E	25.8	—	—

[a] 4-day retention interval

will no longer be available as competitors, creating the reverse in the temporal trend for these two groups.

In summary, little is known about competition, either as a phenomenon or in terms of the mechanisms producing the effect. The data suggest that competition becomes more important on the delayed retention test and that the amount and direction of these trends depend upon conditions of interpolation, e.g., number of alternative responses. There have been no studies concerned with competition in PI. Since the two-factor theory implies that all PI is due to competition factors, experimental effort will have to be directed toward this problem.

DIFFERENTIATION. In view of the fact that the concept of list differentiation has been considered a factor in various discussions of competition, an elaboration of the notion will be given here. As it has been described, differentiation refers to the ability of S to discriminate the list membership of responses he is recalling. Many investigators have asked Ss to indicate list membership following MMFR and have reported an extremely high degree of success on the immediate retention test. Birnbaum (1965), for example, reported 99% correct list designation immediately following 20 $A–C$ trials. This percentage was slightly lower after one day (96%), but significantly reduced after one week (78%). Similar values have been reported by others. These findings indicate that on MMFR, S's ability to discriminate list membership is extremely high initially. However, it is likely that MMFR greatly overestimates the level of differentiation present on the paced-recall test, where instead of unlimited time to discriminate list membership, S has only 2–3 seconds. Perhaps a more realistic estimate of differentiation might be provided by a paced-recogni-

tion test in which S must indicate, within a limited amount of time, the membership of the responses from the two lists.[6]

Whether or not an acceptable measure of differentiation can be devised, there still remains the question of the relationship between differentiation and the production of RI and PI. From the theoretical treatments of list differentiation in the literature, it is not entirely clear as to the exact behavioral consequences brought about by variations in the factor. For instance, list differentiation has been assumed to influence the rate of interlist intrusions but not to affect directly the amount of RI or PI. On the other hand, Underwood (1945) has suggested that high list differentiation may allow the reduction of RI by making more time available for S to produce the correct response during a limited anticipation interval. Barnes and Underwood speculated that immediately following IL, when differentiation is high, nearly all RI is due to unlearning, and that as

[6] There have been two recently reported tests of list differentiation with a recognition-type procedure. McCrystal and Ranken (1966) asked Ss to identify the list membership of all OL and IL responses, presented singly, and found differentiation to decrease over a one-week retention interval. Since their test was relatively unpaced (Ss were allowed up to 12 seconds to respond), it does not provide information concerning differentiation under the pressure of time. Jung (1966), on the other hand, did employ a paced differentiation test in which OL and IL responses were presented at approximately a two-second rate. In this experiment, Jung manipulated paradigm and degree of OL and IL strength; the differentiation test was given immediately following the completion of IL. Results revealed near-perfect differentiation for all experimental groups. This finding provides strong support for the assumption that list differentiation is extremely high at the end of IL for a variety of experimental conditions. Hopefully, interest will be directed toward similar determinations on delayed retention tests.

the retention interval is increased and list differentiation is reduced, response competition increases in importance as a factor in producing RI. In this latter view, it seems that the role of differentiation is largely indirect, holding in check competition when it is high and allowing competition to occur when it is low. If this evaluation is correct, it may be profitable to distinguish between potential competition, the amount of competition in the absence of list differentiation, and *effective* competition, the amount of competition allowed to affect recall at any particular level of differentiation.

As the concept was originally described, differentiation was assumed to increase as OL/IL strengths diverge and to decrease with increases in the interval separating learning and recall (Underwood, 1945). However, little is known about the stimulus characteristics of the notion (cf. Melton, 1961, pp. 184–185). In fact, the question can be raised as to the necessity of the concept. For instance, it could be assumed that response competition is a function of OL/IL strength, increasing as the two lists become equal. This assumption, for example, could explain the increase in competition with time by means of the convergence of OL and IL over this interval (e.g., Koppenaal, 1963). Obviously, the assumption that differentiation decreases with time also leads to a similar expectation. Perhaps it is possible to arrive at a different prediction for the two mechanisms. For instance, the "strength" hypothesis should predict considerable competition on an immediate recall test when OL and IL are of equal strengths, while differentiation predicts minimal competition effects. As it stands, then, differentiation is a possible mechanism to account for temporal changes in RI and PI, but its stimulus properties and its exact contribution to the production of RI and PI remains to be specified.

Evaluation of the two-factor theory

UNLEARNING. There is no question that unlearning is a basic factor in the production of RI. Since competition is also an assumed process in the two-factor theory, it is imperative that estimates of availability are not influenced by response competition. It was this concern that prompted the development of the MMFR test. The fact that various investigators have found only small differences among variations of the MMFR test should not be taken to mean that the test is insensitive to competition under all experimental conditions. It is conceivable that under conditions of high interlist confusion, e.g., the *A–Br* paradigm, or of low list differentiation, e.g., delayed retention test, that differences will emerge.

The elicitation hypothesis offers some promise as an underlying mechanism of unlearning. At present, the notion merely states that unlearning depends upon the implicit intrusion of OL responses during IL. While the hypothesis has been confirmed in a set of reasonably different experimental situations, the precise theoretical details have not been worked out. One problem is that the operation of the process is assumed to be covert. Differences in the numbers of interlist intrusions are cited as evidence for the occurrence or nonoccurrence of OL elicitation, but it is unlikely that these intrusions indicate which OL responses will be unavailable following IL (Keppel and Rauch, 1966). This brings up the question of whether OL elicitation refers to a property of a list or extends to specific pairs within a list. It will be recalled that Postman and Stark (1965) reported a positive correlation between IL rate and OL recall, with the correlation between OL rate and recall controlled. This finding was interpreted in terms of the elicitation hypothesis, i.e., the faster IL is acquired, the less the frequency with which OL responses are evoked during IL. Runquist (1957) has reported comparisons of RI and PI, after 24 hours, as a function of OL and IL/PL item strengths. In this study, items in both lists were ranked for each S in terms of the frequency of correct anticipation and then RI and PI were determined as a function of these ranks. For present purposes, the most striking aspect of the data was the complete lack of relationship between IL item strength and the absolute amount of RI. These findings suggest that the positive correlation between IL and OL recall, found by Postman and Stark, does not extend to variations of IL within Ss.

While no attempt will be made to completely reconcile these discrepant relationships, several speculations can be made. (a) The Postman-Stark analysis controlled for the correlation between OL rate and recall, while Runquist classified his items in terms of IL rank, ignoring the rank of the OL items. Although Runquist did mention a joint classification of OL and IL strengths, these data were not presented. (b) In Runquist's study, recall was by means of a paced-recall test administered 24 hours following learning; Postman and Stark gave an immediate MMFR test. It is conceivable, then, that differences in competition may account for differences in the findings of the two studies. In this regard, Slamecka and Ceraso (1960) mentioned an experiment by Ceraso (1959) in which he has found that degree of IL did not affect OL recall on an immediate MMFR test. However, it is not apparent from their discussion

whether degree of OL strength was controlled. (c) Finally, it is likely that variation in IL rate is considerably greater between Ss than it is within Ss. That is, the very fast and very slow Ss differ widely in the numbers of opportunities for first-list elicitation, while the differences in the number of these opportunities are probably much smaller within any given S. Thus, the failure to find a positive relationship between IL rank and OL recall may, in part, be due to the restricted range of elicitation opportunities inherent in the item analysis. More generally, it may be that implicit elicitation is primarily a function of the characteristics of the list, e.g., response form class or experimental context, or of the S, and that the actual operation of the effect is superimposed upon specific pair relationships. That is, the prediction of unlearning of specific pairs may require a consideration of the characteristics of the list as well as a concern for the properties of the individual pairs involved, e.g., differences in the difficulty of respective OL and IL pairs.

UNAVAILABILITY IN PI. According to the two-factor theory, there is no factor which will account for the occurrence of PI on the MMFR test. In order to test for this possibility, it is necessary to equate the level of learning attained by the control Ss with the level reached by the experimental Ss on the second list. This has been accomplished in three experiments either through the use of equal criteria (Koppenaal, 1963; Koppenaal, Krull, and Katz, 1965) or by the administration of differential numbers of trials (Postman, unpublished). In all three studies, significant PI was found on the MMFR test. In addition, Koppenaal (1963) found a significantly increasing decrement in second-list recall with increases in the length of the retention interval. Two possible explanations suggest themselves. (*a*) The MMFR test is affected by competition factors. If such an explanation is accepted, the theoretical "purity" of the MMFR test as a measure of response availability is immediately brought into question. Evidence presented previously suggested that determinations of OL availability immediately following IL are relatively unaffected by response competition. However, it is still conceivable that estimates of second-list availability (i. e., PI) are. Specifically, if it is assumed that weak items are more susceptible to competition than are strong items, estimates of second-list availability may be reduced due to the larger number of weaker items present for this list. One implication is that as the retention interval is increased and the weaker items are forgotten, susceptibility of the second-list to competition on MMFR should be reduced. (*b*) A second factor producing PI on the MMFR test may involve the differential susceptibility of control and second-list pairs to forgetting during the retention interval. While there are no data to support the hypothesis, it is possible that second-list responses which have either replaced an earlier response or share the stimulus with the first-list response represent associations which are more adversely affected by uncontrolled unlearning during the retention interval than are the associations formed by the control *S*s. In contrast with the first explanation, this factor would be expected to increase in importance as the retention interval is lengthened and uncontrolled forgetting occurs. Whatever the explanation, it is clear that PI can be demonstrated on the MMFR test. Whether this deficit should be interpreted in terms of competition (Factor *a*) or in terms of unlearning (Factor *b*) awaits further research. The possibility of competition

on the MMFR test seriously threatens earlier estimates of response availability obtained with the MMFR test, although it is unlikely that RI estimates will be as strongly affected as are PI estimates, due to considerations of difference in item strengths for the two paradigms. In any case, it is obvious that tests of this potentially ambiguous state of affairs are urgently needed.

EXTINCTION VERSUS UNLEARNING. Attempts to apply principles of classical conditioning to the phenomena of verbal learning have been largely unsuccessful.[7] While the analogy between extinction and unlearning may have been useful in suggesting variables which may be critical for the study of the unlearning phenomenon, the analogy breaks down logically as well as empirically. (*a*) As Barnes and Underwood have noted, the paradigm most closely represented by the *A–B*, *A–C* relationship is that of counterconditioning, where a new CR is learned to the same CS. (*b*) Moreover, there is no evidence that the omission of the response term, i.e., "extinction," produces a decrement in response availability. On the contrary, performance appears to increase (e.g., Buttler and Peterson, 1965; Greenbloom and Kimble, 1965; Richardson and Gropper, 1964). This analogy could be questioned, however, on the grounds that the omission of response terms in paired-associate learning does not actually constitute the same set of operations as those employed in conditioning studies. (*c*) Spontaneous recovery appears to occur under a relatively restricted set of experimental conditions. Furthermore, explanations which have employed spontaneous recovery as an explanatory device, e.g., Underwood, Keppel, and Schulz (1962),

[7] See, for example, Underwood's (1961) discussion of Gibson's (1940) theory of verbal learning.

have not been supported either over short retention intervals (Goggin, 1966) or long retention intervals (Keppel, in press). (*d*) The overt occurrence of a first-list response is not necessary for unlearning to occur (Houston, in press; Keppel and Rauch, 1966). These findings suggest, then, that unlearning is neither operationally nor empirically related to the phenomena of classical conditioning. On the other hand, certain concepts drawn from the conditioning literature, e.g., spontaneous recovery and the elicitation hypothesis, have been useful in accounting for RI and PI phenomena. However, the important question remains as to whether or not unlearning and extinction are produced by the same underlying processes. To the extent that additional failures in the application of the conditioning paradigm to verbal learning and retention are reported, the probability of an affirmative answer to this question is lowered.

RESTATEMENT OF THE TWO-FACTOR THEORY. A revision of two-factor theory which is more parsimonious with the facts involves the restriction of absolute spontaneous recovery to a relatively short time interval, e.g., a few hours. The exact terminal point will undoubtedly be a function of degree of OL and IL. For low degrees of learning (OL = 7 trials; IL = 5 trials), this interval may be as short as 30 minutes (Postman, unpublished). Following the recovery period, OL strength is assumed to be affected only by extra-experimental sources. A reduction in the amount of RI, formally termed "relative" recovery, is assumed to be due to the differential susceptibility of OL items in the control condition to extra-experimental interference (EEI). The restatement of the two-factor theory can now be given as a series of assumptions. (*a*) RI is a function of unlearning and competition and PI is largely a function of competition, although it is not clear whether availability loss is to be attributed to competition on MMFR or to the presence of less stable items. (*b*) Absolute recovery is short-lived, completed within a few hours. (*c*) Rate of forgetting due to EEI is a function of item strength. Due to the effects of IL, the first list suffers less from EEI than does the second list or the control list. (*d*) Competition increases as a function of time due to a loss of list differentiation or to a convergence of first- and second-list strengths, if it is assumed that competition increases as the lists become equal. This assumption is necessary to account for an increase in PI with increases in the length of the retention interval (e.g., Postman, 1962c). An application of these assumptions to the RI and PI paradigms, predicts the following temporal functions with MMFR and paced-recall tests:

1. On the MMFR test, the first-list will initially rise and then decline slowly. The control condition will decrease more rapidly due to the more damaging influence of EEI. Eventually, the two functions will meet and continue to decrease together (cf. Birnbaum, 1965; Koppenaal, 1963).

2. The second list, on the other hand, will show an initial decrement and a continued decline over the retention interval. The second list should remain parallel to the control curve, unless the second-list associations are more susceptible to EEI. In which case, the second list may fall below the first and control lists at the point of their convergence (e.g., Koppenaal, 1963).

3. On the paced test, where competition is added to any loss of response availability, the initial portions of the

first-list curve will be parallel to the availability function. Since the control list will decline over the interval, the *absolute* amount of RI, i.e., $C-E$, will decrease due to the greater effect of EEI on the control. On the face of it, this expectation runs counter to the assumption that competition will increase over the interval due to a loss of list differentiation. It is likely, however, that the assumed loss of differentiation may be obscured by the greater retention loss of the control Ss. If this were the case, it should still be possible to show that the *proportion* of RI attributed to competition is increasing over the interval. At the point of first-list and control-list convergence on the MMFR test, RI on the paced test will be determined primarily by differentiation loss.

4. Recall of the second list on the paced test will continue to decrease over the retention interval. Initially, the increase in absolute PI will be due to the recovery of the first list. After this point PI may continue to increase due to (a) the increasing loss of differentiation and (b) the greater loss of availability of the second list relative to the control. When the two lists are equally available on the MMFR test, RI and PI on the paced test should become roughly equivalent and show the same function from that point on.

ALTERNATIVE EXPLANATIONS OF RI AND PI. Almost all recent attempts to account for RI and PI have been created by interference theorists. The very fact that the phenomena exist immediately rules out a simple theory of trace decay. Criticisms of interference theories have come primarily from the interference theorists themselves, e.g., Postman (1961b, 1963); Underwood and Ekstrand (1966). An exception to this statement is the comments of

Asch, Rock, and their associates, namely, Asch (1964); Asch and Ebenholtz (1962b); Rock and Ceraso (1964). In considering the influence of $A-C$ interpolation on $A-B$ recall, Rock and Ceraso conceived of a failure on MMFR as being the result of either

(a) the unavailability of the memory trace ("trace destruction"), or
(b) the inaccessibility of the memory trace ("trace unavailability"), or
(c) to an operation of both factors.

In this regard, Rock and Ceraso suggested that the matching task provides a means by which the operation of the first factor may be neutralized.

From the exposition presented earlier, it is clear that the Rock-Ceraso theory is closely related to McGovern's theory, which postulates a contextual association which mediates response availability and a specific association which mediates the correct pairing of the stimulus and response terms. In a related argument, Asch and Ebenholtz (1962b) rejected the possibility that any associative unlearning was involved in the production of RI in their free learning experiment and instead suggested that the decrement was due to a reduction in response availability. While the assumption of a loss of response availability is consonant with McGovern's theory, the conclusion that specific associative factors are not responsible for the RI in free learning is questionable since, as noted earlier, there may have been specific stimulus overlap between the nonsense syllable lists. Moreover, their additional speculation that RI in other learning situations, e.g., paired-associate learning, may be wholly due to loss of response availability is clearly not upheld by the data (McGovern, 1964). In short, neither the Rock-Ceraso nor the Asch-

Ebenholtz account represents an approach which is basically different from the explanation of unlearning phenomena offered in the McGovern analysis.

Single-List Retention

It was mentioned earlier that the RI and PI paradigms have been primarily used as a model of the forgetting process. That is, it has been assumed that interference is the major cause of forgetting (cf., Underwood and Postman, 1960) and that this interference can be produced by the presence of conflicting associations learned previously outside of the laboratory, i.e., PI, or by associations learned subsequently during the retention interval, i.e., RI[8]. The phenomena of RI and PI are certainly not restricted to the area of verbal learning and the operations necessary to define these phenomena obviously can be translated into the procedures employed in the study of other types of learning tasks. In fact, there is some indication that phenomena and theory which have been tied closely to verbal learning have been translated directly into studies of animal learning, e.g., Gleitman and Steinman (1963), Kehoe (1963), and Rickard (1965). One of the purposes of this conference is to consider the relationship between specific theories of verbal learning and a general theory of learning. To this end, this last section will consider in detail an attempt to apply an interference theory, based upon the data obtained with RI and PI paradigms, to the processes presumed to be responsible for the forgetting of single lists of verbal

---

[8] Battig, in his paper, has suggested that interference within the learning task should be added as a factor in an interference theory of forgetting.

materials. Following this exposition, the theory will be evaluated, and other explanations will be discussed.

Extra-experimental sources of interference

UNDERWOOD-POSTMAN THEORY. The fact that the amount of forgetting has been shown to be related directly to the number of previously learned verbal tasks (Underwood, 1957) has made more reasonable a theory which is based upon a consideration of extra-experimental interference (EEI). Specifically, rather than being required to account for 80% forgetting over 24 hours, a typical value from the retention studies employing a counterbalanced design, an interference explanation need only account for the approximately 20% forgetting which is shown by Ss naive to verbal learning. The Underwood-Postman (1960) theory, then, represents an attempt to account for this 20% forgetting.

The basic principle underlying the theory is that the learning and retention of a list of verbal materials must be superimposed over the strong linguistic habits (EEI) which S brings with him to the laboratory and which he will experience during the retention interval. While the model specifies a combination of RI and PI, an interference paradigm which has received only a little attention (cf., Koppenaal and O'Hara, 1962), the PI component is assumed to be of greater importance. The reason for this is the higher probability that S will have experienced conflicting linguistic habits prior to the learning of the verbal materials than he will during the relatively short retention interval. In a direct application of two-factor theory, it was assumed that conflicting linguistic habits will

(a) intrude during acquisition,

(b) eventually be unlearned, and

(c) recover over the retention interval to interfere with the recall of the verbal material.

Two sources of EEI were specified, letter-sequence and unit-sequence interference. Letter-sequence interference refers to interference stemming from stronger letter-letter associations than those which will be learned in the experimental situation. For example, a letter sequence $A–X$ is assumed to be interfered with by stronger linguistic associates to A, such as T, B, S, etc. Common indices of letter-sequence habits are the letter-association norms of Underwood and Schulz (1960) and the various scalings of association value. Unit-sequence interference, on the other hand, refers to interference between verbal items which are responded to as units, e.g., words. Both sources of EEI are assumed to be a function of the general dimension of meaningfulness. Letter-sequence interference is thought to be at a maximum at the lowest end of the dimension and to decrease with increases in meaningfulness. Somewhere in the middle of the dimension unit-sequence interference becomes important, reaching a maximum at the highest values of meaningfulness. While it is not clear as to the exact point of overlap of the two gradients of EEI, nor to the extent of this overlap, the theory is clear with regard to a comparison of extreme points on the meaningfulness dimension with midpoints on the dimension, i.e., greater EEI at the ends than in the middle.

EVIDENCE FOR LETTER-SEQUENCE INTERFERENCE. In addition to the explicit prediction as to the effect of EEI on rate of forgetting, the theory leads to certain expectations concerning the influence of EEI on acquisition rate and the production of errors during learning and recall. Specifically, poorly integrated responses should be more difficult to learn, and this deficit should be reflected by the intrusion of the stronger letter sequences during learning. These expectations correspond to the demonstration of negative transfer and the production of interlist intrusions during the learning of IL in the $A–C$ paradigm. At recall, the greater forgetting of the poorly integrated responses should be accompanied by some evidence of the recovery of the unlearned letter associations. Turning first to the acquisition data, it is obvious that the prediction concerning speed of learning has received strong support from the literature (cf., Underwood and Schulz, 1960). In most of these investigations, however, analyses of the specific letter-sequence intrusions have not been reported. Even if such analyses had been reported, there would still remain several problems in the interpretations of these data. The first problem involves a consideration of the types of intrusions possible. For example, if a low list consists of the lowest letter combinations possible (i.e., zero values on the norms), just a random guessing of letters would be sufficient to produce errors of a higher associative value than the prescribed ones, i.e., evidence which would be taken as supporting the theory. A second problem mentioned earlier in the context of RI studies is the possibility that the production of unlearning may be independent of the occurrence of overt errors during acquisition. Evidence from the two-list situation indicates that second-list error rate has very little effect upon the amount of unlearning produced with the $A–C$ paradigm. Finally, it is a well-known fact that Ss restrict their errors to intralist responses and tend not to give importations from outside of the list. This means that while strong letter habits may interfere with learning, the overt indication of this interference will depend upon whether these responses are also present in the list. In short, it is questionable that an analysis of overt errors during learning will provide data which are critical for the Underwood-Postman theory.

There is no ambiguity, however, in the number of correct responses expected by the theory on the recall test, namely, greater forgetting of the poorly integrated verbal units. As is the case in the study of any variable which is thought to influence retention, it is necessary to bring the various conditions to the same level of learning prior to the start of the retention interval (cf., Underwood, 1964). In the experiments to be reported, this has been accomplished by means of a common performance criterion (and an estimate of immediate retention) or through the use of different numbers of trials, chosen to produce equivalent estimates of immediate retention for the various groups. The results of these experiments, in terms of percentage of responses forgotten, are presented in the upper portion of Table 5. Included in this summary are only the studies in which single lists were learned and estimates of immediate retention were available. The values reported for the Underwood-Keppel (1963) study are averages taken over conditions representing equal degrees of learning (see their Fig. 4). In order to simplify the table, only the results for the one-day and one-week intervals are presented. Inspection of the values reported for the 24-hour intervals reveals small and inconsistent differences in the forgetting of poorly and highly integrated responses for a variety of learning tasks (serial, paired-associate, and free-learning). The average percentage forgotten, summing down the seven

independent tests of the theory, is 22.2% for the low meaningful items and 19.8% for the high meaningful items. Similar averages over the 1-week interval are 48.6% and 41.5%, respectively. While these differences are in the expected direction, the differences are small and variable between experiments. In addition, there is some evidence that greater forgetting is found with low meaningful trigrams in the initial and middle portions of a serial list (Underwood and Postman, 1960). In general, though, the overall picture presented in Table 5 is essentially negative, i.e., meaningfulness does not influence rate of forgetting.

As was the case for acquisition, overt errors provide equivocal data. For example, Underwood and Postman reported an increase in the number of letter-sequence errors over the one-week interval for the low trigram list and a decrease for the high trigram list. However, these results may have been influenced by differences in degree of formal intralist similarity. Moreover, the authors noted that very few letters were imported so that the overt index of interference is largely due to intralist intrusions. Underwood and Keppel (1963) reported a strong tendency for *S*s to emit errors which were appropriate to the level of associative strength reflected by the list. These findings again indicate that *S*s do not produce errors randomly but instead restrict themselves to errors which are "reasonably" close to the materials which they have learned. In any case, the retention data are unambiguous: the differences in forgetting predicted on the basis of a consideration of letter-sequence interference are not borne out by the data.

EVIDENCE FOR UNIT-SEQUENCE IN-TERFERENCE. The influence of unit-sequence interference on learning is complicated. It is assumed that as meaningfulness (indexed by word

Table 5

PERCENTAGE FORGETTING (BASED ON ESTIMATES OF IMMEDIATE RETENTION)

| | Retention Interval | | | |
| Letter-Sequence Interference | One Day | | One Week | |
	Low	High	Low	High
Underwood and Richardson (1956)[a]	11.9[e]	17.6	—	—
	23.1[f]	16.8	—	—
Postman and Rau (1957)[a]	26.2	21.3	—	—
	22.0[g]	17.2	—	—
Underwood and Postman (1960)[a]	—	—	57.5	42.6
Underwood and Keppel (1963)[b]	8.8	11.2	39.8	40.4
Underwood (1964)[b]	19.6	21.5	—	—
Ekstrand and Underwood (1965)[c]	43.6	32.9		

| | Retention Interval | | | |
| Unit-Sequence Interference | One Day | | One Week | |
	Low	High	Low	High
Postman and Rau (1957)[a]	18.8	19.6	—	—
	10.9[g]	11.7		
Underwood and Postman (1960)[a]	—	—	42.6	42.4
Postman (1961)[a]	—	—	42.9	57.0
	—	—	16.7[g]	16.0
	—	—	56.0	43.1
Postman (1962)[b, d,]	—	—	52.8[b, h]	45.1
	—	—	48.9[b, i]	43.0
	—	—	10.8[d]	23.9
Ekstrand and Underwood (1965)[c]	44.3	43.1	—	—
	47.5	48.0	—	—

[a] Serial learning
[b] Paired-associate learning
[c] Free learning
[d] Verbal discrimination
[e] Low intralist similarity
[f] High intralist similarity
[g] Free recall
[h] Stimulus frequency
[i] Response frequency

frequency) increases, the number of associations between a word in the list and the other words in the list and words not in the list also increases. However, this increase in frequency should have both positive and negative effects on learning. First, increase in frequency will make the words more available as recallable units (Hall, 1954), accelerating the onset of the associative stage. Second, increases in frequency will produce increases in inappropriate interlist and extralist associations, resulting in a retardation of associative learning. Underwood and Postman acknowledged this problem and presented evidence from a stage analysis and an analysis of intralist errors for the operation of the positive influence of response availability and the negative effect of conflicting interitem associations. These findings indicate that exact predictions concerning the relationship between frequency and learning cannot be made at this time, but that there is some evidence for the increase in associative interference specified by the Underwood-Postman theory.

In the lower portion of Table 5 are summarized the results of various tests of the unit-sequence hypothesis, the prediction being that high frequency lists will be forgotten at a faster rate than will low frequency lists.[9] The average percentage forgotten over 24 hours was 30.4 and 30.6 for low and high frequency lists, respectively; the values over the one-week interval were 39.9 and 39.0 per cent. Again, with only minor variations between studies, the conclusion is clear: meaningfulness does not influence rate of forgetting. Analyses of errors at recall offer some support for the recovery of unit-sequence interference. For example, Postman (1961a) found a greater increase in the frequency of intralist intrusions over a one-week interval for high frequency serial lists. A similar relationship was reported by Underwood and Postman (1960). In contrast to the numbers of intralist intrusions found with serial lists, Postman (1962b) noted that few such responses are found

with paired associates on either the immediate or delayed test, i.e., over 60 per cent of the *S*s do not give any misplaced responses on the recall test.

Extra-experimental interference as a factor in forgetting

The Underwood-Postman theory was an attempt to account for differences in the learning and retention of verbal materials in terms of two sources of interference, both of which were assumed to be a function of meaningfulness. In this section, the Underwood-Postman theory will be evaluated in terms of the assumptions which underlie the theory. The discussion will be followed by a consideration of various attempts which have been offered to account for the failure of the Underwood-Postman theory.

ASSUMPTIONS OF THE UNDERWOOD-POSTMAN THEORY. Underlying the Underwood-Postman theory are three premises, namely, that linguistic habits

(a) are unlearned during acquisition,
(b) recover during the retention interval, and
(c) compete with the prescribed responses at the time of recall.

Although the theory has not been strongly supported by the retention data, it is still possible that there is evidence for the operation of these basic mechanisms. If this evidence is positive, the question then becomes one of specifying why these processes did not affect the rate of forgetting.

1. Are linguistic habits unlearned during acquisition? Evidence for this unlearning has come from an analysis of errors during learning. However, it has already been suggested that the presence of overt errors may be unrelated to the unlearning of the linguistic

[9] Since the Ekstrand-Underwood (1965) study involved free learning, the contribution of unit-sequence interference is probably minimal.

associations. As far as is known, there have been no direct tests of the assumption of linguistic unlearning. Such a test might consist of a free-association test which follows the learning session. Suppose, for example, that S is presented a list of low probability letter-letter pairs to learn and that after acquisition he is asked to give associates to the letter stimuli. The S, of course, would be asked not to give the previously learned response. Evidence for the unlearning of the stronger linguistic associations would be a shift in the normative distribution away from the strongest associates. Another approach is reflected in the work of Saltz (1965). In this study Ss were asked to respond to 20 bigram stimuli with any single-letter response of their choice. The first five trials, on which there was no informative feedback, were used to define "dominant" responses to the bigram stimuli. Following these trials, five bigrams were selected for "extinction" training during which S was told "wrong" whenever he gave a dominant response. Training was continued until S failed to give these responses to the five selected stimuli on two successive trials. After varying periods of time (10 minutes to 24 hours), Ss were presented the stimuli and asked to give the first letter that came to mind. Saltz reported that Ss did learn to avoid giving the dominant responses during extinction, although extinction rates were quite variable, and that there was a recovery of the tendency to give the dominant responses with increases in the "retention" interval. While this study is considerably different from the usual paired-associate experiment, e.g., ambiguous recall instructions and no prescribed response during "learning" and "extinction," the approach may provide a useful tool for the assessment of changes in the strengths of linguistic habits following learning.

2. Do linguistic associations recover during the retention interval? As noted earlier, an analysis of overt errors at recall suffers from the same difficulties as those mentioned for the learning data. For instance, does an increase in intralist errors mean that the influence of linguistic habits is restricted to those associations which are present in the list? Or does it mean that S restricts his guesses to responses which are appropriate to the list? In this regard, it should be recalled that a majority of Ss do not give any overt errors at recall, but instead choose not to respond. In lieu of error analyses, the association techniques mentioned above, if proved successful, may provide relevant data.

3. Do linguistic associations compete at recall? Competition, as it seems to be used, refers to a confusion of linguistic habits with the prescribed associations. This would imply that S's failure to recall correctly is not primarily due to the loss of the prescribed association or response, but rather to a loss of differentiation between linguistic and experimental habits. If it is assumed that the major source of forgetting is from previously acquired associations, it should be possible to show that retention losses are greatly reduced on an unpaced recall test. Presumably, the reduction in loss should be greater for the high competition condition. This conclusion is based upon the same assumption underlying the MMFR test, namely, that if S is given unlimited time to recall responses from both lists, competition factors should be minimized. Competition could be reduced further if S were asked to continue responding with response alternatives until the correct response is given (cf., Brown, 1965). If under these conditions there is still a decrement in recall, it

would seem reasonable to attribute this loss to a noncompetitive factor, such as unlearning.

EVALUATION OF THE UNDERWOOD-POSTMAN THEORY. The original Underwood-Postman theory has been evaluated separately by both Underwood (Underwood and Ekstrand, 1966) and Postman (1963). The analysis by Underwood and Ekstrand is an attempt to specify the reasons for the failure of the theory to predict forgetting rate by focusing upon certain differences between linguistic habits and experimentally acquired habits. Postman, in his paper, suggested several mechanisms which may tend to reduce greatly the extra-experimental interference presumed to be operating during learning and retention. The Underwood-Ekstrand evaluation will be considered first. In their analysis, they noted that there are two main ways in which linguistic associations differ from laboratory ones—conditions of learning and level of learning. Specifically, linguistic habits are acquired under widely spaced conditions of practice, while laboratory associations are generally learned under conditions of massed practice. In addition, linguistic habits represent much higher degrees of learning than do those developed in the laboratory. Since the Underwood-Postman theory was based upon laboratory demonstrations of unlearning, spontaneous recovery, and RI and PI, Underwood and Ekstrand hypothesized that if either of the two differentiating characteristics, distributed practice and degree of learning, were responsible for the failure of the theory to account for forgetting, this same failure should be demonstrable with laboratory associations. In other words, if the reason for the failure were the differences in degree of learning, manipulations of this variable in the laboratory should reduce

the influence of this list $(A-B)$ on the recall of the second list $(A-C)$, i.e., reduce PI at the time of recall. Similarly, if distributed practice were critical, this variable should function to reduce laboratory produced PI. In order to test these hypotheses, Underwood and Ekstrand varied degree of first-list learning (12, 32, 48, or 80 trials) and conditions of practice (first-list learning evenly spaced over four days vs. training all in one day). The second list $(A-C)$ was learned to a criterion of one perfect recitation and then recalled 24 hours later. The results of the paced-recall test showed

(a) significantly less forgetting for the distributed Ss and

(b) an influence of degree of A–B training for the massed Ss, but not for the distributed Ss.

Under the assumption that the distributed condition reasonably simulates the conditions under which linguistic associations are acquired, Underwood and Ekstrand concluded that the failure of the Underwood-Postman theory was due largely to this characteristic of the natural language habits.

One difficulty with this argument is that although the analogy between linguistic associations and laboratory associations acquired under distributed practice holds for the retention data, it is not maintained for the transfer data. Specifically, differences in the strength of inferred linguistic habits, e.g., letter-associations norms, are known to predict rate of acquisition quite well. Thus, verbal materials which correspond to strong linguistic habits are facilitated and materials which do not are inhibited. Said another way, the degree of correspondence between linguistic associations and prescribed associations is positively correlated with learning. By analogy, then, there should have been a negative correlation between degree of first-list learning (increasing noncorrespondence) and transfer in the Underwood-Ekstrand study. That is, *A–C* performance should have *decreased* with increases in *A–B* training. In contrast, neither variable affected second-list performance. (Although a *C–D* control may have shown an increase in negative transfer, it is not apparent whether the linguistic-laboratory analogy would specify differences in transfer, *C–D* vs. *A–C*, or in second-list performance.) Although this finding suggests that the analogy between linguistic and laboratory associations is not perfect, Underwood and Ekstrand have at least indicated a possible explanation of the failure of the Underwood-Postman theory. Of course, it should be realized that while Underwood and Ekstrand have attempted to explain why linguistic habits do not *differentially* affect the retention of high and low meaningful lists, the problem still remains for an interference theory to account for the forgetting which is normally found in laboratory studies of retention. One such attempt will be proposed in a later section.

Rather than questioning the adequacy of the analogy between laboratory phenomena and linguistic associations, Postman (1963) has argued that there are mechanisms which restrict the operation of EEI. In this article, Postman discussed five factors, some or all of which may tend to override interference processes and thus tend to conserve retention. Listed as factors were

(a) differentiation, in which *S*'s ability to discriminate strong competing responses may reduce interference,

(b) the selector mechanism, where effective interference may be restricted to competing associations within the list,

(c) a consideration of functional stimuli which may have different interference characteristics than the nominal ones,

(d) a recoding process by which interference between specific elements may be avoided, and

(e) a covariation of facilitation and interference.

This last factor, as it affects recall, represents a modification of the Underwood-Postman theory and will be elaborated at this time.

In the original statement of the theory, Underwood and Postman acknowledged the fact that increases in word frequency would produce both positive and negative effects in learning. i.e., increased response availability and increased unit-sequence interference. However, no clear statement was made concerning the presence of positive and negative factors at recall. In a paired-associate experiment, Postman (1962b) manipulated stimulus frequency, assuming a covariation of unit-sequence facilitation and interference with variations in stimulus frequency, i.e., the associative paradox (Underwood and Schulz, 1960). Unit-sequence facilitation occurs when the prescribed association corresponds to linguistic habits, while the interference refers to the presence of conflicting linguistic associations. On the assumption of a covariation of unit-sequence facilitation and interference, Postman predicted a curvilinear relationship between forgetting and stimulus frequency, retention being maximum at medium levels of stimulus frequency above which unit-sequence interference begins to outweigh unit-sequence facilitation. The results of the experiment supported these speculations. In another experiment, Postman (in press) compared the learning and retention of serial lists varying in degree of interitem associative strength (high and zero). It was assumed that the presence of interitem associations would facilitate the acquisition and recall of the responses but interfere with the establishment of the prescribed serial order. Acquisition data supported these predictions. In recall, there was significantly greater forgetting for the *zero* list (60.6 per cent) than for the high list (39.4 per cent), but this difference was reversed on subsequent relearning trials. Postman interpreted these data to mean that response availability was facilitated through the recall of the "concept" in the high association lists, and this facilitation successfully counteracted the negative effect of conflicting pre-experimental associations. Thus, as Postman noted, the actual outcome of the retention test depends upon the role of response recall. That is, if the requirement of response recall is minimized, the presence of associative interference should be more strongly revealed. These speculations would imply that a re-ordering test, in which the responses are provided *S* and he attempts to reconstruct serial order, would reverse the Postman results, i.e., a greater loss of serial order for the high association list than for the zero association list.

Presumably, the same rationale can be applied to any serial list in which there may be facilitation in the recall of the responses but interference in the recall of a specific serial order. Support for this speculation is found in a serial experiment (Keppel, 1966) in which high and low frequency serial lists were recalled following unrelated rest activity. Retention of serial order, as measured by the re-ordering test, was significantly greater for the low than for the high frequency list. Thus, it is clear that a manipulation of unit-sequence interference, either by means of word frequency or through the direct manipulation of measured pre-experimental associations, results in a more

complicated picture than was originally conceived by Underwood and Postman. That is, it now appears that manipulation of stimulus frequency will produce both unit-sequence facilitation and interference (Postman, 1962b) and that manipulation of interitem associative strength (Postman, in press) or word frequency (Keppel, 1966) with serial lists will result in the unit-sequence facilitation of the response-recall stage in addition to the assumed interference in the associative stage.

In summary, both Underwood and Ekstrand (1966) and Postman (1963) have acknowledged the failure of the Underwood-Postman theory in predicting rate of forgetting. In contrast with the approach of Underwood and Ekstrand, in which the basic assumptions underlying the theory are questioned, it is Postman's thesis that the original assumptions of the theory may still be tenable but that various performance factors tend to mask the operation of linguistic interference. In addition, he has suggested that the manipulation of unit-sequence interference results in a covariation of positive and negative factors. To the extent that Underwood and Ekstrand's position requires a perfect simulation of phenomena involving linguistic associations, the argument is weakened by their failure to find increasing negative transfer as a function of the number of first-list trials. Postman's argument will gain strength, of course, to the extent that his "principles of conservation" can be manipulated independently of the inferred operation of linguistic interference.

A nonspecific interference theory of forgetting

Considering the lack of success with which specific interference factors have been shown to influence rate of forgetting, the general question can be raised as to the ability of any interference theory to explain the residual amount of forgetting which is found for the unpracticed S. The Underwood-Postman theory stressed the interfering role of previously acquired linguistic habits, although the presumed minor role of the same habits during the retention interval was recognized. The following discussion, on the other hand, will center around an alternative theory of forgetting which emphasizes the retention-interval activity as the major cause of forgetting. It must be realized that these statements are not intended to represent a comprehensive theory of forgetting, but rather to suggest at least the possibility of a simplified interference theory in which *unlearning* becomes the basic process underlying forgetting. While the present theory will be stated in terms of the nonspecific effects of unlearning, it is possible that specific unlearning may occur for one specific interference source, e.g., unit-sequence, but not for the other, e.g., letter-sequence. For the sake of simplicity, however, the theory will be developed completely in nonspecific terms. It is assumed that nonspecific linguistic activity occurring during the retention interval results in the unlearning of the newly acquired material and that the amount of this unlearning will depend largely upon the degree of learning and the amount of postlinguistic activity. Since it is known that degree of learning and rate of forgetting are inversely related (Underwood and Keppel, 1963), it is necessary to assume that unlearning (or forgetting) is also inversely related to OL strength. The amount of postlinguistic activity, e.g., reading, writing, hearing, etc., during the retention interval, is assumed to increase with the length of the interval. These two assumptions make possible

the conclusion that equal degrees of learning will result in equal rates of forgetting. It should be noted that a decay theory can reach the same conclusion by postulating a decay process which increases with time and is inversely related to degree of learning. Fortunately, it is possible to contrast these two theories in terms of implications which may be drawn from them.

A major implication of the interference theory under discussion is that manipulation of the retention-interval activity should produce changes in rate of forgetting, but an equivalent change for materials brought to the same level of learning. Presumably this expectation can be tested through the controlled interpolation of the retention-interval activity. Before these techniques are discussed, however, a few words should be said concerning the hypothesized nonspecific linguistic activity. It is assumed that any type of linguistic activity can produce unlearning. The experimental counterpart in the RI design is the C–D transfer paradigm in which there is assumed to be the unlearning of the contextual association, but not the specific associations. Thus, the single list corresponds to A–B and the nonspecific activity to C–D.

The classic example of the manipulation of general linguistic activity is the sleep-wake experiment, e.g., Jenkins and Dallenbach (1924); van Ormer (1932), in which reduced forgetting was observed when the retention interval was filled with sleep than when it was filled with everyday linguistic activities. These findings have generally been attributed to a reduction in RI, an interpretation which is consonant with the present theory. Underwood (1957), on the other hand, suggested that sleep retards the build-up of PI. Such an explanation is quite plausible since there were apparently large amounts of interlist interference in the sleep-wake studies. As part of a larger experiment, Ekstrand (1966) provided a test of these two interpretations by comparing forgetting after sleep or wake conditions for naive Ss learning and recalling a single list. If the difference between sleep-wake Ss, in the earlier studies, was due entirely to the retardation of PI, there should be no difference in the forgetting of naive Ss under the two interval conditions. The results showed a significant difference in the recall of the single list in favor of the sleep Ss (10.15 vs. 8.80 correct responses). This finding provides support for the contention that a reduction in linguistic activity reduces the amount of forgetting. Moreover, this reduction is not merely a performance phenomenon, since similar differences were found by Ekstrand on an unpaced recall test (11.75 vs. 10.55 correct responses.)

While the sleep-wake study offers a means by which linguistic activity may be manipulated, the data are subject to interpretations other than the RI explanation. Instead of considering the amount of linguistic activity, for example, a decay theorist might explain the same results in terms of a slowing down of metabolic functioning during sleep. A less ambiguous contrast of the interference theory under discussion and decay theory would be an experiment in which nonspecific linguistic activity is controlled directly, through an increased (or decreased) exposure to these sources of interference during the retention interval. While the sensory-deprivation experiment would introduce additional problems of interpretation, a more adequate situation might be one in which all Ss are placed in a restricted environment but one group is presented a large amount of verbal stimulation while another group receives a large amount of nonverbal

stimulation, e.g., music listening or motor tasks.

Assuming that the nonspecific interference theory can handle the retention data, it is still necessary to account for the influence of previously learned linguistic habits in the acquisition of verbal materials which run counter to these habits. In the Underwood-Postman theory this was accomplished by the assumption that the strong linguistic habits interfere with the learning of uncommon linguistic associates and that learning eventually occurs through the unlearning of these incompatible associations. Since the present interference theory does not require the unlearning and recovery of linguistic associations to account for forgetting, there are various other ways in which the acquisition data may be explained. For example, it could be assumed that unlearning of linguistic associations does not imply the same consequences as unlearning in the A–C paradigm, but rather some sort of suppression of the linguistic associations. An alternative explanation would be that low probability units are difficult to acquire just because they are low probability units. That is, these units receive zero transfer from linguistic associations, while the high probability units receive large amounts of positive transfer.

Concluding Remarks

Most of the current research which appears promising represents departures from the typical serial and paired-associate tasks. For example, mention has already been made of the possibility of unconfounding unit-sequence facilitation and interference by means of free-recall and associative-matching tests and of the free-association technique introduced by Saltz (1965). Perhaps it will be possible to overcome the restrictive operation of the "selector mechanism" by incorporating presumably conflicting habits into the materials to be learned, e.g., some sort of "mixed list" consisting of high and low materials. Another potentially fruitful approach, recently reported by Wallace (1966), involves the initial acquisition of a set of paired words (*A–B*), the subsequent presentation of *A* in a recognition-test procedure (cf., Underwood, 1965), with the critical test being a determination of the probability of the false recognition of *B* or a strong free associate of *A*. Control *S*s, who received a prior paired-associate list of *C–B* pairs, tended to falsely select the strong associates over the *B* terms (.13 vs. .07); this finding corroborated the results of Underwood (1965). Experimental *S*s, on the other hand, falsely selected *B* with higher probability (.37) than the free associate (.03). Thus, Wallace was able to modify the false-positive rate for free associates by means of prior paired-associate training. In current work[10], he is testing for the recovery of the linguistic habits by varying the time between learning and the recognition task.

By way of summary, the phenomena of RI and PI were first described with an emphasis being placed upon current research, methodological considerations, and theory which has been developed to account for these phenomena. While the two-factor theory provides a fairly reasonable accounting of the facts, some modifications of the original theory seemed necessary and were discussed. As is typical of verbal learning, the research in this area continues to be strongly data-oriented with theory constantly being tested and revised. In an attempt to apply interference factors to explain extra-experi-

mental forgetting, Underwood and Postman (1960) focused upon interference produced by previously acquired linguistic habits which were unlearned during acquisition and assumed to recover over the retention interval to compete with the conflicting prescribed associations at recall. Although the theory has not been successful in predicting rate of forgetting, its failure has led to a discussion of ways in which linguistic habits differ from experimentally acquired ones (Underwood and Ekstrand, 1966) or their functioning is masked by the presence of factors which tend to decrease extra-experimental interference (Postman, 1963). Obviously, the long-range usefulness of interference theory will depend upon the success with which interference factors influencing forgetting can be identified and manipulated. In this regard, it is most likely that interference theory will continue to derive its main theoretical and empirical support from investigations employing the RI/PI model of the forgetting process.

References

Adams, S., "Temporal Changes in the Strength of Competing Verbal Associates," Unpublished doctoral dissertation, University of California, Berkeley, 1962.

Asch, S. E., "The Process of Free Recall," in C. Scheerer, ed., *Cognition: Theory, Research, Promise*. New York: Harper & Row, Publishers, 1965. Pp. 79–88.

———, and S. M. Ebenholtz, "The Principle of Associative Symmetry," *Proceedings of the American Philosophical Society*, 106 (1962), 135–163 (a).

———, ———, "The Process of Free Recall: Evidence for Nonassociative Factors in Acquisition and Retention," *Journal of Psychology*, 54 (1962), 3–31 (b).

Bahrick, H. P., "Retention Curves: Facts

[10] Personal communication.

or Artifacts?" *Psychological Bulletin,* **61** (1964), 188–194.

Barnes, J. M., " 'Fate' Revisited," Unpublished doctoral dissertation, Northwestern University, 1960.

———, and B. J. Underwood, " 'Fate' of First-List Associations in Transfer Theory," *Journal of Experimental Psychology,* **58** (1959), 97–105.

Bilodeau, I. M., and H. Schlosberg, "Similarity in Stimulating Conditions as a Variable in Retroactive Inhibition," *Journal of Experimental Psychology,* **41** (1959), 199–204.

Birnbaum, I. M., "Long-Term Retention of First-List Associations in the A–B, A–C Paradigm," *Journal of Verbal Learning and Verbal Behavior,* **4** (1965), 515–520.

———, "Unlearning in Two Directions," *Journal of Experimental Psychology,* **72** (1966), 61–67.

Briggs, G. E, "Acquisition, Extinction, and Recovery Functions in Retroactive Inhibition," *Journal of Experimental Psychology,* **47** (1954), 285–293.

Brown, J., "A Comparison of Recognition and Recall by a Multiple-Response Method," *Journal of Verbal Learning and Verbal Behavior,* **4** (1965), 401–408.

Buttler, D. C., and D. E. Peterson, "Learning during 'Extinction' with Paired Associates," *Journal of Verbal Learning and Verbal Behavior,* **4** (1965), 103–106.

Ceraso, J., "An Experimental Critique of Competition of Response and Specific Interference as Factors in Retroactive Inhibition." Unpublished doctoral dissertation, New School for Social Research, 1959.

———, and A. Henderson, "Unavailability and Associative Loss in RI and PI," *Journal of Experimental Psychology,* **70** (1965), 300–303.

Dallett, K. M., and L. D'Andrea, "Mediation Instructions versus Unlearning Instructions in the A–B, A–C Paradigm," *Journal of Experimental Psychology,* **69** (1965), 460–466.

Ekstrand, B. R., "The Effect of Sleep on Retention." Unpublished doctoral dissertation, Northwestern University, 1966.

———, and B. J. Underwood, "Free Learning and Recall as a Function of Unit-Sequence and Letter-Sequence Interference," *Journal of Verbal Learning and Verbal Behavior,* **4** (1965), 390–396.

Gibson, E. J., "A Systematic Application of the Concepts of Generalization and Differentiation to Verbal Learning," *Psychological Review,* **47** (1940), 196–229.

Gleitman, H., and F. Steinman, "Retention of Runway Performance as a Function of Proactive Interference," *Journal of Comparative and Physiological Psychology,* **56** (1963), 834–838.

Goggin, J., "Retroactive and Proactive Inhibition in the Short-Term Retention of Paired Associates," *Journal of Verbal Learning and Verbal Behavior,* **5** (1966), 526–535.

———, "First-List Recall as a Function of Second-List Learning Method," *Journal of Verbal Learning and Verbal Behavior,* in press.

Grayson, T. S., "Unlearning and Competition in the Retention of Verbal Materials." Unpublished doctoral dissertation, University of California, Berkeley, 1966.

Greenbloom, R., and G. A. Kimble, "Extinction of R-S Associations and Performance on Recall Trials without Informative Feedback," *Journal of Verbal Learning and Verbal Behavior,* **4** (1965), 341–347.

Greenspoon, J., and R. Ranyard, "Stimulus Conditions and Retroactive Inhibition," *Journal of Experimental Psychology,* **53** (1957), 55–59.

Hall, J. F., "Learning as a Function of Word-Frequency," *American Journal of Psychology,* **67** (1954), 138–140.

Houston, J. P., "Verbal R-S Strength Following S-R Extinction," *Psychonomic Science,* **1** (1964), 173–174.

———, "First-List Retention and Time and Method of Recall," *Journal of Experimental Psychology,* **71** (1966), 839–843.

————, "Retroactive Inhibition and Point of Interpolation," *Journal of Verbal Learning and Verbal Behavior,* **6** (1967), 84–88.

————, "Supplementary Report: Unlearning and the Unreinforced Evocation of First-List Responses," *Journal of Verbal Learning and Verbal Behavior,* in press.

————, B. E. Garskef, D. E. Noyd, and J. M. Erskine, "First-List Retention as a Function of the Method of Recall," *Journal of Experimental Psychology,* **69** (1965), 326–327.

Irion, A. L., "Retroactive Inhibition as a Function of the Relative Serial Positions of the Original and Interpolated Items," *Journal of Experimental Psychology,* **36** (1946), 262–270.

Jenkins, J. G., and K. M. Dallenbach, "Obliviscence during Sleep and Waking," *American Journal of Psychology,* **35** (1924), 605–612.

Jung, J., "Measurement of Differentiation in the Negative Transfer Paradigm." Paper given at the meetings of the Southwestern Psychological Association, Arlington, Texas, April, 1966.

Kehoe, J., "Effects of Prior and Interpolated Learning on Retention in Pigeons," *Journal of Experimental Psychology,* **65** (1963), 537–545.

Keppel, G., "Retroactive Inhibition of Serial Lists as a Function of the Presence or Absence of Positional Cues," *Journal of Verbal Learning and Verbal Behavior,* **3** (1964), 511–517.

————, "Unlearning in Serial Learning," *Journal of Experimental Psychology,* **71** (1966), 143–149.

————, "A Reconsideration of the Extinction-Recovery Theory," *Journal of Verbal Learning and Verbal Behavior,* in press.

————, and L. Postman, "Studies of Learning to Learn: III. Conditions of Improvement in Successive Transfer Tasks," *Journal of Verbal Learning and Verbal Behavior,* **5** (1966), 260–267.

————, ————, and B. Zavortink, "Response Availability in Free and Modi-

fied Free Recall for Two Transfer Paradigms," *Journal of Verbal Learning and Verbal Behavior,* in press.

————, and D. S. Rauch, "Unlearning as a Function of Second-List Error Instructions," *Journal of Verbal Learning and Verbal Behavior,* **5** (1966), 50–58.

————, and B. J. Underwood, "Retroactive Inhibition of R-S Associations," *Journal of Experimental Psychology,* **64** (1962), 400–404.

————, and B. Zavortink, "Unlearning and Competition in Serial Learning," *Journal of Verbal Learning and Verbal Behavior,* in press.

Koppenaal, R. J., "Time Changes in the Strengths of A–B, A–C Lists: Spontaneous Recovery?" *Journal of Verbal Learning and Verbal Behavior,* **2** (1963), 310–319.

————, A. Krull, and H. Katz, "Age, Interference, and Forgetting," *Journal of Experimental Child Psychology,* **1** (1965), 360–375.

————, and G. N. O'Hara, "The Combined Effect of Retroaction and Proaction," *Canadian Journal of Psychology,* **16** (1962), 96–105.

McCrystal, T. J., and H. B. Ranken, "List Differentiation and Response Recall as a Function of Retention Interval." Paper given at the meetings of the Midwestern Psychological Association, Chicago, Illinois, May, 1966.

McGovern, J. B., "Extinction of Associations in Four Transfer Paradigms," *Psychological Monographs,* Vol. 78, No. 16 (1964), (Whole No. 593).

Mandler, G., and B. Earhard, "Pseudomediation: Is Chaining an Artifact?" *Psychonomic Science,* **1** (1964), 247–248.

Martin, R. B., and S. J. Dean, "Implicit and Explicit Mediation in Paired-Associate Learning," *Journal of Experimental Psychology,* **68** (1964), 21–27.

Melton, A. W, "Comments on Professor Postman's Paper," in C. N. Cofer, ed., *Verbal Learning and Verbal Behavior.* New York: McGraw-Hill Book Company, 1961. Pp. 179–193.

————, and J. M. Irwin, "The Influence of Degree of Interpolated Learning on Retroactive Inhibition and the Overt Transfer of Specific Responses," *American Journal of Psychology*, **53** (1940), 173–203.

————, and W. J. von Lackum, "Retroactive and Proactive Inhibition in Retention: Evidence for a Two-Factor Theory of Retroactive Inhibition," *American Journal of Psychology*, **54** (1941), 157–173.

Murdock, B. B., Jr., "The Retention of Individual Items," *Journal of Experimental Psychology*, **62** (1961), 618–625.

Neimark, E., P. Greenhouse, S. Law, and S. Weinheimer, "The Effect of Rehearsal-Preventing Tasks upon Retention of CVC Syllables," *Journal of Verbal Learning and Verbal Behavior*, **4** (1965), 280–285.

Newton, J. M., and D. D. Wickens, "Retroactive Inhibition as a Function of the Temporal Position of the Interpolated Learning," *Journal of Experimental Psychology*, **51** (1956), 149–154.

Peterson, L. R., and M. J. Peterson, "Minimal Paired-Associate Learning," *Journal of Experimental Psychology*, **63** (1962), 521–527.

Postman, L., "Extra-Experimental Interference and the Retention of Words," *Journal of Experimental Psychology*, **61** (1961), 97–110 (a).

————, "The Present Status of Interference Theory," in C. N. Cofer, ed., *Verbal Learning and Verbal Behavior*. New York: McGraw-Hill Book Company, 1961 (b). Pp. 152–179.

————, "Retention of First-List Associations as a Function of the Conditions of Transfer," *Journal of Experimental Psychology*, **64** (1962), 380–387 (a).

————, "The Effects of Language Habits on the Acquisition and Retention of Verbal Associations," *Journal of Experimental Psychology*, **64** (1962), 7–19 (b).

————, "The Temporal Course of Proactive Inhibition for Serial Lists," *Journal of Experimental Psychology*, **63** (1962), 361–369 (c).

————, "Transfer of Training as a Function of Experimental Paradigm and Degree of First-List Learning," *Journal of Verbal Learning and Verbal Behavior*, **1** (1962), 109–118 (d).

————, "Does Interference Theory Predict Too Much Forgetting?" *Journal of Verbal Learning and Verbal Behavior*, **2** (1963), 40–48.

————, "Studies of Learning to Learn: II. Changes in Transfer as a Function of Practice," *Journal of Verbal Learning and Verbal Behavior*, **3** (1964), 437–447.

————, "Unlearning under Conditions of Successive Interpolation," *Journal of Experimental Psychology*, **70** (1965), 237–245.

————, "The Effect of Interitem Associative Strength on the Acquisition and Retention of Serial Lists," *Journal of Verbal Learning and Verbal Behavior*, in press.

————, and G. Keppel, "Retroactive Inhibition in Free Recall," *Journal of Experimental Psychology*, in press.

————, ————, and K. Stark, "Unlearning as a Function of the Relationship between Successive Response Classes," *Journal of Experimental Psychology*, **69** (1965), 111–118.

————, and L. Rau, "Retention as a Function of the Method of Measurement," *University of California Publications in Psychology*, 8 (1957), 217–270.

————, and D. A. Riley, "Degree of Learning and Interserial Interference in Retention," *University of California Publications in Psychology*, 8 (1959), 271–396.

————, and K. Stark, "Retroactive Inhibition as a Function of Set during the Interpolated Task," *Journal of Verbal Learning and Verbal Behavior*, **1** (1963), 304–311.

————, and ————, "The Role of Response Set in Tests of Unlearning," *Journal of Verbal Learning and Verbal Behavior*, **4** (1965), 315–322.

————, ————, and J. Fraser, "Temporal Changes in Interference," *Journal of Verbal Learning and Verbal Behavior*, in press.

Richardson, J., and M. S. Gropper, "Learning during Recall Trials," *Psychological Reports*, **15** (1964), 551–560.

Rickard, S., "Proactive Inhibition Involving Maze Habits," *Psychonomic Science*, **3** (1965), 401–402.

Rock, I., and J. Ceraso, "Toward a Cognitive Theory of Associative Learning," in C. Scheerer, ed., *Cognition: Theory, Research, Promise*. New York: Harper & Row, Publishers, 1964. Pp. 110–146.

Runquist, W. N., "Retention of Verbal Associates as a Function of Strength," *Journal of Experimental Psychology*, **54** (1957), 369–375.

Saltz, E., "Spontaneous Recovery of Letter-Sequence Habits," *Journal of Experimental Psychology*, **69** (1965), 304–307.

Slamecka, N. J., "Supplementary Report: A Search for Spontaneous Recovery of Verbal Associations," *Journal of Verbal Learning and Verbal Behavior*, **5** (1966), 205–207.

———, and J. Ceraso, "Retroactive and Proactive Inhibition of Verbal Learning," *Psychological Bulletin*, **57** (1960), 449–475.

Taylor, A. B., and A. L. Irion, "Contiguity Hypothesis and Transfer of Training in Paired-Associate Learning," *Journal of Experimental Psychology*, **68** (1964), 573–577.

Thune, L. E., and B. J. Underwood, "Retroactive Inhibition as a Function of Degree of Interpolated Learning," *Journal of Experimental Psychology*, **32** (1943), 185–200.

Tulving, E., "Subjective Organization in Free Recall of 'Unrelated' Words," *Psychological Review*, **69** (1962), 344–354.

———, and G. B. Thornton, "Interaction between Proaction and Retroaction in Short-Term Retention," *Canadian Journal of Psychology*, **13** (1959), 255–265.

Underwood, B. J., "The Effect of Successive Interpolations on Retroactive and

Proactive Inhibition," *Psychological Monographs*, Vol. 59, No. 3 (1945).

———, "Retroactive and Proactive inhibition after Five and Forty-Eight Hours," *Journal of Experimental Psychology*, **38** (1948), 29–38 (a).

———, "'Spontaneous Recovery' of Verbal Associations," *Journal of Experimental Psychology*, **38** (1948), 429–439 (b).

———, "Interference and Forgetting," *Psychological Review*, **64** (1957), 49–60.

———, "An Evaluation of the Gibson Theory of Verbal Learning," in C. N. Cofer, ed., *Verbal Learning and Verbal Behavior*. New York: McGraw-Hill Book Company, 1961. Pp. 197–217.

———, "Degree of Learning and the Measurement of Forgetting," *Journal of Verbal Learning and Verbal Behavior*, **3** (1964), 112–129.

———, "False Recognition Produced by Implicit Verbal Responses," *Journal of Experimental Psychology*, **70** (1965), 122–129.

———, and B. R. Ekstrand, "An Analysis of Some Shortcomings in the Interference Theory of Forgetting," *Psychological Review*, **73** (1966), 540–549.

———, and G. Keppel, "Retention as a Function of Degree of Learning and Letter-Sequence Interference," *Psychological Monographs*, Vol. 77, No. 4 (1963).

———, ———, and R. W. Schulz, "Studies of Distributed Practice: XXII. Some Conditions Which Enhance Retention," *Journal of Experimental Psychology*, **64** (1962), 355–363.

———, and L. Postman, "Extraexperimental Sources of Interference in Forgetting," *Psychological Review*, **67** (1960), 73–95.

———, and J. Richardson, "The Influence of Meaningfulness, Intralist Similarity, and Serial Position on Retention," *Journal of Experimental Psychology*, **52** (1956), 119–126.

————, and R. W. Schulz, *Meaningfulness and Verbal Learning.* Philadelphia: J. B. Lippincott Co., 1960.

van Ormer, E. B., "Retention after Intervals of Sleep and of Waking," *Archives of Psychology*, **21** (1932), No. 137.

Wallace, W. P., "False Recognition Produced by Laboratory-Established Associative Responses." Paper given at the meetings of the Midwestern Psychological Association, Chicago, Illinois, May, 1966.

Wickelgren, W. A., "Acoustic Similarity and Retroactive Interference in Short-Term Memory," *Journal of Verbal Learning and Verbal Behavior*, **4** (1965), 53–61.

Young, R. K., "Tests of Three Hypotheses about the Effective Stimulus in Serial Learning," *Journal of Experimental Psychology*, **63** (1962), 307–313.

The Doctrinal Tyranny of Associationism: or What is Wrong with Rote Learning

9 SOLOMON E. ASCH

There should be currently something of a ferment in the normally staid area of rote learning, for recent investigation has brought forward findings that challenge beliefs of long standing. In the course of a relatively brief period a number of the most basic assumptions in the field have been brought into question. So elementary are the points at issue that one cannot help asking whether the foundations of this intensively cultivated part of psychology are at all secure. In the meantime the entire enterprise has come under attack from the side of linguistics. It may therefore be in order to examine briefly the leading ideas that have been behind this movement for the greater part of a century.

Such an examination needs to consider the claim that the study of rote operations provides the foundations for a psychology of human learning and memory. This claim, which has furnished the impetus for a very considerable experimental effort, is rooted in the premise of associationism, or the assumption that the diverse phenomena of learning and memory are products of one basic process, that of associations. The study of rote learning has been largely the study of associative operations. More important, investigators in this area have generally defined learning in terms of the formation of associations; at least they have admitted no other process.

The Theoretical Background of Rote Learning Studies

Despite this starting point, some students have maintained recently that the customary investigation of rote phenomena implies no particular theoretical commitments. This belief obscures a background that was historically important and that continues to have vitality today despite changes and qualifications. The study of rote phenomena grew out of an empiristic conception of psychological functioning. It presumed an initial condition of lack of order or chaos among the primitive elements of mental life and appealed to habit or the slow accretions of experience as the agency that introduced order among them. Specifically, it assigned to the mechanism of association by contiguity the task of producing coherence among psychological events. First elaborated by the British empiricists, the notion of association also drew upon nineteenth-century conceptualizations of the reflex arc. In this scheme single associations served as the analytical units for the explanation of the modifications that experience produces; the basic terms were discrete elements and connections formed between them. Further, associations were assigned the character of mere bonds that do not alter the terms they join; they were empty connections. This starting point also dictated the conclusion that sequences of psychological events must be treated as chains linked by associations. The import of association is that it was rooted in and was a necessary completion of a particular psychological theory of order, one that admitted no basis of order other than the connections formed between unrelated elements in the course of individual experience. It is this background of meaning that has adhered to association and that the rote learning movement has not questioned, let alone transcended.

There is, however, more than one way of thinking about dependence among psychological events. Gestalt psychology proposed one alternative, which was explicitly opposed to that of associationism. Beginning with observations in perception, it made the point that the properties of units are not identical with those of their separate components, and concluded that these cannot be accounted for in terms of associations between elements. On this ground it rejected the general validity of the elementaristic premise. Its analysis gave central place to autochthonous organizing operations that are dependent upon relations between discrete stimulations. Of consequence in this connection is that organization, which is based on relational determination, is the antithesis of association by contiguity. Subsequently, gestalt psychology extended this analysis to other areas—

to thinking, action, learning, and to associations themselves.

This approach provided the first theoretically motivated critique of associationism and of rote phenomena as an adequate basis for a general psychology of human learning. The main point was that rote operations, which consist largely of the memorization of items, exclude much that is of greatest consequence in the gaining of knowledge, in particular the innovations characteristic of the most commonplace psychological activities (Köhler, 1929; Wertheimer, 1945). Gestalt psychologists concluded that it is misleading to consider rote operations as representative of the effects of experience. On these grounds they also saw a danger in the application of ideas derived from rote learning to education. These considerations may suffice to show that rote learning touches upon central issues of psychology, but they bring us only to the threshold of the problems in this domain. The interest of gestalt critics in rote phenomena proper was at best mild; they were mainly concerned to show that rote operations could not account for the facts of perception and thinking. This is the case also with contemporary linguists. We need therefore to take a closer look at some aspects of rote learning.

Learning and Rote Learning

There is a natural starting point for the study of learning, namely, the examination of the kinds of achievement that experience makes possible. The problems of human learning are part of the inclusive problem of how we come to know, of the capacities we bring to this task, and of the ways in which experience alters them. The operations of knowing are diverse and complex, ranging from the perception of objects to the discovery of general principles. The rote learning movement did not begin with an unprejudiced examination of these phenomena. Basing itself upon the techniques that Ebbinghaus introduced, its procedures exclude from observation numerous effects of experience. It has not concerned itself except in the most marginal way with object-perception, with logical, mathematical, or linguistic operations. Instead the rote learning program has singled out for examination one particular relation between psychological events, that of contiguity; it has concentrated upon the effects that ensue when a learner experiences discrete and unrelated events that are made to occur simultaneously or in close succession. All the experimental procedures that have been elaborated either contain the condition of contiguity or refer to it as fundamental; all questions that have been asked revolve around it.

This emphasis would hardly require notice were it not for the accompanying assumption that association by contiguity is fundamental to all effects of experience. The equation of learning with association by contiguity has, I believe, exerted a restrictive effect; it has been responsible for the neglect of important phenomena, for onesided interpretations of others, and it has obscured the place of associations themselves in psychological functioning.

Relations and associations

Formal investigation is hardly necessary to establish that there are numerous relations between simultaneous and successive events or objects which we are capable of noting and recalling. Thus one event may be experienced as part of another, as the cause or effect of another, as similar to another, and so on. More generally, the ordering of events according to their spatial, temporal, and logical relations comprises an important part of what human beings come to know about their environment and is indispensable in their dealings with it. Further, relations are of theoretical consequence because they refer in the most direct way to phenomena of interdependence. The outstanding character of relations is that they bind terms into a unit. A relation is not another item added to others; the terms with their relation form a unit all parts of which are interdependent.

The major effect of the associationistic premise was to exclude from observation or reduce to an entirely subsidiary position the play of relations in mental life. The procedures of rote learning have involved as a rule the memorization of strings or pairs of arbitrarily joined items. Their aim was to approximate to the condition of sheer contiguity; accordingly they eliminated as far as possible the presence of relations other than contiguity. Thus, of all relations that may obtain between events, investigators singled out for attention that in which two terms have nothing to do with one another except for their being together. The consequence is that the existing body of knowledge and theory refers mainly to the condition of contiguity alone. This emphasis, which is responsible for the systematic neglect of phenomena of interdependence, is a direct consequence of the elementaristic assumption that the coexistence of unrelated events is prior to and more fundamental than relations between them.

The effects of this selectiveness have been far-reaching. One consequence has been to limit investigation largely to connections formed between terms each of which is a distinct and heterogeneous unit, to the neglect of relatedness within units (e.g., Asch, Ceraso, & Heimer, 1960; Asch, 1962). When students of rote learning have addressed themselves to relations, they treated them generally as complications of the presumably more basic condition of sheer contiguity. That relations are derivative cannot be assumed. What is more to the point is that they are phenomena of learning and memory, no less relevant to human functioning than the condition favored in rote learning studies. To ignore them or to treat them as secondary is to lose sight of a range of effects which are important in their own right and which, at least from the standpoint of the learner, are more intelligible. But further, to neglect relations between neighboring events is to eliminate some of the most crucial effects of contiguity.

Perceptual memory effects

One will hardly find any reference to perception in the rote learning literature. Yet the thinnest of lines separates facts of perception from those of memory and learning. The formation of a percept in primary experience is a case of acquisition, and the products of perception form part of the contents of memory. Their relevance to this discussion arises from the fact that many percepts are relationally determined, that they are effects of organization. Indeed, the formation of a unitary percept does not conform to the associative paradigm, which has always referred to a pair of units. At least as instructive are those perceptual facts that depend directly upon the contribution of past experience. All percepts that are built up over time, such as the perception of motion or of auditory configurations, are in-

stances of organization among immediately past and present stimulations; thus they demonstrate short-term memory effects. What is of consequence in these cases is that the memory traces which participate in the process do not simply add their sensory content to the incoming stimulations; rather they impose a particular structure on a percept. The following is a concrete example. An observer views on a translucent screen the rotating shadow of a wire figure. What is presented to him retinally is an ever-changing or deforming plane figure; what he sees is a rigid three-dimensional form in rotation (Wallach and O'Connell, 1953). Each single projection when given alone is seen as two-dimensional when the wire figure is properly chosen; only when it is preceded by other such projections does the experience of depth arise. The perception of depth in this case is an outcome of organization that does not depend on the momentary stimulations alone.

Although students of rote learning have from the first been intensely interested in memory phenomena, they have not concerned themselves with facts of the kind just described, for the understandable reason that these require a specialized background of thinking and techniques. However, no student of memory can afford to ignore the following further observations. Once an observer has seen a figure in the example above as three-dimensional, he will subsequently tend to see a stationary projection belonging to it as three-dimensional after intervals ranging up to a week; the same projection will appear as two-dimensional when it has not previously been part of a three-dimensional organization (Wallach, O'Connell and Neisser, 1953). This is an instance of a long-term memory effect, which illustrates the contribution of past experience to the organization of a percept. It would be easy to ignore this mode of operation of past experience if it were isolated; in fact, it has an impressive range of application. Absolute judgments, which functionally speaking are relative, can only be understood as memory effects. The 'adaptation-level' demonstrates the effect of past stimulations in determining the phenomenal intensity of percepts (Helson, 1964). These instances of organization mediated by memory traces cannot be treated as effects of association in the customary sense.

Rote learning and language

It is hard to ignore the relation between language acquisition and rote learning, if for no other reason than that the area has traditionally concentrated upon 'verbal learning' and 'verbal behavior.' The rote learning perspective admits only one way of treating linguistic phenomena—as products of associative habits. Specifically, it can deal with linguistic events only in terms of step-by-step sequential chaining of words. The assumption that learned sequences are chains of associations has, as we shall shortly see, come into serious question in the course of recent rote learning studies. A far more fundamental critique of associative models of language derives from the analysis of syntax as a system of rules having a hierarchical structure (Chomsky, 1957). The relations between the words of a sentence cannot be handled in terms of associations. Nor can the ability of a speaker to produce new sentences, or to understand new sentences just as well as those he has previously heard, be reconciled with the assumption that sentences are generated on the basis of sequential dependencies of words.

The conclusion I draw from this examination is that association by contiguity excludes far too much to provide a coherent foundation for a psychology of learning and memory. In particular, it makes no provision for the representation of the structure of events. By limiting the contribution of the learner largely to a joining of one item with another, it obscures the variety and complexity of operations that he is capable of performing on what is given. In retrospect one can see how thoroughly the underestimation of the constructive activities of the learner has dictated the course of investigation. Had students of human learning considered the acquisition and recall of perceptual units, they would have been confronting the problems of perceptual organization. Had they chosen to investigate the acquisition and recall of sentences, they would have had to face the problems of syntactic and semantic structure. The neglect of these phenomena and of the issues they pose is not accidental but inherent in the empiristic conception that what is learned is a replica of what is given and in the elementarism that has been a central part of this position.

Stimulus-Response Associationism : Atheoretical Theory

A newcomer who turns from the preceding consideration of neglected questions to the issues that have figured prominently in the territory of rote learning is bound to be surprised. Having heard about the dominance of the empiristic point of view and of the inadequacy of an associative model to the facts of perception, language, and thinking, he is ill prepared for the virtual absence of a theory of rote phenomena or of associations. He will find that the concepts of rote learning consist to a remarkable degree of descriptive statements of empirical relations, with little reference to constructs about underlying processes. Two developments of recent decades contributed to this situation: the adoption in the 1930's of a behavioristic orientation to associative learning, and the concurrent spread of an operationist way of thinking about problems of science.

Classical associationism was mentalistic. The shift to a systematically behavioristic position signaled the abandonment of reference to mental facts and the treatment of learning purely as changes of behavior. It also marked the conceptualization of associations as stimulus-response connections, a shift that coincided with the subsuming of associations under the presumably more fundamental phenomena of conditioning. The paired-associate method, which was increasingly favored as a result of this conceptualization, illustrates the S-R way of looking at the facts of learning. Given a list consisting of pairs of terms to be memorized by the method of anticipation, the first member was described as the stimulus, the second member as the response, and the connection between them as one of conditioning. Errors during learning were thought of in terms of stimulus generalization, their disappearance as a consequence of differentiation, and interference between successive tasks as effects of extinction.

This extrapolation of conditioning concepts has not proven fruitful; it did not illuminate any fact or principle. Its precariousness is becoming increasingly evident, as the discussions of Battig and Keppel make clear. One should not, however, conclude that the effort was wrong in principle; the inadequacies may be attributable to an insufficiently detailed acquaintance with the area of conditioning.

More important for the present examination is the S-R conceptualization of associations (which is logically independent of the conditioning constructs with which it became intertwined) and the operationist temper of thinking which inspired it. What is particularly noteworthy is that its proponents represented this formulation as a methodological statement of the minimal requirements of scientific analysis. They equated the stimulus and response of the S-R formula with antecedent and consequent conditions, respectively. Accordingly, they found it easy to conclude that this formulation was wholly independent of theoretical assumptions and that to question it was tantamount to abandoning the goals of causal analysis. In fact, the S-R formulation served to discourage inquiry about processes underlying empirical observations and prevented a reexamination of the associationistic premise. The following examples may serve as partial illustrations of this contention.

Associative symmetry

The issue of associative symmetry, with which I happen to be personally acquainted, illustrates some of the problems raised by an S-R account of associative learning. For this purpose it is not necessary to assume that the matter is settled; it suffices only to ask why it was necessary to wait 75 years before entertaining the possibility of symmetry. The obvious answer that the "principle" of asymmetry was accepted because it was a summary of empirical findings is correct but not entirely revealing. One can hardly doubt that the deeper reason was the belief that an association is a connection of a response to a stimulus. Indeed, given this assumption, the fact that backward associations occur at all was a puzzling embarrassment; it made no sense. What happened in consequence is quite instructive. On the one hand, students accepted backward associations as a brute fact that could not be denied. At the same time they attempted to reduce the contradiction by reinterpreting backward associations as an effect of incidental learning, the formation of a second association between the same items in reverse order. This effort is a tribute to their consistency and ingenuity more than to their readiness to entertain an unwelcome alternative.

What is at issue in the question of symmetry? In the first place, it makes clear that relations between learning and performance are less direct than had been supposed. Specifically, one must refer to at least two effects of experience in the study of symmetry: interitem associations and item availability. As good experimentalists, students of rote learning have accepted this implication and are themselves energetically pursuing the problem. Second, the formulation that associations are symmetrical is no longer merely a summary of empirical data, although of course it can only be tested by them; it is a construct or a proposition concerning a property of associations. Third, the principle of associative symmetry raises an urgent question about the status of forward and backward associations. In accordance with the prevailing views, investigators concluded that forward and backward associations are distinct events. If, however, associations are symmetrical, and if there are no conditions in which symmetry fails, the distinction between forward and backward associations collapses, which leads to the view that there is one and only one association between a pair of terms.

The principle of associative symmetry, if established, will require the abandonment of the stimulus-response conceptualization of associative learning. Those students of rote learning who saw an incompatibility between backward association and the S-R paradigm were indeed right, although they tried to resolve the difficulty in their own way. The principle of symmetry sharpens the contradiction, since it asserts that the terms entering into association have identical roles in the associative process and thus renders untenable the distinction between stimulus and response. The presupposition embedded in the customary thinking assigned to one pole of an association the character of a stimulus and to the other the character of a response; according to this scheme the response was literally the utterance of a syllable or word. The signal error of this formulation was the failure to consider the alternative that an association is a central process, of which the response is an index. This oversight is all the more strange when one considers that reference to connections between sensory processes is commonplace in discussions of classical conditioning and that there is increasing evidence to support their existence (Asratyan, 1961). Further, acquisition occurring in the absence of responses is well established in animal studies (e.g., Beck and Doty, 1957). There were accordingly impressive reasons to regard associations as instances of S-S connections. If this is indeed the case, the customary formulation embodies a systematic distortion of focus; it purports to deal with sensori-motor action when the phenomena under investigation refer almost entirely to states that precede the motor response.

In classical associationism an association is also a central state; further, it is cognitive in character, in the sense that it provides knowledge of 'what goes with what.' In the light of the preceding discussion, the shift away from the older position was a step in the wrong direction. A mentalistic psychologist could hardly have failed to note that both terms of an association have stimulus properties in equal degree, that their division into stimulus and response terms is arbitrary, that to go backward among one's experiences is quite natural, and that when one moves among one's experiences of the past, the sequence in which they originally occurred is not of much import. In fact, going backwards, in this sense, among one's experiences is essential in an attribution of cause and effect. It is not without interest that Hume clearly enunciated the latter point; he would probably have been most astonished at the thought that an association is a response and not the condition of a response. At this point the behavioristic injunction to disregard phenomenal facts conflicts with the elementary requirement of faithful observation. To be sure, such observations are not proof, but to dismiss them in advance can be a form of self-victimization.

Recognition

Recognition is of consequence because it is a basic effect of past experience and because it appears to present certain contrasts to association by contiguity. There is first the fact that recognition occurs despite tremendous variability in the physical characteristics of an object or event; given the experience of one or a few instances, an indefinite number of other instances are identifiable as similar. This observation points to the operation of an underlying rule that does not appear as an element in the situation but is constructed by the observer.

Second, and related to the preceding point, recognition is, functionally considered, a bridging of events separated in space and time. A face one sees now may appear familiar if one has seen it only once years ago and in a different setting. The point of this example is that the two faces, those of the present and the past, have not occurred in contiguity. The first problem is accordingly to understand how the spatio-temporal gap is overcome.

It is instructive to contrast two attempts to analyze recognition as a process. Some thinkers, foremost among them Höffding (1891), have stressed the role of similarity in recognition. Pursuing this lead, Köhler (1940) proposed an account in terms of the action of memory traces, the physical substratum of memory. It begins with the general proposition that recognition requires memory trace contact that is initiated by stimulation from an external object. The further and main point is that recognition is an instance of memory trace selection by a stimulus of the present on the basis of their distinctive similarity, analogously to grouping according to similarity in perceptual experience. This proposal is admittedly rudimentary, since the mechanism of trace selection and the rules specifying similarity are not known. However, the formulation contains a fundamental implication for the character of associative recall, the critical phenomenon of rote learning investigations. Briefly stated, associative recall involves two steps: trace contact by similarity followed by recall on the basis of an association. Suppose that a learner has formed an association between a and b, corresponding to two external objects A and B, and is subsequently given A under instructions to produce the missing member. The proposal asserts that associative recall at the time of test will occur only if the stimulation proceeding from A will make contact with the corresponding memory trace *a*, and that such contact occurs on the basis of similarity. This is to say that a step involving similarity is a necessary prior condition of associative recall.

In contrast, the treatment of recognition in the rote learning area has been largely dominated by the attempt to subsume it under association by contiguity. At this point the S-R conceptualization has played a prominent part. It begins by describing the occurrence of recognition as a response, the antecedent initiating event as a stimulus, and the connection between them as a standard association. This attempt epitomizes much of the scientific temper of the rote learning area and is for this reason deserving of scrutiny. It simply ignores the analysis that Höffding called into question. But further, the reasoning employs the notions of stimulus and response in a manner that is misleading. The "response of recognition" actually refers to a mental operation denoting a choice the content of which is: "Yes, I have seen this before." As Rock and Ceraso (1964) have pointed out, this "response" surely did not occur at the time of original experience. Had a response of this sort occurred, it would have been to the effect: "No, I have not seen this before." Recognition is, to be sure, dependent upon past experience, but it is not simply a duplication of past experience; the step of recognition occurs at the time of test, not at the time of acquisition. To assimilate this contact between a past and present experience to an association by contiguity does not fit the facts, at least not obviously. The unsupported proposal that it does rests on the questionable assumption that when two events follow each other, and refer in some way to the past, they must have been previously associated. This way of thinking amounts simply to a determination not to admit any relation other than contiguity as the condition of contact between psychological events.

Serial learning

One of the more interesting developments of recent years relates to the problems of serial learning. Beginning with Ebbinghaus it was customary to describe the mastery of lists of items in terms of associations formed between the successive members. This starting point served as the basis for further conclusions about remote associations, the serial position effect, etc. These interpretations were retained intact when serial learning was subsequently described as a chain of S-R units, each member of which was said to be both a stimulus and a response. Recent investigation has cast strong doubt on these formulations. It appears that remote associations may not be a fact (e.g., Slamecka, 1964). Further, one can in part account for the serial position effect in terms of the discrimination of the ends of the series. More important, ingenious investigation has shown that serial learning depends preponderantly not on connections formed between one item and another but rather on connections between items and their temporal position (e.g., Young, 1962; Ebenholtz, 1963). While certain detailed questions still await solution, this conclusion appears well established.

These findings tell heavily against the chaining hypothesis of serial learning, hitherto a central part of the rote learning scheme. They also raise some challenging questions. It might appear that the S-R analysis remains untouched except for one factual revision: associations between items are now replaced in large part by associations between items and their positions. To preserve the S-R analysis, it only suffices, it seems, to treat temporal position as a stimulus and the verbal item as a response. Aside from the dubiousness of this distinction, of which enough has been said earlier, the formulation masks the point that position is a radically different entity from a stimulus in the rote learning sense. First, a stimulus in the latter sense is a concretely appearing item, in contrast to a temporal position which is nonappearing. Second, and connected with the preceding point, a stimulus in the rote learning sense is an isolable item, like a nonsense syllable which may be shifted at will without substantially altering its identity or that of its neighbors. A position is not, however, isolable in this way, and the relation of one position to another is not analogous to the relation between two arbitrarily chosen verbal units. A position is relationally determined, a dependent part of the framework to which it belongs. One may accordingly formulate that the standard serial learning task includes two fundamentally distinct kinds of facts: a *list*, consisting of an arbitrary set or collection of items; and a *series*, consisting of an ordered set of positions. The mastery of such a task involves in large part a coordination between list and series, in contrast with the earlier interpretation of it as sheer list learning (Asch, Hay and Diamond, 1960). One must conclude that despite their best efforts investigators did not succeed in eliminating relations from at least one of the major paradigms of rote learning.

Some implications of this analysis may be briefly noted. First, an explanation of serial learning must include reference to the learner's representation of the series. More specifically, the movement of the learner from one member of a list to another can no longer be treated independently of the relational character of the series.

Presumably the learner progresses along the series from one position to another, but these are not connected associatively, in the usual sense of this term. Second, the presence of a series cannot be reconciled with the fundamental S-R assumption that serial phenomena are built up from pairwise associations. If position is not an element in the customary sense, the representation of the entire series is implied at each step. Third, the decisive effect of instructions in derived-list studies underlines the importance of cognitive operations in serial learning. Hitherto the presence of such operations has been considered incidental to the main issues of serial learning, but their role in transfer between derived lists is altogether too strong to be discounted in this way. Nor are the effects of instructions, as Young has pointed out, compatible with predictions derived from the action of associations. Finally, the evidence increasingly points to the conclusion that the serial learning gradient is a relationally determined effect of position along a dimension, not a standard associative effect (Murdock, 1960; Jensen, 1962; Ebenholtz, 1963). These findings are not reconcilable with an interpretation of verbal connections in terms of S-R contingencies. Since serial learning has an extremely simple structure, it is hardly likely that the far more complex structures of natural language will alter this conclusion.

Summary

The S-R formulation introduced limitations upon thinking while exonerating the limitations. In the main it served to entrench the associationistic premise by protecting it from examination. This outcome owes much to the operationist principle that theoretical statements should be directly reducible to observations. Nowhere is this more evident than in the treatment of association itself. Strictly speaking, one does not find in the area of rote learning a theory of associations (as distinct from a pre-experimental orientation); the term simply names a relation between experimental conditions and an observed outcome. Similarly, the notion "strength of association," second in importance only to that of association, refers simply to the factual relation between practice and increasing likelihood of a response. Other general formulations are equally mere restatements of empirical findings. When investigation showed that associative practice makes possible backward as well as forward recall, students concluded that there are backward as well as forward associations; when forward recall was found to be generally superior to backward recall, they concluded that associations were asymmetrical. There has been a minimum of effort to go beyond the empirical relations in order to arrive at constructs about underlying processes.

This orientation has in effect turned the S-R formulation into a device for analyzing neither the stimulus nor the response. Students of rote learning have generally taken the stimulus for granted. They identified the latter with the external conditions, without inquiring how the psychological stimulus is achieved, or how a sequence of events becomes a unit; in this way they avoided reference to perception. By dealing similarly with responses they eliminated the analysis of action. Even more noteworthy has been the failure to consider the nature of associations, the ostensible object of inquiry in this area. Despite the paramount role assigned to contiguity, there has been no fundamental inquiry of the ways in which events become psychologically contiguous.

The behavioristic injunction to delete reference to phenomenal events has supported the tendencies described above. It has contributed to the neglect of experienced relations and in general of cognitive operations. As stated earlier, it has been responsible for inadequacies in the treatment of recognition. If one is not free to refer to the experience of familiarity, one will be compelled to talk about the response of recognition, thus confusing wholly different categories of events. If one may not say that an experience occurring now resembles one of the past, one is less likely to think of the relation of similarity as a condition of the evocation of past events. Whoever is inclined to question the stringency of this behavioristic rule would do well to seek in the literature of recent decades for any reference to the fact that in remembering we refer to matters of the past *as past*, or that memory is a unique modality of human experience.

Concluding Comments

I cannot do justice to the formidable array of problems and studies that the contributors to this session have examined; instead I will limit myself to the bearing of their discussion on some of the issues considered above.

In the light of what has been said, it will not come as a surprise that I miss in the accounts of Battig, Young, and Keppel an effort to relate the major paradigms they have discussed to learning in its natural habitat. To be sure, this was not their task; nonethless the point is of some relevance. Battig treats the paired-associate paradigm as if it were a fact of nature on a level with the chain of digestive processes; this is the only way I can understand his references to "PA theory" and "PA theorists." In fact, the PA paradigm carries a definite label: manufactured in the laboratory. This is not to deny that it is a useful experimental tool, and of course its components occur under natural conditions. But most of Battig's problems arise from the conglomeration of tasks that are comprised in PA learning. I need to be convinced that nature or society confronts us with such a concatenation of tasks except rarely and under special conditions. The same comment applies to the serial learning task that Young has discussed. Despite the interest that rightly attaches to this paradigm, it is surely not out of place to ask in what ways it is representative of important phases of human learning. On the other hand, the interference phenomena examined by Keppel have great generality. Yet even here it seems pertinent to note that the intense degrees of interference generated under experimental conditions probably have few analogues outside the laboratory. It is not my intention to suggest that experimental situations should duplicate natural situations; the use of special or extreme procedures for purposes of experimental clarification does not stand in need of justification. It does not, however, follow that their relevance to everyday operations of learning and memory can be safely neglected.

I am in sympathy with much of what Battig says about the shortcomings of a simple S-R conditioning model applied to PA learning. His criticism of reinforcement as a condition of PA learning is to me convincing and supports the analysis of Rock and Ceraso (1964). Battig's major point—that PA learning comprises a considerable number of distinct operations and that the association of pairs is only one, and perhaps not the most important, component—is valuable as a reminder of the need to decollapse the global notion of association and as an indication of a number of attractive problems that

emerge when one follows this direction. In one respect I wish that Battig had gone further than he has. It is not clear to me whether his strictures against a simple S-R conceptualization are intended as an argument for a more complex and differentiated S-R analysis of PA learning or whether he sees the need for a different type of theory. Battig has described the components of PA learning in "achievement" terms; this is an excellent way to begin, but it only sets the stage for a theoretical analysis which he does not pursue. I also find a difficulty with one main conclusion that Battig draws from the complexity of PA learning. He appears to think that a complex psychological situation requires correspondingly complex experimentation and theoretical formulations. Thus he argues against associative symmetry not only on empirical grounds but also on the ground of its simplicity, which he takes to be in contradiction with the many-faceted character of the PA task. Surely this conclusion is not necessary; the complexity of PA learning may well be a consequence of the fact that it is an aggregation of different tasks, each perhaps comparatively simple.

Young's account of recent advances in the study of serial learning, to which he has himself made a valuable contribution, is most instructive. He tells an absorbing story of the vicissitudes of a scientific problem. At the same time I must charge him with not being altogether fair to his own findings; to me it seems that Young has not freed himself of a mode of thinking which his own studies have seriously weakened. His main concern is to characterize serial learning so as not to disturb the usual S-R conceptualization, which he takes for granted. This commitment determines his treatment of the positional factor in serial learning; it seems clear that he is uncomfortable with the role of position as long as he cannot convert it to the dimensions of a stimulus in the rote learning sense. Accordingly he fails to consider adequately the relational character of position and sacrifices, in my opinion, an important insight. This orientation is also responsible for the negative conclusion he reaches about the value of the serial learning paradigm for the area of rote verbal learning. Young apparently does not realize that this conclusion only tends to narrow further an area that is already unduly restricted.

My confidence deserts me as I come to Keppel's imposing paper. The study of interference has become a complex and rapidly growing specialty in which I disclaim expertness; I therefore confine myself to one aspect of his analysis, the problem of association with context, which has figured prominently in current interpretations of interference. Since the work of Barnes and Underwood (1959), it has become clear that interpolated activity produces decrement in recall by disrupting the original learning. This unlearning has been conceptualized as associative in character, or produced by conflicting associations. The associative analysis of unlearning has concentrated increasingly, particularly since the work of McGovern (1964), upon the contribution of contextual associations. This analysis raises a number of points that I find puzzling.

Context has been identified with environmental stimuli—the room, the apparatus, the experimenter, etc. Rote learning students will probably be the first to say that context comprises a number of things, as just indicated. This implies that each item forms associations with a number of different objects in the environment. This is a condition productive of interference during acquisition as well as during interpolated learning, yet discussions of

context treat it as a single stimulus. The basis of this assumption deserves to be made clear. To be sure, no one can specify adequately, as Keppel points out, what is meant by context; still a step has intruded into thinking without its being justified or, I suppose, suspected.

The complete identification of item availability with contextual associations exemplifies another aspect of the S-R conceptualization that I find questionable. This interpretation assumes that the sole condition of item availability is ease of access to it and that the content of the item is of no account except as it affects the associative connection. Consider, however, the free recall of a mixed list containing words and nonsense syllables. For the sake of the argument let us suppose that interitem associations do not contribute substantially to recall on the first trial. What compelling reason is there to insist that the words have become more strongly associated with the context than the nonsense syllables and that this accounts fully for their superior recall? Is it all that difficult to conceive of two associations working with full effectiveness, one producing recall and the other not? The assumption that recall of an item is a function solely of its connection with something else is an instance of the slighting of the content of recall for which I can see no adequate justification.

Keppel is right to point out that there may be other as yet unidentified conditions of interference. One source of interference may have its locus in the recognition phase of associative learning. Specifically, the identical first member of a pair in two lists may be represented by distinct memory traces; interference could then result from improper memory trace contact. The customary S-R analysis slights the possibility that the identical objective materials may be represented in psychologically distinct ways.

* * *

The foregoing, admittedly incomplete, examination of the associationistic position in the area of rote learning, has touched mainly on two issues, which will now be summarized.

Associations by contiguity comprise a highly restricted segment of the domain of human learning; the assumption that they are coextensive has imposed a distorted conception of learning. It is at best artificial to divorce the issues of learning and memory from the elementary operations that make for object perception, the acquisition of language, or the grasp of logical connections. An explanation of these achievements must give a central place to constructive and innovative steps. The associationistic emphasis on arbitrary connections is not equipped to treat these phenomena. It slights precisely those effects of experience that produce changed ways of perceiving and understanding.

At the same time recent investigations make it increasingly clear that the paradigms of rote learning are by no means free of relational operations. These advances promise to bridge the gap between rote and other phenomena of learning. They also provide support for a cognitive interpretation of associations. These developments should open the way to a freer examination of the presuppositions that have dominated the rote learning area and of the limited conception of science that it fostered. In general, the erosion of thinking about cognitive processes under the influence of behaviorism is receding. It is becoming easier to reconsider the positivistic equation of a law of nature with an empirical regularity. It is becoming more difficult to

rule out the thought that associative phenomena refer to central processes, not themselves behavior, which control behavior. It may even be in order to entertain the possibility that it is not necessary, nor perhaps fruitful, to be an associationist in the study of associations.

References

Asch, S. E., "A Problem in the Theory of Associations," *Psychologische Beiträge*, **6** (1962), 553–563.

———, and S. M. Ebenholtz, "The Principle of Associative Symmetry," *Proceedings of the American Philosophical Society*, **106** (1962), 135–163.

———, J. Ceraso, and W. Heimer, "Perceptual Conditions of Association," *Psychological Monographs*, Vol. 74, No. 490, (1960).

———, J. Hay, and R. M. Diamond, "Perceptual Organization in Serial Rote-Learning," *American Journal of Psychology*, (1960), 177–199.

Asratyan, E. A., "Some Aspects of the Elaboration of Conditioned Connections and Formation of Their Properties," in J. F. Delafresnaye, ed., *Brain Mechanisms and Learning*. New York: Oxford University Press, Inc., 1961.

Barnes, J. M., and B. J. Underwood, "'Fate' of First-List Associations in Transfer Theory," *Journal of Experimental Psychology*, **58** (1959), 97–105.

Beck, E. C., and R. W. Doty, "Conditioned Flexion Reflexes Acquired During Combined Catalepsy and De-efferentiation," *Journal of Corporation and Physiological Psychology*, **50** (1957), 211–215.

Chomsky, N., *Syntactic Structures*. The Hague: Mouton, 1957.

Ebenholtz, S. M., "Position Mediated Transfer between Serial Learning and a Spatial Discrimination Task," *Journal of Experimental Psychology*, **65** (1963), 603–608

———, "Serial Learning: Position Learning and Sequential Associations,"

Journal of Experimental Psychology, **66** (1963), 353–362.

Helson, H., *Adaptation-Level Theory.* New York: Harper & Row, Publishers, 1964.

Höffding, H., *Outlines of Psychology.* London: Macmillan & Co., Ltd., 1891.

Jensen, A. R., "Temporal and Spatial Effects of Serial Position," *American Journal of Psychology,* **75** (1962), 390–400.

Köhler, W., *Gestalt Psychology.* New York: Liveright Publishing Corp., 1929.

———, *Dynamics in Psychology.* New York: Liveright Publishing Corp., 1940.

———, "On the Nature of Associations," *Proceedings of the American Philosophical Society,* **84** (1941), 489–502.

McGovern, J. B., "Extinction of Associations in Four Transfer Paradigms," *Psychological, Monographs,* **78** (1964).

Murdock, B. B., Jr., "The Distinctiveness of Stimuli," *Psychological Review,* **67** (1960), 16–31.

Rock, I., and J. Ceraso, "Towards a Cognitive Theory of Associative Learning," in C. Scheerer, ed., *Cognition:* *Theory, Research, Promise.* New York: Harper & Row Publishers, 1964.

Slamecka, N. J., "An Inquiry into the Doctrine of Remote Associations," *Psychological Review,* **71** (1964), 61–76.

Wallach, H., and D. N. O'Connell, "The Kinetic Depth Effect," *Journal of Experimental Psychology,* **45** (1953), 205–217.

———, and ———, and V. Neisser, "The Memory Effect of Visual Perception of Three-Dimensional Form," *Journal of Experimental Psychology,* **45** (1953), 360–368.

Werthheimer, M., *Productive Thinking.* New York: Harper & Row, Publishers, 1945.

Young, R. K., "A Comparison of Two Methods of Learning Serial Associations," *American Journal of Psychology,* **72** (1959), 554–559.

———, "Tests of Three Hypotheses about the Effective Stimulus in Serial Learning," *Journal of Experimental Psychology,* **63** (1962), 307–313.

———, E. W., Milauckas, and J. D. Bryan, "Serial Learning as a Function of Prior Paired-Associate Training," *American Journal of Psychology,* **76** (1963), 82–88.

Related Processes

Part III

Concept
Attainment[1]

10 LYLE E. BOURNE, JR.

It is a crass truism to say that there is substantial interplay and communality between the verbal and conceptual processes of human beings. Words and concepts are often inextricably tied. It is difficult to imagine any concept devoid of verbal associations. Not only are most concepts given labels, but some (e.g., "gene," "atom," "economic depression") are employed exclusively in a verbal context—or, in any event, are not easily assignable to empirical referents. More specifically, the well-established tendency to cluster associatively related items in free recall (Bousfield and Puff, 1964), the phenomenon of stimulus selection in paired-associates learning (Underwood, 1963), the facilitative effect of sequential and structural relationships among items in a serial list (Epstein, 1961; Bourne and Parker, 1964), as well as recent evidence of other organizational factors (e.g., Cofer, 1965; Tulving, 1962) suggest the

considerable involvement of conceptual activities in the acquisition and retention of verbal materials. It appears difficult, if not impossible, to avoid the influence of conceptual components in most verbal (and perhaps nonverbal) tasks. This obvious overlapping leads naturally to the expectation that knowledge of conceptual processes will have important implications for and might explicate some of the knotty problems of verbal behavior.

The purpose of this paper is relatively simple—to review data and theory from contemporary research on concept attainment. It will make no serious attempt to consider how this information might contribute to an understanding of verbal learning. That task, despite the prefatory remarks, is far more difficult, for our body of evidence on conceptual processes—particularly the verbal components—is quite primitive. Currently popular experimental procedures typically fail to externalize, indeed often constrain important verbal aspects of problem solving. Therefore, while it is clear on a superficial level that fundamental relationships underlie these forms of behavior, our present factual information can at best sustain only a few tentative guesses about the linkage.

[1] This paper is Publication Number 97 of the Institute of Behavioral Science, University of Colorado. The work was supported by research grants MH 08315 from the National Institute of Mental Health and GB 3404 from the National Science Foundation.

The author is indebted to W. F. Battig and D. R. Justesen for the extensive comments on an earlier version.

General Considerations

There is less than complete agreement on terminology, procedural techniques, and measures in the area of this review. For this reason, it is helpful to begin with an elementary analysis. Although they are unlikely to enjoy universal acceptance or wide popularity, the definitions so provided might make the subsequent discussion somewhat more comprehensible.

Concepts

THE STRUCTURE OF CONCEPTS. Concepts refer to groups, categories, or collections of things, events, or relations. According to Hunt (1962) and Church (1958), a *concept* is best described as the meaning of a name, i.e., a structural description—characteristically verbal—of things to which a given name properly applies. In a slightly different sense, a concept prescribes a set of specific things identified or associated with a name, i.e., the positive instances or the denotation of the name.

Any concept has two critical features. First, and rather obvious, are its *relevant* or defining *attributes*—physical characteristics which underlie the necessary distinctions among things. The second feature can be called a *rule*, i.e., a relation between or an operation on relevant attributes which elaborates a two-class partition of stimulus objects. As a concrete illustration, consider the concept, "all things which are both red and triangular" (or simply "red triangles"). Redness and triangularity are the relevant attributes. The ability to distinguish or discriminate these attributes (or values) from others on the color and shape dimensions is obviously necessary to an understanding of the concept. But the concept is complete only after the proper combination or relation of relevant attributes has been articulated. In the example, the relation or rule is conjunction. Only those things which are red *and* triangular are positive instances of the concept. The same pair of relevant attributes could be related by a different rule, say, disjunction—red or triangle; but this of course is a different concept.

The foregoing is a simple illustration of the distinction between fundamental aspects of concepts. All concepts admit to such an analysis. There are, of course, a wide range of attributes (including those which are characteristic of verbal materials) and a variety of rules which might be involved in the descriptions of classes of things. A more complete listing of common conceptual rules for nominal and deterministic classifications, based on the primitive operators of symbolic logic, has been provided by Hunt (1962; see also Haygood and Bourne, 1965).

A REMARK ON ATTRIBUTES. At the risk of some confusion, it should be noted that any attribute itself will denote a class of things and is therefore a concept. It is based on a single defining feature and a rule which specifies that positive instances shall embody that feature while negative ones shall not. Attributes can be thought of as primitive (unidimensional or Level I; Neisser and Weene, 1962) concepts from which more complicated, multiattribute groupings are constructed. This is the sense in which the term is used in the present discussion.

Conceptual problems

To solve a problem, the subject must somehow learn or discover both the relevant attributes and the rule of the concept. While it is not necessarily the case that subjects approach a conceptual problem analytically, making an independent determination of the attributes and the rule, their eventual solutions must demonstrate sufficient knowledge of both components.

A problem can be simplified by converting one of the unknowns to a "given." The subject might be instructed in detail (and pretrained if necessary) on the rule or the general solution form making the primary task requirement a matter of learning or discovering the relevant attributes. Conversely, the subject might be given the relevant attributes but be required to determine an unknown rule to complete the concept. If there are specifiably different behaviors—strategies, associational processes, information utilization activities—identified with learning the structural components of a concept, then these tasks might provide a valid procedure for their separate and independent study.

It is important to note that most experimental studies of conceptual behavior have employed problems in which the only unknown is the set of relevant attributes. Typically, the general form of solution is a familiar unidimensional or conjunctive arrangement of categories. Only recently has any detectable interest in rules, as components of conceptual tasks, been expressed in the literature (e.g., Hunt, 1962; Neisser and Weene, 1962). Unfortunately, from the present point of view, most of these studies required the subject to learn both rule and attributes in each problem, precluding an independent evaluation of potentially unique behaviors.

Conceptual behaviors

We are in no position to map in detail the structure of conceptual behavior.

However, certain activities which have been discussed rather loosely and without definition heretofore need to be placed in sharper focus.

ATTRIBUTE LEARNING AND UTILIZATION. Knowledge of a concept implies recognition and understanding of its relevant attributes. In the majority of cases the behavior involved is better described as identification or selection rather than as a learning or formative process. The necessary distinctions among attributes are for the most part not dependent on training. This, of course, is not to deny the importance of associational processes involved in labeling the attributes (Goss and Moylan, 1958), the possibility of reducing threshold differences between adjacent values on a dimension through training (Engen, 1960), or the enhanced refinement of a category scale through codification of its subgroups (Brown and Lenneberg, 1954). The claim is merely that most experimental work has used problems for which the requisite discriminations are well formed at the outset. Thus when the solution to a conceptual problem rests solely upon the determination of which attribute or attributes are critical to the positive-negative partition, the behaviors involved are properly called *attribute* (or concept) *identification*.

RULE LEARNING AND UTILIZATION. Confidence about the subjects' prior knowledge of rules is more tenuous. Some rules are well known to adult human beings. If one were to name the relevant attributes, redness-squareness, and ask subjects to sort geometrical designs into two groups in whatever way seemed appropriate, the almost universal result is a conjunctive split—red squares in the positive category, all other designs in the negative category. Interviews with undergraduates who have done this simple task often reveal their considerable bewilderment about other possible sorting arrangements. This illustration further implies that other rules, which seemingly occur with some frequency in the everyday affairs of most adults, are not used efficiently.

Rules for forming concepts, then, differ in difficulty. Indeed, the few data that are available show a remarkably consistent order of difficulty for nominal rules, such as conjunction, disjunction, implication, and the like, derived from symbolic logic (Neisser and Weene, 1962; Hunt and Kreuter, 1962; Haygood and Bourne, 1965). The order, however, is not inflexible. Given practice over a series of problems wherein the relevant attributes are given but the solution form is unspecified, subjects become equally proficient with a variety of rules. The finding is hardly unexpected. It bears notable similarity to the acquisition of learning sets (Harlow, 1959), though, in the present context, the process is called *rule learning*, primarily to emphasize that relevant stimulus attributes do not constitute an unknown in any problem. It is appropriate to consider the learning and subsequent utilization of rules as much an integral part of conceptual behavior as the more commonly studied process of abstracting and identifying relevant attributes.

Concepts and language: an analogy

The foregoing analysis suggests a tempting though naive analogy and some points of contact between a language and a system of concepts. The lexicon of a language consists of words (or morphemes) which function as a type of behavioral responses to discriminable features of the environment. These words are coded reactions to stimulation which represent a con-

sensually valid mapping of nonverbal stimulation into words. Within the domain of concepts, perceptual attributes (or their associated identifying responses) play a similar role; they comprise in a sense the lexicon from which complex concepts are constructed.

But a language, of course, is more than a list of names. There are semantic principles which operate on individual members of the lexicon so as to modify their meaning or implication. Further there are syntactic principles which govern the ways in which a group of terms is ordered or arranged in expressions of actions, functions, relations, and the like. To implement these principles, the language contains bounded morphemes—$/s/$, $/z/$—and free morphemes—prepositions, conjunctions—which lack lexical or naming properties. Conceptual rules provide the semantic and syntactic functions within a system of concepts. Such a rule can operate on a single attribute or prescribe a relationship among attributes, thus generating a specific, meaningful grouping of objects. Attributes are the particular, usually denotable qualities of things; their signs or labels are words. A conceptual rule is a vehicle for generating sensible stimulus groupings, given a set of attributes; analogously, semantic or grammatical rules govern the meaning either of single words or of word sequences.

Discriminations among attributes are likely in part to be learned, much as the distinctions among and the ability to produce speech sounds and their written counterparts are learned. Once acquired, both attributes and words can enter into the formation of more complex conceptual and linguistic structures. As a consequence of attaining specific structures, an individual develops facility with more general principles which might be common to several.

On the one hand, solutions to conceptual problems are attained with increasing speed as a function of the number of preceding problems encountered which are based on the same rule (Haygood and Bourne, 1965; Shepard, Hovland and Jekins, 1961). Similarly, perception, memorization, and utilization of word transformations and sequences are directly related to their conformance with semantic and grammatical principles (Brown and Fraser, 1963; Epstein, 1961; Marks and Miller, 1964; Miller, 1959; Miller and Isard, 1963; Tulving and Gold, 1963). Just as linguistic rules, once learned, provide a means for generating and for understanding completely new and unpracticed words or sentences, conceptual rules are likely to underlie the production of new concepts which are nonetheless appropriate in novel situations and problems.

The analogy, as presented, suggests that the capabilities for verbal and conceptual behavior develop along parallel paths. But it must also be clear that there are important interactions. Words serve as labels (one type of identifying response) for attributes and more complex conceptual groupings. Indeed the language might in some sense impose conceptual groupings, when for lack of a sufficiently differentiated lexicon, detectably different stimuli, e.g., shades of red or varieties of snow, are tagged with the same label (Brown and Lenneberg, 1954). Studies of concept formation, then, seem a potentially valuable source of knowledge about the acquisition of word meaning, particularly denotative meaning; the behaviors involved are so closely intertwined that it becomes virtually impossible to distinguish between them. Finally, of course, conceptual rules themselves can be coded and expressed verbally, perhaps as Dulany (1965) has suggested in the form of propositions

which provide a "cognitive" control of overt behavior.

Like all analogies, the one drawn here can easily be overextended. Its force is limited by a lack of research on conceptual rules, particularly those with sequential properties (Simon and Kotovsky, 1963) which seem most closely related to syntactical principles. Further, no implication of an identity of linguistic and conceptual systems is intended, although neither is that possibility totally ruled out. The analogy is meant primarily to point up (*a*) the basic similarities of verbal and conceptual structures and their acquisition and (*b*) the symbolic and overt response system provided by language within which conceptual behavior may express itself.

Current Research

The remainder of this paper is concerned strictly with research on conceptual processes. It is organized around theoretical orientations, with the results of empirical work serving as a basis for evaluating these systems.

General outline

Contemporary theories of concept attainment, not unlike those of verbal behavior, are largely derivative from classical learning theory. Conceptual behavior is often treated by the theorist as a complication of some basic learning process.

Two main lines of development seem to characterize several currently popular theoretical descriptions. (It is of some interest to note that these possibilities were recognized even by the earliest researchers (Heidbreder, 1924; see also Woodworth, 1938.) According to an associationistic point of view, concepts are attained gradually over a series of encounters with positive and negative instances. The process is usually assumed to involve repeated and consistent reinforcement of differential responses to attributes arising from relevant stimulus dimensions. Each reinforcement produces a measurable increment in correct response tendencies. In its simplest form, this type of theory asserts nothing about internal activities or conditions of the organism except for some form of memory trace of previous stimuli. The subject is merely a passive recipient of information and does not operate on it in any significant manner. Concept attainment, like simpler forms of learning, is viewed as a process wherein stimuli become associated gradually with responses.

The second and contrasting theoretical development describes the subject as an active participant in the process of forming concepts. It asserts, in general, that an organism always entertains some hypothesis about the unknown concept. Each presented example and nonexample provides a test of the current hypothesis. Over a sequence of examples several hypotheses might be infirmed, but eventually the subject hits on the correct one, thus solving the problem. In this theory the subject does more than merely register external events. He is assumed to use incoming information first as a check on his current hypothesis and then as a basis for modifying that hypothesis if it is incompatible with available evidence.

Both orientations have merits. Both seem adequate as descriptions of certain facets of conceptual behavior—and woefully inadequate in other circumstances. The full range of conceptual behavior is surely too complex for either to represent fully. While it is easy to criticize these theoretical ideas, replacing them with a better system is entirely a different matter. There is,

however, some recent evidence to suggest that a more elaborate, multiprocess theory—one which accomodates both associational and selection-and-test processes, with the latter developmentally and sequentially contingent on the former—might provide the rudiments of a more general, yet exacting account. Specifically, the current trends in S-R theory, which allow for an internalized representation of associations acquired in the past as mediational links in a behavioral sequence, offer considerable promise. If mediators (or symbolic analogs of overt behavior) can function as hypotheses in new problems, a basis for reconciling a fair number of seemingly discrepant observations is provided. In any case, some such more liberal approach to theory construction is an absolute necessity if interpretations are to keep pace with and make sense of the data.

There is more to be said about multistage or multiprocess theories. But we turn first to a consideration of formalized illustrations of the basic S-R associational and the "hypothesis-testing" notions.

S-R associational theory

BASIC NOTIONS. Associationistic descriptions almost invariably picture concept formation as a complex form of discrimination learning, i.e., as some elaboration of the processes of detecting and labeling discriminable aspects of stimulus patterns. The complication arises because conceptual problems, unlike simple discriminations, require that differential responses be associated only with certain "relevant" features which might appear in a large number of otherwise different patterns. This discrimination process leads to the abstraction of an element or combination of elements common to a variety of stimuli. The necessary discriminations are based on a direct, or one-stage, conditioning of the conceptual or categorizing response to the common stimulus elements (or to their internalized representations). Associations are said to develop such that whenever the critical element occurs, even within the context of an entirely new stimulus pattern, the conceptual response tends to be elicited.

There are, of course, many subvarieties of S-R associational theory—clearly more than can be reviewed here. Most of the basic ideas and principles, however, can be traced to the work of Hull (1952), Spence (1957), and Guthrie (1935). The main distinction between these theorists to be noted for present purposes concerns the notion of associative bonds. Whereas Hull and Spence postulate a continuum of habit strength which changes incrementally with each reinforced response, Guthrie assumes a quantum process whereby some proportion of a population of hypothetical stimulus elements becomes conditioned, all at once, on each trial. Nonetheless, the two positions agree that changes in overt behavior and improvement in performance are gradual.

The fundamental principles of associational theory were developed in the context of simple learning situations. Hull, Spence, and Guthrie made no explicit attempt to extend the system to the phenomena of concept attainment. In fact, both Hull and Spence suggested important constraints and boundary conditions of their models and warned that complex behavioral processes might demand quite different assumptions. Still, some attempts have been made—with significant success— to extrapolate from these primitive notions to the behaviors involved in concept attainment.

A MATHEMATICAL MODEL OF ASSO-CIATION FORMATION. One attempt to extend the notions of associational learning to conceptual behavior was made by Bourne and Restle (1959). These authors amended and elaborated Restle's (1955) theory of discrimination learning to provide a quantitative account of data collected in a number of experimental studies of concept (attribute) identification. Concept identification problems are interpreted as follows within the amended theory. Each stimulus pattern (example or nonexample of the concept) presents the subject with a sample from a population of hypothetical cues or elements. Each stimulus dimension contributes a set of cues, termed relevant or irrelevant (depending on the relation of the dimension to the concept). A residual set of irrelevant cues, of unspecified origin, is introduced to take account of incidental (adventitious) stimulation which might affect performance. The intention is to be entirely inclusive; anything the subject can use as a basis of response is part of the total population of cues. The size of the cue-set arising from any dimension is, roughly, a measure of the saliency of that dimension and can be calibrated from appropriate data. For simplicity here we shall assume that the various dimensions produce equal-sized sets of cues so that the measure of relevant cues is proportional to the number of relevant dimensions.

The identification of a concept is based, by assumption, on two processes: (*a*) the conditioning of relevant cues— cues which arise from an attribute which is consistently paired with a particular category—to proper responses. In this respect the theory is like Estes' formalization (1950) of Guthrie's description. (*b*) In addition, irrelevant cues, which are not consistently associated with any available response category, are rendered ineffectual, *adapted* or *neutralized*. Conditioning and adaptation proceed regularly, simultaneously and at the same rate over trials. The main structural parameter in the theory is the proportion of relevant cues in the entire cue population. By assumption this parameter controls the rates of cue-conditioning and adaptation. The probability that a subject will make a correct category response on any trial is a function of the proportion of unadapted cues which at that moment are in the "conditioned" state.

The theory, in more explicit form, states that when the correct category response is indicated on any trial n, there is some probability, θ, that relevant cue, k, will be present in the effective stimulus sample and will be conditioned. Letting $C(k, n)$ represent the probability that k is conditioned on trial n, we can write, by assumption, $C(k, n) = C(k, n - 1)(1 - \theta) + \theta$. Irrelevant cues are adapted with an independent, similarly derived probability. Thus, $A(k', n) = A(k', n - 1)(1 - \theta) + \theta$ where k' is some irrelevant cue. These equations have well-known general solutions specifying the probabilities of conditioning and adaptation for any cue on trial n, given only the corresponding initial probabilities. Since the probability of a correct response on trial n, $P(n)$, is assumed to be the proportion of nonadapted cues which are properly conditioned, we can write

$$P(n) = \frac{\Sigma\{C(k, n)[1 - A(k', n)]\}}{\Sigma[1 - A(k', n)]}$$

where the summation is taken over the entire cue population.

Making the necessary substitutions for $C(k, n)$ and $A(k', n)$,

$$P(n) = 1 - \frac{1}{2} \frac{(1 - \theta)^{n-1}}{\theta + (1 - \theta)^n}$$

Summing $1 - P(n)$, the probability of an error on trial n, gives an expectation for number of errors, $\bar{E}$, prior to solution of any single-attribute problem. An approximate solution for this summation is

$$\bar{E} \cong \frac{1}{2} + \frac{1}{2} \frac{\log \theta}{(1 - \theta) \log (1 - \theta)} \quad [1]$$

Thus, quantitative predictions of one common measure of overall performance in concept identification tasks can be accomplished.

In the simplest case, θ, the learning rate, is set equal to the proportion of relevant cues, say r. The exact value of r, while unknown, is a function of the proportion of relevant dimensions and can be estimated from calibration data. Let the measure of cues contributed by each dimension be 1, I be the number of irrelevant dimensions, k be a proportionality constant and B represent the total of all irrelevant cues arising from background sources. Then,

$$r = k\left(\frac{1}{1 + I + B}\right)$$

for a two-category problem with one relevant dimension. But θ is also determined by various experimental manipulations affecting the consistency of cue-category assignments. Suppose, for example, informative feedback is omitted on some trials. In this case, θ is defined by the product of independent probabilities r and α where α is the relative frequency of trials with feedback; that is,

$$\theta = r \cdot \alpha$$

An Illustrative Application. The foregoing description has been used to interpret a wide range of experimental results. Theoretical analysis of the effects of delayed feedback, probabilistic feedback, number of irrelevant dimensions, and several other variables were presented by Bourne and Restle (1959). To demonstrate the use of the model, we consider here an unpublished study of the effects of varying cue validities in concept identification (Bourne, 1963; the experiment is an essential replication of one part of a study reported by Bourne and Haygood, 1960).

Subjects solved two-category concept problems, containing one relevant (R), one partially relevant (PR) and one, three, or five irrelevant (I) dimensions. The correlation between dimensions R and PR was the main manipulated variable. This correlation was such that, for different groups of subjects, responses consistent with dimension PR were correct on 50, 60, 70, 80, 90 or 100 per cent of the trials. In Condition 50 per cent, clearly, dimension PR is completely irrelevant. The remaining conditions provide problems wherein two dimensions are associated with nonzero validities as cues to correct responses. In Condition 100 per cent, dimension PR is fully relevant and therefore redundant with dimension R.

In theory, dimension PR contributes to the proportion of relevant cues in accord with its validity. Performance, therefore, should improve with degree of correlation between this dimension and the sequence of correct responses. To apply the theory, a method for evaluating the contribution of dimension PR is needed. After Restle (1957), assume that the validity coefficient, V_π, associated with dimension PR may be described as

$$V_\pi = 4\pi^2 - 4\pi + 1$$

where π is the percentage of trials on which the dimension is consistent with informative feedback. The adequacy of this assumption is well documented in a review of empirical work on probabilistic reinforcement presented by Restle (1957). Then, since cues arising from different dimensions are assumed to be additive

$$r_\pi = \left(\frac{k}{2 + I + B}\right) + V_\pi\left(\frac{k}{2 + I + B}\right)$$

where r_π is the proportion of relevant cues available in any condition of the experiment.

Thus, it is clear that

$$r_{50} = \frac{k}{2 + I + B}$$

In Condition 50 per cent, the validity dimension PR is zero and its cues are completely irrelevant. Further,

$$r_{100} = \frac{2k}{2 + I + B}$$

In Condition 100 per cent, dimensions PR and R contribute equivalently to the total subset of relevant cues. In general, r_π increases, and therefore performance should improve, as the validity of dimension PR increases.

The results of the experiment are summarized in Table 1; as can be seen, performance does show the expected changes. To provide a quantitative account, we can evaluate the empirical constants, k and B, using data from two conditions and then "predict" the results of other groups. Instead, a simpler test is presented. Estimates of the proportion of relevant cues for all conditions, $\hat{r}_\pi$, are made using the

Table 1

MEAN NUMBER OF ERRORS TO SOLUTION OF TWO-CATEGORY
CONCEPT IDENTIFICATION PROBLEMS

Number of Irrelevant Dimensions	Per Cent Reinforcement of the PR Dimension					
	50	60	70	80	90	100
1	7.35	7.02	6.25	6.00	5.01	3.52
3	11.98	10.00	7.77	6.72	5.95	4.89
5	15.10	13.66	12.09	10.11	7.98	6.02

obtained error means and Equation 1. Values of $\hat{r}_\pi$ should increase linearly with V_π for each level of task complexity (i.e., number of irrelevant dimensions). These values are plotted in Figure 1. As the theory implies, trends are fit fairly well by three parallel straight lines.

tions, in an indirect way. It assumes that the various relevant attributes are associated independently with response categories according to the forego-

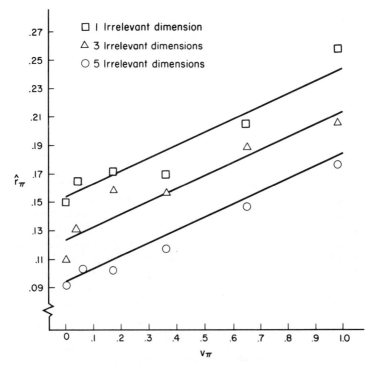

Figure 1. Estimated proportions of relevant cues, $\hat{r}_\pi$, as a function of the number of irrelevant dimensions and the validity of a partially relevant dimension in two-category concept identification tasks. Straight lines are fitted by inspection. For an explanation, see text.

dimensions). These values are plotted in Figure 1. As the theory implies, trends are fit fairly well by three parallel straight lines.

CONCLUDING COMMENTS. The development outlined thus far describes the identification of a single relevant attribute, though as noted it is easily extended to those cases in which two or more attributes *redundantly* define a concept or conceptual system. The Bourne-Restle theory treats multiattribute concepts, such as conjunc-

ing conditioning-adaptation principles. That is, a two-dimensional conjunctive problem is envisioned as two independent unidimensional problems which are solved separately and simultaneously. The probability of a correct response on any trial is a product of the corresponding probabilities for each of the two subproblems. The concept is attained only after the attributes of both relevant dimensions have been conditioned and all other dimensions neutralized. While it is impossible to present documentation here, there is considerable empirical support for a principle of independent subproblems (Bourne and Restle, 1959; Trabasso and Bower, 1964a).

As the theory has been presented, conceptual rules are ignored except insofar as they determine the program of informative feedback (or reinforcement) specifying attribute-to-category assignments. The rule is not treated as a separate component of the concept. Thus, the theory encounters potentially grave difficulties in data which demonstrate marked improvement over a series of problems based on the same rule (e.g., Haygood and Bourne, 1965). Theoretical assumptions could be elaborated to include a set of "abstract cues"—cues which are valid across all problems of a given type and, as such, represent the rule. Restle (1958) has proposed this possibility in his account of learning set data. But the implications of such a development for conceptual rule learning have not been explored. Thus, at present, the theory is limited to attribute identification problems with rates of conditioning and adaptation dependent in some unspecified way on previous experience with problems based on the same rule.

" Hypothesis-testing " theories

In general, S-R associational theories assume that learning is a passive, somewhat automatic stamping-in of connections between stimulus events and responses. When stimulus and response occur contiguously with reinforcement or informative feedback, an association develops. Though these associations presumably exist within the organism, there is no important internal monitoring or control mechanism.

Hypothesis-testing theories make quite different assumptions. For one thing, the performing organism is presumed to operate actively on the information supplied by the environment. He might not respond, even at the outset, to all available stimulus features but rather select and attend only to certain aspects, which, because of some hypothesis, are considered relevant. He decides upon and executes an overt response, in conformance with the hypothesis, which serves as a test of its adequacy. Typically, these theories view any associational process, say, between critical stimulus attributes and response, as trivial. While such associations might develop, they are merely by-products of selection and test routines. Moreover, by the very nature of these routines, associations are presumed to develop quickly, perhaps in a single trial. The important "learning" does not involve S-R associations but rather the discovery and verification of a principle required by the task. In contrast to the associational orientation, one of the most unique characteristics of hypothesis theory is its assumption that reinforcement or feedback affects the selection and maintenance of internalized hypotheses rather than the strength of S-R connections.

As was the case with S-R accounts, hypothesis theories were first proposed and evaluated in the context of tasks, like discrimination learning (for an early example, see Krechevsky, 1932), which are simpler than conceptual problems. But their usefulness transcends these situations, as several attempted extensions of the basic notions demonstrate.

SPECIFIC MODELS. A number of descriptive models of concept learning fall under the general rubric of hypothesis theory. For example: Levine (1959, 1963) adopted certain features of Krechevsky's analysis and coupled them with Harlow's (1959) error factor notions. Like Harlow, Levine assumes that many environmental factors compete for the subject's attention and that problem solving consists primarily of testing and eliminating hypotheses based on all factors which are more powerful than the correct one. One of the major contributions of Levine's work is the development of procedures and measures for evaluating the nature and potency of internalized hypotheses adopted and used by subjects (Levine, 1964).

Though less formal in structure, the analysis by Bruner, Goodnow and Austin (1956) is also predicated essentially on hypothesis-testing assumptions. These authors describe the concept attainment process as the product of an underlying plan of attack or strategy which prescribes a regular sequence of decisions based on trial-by-trial information about the correctness of potentially-valid hypotheses. Not unlike the description by Bruner, *et al.*, is an "information-processing model" constructed by Hunt (1962). This theory attributes to the learner certain primitive procedures for receiving, organizing and interpreting stimulus and feedback inputs from the environment (called information-processing units) in such a way as to define a conceptual grouping. The model, realized in a computer program, embodies a minimal repertoire of routines sufficient to simulate the behavior of real subjects. Perhaps the most important distinguishing feature of this model is its ability to accomodate concepts of a wide range of complexity based on a variety of nonconjunctive rules (Hunt and Kreuter, 1962).

Space prohibits a detailed examination of the various hypothesis theories. Rather, we shall outline a current development which has certain parallels to the cue-conditioning model of Bourne and Restle (1959).

A MATHEMATICAL MODEL OF HYPOTHESIS BEHAVIOR. Restle (1962) and

Bower and Trabasso (1963a) have proposed explicit quantitative descriptions of hypothesis-testing which supply at least the rudiments of a rigorous theory. Restle assumes that any problematic situation defines for the subject a pool of hypotheses. Presumably each hypothesis could be identified with one or a combination of stimulus attributes, though in theory they are left unspecified. Most of these hypotheses are incorrect; some lead the subject always to make a wrong response while others produce wrong responses at a chance rate (50 per cent in the typical two-category situation). One or more hypotheses in the pool are correct and provide the basis for solution. If and when a correct one is sampled by the subject, he will make no errors in classifying the stimulus patterns.

Hypotheses from the pool can be sampled and tested in one of three ways, each of which amounts to a particular strategy. (*A*) Hypotheses are selected randomly, one at a time. The chosen hypothesis is held until an incorrect category response is made, at which time it is returned to the pool and a new one is sampled. The procedure continues until, by random choice, a correct hypothesis is obtained. (*B*) The subject begins by considering all possible hypotheses at once. Given the first stimulus, some proportion of hypotheses will indicate "positive instance" and others "negative instance." The response made by the subject is determined by the larger of these two proportions. If the response is correct, all hypotheses leading to the contrary response are eliminated, and the subject begins to close in on the correct hypothesis. By a process of elimination, the subject ends with the correct hypothesis. (*C*) The subject presumably begins with a random sample, greater than one but less than all, from the pool of hypotheses. Again the process is one of elimination until a correct hypothesis in the sample is located or the sample is exhausted. In the latter case, the subject returns to the pool for a new sample.

Strategies A and B above are special cases of strategy C; in case A the sample size is one, and in case B the sample size is the entire pool. Further, all three strategies lead to the same expectations in the data. Thus, although formally different behavioral processes are assumed, the efficiency of problem solving is presumed not to differ. While this proposition is intuitively uncomfortable, there are no data strictly to the contrary.

The theory provides an all-or-none description of performance changes and learning. That is, prior to that trial (under strategy A) on which a correct hypothesis is sampled—the last error trial—response probabilities are stationary at a chance level. Suppose that in the pool of hypotheses the proportion which are relevant (there may, of course, be only one) is c. The probability of sampling one of these on any trial n (including trial 1) is c. Therefore, the probability of exactly n errors is $c(1 - c)^n$, the product of independent probabilities representing n incorrect and one correct hypothesis selection. The probability distribution of errors is geometric

$$P\{E = n\} = c(1 - c)^n$$

and has a well-known expectation

$$\bar{E} = \frac{1 - c}{c} \qquad [2]$$

Thus, the average number of errors ($\bar{E}$) is the ratio of $1 - c$ (the proportion of incorrect hypotheses) to c (the proportion of correct hypotheses). To predict mean errors for any problem, it is necessary only to know c.

Formally, this description is based on a theory of uncertain recurrent events (Feller, 1957). Because the sub-

ject samples randomly from the pool of hypotheses, with no memory for previously rejected hypotheses, he must begin the problem solving processes anew after each incorrect response and accompanying error signal.

Without asserting a strict identification of each hypothesis with some distinguishable facet of the problematic situation, it is impossible to determine c by "counting" the number of correct and incorrect hypotheses available to the subject. The typical evaluative procedure is to "calibrate" a problem by using the data from one or more control groups of an experiment (and Equation 2) to obtain an estimate of c. (Recall that precisely the same technique is employed to evaluate learning rate parameters in the cue-conditioning model.) Data of the remaining conditions of the study are then "predicted," using the obtained c plus other theoretical considerations pertaining to procedural differences among experimental treatments.

Many of the same assumptions are adopted by Bower and Trabasso (1963a), although the behavioral implications of their work are slightly different. These authors propose a stimulus selection process by which the subject is said to attend only to the attributes of a single stimulus dimension. Dimensions are selected randomly and rejected on the basis of error signals. Once the relevant dimension is selected, its attributes are conditioned to their assigned responses. Because the number of responses in concept problems is small, the conditioning process is rapid (occurring in a single trial). Thus, the primary behavioral component of concept identification is selection. The mathematical characteristics of the selection process are virtually indistinguishable from Restle's model.

For present purposes, it is interesting

to note that the Bower-Trabasso notions represent an extension of a theory of paired-associates learning (Bower, 1962) by the addition of a stimulus selection phase. They point out that the relative importance (and difficulty) of the selective and associative (or conditioning) phases can probably be manipulated experimentally. To lengthen the paired-associates component, one could increase the number of attributes arising from the relevant dimension and require a unique categorizing response for each. Correspondingly, the difficulty of stimulus selection can be varied by changes in the number of irrelevant dimensions. The limiting cases, of course, are, on the one hand, the usual paired-associates task in which there are no irrelevant dimensions and the single task for the subject is to form one-to-one S-R connections and, on the other, the usual two-category concept identification problem. The theory, then, specifies a range of experimental tasks and, although no extensive evidence is available, presumably enjoys some degree of general applicability over that range.

SOME EXPERIMENTAL EVIDENCE. A number of ingenious and detailed tests of hypothesis and selection theories have been reported. Particularly noteworthy is a series of studies by Bower and Trabasso (1963b; Trabasso and Bower, 1964b) using two-category concept identification problems wherein the solution is shifted after error trials without the subject's knowledge. The fact that these repeated shifts result in little or no performance decrement is at once a striking confirmation of an all-or-none model and a source of some discomfort for incremental theories. While the evidence is not entirely consistent nor the analytic techniques free from bias (Suppes and Ginsberg, 1963), the frequently reported (Bower and Trabasso, 1963a; Guy, Van Fleet and

Bourne, 1966) tendency for response probabilities in two-category problems to remain stationary prior to the last error trial also supports the model. Apparently, concept problems with structurally simple solutions can be mastered rapidly, perhaps in a single trial.

Still, the model embodies some doubtful features. Most apparent are its assumptions about hypothesis (or stimulus) sampling and the occasions for hypothesis rejection and resampling. By assuming sampling with replacement (i.e., no memory for preceding events), hypothesis models imply a constant proportion of relevant hypotheses in the pool across presolution trials. Testing this assumption with the multiple solution shift procedure mentioned above, Trabasso and Bower (1965) observed performance effects which could be accounted for only by revising the model to allow for memory of at least one stimulus-feedback event over several trials. Similarly, Guy, Van Fleet and Bourne report significant performance differences when the solution to a two-category problem is shifted to a formerly redundant, to a formerly irrelevant, or to a novel stimulus dimension. The result implies that hypotheses, if they exist, are sampled in accord with their previous history in the problem.

In theory, hypotheses are rejected only on the occasion of an error trial. To the contrary, both Levine (1964) and Suppes and Schlay-Rey (1965) have shown evidence of hypothesis changes on correct response trials. Clearly some subjects learn from both infirming and confirming information, a result which is difficult to rationalize with the Bower-Trabasso model but is quite basic to all known incremental theories.

COMMENTS. The available evidence is hardly decisive. While many characteristics of performance in simple conceptual tasks are well described by hypothesis theory, others pose difficulties for the models as formally stated. Characteristically, in the experimental tasks used to explore the formal all-or-none models

(a) the stimulus dimensions are familiar,

(b) the levels within dimensions are quite discriminable and

(c) have common pre-established labels,

(d) the responses are primitive and highly integrated,

(e) the solution is simple, involving the identification of a single relevant dimension and

(f) preliminary instructions and practice problems designed to emphasize the necessary form of solution are given.

When any or all of these conditions fail, learning might not only be slowed down, but also might become gradual. All-or-none hypotheses theories are attractively simple and a rich source of testable ideas. On the other hand, their boundary conditions might be fairly narrow. What is needed, of course, is empirical and theoretical work to establish more clearly their range of generality and applicability.

One final comment: Like cue-conditioning theory, quantitative notions of hypothesis testing apply directly only to attribute identification problems. The essential concern is with the manner in which subjects discover which of several variable stimulus features relate to response categories. The model is tacit on rules—both the processes involved in their acquisition and their relation to the structure of hypotheses are formulated for test. Other than unidimensional concepts, the model has been seriously applied only to a four-category conjunctive

system (Trabasso and Bower, 1964a). There, as in the corresponding analysis supplied by cue-conditioning theory, it is assumed that the subject attacks the problems as two independent subproblems, each based on one of the relevant stimulus dimensions. This analysis, it might be noted, encountered serious discrepancies between data and theory. While these discrepancies might be a product of peculiar memory and response characteristics of four-category tasks, they might also arise from gradual associative processes required by complex problems.

General comments

The simplest associational theories visualize concept attainment as a learning process wherein new linkages gradually develop between distinguishable features of an external stimulus and an overt response. Hypothesis theories assert that the linkages, if indeed there are any, either already exist or are formed instantaneously and that the basic problem for the subject is discovering which linkage (hypothesis) works. The descriptions are different but not necessarily incompatible or irreconcilable.

Theories considered in the preceding section simply assume that hypotheses exist and do not address the question of their origin. Yet the existence of hypotheses logically compels some assumptions about capabilities, past experiences, and training. It seems only reasonable that the subject must have encountered and learned to differentiate potentially important stimulus attributes before he can use them as hypotheses. Furthermore, it is likely that a hypothesis involving two or more attributes can arise only from prior learning of conceptual rules. The same argument holds even more strongly for integrated series of hypotheses, i.e., strategies. Hypothesis-testing and more general strategic behavior appear to be relatively sophisticated kinds of performance, not likely to characterize the behavior of young, naive, or stupid organisms. Rather, performance of this order depends on a backlog of training and experience which is transferable to new conceptual problems.

The prior learning requisite for hypothesis behavior might derive partly from the acquisition of associations among stimulus attributes and responses. The totally naive subject must begin by learning stimulus discriminations and responses for the discriminated attributes. These associations, supplemented perhaps by more generic rules for grouping, such as conjunction, provide the raw materials from which hypotheses are formed or invented and on which more complex conceptual behavior is predicated. A solution to the problem of how simple associations are transformed into hypotheses is suggested by recent elaborations of S̆-R associational theory.

Multistage associational theory

Even to most S-R theorists, an explanation of the acquisition of stimulus groupings based on the discrimination of some property or properties of physical stimuli which set apart positive from negative instances is far too simple to handle many of the phenomena of concept attainment. If an example is needed, consider the learning of fairly simple concepts (e.g., "food") in which no element or combination of elements is common to all positive instances. An ancient suggestion, recently rejuvenated (Goss, 1961; Kendler, 1960), is that the basis of such groupings lies less in the characteristics of external stimulus objects and more in the internal (to the organism) activities they initiate. This possibility, of course, attributes important functional significance to an intervening mediational process in the chain of associations between external stimulus and overt response.

Mediational accounts of conceptual behavior tend to assume the basic validity of Hull's discrimination-abstraction theory. Concepts are learned through a conditioning process which links two or more stimuli with a common response. However, the common response in mediational theory has an internal as well as an external representation. Thus, rather than a direct association between common features of physical stimuli and an overt act of behavior, there develops a complex (at least two-stage) chain of connections involving internal and external stimulus and response events.

Hull (1930), of course, was among the first to use the mediational construct explicitly. According to him, external stimulation can initiate within the organism an event called the "pure stimulus act," a response functioning solely to produce additional stimulation which serves as a cue for overt responses. The cue-producing function of the mediator can itself be learned. Thus this notion allows for the entry of prior learning, stored in memory, into a new associational process.

Within this theory, concept learning is the acquisition of a categorizing response to common mediators evoked by various otherwise unique stimulus patterns. Conceptual behavior is thus a special, mediated chain involving multiple converging linkages between external stimuli and responses, through a discriminatory mediational process.

EXPERIMENTAL EVIDENCE. The descriptive and explanatory values of mediators insofar as conceptual behavior is concerned is most clearly seen in problems which require solution shifts. In the typical experiment, the subject solves two unidimensional concepts in succession. For example, concept 1 might require sorting on the basis of color—red patterns are positive and green negative. Once the subject has made some arbitrary number of consecutively correct sorts, the solution is changed. Neither is there an interruption at this point nor is the subject forewarned of the impending shift.

Two basic types of shift are used. For a reversal shift, the subject must learn to assign all formerly positive instances to the negative category and vice versa. The same stimulus dimension is relevant to both concepts, but the stimulus-to-category assignments are reversed. A nonreversal shift requires the subject to sort stimuli on the basis of a different relevant dimension.

If concept attainment is a process of associating physical stimulus attributes with overt category responses, it is easily seen that the reversal shift should be more difficult than the nonreversal. This follows from the fact that some proportion of the associations learned in the first concept are valid after the nonreversal shift. Reversal shifts, in contrast, require a change in all initially acquired associations. Thus, if the number of new associations to be formed (and/or old ones to be extinguished) is a measure of problem difficulty, reversal shifts should take longer to complete than nonreversals.

Whereas the prediction holds when problems of this sort are given to preverbal children and lower organisms, just the opposite is true for adult human subjects (Kendler and Kendler, 1962). This inversion in problem difficulty is taken to imply the acquisition by adult subjects of both the mediating response of orienting or attending to the relevant stimulus dimension (abstraction) and the overt category responses necessary to identify any instance as positive or negative. In a reversal shift, the relevant dimension and therefore the mediating process remain unchanged. In a nonreversal, however, a new mediational link must develop. The relative ease of reversal shifts for adult subjects is thus attributed to the availability of the appropriate mediational process for the second concept.

On the assumption that internal (symbolic) behavior has essentially the same properties as overt behavior, mediational events are commonly described in S-R language. There is, however, no universal agreement about the defining characteristics of the mediational process. From the data on reversal and nonreversal shifts, it seems reasonable to suppose that implicit verbal activities are involved. Preverbal children and lower organisms (who perform better on nonreversal shifts) are surely capable of physical orientation but cannot vocalize, either overtly or covertly. Kendler and Kendler (1962) have suggested that internalized verbalization acts as a self-generated, cue-producing response which guides orientation toward the relevant attributes.

No attempt will be made to present the full range of complexity and implications of the mediational construct. Rather the concern is primarily with the specific relation of mediational theory to conceptual behavior, its suggested solution to the origin and genesis of hypothesis, and its contribution to a rapprochement of hypothesis-testing and associational theories.

THE ORIGIN OF MEDIATORS. Mediators are in part a product of learning. Mandler (1954, 1962) has described the process in the following way. In those situations which demand "new" behavior, an organism makes discrete, perhaps primitive and disorganized responses, some of which might be appropriate and others not. To the extent that the task resists generalization and transfer of prior training, the learning process is purely associational. With practice, however, errors are eliminated and the proper response or response sequence becomes relatively stable. Where there are several distinct motor components required by the task, the learning process results in the development of interassociations among response elements such that an entire sequence comes to function as a unit. This aspect of the process has been called response integration or response learning (Mandler. 1954). Once integrated, the response develops a structural representation—an internalized analog—which can function independently of overt behavior. Mandler calls the internalized habit a symbolic analog or analogic structure, but it has the essential characteristics of a mediational response unit.

Mediators and hypotheses

Analogic structures or mediational responses are the substance of covert behavior; they provide for "cognitive" control of overt activities. Given the fact that many mediators might be elicited in any stimulus situation, we can imagine that overt responses are guided by one then another mediator, in an order determined by their relative strengths and by stimulus generalization. Incorrect mediators might be rejected (momentarily suppressed or extinguished) on the basis of informative feedback, nonreinforcement or negative reinforcement. Eventually, the appropriate mediational sequence for the problem will become dominant, activated, reinforced and thereby sustained or strengthened.

If this is true, the learning process might appear to be discontinuous—

essentially an all-or-none type shifting from one response base to another. But, as Mandler suggests, this discontinuity is illusory. The response bases themselves arise from the prior establishment of S-R associations by a continuous, incremental process. Only after these are firmly established is there evidence of cognitive control. This analysis leads rather directly back to a consideration of hypothesis-testing theories. It is an easy step from mediator to hypothesis. Whether there is any useful distinction is doubtful. Mediational and hypothesis-testing theories seem to differ mainly in technical language. Except for the manner in which internal processes are initiated—mediators through some stimulus cuing event and hypotheses by a subject-determined selection mechanism—these theories are almost directly translatable.

EXPERIMENTAL EVIDENCE. Both mediational and hypothesis behavior are probably limited to sophisticated organisms, characterized on the one hand by high-order intellectual capacity and perhaps also the ability to verbalize and on the other by a certain amount of relevant past experience. Notably suggestive of this conclusion are three sets of empirical results. First of all, Kendler and Kendler (1962) have shown that verbal childern solve reversal shift problems more rapidly than nonreversal shifts, whereas just the opposite result obtains for preverbal children. Secondly, the Kendlers (1959, 1962) found a similar performance difference on shift problems between faster and slower learners among a group of young children. As noted, a simple, nonmediated S-R description accounts quite well for the behavior of preverbal or slow learners. However, the performance of faster, verbal subjects compels a more elaborate, possibly mediational interpretation. Further, the data seem clearly to implicate both verbal processes and (at the age of these subjects) a better than average facility with concept problems in the capacity for symbolic functioning. According to the Kendlers, the better problem solvers in these experiments acted on the basis of internal, mediational processes (hypotheses?) during shift problems. They reasoned that all human beings eventually develop the capacity for mediational behavior but that the children used in these experiments were of an age at which mediational activities appropriate to the task were just beginning to take shape. Some subjects (i.e., the faster, more verbal individuals) were further along in this development than others.

Finally, a related result was reported by Osler and Fivel (1961). These experimenters observed that some of their subjects—children between 6 and 14 years of age—showed gradual improvement in performance over a series of trials in a concept problem while others solved suddenly, in an almost insightful fashion. This was taken as an indication that some subjects learned through the strengthening of S-R associations and others attained solution by testing hypotheses. The relative frequency of gradual and sudden learners was a function of intelligence. At all ages, the number of sudden learners was significantly larger among high than among low IQ children. According to the authors, this finding might mean that brighter children are relatively better able to use symbolic or mediational processes in their efforts to solve conceptual problems. Whereas normal (and subnormal) subjects at these ages might learn by gradual acquisition of associations, more intelligent individuals presumably use the higher-level approach of actively formulating and testing hypotheses.

These data, taken as a whole, demonstrate that the utilization of mediational activities during concept learning—which results in significant differences in overt behavior and in the way a problem is solved—is characteristic of fast-learning, intelligent, and verbal subjects. Thus, it might be the case that naive or unsophisticated subjects learn stimulus discriminations and responses for discriminated attributes in a direct and gradual fashion. But, given these associations, particularly if they have somehow been internalized as mediational linkages, the subject has the raw material for forming simple hypotheses. Any problem which has as its solution a well-established, prior association (e.g., $\Delta \rightarrow$ "triangle") may be solved rapidly, in an all-or-none fashion, as if by hypothesis-testing, for the required categorization merely involves the association $\Delta \rightarrow$ "positive instance" mediated by the well-learned label "triangle." But if the same problem was given to a naive subject— one who had not learned the association between Δ and "triangle"—or if a formally identical problem was constructed with unfamiliar nonsense shapes, one might very well observe gradual learning; here truly new associations, unmediated by any relevant prior learning, might be required.

Concluding remarks

The structure of mediational or cognitive behavior is undoubtedly more complex than a set of first-order associations or single attribute hypotheses. It should be clear that complex hypotheses, involving several stimulus features and rules for combining them, are characteristic of human conceptual processes. Interestingly, these tentative concepts are often totally novel inventions based on an integration of known but formerly unconnected attributes and rules. The analogy to human verbal behavior, especially sentence production, is obvious (Brown and Fraser, 1963). Even more complicated than hypothesis formation are the problem solving strategies described by Bruner, Goodnow, and Austin (1956). But neither strategies or hypotheses are to be thought of as fixed, unalterable devices. They depend on a variety of factors determined by the problem and the conditions under which it is solved and are subject to continual modification through learning.

How complex hypotheses, strategies, and, in general, rule-governed behavior are learned is a question only future research can answer. To date, little effort has been invested in attempts to find out. One reasonable lead for such research comes from the studies of learning set formation, for the strategies discussed by Bruner, *et al.*, though befitting more complex problems than simple discrimination or oddity learning, can be interpreted, like Harlow's learning sets, as generic behavioral principles which are applicable in a variety of problematic situations. Just as the oddity learning set guides the subject in his selection of the unique member of any stimulus array, conservative focusing directs a sequence of stimulus selections necessary to pinpoint some conjunctive combination of relevant attributes. Both devices are "independent" of the particular stimulus features within which a given problem is cast. Both implement the utilization of some rule (oddity, conjunction, or otherwise).

Using essentially the paradigm of learning set research, Haygood and Bourne (1956) uncovered evidence of the gradual evolution ·of a rather general strategy for solving conceptual problems which require either the identification of a known bidimensional rule or the invention (or rapid acquisition) of a new one. The strategy, while used by subjects in a more or less intuitive fashion, bears notable resemblance to a deductive device known as the truth-table. That is, with training subjects came to collapse a potentially unlimited population of stimulus objects to four classes based on the presence or absence of two relevant attributes. (In accord with the previously described procedures for rule learning tasks, these attributes were known to the subject at the outset.) Learning a new conceptual rule of the same nominal, bidimensional form or identifying one of several familiar rules then became simply a matter of learning or discovering the assignments of four stimulus classes to two response categories, positive and negative instances. Later evidence (Dodd and Bourne, 1965) has shown the utilization of a cognate strategy for identifying the relevant attributes of a concept for which the rule is given. Acquisition of these strategies, which greatly reduces problem difficulty, is apparently quite common. We have yet to find a college student whose behavior, after sufficient rule training, deviates markedly from this description. This research, although admittedly primitive and exploratory, is at least suggestive that the learning of complex conceptual behaviors is potentially accessible to experimental analysis.

The learning and utilization of higher-order response units, such as complex hypotheses and strategies, might not constitute an essential falsification of an associational or any other known theory of behavior. However, along with the broader field of research on human concept attainment, they do embody important implications for a general descriptive system within the S-R framework. Three points are worth mentioning briefly. First, an adequate account must make allowances for the nonindependence of associative relationships. There is an abundance of recent evidence that categorizing or grouping items into classes on the basis of communalities, similarities or more subtle relationships is a frequent component of many verbal tasks, which can result in massive facilitating or interfering effects on performance. The activities involved must be similar to, if not the same as, those of primary concern in this paper. Together, these observations point up the total inappropriateness of assuming independent, noninteracting associations between different stimulus-response pairs. "Organizational" factors can easily be accomodated within an S-R analysis, and, in light of the evidence, there seems to be no defensible reason for omitting them.

Second, while simplicity, parsimony, and elegance are creditable goals, they do not justify the omission from theory of demonstrably important process variables. To ignore memory (Cahill and Hovland, 1960), perceptual (Kendler, Keston and Glucksberg, 1961), intellectual (Osler and Fivel, 1961) and other factors, simply because in a certain set of experimental results their contribution is minimal, is entirely self-defeating in any useful description of behavior. Yet many associational (Bourne and Restle, 1959) and hypothesis (Restle, 1962) theories do not afford a natural interpretation of these effects. An argument can be made for limited but precise models, later perhaps to be elaborated as new data are collected. But when the evidence is already available and the discussion concerns general behavior theory, some reasonable attempt to represent the responsible variables is obligatory.

Finally, and by way of brief summary of what has been said before, studies of concept attainment suggest the potential advantage for a general theory of admitting a more liberal

multistage or multiform interpretation of responses. In a sense, it is possible to think of simple S-R association, multistage association, hypothesis-testing and some higher-order theory yet to be formalized (possibly based on propositional control, as in Dulany and O'Connell, 1963), as descriptions of differing locations on a continuum of behavioral development, sophistication, and competence. Depending on the age, intelligence, and relevant experience of a subject and on the task conditions, the behavior we observe may take on a variety of forms. Viewed as miniaturized and bounded models, applicable only to limited (and largely exclusive) domains of behavior, the theoretical interpretations discussed here are neither incompatible nor irreconcilable. As an integrated system, they might provide a coherent and general account of conceptual and nonconceptual behavior over a wide range of organismic and environmental conditions.

References

Bourne, L. E., Jr., "Effects of Intermittent Reinforcement of an Irrelevant Dimension on Concept Identification," dittoed, University of Utah, 1963.

——, and R. C. Haygood, "Effects of Intermittent Reinforcement of an Irrelevant Dimension and Task Complexity upon Concept Identification," *Journal of Experimental Psychology*, **60** (1960), 371–375.

——, and B. K. Parker, "Interitem Relationships, List Structure and Verbal Learning," *Canadian Journal of Psychology*, **18** (1964), 52–61.

——, and F. Restle, "Mathematical Theory of Concept Identification," *Psychological Review*, **66** (1959), 278–296.

Bousfield, W. A., and C. R. Puff, "Clustering as a Function of Response Dominance," *Journal of Experimental Psychology*, **67** (1964), 76–79.

Bower, G., "An Association Model for Response and Training Variables in Paired-Associates Learning," *Psychological Review*, **69** (1962), 34–53.

————, and T. Trabasso, "Concept Identification," in R. C. Atkinson, ed., *Studies in Mathematical Psychology.* Stanford: Stanford University Press, 1963.

————, and ————, "Reversals Prior to Solution in Concept Identification," *Journal of Experimental Psychology*, **66** (1963), 409–418.

Brown, R. W., and C. Fraser, "The Acquisition of Syntax," in C. N. Cofer and B. S. Musgrave, eds., *Verbal Behavior and Learning.* New York: McGraw-Hill Book Company, 1963.

————, and E. H. Lenneberg, "A Study of Language and Cognition," *Journal of Abnormal and Social Psychology*, **49** (1954), 454–462.

Bruner, J. S., J. J. Goodnow, and G. A. Austin, *A Study of Thinking.* New York: John Wiley & Sons, Inc., 1956.

Cahill, H. E., and C. I. Hovland, "The Role of Memory in the Acquisition of Concepts," *Journal of Experimental Psychology*, **59** (1960), 137–144.

Church, A. A., *Introduction to Mathematical Logic.* Princeton: Princeton University Press, 1958.

Cofer, C. N., "On Some Factors in the Organizational Characteristics of Free Recall," *American Psychologist*, **20** (1965), 261–272.

Dodd, D. H., and L. E. Bourne, Jr., "Attribute Identification and Rule Learning." Unpublished data, 1965.

Dulany, D. E., Personal communication, 1965.

Dulany, D. E., Jr., and D. C. O'Connell, "Does Partial Reinforcement Dissociate Verbal Rules and the Behavior They Might Be Presumed to Control?" *Journal of Verbal Learning and Verbal Behavior*, **2** (1963), 361–372.

Engen, T., "Effect of Practice and Instruction on Olfactory Thresholds," *Perception and Motor Skills*, **10** (1960), 195–198.

Epstein, W., "The Influence of Syntactical Structure on Learning," *American Journal of Psychology*, **74** (1961), 80–85.

Estes, W. K., "Toward a Statistical Theory of Learning," *Psychological Review*, **57** (1950), 94–107.

Feller, W., *An Introduction to Probability Theory and Its Applications*, Vol. I (2nd ed). New York: John Wiley & Sons, 1957.

Goss, A. E., "Verbal Mediating Response and Concept Formation," *Psychological Review*, **68** (1961), 248–274.

————, and M. C. Moylan, "Conceptual Block-Sorting as a Function of Type and Degree of Mastery of Discriminative Verbal Responses," *Journal of General Psychology*, **93** (1958), 191–198.

Guthrie, E. R., *The Psychology of Learning.* New York: Harper & Row, Publishers, 1935.

Guy, D. E., F. Van Fleet, and L. E. Bourne, Jr., "Effects of Adding a Stimulus Dimension Prior to a Nonreversal Shift," *Journal of Experimental Psychology*, **72** (1966), 161–168.

Harlow, H. F., "Learning Set and Error Factor Theory," in S. Koch, ed., *Psychology: A Study of a Science*, Vol. I. New York: McGraw-Hill Book Company, 1959.

Haygood, R. C., and L. E. Bourne, Jr., "Attribute and Rule Learning Aspects of Conceptual Behavior," *Psychological Review*, **72** (1965), 175–195.

Heidbreder, E., "An Experimental Study of Thinking," *Archives of Psychology*, Vol. 11, No. 73 (1924).

Hull, C. L., "Knowledge and Purpose as Habit Mechanisms," *Psychological Review*, **57** (1930), 511–525.

————, *A Behavior System.* New Haven: Yale University Press, 1952.

Hunt, E. B., *Concept Learning: An Information Processing Problem.* New York: John Wiley & Sons, 1962.

————, and J. M. Kreuter, *The Development of Decision Trees in Concept Learning: III. Learning the Connectives.* Los Angeles: Western Management Sciences Institute, 1963.

Kendler, H. H., S. Glucksberg, and R. Keston, "Perception and Mediation in

Concept Learning," *Journal of Experimental Psychology*, **61** (1961), 186–191.

——, and T. S. Kendler, "Vertical and Horizontal Processes in Problem Solving," *Psychological Review*, **69** (1962), 1–16.

Kendler, T. S., "Learning, Development and Thinking," in E. Harms, ed., Fundamentals of Psychology: The Psychology of Thinking. *Annals of the New York Academy of Science*, **91** (1960), 52–56.

——, and H. H. Kendler, "Reversal and Nonreversal Shifts in Kindergarten Children," *Journal of Experimental Psychology*, **58** (1959), 56–60.

Krechevsky, I., "'Hypotheses' in rats," *Psychological Review*, **38** (1932), 516–532.

Levine, M., "A Model of Hypothesis Behavior in Discrimination Learning Set," *Psychological Review*, **66** (1959), 353–366.

——, "Mediating Processes in Humans at the Outset of Discrimination Learning," *Psychological Review*, **70** (1963), 254–276.

——, "Hypothesis Behavior by Humans during Discrimination Learning." Paper read at Psychonomic Society Meeting, 1964.

Mandler, G., "Response Factors in Human Learning," *Psychological Review*, **61** (1954), 235–244.

——, "From Association to Structure." *Psychological Review*, **69** (1962), 415–427.

Marks, L. E., and G. A. Miller, "The Role of Semantic and Syntactic Constraints in the Memorization of English Sentences," *Journal of Verbal Learning and Verbal Behavior*, **3** (1964), 1–5.

Miller, G. A., "Free Recall of Redundant Strings of Letters," *Journal of Experimental Psychology*, **56** (1958), 485–491.

——, and S. Isard, "Some Perceptual Consequences of Linguistic Rules," *Journal of Verbal Learning and Verbal Behavior*, **2** (1963), 217–228.

Neisser, U., and P. Weene, "Hierarchies in Concept Attainment," *Journal of Experimental Psychology*, **64** (1962), 644–645.

Osler, S. F., and M. W. Fivel, "Concept Attainment: I. The Role of Age and Intelligence in Concept Attainment by Induction," *Journal of Experimental Psychology*, **62** (1961), 1–8.

Restle, F., "A Theory of Discrimination Learning," *Psychological Review*, **62** (1955), 11–19.

——, "Theory of Selective Learning with Probable Reinforcements," *Psychological Review*, **64** (1957), 182–191.

——, "Toward a Quantitative Description of Learning Set Data," *Psychological Review*, **65** (1958), 77–91.

——, "The Selection of Strategies in Cue Learning," *Psychological Review*, **69** (1962), 329–343.

Shepard, R. N., C. I. Hovland, and H. N. Jenkins, "Learning and Memorization of Classifications," *Psychological Monographs*, Vol. 75, No. 13 (1961).

Simon, H. A., and K. Kotovsky, "Human Acquisition of Concepts for Sequential Patterns," *Psychological Review*, **70** (1963), 534–546.

Spence, K., *Behavior Theory and Conditioning*. New Haven: Yale University Press, 1957.

Suppes, P., and R. Ginsberg, "A Fundamental Property of All-or-None Models, Binomial Distribution of Responses Prior to Conditioning, with Application to Concept Formation in Children," *Psychological Review*, **70** (1963), 139–161.

——, and M. Schlag-Rey, "Observable Changes of Hypotheses under Positive Reinforcement," *Science*, **148** (1965), 661–662.

Trabasso, T., and G. Bower, "Component Learning in the Four-Category Concept Problem," *Journal of Mathematical Psychology*, **1** (1964), 143–169.

——, ——, "Presolution Reversal and Dimensional Shifts in Concept Identification," *Journal of Experimental Psychology*, **67** (1964), 398–399.

——, and ——, "Presolution Dimensional Shifts in Concept Identification:

A Test of the Cue-Sampling Axiom," mimeo: University of California, Los Angeles, 1965.

Tulving, E., "Subjective Organization in Free Recall of 'Unrelated' Words," *Psychological Review*, **69** (1962), 344–354.

————, and C. Gold, "Stimulus Information and Contextual Information as Determinants of Tachistoscopic Rec-ognition of Words," *Journal of Experimental Psychology*, **66** (1963), 319–327.

Underwood, B. J., "Stimulus Selection in Verbal Learning," in C. N. Cofer, and B. S. Musgrave, eds., *Verbal Behavior and Learning*. New York: McGraw-Hill Book Company, 1963.

Woodworth, R. S., *Experimental Psychology*. New York: Holt, Rinehart & Winston, Inc., 1938.

Verbal Conditioning: A Review of Its Current Status[1]

11

FREDERICK H. KANFER

In view of the central role of verbal behavior in human relationships, it is not surprising that personality theories and research on social behavior have leaned heavily on the content of verbal reports as a primary datum for theory construction. Early psychophysical experiments, perception research, psychoanalytic interviews, and studies of emotions all shared the methodological error of confounding the subject's verbalizations with actual or imagined events to which the content referred. Bergman concisely presents the problem of separating the verbal response of the subject from the protocol sentences of the scientist by the assertion that "the behavior scientist and his subjects do not, in principle, speak the same language" (1950, p. 485). Most psychologists working with human subjects have taken care to differentiate between language as the primary datum and as correlates of other response events. But when verbal behavior is the subject of inquiry, further problems are introduced by the similarity in form of the subject's response and the experi-

menter's record of the response, and the distinction between data language and the vernacular is difficult to maintain.

Classical theories of psycholinguistics have constructed dualistic models which circumvent the problem of correspondence between language responses and events. These theories of language hold that a relationship between a symbol and its referent is mediated by an intervening "thought" process or that thoughts are elements of the mind which are "expressed" in language. In a careful analysis of psycholinguistic theories, Pronko (1946) has shown the implications of different basic models of language for conceptualization and research on the problems of acquisition and production of verbal acts. He contrasted the mentalistic view of the symbol expression theories with the behavioristic view. Behaviorists are interested in the total (verbal and nonverbal) interactional episode, the consequence of a verbal response and the social setting in which it is acquired or emitted. Classical psycholinguistics, on the other hand, are mainly concerned with discovery of the relationship between phenomenal experiences and words or meanings of symbols. Any research effort based on a dualistic theory of language, one which

[1] This paper was written in conjunction with research supported in part by Research Grants MH 06921–04 and MH 06922–04 from the National Institute of Mental Health, United States Public Health Service.

permits words the status of sole indices of other (nonphysical) events inside the subject's skin, must ultimately return to the question of defining the bond between the observable verbal datum and the hypothetical, unobservable counterpart in the subject's mind. Similar considerations aimed at avoiding the pitfalls of introspection in psychophysics led to a reformulation of psychophysical methods (Johnson, 1929; Graham, 1950; Goldiamond, 1958; Goldiamond and Hawkins, 1958) from a behavioral viewpoint.

In the study of language psychology there were few proponents of the behavioristic view. Watson (1930) treated words as conditioned responses, substitutes for objects which become organized into interdependent sequences. The limitations of this approach, and several later attempts by other S-R theories to treat verbal responses as simple conditioned substitutes for object-referents, are all too obvious. Classical conditioning may play a role in language acquisition, but this approach provides only minimal explanation for response emission or for the complex innovations and constant reorganization of spoken language.

A functional approach to verbal behavior was suggested by J. R. Kantor (1949) within an interbehavioral framework. Kantor carefully differentiated between language as a psychological behavior, as a cultural product, and as a fixed system of conventional sounds and symbolizations. He noted that

. . . from the psychological standpoint language comprises various sorts of adjustmental behavior, diverse forms of adaptations to surrounding stimuli. Such reactions in common with other types of psychological response, serve as definite means of accomplishing specific results. In consequence, for the psychologist language reactions are

unique, personal, and sometimes practically serviceable or expressive reactions . . . . Whatever is common or standard about such behavior is due entirely to the commonness in the institutional character of the stimuli which condition the acquisition of the specific phases of language reactions and call them out when they are acquired (1949, p. 210).

The functional approach was further developed by Skinner (1957) in an attempt to treat verbal behavior as highly complex human reactions which are, nevertheless, subject to modification and influences of the same sets of variables as affect nonverbal responses. The underlying distinction between these approaches and the traditional formulations of theories of verbal behavior lies in the emphasis of the former on the modifiability of the verbal response by the social community. While the requirements for social intercourse necessitate some correspondence between external stimulus events and verbal responses and some adherence to conventional rules of grammar, emission of verbal responses ". . .is shaped and sustained by a verbal environment—by people who respond to behavior in certain ways because of the practices of the group of which they are members. These practices and the resulting interaction of speaker and listener yield the phenomena which are considered here under the rubric of verbal behavior" (Skinner, 1957, p. 226).

It is against the pervasive treatment of verbal behavior from a mentalistic viewpoint and the earlier failure of Watson to have moved beyond a rudimentary approach to the analysis of language that one can understand the enthusiasm generated by a series of experiments around 1950. These studies attempted to test the feasibility of extending Skinner's methodological analysis, based then almost exclusively on observation of laboratory animals, to motor and verbal human behavior (cf. Estes, 1945; Fuller, 1949; Hovorka, 1950). Among the experiments which received the widest popular attention was one carried out by Greenspoon around 1949 and first published in 1951. Greenspoon investigated the effects of introducing a brief verbal response by the experimenter (E) on the frequency of occurrence of a verbal response class in continuous verbal responding. The implications of this study were almost immediately taken to the clinical field by Dollard and Miller (1950). While Greenspoon (1955) emphasized the paradigm as an analogue to animal operant conditioning, Dollard and Miller stressed the automatic, unconscious aspects of the effects of reinforcement and the potential applications of this line of research to clinical psychology.

A second basic paradigm was developed from Taffel's (1955) sentence construction procedure. Taffel's method introduced increased stimulus control by use of discrete trials, but this change also modified the analogue from that of a free operant to a discrimination task. In contrast to Greenspoon, Taffel utilized this modified operant conditioning paradigm as a test of the assumption that verbal behavior in clinical interviews is subject to modification by conditioning and underlined his clinical interests by use of a psychiatric subject population. The similarities between these paradigms and clinical interviews were quickly seen by clinical psychologists, and the area to be called "verbal conditioning" became a vehicle for tests of hypotheses derived from clinical practice and theory.

In this paper I will not attempt to cover the empirical findings of the vast literature which has accumulated, since several excellent reviews are available (Greenspoon, 1962; Krasner, 1958;

Salzinger, 1959; Williams, 1964). After a brief discussion of research trends over the last decade and a half, I will turn to consideration of the heuristic contributions toward clinical practice. This will be followed by a comparison of the verbal conditioning paradigm to animal operant conditioning. The subsequent section will deal with research areas that have developed out of verbal conditioning research, notably those concerned with categorizing effectiveness of reinforcing stimuli, and the consequences of self-regulation in response emission. The last section will be devoted to a discussion of several theoretical issues which have been raised with regard to verbal conditioning.

Stages in Verbal Conditioning Research

It is possible to categorize verbal conditioning studies with regard to four major purposes. Although there is continuing overlap between studies, the bulk of experiments show a trend of increasing shifts toward the latter categories. It seems that research on verbal conditioning has undergone the following four stages:

(1) a *Demonstration* stage;
(2) a *Re-evaluation* stage;
(3) an *Application* stage; and
(4) an *Expansion* stage.

(1) *Demonstration stage*—Studies of the early 1950's mainly purported to demonstrate that various modifications of the basic operant conditioning paradigm can be fruitfully applied to human behavior and that response classes of varying complexity are sensitive to reinforcing operations. These studies attempted to show that at least some of the variables found to be effective in modifying animal be-

havior might be applied to human verbal responses. The repeated demonstrations of the modifiability of verbal behavior by systematic application of stimuli known to have reinforcing properties can leave no doubt that such a demonstration has been successful. While it is always possible to use an endless variety of verbal response classes, with innumerable variations in the setting and in the reinforcing operations, the continued demonstration of the effectiveness of conditioning techniques with different verbal behaviors is no longer of great significance.

(2) *Re-evaluation stage*—Verbal conditioning paradigms originally had been hailed for their apparent simplicity in an approach to understanding human verbal behavior. The accumulating evidence made it clear that the typical verbal conditioning experiment, despite its minimal requirements of materials, equipment or experimenter skill, is highly sensitive to the influence of a wide variety of variables. As has been pointed out (Kanfer and Marston, 1961; Kanfer, 1965), the unstructured nature of the task permits full play for most of the variables usually affecting human behavior in novel situations. Early findings of large variabilities in group data also suggested that S's performance may be affected by many of his past experiences, including those related to his participation in the psychological experiment, to his attitude toward E, to his past history with the task materials, and to his general style of approaching problem-solving situations. Numerous studies demonstrated the effects with different task variables (e.g., Quay, 1959; Portnoy and Salzinger, 1964; McNair, 1957), and for variations in reinforcing stimuli, (e.g., Buss, Braden, Orgel, and Buss, 1956; Sidowski, 1964; Kanfer and Marston, 1961), social settings (e.g., Binder, McConnell, and Sjohelm, 1957; Solley

and Long, 1958; Weiss, Krasner, and Ullmann, 1960), subject populations (e.g., Johns and Quay, 1962; Leventhal, 1959; Slechta, Gwynn, and Peoples, 1963), and interactional variables (e.g., Sapolsky, 1960; Sarason, 1958). The multiplicity of relevant variables suggests caution for the generalization of findings from the verbal conditioning studies to other situations unless all of these factors were taken into account.

(3) *Application stage*—With little direct interest in the theoretical problems created by the re-evaluation of the original verbal conditioning paradigm, investigators have gone on to use the procedures for the evaluation of hypotheses about social behavior, personality, or other topics of their interest, In these studies, the verbal conditioning procedure has simply been used as a tool, as might be other learning procedures, to establish differences between values of independent variables. The potential for tests of specific and limited hypotheses about the effects of many independent variables is enhanced by the fact that the very ambiguity of the paradigms and the sensitivity of response measures to clinically relevant factors parallels many clinical interactions. In this sense, verbal conditioning methods represent excellent laboratory analogues to the clinical interview and to other psychotherapeutic procedures. Further, the identity of the experimental purpose and the goal of interview therapies to change verbal behavior has led to utilization of the verbal conditioning paradigm as a treatment procedure (e.g., Isaacs, Thomas and Goldiamond, 1960; Sherman, 1965). Verbal conditioning studies have also become vehicles for the investigation of the comparative effect of different reinforcing stimuli. In this category fall the numerous studies comparing verbal and nonverbal reinforcing stimuli,

different classes of experimenter statements, aversive and nonaversive stimuli, and many others.

Another group of studies with clear implications for clinical practice has the goal of testing the effectiveness of various clinical procedures. Among these studies are those which attempt modification of interviewee behavior, group therapy behavior or other small group interactions (e.g., Levin and Shapiro, 1962; Oakes, Droge, and August, 1961; Dinoff, Horner, Kurpiewski, and Timmons, 1960; and others).

A final line of research is concerned with the applicability of verbal conditioning techniques toward modification of different verbal response classes. In this group one finds studies comparing modifiability of hostile and nonhostile, emotional and neutral, socially acceptable and unacceptable, subject compatible and subject incompatible words with regard to their susceptibility to reinforcement.

(4) *Expansion stage*—The researcher who has become interested in verbal conditioning because of its promise to approach verbal behavior within a simple S-R framework has discovered that the procedure also lends itself to investigation of theoretical issues related to the capability of human *S*s for self-regulation. This human characteristic tends to attenuate predictability of behavior from simple knowledge of input-output relationships. Therefore, some researchers have used the verbal conditioning procedure as a starting point for the study of complex verbal processes. Others have seen the richness of problems encountered in verbal conditioning not as a challege to their solution but as an opportunity to attack once again the feasibility of an S-R approach to complex behavior. Still others have made the point that the discovery of effective variables, not currently under *E*'s control in the

verbal conditioning paradigm, is sufficient ground for rejecting all the empirical relationships which had been demonstrated in the verbal conditioning literature, on the basis of the fact that the paradigm did not turn out to be a simple, "automatic" procedure for behavior modification.

In this stage, experimenters have increasingly modified the original paradigms to study such processes as vicarious learning, the role of awareness in learning, variables affecting self-reinforcing and self-control, the associative relationship of words, and many others. Eventually, this phase should lead to efforts toward integration of the verbal conditioning literature with other verbal learning paradigms.

Heuristic Contributions

In the analysis of clinical processes and social interactions it has often been assumed that *S*'s verbal productions or his interpersonal behaviors reflect primarily long-established and well ingrained behavior patterns which are relatively invariant under minor changes in the environmental setting. This assumption is held especially with regard to the interview and the projective tests. Results from verbal conditioning studies clearly made it necessary to re-examine this assumption and to pay increasing attention to the full range of potential variables of which the response must be considered a function.

The generalization of findings from verbal conditioning studies to interview conduct are facilitated by many similarities in the two situations. The *S*'s dependence on rules established by *E*, the lack of specific instructions concerning the task, and the verbal nature of the interaction with its implicit consequence of heavy use of generalized verbal reinforcers provide an excellent parallel between the interview and the verbal conditioning situation. It is not surprising, therefore, that many studies have contributed to a better understanding of the mechanics of the interview process. Many of the variables believed to affect an interviewee's behavior have been examined carefully in studies using modified verbal conditioning procedures. Krasner (1962) has given an excellent summary of the research findings and their implications. Probably the most important contribution in this area has been the increased recognition by interviewers of their own capacity for systematically biasing the rate, volume, or content of patient productions.

Hildum and Brown (1956) sounded an early warning about interviewer control on the basis of their finding that the interpolation of "good" following opinion statements in a telephone survey resulted in significant opinion influence. They suggest that "it may eventually prove to be necessary to train interviewers to control their specific reactions to the content received from an informant" (1956, p. 111). Quay's study (1959), in which reports on early childhood experiences were differentially reinforced, carries a message for those who assume that memories produced in the psychoanalytic hour are mainly determined by past events or by intrapsychic processes. The strong effect of interviewer behavior on the content of subject productions has also been demonstrated by Rogers (1960), Adams and Hoffman (1960), Kanfer and McBrearty (1962), Salzinger and Pisoni (1958, 1960), Waskow (1962), Krasner (1958), and many others.

While these findings may help therapists to become more aware of the influence of their own behavior on the patient, there has not yet been devel-

oped a systematic "rule book" which would permit therapists to conduct their interviews to the degree of systematization that Krasner (1962) foresees. The many research findings will eventually need to be integrated so that an interviewer could predetermine his effectiveness on the basis of knowledge of the interactions between subject characteristics, his own characteristics and the situational variables. To date only a beginning toward such an integration has been made. More importantly, verbal conditioning research has helped professional people in many fields to re-examine their interviewing techniques and to approach verbal behavior not as an expression of the interviewee's thought processes, but as interactional behavior which can be systematically influenced by environmental variables. For this reason alone the broad impact of verbal conditioning studies cannot be underemphasized. There is increasing reference in the clinical literature to these research findings with the inevitable consequence of re-examination of traditional approaches to verbal behavior and to behavior modification in general. Reports of failures to affect interviewee productions have more clearly delineated variables to be considered in order to attain greater effectiveness in behavior influence. For example, difficulties of obtaining lasting learning effects with schizophrenics, the demonstration of the importance of the relationship between S and E, and the interaction between response to rewards and psychological adjustment, are among the findings which raised new questions in areas only distantly related to verbal behavior.

A second consequence of verbal conditioning studies for clinical psychology has been the provision of an experimental analogue for therapeutic intervention. The paradigm is a convenient vehicle for testing the effect of innumerable variables relating to technique, to doctor-patient relationships, and to population characteristics. It has been used in clinical psychology on the assumption that many of the source variables acting in both situations are similar. The experimental paradigm permits introduction of each of the elements suspected to act in therapy singly and with increased control.

Findings from verbal conditioning studies have also served to stimulate new approaches to group therapy. In the studies on which these innovations are based, evidence is given for the modifiability of verbal content, and also of social-verbal interactions among group members. Coupled with the studies on the effect of vicarious reinforcement in groups, this body of data should be of value to social psychologists concerned with group dynamics, conformity, and interpersonal behavior.

Another area in which the impact of verbal conditioning research has been noted is that of projective testing. In the testing area the verbal response has often been considered as a description of actual internal events of the respondent. Many projective tests, in fact, have emphasized that instructions and situational variables *should* be varied to suit the particular situation. Studies by Fahmy (1953), Gross (1959), Simkins (1960) and others have clearly demonstrated that cues given by the examiner influence the production of projective test protocols in a predetermined direction. Such findings, together with emphasis on situational variables in test situations from other quarters (e.g., Rotter, 1960) have contributed to the declining faith in projective test protocols as manifestations of invariant patient characteristics. In this area too, the consequence has been an increasing recognition of the functional nature of verbal behavior and its susceptibility to

interpersonal and other situational variables.

Another series of studies using the verbal conditioning paradigm have been of interest because of their attempts to validate hypotheses about psychopathological processes in a learning framework. For instance, predictions of differential responses have been made for subjects of such diverse diagnostic groups as psychopaths, normal, neurotic, and schizophrenic subjects.

In addition, there are studies which have attempted to use the verbal conditioning procedure as a treatment variable. Such a strategy is implicit in the belief of many writers that the process of psychotherapy involves the modification of verbal behavior by therapist intervention and the subsequent change of other behavior which is contingent on such verbal statements. Some implications of this trend have been discussed by Greenspoon (1962), Krasner (1962), and others.

Outside the clinical and social areas, there has been remarkably little attention paid to this body of research. For example, in a recent volume devoted to the psychology of human learning (Melton, 1964), there is only a brief reference to this area. The conceptual issue of awareness has been of some interest, as have a few single studies on such parameters as reinforcement schedules or instruction effects. At this stage it is difficult to speculate about the reasons for this isolation, although the main concern of researchers with clinical rather than learning-process variables makes it easier to understand why this area has remained on the periphery of traditional verbal learning research.

In this section we have attempted to summarize the heuristic value of verbal conditioning research for clinical psychology. If the value of a particular experimental procedure and its underlying rationale can be measured at all, it is only with regard to the amount of additional work generated by it and often by the number of additional problems raised as a consequence. By this measure, verbal conditioning seems to have accomplished its purpose in introducing a new approach to verbal behavior in clinical quarters where a mentalistic, symbolic-expressive theory of language had been most deeply entrenched. However, to date, little cognizance has been taken of this area by workers in the field of experimental verbal learning and by the majority of more than 300 verbal conditioning studies that have appeared in journals dealing with clinical, social, and developmental psychology.

Verbal and Animal Conditioning Compared

When a laboratory phenomenon is the basis of an analogue for further research exploration in a different species, it is essential to recognize that inherent species differences may necessitate methodological and conceptual adjustments. Before the general principles of the underlying theoretical framework can be extended, it must be first ascertained whether or not the necessary changes or transformations can be accommodated. This adjustment may create new problems for the more limited theoretical framework, but the expansion can hold the promise for increased coverage and for more stringent tests of the framework.

In verbal conditioning research the parallel to animal work rested mainly on the following elements of operant conditioning:

1. Operant conditioning is characterized by an initial lack of congruence of the response with a particular eliciting stimulus. Therefore, any response class can be chosen if it has

a moderate rate of occurrence in an environment, even when the eliciting stimulus is unknown.

2. Response classes of varying sizes can be chosen with reference to their functional similarity, as long as it is known that they have the potential for increase.

3. Response frequencies can be changed by administration of any stimulus known to have reinforcing properties, closely following emission of the critical response.

4. Empirical relationships can be described in terms of the systematic application of reinforcing stimuli and response rate, generally with the assumption that no other systematic organismic changes occur in S during acquisition.

In applying this paradigm to verbal behavior, additional considerations are required because of the species differences between rats, pigeons, and men, and because human experimentation requires certain methodological changes due to the characteristics of Ss. It is obvious that the greater the number of modifications made in the human study, the more variables need to be accounted for, and the more distant becomes the comparison with the animal analogue. A point may be reached where sufficient differentiation between the two experimental methods may tax the underlying theory to the degree that drastic changes become necessary. In fact, as has been the case in the area under discussion, entirely new research areas may develop out of the problems posed by the expansion of the analogy. A review of verbal conditioning studies suggests the following among the main differentiating features of the verbal procedure.

Habituation

In animal work Ss are usually exposed to the experimental apparatus for several sessions before the actual experimental design is introduced. During this habituation period animals manifest individual differences in their preferences for various motor responses, for various locations of a cage, or for activities involving different parts of their bodies. Upon their first experience in a Skinner box, many animal Ss also show a somewhat higher rate of "emotional" responses, including rapid movement, bar-biting, defecation, and urination. While we do not know to what specific stimuli these animals are responding, nor what their behavioral intentions may be, the habituation period serves to reduce individual differences and behavior fluctuations in order to permit observation of a stable base rate prior to introduction of independent variables. If animals seem to be oriented away from the manipulandum, some shaping often is carried out to speed up the response to the manipulandum and the food trough. If any consistent response-reinforcement contingencies are set up at all during this pretraining phase, they are not identical to training conditions. With simultaneous extinction of many initial exploratory or emotional responses, the animal is better prepared and more easily controlled by the subsequent experimental manipulations.

In the human experiment, the habituation procedure is usually absent or of brief duration. Considerable variability in verbal behavior has often been noted during the initial few minutes of the experiment. However, only a few studies parallel the essential preparation of an animal for an acquisition experiment by use of repeated sessions with human Ss over an extended period of time. To preserve a closer analogy to animal conditioning, it would be more appropriate to conduct verbal conditioning procedures only after variability has been reduced and S has shown relatively stable behaviors, in an environment which he has had time to evaluate,

scrutinize, and test out. As it stands, although animal studies involve organisms with a much more limited response repertoire, a relatively simple history, and less potential for interaction with the environment, animal Ss are carefully handled in sound-proofed, air-conditioned, humidity-controlled, and light-controlled boxes to avoid adventitious learning. In contrast, human Ss with their rich verbal and motor repertoire and great sensitivity to environmental stimuli are seen in offices, laboratories, home environments, or called over the telephone, and observation of operant rate is often begun at once and followed immediately by an acquisition procedure.

When care is taken to pretrain human Ss, much of the variability and the problems of self-instructions, hypothesis testing, or other "game playing" disappear and S's behavior comes under increased control of E's experimental manipulation. In verbal conditioning, cumulative records of S's working under different reinforcement schedules after six hourly sessions on consecutive days show highly regular response curves and greatly reduced inter-individual differences (Kanfer and Marston, 1962). In fact, S's attitudes toward E, his awareness of the response-reinforcement contingency and many other interesting but tangential variables seem to lose their impact. It is only under such conditions of sustained performance that verbal response measures may approximate the regular patterns obtained with nonverbal operant responses reported by Lindsley (1960) with psychotics, by Long, Hammack, May, and Campbell (1958) with children, and by many other investigators.

Available reinforcers

In tests of particular hypotheses in animal operant conditioning, stimuli are used which have such well-established reinforcing properties as food or shock, in conjunction with operations insuring their effectiveness, e.g., food deprivation. If a study tests the effectiveness of differing stimuli as reinforcers, care is taken to select response classes and experimental parameters which have been well explored in other studies to provide easy comparability of findings and to avoid ambiguity of conclusions due to interactions among other variables. Frequently, a new reinforcing stimulus is first tested for its effectiveness in a close replication of a widely accepted basic experiment. With human *S*s this rigorous procedure has usually not been followed. On the basis of Skinner's theoretical analysis (1953) and the early findings of the effectiveness of minimal verbal cues in group data, many researchers have continued to presuppose that simple verbal responses by *E* can equally serve as reinforcers for all *S*s.

Mandler and Kaplan (1956) were among the first to point out that human *S*s differ greatly in their responsiveness to the reinforcing properties of verbal stimuli. Following the Greenspoon procedure, Mandler and Kaplan separated their *S*s on the basis of a postexperimental questionnaire. Those *S*s who thought the reinforcer had positive aspects showed significant increases in plural noun production, while those who thought that *E*'s "Mm-hmm" meant that they were giving the wrong words or were going too fast actually decreased in plural rate. Spielberger, Levin, and Shepard (1962), following a Taffel procedure, determined *S*'s attitudes toward reinforcement by the postexperimental question: "Would you say you wanted me to say 'good'?" They found that *S*s who stated they wanted very much to receive the reinforcement showed a significantly greater acquisition rate than did *S*s with less positive attitudes toward reinforcement. It is of interest to note that these studies have not led to efforts toward *independent* verification of *S*'s responsivity to the experimental reinforcing stimulus. While assessment of reinforcing properties of a stimulus *post hoc* may be better than total disregard of this variable, this practice raises serious methodological problems. The conduct of a preference test for different food substances as a basis for splitting experimental groups with animals who have just completed experimental runs in which food reward was offered would parallel the postexperimental inquiry. This difference of *prior* testing of the reinforcing stimulus versus *post* testing is one notable factor encountered in comparing the animal and human research paradigms.

Response acquisition versus response discrimination

In animal studies a differentiation is usually made between learning experiments in which some cue to impending reinforcement is presented by *E* prior to response emission and those experiments in which only reward follows selected responses. Grant (1964) has differentiated these classes of experiments by calling the former discriminated operant conditioning, and the latter reward training. In animal studies these are clearly separated by presentation of S^D and S^Δ on discrete trials. The Greenspoon procedure more closely fits the reward training paradigm whereas the Taffel procedure approximates the discriminant operant training paradigm (Greenspoon, 1962). Skinner (see Spielberger, 1962) has suggested that the "good" following a response may also have discriminative properties associated with *S*'s history. The distinction between reward and discriminated operant training may be more difficult to maintain in verbal learning.

With human Ss the situation is further complicated because of S's response to his own behavior and the known tendency of human Ss to attempt categorization of their own responses. Verbal conditioning research presents Ss with the problem of either *concept formation*, or *concept identification*, or both (Kendler and Kendler, 1962). Animal research generally distinguishes more clearly between these two types of tasks on the basis of knowledge of the animal S's history and repertoire.

It is customary to test the discriminability of S^D and S^Δ in animal discriminated operant training for four reasons:

1. to establish the capacity for making the discrimination;
2. to be sure that the animal discriminates differences in stimulus sets on the basis of the same dimension as the one used by E to prepare the stimulus set;
3. to ascertain whether S has prior preferences for one set of stimuli or the other; and
4. to discover whether the task is one in which the animal is learning to discriminate among classes of stimuli or whether the task requires only emission of a response to a previously established discrimination.

These procedures are essential for E's understanding and definition of the experimental task. In the human experiments, limited attention has been paid to these distinctions. S's capacity for achieving the discrimination is usually based on E's assumption that Ss are very much like himself, or this assumption is put to the test in the very experiment in which the effects of other independent variables are also investigated. Failure by some Ss to show learning then requires speculation about the "cause" of nonlearning. The basis of the discrimination, if at all tested, is usually ascertained from postexperimental verbal reports. These reports are categorized as hypotheses of varying correspondence with E's stimulus classification. Preference for stimulus sets is frequently obtained during an operant phase, and Ss are then usually assigned to treatments which aim to condition the nonpreferred class (a procedure parallel to some animal work).

The individual differences in learning due to prior experiences with the critical response class have been of interest to some investigators because of their implications for personality theory. However, when groups of normal human Ss are studied, these differences may lead to problems in generalizing from group data. For example, depending on their prior experiences and their current set, some human Ss may respond to the identical set of presented stimuli by formation of a concept, while others may be at a level of identification of an established concept. Research in stimulus predifferentiation and in the "perceptual defense" area makes it clear that verbal labels and other prior verbal experiences facilitate discriminations. These differences among Ss are rarely verified in verbal conditioning studies. The problem is magnified because studies differ with regard to the degree to which special pretraining or prior histories may be helpful to Ss. The required discriminations range from simple discriminations of personal pronouns (primarily an identification task) to complex discriminations requiring the differentiation of therapist operations (e.g., Kanfer and Pomeranz, 1965; Adams and Frye, 1964), hostile and nonhostile responses (Buss and Durkee, 1958), specific verbal content such as personality test items (Nuthman, 1957; Staats, Staats, Heard and Finley, 1962), affect responses (Salzinger and Pisoni, 1958,

1960), and many others. These difficult tasks may require discriminations which (a) are difficult to label, and (b) may not have been predifferentiated equally by all Ss. To the less trained S they would represent concept acquisition tasks, requiring different behaviors during acquisition than for the more sophisticated S.

Task requirements

In an effort to provide comparability with animal research, verbal conditioning studies usually have given Ss limited or misleading instructions about the task. In a sense, both animal and human Ss are informed of the task by E's manipulation of their environment. It is pretty clear, however, that the analogue breaks down rapidly when one considers the propensity of human Ss for defining their job not only on the basis of environmental cues, but also on the basis of their diverse past experiences. Although several writers (e.g., Krasner, Knowles, and Ullmann, 1965; Kanfer and McBrearty, 1961; Greenspoon, 1962; Verplanck, 1962; Spielberger, 1962; and Kanfer and Marston, 1961) have recognized the importance of the demand characteristics of the experimental situation in determining S's behavior, and Orne (1962) has made an excellent case for careful investigation of S's attitudes toward the entire research setting, few of the facets of this problem have been explored. In contrast to animal work, the human S appears to be faced with the problem of discovering what E wishes him to do, with the task of following instructions, and with other self-imposed tasks which affect the result, often in unknown ways. The complexity of variables controlling the behavior of human Ss in a one-hour experiment, with a strange E, in a novel experimental setting, and with an ambiguous task further attenuates direct and simple comparison with animal research.

The preceding points have focused mainly on methodological differences. The following points are related to inherent differences in the human laboratory setting, to specific species differences, and to the relevance of individual histories to the task. These are generally of lesser importance in animal work and few direct comparisons can be drawn.

Interaction of S and E

Several studies have shown the importance of the social characteristics of both S and E and their interactional relationships in verbal conditioning (Kanfer and Karas, 1959; Sapolsky, 1960; Binder, McConnell and Sjohelm, 1957; and others). When two of these three sets of variables are under experimental control, the effect of the third can be clearly demonstrated. However, such control is not easily accomplished, nor does it eliminate the continuous impact of these variables even in those studies in which they are not under direct experimental scrutiny. The importance of the S-E relationship may also enhance any differences among Es in their handling of Ss and in their effects due to their own personal histories. Coupled with the fact that the definitions of the response classes are usually based on human judgments, interactions between the S-E and E variables and the task variables can further be expected (Rosenthal, 1964). To achieve increased control and better understanding of these variables, investigators can either limit their studies to situations in which most of the variance is controlled, or they can turn to representative designs, in which wide stimulus populations are sampled for the same or similar Ss.

Human self-regulation

In addition to the consequences of the wider range of responsiveness by human *S*s to environmental stimuli, human *S*s also are characterized by their capacity for self-evaluation and for self-regulation which alter the direct consequences of input variables under many circumstances. The verbal conditioning procedure shares with other problem-solving research (Duncan, 1959) the susceptibility to manifestations of individual differences, of attitudinal biases, and of other modifying influences which are of little consequence in animal work. While the opportunity for manifestation of such behaviors is enhanced by the ambiguity and general task complexity, its very difference from animal operant research has suggested a possibility of studying personality variables and self-regulatory mechanisms within the paradigm.

Verbal response classes

In animal work the critical response is usually defined with sufficient clarity so that its occurrence can trigger off a mechanical reinforcing mechanism. The selection of verbal behavior for modification immediately carries with it the problem of analysis of such a behavior along some dimensions. Difficulties of defining a verbal response class have been extensively discussed by Salzinger (1965) and others. The choice of the verbal response mode is further complicated by the fact that verbal conditioners seek to isolate *functional* response units. In distinction to other areas of verbal learning, this choice limits use of structural (grammatic or semantic) word categories. The richness of the verbal repertoire may also affect the rate of learning and the ease of forming conditionable response classes. Salzinger,

Feldman, and Portnoy (1964) found that verbal members conditioned as a single response class and at a faster rate than nonverbal members, which tended to be conditioned separately. The importance of the characteristics of other items in which the class is embedded on presentation has been demonstrated by Kanfer and McBrearty (1961), and Marston, Kanfer, and McBrearty (1962), and McBrearty, Kanfer, Marston, and Evander (1963).[2]

Some Problem Areas

The verbal conditioning paradigms pave the way for renewed investigation of other areas which may contribute toward understanding the human learning process. Among the many questions posed by the findings of great individual differences in verbal conditioning, and still only partially answered, are those relating to the effectivenes of different reinforcing stimuli for individual human *S*s and to the role of self-regulatory processes in the acquisition and maintenance of verbal behavior.

Effectiveness of reinforcing stimuli

In his discussion of motivational variables in learning, Farber (1955) differentiates between nonassociative (drive) properties and associative properties of motivational variables. This distinction is of special importance in verbal conditioning. Particular reinforcing stimuli may have properties which serve a directive function in conveying information to *S* about the task at hand, or an energizing function in

---

[2] The identical linguistic form of stimulus and response creates the problem of distinction between *E*'s presentation of words as stimuli and *S*'s textual verbal responses. Technically, it is the response class, rather than the groupings of S^D and S^Δ items to which we refer here.

increasing the probability of responding without yielding additional information about the task.

Proper experimental design would require independent verification of the effectiveness of the reinforcer and its motivational and informational properties prior to its utilization in an experiment. While many reinforcing stimuli are known to have similar effects on most members of a species, e.g., food, oxygen deprivation, intense electric shock, etc., the same verbal stimulus or the context in which it occurs may result in different effects on individual *S*s. In verbal conditioning paradigms the procedure makes it more difficult to distinguish between the informational and motivational aspects of the reinforcing stimulus due to use of verbal reinforcers which frequently incorporate both aspects. Therefore, it appears necessary to ask first whether different reinforcing stimuli vary in the extent to which they provide specific information or incentive, and whether they do so to differing degrees in individual *S*s.

In extending the Skinnerian framework to verbal behavior, one problem which threatens to have nearly unmanageable proportions at the human level is the establishment of transsituational verbal reinforcers. In human *S*s it appears that particular environmental changes, verbal and others, not only interact with *S*'s history, his personality, the prior instructions and experiences with laboratory procedure, but also with *E* and with the particular task for which the reinforcer is applied. Broad hierarchies of effective reinforcing stimuli in human *S*s have not yet been established. Verbal conditioning research suggests the need for categorization of such stimuli, not on the basis of their verbal content or form, but on the basis of their functional consequences and the conditions under which they are effective.

There are numerous studies which have compared the effectiveness of reinforcing stimuli for groups of *S*s under similar experimental conditions. For example, Simkins (1961) found that points associated with pennies served as reinforcers for college *S*s, while the verbal statements "good" and "that's fine" effectively modified a critical response class only in interaction with the nature of *S*'s prior experience with *E*. Adams and Frye (1964) used minimal social reinforcement, clinical interpretations, reflective sentences, and hostile statements, following a critical response. While the former two stimuli increased the critical class, the last two decreased the same class. Golightly and Byrne (1964) followed the critical response with an attitude statement by *E*, either similar or dissimilar to *S*'s previously established attitudes. They found that similar attitudes significantly changed response frequency. Krasner and Ullmann (1963), with psychiatric patients in a story-telling task, found that "Mm-hmm" effectively served as a reinforcing stimulus while a click and advance on a counter did not affect response frequency. Kanfer and Marston (1961) varied task information by instructing *S*s that the reinforcing stimulus indicated a point score in combination with "good," or a green signal light following critical responses. While increased task information increased learning, the use of "good" or the light interacted both with task information and degree of stimulus discriminability. With psychiatric patients, Gross (1959) found no difference in the effectiveness of "good" versus head-nodding in modifying a class of responses to the Rorschach Test. In a motor operant task, Munsinger (1964) found that meaningfulness, predefined by association frequency, evaluation, and prepotency, was a significant dimension of verbal reinforcing stimuli.

In addition to the reports of differential effects among different reinforcing stimuli in the same study, there is evidence that even under the same conditions Ss differ in performance in relation to the desirability of the reinforcing stimulus, measured by post-experimental inquiry. For example, Barik and Fillenbaum (1961) found that repetition of presentation of the same stimulus item did not have the predicted aversive effect, although "85 percent of the experimental Ss reported a dislike for the procedure" (p. 112). On the other hand, Spielberger (1965) and his coworkers (Spielberger, Berger, and Howard, 1963; Spielberger, Bernstein, and Ratliff, 1966) have reported several studies in which learning differences were obtained, associated with S's post-experimental statements about the degree to which he wanted the presumed reinforcing stimulus.

These findings suggest that, in addition to the informational contribution of a stimulus following the critical response, some motivational characteristics are inherent in a wide range of previously used reinforcing stimuli. To maintain equivalent reinforcer effectiveness for all Ss in a given study, it may be necessary to pretest Ss in an independent experimental task. Greenspoon (1965, *personal communication*) used a procedure in which he found that Ss differed in response to such stimuli as "good," "fine," "excellent," and others, which have often been combined into one class. A similar procedure has been used with non-verbal reinforcers by Kanfer (1960) in a study on the incentive value of generalized reinforcers.

The consequences of self-regulation

A second problem highlighted by verbal conditioning research has been the difficulty of evaluating the effects of human self-regulation on verbal behavior. This issue has arisen out of attempts to attack directly the intervening and normally covert behaviors which may have some relationship to performance or to verbal reports. It has stimulated investigations of the process of self-reinforcement and self-control, and of vicarious learning. Several studies have suggested that Ss may provide feedback about their own behavior in the absence of external feedback and that these responses tend to maintain their performance. In a series of studies from our own laboratories (e.g., Kanfer and Marston, 1963) a paradigm was used in which Ss learned a verbal task to a low criterion of acquisition. Ss were asked to take over E's control in the administration of a reinforcing stimulus and to activate such reinforcement when they thought that their response had been correct. Further studies by Kanfer and Marston (1963, a, b), and Marston (1965) have shown that such self-reinforcing behavior reflects S's pretraining, instructions and that it follows a fairly constant response pattern over various tasks. Bandura and Kupers (1964) have also shown that such self-reinforcing behavior is subject to modification by modeling and that it can be easily established in children. The clear demonstration of reinforcing effects of such behavior is difficult to obtain, because human Ss frequently make such responses covertly, even when assigned to control groups. Self-reinforcement research has implications for verbal learning because it explores an area in which variables are suspected to alter S's performance by supplementing or opposing the effects of the variables controlled by E. The effects of such behaviors would be expected to increase as the specificity of the task and feedback from E decreases. This research area is also of interest because it suggests one methodological approach toward direct exploration of some aspects of human behavior which have previously been handled by postulation of hypothetical processes.

A direct experimental attack on behavioral processes, normally occurring "under *S*'s skin" and presumed to constitute mediating links in the chain of human behavior, has been attempted by Verplanck (1962). An accumulation of evidence on the modifiability of such behaviors and their influence on *S*'s instrumental performance should eventually indicate which of the following theoretical constructions provide the best model for description of internal verbal processes and whether or not different models are needed for different conditions. The choices for description of the hypothesized verbal processes consist of a sequentially-dependent chain model, a parallel-independent model, or a complex-interactional model.

Another situation in which self-regulating behavior must be taken into account is vicarious learning. Apart from its intrinsic interest, this experimental situation is of relevance because it may parallel the process of *S*'s self-observation or feedback of his own actions in a setting where the model's performance can be controlled. Studies with children by Bandura and his associates (1962) and by Kanfer and his coworkers (1965) in verbal conditioning procedures show that human *S*s can learn by observation of models without direct reinforcement or overt responding. Such vicarious or no-trial-learning together with research on incidental learning further point to the need for a better understanding of *S*'s covert and frequently self-instructed verbal activities before a full account of complex verbal learning can be given.

Theoretical Issues

Although most studies have addressed themselves to pragmatic issues, two theoretical issues have arisen in conjunction with verbal conditioning studies. The first point of contention among the different positions is centered on the necessity for constructing a theoretical framework to account for covert or mediating mechanisms in verbal conditioning and, if one is needed at all, on the choice and type of constructs to be employed. The second issue is methodological and closely related to the first. It concerns the status of post-experimental verbal reports as valid evidence about *S*'s nonobservable "private" behavior. The issues have been sharpened by the introduction of wider epistemological issues and polarization of the contrasting views into the cognitive and behavioristic camps (Spielberger, 1965). This section will summarize the different positions on each of the issues.

Intervening processes

From our foregoing discussion it is apparent that a simple linear input-output model does not cover verbal conditioning data adequately. Consequently, explanatory schemes have been introduced ranging from simple S-R chaining models to complex theories. In verbal conditioning, the most complex theoretical network has been advocated by Dulany (1961, 1962). The hypotheses are based on the findings of some studies that *S*s do not show performance increments unless they report knowledge of the correct response class and reinforcing stimuli, and intention to act on this knowledge. The postulated network states relationships between the following constructs: (a) Reinforcement hypotheses (RH), (*S*'s speculations about the consequences); (b) Behavioral hypotheses (BH), (*S*'s speculations about the correct class); and (c) Behavioral intentions (BI), (*S*'s reported intentions to produce the correct response). These are measured by S's postexperimental verbal reports. Jointly with other constructs, subjective incentive value (I), drive (D), and habit (H), they determine S's performance. Dulany argues that inclusion of these constructs is essential for explanation of performance variability in Ss. He also holds that the network provides "... handling the subjects' reports by treating report validity as an inductively confirmable hypothesis" (1962, p. 127). This is accomplished by its initial acceptance into the theoretical network and its verification through achievement of empirical outcomes, predicted from the total network. Finally, "it provides a conception of awareness that relates awareness to response selection" (1962, p. 127). Since Dulany found experimental evidence for performance differences correlated with those report categories which served as measures for the constructs, he is led to conclude that no conditioning without awareness was found. He argues that "... Certainly it is possible that with somewhat different conditions—perhaps longer series of trials, more potent reinforcers, or less figural response classes—we would have found it. But if this kind of learning or conditioning without awareness is to have the social generality commonly imputed to it (as by Dollard and Miller, 1950, for example), it seems likely that we would have found it in some of these experiments" (1962, p. 126). The view is used as a basis for an attack on operant conditioning for its failure to account for performance differences ascribed by Dulany to the action of cognitive mediating mechanisms.

Spielberger (1965) and Spielberger and DeNike (1966) put the current debate on a broader basis by spelling out the opposing assumptions. In brief form, the cognitive position maintains that "cognitive processes such as thoughts, ideas, and hypotheses exist

... (and that) although cognitive processes are not directly observable, they may be inferred, albeit imperfectly, from the subject's verbal responses to interview questions" (Spielberger, 1965). Cognitive interpretations further propose that affective and conative states are influenced by various variables and, in turn, contribute to S's hypothesis-testing behavior. When a response is followed by reinforcement, the hypothesis is confirmed and the response class is strengthened, provided that S has had a tentative hypothesis about this class and desires the offered reinforcement. The various internal states are related to experimentally controlled manipulations, to S's verbal reports, and to predicted performance outcomes.

This position utilizes S's verbal reports as indices of mediating states and requires that performance data be analyzed as a function of such indices as if they were empirical, independent variables. What is learned in verbal conditioning is thus held to be the correct response-reinforcement contingency, and no learning occurs unless a correct or correlated hypothesis is present (Spielberger, 1962). As a consequence of this orientation, a major effort has been made to lengthen and refine the postexperimental questionnaire so that a larger sample of scorable verbal responses could be obtained. These samples are taken as a more complete index of the "awareness" construct. The emphasis on mediating cognitive states by necessity shifts the focus of study to the relationship between post-experimental verbal reports and performance. The experimental treatment variables serve mainly as auxiliary operations aimed at modifying the mediating states, and cognition is used, in turn, as an independent variable (e.g., DeNike and Spielberger, 1963).

The behavioristic position of writers

in verbal conditioning is characterized by the general assumption that the determinants of performance can be isolated experimentally without recourse to complex theoretical constructs. A Skinnerian view of self-reports in verbal conditioning studies regards them as verbal behaviors in their own right and subject to all the same variables as other behaviors. They differ from the conditioning response only in the discriminative (instructional) and historical stimuli controlling their emission. Self-reports cannot be given special status as indices of *other* events, any more than acquisition responses or any other observed behavior. Therefore, their validity is not questioned. These reports can only be treated as a dependent variable related to operations. Or if, indeed, they would be directly manipulated *separately* from performance, they could be viewed like other responses with cue properties, as independent variables affecting subsequent behavior.

It was recognized in early studies that *S*s in verbal conditioning engage in problem-solving activity. Investigators did not take the now obvious step of controlling or eliminating such behavior by habituation or other modifications in procedure. Instead, they looked for ways in which to account for this experimentally uncontrolled behavior. In the behavioristic approach an intermediate process is not postulated as a *necessary* condition for learning, nor is an invariant relationship between performance and verbalizations assumed to hold for wide ranges of parameters of the task, experimental setting, subject population, etc. In this regard it is similar to the approach to problem-solving by Kendler and Kendler (1962), who propose a two-part model of horizontal (chaining) and vertical (parallel, concurrent) behaviors which may or may not be interrelated under specified

conditions. If *S*'s reports are used at all, they are generally treated as dependent variables, subject to control by similar factors which affect *S*'s performance on the conditioning task. Thus the verbal reports are treated functionally, i.e., as responses to *E*'s questions, following an experimental session. This is to distinguish them from possible antecedent verbal responses which *may* affect performance but have been isolated only under special conditions (e.g., Verplanck, 1962; Marston and Kanfer, 1963; Kanfer and Marston, 1963) when these processes were themselves under investigation.

On the basis of his extensive review of empirical findings, Krasner (1962) concluded that

> (a) Conflicting reports on the relationship between reported awareness and conditioning reflect conceptual confusion with regard to the role of reported awareness in performance. (b) *S*s' awareness of the reinforcing contingency will affect performance in verbal conditioning experiments when awareness is made an integral part of *S*s' task. (c) The specific effect that awareness will have on performance depends on subject-determined variables, e.g., *S*s' emotional attitude toward *E* (1962, p. 80).

Verplanck (1962) suggests specific terms for the verbal response classes in the total behavior chain. The *notants* describe verbal responses whose referents are environmental relationships. These, in turn, are often the S^Ds for *monents*, self-administered instructions which may serve as S^Ds for further action. This model is similar to one proposed by several writers for perceptual processes (e.g., Kanfer, 1956; Wyckoff, 1952), in which a simple discrimination response, an observing response, is made and often is followed by an instrumental response. While the simple discrimination can be put under close control of environmental stimuli, the latter response is a function of instructions, intraverbal associations, competing response variables, and variables relating to the task and the condition under which it is performed. The status of these responses is not that of intervening variables, as in the cognitive view, but of definitional constructs with provision for direct observations under specified experimental conditions. As Verplanck said, ". . . these verbal behaviors are not theoretically inferred, or indirectly manipulated, but rather are subject to direct experimental investigation" (1962, p. 157).

The mediational construct most frequently proposed in verbal conditioning has been "awareness." Several authors have used this term with the specific and definitional referent as the verbalization of a response-reinforcement contingency on a postexperimental inquiry. In retrospect, this practice may have been unfortunate for it has not avoided the difficulty of carrying along its surplus meaning. The term has been used by investigators to describe *S*'s verbal behavior about the experiment, and it has been suggested that these statements by *S*s be considered separate from (though related to) performance (Krasner, 1965; Kanfer and McBrearty, 1961; Kanfer and Marston, 1961; Krasner, Weiss, and Ullmann, 1961, and others).

The methodological issue of awareness

Since the cognitive view postulates a mediating process of awareness, use of operations for testing this theoretical assertion becomes an intrinsic feature of the theoretical issue. The cognitive view has shifted interest from the verification of relationships between manipulated conditions and performance to one in which *S*'s reports take

a central position. In fact, as Spielberger and DeNike (1966) suggest, "the most significant contribution of verbal conditioning research has been the stimulation of interest in verbal report procedures and in concepts such as awareness. . ."

Almost all investigators in the area have asked *S*s questions about their performance, following or during the experiment. The protagonists of a cognitive view have used the replies as a basis for splitting experimental groups for further statistical analyses using the questionnaire data as an independent variable. The behavioristic group has treated these data as a dependent variable and related them to different group treatments or correlated them with performance. The problems associated with postexperimental inquiries as operations for investigating "awareness" have been acknowledged by both groups (Greenspoon, 1963; Krasner, 1962, 1965; DeNike, 1964; Matarazzo, Saslow, and Pareis, 1960; Kanfer, 1965, and others).

Cognitive theorizing also has required the continuous improvement and revision of questionnaires, since there is always the possibility that "awareness" was not found in *S*s who have it but who were not questioned sufficiently.

Some Comments on the Cognitive Position

The main contributions of the cognitive view have been to stress the central role of awareness in verbal conditioning, to propose the use of verbal reports as the measuring instruments of awareness, and to offer theoretical models aimed at remedying the insufficiencies of S-R approaches with respect to mediational constructs. This section attempts to show that some of the problems remain unsolved because of the questionable status of verbal reports and the complexity of cognitive constructional frameworks.

The verbal report

When S's verbal or written reports are treated as indices or correlates of hypothesized internal processes, the full range of problems associated with introspectionism again beclouds the issue. There is much merit in gaining information from Ss about their attitudes and descriptions of the experimental procedures. This information can provide a rich field for hypotheses to be tested in subsequent studies and yields many insights useful for the design of fresh experiments. The major difficulty lies in the temptation to handle these verbal reports as substitutes for the events which they describe. It is for these reasons that most researchers in other areas of verbal learning have avoided their use.

Duncan (1959) considers that it would be more fruitful to determine functional relationships between environmental or task variables on the one hand, and performance or products on the other, than to continue research attacks on the *processes* of problem solving. Kendler and Kendler (1962) note that "it would be unwise, and strategically short-sighted, to *identify* mediational events with introspective reports or language behavior, or other observable events" (p. 7). The Kendlers report their observation of frequently obtained spontaneous verbalizations of correct solutions with simultaneous incorrect choices in discrimination experiments with children. They state that "these observations and their interpretations of non-interacting parallel processes point to the complex interrelationship existing between verbal behavior on the one hand and problem solving on the other" (p. 9). In an

analysis of problem-solving behavior, Marx (1958) describes two risks in the use of self-reports as reflections of ongoing thinking processes. First, social pressures and S's eagerness to report may distort his statements. Second, the subject may not be sufficiently skilled to select important and relevant parts of the reported process. Marx concludes that response measures not primarily dependent on verbal self-reports offer a more promising avenue to effective representation of thinking. Perhaps the most significant note of caution about use of verbal reports as reflections about S's state of awareness rather than as functional responses comes from the findings of verbal conditioning researchers themselves. That these reports cannot be treated solely on the basis of verbal content has been shown by results which demonstrate their great susceptibility to many variables associated with the social setting of the experiment, the number and type of questions asked, and the experimental task.

In a thoughtful and detailed analysis of this problem, Spielberger and DeNike (1966) summarize the main criticism by noncognitive researchers of the use of verbal reports under four headings:

1. the procedure suggests awareness;
2. awareness follows learning;
3. awareness facilitates later learning during acquisition; and
4. awareness may be a behavior concurrently strengthened during acquisition.

Partial remedies are proposed by the authors and have been utilized in studies coming from their laboratories. The first criticism can be attenuated by careful phrasing of questions or use of written questionnaire responses, although Spielberger and DeNike note that a standardized written procedure may not be sufficiently complete or clear to elicit full reports. We would be inclined to question whether or not a change in the written mode of response eliminates the influence of the experimental setting on the content of these replies, even though the personal interaction with E is reduced.

In attempting to overcome the second criticism, concerned with the temporal relationship between conditioning and the verbal report, DeNike (1964) and Spielberger, Bernstein, and Ratliff (1966) asked Ss to write their thoughts about the experiment after each block of 25 trials *during* conditioning. This procedure does bring the report temporally closer to the performance. Nevertheless, the report still deals with the *preceding* trial blocks. This procedure would also be expected to influence performance on subsequent blocks, because the request of S to evaluate his behavior should enhance the problem-solving aspect of the task. The possible contamination of the verbal report by the preceding learning experience may pose an unsolvable dilemma. This apparent impasse is not only based on epistemological grounds, as Spielberger (1965) suggests, but also on the practical problem of defining independently an antecedent condition, subsequent to the occurrence of the response. The cognitivists' rebuttal of these criticisms is tantamount to arguing independence for two operationally interdependent responses. The last two criticisms noted by Spielberger and DeNike (1966) appear to be based on the differences in theoretical orientations and represent the core of the disagreement.

The criticism of the use of the verbal report should not be construed to deny that relationships can be established between specific experimental operations (such as giving information about the task or about the response-reinforce-

ment contingency in instructions) and performance. There is good evidence that such information does, in fact, facilitate learning. The crux of the behavioristic criticism of the cognitive position, however, lies in the fact that such information cannot be inferred to mediate learning when it is obtained in postlearning reports.

Another problem encountered in the use of verbal reports lies in the fact that it demands a special verbal repertoire. Accurate discriminations of complex problems often occur in the absence of S's ability to verbalize the characteristics of the two discriminated classes. On the response side, differences in Ss' histories, training in stimulus predifferentiation, and other variables affect the emission of the verbal report. In verbal conditioning, the particular stimulus dimensions selected for discrimination may affect not only S's performance, but also his verbalizations (Martin and Dean, 1965). While personal pronouns are easily labeled, such other discriminated classes as affective responses, (Salzinger, 1958, 1960), self-references (Adams and Hoffman, 1960), or classes of therapist operations (Kanfer and Pomeranz, 1965) may not be easily describable by Ss who are unfamiliar with the appropriate terms used by E in forming these classes. Although comparisons have been made among verbal conditioning studies with different tasks, the kind of discrimination required of S could be a critical variable for verbal statements about the response-reinforcement contingencies (awareness). Salzinger (1965) has criticized the cognitive position on the basis that the studies from which it draws support have been carried out mainly in modifications of the Taffel procedure, which restricts the number of members in the response class to one or two pronouns. Since reports of the response-reinforcement contingency are related to the number of response class members, the Taffel procedure would be most likely to produce correct verbal reports and would lend itself best to findings of correlations between verbal reports and learning.

Although it is not uncommon in social and clinical psychology to use *S*'s response to a questionnaire or test as a basis for assigning *S*s to different treatment groups, the practice of separating *S*s on the basis of postexperimental questionnaires has many drawbacks which it shares with other experiments growing out of cognitive theories. The design of such studies produces unequal *N*s in the split groups and the temptation to compare data curves from groups ranging from an *N* of one up to 29 (e.g., Dulany, 1962). In addition, the *post hoc* nature of the design has often led investigators to make analyses and comparisons arising from the initial findings. While such data may aid the researcher to plan his further strategy, their *post hoc* origin demands caution in interpretation.[3]

[3] The experimenter obtains two task-relevant responses from *S*, a conditioning score and a verbal report. Unlike other situations in which postperformance tests (e.g., of personality) are given, there is little reason to assume that the verbal report represents a more durable or prior characteristic than the performance score. The choice of the "independent" variable for an analysis of variance design is made mainly on the basis of cognitive theory and "common sense." An equally admissible procedure, based on the "common sense" rule of taking chronologically earlier observations as the "causal" factor, would split *S*s by learning scores and examine differences in verbal report scores. The former choice has the implication of accepting *S*'s report content about the temporal sequence of which came first, *S*'s "awareness" or his performance. Although analyses of variance on aware vs. unaware *S*s have been reported in many investigations (including a study by this writer), we now view correlational techniques as more appropriate.

When groups must be divided on the basis of postexperimental questionnaires to test uncontrolled or uncontrollable variance, it is apparent that the experimental manipulations were not sufficiently defined nor powerful enough to affect the behavior of all *S*s without recourse to supplementary response inferred variables. Such a failure to bring about consistency in emission of verbal reports within treatment groups justifies further refinement of the variables or the procedure. But the situation is not remedied by *post hoc* group splitting. It should be noted that the practice of splitting groups on the basis of the verbal reports has been common among adherents of both theoretical persuasions, although the cognitive group has tended to treat these data as independent variables, while others have generally used them for inferences of correlations or have reported them separately.

The problem of acceptance of verbal reports as awareness indices is illustrated in Dulany's categorization of verbal reports for measuring behavioral intentions (BI). One response category (Dulany, 1962, p. 114) classifies an *S* who reports intentions to produce some response class that is negatively correlated with the correct response class. If one performs experimental manipulations producing such a report, e.g., by asking *S* not to cooperate with *E*, or by a hostile set, it would logically follow that such an *S* might respond with falsehoods to the questionnaire. If he does so, such a stated intention should also affect his response to the questionnaire (e.g., by denying knowledge of the response-reinforcement contingency or misrepresenting his attitudes), as well as his performance on the conditioning task.

The case of the "lying subject" raises the problem of categorizing the verbal report by its content when suppressive factors may be operating. One could argue that other conditions not as extreme as lying, such as the induction of a hostile set or personality variables associated with hostility, would influence the report in a predetermined nonveridical or *E*-antagonistic direction. It is interesting to note that Krasner, Weiss, and Ullmann (1961) found that college *S*s who had undergone hostility induction by a preexperimental negative interaction with the examiner reported fewer awareness responses than those *S*s who had not been made hostile. Further, *S*s who did not report awareness were significantly more hostile on two different test measures of hostility than *S*s who did report awareness.

The criticisms concerning the status of verbal reports should not be interpreted to suggest that they have no heuristic value in generating new research hypotheses. However, when a theoretical position is strongly anchored in these reports and their use becomes a base for rejecting other research strategies, it is most critical to avoid building a theoretical formulation mainly on response dimensions which have equivocal status.

The mediational constructs

The use of mediational or multiple-stage accounts of verbal behavior is not inconsistent with S-R theory. In association learning, problem solving, thinking, and in concept formation, mediators of some kind have been suggested by Hull, Osgood, Kendler, Verplanck, Staats, and others. It is therefore more useful for expository purposes than it is accurate to contrast the cognitive and S-R positions with regard to presence or absence of mediators. In general, the behavioristic group, once seduced to use the term "aware-

ness," has attempted to stay close to operational definitions, mainly by content of a verbal report. Cognitive writers have used the same term to describe a construct at a much higher level of abstraction, with theoretical as well as empirical implications. In verbal conditioning the extremes of the continuum are encountered, since the phenomenon has been often regarded either as "pure" operant conditioning or hypothesis-learning. The major distinction therefore lies in the type of assumptions and the complexity of meaning assigned to the awareness construct.

Even within the S-R camp, differences in complexity of the mediational chain appear. Gough and Jenkins (in Marx, 1958) succinctly summarize the difference between mediation hypotheses like that of Osgood (1953) and Skinner's view. The covert responses of Skinner are not some fractional component of a total response, nor are they implicit associates evoked by verbal stimuli. "Covert behavior is, according to Skinner, overt behavior which has receded, and this process itself is open to description. Covert behavior, its antecedents, and its controlling conditions are describable in exactly the same terms as overt behavior" (Gough and Jenkins, 1963, p. 172). This position is not without problems. It is parsimonious in assuming the same general relationships between variables for accessible and inaccessible behaviors. But it does raise the methodological problem of "making the private public." Skinner (1953) has discussed this problem in detail and appears to consider it mainly a technological one.

The mediators proposed by Dulany and Spielberger for verbal conditioning are complex constructs related to behavior only through a theoretical framework. This position calls as heavily on rules of theory construction as it does on empirical findings. An examination of Dulany's theory of propositional control illustrates some of the grounds on which complex mediational models have been rejected as underlying research strategies by the behavioristically inclined investigators. The strategy of constructing a complex nomological net to establish construct validity for its components is not entirely without hazards. Bechtoldt (1959) has pointed out that a response-defined variable approach encounters difficulties because a given behavior can arise from many different combinations of experimental conditions. Therefore, any one of numerous sets of explanatory constructs can be postulated and be "correct" in terms of agreement between prediction and observation. Use of the construct validity approach also presents the danger of forcing complex meanings into simple phenomena, more parsimoniously handled by description of empirical relationships.

Another difficulty in use of a nomological net is the burden of the theoretician to demonstrate that *each* of the constructs in the net is, in fact, necessary to account for the data and that *each* given concept enters into the specified relationships (Bechtoldt, 1959). Dulany argues that the validity of the verbal report can be established by its acceptance as an hypothesis within the network and verification of predicted outcomes. Tests of report validity have not yet been made separately from simultaneous tests of other hypotheses, into which enter all the other constructs in the net. The validity of the verbal report can, of course, never be established in the sense of its "truth" but only in terms of the pragmatic utility of its acceptance.

If the main focus of the cognitive researchers is on the role of awareness in learning, it is surprising that the studies in support of the mediational view have all used the same general procedures, even to the point of several replications of previously reported research. From a theoretical view, it would seem important to ascertain the independence of the theoretical formulations from the methods of verbal conditioning. Campbell and Fiske (1959) note the importance of establishing both convergent and discriminant validation for gaining confidence in the adequacy of a set of operations as a construct-related measure. It is in this regard, that experiments testing Dulany's network in other complex verbal learning tasks might provide a bridge between verbal conditioning and problem-solving or concept-formation studies. Spielberger and De-Nike's (1966) schema of proposed mediating cognitive states similarly appear to have sufficient generality for their application in other situations.

Dulany's proposed network raises the practical question how to measure BH, RH, and BI independently. It is difficult to conceive of an S who can state that a reinforcing stimulus has some selective function or informative value about the preceding response (RH) without some statement of the characteristics of that response (BH). It would also seem that a reported intention (BI) to produce the response class that E designated as correct would not be independent of S's report that he does or does not know the correct response class (BH).

Some Comments on the Non-Cognitive Position

Much of the controversy in the verbal conditioning literature has resulted from the limitations of the operant conditioning paradigm to account for variability among Ss due to factors not under E's control. While such issues as the role in learning of S's covert verbalizations can be temporarily postponed, the problems cannot be resolved by ignoring them. At this time the behavioristic approach cannot offer adequate experimental support for a description of human self-regulatory processes, their development, or their relationship to thinking and problem-solving. The statement that response learning and learning of rules or other verbal behaviors occur concurrently and may be parallel or interdependent is a tentative formulation until the conditions are worked out which describe these relationships and provide a basis for higher-order generalization.

The early experiments in verbal conditioning had hoped to avoid the very problem of inference from verbal reports by introduction of the operant conditioning paradigm. And the approach has been, and can continue to be, of value in examining empirical relationships without attempting to resolve the process-issue. This approach has faith in the feasibility of eventually attacking these "processes" directly as behavioral events which can be observed, at least under special laboratory conditions, and related to other variables. Progress in this direction has been made in several research areas, growing out of the Skinnerian system. For instance, the relationship of verbal and nonverbal behavior has been studied by Lovaas (1961; 1964), who found evidence for increase in aggressive nonverbal behavior following reinforcement of aggressive verbal behavior. Lovaas also demonstrated a change in food selection as a result of conditioning of food-denoting verbal responses. Verbal control over a motor response (squeezing a dynamometer) has also been reported by Krasner, Knowles, and Ullmann (1965) by means of conditioning attitudes toward medical research. This inductive route

may be more tedious because of the requirement for accumulation of a large body of data before generalizations can be formed. Preference for this strategy is based on the conviction that premature theorizing may be more hazardous than acceptance of several temporary and limited descriptive hypotheses.

The operant-conditioning model has fallen short of expectations because too much has been expected too soon. In addition to the puzzling problem of handling covert links in a complex chain of verbal responses, the introduction of hypotheses from the clinical and social areas has yielded a mixture of findings with pragmatic clinical value in which the substantive contributions to a Skinnerian framework tend to be overlooked. For example, such variables as reinforcement schedules (Simkins, 1962; McNair, 1957; Webb, Bernard, and Nesmith, 1963; Kanfer, 1954, 1958), or delay of reinforcement (Lublin, 1965; Hare, 1965), and others of traditional interest in learning have not been separated from studies in which personality or interactional variables are examined.

In attacking the behavioristic approach to verbal conditioning, Spielberger (1965) quotes Chomsky's review to bolster the argument that "lack of interest in internal processes is strikingly evident in the proportion of verbal conditioning experiments in which the awareness issue is simply ignored, and in the operations by which awareness is evaluated in most of the remaining studies." The arguments by Spielberger and his colleagues are based heavily on the assumption that verbal conditioning in the hands of Skinnerians presumes an "empty box" organism. This oversimplification can easily be remedied by reference to Skinner's own view that the individual does take an active role with regard to the variables affecting him. Specifically referring to such behaviors which have often been called "self-determination" Skinner writes,

> any comprehensive account of human behavior must, of course, embrace the facts referred to in statements of this sort. But we can achieve this without abandoning our program. When a man controls himself, chooses a course of action, thinks out the solution to a problem, or strives toward an increase of self-knowledge, he is behaving. He controls himself precisely as he would control the behavior of anyone else— through the manipulation of variables of which behavior is a function. His behavior in so doing is a proper object of analysis and eventually it must be accounted for with variables lying out-side the individual himself (1953, pp. 228–229).

Skinner devotes an entire section of *Science and Human Behavior* to an analysis of the manner in which "the individual acts to alter the variables of which other parts of his behavior are functions."

Skinner's solution has its difficulties. The philosophical weaknesses of be-haviorism *and* phenomenology are well illustrated in a recent Rice University Symposium (Wann, 1964). The crux of the problem is presented perhaps most clearly by Malcolm who notes that

> the notion of verification does not apply to a wide range of first person psy-chological reports and utterances. An-other way to put the point is to say that those reports and utterances are *not based on observations*. The error of introspectionism is to suppose that they are based on observations of the inner, mental events. The error of behaviorism is to suppose that they are based on observations of outward events or physical events inside the speaker's skin. These two philosophies of psychology share a false assumption,

namely, that a first person psychological statement is a report of something the speaker has, or thinks he has, observed (p. 151).

It seems proper to criticize both the behavioristic and phenomenological positions for their failure to have re-solved the puzzle on how to deal with "subjective" verbal content. However, it is not proper to contrast behavioristic and cognitive approaches to verbal conditioning on the basis that the former denies that complex processes may intervene between stimulus input and response, while the latter offers an adequate account of these processes.

The area of verbal conditioning has introduced Skinner's functional analysis to verbal learning, but it has not con-tributed significantly to the construc-tion of a good model for analysis of verbal content, verbal associations, and the semantic aspects of language. The Skinnerian schema (1957) for classifying verbal operants into tacts and mands and his analysis of the autoclitic and of the variables of self-control in verbal behavior has remained a guiding framework, but it has not stimulated the massive research efforts which would demonstrate its contribu-tion to the traditional areas of verbal learning. While the interest of the Skinnerian approach is avowedly in "natural" verbal interactions and not in understanding either the serial or paired-associates learning to nonsense syllables or specific language units, it would be very comforting to see both the traditional associationistic and the Skinnerian view attacking similar problems in human learning.

Staats (1961) has made an interesting attempt to integrate operant condi-tioning into a Hullian model for the development of meaning and intraver-bal associations. Staats appears to accept operant conditioning as a method by which response emission can be modified, but classical conditioning is involved in the learning of (implicit) meaning responses, and reinforcement of a given response affects both the meaning response (rm) as well as the verbal response itself. It is the strengthening of the common anticipatory meaning response in the habit-family that mediates strengthening of the responses in the class defined by E. This view suggests that effectiveness of verbal conditioning procedures is related to S's particular verbal habit-families and to variables associated with meaning components of a given word class. Lack of congruence between E's and S's response classes could occur when reinforcement of a subset in a class strengthens all the meaning components so that only the subset responses are given.

This view of "what is reinforced" in verbal conditioning differs from Salzinger's (1959) suggestion that verbal response classes can be defined on a functional basis, i.e., by the variables controlling the class members, and that generalization accounts for strengthening of other response class members which share some property with the reinforced response. Among some of the dimensions for categorizing verbal responses are the communalities of effects on the environment, controlling stimuli, response topographies, etc.

The case for concurrent learning

The behaviorally oriented group has taken the position that verbal reports and task responses are functions of the experimental variables and that concurrent interdependent learning occurs as a consequence of such factors as the characteristics of the experimenter, the subject, the task, and of the interaction of these three (Krasner, 1965).

This position has been supported by repeated findings that different experimental treatments yield differences in the extent of correlation between these two sets of responses. The more frequently encountered reports illustrate a portion of this thesis, namely that experimental treatments affect verbal reports and that they seem to do so with some consistency in the direction of more frequent awareness reports with favorable Es, simple discriminations, nonemotional task variables, increased relevant task information, and with Ss who were generally disposed to please E.

Tatz (1960), Krasner and Ullmann (1963), Simkins (1963), Kanfer and Marston (1961), and others found increased awareness reports with more task information. Binder and Salop (1961) found more awares among Ss who were given "good" as a reinforcing stimulus than in Ss who received a mild shock. Gerstein (1961) found increasing reports of awareness as a function of systematic variation of the schedule of reinforcement. Farber (1963) reported fewer aware Ss in a group with a failure experience (and a "nasty" E) than in a neutral control group. The effect of stimulus characteristics on awareness reports has been demonstrated by Martin and Dean (1965), Kanfer and McBrearty (1961), Marston, Kanfer, and McBrearty (1962), and others.

Differences in verbal reports also appear related to S characteristics. For example, Buss, Gerjuoy, and Zusman (1958) found more awareness reports on the same task in college students than in psychiatric patients. Epstein (1964) found an interaction between need for approval and reinforcement conditions upon level of awareness in children.

Any comparison of studies must take into account the findings of Rosenthal (1963) in other settings and of Rosenthal, Persinger, Vikan-Kline and Fode (1963) in verbal conditioning. These authors found that *E*s who expected high rates of awareness obtained it, compared to *E*s with low-awareness expectancies. If such bias is operating in the published studies, their discrepant findings would be less puzzling. For example, Spielberger and Levin (1962) found no difference in awareness as a function of relevant instructions, nor was a difference in frequency of awareness reports found as a function of high or low need for approval scores (Spielberger, Berger, and Howard, 1963). In addition to possible subtle variables which may predetermine outcome, studies also vary in treatment procedures and methods for eliciting verbal reports. Therefore, these discrepancies cannot be attributed to any single factor. Even studies by the cognitive group (Spielberger, 1965) demonstrate, however, that verbal reports can be affected by experimental conditions. Thus, the weight of this evidence suggests strongly that reports rated as "awareness" are not solely determined by internal processes, and can be treated as any other dependent variable.

A ubiquitous correspondence between learning and reports of awareness has not been universally reported, even by investigators who thoroughly probed for awareness. Levin (1961) used psychiatric patients with a Taffel procedure and gave an extensive interview to obtain reports of awareness. Levin demonstrated that an extended interview resulted in increased numbers of scorable awareness responses. Further, Levin stated that the evidence for conditioning without awareness was found to have been largely accounted for by *S*s whose awareness has been demonstrated only by the extended procedure. Nevertheless, "there was also limited evidence for conditioning

without awareness in that a group of *S*s who were unaware of the reinforcer, in addition to being unaware of a correct contingency, showed as much conditioning as *S*s who were aware of a correct contingency" (1961, p. 74). Bryan and Lichtenstein (1966) studied the effects of attitudes of *E*s and *S*s toward one another in a Taffel task. Differences were found related to *S*'s stated desire for the reinforcement, and a significant interaction with trials suggested that hostile *E*s inhibited conditioning. Following Spielberger's interviewing procedure (1962), awareness reports were obtained. It was found that awareness was not related to *E* attitudes, contrary to Farber's findings (1963). Aware and unaware *S*s were found to condition equally well.

Mandler and Kaplan (1956) used a Greenspoon procedure and thirty postexperimental questions. They found that subjective evaluations of the reinforcing stimulus significantly affected learning, while both the positive and negative groups had equal awareness ratings. The authors state that "since there are no differences in the awareness of the subjects in the two groups, this effect cannot be simply ascribed to some cognitive response to the contingency in one group which is absent in the other. It is also difficult to ascribe the difference between the two groups to some simple mediating judgments" (1956, p. 582). Simkins (1963) used a Taffel procedure to study the effects of instructions and types of reinforcers on verbal reports and conditioning. He found differences in conditioning related to the degree of information given in the instructions. In experimental groups which received only partial information, *S*s who received points conditioned better than *S*s who received "good" even though there were no differences in reported awareness levels.

Sidowsky and Naumoff (1964) compared *S*s who were either paced by a signal light flash or who said words at their own rate. The amount of information about the task by instructions was also varied. In this procedure with college students it was found that increased information resulted in improved learning. However, while experimental conditions affected the frequency of stating the correct response-reinforcement contingency, *S*s were found who learned but who did not state a word-association hypothesis.

These examples of reported research findings illustrate the complexity of the interactions between experimental variables on the one hand and correlations between verbal reports and task learning on the other. A few studies have reported specific correlations between verbal reports and learning scores. Kanfer and McBrearty (1961) used a Taffel procedure with stimulus pairs consisting of a neutral word, and either a mildly hostile or an intensely hostile word. When more easily discriminable word pairs (intensely hostile vs. neutral) were presented, significantly greater verbalization of the response-reinforcement contingency was obtained. Further, point-biserial *r*'s were run between awareness ratings and learning scores. While an *r* of 0.07 showed no relationship in the mildly hostile groups, an *r* of 0.32 revealed a significant correlation between awareness scores and learning scores, but only for *S*s presented with the highly distinctive stimulus pairs.

Kanfer and Marston (1961) used a Taffel procedure in a $2 \times 2 \times 2$ factorial design in which ambiguity was varied with regard to (a) information about the task, (b) nature of the reinforcing stimulus, and (c) ease of discriminability of the stimuli. To differentiate between "pure" operant conditioning and discrimination

learning, a transfer task was then administered requiring the same discrimination but with a different set of stimuli. Seven postexperimental questions were given to obtain *S*'s verbal report. If similarity or identity of processes which mediate discrimination and verbal awareness are assumed, a high correlation between transfer scores and awareness ratings would be expected. A product moment *r* of 0.32 was obtained. On the original learning list, a significant correlation of 0.52 was obtained between *S*'s linear coefficients and their awareness ratings. However, these correlations differed for each of the groups, and ranged from 0.34 for groups with minimal information about the task to 0.63 for groups with the greatest stimulus discriminability. The authors suggested that these data demonstrate that learning and verbal reports can be treated as separate dependent responses which may or may not covary in any one situation.

When treating awareness responses as concurrent behavior, the experimental questions posed concern the degree of relationship with experimental conditions, personality variables, or other factors expected of affecting the learning-awareness relationship. This contrasts with the view which assumes that verbalization of correct response-reinforcement contingencies *necessarily* act as mediating responses (1961, p. 473).

An interesting example of the fact that correct response-reinforcement contingencies may be offered by an *S* on the basis of his guesses regarding what the experiment *might* be about is given by Marston, Kanfer, and McBrearty (1962). In a verbal conditioning study nonsense syllables of equal or unequal association values were paired in different groups. *S*s were reinforced for selection of the syllable with the lower association value of a pair. In a control group, syllables with equal association values were paired and the group was given random reinforcement in an impossible discrimination. In the postexperimental inquiry, 53 percent of the *S*s in this control group verbalized awareness of the dimension which had, in fact, been correct for the experimental groups, but not for their own. This group, of course, did not show any learning.

In a direct test of the mediational hypothesis, Dixon and Oakes (1965) reasoned that hypothesis formulation would require time and should be facilitated by rehearsal between trials. The cognitive position would predict reduced conditioning in a group which had a filled inter-trial interval, but the same relationship between learning scores and awareness scores would be expected in these groups and the control group. The behavioristic position would predict no effect on the results with respect to conditioning but would predict a reduction in the positive relationship usually found between verbal reports and conditioning scores in the interference group. The results indicated that both groups conditioned significantly. However, while a significant correlation between conditioning and statement of the reinforcement hypothesis (after Dulany's RH) of 0.66 was found in the group which had a ten-second uncontrolled intertrial interval, the interference group, which named colors during the interval, showed a nonsignificant correlation (0.06) between learning scores and awareness reports.

Concluding Remarks

Our review of verbal conditioning is an attempt to show the development of a research area which had as its intent the demonstration of the utility of a functional-behavioral analysis for verbal interactions. The implications of the effectiveness of social reinforcement in modifying verbal responses were quickly grasped by the clinical researcher. Not inconsistent with the spirit of other work growing out of Skinner's system, the verbal conditioning paradigm was extensively used in the area of engineering verbal behavior, especially for attack on clinical problems. This significant contribution can be measured only by its heuristic value.

For purposes of theorizing, even at the level of limited inductive generalizations, the research findings have been difficult to evaluate. Even though only two basic procedures have been used, studies are not often comparable because of the differences in several variables, in addition to the specific treatment variable under experimental investigation. Among these are:

1. population differences: inclusion of psychiatric patients, college students, children or "normal" volunteer *S*s;
2. the stimulus and response content, method of presentation, timing, and other parameters of the task;
3. the financial or other type of compensation for *S*s and the method of recruitment and selection;
4. the instructions;
5. the criteria for learning;
6. the degree of control over the reinforcing stimulus; and
7. the presence, manner and use of postperformance inquiries.

Contrasting findings such as the ones cited here appear to be sufficient reason to view the current research in verbal conditioning as pretheoretical. The data do warrant the conclusion that the paradigm covers a complex human activity, related to the areas traditionally subsumed under problem-solving rather than conditioning. However, it is also clear that a "conditioning" or S-R approach, wiser and older by a half a century than Watson's view (with which it is often compared) may now be able to attack these complex behaviors more effectively. Serving as a point of departure, the introduction of a functional Skinnerian approach has already had its impact not only in clinical research but also in the study of self-regulatory behavior, which is undoubtedly involved in verbal conditioning.

The problem of dealing with personal, covert, or self-observed experiences has slipped into the area by way of the "awareness issue." That this issue has not yielded to solution by decrees of exclusion, or dualism, or operational definitions is a well-known and often deplored fact. However, it would be burdening the limited verbal conditioning procedure too much to make it the arena for testing these philosophical issues. The same issues are encountered in much of human psychology. As Feigl (1959) has suggested, the very definition of psychology's subject matter is painfully uncertain until there is some resolution of the "nothing but" vs. the "something more" view of behavior. The choice of research strategy is partly determined by the investigator's interest and his estimate of the ultimate utility of his approach. In verbal conditioning the wider contributions so far seem to have come from the behavioristic camp, if the disclosure of new research areas is taken as a criterion.

Neither the cognitive nor the S-R views have answered the question of "what is learned" or "how is it learned," but these questions also underlie a large proportion of the research in contemporary American psychology. What contribution has been made by verbal conditioning studies comes from isola-

tion of some relevant variables, not from any new theoretical formulations. It is probable that verbal conditioning will gradually be absorbed into the psychology of verbal behavior as a useful laboratory procedure. Greater interest in nonclinical variables might also lead to several modifications in procedure which would reduce *S*s' variability, the importance of prior experiences, and the problem-solving behavior of *S*s. These changes could make the paradigm more manageable for research on basic verbal learning principles. The contributions to the structure of interverbal associations has been limited, as has been the use for the study of language acquisition. Perhaps some progress toward a comprehensive behavior theory has been made, after all, when we note that the simple conditioning paradigm (dervied from the animal laboratory, at that) has been of service in testing the wide range of hypotheses and empirical relationships represented by the literature in this area.

References

Adams, H. E., and R. L. Frye, "Psychotherapeutic Techniques as Conditioned Reinforcers in a Structured Interview," *Psychological Reports*, **14** (1964), 163–166.

Adams, J. S., and B. Hoffman, "The Frequency of Self-Reference Statements as a Function of Generalized Reinforcement," *Journal of Abnormal and Social Psychology*, **60** (1960), 384–389.

Bandura, A., "Social Learning through Imitation," in M. R. Jones, ed., *Nebraska Symposium on Motivation*. Lincoln: University of Nebraska Press, 1962.

———, and Carol J. Kupers, "The Transmission of Patterns of Self-Reinforcement," *Journal of Abnormal and Social Psychology*, **69** (1964), 1–9.

Barik, H. C., and S. Fillenbaum, "Negative

Reinforcement of Two Grammatical Response Classes," *Canadian Journal of Psychology*, **15** (1961), 107–115.

Bechtoldt, H. P., "Construct Validity: A Critique," *American Psychology*, **14** (1959), 619–629.

Bergman, G., "Semantics," in *A History of Philosophical Systems*. New York: Philosophical Library, 1950.

Binder, A., D. McConnell, and N. A. Sjohelm, "Verbal Conditioning as a Function of Experimenter Characteristics," *Journal of Abnormal and Social Psychology*, **55** (1957), 309–314.

——, and Phyllis Salop, "Reinforcement and Personality Factors in Verbal Conditioning," *Journal of Psychology*, **52** (1961), 379–402.

Bryan, J. H., and E. Lichtenstein, "The Effects of Subject and Experimenter Attitudes in Verbal Conditioning," *Journal of Personal and Social Psychology*, **3** (1966), 182–189.

Buss, A. H., W. Braden, A. Orgel, and Edith H. Buss, "Acquisition and Extinction with Different Verbal Reinforcement Combinations," *Journal of Experimental Psychology*, **52**, (1956), 288–295.

——, and Ann Durkee, "Conditioning of Hostile Verbalizations in a Situation Resembling a Clinical Interview," *Journal of Consulting Psychology*, **22** (1958), 415–418.

——, Irma R. Gerjuoy, and J. Zusman, "Verbal Conditioning and Extinction with Verbal and Nonverbal Reinforcers," *Journal of Experimental Psychology*, **56** (1958), 139–145.

Campbell, D. T., and D. W. Fiske, "Convergent and Discriminant Validation by the Multitrait-Multimethod Matrix," *Psychological Bulletin*, **56** (1959), 81–105.

DeNike, L. D., "The Temporal Relationship between Awareness and Performance in Verbal Conditioning," *Journal of Experimental Psychology*, **68** (1964), 521–529.

——, and C. D. Spielberger, "Induced Mediating States in Verbal Conditioning," *Journal of Verbal Learning and Verbal Behavior*, **1** (1963), 339–345.

Dinoff, M., R. F. Horner, B. S. Kurpiewski, and E. O. Timmons, "Conditioning Verbal Behavior of Schizophrenics in a Group Therapy-Like Situation," *Journal of Clinical Psychology*, **16** (1960), 367–370.

Dixon, P. W., and S. F. Oakes, "Effect of Intertrial Activity on the Relationship between Awareness and Verbal Operant Conditioning," *Journal of Experimental Psychology*, **69** (1965), 152–157.

Dollard, J., and N. E. Miller, *Personality and Psychotherapy: An Analysis in Terms of Learning, Thinking, and Culture*. New York: McGraw-Hill Book Company, Inc., 1950.

Dulany, D. E., Jr., "Hypotheses and Habits in Verbal 'Operant Conditioning,'" *Journal of Abnormal and Social Psychology*, **63** (1961), 251–263.

——, "The Place of Hypotheses and Intentions: An Analysis of Verbal Control in Verbal Conditioning," in C. W. Eriksen, ed., *Behavior and Awareness*. Durham, N. C.: Duke University Press, 1962.

Duncan, C. P., "Recent Research on Human Problem Solving," *Psychological Bulletin*, **56** (1959), 397–429.

Epstein, R., "Need for Approval and the Conditioning of Verbal Hostility in Asthmatic Children," *Journal of Abnormal and Social Psychology*, **69** (1964), 105–109.

Estes, Katherine W., "Some Effects of Reinforcement upon Verbal Behavior of Children." Unpublished doctoral dissertation, University of Minnesota, 1945.

Fahmy, Sumaya A., "Conditioning and Extinction of the Referential Verbal Response Class in a Situation Resembling a Clinical Diagnostic Interview." Unpublished doctoral dissertation, Indiana University, 1953.

Farber, I. E., "The Role of Motivation in Verbal Learning and Performance," *Psychological Bulletin*, **52** (1955), 311–327.

——, "The Things People Say to Themselves," *American Psychology*, **18** (1963), 185–197.

Feigl, H., "Philosophical Embarrassments of Psychology," *American Psychology*, **14** (1959), 115–128.

Fuller, P. R., "Operant Conditioning of a Vegetative Human Organism," *American Journal of Psychology*, **62** (1949), 587–590.

Gerstein, A. I., "The Effect of Reinforcement Schedules on Meaning Generalization and on Awareness of the Purpose of the Experiment," *Journal of Personality*, **29** (1961), 350–362.

Goldiamond, I., "Indicators of Perception: I. Subliminal Perception, Subception, Unconscious Perception: An Analysis in Terms of Psychophysical Indicator Methodology," *Psychological Bulletin*, **55** (1958), 373–411.

———, and W. F. Hawkins, "Vexierversuch: The Log Relationship between Word-Frequency and Recognition Obtained in the Absence of Stimulus Words," *Journal of Experimental Psychology*, **56** (1958), 457–463.

Golightly, Carole, and D. Byrne, "Attitude Statements as Positive and Negative Reinforcements," *Science*, **146** (1964), 798–799.

Gough, P. B., and J. J. Jenkins, "Verbal Learning and Psycholinguistics," in M. H. Marx, ed., *Theories in Contemporary Psychology*. New York: The Macmillan Company, 1963.

Graham, C. H., "Behavior, Perception and the Psychophysical Methods," *Psychological Review*, **57** (1950), 108–120.

Grant, D. A., "Classical and Operant Conditioning," in A. W. Melton, ed., *Categories of Human Learning*. New York: Academic Press, 1964.

Greenspoon, J., "The Effect of Verbal and Nonverbal Stimuli on the Frequency of Members of Two Verbal Response Classes." Unpublished doctoral dissertation, Indiana University, 1951.

———, "The Reinforcing Effect of Two Spoken Sounds on the Frequency of Two Responses," *American Journal of Psychology*, **68** (1955), 409–416.

———, "Verbal Conditioning and Clinical Psychology," in A. J. Bachrach, ed., *Experimental Foundations of Clinical Psychology*. New York: Basic Books, Inc., Publishers, 1962.

———, "Reply to Spielberger and DeNike: 'Operant Conditioning of Plural Nouns—A Failure to Replicate the Greenspoon Effect,' " *Psychological Reports*, **12** (1963), 29–30.

Gross, L. R., "Effects of Verbal and Nonverbal Reinforcement in the Rorschach," *Journal of Consulting Psychology*, **23** (1959), 66–68.

Hare, R. D., "Suppression of Verbal Behavior as a Function of Delay and Schedule of Severe Punishment," *Journal of Verbal Learning and Verbal Behavior*, **4** (1965), 216–221.

Hildum, D. C., and R. W. Brown, "Verbal Reinforcement and Interviewer Bias," *Journal of Abnormal and Social Psychology*, **53** (1956), 108–111.

Hovorka, E. J., "An Application of the Operant Conditioning Paradigm to Human Studies," *Proceedings of the Indiana Academy of Science*, **59** (1950), 288.

Isaacs, W., J. Thomas, and I. Goldiamond, "Application of Operant Conditioning to Reinstate Verbal Behavior in Psychotics," *Journal of Speech and Hearing Disorders*, **25** (1960), 8–12.

Johns, J. H., and H. C. Quay, "The Effect of Social Reward on Verbal Conditioning in Psychopathic and Neurotic Military Offenders," *Journal of Consulting Psychology*, **26** (1962), 217–220.

Johnson, H. M., "Did Fechner Measure Introspectional Sensation?" *Psychological Review*, **36** (1929), 257–284.

Kanfer, F. H., "The Effect of Partial Reinforcement on Acquisition and Extinction of a Class of Verbal Response," *Journal of Experimental Psychology*, **48** (1954), 424–432.

———, "Perception: Identification and Instrumental Activity," *Psychological Review*, **63** (1956), 317–329.

———, "Verbal Conditioning: Reinforcement Schedules and Experimenter Influence," *Psychological Reports*, **4** (1958), 443–452.

———, "Incentive Value of Generalized Reinforcers," *Psychological Reports*, 7 (1960), 531–538.

———, "Vicarious Human Reinforcement: A Glimpse into the Black Box," in L. Krasner and L. P. Ullmann, eds., *Research in Behavior Modification: New Developments and Their Clinical Implications.* New York: Holt, Rinehart and Winston, Inc., 1965.

———, and Shirley Karas, "Prior Experimenter-Subject Interaction and Verbal Conditioning," *Psychological Reports*, 5 (1959), 345–353.

———, and A. R. Marston, "Verbal Conditioning, Ambiguity and Psychotherapy," *Psychological Reports*, 9 (1961), 461–475.

———, and ———, "Control of Verbal Behavior by Multiple Schedules," *Psychological Reports*, 10 (1962), 703–710.

———, and ———, "The Effect of Task-Relevant Information on Verbal Conditioning," *Journal of Psychology*, 53 (1962), 29–36.

———, and ———, "Conditioning of Self-Reinforcing Responses: An Analogue to Self-Confidence Training," *Psychological Reports*, 13 (1963), 63–70.

———, and ———, "Determinants of Self-Reinforcement in Human Learning," *Journal of Experimental Psychology*, 66 (1963), 245–254.

———, and J. F. McBrearty, "Verbal Conditioning: Discrimination and Awareness," *Journal of Psychology*, 52 (1961), 115–124.

———, and ———, "Minimal Social Reinforcement and Interview Content," *Journal of Clinical Psychology*, 18 (1962), 210–215.

———, and D. Pomeranz, "Conditioning and Transfer of Therapist Operations," *Psychological Reports*, 16 (1965), 593–602.

Kantor, J. R., *Principles of Psychology.* Vol. II. New York: Alfred A. Knopf, Inc., 1926; reprinted Bloomington, Ind.: Principia Press, 1949.

Kendler, H. H., and Tracy S. Kendler, "Vertical and Horizontal Processes in Problem Solving," *Psychological Review*, 69 (1962), 1–16.

Krasner, L., "A Technique for Investigating the Relationship between the Behavior Cues of the Examiner and the Verbal Behavior of the Patient," *Journal of Consulting Psychology*, 22 (1958), 364–366.

———, "Studies of the Conditioning of Verbal Behavior," *Psychological Bulletins*, 55 (1958), 148–170.

———, "The Therapist as a Social Reinforcement Machine," in H. H. Strupp and L. Luborsky, eds., *Research in Psychotherapy*, Vol. II. Baltimore: The French-Bray Printing Company, 1962.

———, "Verbal Conditioning and Awareness," Paper presented at APA, St. Louis, August 1962.

———, J. B. Knowles, and L. P. Ullmann, "Effect of Verbal Conditioning of Attitudes on Subsequent Motor Performance," *Journal of Personal and Social Psychology*, 1 (1965), 407–412.

———, and L. P. Ullmann, "Variables Affecting Report of Awareness in Verbal Conditioning," *Journal of Psychology*, 56 (1963), 193–202.

———, R. L. Weiss, and L. P. Ullmann, "Responsivity to Verbal Conditioning as a Function of 'Awareness,'" *Psychological Reports*, 8 (1961), 523–538.

Leventhal, A. M., "The Effects of Diagnostic Category and Reinforcer on Learning without Awareness," *Journal of Abnormal and Social Psychology*, 59 (1959), 162–166.

Levin, G., and D. Shapiro, "The Operant Conditioning of Conversation," *Journal of Experimental and Analytical Behavior*, 6 (1962) 309–316.

Levin, S. M., "The Effects of Awareness on Verbal Conditioning," *Journal of Experimental Psychology*, 61 (1961), 67–75.

Lindsley, O. R., "Reduction in Rate of Vocal Psychotic Symptoms by Differential Positive Reinforcement," *Journal of Experimental and Analytical Behavior*, 2 (1960), 269.

Long, E. R., J. T. Hammack, F. May,

and B. J. Campbell, "Intermittent Reinforcement of Operant Behavior in Children," *Journal of Experimental and Analytical Behavior*, 1 (1958), 315–339.

Lovaas, O. I., "Interaction between Verbal and Nonverbal Behavior," *Child Development*, 32 (1961), 329–336.

———, "Control of Food Intake in Children by Reinforcement of Relevant Verbal Behavior," *Journal of Abnormal and Social Psychology*, 68 (1964), 672–678.

Lublin, I., "Sources of Differences in Effectiveness among Controllers of Verbal Reinforcement." Paper presented at APA, Chicago, 1965.

Mandler, G. and W. K. Kaplan, "Subjective Evaluation and Reinforcing Effect of a Verbal Stimulus," *Science*, 124 (1956), 582–583.

Malcolm, N., "Behaviorism as a Philosophy of Psychology," in T. W. Wann, ed., *Behaviorism and Phenomenology*. Chicago: The University of Chicago Press, 1964.

Marston, A. R., "Imitation, Self-Reinforcement, and Reinforcement of Another Person," *Journal of Personal and Social Psychology*, 2 (1965), 255–261.

———, and F. H. Kanfer, "Human Reinforcement: Experimenter and Subject Controlled," *Journal of Experimental Psychology*, 66 (1963), 91–94.

———, ———, and F. J. McBrearty, "Stimulus Discriminability in Verbal Conditioning," *Journal of Psychology*, 53 (1962), 143–153.

Martin, R. B., and S. J. Dean, "Word Familiarity and Avoidance Conditioning of Verbal Behavior," *Journal of Personal and Social Psychology*, 1 (1965), 496–499.

Marx, M. H., "Some Suggestions for the Conceptual and Theoretical Analysis of Complex Intervening Variables in Problem-Solving Behavior," *Journal of General Psychology*, 58 (1958), 115–128.

Matarazzo, J. D., G. Saslow, and E. N. Pareis, "Verbal Conditioning of Two Response Classes: Some Methodological Considerations," *Journal of Abnormal and Social Psychology*, 61 (1960), 190–206.

McBrearty, J. F., F. H. Kanfer, A. R. Marston, and Deanne Evander, "Focal and Contextual Stimulus Variables in Verbal Conditioning," *Psychological Reports*, 13 (1963), 115–124.

McNair, D. M., "Reinforcement of Verbal Behavior," *Journal of Experimental Psychology*, 53 (1957), 40–46.

Melton, A. W., ed., *Categories of Human Learning*. New York: Academic Press, 1964.

Munsinger, H. L., "Meaningful Symbols as Reinforcing Stimuli," *Journal of Abnormal and Social Psychology*, 68 (1964), 665–668.

Nuthman, Anne M., "Conditioning of a Response Class on a Personality Test," *Journal of Abnormal and Social Psychology*, 54 (1957), 19–23.

Oakes, W. F., A. E. Droge, and Barbara August, "Reinforcement Effects on Conclusions Reached in Group Discussion," *Psychological Reports*, 9 (1961), 27–34.

Orne, M. T., "On the Social Psychology of the Psychological Experiment: with Particular Reference to Demand Characteristics and Their Implications," *American Psychology*, 17 (1962), 776–783.

Osgood, C. E., *Method and Theory in Experimental Psychology*. New York: Oxford University Press, Inc., 1953.

Portnoy, Stephanie, and K. Salzinger, "The Conditionability of Different Verbal Response Classes: Positive, Negative, and Non-Affect Statements," *Journal of General Psychology*, 70 (1964), 311–323.

Pronko, N. H., "Language and Psycholinguistics: A Review," *Psychological Bulletin*, 43 (1946), 189–239.

Quay, H., "The Effect of Verbal Reinforcement on the Recall of Early Memories," *Journal of Abnormal and Social Psychology*, 59 (1959), 254–257.

Rogers, J. M., "Operant Conditioning in a Quasi-Therapy Setting," *Journal of Abnormal and Social Psychology*, 60 (1960), 247–252.

Rosenthal, R., "On the Social Psychology of the Psychological Experiment: The Experimenter's Hypothesis as Unintended Determinant of Experimental Results," *American Science*, **51** (1963), 268–283.

———, "Experimenter Outcome-Orientation and the Results of the Psychological Experiment," *Psychological Bulletin*, **61** (1964), 405–412.

———, G. W. Persinger, Linda L. Vikan-Kline, and K. L. Fode, "The Effect of Experimenter Outcome-Bias and Subject Set on Awareness in Verbal Conditioning Experiments," *Journal of Verbal Learning and Verbal Behavior*, **2** (1963), 275–283.

Rotter, J. B., "Some Implications of a Social Learning Theory for the Prediction of Goal Directed Behavior from Testing Procedure," *Psychological Review*, **67** (1960), 301–316.

Salzinger, K., "Experimental Manipulation of Verbal Behavior: A Review," *Journal of General Psychology*, **61** (1959), 65–94.

———, "The Problem of Response Class in Verbal Behavior." Paper presented at the Verbal Behavior Conference, New York City, September, 1965.

———, R. S. Feldman, and Stephanie Portnoy, "The Effects of Reinforcement on Verbal and Non-Verbal Responses," *Journal of General Psychology*, **70** (1964), 225–234.

———, and Stephanie Pisoni, "Reinforcement of Affect Responses of Schizophrenics during the Clinical Interview," *Journal of Abnormal and Social Psychology*, **57** (1958), 87–90.

———, and ———, "Reinforcement of Verbal Affect Responses of Normal Subjects during the Interview," *Journal of Abnormal and Social Psychology*, **60** (1960), 127–130.

Sapolsky, A., "Effect of Interpersonal Relationships upon Verbal Conditioning," *Journal of Abnormal and Social Psychology*, **60** (1960), 241–246.

Sarason, I. G., "Interrelationships among Individual Difference Variables, Behavior in Psychotherapy, and Verbal Conditioning," *Journal of Abnormal and Social Psychology*, **56** (1958), 339–344.

Sherman, J. A., "Use of Reinforcement and Imitation to Reinstate Verbal Behavior in Mute Psychotics," *Journal of Abnormal Psychology*, **70** (1965), 155–164.

Sidowski, J. B., "Influence of Awareness of Reinforcement on Verbal Conditioning," *Journal of Experimental Psychology*, **48** (1964), 355–360.

———, and H. Naumoff, "Pacing, Problem-Solving Instructions, and Hypothesis Testing in Verbal Conditioning," *Psychological Reports*, **15** (1964), 351–354.

Simkins, L., "Examiner Reinforcement and Situational Variables in a Projective Testing Situation," *Journal of Consulting Psychology*, **24** (1960), 541–547.

———, "Effects of Examiner Attitudes and Type of Reinforcement on the Conditioning of Hostile Verbs," *Journal of Personal and Social Psychology*, **29** (1961), 380–395.

———, "Scheduling Effects of Punishment and Nonreinforcement on Verbal Conditioning and Extinction," *Journal of Verbal Learning and Verbal Behavior*, **1** (1962), 208–213.

———, "Instructions as Discriminative Stimuli in Verbal Conditioning and Awareness," *Journal of Abnormal and Social Psychology*, **66** (1963), 213–219.

Skinner, B. F., *Science and Human Behavior*. New York: The Macmillan Company, 1953.

———, *Verbal Behavior*. New York: Appleton-Century-Crofts, 1957.

Slechta, Joan, W. Gwynn, and C. Peoples, "Verbal Conditioning of Schizophrenics and Normals in a Situation Resembling Psychotherapy," *Journal of Consulting Psychology*, **27** (1963), 223–227.

Solley, C. M., and J. Long, "When is 'Uh–Huh' Reinforcing?" *Perceptual Motor Skills*, **8** (1958), 277.

Spielberger, C. D., "The Role of Awareness in Verbal Conditioning," in C. W. Eriksen, ed., *Behavior and Awareness*. Durham, N. C.: Duke University Press, 1962.

———, "Theoretical and Epistemological Issues in Verbal Conditioning," in S. Rosenberg, ed., *Directions in Psycho-*

linguistics. New York: The Macmillan Company, 1965.

————, A. Berger, and Kay Howard, "Conditioning of Verbal Behavior as a Function of Awareness, Need for Social Approval, and Motivation to Receive Reinforcement," *Journal of Abnormal Social Psychology*, **67** (1963), 241–246.

————, I. H. Bernstein, and R. G. Ratliff, "The Information and Incentive Value of the Reinforcing Stimulus in Verbal Conditioning," *Journal of Experimental Psychology*, **71** (1966), 26–31.

————, and L. D. DeNike, "Descriptive Behaviorism Versus Cognitive Theory in Verbal Operant Conditioning," *Psychological Review*, **73** (1966), 306–326.

————, and S. M. Levin, "What is Learned in Verbal Conditioning?" *Journal of Verbal Learning and Verbal Behavior*, **1** (1962), 125–132.

————, ————, and Mary C. Shepard, "The Effects of Awareness and Attitude Toward the Reinforcement on the Operant Conditioning of Verbal Behavior," *Journal of Personality*, **30** (1962), 106–121.

Staats, A. W., "Verbal Habit-Families, Concepts, and the Operant Conditioning of Word Classes," *Psychological Review*, **68** (1961), 190–204.

————, C. K. Staats, W. G. Heard, and J. R. Finley, "Operant Conditioning of Factor Analytic Personality Traits," *Journal of General Psychology*, **66** (1962), 101–114.

Taffel, C., "Anxiety and the Conditioning of Verbal Behavior," *Journal of Abnormal and Social Psychology*, **51** (1955), 496–501.

Tatz, S. J., "Symbolic Activity in 'Learning without Awareness,'" *American Journal of Psychology*, **73** (1960), 239–247.

Verplanck, W. S., "Unaware of Where's Awareness: Some Verbal Operants—Notates, Monents, and Notants," in C. W. Eriksen, ed., *Behavior and Awareness*. Durham, N. C.: Duke University Press, 1962.

Wann, T. W., ed., *Behaviorism and Phenomenology*. Chicago: The University of Chicago Press, 1964.

Waskow, Irene E., "Reinforcement in a Therapy-like Situation through Selective Responding to Feelings or Content," *Journal of Consulting Psychology*, **26** (1962), 11–19.

Watson, J. B., *Behaviorism*. New York: W. W. Norton & Company, Inc., 1930.

Webb, R. A., J. L. Bernard, and C. C. Nesmith, "Reinforcement Ratio, Spontaneous Recovery and Suggestibility as a Control in Verbal Conditioning," *Psychological Reports*, **12** (1963), 479–482.

Weiss, R. L., L. Krasner, and L. P. Ullmann, "Responsivity to Verbal Conditioning as a Function of Emotional Atmosphere and Pattern of Reinforcement," *Psychological Reports*, **6** (1960), 415–426.

Williams, Juanita H., "Conditioning of Verbalization: A Review," *Psychological Bulletin*, **62** (1964), 383–393.

Wyckoff, L. B., Jr., "The Role of Observing Responses in Discrimination Learning, Part I," *Psychological Review*, **59** (1952), 431–442.

Theoretical Conceptions
of Semantic Conditioning
and Generalization [1]

12

IRVING MALTZMAN

In order to evaluate the effectiveness of
S-R theory in accounting for semantic
conditioning and generalization, it is
first necessary to clarify the usage of
"S-R theory." It may be interpreted,
on the one hand, as equivalent to
methodological behaviorism, a prescription for the introduction and usage of
concepts in psychology. It says that no
matter how "abstract" or removed
from immediately observable events, a
concept must be relatable to antecedent
observable stimulus conditions and
consequent observable responses or
behavior. It is just good psychological
science to specify the antecedent and
consequent conditions under which a
concept is being used, if that concept
is to have empirical meaning. Such a
methodological position for psychology
is simply an extension of logical empiricism (Bergmann, 1951, 1957). It asserts
that the basic undefined terms of
science refer to properties of physical
objects and their simple spatial and
temporal relations. Psychology and
physical science have the same subject
matter.

[1] This study was made possible in part by
funds granted by the Carnegie Corporation
of New York and PHS Research Grant
MH 04684 from the Institute of Mental
Health.

Such a prescription, or systematic
position, is neither true nor false, but
a volitional decision (Reichenbach,
1938) as to how one should go about
introducing and using terms in psychology. As a decision it entails further
consequences; the problems investigated
and the methods employed are influenced by the position adopted. Continued acceptance of the S-R methodology depends upon its fruitfulness, the
extent to which it generates research,
principles, and theories, and undoubtedly the extent to which it withstands
the challenge of alternative volitional
decisions. In this regard I think that
it has been rather successful. Alternative
approaches such as the older mentalism
in which basic concepts referred to
immediate experience and were undefined in terms of antecedent and consequent conditions have not been
viable.

Another procedure for introducing
concepts into science is via the use of
partially interpreted axiomatic systems.
It has been highly successful in certain
areas of physical science (Bergmann,
1943) and is characterized by general
as well as precise mathematical statements. Proponents of the use of this
method for psychology (Carnap, 1956;
Sellars, 1956) fail to consider the

marked difference in the present state of development of psychology and physics. Use of this powerful method of theory formation is not incompatible with behaviorism if the definitions coordinating parts of the axiomatic systems include terms referring to observable environmental and behavioral or physiological conditions.

Watson's (1913) brilliant paper "Psychology as the Behaviorist Views It" rather clearly and convincingly stated the position of methodological behaviorism, the systematic position of S-R psychology. However, in this and subsequent work he promulgated a variety of theories concerning learning, thinking, emotions, child rearing, etc. By "theory" we mean a falsifiable set of assertions regarding, for example, the conditions under which learning, the acquisition of associations, occurs. Obviously, there may be alternative S-R theories of learning, as there have been. Although each introduces its concepts in the same methodological fashion, they posit different conditions as critical for learning.

A characteristic of much of Watson's theorizing was his emphasis upon peripheral responses, eschewing the CNS, as though the further one penetrates under the skin the greater the likelihood of involving the mind. There was some justification for avoiding speculation of a pseudophysiological sort in Watson's time and therefore couching theories in terms of peripheral response changes. This tendency, unfortunately, still persists among most methodological S-R psychologists. However, the question of centralism vs. peripheralism is a matter of fact, an empirical problem, and not a methodological or systematic issue. Watson's espousal of a systematic S-R position as well as specific hypotheses formulated in S-R terms has resulted in the unfortunate confusion of the systematic

position and falsifiable empirical hypotheses.

In terms of the latter criterion, S-R theories of semantic conditioning and generalization are falsifiable, and they are false or faulty, as we shall try to indicate. Despite more than 25 years of activity, semantic conditioning and generalization are not adequately accounted for in detail by current S-R theories. This failure suggests that basic assumptions are at fault. It is engendered in part by the fact that S-R theories of semantic conditioning and generalization presuppose an inadequate conception of simple conditioning. A basic prerequisite for an adequate formulation of simple, as well as of semantic conditioning and generalization, is a recognition of the fundamental role of attention as represented by the concept of the orienting reflex (OR). In the case of extended training with a noxious US the added complexity introduced by the development of defensive reflexes (DR) must also be considered. After reviewing S-R formulations of semantic conditioning and generalization, and the problems encountered by them, we shall outline an attempt at a more adequate formulation of semantic conditioning and generalization—and the simple conditioning from which they are derived.

The Origins of S-R Theories of Semantic Conditioning Generalization[2]

Razran (1939, 1961) who introduced the term "semantic conditioning" de-

---

[2] No attempt will be made to cover exhaustively the relevant experimental literature in this country or the Soviet Union. Recent reviews have already accomplished this task (Feather, 1965; Hartman, 1965; Razran, 1961).

fines it "as the conditioning of a reflex to a word or sentence irrespective of the particular constituent letters or sounds of the word or the particular constituent words of the sentence . . . " (1961, p. 99).

Although Razran has been the most active investigator in this particular area, current S-R theories of semantic conditioning and generalization stem largely from the formulations of Hull developed during the 1930's and 1940's (Hull, 1934, 1943). Goss (1961) has described the development of theories of mediated behavior prior to Hull, indicating quite clearly that Hull did not originate such conceptions, but because of his apparent explicitness he greatly influenced subsequent theorizing.

The experimental bases for these theoretical formulations stem largely from a series of conditioning studies by Shipley (1933, 1935), an abstract of a study by Lumsdaine (1939), and an unpublished doctoral dissertation by Birge (1941) employing a more complex learning task. The Shipley-Lumsdaine experiments employed a variation of classical conditioning with nonverbal stimuli. Basing theories of semantic conditioning and generalization upon such experiments involves the assumption that the addition of verbal stimuli does not result in the introduction of new principles. Generality of the theory is gained, of course, by showing the continuity between the two types of procedures, and it permits the deduction of semantic generalization as a special case of nonverbal mediated generalization.

THE SHIPLEY-LUMSDAINE EXPERIMENTS. The following is a brief description of the series of experiments conducted by Shipley (1933, 1935) and the one briefly reported by Lumsdaine (1939).

Shipley reported the results of nine

different conditions in which independent groups of approximately ten subjects each were used. On the basis of the pattern of results he suggested that transfer or generalization of a response from one stimulus to another physically different stimulus occurred as the result of the formation of a response chain, mediated generalization.

In the first series of three experiments (Shipley, 1933) the following critical experimental phases, among other variations, were introduced during the course of three days of experimentation.

(*1A*) A dim light flash was paired with a sharp rap on the cheek provided by a padded hammer striking the cheek below the eye which produced an eyeblink. The hammer strike was then paired with an electric shock to a finger producing finger withdrawal and, as subsequently hypothesized, an eyeblink as well. Mediated generalization was tested by giving two trials on which the light flash alone was presented. Nine of 15 subjects gave one or more finger withdrawals, showed mediated generalization. Panel 1A in Figure 1 shows the three experimental phases and the hypothesized S-R associations. Since test trials were not administered during the first two training phases, it must be assumed that conditioning was established prior to the test phase.

(*1B*) Subjects in this condition were treated in the same fashion as in 1A except that wherever subjects in 1A received the light-strike combination, subjects now received only the strike. None of the ten subjects showed evidence of mediated generalization. Panel 1B in Figure 1 illustrates the major phases in this condition; the X in stage III indicates that transfer did not occur.

(*1C*) These subjects received only the shock where group 1A received the strike-shock combination. One of 11

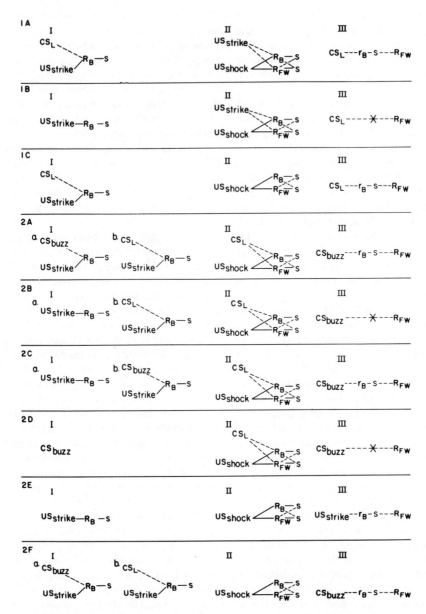

Figure 1. Theoretical interpretation of conditions employed in Shipley's (1933, 1935) experiments. Lumsdaine (1939) repeated condition 1A.

subjects showed mediated finger withdrawal. Panel 1C in Figure 1 illustrates the principal phases in this condition. Results from the following six groups were reported in a second study by Shipley (1935).

(24) A light was paired with the strike on some trials while on other trials a buzz was paired with the strike. Presumably, the light and the buzz were each conditioned to the eyeblink. The light was then paired with shock

to the finger for the conditioning of finger withdrawal. The test of mediated generalization was administered by presenting the buzz alone. Six of ten subjects showed generalization. Panel 2A in Figure 1 illustrates the principal phases in this variation.

(*2B*) The same conditions were employed here as in 2A except that strike alone was administered wherever the buzzer-strike combination was used in 2A. None of the ten subjects showed mediated generalization. Panel 2B in Figure 1 illustrates the principal phases in this condition.

(*2C*) The procedure was the same as in 2A except that the strike was given alone wherever the flash-strike combination was administered in 2A. The buzz was conditioned to the eyeblink; the light flash was conditioned to finger withdrawal while the mediation test consisted of the buzz alone. Seven of 10 subjects showed finger withdrawal, mediated generalization. Panel 2C in Figure 1 illustrates the principal phases in this condition.

(*2D*) Thirty presentations of the buzz alone were given on the first day of experimentation. Twenty-five flash-shock presentations were administered on the second day followed by test trials of buzz alone. None of the ten subjects showed mediated generalization. Panel 2D in Figure 1 illustrates the major phases in this condition.

(*2E*) Twenty-five presentations of the strike alone were administered on the first day of experimentation. Twenty-five presentations of shock alone were administered on the second day followed by test trials presenting the strike alone. One subject showed finger withdrawal on the test trials. Panel 2E in Figure 1 illustrates the major phases in this condition.

(*2F*) The procedure here was the same as in 2A except that shock alone was administered instead of the strike-shock combination: Again, presentation of the buzz alone constituted the test for mediated generalization. Two of the ten subjects showed mediated transfer. Panel 2F in Figure 1 illustrates the major phases in this condition.

Shipley (1935) formulated a "conditioned-chain-reflex" hypothesis to account for the occurrence of mediated generalization of finger withdrawal. It assumes that the shock to the finger evokes an eyeblink as well as finger withdrawal, and the kinesthetic cues from each of these responses may be conditioned to the other response. Backward as well as forward conditioning may occur. Although backward conditioning may seem to be a tenuous assumption, there is considerable Soviet evidence (Asratyan, 1961) to indicate that two-way connections, simultaneous forward and backward connections, do occur. Figure 1 illustrates the assumed associations between the response-produced cues from the eyeblink and finger withdrawal which provide the response chain necessary for mediated generalization. Shipley (1935) indicated that the recording apparatus he employed was not sensitive enough to record the occurrence of the mediating eyeblinks in the test phase, evidence which he believed to be necessary for the substantiation of his hypothesis.

Evidence apparently supporting the mediation hypothesis came from a brief abstract of a paper reported by Lumsdaine (1939), who repeated condition 1A of Shipley's experiment. In the test phase "conditioned finger withdrawals occurred in an appreciable proportion of subjects in addition to conditioned eyelid responses, although the light had never before occurred in conjunction with the finger response. The finger response was absent if the lid response failed to appear. Photographic recording made detailed analysis possible. These results support the hypothesis that such 'indirectly' conditioned finger responses may be mediated by the concomitants of the eyelid response which is a common feature of the 2 conditioning stages" (Lumsdaine, 1939, p. 650). Unfortunately, a more detailed report of the experiment has not been published. It is apparent that a very extensive theoretical structure has since developed even though only the most fragmentary kinds of evidence were available to support the basic hypotheses.

Hull's influential account of the transfer effect obtained in Shipley's experiments is as follows:

An apparent case of secondary stimulus generalization has been reported by Shipley . . . and verified by Lumsdaine. . . . These investigators presented a subject with a flash of light followed by the tap of a padded hammer against the cheek below the eye, thus conditioning lid closure to the light flash. Next, the same subject was repeatedly given an electric shock on the finger. This evoked not only a sharp finger withdrawal from the electrode, but lid closure as well. Finally the flash of light was delivered alone. It was found in a considerable proportion of the subjects of both experiments that during this latter manoeuvre the light evoked finger retraction *even though the former had never been associated with either the shock or the finger retraction.* The interpretation is that the light evoked the lid closure, and the proprioceptive stimulation produced by this act (or some other less conspicuous act conditioned at the same time) evoked the finger retraction.

Lumsdaine's photographic records . . . of the process tend to support the view that in this experiment the wink reaction served as a mediating agent, since they show that, typically, when the light evoked finger retraction the lid closure usually took place between the flash of the light and the finger movement. Occasionally, however, the two reactions occurred at the same time, and sometimes the finger movement even preceded the blink. This, of course, could not have happened if the finger retraction was evoked by the proprioceptive stimuli arising from the lid closure. It is possible, however, that numerous other reactions were conditioned at the same time as the wink, and that proprioceptive stimuli from all of them became conditioned to finger retraction. If occasionally the lid closure should have occurred later than the other reactions, the proprioception from the latter might easily have evoked the finger reaction alone (Hull, 1943, pp. 192–93).[3]

For Hull, secondary stimulus or mediated generalization occurred primarily on the basis of peripheral response-produced stimulation. Hilgard and Marquis (1940) were somewhat less certain that the empirical phenomenon of mediated generalization was a consequence of peripheral response produced stimulation.

In recent years Grice and his students have conducted a series of carefully designed experiments which pertains to the assumption that mediated generalization is in fact mediated by movement-produced stimuli (Grice, 1965; Grice and Davis, 1958, 1960; Grice and Hunter, 1963; Grice, Simmons, and Hunter, 1963). In general, their results do not provide clear evidence in support of the traditional S-R position.

A fundamental difficulty is present which cannot be avoided by even the most careful control and measurement of the assumed mediating response in such experiments. Finding, for example, in Shipley's experiment that the eyeblink, the assumed mediator, always occurred prior to the finger withdrawal, and in the absence of eyeblinks transfer

---

[3] Hull has incorrectly described the conditions in Lumsdaine's experiment. Lumsdaine repeated condition 1A and not condition 1C, which Hull describes here and where only one of 11 subjects showed transfer.

of finger withdrawal did not occur, is not unequivocal evidence for movements and their kinesthetic stimuli as mediators. It is always possible that the occurrence of the assumed mediating response and the test response covary because of a partial correlation. They are both due to a common variable. The obvious source of partial correlation is the central nervous system, particularly processes in the cerebral cortex. The assumption that the transfer of finger withdrawal is accomplished on the basis of kinesthetic stimulation stemming from an eyeblink seems quite unreasonable on the face of it. Such a position also assumes that conditioning occurs in a particular fashion. It assumes that peripheral responses are directly conditioned to environmental stimuli or their effects and that their kinesthetic stimuli in turn are conditioned to other responses. Establishment of conditioned responses in deafferentated primates (Taub, Ellman, and Berman, 1966) suggests that the importance of afferent feedback has been greatly overemphasized. There is considerable additional evidence which we shall present later that further contradicts a peripheralistic S-R position with respect to simple classical conditioning. If simple classical conditioning does not occur in the manner assumed by S-R theories of mediated and semantic generalization, then the latter likewise cannot occur in the manner assumed.

BIRGE'S MEDIATED GENERALIZATION STUDY. Birge's (1941) unpublished dissertation is one of the first studies in this country using a mediated generalization procedure other than classical conditioning. It will be discussed at some length because it employed a relatively simple procedure which is open to several of the possible theoretical interpretations which may be offered to account for conditioned generalization.

She used third, fourth, and fifth grade elementary school pupils as subjects in her experiments. In one series she determined whether a verbal response, a nonsense name, would serve to mediate an instrumental response and also whether overt verbalization would facilitate the transfer process. In a second study she determined whether or not an instrumental response would mediate the transfer of a verbal response. Positive results were obtained in both studies, but only the principal portion of the first experiment will be described here. The children were individually shown four identical boxes in serial order with different nonsense shapes drawn on each of their covers. These are stimuli S_1, S_2, S_3, and S_4. In this first phase of the experiment, name learning, a common response, for example, "Towk," was learned to boxes S_1 and S_3, and the common name "Meef" was learned to S_2 and S_4. Phase I of Figure 2 indicates the stimulus-response associations established at the conclusion of this name learning phase of the experiment.

A discrimination-learning, candy-finding phase constituted the next stage in the experiment. S_1 and S_2, for example, were presented to the children with the former positive and the latter negative. Candy was always found under S_1, "Towk," regardless of its spatial position. The response of reaching, R_r, for S_1 was reinforced while the response of reaching for S_2 was extinguished, since candy was never found under the box labeled "Meef." Phase II in Figure 2 indicates the stimulus-response associations established at the conclusion of the candy-finding phase of the experiment.

Immediately after a child learned to reach consistently for S_1 and not S_2,

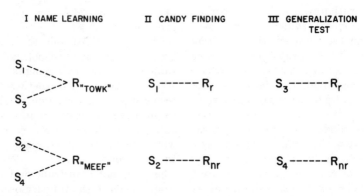

Figure 2. Stimulus-response associations present at the conclusion of the training and test phases of Birge's (1941) experiment

he was presented with boxes S_3 and S_4 in place of the previously discriminated boxes. The test phase was designed to determine whether or not the reaching response, R_r, associated with S_1 would now transfer to S_3. Significantly more

"Towk," which presumably produces an internal stimulus s_T. At the same time S_2 and S_4 have been associated with $R_M - s_M$. Response produced stimuli produced by the verbal labels are the only additional assumption in

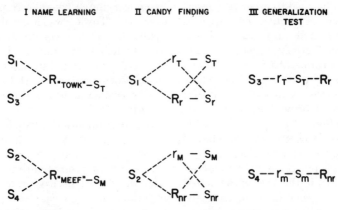

Figure 3. Theoretical interpretation of mediated generalization in Birge's (1941) experiment

children did respond by reaching for S_3 than S_4. Empirically, conditioned or mediated generalization has occurred, as indicated in Phase III of Figure 2.

Figure 3 shows the usual S-R interpretation of mediated generalization as it developed in the Birge experiment. In the name-learning phase two qualitatively different stimuli S_1 and S_3 are associated with the verbal response

this phase as compared to the observed conditions described in the first phase of Figure 2. In the second phase of the procedure for producing mediated generalization S_1 is associated with a reaching response, Rr, which in turn produces s_r. It is assumed that presentation of S_1 results in the arousal of some fractional component of $R_T - s_T$. The concurrence of $Rr - s_r$ and $r_T - s_T$

results in the association of the response from one segment with the response produced stimulus of the other.

In the final test phase S_3 and S_4 are presented and the former stimulus is followed by the correct choice, Rr, even though they have not previously been associated. The response Rr has become part of a new response chain with $r_T - s_T$ as its mediating link. Subsequently when $r_T - s_T$ is elicited by its previously established cue, the remainder of the chain is run off providing for the observable occurrence of R_r.

Four different subgroups were present in the experiment:

1. children instructed to pronounce the names of the boxes while learning to find the candy and when tested for generalization,
2. children pronouncing the names only during the candy-finding phase,
3. children pronouncing the names only during the generalization test phase, and
4. children who did not pronounce the names during either the candy-finding or the test phases.

The percentage of children choosing the critical box was 85, 77, 62, and 54 respectively. Only the first two groups showed a significant deviation from chance.

Increased transfer with verbalization may be due to any one of several factors, none of which can be determined from this experiment. Overt verbalization increased the vigor or amplitude of the assumed mediating response, insured the occurrence of the verbal mediator on each trial; or the increased mediation effect may not have been related to the verbalization and the verbal mediator at all. The instructions to verbalize and the necessity of verbalizing correctly may have forced the child to orient in a more appropriate manner, evoking correct observing responses and aug-menting the orienting reflex (Maltzman and Raskin, 1965) which facilitated learning.

Birge (1941) conducted another experiment in which the candy-finding and naming phases were reversed. Children first learned to pick up one of a pair of boxes to find candy and when presented with a second pair of different boxes, to pick one of these boxes. Following candy-finding, the second phase of name learning was instituted. The children learned, for example, to call one of the correct boxes "Towk" and one of the incorrect boxes "Meef." They were then asked which name goes with which of the boxes previously unnamed. Seventy-five per cent of the children transferred the names to the boxes evoking the same instrumental response, a highly reliable result.

Another rather different although not necessarily incompatible interpretation of mediated generalization is possible under Birge's experimental conditions. This second interpretation is based upon the notion of observing responses (Kanfer, 1956; Kurtz, 1955; Mandler, 1954; Murdock, 1952; Spence, 1940; Wykoff, 1952) and parasitic reinforcement (Bousfield, Whitmarsh, and Danick, 1958; Morgan and Underwood, 1950). Parasitic reinforcement in particular may seem more obvious when the stimulus materials are words, but it may also operate in a situation such as the one employed by Birge. This second interpretation of mediated generalization assumes that any stimulus evokes implicit differential observing responses. These responses may be verbal or nonverbal. When the stimuli are words, they are assumed to be implicit verbalizations of the stimulus word and an increased disposition for its associates to occur. A nonverbal stimulus may evoke verbal or nonverbal responses. In Birge's experiment each of the stimuli are assumed to evoke

I NAME LEARNING   II CANDY FINDING   III GENERALIZATION TEST

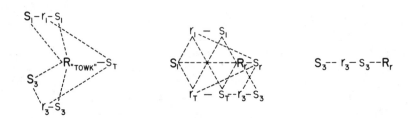

Figure 4. An alternative theoretical interpretation of Birge's mediated generalization experiment based upon observing responses

differential implicit observing responses as illustrated in Figure 4.

During the name-learning phase of the experiment the observing responses become associated to the verbal label learned to each nonsense figure. In the candy-finding phase of the experiment the reaching response, Rr, is associated with S_1, the observing response it evokes, $r_1 — s_1$, and as the result of a two-link implicit chain, the observing response of S_3, $r_3 — s_3$. In the third stage S_3 is followed by R_3 as the result of mediation by the observing response $r_3 — s_3$ previously associated with Rr during the candy-finding phase of the experiment. Although this is a different interpretation from the first offered, stressing the association of the instrumental response and the mediating response produced stimulus in the second phase of the experiment rather than generalization in the final test phase, there is no logical reason why both sorts or processes may not be occurring. The fact that the locus of generalization is still a matter of doubt —it may occur either during conditioning (Mink, 1963), testing (Razran, 1949a, 1949b), or in both places (Brotsky, 1964; Kurcz, 1964; Moss, 1960)— indicates that the bases for mediated and semantic generalization are still not well understood.

Birge's first experiment is a transition between mediated and semantic generalization in that the mediator was a verbal response, although not a word, while the stimuli were nonsense figures.

A semantic conditioning experiment employing the classical conditioning of the GSR by Martha Mednick (1957) illustrates semantic generalization and incorporates an important innovation, the use of word association norms to provide an independent measure of the extent to which generalization may occur between words. She attempted to manipulate the anterior segment of the response chain by selecting test words from the Minnesota norms of the Kent-Rosanoff word association test (Russell and Jenkins, 1954). Four words were selected — "dark," "lamp," "heavy," "soft"—each of which evoked the response "light" with a different frequency. The percentage of normative subjects giving the response "light" to the above words was 83, 63, 58, and .86 respectively. It is assumed that the probability of these words evoking "light" in any given experimental subject would correspond to the normative frequencies. Figure 5, Part I indicates the convergent mechanism, the different stimuli having varying dispositions for the elicitation of the response "light," as implied by the

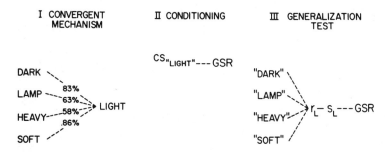

Figure 5. Theoretical interpretation of semantic generalization in Mednick's (1957) experiment

association norms. Part II in Figure 5 shows the usual classical conditioning paradigm with "light" presented orally as the conditioned stimulus evoking the galvanic skin response. Part III of Figure 5 indicates the conditions in the generalization test situation where the anterior segments of the response chains evoked by the respective test stimuli differ in associative strength. Neutral words were also presented during the training and test situations which did not evoke "light" in their association norms. Each of the test

normative frequencies were not significant.

An alternative associationistic interpretation of Mednick's study is indicated in Figure 6. This interpretation assumes that the locus of generalization is in the conditioning phase of the experiment. Presentation of the CS word "light" implicitly evokes its associates which are then conditioned to the GSR, a situation analogous to the observing response interpretation offered for Birge's results, but in this case substituting verbal for nonverbal

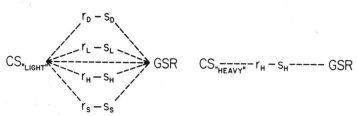

Figure 6. An alternative theoretical interpretation of semantic generalization in Mednick's (1957) experiment based upon implicit associates evoked during conditioning

words evoked a greater response on the test situation than a selected neutral word, and except for "dark" the rank order of the generalized responses corresponded to the associative frequency of the normative data. However, the differences among the test words corresponding to the order of

responses. Of course it could be argued that nonverbal observing responses as well as verbal associates are functioning to determine the course of semantic generalization. However, a serious shortcoming of the observing response hypothesis in experiments of this kind is that it does not provide a measure of the observing response which is independent of the response change it is assumed to explain. Under appropriate conditions, however, independent measures of observing responses may be possible.

Osgood's (1953) theory assumes that semantic generalization of the GSR, other things being equal, occurs on the basis of the similarity between the representational mediational process, $r_m - s_m$, of "light" and the various test words. The theory does not specify the locus of generalization. Finally, Razran (1949a) would interpret the semantic generalization as occurring in the test situation as the consequence of a "judgment of similarity" between the CS and test words.

We will turn now to a more detailed discussion of the principal S-R theories of semantic conditioning and generalization.

S-R Theories of Semantic Generalization

BOUSFIELD. The type of theoretical interpretation described in connection with the experiments by Shipley, Birge, and Mednick has undergone several modifications. Bousfield has provided a more sophisticated variation of the Shipley-Hull chaining hypothesis in accounting for semantic generalization (Boúsfield, 1961; Bousfield, Whitmarsh, and Danick, 1958). His theory contains features similar to an observing response theory, substituting a specific verbal response for nonverbal observing responses similar in part to Figure 6. Both types of theory assume conditioning of the potential mediators to the criterion response during training.

Bousfield's theory in large measure stems from his method of measuring the associative strengths between words, i.e., his index of generalization (IG).

The theory and the method of measurement assume that each stimulus word when presented to a subject evokes a representation of itself, the representational response. The extent to which semantic generalization occurs between two words is the consequence of the extent to which the two words share associates.

However, the sum of the common associates to each of the two words need not be the same. Bousfield (1961) gives as an example the words "needle" and "scissors." Common associates to "needle" and their frequency of occurrence for the normative 1008 subjects are as follows: sharp (55), thread (464), sew (64), sewing (8), with a sum of 591. Common associates for "scissor" are: sharp (90), thread (13), needle (9), sew (8), sewing (8), with a sum of 128. The IG for a given word is its common associates divided by the total number of normative associates.

In order to obtain an adequate measure of associative strength in terms of common associations between two words, it is necessary to include the representational response to a stimulus so that it can be counted as a common associate in the hierarchy of a second stimulus word. The representational response "needle" could not otherwise be counted as a common associate to "scissors." Also worth noting is that the IGs for the two words differ; unidirectional associative effects may therefore be predicted under appropriate conditions.

Evidence for the utility of the index is indicated by the reliable correlations obtained between the IG and measures of mediated generalization in a paired-associate task (Bousfield, Whitmarsh, and Danick, 1958). Striking evidence for the role of associative strength in semantic generalization and the utility of the IG is indicated by the correlation of .70 between the IG and Razran's

(1949a) measure of semantic generalization of the salivary response (Whitmarsh and Bousfield, 1961).

These results indicate that the IG may be used as an independent measure of associative connections between words and provides a basis for predicting the extent of semantic generalization of a new response between words. How much better the IG predicts semantic generalization as compared to a simple measure of the frequency that the words are associates of each other—for example, as used by Mednick (1957) —is not known. Likewise, the relative utility of other measures of associative strength (Marshall and Cofer, 1963) for predicting semantic generalization has not been adequately explored.

Although the index of generalization is useful as an independent measure for predicting the extent of semantic generalization between words, it does not follow that the theory of semantic generalization related to the measurement technique is a good one. I find it rather unsatisfactory. Bousfield (1961) assumes that the conditioning of the mediator to the test response occurs during training, as does Mink (1963) and various forms of the observing response hypothesis (Murdock, 1952). Presentation of the auditory CS "needle" to a subject results in the evocation of its representational response, needle, which in turn evokes all of its possible associates which, since they occur in the presence of the UCR, become conditioned to that response. On a semantic generalization test, presentation of the word "scissors" evokes its representational response, scissors, which in turn evokes all of its associates. Since some of these were conditioned to the GSR during conditioning, when they were evoked by the representational response of the CS word, semantic generalization occurs.

According to Bousfield the implicit associations to the test word, the IG of the test word, determines the extent of generalization, not the IG of the training word, even though the conditioning necessary for the transfer occurred during the original conditioning trials. Bousfield suggests that during conditioning the implicit associations to the representational response are repeatedly aroused. Assuming a negatively accelerated curve of associative strength, the weak associates gain more in strength than the strong associates. The probabilities for evoking the different associates are equalized during conditioning. In the test situation, in contrast, the probability of occurrence of the different associates to the representational response of the test word still corresponds to the normative index. The extent to which semantic generalization occurs and the kind of gradient obtained are therefore predictable from the IG of the test word even though the actual association between the mediators and the observable test response was established during the conditioning phase of the experiment.

Bousfield's theoretical account of semantic generalization is unreasonable in several respects. The usual semantic conditioning and generalization study in this country employs relatively few trials, approximately five to ten. A CS word, assuming that it primes or evokes associates, can do this for a very large number of potential associates, many more than the few that are shared with the unknown test word yet to come. Since many of the associations shared with the test word are of low frequency, it is highly improbable that they would occur even once, much less reach asymptotic strength with dominant associates. That all possible associates of a word are implicitly evoked or even primed whenever a subject is stimulated by a word seems most unreasonable and chaotic. Implicit associates evoked by a word in an experiment, if they occur at all, will primarily be determined by the conditions present in the experiment. If subjects are not instructed to free-associate to each word during the experiment, such behavior will be rather uncommon.

At the conclusion of our experiments on semantic conditioning and generalization we ask our subjects, as part of an extensive questionnaire, what they were thinking about during the experiment when they heard the CS word. By far the most frequent answer given by subjects is that they thought about the US that would follow. Few subjects reported that they thought of words or activities related to the CS word. In view of the general consistency of the verbal report of the subjects in our experiments, it is difficult to reconcile such behavior with Bousfield's formulation and the similar assumption made by Mink (1963) that the CS word evokes implicit verbal associates that are then and there conditioned to the observable response which serves subsequently as the transferred response. Although we would not exclude the possibility under certain conditions of associative priming as described by Bousfield, it seems to be an unlikely occurrence in classical conditioning with noxious stimuli. A more likely form of prompting would be the increased probability of occurrence of the CS word as an associate of the test word, an effect in accord with Storms' (1958) findings on prompting and backward associations. The latter effect would favor the test situation as the locus of generalization.

OSGOOD'S THEORY. According to Osgood, mediation may be understood in the following terms: "Whenever some originally neutral stimulus (sign-to-be) . . . is repeatedly contiguous with another stimulus (significate) . . . which regularly and reliably elicits a particular

pattern of total behavior . . . the neutral stimulus will become associated with some portion . . . of this total behavior as a representational mediation process" (Osgood, 1963, p. 740).

The mediating response is not the implicit occurrence of some fractional component of a specific verbal response. Each verbal stimulus evokes a characteristic representational mediation process, a "meaning" response. The extent to which semantic generalization occurs between two words is a function of their similarity in meaning, the similarity between their representational mediating processes, more specifically the response produced stimulus s_m. In terms of the operations and results of semantic differential ratings, meaning is defined as a point in a Euclidean semantic space. Each point may vary in its direction and its distance from the origin. These properties are coordinated with the quality and intensity of meaning in terms of the checking operations on a bipolar scale, with quality corresponding to which end of the scale is checked, and intensity corresponding to the extremeness of the rating. These characteristics of the scale factors and their measurement operations are placed in correspondence with the hypothesis of representational mediation processes. Each representational mediation process is composed of a limited number of pairs of antagonistic mediating reactions. The number of pairs of antagonistic mediators corresponds to the number of independent factors of meaning or dimensions in semantic space. The direction checked on a bipolar scale is a function of which member of the relevant pair is evoked, and the intensity of this component mediator is related to the extremeness of the judgment.

Osgood (1961) has also agreed that semantic generalization may occur on the basis of verbal response chains in the manner generally described by Bousfield (1961) and Jenkins (1963) as well as on the basis of similarity of meanings. Semantic generalization may occur between opposites, words maximally dissimilar in meaning. Unidirectional semantic generalization can be obtained (Mink, 1963; Razran, 1949a), whereas similarity of meaning between words as defined by the semantic differential implies that only bidirectional effects can be obtained. In addition, research on mediated generalization employing the paired-associates method has obtained reliable evidence of mediation between words possessing associative connections but little or no similarity in meaning (Bastian, 1961; Ryan, 1960).

Presumably, in cases where no associative connections are present, for example, as measured by the IG, the basis for generalization is similarity of meaning. Generalization based upon connotative similarity, $r_m - s_m$, would be the basic process involved for words such as "home" and "nurse," where it is likely that neither is an associate of the other, nor are there appreciable common overlapping associates (Baxter, 1962).

Examination of Osgood's theory even under these more restricted conditions suggests that it cannot adequately account for semantic generalization or that it implies a nonobvious consequence that is either a *reductio ad absurdum* or has received striking confirmation. We believe the former is the case. The basis for my belief that connotative similarity cannot account for semantic generalization is as follows.

Words can be selected that have no associative communality according to association norms and are similar in only one respect, similar positive evaluative ratings. Generalization must occur on the basis of similarity in this one component of the representational mediation process. Pairing the CS word

with a noxious US in a classical conditioning paradigm results in the conditioning of "detachable" components of the total response evoked by the US to the representational process of the CS word. This means that the negative evaluative component of the CS word will be strengthened.

In the semantic generalization test situation a word is presented which, on the basis of semantic profiles obtained prior to the start of conditioning, was highly similar in evaluative meaning but dissimilar in all other respects. A semantic differential rating of the CS word after conditioning would indicate that the meaning of the CS word had become highly negative. In the semantic generalization test situation a word is presented which prior to the experiment had a similar positive evaluative rating as the CS word prior to conditioning but differed in all other respects (no associative communality, dissimilar potency and activity ratings). Osgood's theory would require that no semantic generalization would occur between the two words, since the CS and test words are now quite dissimilar. This obviously is not what Osgood thinks will happen since he cites studies of semantic generalization as support for his formulation (1961). Of course, it may be argued that semantic generalization actually occurs during the conditioning situation but is only manifested in the test situation. This assumption, aside from the contrary evidence in classical conditioning, is of no help. Changes in rated meaning are a function of the number of conditioning trials (Brotsky, 1964). Thus a word with a highly positive evaluation will become increasingly negative as a function of conditioning trials. If generalization occurs during conditioning, then all words from those with ratings corresponding to the initial rating of the CS word prior to the start of conditioning to those corresponding to the final rating of the CS word at the conclusion of conditioning will have their evaluative ratings changed. All words would show semantic generalization, the degree would depend upon the number of conditioning trials, but the generalization test word would not show greater transfer than control words. On the other hand, a negatively evaluated word paired with a noxious stimulus would only become more negatively evaluated. In this case a test word similar in connotative meaning to the training word, maximally negatively evaluated, would show the greatest amount of semantic generalization. A monotonic gradient of semantic generalization as a function of semantic distance should be obtained.

A study by Baxter (1962) would seem to offer striking confirmation of the above interpretation of Osgood's theory of semantic generalization. Words were selected over a wide range of connotative meaning. Ratings for the words were obtained from each experimental subject. One group of subjects was then conditioned to one of the words randomly selected and tested for generalization on the remaining five words. No evidence of semantic generalization of the GSR was obtained with this group. A second group of subjects was conditioned on the particular words for which they gave the highest positive evaluative rating and tested on the remaining words. A third group was conditioned on the word for which they gave the most extreme negative evaluative rating and tested on the remaining words. The semantic generalization gradients for the GSR obtained for the latter two groups intersected. The group conditioned on the negatively evaluated word showed smaller GSRs to the other words as a function of semantic distance. The group conditioned on the positively evaluated word showed smaller GSRs to similar rated words

than to less similar words. Negatively evaluated words showed greater responsivity than positively evaluated words. It is unfortunate that Baxter did not obtain postexperimental ratings of the conditioning and test words in order to determine whether or not similar results were obtained in terms of semantic differential ratings.

Osgood (1961) interpreted the interaction between semantic generalization gradients obtained by Baxter as support for his notion of reciprocally antagonistic mediation processes. For the subjects receiving a negatively evaluated word as a CS

> we get an almost perfect generalization gradient as a function of semantic distance. Now, recalling that the unconditioned stimulus here was a just barely bearable shock and realizing that the training situation is precisely that in which Arthur Staats would talk about the 'conditioning of meaning' ... it becomes evident that here Baxter was intensifying an already negatively evaluative representational process and recording GSR as an index of it. This is a semantically uncomplicated situation. Now look at the results ... where the most positively evaluated word was associated with shock: here the most similar word in meaning shows the least generalization, while the words which already had a negative evaluation show more generalization. Here we have a complicated semantic situation, in which an opposite meaning is being foisted upon the training stimulus.
>
> Is such evidence sufficient to justify postulation of a semantic generalization mechanism as separate from verbal response chaining? I think it is ... (Osgood, 1961, pp. 96–97).

I do not believe such evidence is sufficient to postulate a mechanism of meaning. The data from the conditioning phase of Baxter's experiment, apparently not available at the time Osgood commented on the generalization test, does not support the notion of reciprocally antagonistic mechanisms operating in the conditioning of a positively evaluated word with a noxious US. Such a conception implies that conditioning would be more difficult with the positive word than with the negatively evaluated word. There was no such evidence. Unfortunately, Baxter (1959, 1962) did not compare the two CRs directly, but their difference scores obtained in comparison with a control stimulus indicate that the positively evaluated CS word showed slightly better conditioning than the negatively evaluated word, contrary to the conception of reciprocally antagonistic mechanisms operating in one case but not the other.

An experiment by Acker and Edwards (1964) provides additional evidence contrary to the conception of reciprocally antagonistic mediation processes. Using highly noxious white noise as the US, they conditioned peripheral vasoconstriction to the word "good" in one group of subjects and "bad" in another group. The presentation of words previously rated as positive or negative on an evaluative scale of the semantic differential evoked the appropriate differential vasomotor response in the two groups. Subjects conditioned with "good" showed larger responses to positively evaluated than negatively evaluated or neutral words while the subjects conditioned with "bad" showed larger responses to negatively evaluated than positively evaluated or neutral words. Semantic generalization of the vasomotor response was obtained. However, semantic differential ratings of the test words at the conclusion of the experiment did not show the interaction predicted by Osgood. Both positively and negatively evaluated words as determined by ratings prior to the experiment showed a regression toward neutrality. The regression toward neutrality in the

ratings, the fact that "good" could be readily conditioned using a noxious stimulus, and positively as well as negatively evaluated words showed semantic generalization all contradict Osgood's formulation.

This still leaves the interpretation previously given, an interpretation that does not imply differential conditioning effects as a consequence of reciprocally antagonistic mediation processes, only differential generalization effects. Despite the apparent accord between the nonobvious implications of the interpretation of Osgood's theory and Baxter's generalization gradients, I do not believe that the data can be accepted as supporting the implications of the theory.

Baxter's results, I suspect, are artifactual. The generalization gradients he obtained are highly contaminated with effects of the orienting reflex (OR). Conditioning was conducted by repeatedly presenting only one word, the CS word, interspersed with blank slides; without interruption the test series words were introduced. Appearance of a different word after 12 presentations of the CS word would evoke an OR. Successive presentations of the different test words would result in habituation of the OR as evidenced by decreased GSRs. Baxter (1962) states that the test words were presented in random order for each subject, but unfortunately he did not analyze order effects. I am suggesting that the gradients obtained are primarily a manifestation of the OR as a function of the presentation order. Such an interpretation sounds highly improbable, since the words were presented in random orders. However, it must be noted that the adjacent points in his gradients are not likely to be significantly different from each other. It would take only the disproportionate occurrence of a few words in a given order to produce the gradients obtained.

At the very least it can be said that the experiment does not adequately control for contamination of the generalization gradient by the OR. In the absence of information on order effects it is extremely hazardous to interpret Baxter's generalization data as providing differential support for a particular theoretical formulation of semantic generalization.

Osgood (1961) has also cited an experiment by Dicken (1961) using the Mink procedure of operant conditioning for studying semantic generalization as providing support for his formulation as opposed to the verbal chaining interpretation. Subjects during training were presented with critical words that were high on the positive end of the evaluative scale, words that were high on the negative end of the scale, and neutral filler words. The critical word clusters were selected so that within a culster they were highly similar on the semantic differential but were not associated with each other in terms of word association norms. In the test situation the critical words were presented along with additional new critical words from each cluster and new filler words. The subjects made more recognition errors to the new critical words than the new filler words. What appeared to be reliable evidence of semantic generalization was obtained on the basis of semantic similarity and in the absence of evidence of existing interverbal associations.

Mrs. Luann Campeau has repeated this study in my laboratory as her doctoral dissertation. She recorded measures of the OR continuously and in addition used a control group which received the same test list as the experimental group used by Dicken but the training list contained only neutral words. Mrs. Campeau replicated Dicken's results in her experimental condition. Reliably more responses occurred to the new critical words than the filler words. However, the control group manifested the same tendency. A mixed-design analysis of variance indicated that the experimental group did not obtain a reliably greater difference between critical and filler words than the control group. Selection of the new critical words on the test list was not due to semantic generalization produced by training on the test list, but a disposition, for some presently unknown reason, to respond to words rated at the extremes of the evaluative scale as compared to neutrally rated words.

General criticisms of S-R theories

Two basic shortcomings of the S-R theories previously discussed are responsible for their limited effectiveness in accounting for phenomena of semantic conditioning and generalization. First, they have adopted an S-R theory of peripheralism in addition to an S-R methodological position. Second, their formulations lack a number of available concepts that are necessary for an adequate theory of simple conditioning as well as semantic conditioning and generalization.

In Watson's time peripheralism had some justification. Relatively little was known about the CNS in relation to behavior. Emphasis upon peripheral responses avoided pseudophysiological speculation and the reintroduction of mentalistic concepts. Reasons of this kind are no longer justifiable grounds for adopting naive peripheral theories of learning. The associative basis, temporary connections, or learning underlying semantic conditioning performance indubitably occurs in the brain, primarily the cerebral cortex, not in the skin or the heart. Current S-R theories are largely formulated as though the college sophomore were an empty shell. Theorists make perfunctory disclaimers: representational me-

diating responses may be either peripheral or central, and they are talking
about constructs. Nevertheless, when
it comes to actual theorizing about
experimental results, the theoretical
statements are obviously referring to
peripheral responses.

The bias towards peripheral theory is
evident, for example, in the manner in
which Staats and Staats (1963) discuss
an experiment they conducted (Staats,
Staats, and Crawford, 1962) in which
the GSR was conditioned to a word and
semantic generalization tested to a
synonym. They found that the magnitude of the conditioned GSR was
significantly correlated with the degree
of negative evaluation of the word on
the semantic differential. They interpret
the results of conditioning as follows:

> the findings indicate that conditioned
> autonomic responses may, at least in
> part, constitute the meaning of a
> word. . . . It is thus suggested that
> word meaning may be classically
> conditioned through pairing a word
> stimulus with another stimulus-speci-
> fically, a US for some response. Since
> the conditioned response is the word
> meaning, it may be called a conditioned
> 'meaning' response. Considered in this
> manner, it would be expected that the
> various principles which apply to the
> conditioning of responses in general
> would also apply to the acquisition of
> word meaning, for example, the greater
> the number of pairings of the word
> stimulus and the US, the stronger the
> meaning (Staats and Staats, 1963,
> pp. 142–43).

It should be noted that the authors
failed to obtain evidence of semantic
generalization either in terms of the
GSR measure or semantic differential
ratings, results hardly providing support
for the theory they are espousing. Our
concern, however, is not with the
failure to obtain or note the results of
the semantic generalization test, but
the nature of the theorizing.

First, I would insist that "meaning"
is a defined concept, not part of the
observation or "thing" level of language. "Meaning" is not a response, but
a theoretical term. Osgood's (1961)
insistence that meaning is the critical
problem in psychology is misplaced.
The critical problem is to explain,
predict, and deduce complex empirical
phenomena of generalization or transfer
from established principles. Meaning
theory is one attempt to do this. But
the problem is to predict and explain
the observed phenomena, not a particular concept.

Second, it is difficult to imagine how,
even in part, complex processes such as
semantic conditioning and generalization are dependent upon peripheral
autonomic responses; even though such
responses may provide proprioceptive
stimulation, they themselves are a
consequence of complex events occurring in the CNS. An autonomic response
such as the GSR is a dependent variable
in a conditioning experiment which is
a function of a multiplicity of different
antecedent and environmental conditions and physiological processes (Maltzman and Raskin, 1965).

Two conditions have contributed to
the grossly erroneous kind of theorizing
represented by the assumption that
peripheral responses in some sense are
directly conditioned and that, in this
case, they are meaning responses. First
is a rigor mortis of theorizing stemming
in part from the failure to distinguish
the systematic and theoretical elements
in Watson's formulations (Bergmann,
1956). A second contributing factor is
the oversimplification of most experimental studies of semantic conditioning
conducted in this country. Parametric
studies are rarely conducted, and more
than one response measure is rarely
employed. When studies employing
multiple measures are conducted, it
becomes readily apparent that "meaning" cannot be a conditioned autonomic

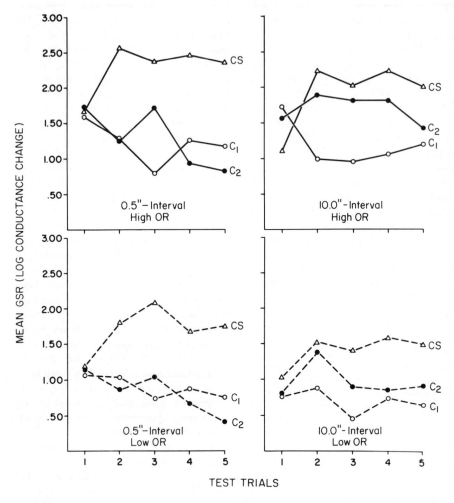

Figure 7. Mean GSR on five conditioning test trials to the CS and preceding (C_1) and following (C_2) test words obtained by High and Low OR groups under two CS-US intervals

response. Likewise, multiple response criteria indicate that covariation between ratings on the semantic differential and a physiological measure is not due to a common determiner such as "meaning" or a representational mediation process. These conclusions are based upon a number of studies conducted in my laboratory.

For example, we have repeated, although not in all details, Martha Mednick's (1957) experiment several times.[4] In one study two different

[4] I am greatly indebted to the students who made this and other research reported here possible: D. Feeney, J. Gould, Ola Johnson, B. Langdon, D. C. Raskin, J. Schull, and M. Smith. I am further indebted to D. Feeney, J. Gould, Mary Mandell, and J. Senf for their critical comments on the present paper.

For the analyses of the results of experiments reported here computing assistance was obtained from the Health Sciences Computing Facility, UCLA, Sponsored by NIH Grant FR-3.

groups of 30 subjects each were conditioned under either a .5-second CS-US interval or a 10-second CS-US interval with a 110-decibel white noise as the US. Palmar GSR and peripheral vasomotor responses were recorded. Subjects were divided into high and low orienters in terms of the magnitude of their response to the first US.

Figures 7 and 8 show the results from the conditioning test trials. In terms of the GSR, reliably better semantic conditioning occurred under the .5-second interval than under the 10-second interval. However, the opposite effect was obtained with the finger vasomotor response. Reliably superior conditioning was obtained under the relatively long, as compared to the short interval.

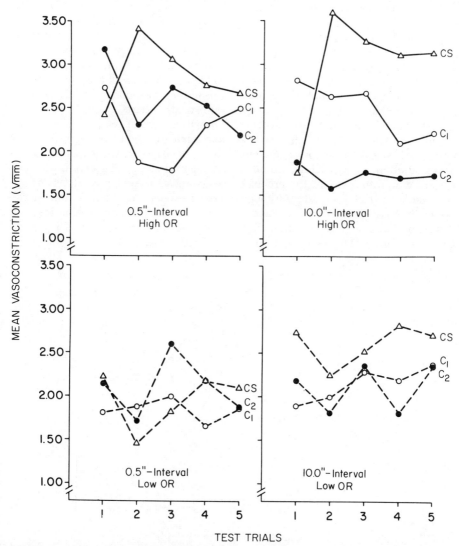

Figure 8. Mean peripheral vasomotor response to the CS on five conditioning test trials and preceding (C₁) and following (C₂) test words obtained by High and Low OR groups under two CS-US intervals

Figure 9 shows the GSR semantic generalization gradient obtained with the test words ordered from high to low in terms of their associative connection with " light."

Reliable semantic generalization was obtained only under the .5-second interval with the GSR in the present experiment. Reliable evidence of semantic generalization was not obtained with the vasomotor response under either CS-US interval.

Results from the conditioning and generalization phases of the experiment indicate, among other things, a considerable degree of response specificity. If the vasomotor response alone were used, it would be concluded that semantic generalization was not obtained.

Another study in my laboratory found that almost any shape of gradient could be obtained with these stimulus materials as a function of the order of the words in the test list. Although associative strength is an important determiner of semantic generalization between words, the response change

observed is affected by a host of other variables. Some of these are peculiar to the response measure employed while others are related to the stimulus sequence.

In another study five different groups of college students ($N = 200$) received a CS word, "plant," interspersed among unrelated words and followed after varying intervals of time by a US of 110-decibel white noise. Different groups received CS-US intervals of .5, 5.5, 10.5, 15.5, or 20.5 seconds. A semantic generalization test followed without interruption, consisting of a single presentation of the word "stem"; this in turn was followed by five extinction trials where the CS word was presented interspersed among other unrelated words but without a US. At the conclusion of the experiment the subjects rated the CS, generalization test word, and neutral filler words on an evaluative scale of the semantic differential.

Results from the extinction test and semantic differential ratings are summarized in Table 1.

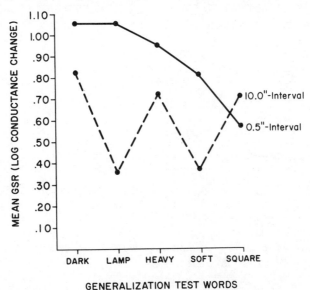

Figure. 9. Semantic generalization of the GSR following conditioning under two CS-US intervals

Table 1

MEAN CONDITIONED GSR AND PERIPHERAL VASOMOTOR RESPONSE (VMR) DURING EXTINCTION, AND EVALUATIVE SEMANTIC DIFFERENTIAL RATINGS OF CS, SEMANTIC GENERALIZATION TEST WORLD (SG), AND CONTROL WORDS AS A CONSEQUENCE OF SEMANTIC CONDITIONING UNDER DIFFERENT CS-US INTERVALS. A RATING OF 1 IS UNPLEASANT AND 7 IS PLEASANT.

	Interval (seconds)				
	0.5	5.5	10.5	15.5	20.5
Extinction					
GSR	1.88	1.34	1.44	1.20	1.45
VMR	1.59	1.90	2.13	1.71	2.04
Semantic Differential Ratings					
CS	1.80	1.55	1.63	1.72	1.68
SG	2.93	3.10	3.13	2.85	2.95
Control	4.39	4.31	4.34	4.21	4.27

For the GSR the shorter the CS-US interval the greater the resistance to extinction. For the peripheral vasomotor response (VMR) the shorter the CS-US interval, by and large, the poorer the resistance to extinction. The .5-second CS-US gave the greatest resistance to extinction in the GSR measure and the poorest for the VMR. The main effects of CS-US conditions were significant for both measures. Significant evidence of semantic conditioning and semantic generalization was obtained on the semantic differential for all intervals, and the intervals did not differ reliably. Thus, three different response measures employed in this experiment revealed three different functional relationships with CS-US interval. It is also worth noting that individual differences in the magnitude of the orienting reflex, as determined at the start of the conditioning experiment, produced a reliable main effect on the semantic differential ratings. Subjects above the median OR level gave reliably more extreme ratings than subjects below the median.

Granted that there are many problems involved in comparing condition- ing under different CS-US intervals and for different measures, the results certainly do not support a conception which makes meaning at least in part an autonomic response. Much of the difficulty is due to the fact that theoretical and experimental studies of semantic conditioning and generalization have tended to ignore the distinction between learning and performance or the possibility that results obtained with a given response measure may reflect parameters peculiar to that response. Ignoring the distinction results in the implication that every reliable change in the CR is a reliable change in meaning, a clearly untenable position. Accepting some such notion as the distinction between learning and performance or parameters specific to response measures and general learning parameters requires giving up the notion of meaning as a response and meaning as the detachable portion of the response to the unconditioned stimulus. A further implication of response specific conditioning and transfer effects is that the peripheral response is not itself conditioned, associated with the stimulus, and transferred.

Theoretical interpretations of the "operant" procedure for studying semantic generalization devised at Minnesota also have difficulty in relating learning to performance due to the assumption of S-R peripheralism (Dicken, 1961; Jenkins, 1963; Mink, 1957, 1963). In these studies subjects are instructed to press a lever to each word in a training list. After several presentations of the training list, a test list is presented containing original training words, new associates of the training words, and new unrelated control words. The subjects are instructed to press the lever to words that they recognize as belonging to the training list. Semantic generalization is evidenced by a greater number of lever presses evoked by associates of the training words than by unrelated control words. It is assumed that the training words evoke their implicit associates which are conditioned to the lever press response during training. When the implicit associates of the training words are presented as stimuli in the semantic generalization test, the previously conditioned lever press occurs.

Contrary to results reported by Jenkins (1963), we found (Maltzman and Belloni, 1964) reliable evidence of semantic generalization when there was no opportunity for the association of the test response to the training words or their implicit associates. In a group situation subjects were presented with the training words to which they made no overt response. They were then given answer sheets where they checked off whether or not words on the test list had previously been presented. They checked off reliably more associates than control words as having previously been on the training list, showing semantic generalization of an "operant" response which had not previously been associated with the words. Semantic generalization under

such conditions was not reliably different from the more usual condition where an overt response occurred to the training words.

A serious shortcoming of S-R theories of semantic conditioning and generalization is the underlying assumption that learning somehow involves the association of stimuli or their traces and overt or covert motor activity. The experimental evidence is overwhelmingly contrary to such an hypothesis.

The Nature of Classical Conditioning

Research, primarily by physiologists, in the Soviet Union as well as in Western Europe and the United States, rather clearly indicates that classical conditioning is considerably more complex than assumed by S-R conceptions underlying current theories of semantic conditioning and generalization.

S-S vs. S-R conditioning

Theories of semantic conditioning and generalization previously considered imply that a peripheral motor response is conditioned to, associated with, a stimulus. Although theorists say that the responses may be peripheral or central (Osgood, 1953, pp. 697–98; Bousfield, 1961, p. 82), they talk as if, and present diagrams depicting, peripheral responses associated to stimuli. Discussions of meaning usually gravitate to statements about autonomic responses, e.g., GSR, as part of the meaning response, etc., as though the central nervous system can somehow be circumvented or is nonexistent.

For many years the experiment by Loucks (1935) in which direct stimulation of the motor cortex paired with a CS failed to show conditioning has been taken as a major source of evidence supporting an S-R reinforcement position (Spence, 1951). More recently Doty and Giurgea (1961) and Kogan (1960) have reported that conditioning can be obtained by direct stimulation of the cortex. Doty and Giurgea (1961) paired direct electrical stimulation of a sensory area of the cortex with stimulation of a motor area that also led to evocation of a motor response. After such pairings stimulation of the sensory area alone evoked the motor response. Conditioning was thus demonstrated in the absence of an exteroceptive stimulus, as well as in the absence of externally administered reinforcement. Apparently the earlier attempt by Loucks (1935) to obtain conditioning by stimulation of the motor cortex failed because his shorter intertrial intervals were not optimal.

Beck and Doty (1957) have obtained evidence that the elicitation of the motor response is unnecessary for conditioning. Paired presentations of a CS and US, shock to a limb, were presented to cats following de-efferentation of the limb by crushing its ventral roots. In addition, the cats were in a cataleptic state induced by bulbocapnine during conditioning. Following reinnervation of the limb, tests showed that a conditioned leg flexion response had been acquired in the absence of an overt unconditioned response.

These studies demonstrate that neither the external stimulus nor the overt motor response is necessary for conditioning. Transfer to the normal state of discriminative conditioning established in dogs paralyzed by D-tubocurarine is further evidence that conditioning may occur in the absence of a peripheral motor response (Solomon and Turner, 1962). It would seem possible to have the smile without the Cheshire cat, the "-" without the S and R.

Learning without prior performance

Some time ago Thorndike (1946) proposed a test of S-S vs. S-R learning theories: transport animals through a maze to a goal object. Having no opportunity to perform instrumental responses that are reinforced, S-R theories would be forced to predict that such animals would learn the maze no more rapidly than animals without the prior experience. S-S learning theory would predict that prior exposure to the maze would facilitate subsequent performance. Gleitman (1955) and McNamara, Long, and Wike (1956) found that transported rats could learn when extramaze cues were available. When extramaze cues were reduced, prior exposure to the situation did not result in learning (McNamara, Long, and Wike, 1956).

The latter results are superficially in contradiction to the extensive research of Beritoff (1965) who found that learning occurs in transported dogs even under severely restricted stimulus conditions. But this may be a species difference. Quite independently of the theoretical controversy in this country, Beritoff for many years has been conducting experiments of this sort. He has repeatedly found that after being transported in a cage to food along a circuitous route only once, dogs can readily find their way back to the goal. Based upon extensive research, Beritoff believes that when the animals are transported along a path they acquire an image of the geographical location of the food. The image is established primarily from labyrinthine stimulation. Elimination of visual, auditory, and olfactory cues, does not prevent the dog from successfully attaining the goal object. According to Beritoff, images are a consequence of activity in the large stellate cells in the third and fourth layers of the neocortex. Images are defined in terms of the neurophysiological state of the organism, not its immediate experience.

Sensory-sensory conditioning

It has been known for many years that classical conditioning of cortical alpha blocking can be obtained as a result of the pairing of an innocuous light serving as the US for desynchronization of alpha and a tone as the CS (Morrell, 1961b). After repeated pairings the tone itself evokes alpha blocking.

Unless it is assumed that such conditioning is artifactual, e.g., due to changes in respiration, or that it is an epiphenomenon, unrelated to behavioral changes, such simple experiments with human subjects quite clearly indicate that the acquisition of associative connections need not involve the occurrence of overt peripheral responses or reinforcement, as ordinarily conceived. That learning of overt responses has occurred without their evocation during conditioning could be made readily apparent. There is little doubt that, if questioned, most subjects could report that a tone was followed by a light.

An interpretation of classical conditioning

Pavlov was explicitly a so-called S-S theorist. A temporary connection or association is not formed between conditioned stimulus and salivary response. Associative connections are formed between the foci of excitability, primarily in the cortex, induced by the CS and the US.

The fundamental mechanism for the formation of a conditioned reflex, wrote Pavlov, is the meeting, the coincidence of the stimulation of a definite centre in the cerebral cortex with the stronger stimulation of another centre, probably also in the cortex, as a result of which, sooner or later, an easier path is formed between the two points, i.e., a connection is made.

Pavlov's views on the intrinsic mechanism of formation of a conditioned connection changed in the course of the development of the conditioned reflex theory. (He at first considered that the strongly excited unconditioned reflex centre attracts the stimulation from the feebly excited centre of the extraneous stimulus, whereas subsequently he considered it to be more likely that the excitatory waves irradiated from both centres meet.) This, however, did not touch the fundamentals of his concept, namely, that a connection is established between the nervous centres. (Asratyan, 1953, p. 90).

Support for the hypothesis that temporary connections are established between foci of excitability in the cortex has been reported by Livanov (1960). Using a toposcope, a 100-lead electroencephalogram, he is able to demonstrate that the presentation of a CS and a US results in the establishment of centers of excitability corresponding to the CS and US. There is widespread bioelectrical activity in the cortex at the outset of conditioning, a state corresponding to the generalized orienting reflex. With repeated conditioning trials, the waves of excitability become restricted to channels between foci in the occipital-parietal and frontal areas. With further trials the motor response, leg flexion, to the CS occurs.

These results support Pavlov's general conception that the temporary connection is formed between foci of excitability induced by the CS and US. The temporary connection in the brain which is manifested as a conditioned response does not occur between events initiated by the CS and the motor representations of the overt response. It is not S-R.

However, Livanov's data as well as other physiological studies of conditioning (Morrell, 1961b) do not confirm S-S behavior theory. The widespread presence of pyramidal and extrapyramidal cells in the cortex, the presence of subcortical as well as transcortical connections even in the conditioning of a single neural cell (Morrell, 1961a) means that the foci of excitability induced by the CS and US include efferents as well as afferents. Such findings as Livanov's contradict a peripheralistic S-R theory which requires the occurrence of overt motor activity as necessary for conditioning and which assumes that the temporary connection is between a sensory and motor center. In the central nervous system conditioning is neither simple S-S nor S-R.

Preliminary theoretical consideration: Orienting and defensive reflexes

A second source of difficulty encountered by current S-R theories of semantic conditioning and generalization, particularly when physiological response measures are employed, is that the complex nature of the dependent variable has not been adequately considered. Related to this problem and a deficiency of more general proportions because it has retarded an adequate development of S-R theories of simple conditioning as well, is the lack of familiarity with the concepts of the orienting (OR) and defensive (DR) reflexes that have been developed in the Soviet Union and demonstrated widely (Anokhin, 1961; Berlyne, 1960; Luria and Vinogradova, 1959; Maltzman and Raskin, 1965; Morrell, 1961b; Razran, 1961; Sokolov, 1960, 1963a; 1963b; Voronin and Sokolov, 1960).

Since most of the experimental studies of semantic conditioning and generalization conducted in this country involve effects of the OR and DR which have not been adequately recognized, we must briefly indicate the characteristics and implications of these concepts. To some extent we have covered this ground elsewhere (Maltzman and Raskin, 1965).

According to Soviet investigators, any stimulus change may evoke an OR, an observation readily corroborated by investigators in this country who have employed the GSR. Quantitative, qualitative, and temporal changes may serve as the antecedent conditions while there is a syndrome of consequent conditions which includes the GSR, cortical alpha blocking, respiratory changes, pupillary dilation, and a complex of peripheral vasoconstriction with cephalic vasodilation. The "orienting reflex" is a defined concept and is not equivalent to any one of these dependent variables.[5] We might add that "emotion," "anxiety," "meaning," etc., are all defined concepts, not directly observable, but definable in terms of observable antecedent conditions and consequences. The GSR, for example, is a dependent variable and not anxiety or meaning. It may be used as a response measure to define such concepts if one so desires. This can be done successfully, if the antecedent conditions under which the response measure is obtained are clearly specified. Whether such defined concepts are useful or not depends upon the lawful relationships developed, the extent to

---

[5] This usage should be distinguished from the more familiar concept in this country of the observing response or receptor-adjustor act (Spence, 1937, 1940; Wykoff, 1952). The latter refers to instrumental acts which affect stimulus reception while the OR as employed here is defined by respondents. Soviet investigators tend to use the orienting reflex concept to refer to both operants and respondents. The intimate relationship between the two kinds of behavioral measures is in urgent need of detailed study.

which the concepts acquire significance (Bergmann, 1957).

Measures of the orienting reflex may be obtained not only when there are changes in the parameters of physical stimuli, such as intensity and frequency of auditory stimuli, but as a consequence of more complex verbal stimulus changes as well, changes that presuppose prior learning histories, e.g., shifting from one kind of word class to another.

Another characteristic of the orienting reflex is its nonspecificity. Similar response changes occur regardless of the type of stimulus change. A qualitative or quantitative change in visual stimuli will evoke an OR in the same fashion as a change in auditory stimuli, although the magnitude of the OR will vary with the amount of stimulus change involved.

Habituation of the OR may be readily produced, as indicated by the decrement in magnitude of its response measures with repeated stimulation of an unvarying sort. The OR may be evoked again when the pattern of stimulation is changed. According to Soviet theorists (Anokhin, 1961; Sokolov, 1963b), a discrepancy between present stimuli and traces of past stimuli gives rise to an OR. Thus an OR may occur to the absence of a stimulus when a pattern of stimulation has repeatedly occurred. Therefore phenomena that Grings (1960) has interpreted in terms of a perceptual disparity response represent a special case of the orienting reflex.

Although the OR may habituate, its conditioning and maintenance is also possible. Giving a stimulus significance, in the terminology of Soviet investigators (Luria and Vinogradova, 1959) may maintain an OR at a given level or retard the rate at which it habituates (Maltzman and Raskin, 1965). Reinforcing a conditioned stimulus as in classical conditioning not only may retard the rate of habituation, but results in increased magnitude of its OR, produces a conditioned OR.

Measurement of the defensive reflex (DR) in many situations is as vitally important as the recording of the OR. Other things being equal, the greater the stimulus intensity or stimulus change, beyond some point above a near threshold value, the larger the magnitude of the OR (Sokolov, 1963b). The "law of strength" holds. But beyond some point further increases in intensity of stimuli, or repeated presentations of a given stimulus, may give rise to a DR. In terms of most peripheral physiological measures, the qualitative change in the reflex evoked may not be apparent, so that a similar GSR will be evoked when a DR as well as an OR is elicited by a stimulus. The measure which differentially defines the two reflexes is the cephalic vasomotor response, vasodilation in the case of an OR and vasoconstriction in the case of a DR.

Use of the cephalic vasomotor response as the differential measure of an OR and DR is of vital importance, because it is not possible to predict accurately at present whether an OR or DR will be evoked by a given stimulus intensity. The functional relationships between stimulus intensity, stimulus repetitions, and OR and DR magnitudes reported by Sokolov (1963b) hold only for stimuli presented in isolation. We find marked differences in whether an OR or DR will occur when stimuli are used in a conditioning situation, when the stimuli "acquire significance," as well as marked individual and population subject differences in the tendency for a given stimulus intensity to evoke an OR or DR.

Simply as peripheral response measures these physiological changes are relatively trivial, just as by themselves operationally defined concepts of an OR or DR are trivial. Their importance stems from their lawful relations with other kinds of behavior, concepts, and experimental variables.

According to Soviet investigators (Sokolov, 1960, 1963b) the importance of the OR stems from its functional relationships with learning and perception. Occurrence of an OR facilitates the acquisition of temporary connections, learning, and tunes the sensory analysers, i.e., lowers sensory thresholds. Conditions under which the OR occurs, and the consequences obtained, correspond in part to the usage of the older concept of "attention," as it was used in consciousness-centered psychology (Maltzman and Raskin, 1965; Pillsbury, 1908). We would add another important function of the OR. It is a reinforcer. In other words, stimuli that are labeled as reinforcers because the responses they follow show an increased probability of occurrence, particularly so-called secondary reinforcers at the human level, are reinforcing because they evoke an OR.

Conditioning of a response to a word and the subsequent generalization of that response to another word is considerably more complex than conceptualized by current S-R theories of semantic conditioning, particularly when a noxious US is employed. A response such as the GSR is not simply conditioned to the representational process or the CS word. The nature of the physiological processes induced by the US may change radically during the course of an experiment, from cephalic vasodilation to vasoconstriction, orienting to defensive reflex.

In semantic conditioning with a noxious stimulus the CS and the filler words initially evoke ORs. The extent to which the CS evokes an OR on the first conditioning trial, prior to the

first pairing with the US, will vary with the number of habituation words, the interword interval, and individual subject differences. Ordinarily, for successful conditioning of a DR, a conditioned OR must first occur, a differentially larger OR to the CS than to the filler words. Eventually, the conditioned OR will be replaced by a conditioned DR. Prior to a stable conditioned DR, the US will evoke an OR, and then shift to a DR. The CS may evoke a conditioned OR while the US on that same trial evokes a DR. There may be oscillation between OR and DR on different trials to both stimuli until finally they both evoke a DR relatively consistently. Many trials may be required, if the subjects are college students, before stable defensive reflexes are evoked. Nonstudents may show conditioned defensive reflexes much more readily, we have found. The reason for this difference may be that college students are a highly select group, intelligent, highly verbal, and suspicious. They have relatively strong ORs; they are constantly trying to discover the purpose of the experiment, and therefore it is difficult to establish DRs. A conditioned OR, on the other hand, is readily established with a noxious US. In terms of the number of conditioning trials ordinarily employed in semantic conditioning experiments in this country, we would guess that no published study employing college students as subjects has yielded stable conditioned DRs.

Figure 10 shows the peripheral and cephalic vasomotor records from two subjects in an experiment similar to the one reported by Martha Mednick (1957). A 10-second CS-US interval was used with a highly noxious 110-decibel white noise as the US. The upper tracings are from a "poor" record, the lower from a "good" record which clearly shows peripheral vasocon-

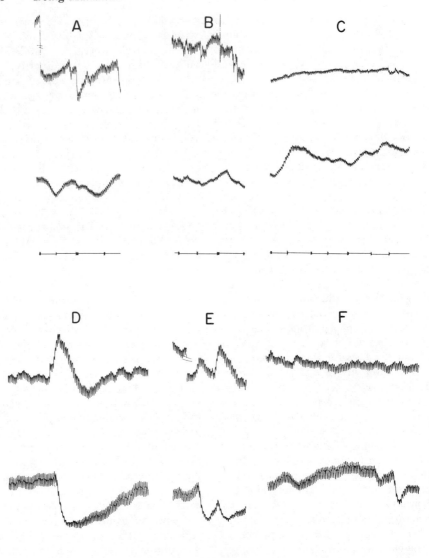

Figure 10. Vasomotor responses in head and finger from a "poor" record classified as a Low Orienter, sections *A, B,* and *C,* and a "good" record representing a High Orienter, sections *D, E,* and *F.* Sections *A* and *D* show the response to the first US; *B* and *E* show the seventh conditioning trial; sections *C* and *F* show the generalization test. Hash marks in the third and sixth tracing indicate the occurrence of words and the US.

striction and cephalic vasodilation to the US, conditioned peripheral vasoconstriction and cephalic vasodilation to the CS word "light," and semantic generalization of these responses to one or more of the generalization words, "dark," "lamp," "heavy," and "soft," and no response to "square." The "poor" record shows some evidence of cephalic vasoconstriction, but a consistent defensive reflex was not established.

Although semantic conditioning with noxious stimuli is complex, in the sense that many different response changes are occurring, semantic generalization is even more complex. As indicated by the description of the results obtained by Luria and Vinogradova (1959), and as indicated by our own research, the kind of reflex that is generalized depends upon the stage of training and the type of connection between the test words and the CS word. Relatively early in conditioning when the CR is an OR, the OR will show semantic generalization. After the DR has been established as the CR, either an OR or DR or both may show semantic generalization depending upon the relationship between the CS and test word and the stage of conditioning attained.

After establishing a conditioned DR to the word "violin," Luria and Vinogradova (1959) found that words closely related, on a common sense basis, such as the names of other stringed instruments, also evoked a DR. Words somewhat more remotely related, such as names of wind instruments, type of music, or similar sounding words, evoked an OR. Unrelated words evoked no response. With additional conditioning trials this "semantic structure" showed a further change. None of the test words evoked a DR. Words previously evoking a DR now evoked an OR while words previously evoking an OR evoked no response. Finally, after still more conditioning trials, semantic generalization no longer occurred. None of the test words evoked a response.

Unfortunately, details of the experimental procedure are lacking, so that it is not known whether or not the same subjects were repeatedly tested for semantic generalization after different stages of training and whether or not the same or different words were used at each generalization test.

Studies conducted in my laboratory have obtained semantic generalization of the OR and the DR, but not in the same experiment. This may be due to the less elaborate "semantic structures" we have employed, i.e., at best only a few different generalization test words and an insufficient number of conditioning trials. Although it is not possible to formulate precisely a theory of semantic generalization of the OR and DR on the basis of the results reported by Luria and Vinogradova, their results are clearly beyond the explanatory power of current S-R theories.

Towards a Theory of Semantic Generalization

S-R theories of instrumental and trial and error learning (Hull, 1943; Spence, 1956) have recognized some of the complexities involved in behavior in such situations by positing an anticipatory response mechanism. Classical conditioning theory has been grossly oversimplified in this respect. In contrast, many current Soviet theorists include a conception of anticipation as basic to behavior in classical as well as instrumental conditioning situations (Anokhin, 1961; Beritoff, 1965; Sokolov, 1963b). Evidence for the role of anticipation in semantic conditioning is available in a number of our experiments. We find, for example, that under certain conditions the control words immediately preceding, C_1, and the control words immediately following, C_2, the CS show characteristic reliable trends over conditioning trials. The response to the preceding word, which is different on each trial, shows a reliable increase, while the succeeding word, also different on each trial, shows a decrement over trials. These trends

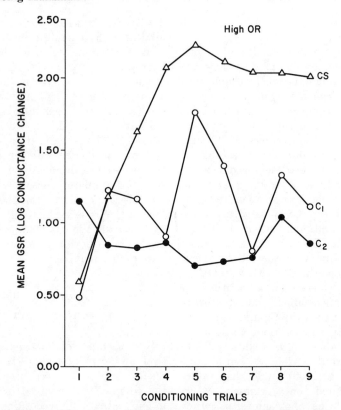

Figure 11. Mean GSR during conditioning of High OR subjects to the conditioned stimulus word (CS), and the neutral control words preceding (C_1) and following (C_2) the CS word on each conditioning trial.

are illustrated in Figures 11 and 12. The conditioning curves are for high and low OR subjects classified on the basis of their response magnitude to the first word in the habituation list prior to the start of conditioning. They represent the average GSR for the four longer CS-US intervals in the experiment previously described. The subject learns to anticipate the occurrence of the CS and US, and the anticipation is based upon the overall pattern of stimulation in the experimental situation. If an anticipation is not fulfilled, a present stimulus is not in accord with the past pattern of stimulation, then an OR may occur. This is probably the reason for the augmented C_1 response

preceding the fifth trial, since it occurred after a larger than usual number of filler words; the CS word was anticipated earlier but a control word occurred in its place.

When the US is omitted, as when extinction begins, in place of the US another filler word, C_2, eventually occurs. As a consequence of the discrepancy between the past pattern of stimulation and the present one, the change from US to C_2, within limits, an exaggerated response representing an OR occurs to the control word. The effect habituates with repeated extinction trials, with the establishment of a new pattern of stimulation.

Semantic conditioning and generali-

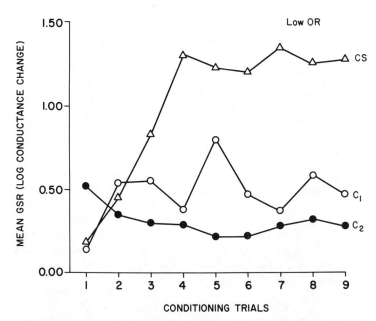

Figure 12. Mean GSR during conditioning of Low OR subjects to the conditioned stimulus word (CS), and the neutral control words preceding (C_1) and following (C_2) the CS word on each conditioning trial.

zation is affected by certain standing conditions of the experiment which are not as yet clearly specified, conditions that establish dispositions, anticipations, or habit family hierarchies, that determine in part the course of behavior in the experiment. Results in accord with this supposition have been reported by Razran (1949b). He found that the nature of controlled associations evoked prior to an experiment reliably affected the kind of semantic generalization of the salivary response subsequently obtained.

Semantic generalization, as measured in my laboratory as well as by many other investigators, cannot be due to a failure to associate, or a failure to discriminate, bases for generalization ascribed to by Lashley and Wade (1946), since a differential response criterion is employed. The response to the test word must be reliably larger than the response to filler words. For

semantic generalization to occur test words must be discriminated as different from control filler words and as related to the training word. According to Razran (1949c)

> when human beings or dogs that have been conditioned to some stimulus or object are confronted with some new non-conditioned but in some way related stimulus or object, they categorize or rate the new stimulus on some sort of crude similarity-dissimiliarity scale. With human subjects, introspections actually reveal such categorizing attitudes as "similar," "very similar," "not so similar," "somewhat similar," "dissimilar," "very dissimilar" and the like—attitudes that apparently control or even initiate the generalization responses. (p. 362).

Razran qualifies the above formulation in the following manner:

> Other *S*s, however, failed to report such introspections, and it appears . . . that

such categorizing behavior may in time well become automatic, an integral part of the individual's learned habits and capacities, and barely conscious . . . present evidence warrants the assumption that CR generalization is much more a function of *automatized* attitudes than of *automatic* reflexive or conditioned reflexive reactions. (1949a, p. 827).

Although Razran's formulation offers a description of what happens in a semantic generalization test situation of the kind he employs, the problem still remains of determining the principles governing such "categorizing behavior." The available evidence strongly suggests that ratings of similarity are at least in part a function of associative strength between the stimulus words rated (Whitmarsh and Bousfield, 1961; Bousfield and Puff, 1965; Mink, 1957; Kurcz, 1964). It is also necessary to note that the gross nature of generalization is in part a characteristic of the particular response measure employed and not necessarily a characteristic of some more basic process. The crudeness of the gradient of generalization may be due in part to the diffuse nondifferentiated nature of the autonomic response measure employed. A distinction analogous to that between learning and performance is necessary. The subject's verbal behavior usually can make finer distinctions, provide more steps in a gradient, than the physiological response (Chatterjee and Eriksen, 1960). Nevertheless, in principle Razran's description is correct; there is some kind of categorization or discrimination that the test word is similar to the CS word. Its basis, I believe, is the orienting reflex.

Presentation of a test word represents a change from the past situation of CS, US, and neutral filler words which the subject comes to anticipate. An OR to the test word results. The test word represents a change in that it is associated with the CS word while the control words are unrelated. When a measure such as the GSR is the dependent variable in the semantic conditioning and generalization experiment, generalization is directly manifested in terms of the response criterion of the OR. When some other response measure such as salivation is the dependent variable, as in Razran's experiments, occurrence of an OR results in increased cortical excitability which activates the dominant focus established by the US (John, 1962; Morrell, 1961a). A response corresponding to the UR results. Elicitation of the OR also primes the second signal system, speech, so that the subject verbalizes that he anticipates the US after the test word in the same fashion as he anticipates the US after the CS word.

Evidence that would provide differential support for the hypothesis that semantic generalization may occur as the result of a "judgment of similarity" which is a consequence of an OR would require semantic generalization in the absence of any possibility of associative connections or similarity of representational processes. Support of this kind stems from part of the extinction phase of a semantic conditioning experiment that we have conducted. Following semantic conditioning with the CS word "plant," different subgroups were given five extinction trials with an associated word, either "stem" or "tree" or an unrelated word "music." Different US conditioning groups were represented proportionately among these three extinction groups.

Figure 13 shows the GSR during extinction to the C_1, critical words, and C_2. The striking result obtained is that instead of a decrement in responsivity, the response to the critical words shows a reliable increase. At the conclusion of the experiment subjects

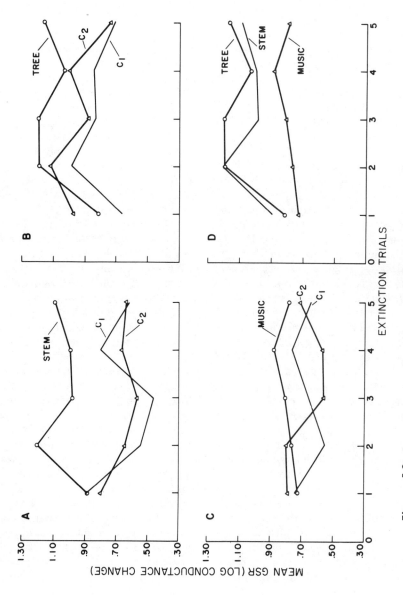

Figure 13. Semantic generalization of the GSR based upon similarity with the CS due to repeated presentations

were given a questionnaire similar to the one employed by Chatterjee and Eriksen (1960). Critical and filler words were presented and the subject was asked to indicate whether the US occurred after the word, or he expected it to occur, etc. Ratings on an evaluative scale of the semantic differential were also obtained for these words.

Results from these measures suggest the basis for the increasing magnitude of the GSR to the unrelated word "music" as well as the associated words "stem" and "tree." Subjects reported that they expected the US to follow the critical words because they were repeated, and the only other word that was repeated, "plant," was followed by the loud noise. Negative evaluations of the critical words were justified in a similar fashion by the subjects.

Semantic generalization of the physiological response and the verbal report occurred on the basis of similarity established in the test situation, a similarity based upon a complex relation, repetition of a word in contrast to nonrepetition of all other words. Development of an OR to the critical words on the basis of their difference from other filler words is responsible for the semantic generalization of the GSR and the verbal report and ratings. That associative strength plays a role in the "categorization" is indicated by the difference in the trends of the associated as compared to the nonassociated word.

It must be admitted, however, that the above results were not anticipated. The experimental conditions were designed to investigate the semantic generalization of extinction effects in a subsequent phase of the experiment. For this reason the results as well as the interpretation must be accepted with caution and require further replication with additional control conditions. Since Chatterjee and Eriksen (1960)

have reported a similar effect, however, there is good reason to assume that the results are reproducible.

A fundamental difference between the S-R theory proposed here and other S-R theories of semantic generalization is that the present theory does not assume a common, relatively specific, mediating response. The OR, which corresponds in part to the common sense notion of attention, is quite nonspecific. The present formulation also assumes that while prior established associations between words are an important determiner, semantic generalization may occur as a consequence of relations between stimuli which evoke an OR in the absence of specific associative connections.

A fundamental difference between the present S-R theory and cognitive theories (Wallach, 1958) is that in the latter "judgment of similarity" or "classification rule" are basic concepts whereas in the present formulation they are defined in terms of measures of the OR. The cognitive formulation suffers from two serious defects. First, a concept such as "classification rule" has no independent measure. It is "inferred" from the very same behavior which it is presumed to explain. Second, such cognitive concepts are not related to established principles of behavior. Deriving judgments of similarity or classification rules from principles of the OR avoids these difficulties. It is a relatively simple matter to conduct semantic generalization experiments in which the measure of semantic conditioning and generalization is different from the measure of the OR. Many principles of the OR are known as well as its relationships with other kinds of behavior (Sokolov, 1960, 1963a, 1963b), although certainly much remains to be done, particularly in the area of semantic conditioning and generalization, and learning in general.

Theoretical issues

Two problems confront every theory of semantic conditioning and generalization. One is peculiar to generalization while the other is of a more general nature: the locus of generalization and the role of awareness.

THE LOCUS OF GENERALIZATION. Razran (1949a, 1949b, 1949c) has maintained that the locus of generalization is the generalization test, not the conditioning situation. He holds this subsequent testing hypothesis for both primary stimulus generalization and semantic generalization. In the case of primary stimulus generalization this hypothesis stands opposed to the Pavlovian and Hullian hypotheses of the spread of excitatory or associative strength from the CS to other similar stimuli. But in the case of semantic generalization Razran's hypothesis is in essential agreement with the Hullian formulation of verbal chaining as represented by the Shipley-Lumsdaine paradigms.

Two kinds of evidence obtained by Razran lend support to his hypothesis that the critical variables determining the development of semantic generalization occur in the generalization test situation. The first (Razran, 1949a) is based upon unidirectional grammatical relationships or unidirectional associative strengths, which appear to be the basis for his obtained effect (Whitmarsh and Bousfield, 1961), while the second is based upon experimental variations (Razran, 1949b).

The first and more familiar source of support stems from the different amounts of semantic generalization obtained, e.g., when the word "doodle" is the CS word and "Yankee" the generalization test word as compared to the condition where the salivary response is first conditioned to "Yankee" and the semantic generalization test is with "doodle." "Yankee-doodle" yielded 13.1 per cent specific generalization while "doodle-Yankee" yielded 57 per cent specific generalization. Such an effect seems reasonable in terms of the verbal chaining hypothesis, since "Yankee" as the test word would evoke the implicit response "doodle" which was previously conditioned to the response; but "doodle" as the test word would not evoke "Yankee" as an implicit response, since the mediator necessary for the elicitation of the generalized response does not occur. But if "Yankee" evokes "doodle" in the test situation, why should it not do so when it, "Yankee," is presented during conditioning? If it did, then the implicit response "doodle" would be conditioned to the response measure. The locus of generalization should be both in the training and the test situation. However, evidence such as that obtained by Razran suggests that the locus is in the test. Occurrence of the implicit mediator in the test situation and not the training situation, it could be argued, is due to the differential effects of prompting (Storms, 1958). "Yankee" or any other CS word may evoke a vast number of implicit associations, and many classes, habit families, of associates. The probability of any one associate occurring and subsequently appearing as the test word is very remote. However, when "Yankee" is presented as the test for semantic generalization, the repeated occurrence of "doodle" during training raises the probability of its occurrence as an implicit response to the test word.

Although the prompting hypothesis seems to be a reasonable S-R interpretation, it is contradicted, or has limited generality, as indicated by the results obtained in the Mink type semantic generalization situation (Maltzman and Belloni, 1964; Mink, 1957, 1963; Moss, 1960).

Another experiment by Razran (1949b) provides striking evidence that semantic generalization can be obtained when the only possible locus is the test situation. There were four CS words with a set of three generalization test words for each CS. Four groups of subjects were employed. One group was told the meaning of the training word prior to conditioning. They were told it is equivalent to one of the test words. A second group was told the meaning of the CS word just prior to the generalization test. A third group was told the meaning of the CS word prior to the start of conditioning, and then prior to the test they were told that the CS word really had a different meaning, was the equivalent of a different word. A final control group was not told the meaning of the CS words.

For example, subjects were conditioned to the Russian word "Dolgo," with which they had no prior familiarity, and tested on the words "long," "short," and "dolphin." The word "long" is the English equivalent of the CS word; "short" is an associate, and "dolphin" is phonetographically similar. Just before the generalization test, after conditioning was complete, subjects were told, for example, that "dolgo" means long. The experimenter's sentence associated "dolgo" and "long," and semantic generalization occurred. Subjects in the condition that were told that the CS word means one English word prior to conditioning and then prior to the test told that it means a second word, showed generalization to the second word comparable to the generalization manifested by the first group. These results indicate that semantic generalization may develop solely in the test situation.

Although Razran has obtained convincing evidence that the locus of generalization is in the test situation, the conditions responsible for the differential development of generalization in the test and not the training situation are relatively specific to his experimental procedure.

Using the operant response type procedure previously described, Mink (1957, 1963) obtained evidence that the locus of generalization is in the training phase. He employed unidirectional associates such as eagle—bird, where free association norms indicate that there is a relatively strong tendency for "eagle" to evoke "bird," but not for "bird" to evoke "eagle." Given word pairs with unidirectional associative strengths, generalization occurs for example when "eagle" is the training word and the "bird" is the test word, but not when "bird" is a training word and "eagle" the test word. These results indicate that the locus of generalization is in the training situation, quite the opposite of Razran's finding that supraordinates yield less generalization than subordinates. Mink's results have been substantiated by various experimenters using different word pairs or different procedures (Maltzman and Belloni, 1964; Moss, 1960).

It might be assumed that these different results pertaining to the locus of generalization are in some manner related to the nature of the experimental procedure, Razran employing classical conditioning and Mink operant conditioning. However, Kurcz (1964) found some evidence for both loci, although her results may be a function of specific features of the Polish language. Brotsky (1964) in a study conducted in my laboratory failed to find evidence for a differential locus of generalization. Her results indicate that the variables responsible for the development of semantic generalization are not generally determined by whether conditioning is operant or classical. As part of a larger study of semantic conditioning and generalization of the GSR, she conditioned one group of subjects to the word "car," which was interspersed among unrelated filler words, and tested for semantic generalization on "Oldsmobile." A second group was conditioned with "Oldsmobile" and tested with "car." Both groups showed reliable evidence of semantic generalization, reliably greater responsivity to test than control words, and the amount of generalization did not differ reliably between the groups. Word association norms indicated the expected unidirectional effect. "Oldsmobile" elicited "car" as a common associate, but "car" did not elicit "Oldsmobile." It is possible, of course, that the discordant results are due in part to peculiarities of word pairs employed in the various experiments, a word by task interaction; however, such interactions seem to be a rather remote possibility. If it is reasonable to generalize from only one word pair, Brotsky's results indicate that unidirectional word associates can be used in classical conditioning to produce semantic generalization in either associative direction.

If, of course, all of the variables determining semantic conditioning and generalization were known, the problem of the peripatetic locus of generalization would be solved. At present we can offer only the usual soporific that more research is needed on the problem. A fruitful approach would include a wide variety of word pairs, including those already found showing unidirectional effects in different experiments of classical and operant conditioning. It would also be useful to combine the operant and classical procedures, a technique that we have employed in my laboratory, although not on this particular problem. It is particularly important to obtain measures of the orienting reflex in such situations in order to determine whether it is differentially evoked in the training or test situation. Assuming, as we do, that the shifting locus of generalization in different kinds of semantic generalization studies is due to the varying arousal of the OR, the problem is to specify the conditions responsible for the differential arousal of the OR, sometimes during training and other times during testing.

AWARENESS. The problem of the relationship between "awareness" and semantic conditioning and generalization is part of the general problem of "awareness" and learning that has been the subject of considerable discussion and research in recent years (Eriksen, 1962a; Farber, 1963).

For methodological behaviorism, "awareness" must be a defined concept. Ordinarily, its antecedent conditions are the stimulus contingencies relevant to learning while its consequent conditions are verbal reports, behavior, which refer to those antecedent conditions. To be useful, to be a significant concept, "awareness" defined in this manner must be lawfully related to other kinds of behavior. The significance of "awareness," according to Bergmann, (1957) stems from its relationship to other measures of learning such as the conditioned GSR or heart rate, etc., in semantic conditioning, or the frequency of personal pronouns in verbal conditioning.

This systematic position of S-R psychology may be contrasted with an alternative cognitive approach. The latter must also use the verbal report and, implicitly, its antecedent conditions, for specifying "awareness." But the typical cognitive psychologist asserts that "awareness" means something more than its defined usage. For the behaviorist, "awareness" may also mean more than its operational definition. However, the cognitive psychologist fails to understand that all concepts may have significance or he believes that the additional source of meaning is not available to the behaviorist, since this additional source of meaning of "awareness" stems from the characteristics of phenomenological experience to which "awareness" is assumed to refer.

Neither position, the behavioristic or cognitive, is falsifiable, because they rest upon decisions as to how concepts may be introduced and employed in psychology. The basis for deciding between them is the fruitfulness of theories adopting one or the other methodological position, the extent to which they promote research that yields general principles, and the extent to which they permit the explanation of diverse phenomena.

Technical philosophy, epistemological analysis, suggests that phenomenological experiences are not entirely equivalent to operational or explicit definitions containing words referring only to things and simple relations (Bergmann, 1951). That behaviorism does not afford a completely satisfactory epistemology is a problem for technical philosophy. That it does not afford a satisfactory systematic position for an empirical science of psychology has not been demonstrated. It would be demonstrated if an alternative approach developed laws which led to the deduction, explanation, and prediction of behavior or phenomena judged to be important which could not be accounted for by a systematic S-R position. Methodological S-R psychology can only be replaced by a more successful systematic position.

Some investigators seem to suggest that "awareness" and the failure to be concerned with its role in learning and conditioning represents a failure of just such a fundamental sort, demonstrating the necessity for some kind of "cogni-

tive" approach which treats the role of awareness in behavior more adequately than S-R psychology. However, the failure in the past of some S-R psychologists to deal adequately with the role of "awareness" is not a systematic issue or a necessary consequence of a systematic position, but an individual failing, and one which is usually a consequence of a grossly oversimplified theory. On the other hand, investigators who seem to believe that "awareness" "means" more than an S-R psychologist would be willing to admit (Spielberger, 1962) have not made any discoveries, obtained empirical relationships, which logically could not be treated within some behavioristic S-R theory.

In contrast to the area of verbal conditioning, where there has been considerably more research, the problem of "awareness" in semantic conditioning and generalization has not assumed the air of a major controversial issue. Relevant evidence in experiments on semantic conditioning and generalization, however, at first glance does appear to be somewhat contradictory. This is due, in large part, to the relative lack of detailed and sophisticated attempts to obtain measures of verbal reports in earlier experiments in contrast to more recent attempts in the area of semantic as well as verbal conditioning.

Many early studies apparently did not question the experimental subjects in detail, nor are the procedures by which the verbal report was obtained indicated. This is the case in the provocative but poorly designed and reported study by Diven (1937). The repetition of Diven's study by Lacey and Smith (1954) and their experimental manipulation of "awareness" (Lacey, Smith, and Green, 1955) represents an improvement over Diven in their method of establishing a physiological response measure. But since their general experimental procedure was the same as Diven's, these studies also suffer from serious inadequacies in experimental design. Some of these deficiencies have been noted elsewhere (Chatterjee and Eriksen, 1960; Lang, Geer, and Hnatiow, 1963). Nevertheless, Lacey and Smith (1954) report that 22 of 31 subjects were "unaware" of the relevant experimental contingencies.

In a second experiment (Lacey, Smith, and Green, 1955) these 22 "unaware" subjects were compared with 20 "aware" subjects who were instructed that the shock would follow a particular word. "Aware" subjects showed a much greater magnitude of response during conditioning and extinction, although it was a decreasing trend throughout. Semantic generalization was also obtained although it was less than in "unaware" subjects.

Chatterjee and Eriksen (1960) were able to replicate Lacey and Smith's study showing that the majority of subjects when questioned in the usual fashion were classifiable as "unaware." These subjects also showed some evidence of conditioning and generalization. However, a simple but detailed additional questionnaire indicated little basis for the inference that the subjects could not verbalize the relevant stimulus contingencies. At the conclusion of the experiment each of the words presented in the experiment was presented to the subject and he was asked whether or not the word was followed by the shock and how certain he was of the contingency. The physiological response to the CS word did not differ reliably from the response magnitude to all other words which the subject indicated might have been followed by shock. Further analyses indicated no evidence of conditioning "without awareness." Chatterjee and Eriksen

also found that subjects expected shock for control words that were repeated six times, the same number of repetitions as the CS word, but that they did not expect shock after other control words, a finding in accord with the results of our semantic generalization experiment previously described.

In other studies producing information on awareness, Luria and Vinogradova (1959) asserted that they obtained "unconscious conditioning." But their results are probably based upon interviews that were not sufficiently detailed. Mednick (1957) reported that 89 of her 90 subjects verbalized that the CS word was followed by the US. Details of the questionnaire were not given. Branca (1957) found that every subject showing semantic conditioning and generalization said that he expected the given test word to be followed by shock. However, not every subject verbalizing the critical contingencies showed reliable evidence of conditioning.

Razran's (1949a, 1949b, 1955) position on awareness occasionally has been misconstrued. He arranges the semantic conditioning experiment and designs the instructions to mislead the subjects concerning the nature of the experiments (that they are studies of conditioning). In this way he attempts to avoid negative attitudes, resentment against being manipulated, etc. However, if subjects verbalize, come to be "aware" of the stimulus contingencies in the experimental situation, their salivary conditioning and generalization is enhanced as in other kinds of semantic conditioning and generalization experiments.

The results obtained by Chatterjee and Eriksen (1960) thus appear to be generalizable. Interpretations of this covariation between the verbal report and semantic conditioning and generalization have been varied. Farber (1963) has suggested that several positions have been taken on this issue.

Recourse to one position, the assumption that "awareness" is more than a defined concept, that it refers to a mental state, apparently has considerable appeal. Resorting to concepts that refer to mental states is a decision of the investigator and represents a systematic position that is neither true nor false. The only criticism that can be raised—and it is a telling one—is the lack of usefulness of such mentalistic concepts. What laws are there of awareness that are different from those pertaining to verbal behavior? What are the antecedent conditions of awareness as distinguished from verbal behavior, and how does awareness vary as a function of these antecedent conditions independently of the possible relationship verbal behavior may have with these antecedent conditions? There is no reliable evidence of such relationships. Until "awareness" used as an index of a mental state is shown to yield new and fruitful empirical relationships that are peculiar to it, there is nothing to be gained by using the concept in such a manner. Nothing is gained because the assumption of mental states does not result in added significance. It does not become part of a viable theory or network of empirical principles.

Adopting a behavioristic definition of "awareness" results in immediate gains, since now the concept may be related to other S-R principles and investigated in terms of available techniques. On the basis of work that we have done to date, it would appear that "awareness" is governed by the same kinds of principles governing other kinds of learned behavior.

Nevertheless, there are some fundamental differences between verbal report behavior and other kinds of response measures. Recalling that there are also characteristic differences between, for example, the GSR and vasomotor responses, the special features of verbal responses are not sufficient grounds for assigning them some unique status such as the mirror of the mind. Subjects may verbalize the relevant stimulus contingencies, show semantic conditioning and generalization in their verbal responses, but not in their physiological measures, while the opposite occurs rarely if at all in college students. Appropriate verbal responses occur more readily than the appropriate physiological responses because the subjects enter the laboratory with a highly differentiated verbal response system and a relatively undifferentiated physiological response system. He already has available the differential representational verbal response "Yankee," "light," etc., but these verbal stimuli do not evoke differential physiological responses prior to conditioning.

Verbal responses differ from other responses in another respect. As Pavlov puts it, they constitute a second signal system; they provide signals of signals, permitting abstraction and conceptualization. The basis, in part, for this special characteristic is the huge network of interverbal associations in which each verbal response is embedded.

Using a procedure similar to the one employed by Chatterjee and Eriksen (1960), studies conducted in my laboratory indicate that "awareness" varies according to the usual principles of behavior. Thus Brotsky (1964) found that awareness increased as a function of the number of conditioning trials, corresponding to the growth of semantic conditioning. The greater the number of conditioning trials, the greater the number of subjects able to verbalize the contingency between CS and US.

In a study in which different kinds

and intensities of US were employed, awareness varied in the same fashion as other behavioral measures obtained, CR, UR, semantic generalization, and ratings of the words and US on the semantic differential. The mean response measures and the percentage of aware subjects in each condition are shown in Table 2. A chi-square test of independence indicated that the percentage of verbalizers in the US conditions differed reliably.

Figure 14 shows the GSR conditioning of verbalizers and nonverbalizers in the above experiment with different US intensities. Subjects in the different

Table 2

MEAN CR, UR, AND SEMANTIC GENERALIZATION (SG) OF THE GSR, AND RATINGS OF THE CS, SG, CONTROL WORDS, AND US ON AN EVALUATIVE SCALE OF THE SEMANTIC DIFFERENTIAL AS A CONSEQUENCE OF CONDITIONING WITH DIFFERENT KINDS AND INTENSITIES OF US. A RATING OF 1 IS UNPLEASANT AND 7 IS PLEASANT.

| US | Mean GSR | | | Per Cent Verbalizers |
	CR	SG	UR	
110-decibel noise	1.71	1.29	2.37	95
95-decibel noise	1.21	0.62	1.97	83
80-decibel noise	0.81	0.55	1.32	83
110-decibel tone	1.23	0.82	1.84	83
80-decibel tone	0.50	0.49	0.55	68

| | Semantic Differential Ratings | | | |
	CS	SG	Control	US
110-decibel noise	1.75	2.89	4.33	1.35
95-decibel noise	2.50	3.40	4.32	1.63
80-decibel noise	3.45	3.78	4.32	2.25
110-decibel tone	2.65	3.44	4.47	1.58
80-decibel tone	3.98	4.36	4.43	3.38

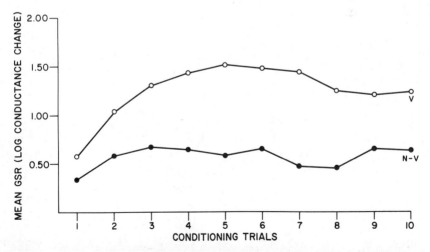

Figure 14. Semantic conditioning of the GSR in verbalizers and nonverbalizers

conditions were randomly discarded to make verbalizers and nonverbalizers proportional within each US condition. The 110-decibel noise group is excluded, because almost all the subjects in this group could verbalize the conditioning contingency. It is apparent from Figure 14 that verbalization is reliably related to semantic conditioning of the GSR. However, the fact that verbalization of stimulus contingencies and extent of semantic conditioning covary does not necessarily mean that the conditioning occurred *because* the subjects verbalized, the position apparently adopted by such cognitive psychologists as Spielberger (1962).

Elsewhere we have indicated that subjects who verbalize the contingency between conditioning and generalization test words as compared to nonverbalizers may manifest reliably larger ORs as measured by the peripheral vasomotor response at the start of conditioning (Maltzman and Raskin, 1965). They were also reliably superior during conditioning, prior to the occurrence of the critical stimulus contingency. Thus individual differences in verbal reports taken as indices of awareness were related to individual differences in conditionability and the OR. Our hypothesis is that individual differences in the OR are responsible, at least in part, for individual differences in conditioning and awareness. Learning as measured by a CR and by a verbal report are both influenced by the OR. Finding such relationships between the OR and "awareness" is in accord with Eriksen's (1962b) suggestion that "attention is inextricably interwoven with awareness."

But the GSR and peripheral vasomotor response are relatively uninformative measures when a noxious US is employed, because they do not adequately differentiate between the OR and DR. When the cephalic vaso-motor response is examined in verbalizers and nonverbalizers, qualitative differences appear in the kind of vasomotor response evoked that are of considerable theoretical interest.

The verbalizers in Figure 14 showed reliable conditioned vasodilation in addition to their conditioned GSR. They manifested differentially larger ORs to the CS than the filler words. Nonverbalizers did not show reliable differential vasodilation to their CS word. Analyses of cephalic vasoconstriction, the measure of the DR, produced different results. Verbalizers did not show conditioning of the DR, nor did nonverbalizers. However, the overall level of DR to all words was reliably greater in nonverbalizers than verbalizers. Nonverbalizers, failing to discriminate between CS and control words, manifested relatively large nondifferential DRs to all words. Verbalizers, discriminating between CS and filler words and showing a differential OR to the CS, manifested relatively small DRs to all words. Verbalizers also gave reliably more extreme negative evaluations of the US on the semantic differential than nonverbalizers. Subjects who were "aware" rated the US as more unpleasant than "unaware" subjects. Verbalizers primarily manifested ORs to the US while nonverbalizers showed DRs.

The general pattern of results suggests that differences in the magnitude of the OR, whether due to experimental variations or individual subject differences, are an important determiner of differences in conditioning, awareness, and ratings of stimuli on the semantic differential.

Conclusions

Theory in the area of semantic conditioning and generalization has been primarily S-R in nature. The principal protagonists have been alternative S-R associative theories of mediation. While these theories have generated some research, the amount seems scarcely commensurate with the assumed basic importance of the problem. Skinner's (1957) formulation of verbal behavior also belongs in this category since he assumes mediating responses in his analysis of verbal behavior, although this aspect of his formulations has neither been developed nor influential in stimulating research. Razran's is the one interpretation which has not assumed common mediating responses in its account of semantic generalization. An account was outlined which stresses the role of the nonspecific orienting reflex as the basis for "judgments of similarity."

A survey of the mediational theories of semantic generalization indicates that they have serious shortcomings. They assume an antiquated S-R peripheralistic theory of learning, and oversimplify the great complexity of classical conditioning. An adequate theory of semantic conditioning and generalization, as well as classical conditioning generally, must recognize the changing role of the orienting and defensive reflexes during the course of an experiment. A preliminary attempt at such a formulation was presented.

All of the above formulations are S-R in a methodological sense. Alternative detailed theories of semantic conditioning and generalization based upon different methodological decisions have not been forthcoming. Cognitive interpretations of similarity and awareness are seriously deficient in that referring these concepts to immediate experience has added nothing to the significance of the concepts. Cognitive psychologists have not developed new and interesting principles that are peculiar to their methodological position and have contributed very little

to the field of semantic conditioning and generalization.

References

Acker, L. E., and A. E. Edwards, "Transfer of Vasoconstriction over a Bipolar Dimension," *Journal of Experimental Psychology*, **67** (1964), 1–6.

Anokhin, P. K., "A New Conception of the Physiological Architecture of Conditioned Reflex," in J. F. Delafresnaye, ed., *Brain Mechanisms and Learning*. Oxford: Blackwell, 1961. pp. 189–229.

Asratyan, E. A., *I. P. Pavlov: His life and Work*. Moscow: Foreign Languages Publishing House, 1953.

——, "Some Aspects of the Elaboration of Conditioned Connections and Formation of Their Properties," in J. F. Delafresnaye, ed., *Brain Mechanisms and Learning*. Oxford: Blackwell, 1961. pp. 95–113.

Bastian, J., "Associative Factors in Verbal Transfer," *Journal of Experimental Psychology*, **62** (1961), 70–79.

Baxter, J. C., "Mediated Generalization as a Function of Semantic Differential Performance," Unpublished doctoral dissertation, University of Texas, 1959.

——, "Mediated Generalization as a Function of Semantic Differential Performance," *American Journal of Psychology*, **75** (1962), 66–76.

Beck, E. C., and R. W. Doty, "Conditioned Flexion Reflexes Acquired during Combined Catalepsy and De-efferentation," *Journal of Comparative and Physiological Psychology*, **50** (1957), 211–216.

Bergmann, G., "Outline of an Empiricist Philosophy of Physics," *American Journal of Physics*, **11** (1943), 248–258; 335–342.

——, "The Logic of Psychological Concepts," *Philosophy of Science*, **18** (1951), 93–110.

——, "The Contribution of John B. Watson," *Psychological Review*, **63** (1956), 265–276.

——, *Philosophy of Science*. Madison: University of Wisconsin Press, 1957.

Beritoff, J. S., *Neural Mechanisms of Higher Vertebrate Behavior*. Boston: Little, Brown And Company, 1965.

Berlyne, D. E., *Conflict, Arousal and Curiosity*. New York: McGraw-Hill Book Company, 1960.

Birge, Janet S., "The Role of Verbal Responses in Transfer," Unpublished doctoral dissertation, Yale University, 1941.

Bousfield, W. A., "The Problem of Meaning in Verbal Learning," in C. N. Cofer, ed., *Verbal Learning and Verbal Behavior*. New York: McGraw-Hill Book Company, 1961. pp. 81–91.

———, and C. R. Puff, "Relationship Between Free Associational and Judgmental Measures of Word Relatedness," *Psychological Reports*, 16 (1965), 279–282.

———, G. A. Whitmarsh, and J. J. Danick, "Partial Response Identities in Verbal Generalization," *Psychological Reports*, 4 (1958), 703–713.

Branca, A. A., "Semantic Generalization at the Level of the Conditioning Experiment," *American Journal of Psychology*, 70 (1957), 541–559.

Brotsky, S. Joyce, "The Classical Conditioning of the Galvanic Skin Response to Verbal Concepts," Unpublished doctoral dissertation, University of California, Los Angeles, 1964.

Carnap, R., "The Methodological Character of Theoretical Concepts," in H. Feigl and M. Scriven, eds., *Minnesota Studies in the Philosophy of Science*. Vol. I. Minneapolis: University of Minnesota, 1956. pp. 38–76.

Chatterjee, B. B., and C. W. Eriksen, "Conditioning and Generalization of GSR as a Function of Awareness," *Journal of Abnormal and Social Psychology*, 60 (1960), 396–403.

Dicken, C. F., "Connotative Meaning as a Determinant of Stimulus Generalization," *Psychological Monographs*, 75 (1961), (1, Whole No. 505).

Diven, K. E., "Certain Determinants in the Conditioning of Anxiety Reactions," *Journal of Psychology*, 3 (1937), 291–308.

Doty, R. W., and C. Giurgea, "Conditioned Reflexes Established by Coupling Electrical Excitations of Two Cortical Areas," in J. F. Delafresnaye, ed., *Brain Mechanisms and Learning*. Oxford: Blackwell, 1961. pp. 133–151.

Eriksen, C. W., ed., *Behavior and Awareness*. Durham: Duke University Press, 1962.

———, "Figments, Fantasies, and Follies: A Search for the Subconscious Mind," in C. W. Eriksen, ed., *Behavior and Awareness*. Durham: Duke University Press, 1962. pp. 3–26.

Farber, I. E., "The Things People Say to Themselves," *American Psychologist*, 18 (1963), 185–197.

Feather, B. W., "Semantic Generalization of Classically Conditioned Responses: A Review," *Psychological Bulletin*, 63 (1965), 424–441.

Gleitman, H., "Place Learning without Prior Performance," *Journal of Comparative and Physiological Psychology*, 48 (1955), 77–79.

Goss, A. E., "Early Behaviorism and Verbal Mediating Responses," *American Psychologist*, 68 (1961), 248–274.

Grice, G. R., "Do Responses Evoke Responses?" *American Psychologist*, 20 (1965), 282–294.

———, and J. D. Davis, "Mediated Stimulus Equivalence and Distinctiveness in Human Conditioning," *Journal of Experimental Psychology*, 55 (1958), 565–571.

———, and J. D. Davis, "Effect of Concurrent Responses on the Evocation and Generalization of the Conditioned Eyeblink," *Journal of Experimental Psychology*, 59 (1960), 391–395.

———, and J. J. Hunter, "Response Mediation of the Conditioned Eyelid Response," *Journal of Experimental Psychology*, 66 (1963), 338–346.

———, H. J. Simmons, and J. J. Hunter, "Failures to Obtain Mediated Generalization Effects in Eyelid Conditioning," *Journal of Experimental Psychology*, 65 (1963), 485–489.

Grings, W. W., "Preparatory Set Variables Related to Classical Conditioning of Autonomic Responses," *Psychological Review*, **67** (1960), 243–252.

Hartman, T. F., "Dynamic Transmission, Elective Generalization, and Semantic Conditioning," in W. F. Prokasy, ed., *Classical Conditioning: A Symposium*. New York: Appleton-Century-Crofts, 1965. pp. 90–106.

Hilgard, E. R., and D. G. Marquis, *Conditioning and Learning*. New York: Appleton-Century, 1940.

Hull, C. L., "The Concept of the Habit-Family Hierarchy and Maze Learning," *Psychological Review*, **41** (1934), 33–54; 134–152.

——, *Principles of Behavior*. New York: Appleton-Century, 1943.

Jenkins, J. J., "Mediated Associations: Paradigms and Situations," in C. N. Cofer and Barbara S. Musgrave, eds., *Verbal Behavior and Learning*. New York: McGraw-Hill Book Company, 1963. pp. 210–245.

John, E. R., "Some Speculations on the Psychophysiology of Mind," in J. M. Scher, ed., *Theories of the Mind*. New York: Free Press of Glencoe, Inc., 1962. pp. 80–121.

Kanfer, F. H., "Perception: Identification and Instrumental Activity," *Psychological Review*, **63** (1956), 317–329.

Kogan, A. B., "The Manifestations of Processes of Higher Nervous Activity in the Electrical Potentials of the Cortex during Free Behavior of Animals," in H. H. Jasper and G. D. Smirnov, eds., *The Moscow Colloquium on Electroencephalography of Higher Nervous Activity*. Montreal: The EEG Journal, 1960. pp. 51–64.

Kurcz, Ida., "Semantic and Phonetographic Generalization of a Voluntary Response," *Journal of Verbal Learning and Verbal Behavior*, **3** (1964), 261–268.

Kurtz, K. H., "Discrimination of Complex Stimuli: The Relationship of Training and Test Stimuli in Transfer of Discrimination," *Journal of Experimental Psychology*, **50** (1955), 283–292.

Lacey, J. I., and R. L. Smith, "Conditioning and Generalization of Uncon-

scious Anxiety," *Science*, **120** (1954), 1045–1052.

——, ——, and A. Green, "The Use of Conditioned Autonomic Responses in the Study of Anxiety," *Psychosomatic Medicine*, **17** (1955), 208–217.

Lang, P. J., J. Geer, and M. Hnatiow, "Semantic Generalization of Conditioned Autonomic Responses," *Journal of Experimental Psychology*, **65** (1963), 552–558.

Lashley, K. S., and M. Wade, "The Pavlovian Theory of Generalization," *Psychological Review*, **53** (1946), 72–87.

Livanov, M. N., "Concerning the Establishment of Temporary Connections," in H. H. Jasper and G. D. Smirnov, eds., *The Moscow Colloquium on Electroencephalography of Higher Nervous Activity*. Montreal: The EEG Journal, 1960. pp. 185–198.

Loucks, R. B., "The Experimental Delineation of Neural Structures Essential for Learning: The Attempt to Condition Striped Muscle Responses with Faradization of the Sigmoid Gyri," *Journal of Psychology*, **1** (1935), 5–44.

Lumsdaine, A. A., "Conditioned Eyelid Responses as Mediating Generalized Conditioned Finger Reactions," *Psychological Bulletin*, **36** (1939), 650.

Luria, A. R., and Olga S. Vinogradova, "An Objective Investigation of the Dynamics of Semantic Systems," *British Journal of Psychology*, **50** (1959), 89–105.

McNamara, H. J., J. B. Long, and E. L. Wike, "Learning without Response under Two Conditions of External Cues," *Journal of Comparative and Physiological Psychology*, **49** (1956), 477–480.

Maltzman, I., and Marigold Belloni, "Three Studies of Semantic Generalization," *Journal of Verbal Learning and Verbal Behavior*, **3** (1964), 231–235.

——, and D. C. Raskin, "Effects of Individual Differences in the Orienting Reflex on Conditioning and Complex Processes," *Journal of Experimental Research in Personality*, **1** (1965), 1–16.

Mandler, G., "Response Factors in Human Learning," *Psychological Review*, **61** (1954), 235–244.

Marshall, G. R., and C. N. Cofer, "Associative Indices as Measures of Word Relatedness: A Summary and Comparison of Ten Methods," *Journal of Verbal Learning and Verbal Behavior*, **1** (1963), 408–421.

Mednick, Martha T., "Mediated Generalization and the Incubation Effect as a Function of Manifest Anxiety," *Journal of Abnormal and Social Psychology*, **55** (1957), 315–321.

Mink, W. D., "Semantic Generalization as Related to Word Association," Unpublished doctoral dissertation, University of Minnesota, 1957.

——, "Semantic Generalization as Related to Word Association," *Psychological Reports*, **12** (1963), 59–67.

Morgan, R. L., and B. J. Underwood, "Proactive Inhibition as a Function of Response Similarity," *Journal of Experimental Psychology*, **40** (1950), 592–603.

Morrell, F., "Effect of Anodal Polarization on Firing Pattern of Single Cortical Cells," in N. S. Kline, ed., "Pavlovian Conference on Higher Nervous Activity," *Annals of the New York Academy of Sciences*, **92** (1961), 860–876.

——, "Electrophysiological Contributions to the Neural Basis of Learning," *Physiological Reviews*, **41** (1961), 443–494.

Moss, S., "A Study of the Semantic Generalization Effect," Unpublished doctoral dissertation, University of California, Los Angeles, 1960.

Murdock, B. B., Jr., "The Effects of Failure and Retroactive Inhibition on Mediated Generalization," *Journal of Experimental Psychology*, **44** (1952), 156–164.

Osgood, C. E., *Method and Theory in Experimental Psychology*. New York: Oxford University Press, Inc., 1953.

——, "Comments on Professor Bousfield's Paper," in C. N. Cofer, ed., *Verbal Learning and Verbal Behavior*.

New York: McGraw-Hill Book Company, 1961. pp. 91–109.

——, "On Understanding and Creating Sentences," *American Psychologist*, **18** (1963), 735–751.

Pillsbury, W. B., *Attention*. New York: The Macmillan Company, 1908.

Razran, G., "A Quantitative Study of Meaning by a Conditioned Salivary Technique (Semantic Conditioning)," *Science*, **90** (1939), 89–91.

——, "Semantic and Phonetographic Generalization of Salivary Conditioning to Verbal Stimuli," *Journal of Experimental Psychology*, **39** (1949), 642–652.

——, "Some Psychological Factors in the Generalization of Salivary Conditioning to Verbal Stimuli," *American Journal of Psychology*, **62** (1949), 247–256.

——, "Stimulus Generalization of Conditioned Responses," *Psychological Bulletin*, **46** (1949), 337–365.

——, "A Direct Laboratory Comparison of Pavlovian Conditioning and Traditional Associative Learning," *Journal of Abnormal and Social Psychology*, **51** (1955), 649–652.

——, "The Observable Unconscious and the Inferable Conscious in Current Soviet Psychophysiology: Interoceptive Conditioning, Semantic Conditioning, and the Orienting Reflex," *Psychological Review*, **68** (1961), 81–147.

Reichenbach, H., *Experience and Prediction*. Chicago: University of Chicago Press, 1938.

Russell, W. A., and J. J. Jenkins, "The Complete Minnesota Norms for Responses to 100 Words from the Kent-Rosanoff Word Association Test," *Technical Report No. 11, Contract No. N8 onr-6616*, Office of Naval Research and University of Minnesota, 1954.

Ryan, J. J., "Comparison of Verbal Response Transfer Mediated by Meaningfully Similar and Associated Stimuli," *Journal of Experimental Psychology*, **60** (1960), 408–415.

Sellars, W., "Empiricism and the Philosophy of Mind," in H. Feigl and M. Scriven, eds., *Minnesota Studies in the*

Philosophy of Science. Vol. I. Minneapolis: University of Minnesota, 1956. pp. 253–329.

Shipley, W. C., "An Apparent Transfer of Conditioning," *Journal of General Psychology*, 8 (1933), 382–391.

——, "Indirect Conditioning," *Journal of General Psychology*, 12 (1935), 337–357.

Skinner, B. F., *Verbal Behavior.* New York: Appleton-Century-Crofts, 1957.

Sokolov, E. N., "Neural Models and the Orienting Reflex," in Mary A. B. Brazier, ed., *The Central Nervous System and Behavior.* New York: Josiah Macy, Jr. Foundation, 1960. pp. 187–276.

——, "Higher Nervous Functions: The Orienting Reflex," *Annual Review of Physiology*, 25 (1963), 545–580.

——, *Perception and the Conditioned Reflex.* New York: The Macmillan Company, 1963.

Solomon, R. L., and Lucille H. Turner, "Discriminative Classical Conditioning in Dogs Paralyzed by Curare Can Later Control Discriminative Avoidance Response in the Normal State," *Psychological Review*, 69 (1962), 202–219.

Spence, K. W., "The Differential Response in Animals to Stimuli Varying within a Single Dimension," *Psychological Review*, 44 (1937), 430–444.

——, "Continuous versus Noncontinuous Interpretations of Discrimination Learning," *Psychological Review*, 47 (1940), 271–288.

——, "Theoretical Interpretations of Learning," in S. S. Stevens, ed., *Handbook of Experimental Psychology.* New York: John Wiley & Sons, Inc., 1951. pp. 690–729.

——, *Behavior Theory and Conditioning.* New Haven: Yale University Press, 1956.

Spielberger, C. D., "The Role of Awareness in Verbal Conditioning," in C. W. Eriksen, ed., *Behavior and Awareness.* Durham: Duke University Press, 1962. pp. 73–101.

Staats, A. W., and Carolyn K. Staats, *"Complex Human Behavior.* New York: Holt, Rinehart and Winston Inc., 1963.

——, ——, and H. L. Crawford, "First-Order Conditioning of Meaning and the Parallel Conditioning of a GSR," *Journal of General Psychology*, 67 (1962), 159–167.

Storms, L. H., "Apparent Backward Association: A Situation Effect," *Journal of Experimental Psychology*, 55 (1958), 390–395.

Taub, E., S. J. Ellman, and A. J. Berman, "Deafferentation in Monkeys: Effect on Conditioned Grasp Response," *Science*, 151 (1966), 593–594.

Thorndike, E. J., "Expectation," *Psychological Review*, 53 (1946), 277–281.

Voronin, L. G., and E. N. Sokolov, "Cortical Mechanisms of the Orienting Reflex and Its Relation to the Conditioned Reflex," in H. H. Jasper and G. D. Smirnov, eds., *The Moscow Colloquium on Electroencephalography of Higher Nervous Activity.* Montreal: The EEG Journal, 1960. pp. 335–346.

Wallach, M. A., "On Psychological Similarity," *Psychological Review*, 65 (1958), 103–116.

Watson, J. B., "Psychology as the Behaviorist Views It," *Psychological Review*, 20 (1913), 158–177.

Whitmarsh, G. A., and W. A. Bousfield, "Use of Free Associational Norms for the Prediction of Generalization of Salivary Conditioning to Verbal Stimuli," *Psychological Reports*, 8 (1961), 91–95.

Wyckoff, L. B., Jr., "The Role of Observing Responses in Discrimination Learning, Part I," *Psychological Review*, 59 (1952), 431–442.

Awareness, Rules, and Propositional Control: A Confrontation with S-R Behavior Theory[1]

13

DON E. DULANY

Imagine that you are seated in a controlled environment kept at a constant temperature of 110° and 35 per cent humidity—as were my experimental subjects. Imagine, too, that you are asked to look at both of these sentences on a card and then read one aloud:

The frog suddenly hopped along a slick log and disappeared into a pond.

The frog quickly hopped over the slippery log and vanished into a pool.

You are to do the same with a second pair of sentences:

The frog quickly hopped along the slick log and disappeared into the pool.

The frog suddenly hopped over a slippery log and vanished into the pond.

And so on through a hundred cards and pairs of sentences.

[1] The work presented here was supported by a grant from the National Institute of Mental Health, Grant No. USPHMH 06836. For collection and analysis of the data from Experiments I and II, I am indebted to Neil Carlson, Charlotte Childers, Steven Schwartz, and Clinton Walker. Stephen Carmean collaborated with me in developing and examining the task in a prior methodological study, and Steven Schwartz helped clarify the validity scale for such tasks. William Batchelder helpfully criticized an earlier draft.

Sometimes after reading a sentence a stream of air blows across your face, and sometimes not. For some of you the air is 40° cooler; for others, at chamber temperature; and for others, 40° hotter; and it happens in all cases that the air comes after reading a sentence with the article "a" before "slippery" or "slick."

Now in this unlikely circumstance what *might* you, or my subjects, become "aware of"—or know, or believe in some degree? No conclusions or even hypotheses at this point; let us simply forebear to flout our common sense in the crude recognition of a problem. You might, I think, come to believe that the stream of air means that the sentence you choose is correct, or incorrect, or neither. Certainly you should be aware that the stream of air feels neutral, or pleasant, or unpleasant in some degree. You might even be aware that you want to say whatever you are supposed to say. And you might, or might not, believe that you are supposed to say, or avoid saying, sentences containing some one of these words. Furthermore, as a consequence of some of these beliefs you might very well consciously *try* to say or avoid saying some of the sentences. After all, why not? Aren't we accustomed to letting what we think, know, and feel have some influence on what we try to do?

At this point, and before we get on to some of the more formal business of theory and experimentation, I invite you to join me in an intuitive exercise:

1. At this moment I am aware, conscious, experiencing; there are many things that I am aware of, that I sense or know or believe in some degree. In a changing and uncertain world there really is nothing of which I can have more conviction. If contrast will illuminate, let me say that I am neither dead nor asleep nor totally ignorant and insensate. At this rather simple and general bedrock I would not quibble over the meaning of any of these words, because I would insist that you know well enough what I mean. And I would so insist because:

2. I grant the same capability for awareness—consciousness, experiencing—to each of you and to my experimental subjects. We are all very much the same kind of organism, and if I am capable of conscious experience, so, with great probability, are others. Furthermore, this analogical inference that is so reasonable to me, I believe will be reasonable to you.

3. I recognize that I as experimenter do not have observational access to your awareness or my subjects' awareness. This is merely to say that there is no known way that stimulus energies emanating from those conscious experiences can activate my receptors.

4. I extend the heuristic assumption of determinism to these conscious, experiential events; I assume that aspects of this awareness may be represented as lawfully related among themselves and to antecedent and consequent experimental variables within the range of my own observation.

We might suspect, by the way, that these laws would be neither weak nor trivial. In a verbal conditioning experiment, for example, we may reinforce subjects for scores of trials and be pleased to observe a barely significant influence on their responses. If we simply tell them what they are supposed to do and the value of their doing so, their behavior is rather powerfully controlled. In fact, they will even move across the room—or leave and come back next week. For that matter, let me be a subject in virtually any of your verbal conditioning or concept attainment or semantic conditioning and generalization experiments, let me know your hypothesis, and I wager that I can behave contrary to it—consciously, intentionally, willfully.

All this is to identify and begin to formulate a problem—the problem of the instrumental or causal effect, if any, of certain private experiential processes or states or entities upon response selection in a number of basic experimental paradigms. I could have extracted the problem from our own early experiments, but I have already done that (Dulany, 1962a), and the parallel exercise sharpens the problem somewhat. It is out of the problem just raised that I believe a confrontation with S-R theory comes. The problem divides into several kinds of questions, all raised in one way or another by the valuable papers of Bourne, Kanfer, and Maltzman:

1. Is there a domain in which a theory encompassing conscious, volitional processes may be seriously competitive with S-R behavior theory?

2. What are some of the relative advantages of seeking S-R and R-R laws in this domain (the question of research strategy)?

3. How are we to accord empirical meaning to a vocabulary of experiential terms, and how are we to investigate the processes they may designate?

The questions are interdependent, of course, and the status of the subject's private reports is a part of them all.

Raise these questions and the confrontation is not merely with S-R theory as theory, but also with its protective research strategy and methodology in the epistemological sense. Confront S-R theory with the problem of awareness, rules, and propositional control, and the S-R theorist sees his historically linked behaviorism on trial. Maltzman comes to the defense of Bergman's (1957) methodological behaviorism and elaborates his symposium paper with another entitled, "Awareness: Cognitive Psychology vs. Behaviorism," (Maltzman, 1966). Kanfer passes with disapproval over "dualistic models" and the "mentalistic viewpoint," then emphasizes that "The behavioristic position is characterized by the general assumption that the determinants of performance can be isolated experimentally without recourse to complex theoretical constructs." And Osgood, in a little different context, worries that, "It is one thing to use notions like 'competence,' 'knowledge,' and 'rules' as heuristic devices, as *sources* of hypotheses about performance; it is quite another thing to use them as *explanations* of performance—unless, of course, one is ready to give up his behavioristic moorings entirely in exchange for a frankly dualistic mentalism."

What I would say about these matters comes in the form of a theoretical and experimental analysis of propositional control, an analysis embodying a particular methodology and strategy of research. It is only on this analysis that I can discuss these theoretical, strategic, and methodological questions—with the panelist's papers as stimulus and pretext. To me there seems something terribly wrong with the conventional wisdom expressed in two of these papers, much that is

sensible in a third, and much more to be said. My answers to these questions are not those of the panelists nor, I am afraid, very brief.

Theory of Propositional Control

As shown in Figure 1, the theory forms a network of sentences interrelating response selection, instructions, reinforcement parameters, habit, a number of states of awareness, and their reports. Out of a common sense analysis of what I, or my subjects, might think and do, the theory has moved by refinement over a series of experiments and earlier stages (Dulany, 1961, 1962a, 1964) to its present form. The result has obvious and welcome similarities in certain particulars or general form to more than I can detail here—from James (1890) through Tolman (1959) and Brunswik (1955) to Miller, Galanter, and Pribram (1960). Suffice it to say here that I have borrowed along the way, and the occasional sense of originality has faded on a little better scholarship.[2]

Propositional constructs

As a first step in the refinement, let us recognize that to be aware that ———, to know that ———, to believe in some degree that ———, may be represented as a *proposition*, Consider, for example: "Sentences with 'a' are followed by the stream of air," a

[2] From Bergmann (1954), Feigl (1959), and Sellars (1956) there is the suggestion that interrelations among private reports could be used in an analysis of mental states. Rozeboom (1961) has proposed a propositional form for learning constructs; O'Neal (1958) and, by implication, Garner (1966), for perceptual constructs; and Piaget (Flavell, 1963), of course, has made interpropositional thinking a central feature of his theory of mature formal thought.

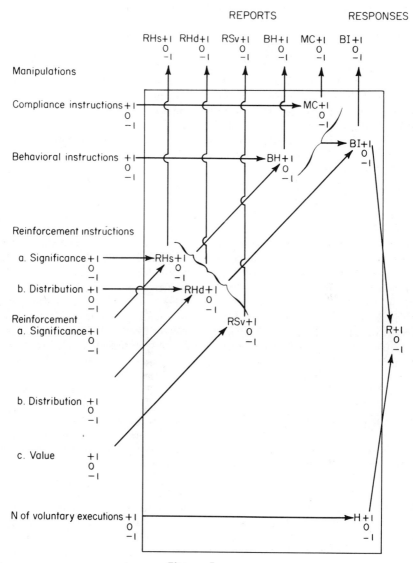

Figure 1

propositional form that could fill any one of these blanks.

1. The proposition (as well as the particular sentence) predicates some property of a subject; it makes an assertion. Unlike a pigeon's peck, a left turn, or a cognitive hiccup, it says something.

2. The proposition—what is as-serted—remains constant, regardless of whether it is articulated in any of a number of alternative stimulus or response sequences. "Sentences with 'a' are followed by the stream of air," "The stream of air followed sentences with 'a'," "Whenever sentences with 'a' occurred, there followed a stream of air," etc., are all different sentences, of

course, different sequences of stimuli or responses but are nevertheless instances of the same proposition. Not only do we judge those sentences to make the same assertion, we now know that these sentences, and many other comparable sets of sentences in the form of instructions or reports, enter into the same relationships with other variables (Dulany, 1961, 1962a, 1964). And that is the useful standard of sameness for scientific constructs.

3. Propositions and the particular sentences that illustrate them combine by laws of logical or quasi-logical inference. If "Sentences with 'a' are followed by the stream of air" and "The stream of air means that I have just said what I am supposed to say," it is logical to infer that "Sentences with 'a' are what I am supposed to say." If "Sentences with 'a' are followed by the stream of air" and "The stream of air feels pleasant," there is an analogous quasi-logic in the conclusion that "Sentences with 'a' are what I will try to say."

The idea of a rule

A second step in the refinement is the recognition that some of the propositions we wonder about seem to be rules. By "rule," I think we generally mean these three things:

1. A proposition that is a rule predicates some property, including an operation, over what is a *class* of events in a specifiable sense. The subject names a class defined by some single attribute or relation of two or more attributes—conjunction, disjunction, implication, equivalence, oddity, causality, progression, serial order, a mathematical function, etc.—which *selects* from the totality of attributes that make each member of the class a unique event. In this sense, the subject of a rule expresses an abstraction.

2. A proposition that is a rule has one of these sources: some kind of inductive inference from a finite set of instances, deductive inference from another rule and a second proposition as premises, or an instruction—someone told us the rule with an instruction that is a rule.

3. A proposition that is a rule has indefinite, perhaps infinite, applicability beyond any finite set of instances from which it may have been induced. The infinite applicability of a rule is most compelling, perhaps, where the connection between a correct attribute relation and a correct response can be expressed by a mathematical equation. In McHale (1965), for example, reinforcement followed a numerical value for k which satisfied the equation, $k = 2$ (the numerical order of the column of figure A) + (the numerical order of the row of figure B). Thus the values taken by k comprised the correct response class, and the right side of the equation comprised the rule subject. Obviously the set of values that will satisfy this equation is infinite, experimentally limited only by practical restrictions on the size of the stimulus matrix. A rule may predicate a property over an infinite set.

But all this must be represented and further refined in the scales and theoretical sentences that comprise a theory.

METRICAL VALUE FOR RULES: THE PRODUCT OF THE VALIDITY OF THE SUBJECT AND PREDICATED CRITERIALITY. Consider these three instances of rules at some value: "Response class x is followed by reinforcement" we may term a Hypothesis of the Distribution of Reinforcement (RHd); it is a rule of reinforcement. "Response class x is what I am supposed to do," is a Behavioral Hypothesis (BH), a rule of social expectation. "Response class x is what I am trying to do" is a Behavioral Intention (BI), a rule of operation.

Table 1

THE DEFINING RELATION FOR A
CORRECT RESPONSE CLASS AND ITS TWO SUBCLASSES

		Defining Attribute or Defining Attribute Relation Satisfied		
		Absent	Present	
			(Scored correct)	
	Present	0	u	a+c
Response to (or with)		c	a	
		(Scored correct) b	d	
	Absent	u'	0	b+d

If x is to be a quantitative variable, we must array response classes on some dimension, and we begin with a familiar anchor point, the response class we score correct. Wherever we have a correct response class, we have a set of responses that we, as experimenters, can sort from others and call "correct"; and we do so on the basis of some attribute or attribute relation that we select and abstract from the cluster of attributes that is each response made or stimulus responded to. Put a little differently, a correct response class is defined by a perfect *relation*—a perfect relation of presence or absence of some response to (or with), and presence or absence of a defining attribute or attribute relation. The attribute(s) may be either properties of the responses or of the stimuli responded to. In Table 1 we see this defining relation and the two subclasses of a correct response class, each of which may be expressed by a conditional probability: P (presence of response to—or with—| presence of defining attributes) $= a/a + c = 1$; and P (absence of response to—or with—|absence of defining attributes) $= b/b + d = 1$. This relation has a composite probability value, $a + b/a + b + c + d$, which is also 1.

Put in this rather labored way, it becomes clear that every other response class must also have some quantitative value—a value that describes the relation of presence and absence of the attributes defining that response class to presence and absence of the attributes defining the correct response class. It is a relation with a composite probability and presence and absence probability components that can take any value from 0 to 1. And this relation can derive from the organization of attributes in a stimulus array (as in Dulany, 1964), the organization of prior habits (as in Dulany, 1961) or, I would think, the anatomical organization of the musculature. The value of a rule subject, we shall say, is the value of the response class or subclass it names, in the sense of its *validity* for predicting the correct response class or subclass.

In the task of our first example, and our experiments, the subject views the sentences as stimuli and speaks them as responses. Thus the attributes are conveniently a property of both. Thus, too, the task belongs to the domains of both verbal conditioning and concept attainment—of general instrumental learning with a systematic organization of the array of attributes. The article "a" defines the class of correct sentences, but for each of the other word attributes, there is a known and scaled probability of occurrence of the correct attribute

posite validity," all of which are equal in the present balanced, two-alternative case with one attribute defining. The quadrants in the off-diagonal express a degree of error, or nonvalidity, of the attribute named, and take values of $1-p$. Table 3 gives the probability value

Table 2

VALIDITY OF RULE SUBJECTS

| | | Defining Attribute or Attribute Relation Satisfied | | |
		Absent	Present	
Attribute or Attribute Relation Named in Rule Subject	Present	c	a	a+c
	Absent	b	d	b+d

Presence validity: p (Defining attribute is present | Attribute named in rule subject is present) $= a/(a + c)$

Absence validity: P(Defining attribute is absent | Attribute named in rule subject is absent) $= b/(b + d)$

Composite validity $= (a + b)/(a + b + c + d)$

in a sentence, given occurrence of each attribute, and the probability of nonoccurrence of the correct attribute, given nonoccurrence of each attribute. Table 2 provides a four-fold table for computing such "presence validities" and "absence validities," as well as a "com-

Table 3

VALIDITIES OF ATTRIBUTES

Attributes	Probability Value	Relational Value
a	+1.0	+1.0
suddenly	.9	+ .8
along	.8	+ .6
slippery	.7	+ .4
pool	.6	+ .2
disappeared	.5	0.0
vanished	.5	0.0
pond	.4	− .2
slick	.3	− .4
over	.2	− .6
quickly	.1	− .8
the	0.0	−1.0

for each of the attributes and possible rule subjects in this task. With the linear transformation, Relational Value $= 2P - 1$, we arrive at a *relational* scale with the very useful properties, as we shall see, of an inert midpoint, 0, and extremes of equal and opposite values.

To obtain a metric for *rule predicates* we begin with the familiar idea of criteriality (Bruner, Goodnow, and Austin, 1956), or utility (Brunswik, 1955) of cues or attributes. By criteriality of an attribute (or attribute relation), we mean the degree of association of presence and absence of the attributes with presence and absence of *response* to (or with) the attributes, as might be expressed in Table 4. Where the criteriality is perfect, all and only those instances with the attribute or satisfying the attribute relation are responded to, or all responses within a set possess the attribute or satisfy the attribute relation. Now rules mention

Table 4

CRITERIALITY OF RESPONSE CLASS

		Response to (or with) Presence or Absence of a Given Attribute or Satisfaction of an Attribute Relation	
		Absent	Present
Attribute or Attribute Relation	Present	c $\quad$ a	$a+c$
	Absent	b $\quad$ d	$b+d$

attributes or attribute absences in their subjects and then predicate some direction of activity, "use" or "avoid," "occurence" or "nonoccurence," either exclusively or in some imperfect degree. Furthermore, each rule type does so for some characteristic *mode of activity*: "try to..." for a behavioral intention,

For a rule naming a subclass of response, cell frequencies come from one of two sources: (*1*) The predicate of a single rule covering some two or more trials may be qualified with a frequency. For example: "Sentences containing 'a' are followed by a stream of air on eight of ten trials." (*2*) Where trial by trial

Table 5

PREDICATED CRITERIALITIES

		Predicated Occurrence of Activity for Any Predicated Mode of Activity: "tried to...," "supposed to...," "...followed by consequence."	
		Absent ("Avoid") ("Nonoccurrence")	Present ("Use") ("Occurrence")
Expressed Occurrence of Attribute or Attribute Relation in Rule Subject	Present (Response to or with)	c $\quad$ a	$a+c$
	Absent (Nonresponse to or with)	b $\quad$ d	$b+d$

"supposed to..." for a behavioral hypothesis, and "... followed by consequence" for a hypothesis of a distribution of reinforcement.

Just as for subject validities, this relationship and the component conditional probabilities may be expressed in a four-fold table such as Table 5.

statements of rules are obtained (as in Dulany and O'Connell, 1963; O'Connell, 1965, 1967; Schwartz, 1966a and b), the frequency entry is the number of trials on which the rule is stated. As for the validities of subjects, we may compute presence, absence, and composite criterialities of predicates and again transform them by $2p - 1$ to arrive at a scale running from -1 through 0 to $+1$.

Scaling subjects and predicates in this way, we see that

$$\text{Rule Value} +1 = $$
$$0$$
$$-1$$

$$\text{(Subject Validity } +1) \times$$
$$0$$
$$-1$$

$$\text{(Predicate Criteriality } +1)$$
$$0$$
$$-1$$

For example, the rule, "Sentences with 'suddenly' $(+.8)$ are what I am trying to use" (formulated on 16 of 20 trials) $(+.6)$ takes a relational value of $+.48$. The ultimate defense of this scale must come from the relations it enters into, of course. But taking the product of these relational values may seem more reasonable if we remember that the number we get is a transform of the probability of correct responses over those 20 trials where an attribute of that validity has that criteriality for response. It is a scale of distance from perfect correctness, running from $+1$ to -1.[3]

In short, we begin with the ideas of validity and criteriality of attributes and generalize these ideas to constitute variables. Then we transform and combine those variables to arrive at a scale on which to array the propositional rules that speak of response classes defined by those attributes.

THE IDEA OF AN ASCRIPTOR AND ITS METRIC. Some propositions we wonder about seem to be something other than rules. They ascribe a property to a subject, but the subject and predicate fall, not on scales of validity and criteriality, but rather naturally on analogous scales ranging over $+$, 0, and $-$ values.

Consider "Occurrence (nonoccurrence) of the consequence meant that I had just done what I was supposed to do (not supposed to do, or neither supposed to do nor avoid doing)" and call this Hypothesis of the Significance of a Reinforcer, (RHs). "Occurrence (or nonoccurrence) of the consequence felt pleasant (or neutral, or unpleasant)" may be called Subjective Value of a Reinforcer (RSv). "Whatever I am supposed to do (not supposed to do) I want (neither want nor want not, want not) to do" is what we term Motivation to Comply (MC).

Now let the propositional subjects "occurrence" and "whatever supposed to do" take the value of $+1$, and "nonoccurrence" and "whatever supposed to avoid doing" take the value of -1. Let "supposed to," "neither supposed to do nor avoid doing," and "not supposed to" take the values $+1$, 0, and -1, respectively. And let "very pleasant" to "very unpleasant" and

---

[3] To be convinced of this we need only go back to the probability values for a correct response given "suddenly," .9, and for use of "suddenly," .8, in this example. The probability of correct response over those 20 trials would be $(P_{\text{validity}})(P_{\text{use}}) + (1 - P_{\text{validity}})(1 - P_{\text{use}}) = (.9)(.8) + (.1)(.2) = .74$. Transforming this value by $2p - 1$ we arrive at .48. This manner of scaling is general to cases with k alternatives, one or more alternatives per trial, equal or unequal marginal frequencies in either validity or criteriality tables, and simple or relational

concepts. Where attributes are continuous rather than discrete (as in McHale, 1965), validity of an attribute is given by the regression of that attribute on the correct attribute, and the criteriality by the regression of that attribute on frequency of the relevant event—response, reinforcement, or predication of one of the three characteristic modes of predication for rules.

For other related uses of validity and/or criteriality dimensions, see especially Smedslund (1955), Bruner, Goodnow, and Austin (1956), Azuma and Cronbach (1966), and Hursch, Hammond, and Hursch (1964).

"very much wanted to" to "very much did not want to" range continuously over a scale running from $+1$ through zero to -1. Then we can also say that

$$\text{Ascriptor Value} \begin{matrix} +1 \\ 0 \\ -1 \end{matrix} =$$

$$(\text{Subject Value} \begin{matrix} +1 \\ 0 \\ -1 \end{matrix}) \times$$

$$(\text{Predicate Value} \begin{matrix} +1 \\ 0 \\ -1 \end{matrix})$$

Theoretical sentences and commentary

RESPONSE SELECTION. What a subject thinks he should do should follow by inference from what he thinks a reinforcer follows and what he thinks it means. To be more precise,

$$(\text{RHd} + 1) (\text{RHs} + 1) \longrightarrow \begin{matrix} 0 & 0 \\ -1 & -1 \\ & \text{BH} + 1 \\ & 0 \\ & -1 \end{matrix} \quad (1a)$$

where BH is his behavioral hypothesis, RHd is his hypothesis of the distribution of reinforcement, RHs is his hypothesis of the significance of a reinforcer, and "————→" is read as "influences." In the common case of no antagonistic behavioral instructions, (see Figure 1) and control of other possible sources of BH, this relationship may be written in the stronger form of

$$\text{BH} + 1 = (\text{RHd} + 1) (\text{RHs} + 1) \begin{matrix} 0 & 0 & 0 \\ -1 & -1 & -1 \end{matrix} (1b)$$

If the subject believes that occurrence of a consequence meant he was correct, he should infer that he is supposed to use whatever response class he believes it follows. If both RHs and RHd are

positive, he should arrive at a positive behavioral hypothesis of like degree. If he entertains reinforcement hypotheses of opposite sign, he should reasonably, and algebraically, arrive at a negatively correlated behavioral hypothesis. And if he fails to hypothesize either a significance or a correlated distribution, if he is zero on either, he should have no basis for inferring a correlated behavioral hypothesis and ought very well to be zero on that, too.

In all cases the new kind of rule is yielded as new *mode* of predication is yielded—from "followed by consequence" to "supposed to." And whenever the ascriptor takes a value other than $+1$, a rule of new value is yielded, by yielding a new value for either subject validity or predicated criteriality. Something new may become correct or something old may become incorrect.

Written in this form, the equation can be interpreted in two ways: (*a*) it expresses a linear relation of BH to the multiplicative aggregate (RHs) (RHd), with slope of 1 and zero intercept understood. (*b*) It expresses a family of linear relations of BH to either RHd or RHs, with the other as a slope parameter taking values from $+1$ to -1, again with an intercept of zero understood. This simplicity follows from the manner of scaling the variables.

In an analogous way, what a subject tries to do, and in what degree, should be influenced by what he thinks a reinforcer follows and how it feels, or more generally, how he values it. In a more general and precise form,

$$(\text{RHd} + 1) (\text{RSv} + 1) \longrightarrow \begin{matrix} 0 & 0 \\ -1 & -1 \\ & \text{BI} + 1 \\ & 0 \\ & -1 \end{matrix} \quad (2a)$$

where RSv is the subjective value of

the reinforcer and BI is the behavioral intention.

When the subject holds a positive distributional hypothesis, he should tend to form a positive intention if evaluation of the reinforcer is positive, and negative if it is negative. And if he is zero on either—if he either knows no correlated distribution or places no positive or negative value on the consequence—his intentions should be zero, regardless of the value taken by the other term. Again an ascriptor, RSv, combines with a rule, RHd, to yield a new rule, BI, by yielding a new mode of predication—from "followed by" to "try to." Again, too, as the ascriptor takes a value other than +1, a rule of new value is yielded, by yielding a new subject validity or a new predicated criteriality. When a reinforcer is unpleasant, for example, one may try either to do something else or to do less often what is reinforced.

On the appeal of analogical balance, I would suggest that what a subject thinks he is supposed to do and his desire to do it will combine in the same way to influence what he tries to do:

$$(BH + 1)(MC + 1) \longrightarrow$$
$$\begin{array}{cc} 0 & 0 \\ -1 & -1 \end{array}$$
$$BI + 1$$
$$\begin{array}{c} 0 \\ -1 \end{array} \qquad (2b)$$

where MC is motivation to comply.

When either the behavioral hypothesis or motivation to comply is positive, intentions should vary directly with the value of the other term. When either is negative, intentions should vary inversely with the value of the other term. And neutrality on either— he doesn't know or doesn't care—should tend to produce a neutral intention, regardless of the value of the other. As before, an ascriptor combines with a rule to yield a new rule with a new

mode of predication—from "supposed to" to "try to." Once more the ascriptor may operate to modify the value of either the subject validity or the predicated criteriality.

Putting these two influences on BI together in a linear regression equation, we may write:

$$BI + 1 =$$
$$\begin{array}{c} 0 \\ -1 \end{array}$$
$$[(RHd + 1)(RSv + 1)]w2 +$$
$$\begin{array}{cc} 0 & 0 \\ -1 & -1 \end{array}$$
$$[(BH + 1)(MC + 1)]w3$$
$$\begin{array}{cc} 0 & 0 \\ -1 & -1 \end{array} \qquad (2c)$$

where an intercept of zero may again be understood and the weights (and also intercept) may be estimated within a standard multiple regression analysis.

But there is important reason to think of RHd as a "cardinal rule," a critical awareness. Notice that if we use Equation 1b as a basis for factoring RHd in Equation 2c, we obtain

$$BI + 1 =$$
$$\begin{array}{c} 0 \\ -1 \end{array}$$
$$RHd + 1 [(RSv + 1)w2 +$$
$$\begin{array}{cc} 0 & 0 \\ -1 & -1 \end{array}$$
$$(RHs + 1 \times MC + 1)w3]$$
$$\begin{array}{cc} 0 & 0 \\ -1 & -1 \end{array} \qquad (2d)$$

which predicts BI from the product of only one rule, RHd, and an aggregate containing all three controlling ascriptors. Thus when RHd = 0 the entire right side of this equation should go to 0, and these ascriptors—and their antecedents—should no longer control intentions.

With experimental conditions that remove physical impediments, a subject should tend to do what he tries to do:

$$BI + 1 \longrightarrow R + 1$$
$$0 \qquad\qquad\quad 0$$
$$-1 \qquad\qquad\quad -1 \quad (3a)$$

where every value of "R" is the product of the validity and criteriality of a response class. With Habit, a second influence on "R" (Figure 1), at some constant, usually asymptotic, value across the alternative response classes, we may also rewrite this relationship in the strong form,

$$R + 1 = BI + 1$$
$$0 \qquad\qquad 0$$
$$-1 \qquad\qquad -1 \quad (3b)$$

where a slope of one and intercept of zero may again be understood.

Given the scaling of these variables, the equation summarizes several types of relationships: (*a*) The validity of a response class varies with the validity of the subject of a behavioral intention. The response tried is the response used. (*b*) The criteriality of a response class varies with the criteriality of a behavioral intention. The number of times a response is tried is the number of times it is used. (*c*) Frequency of members of the *correct* response class varies with the validity of the behavioral intention. (*d*) Frequency of members of the *correct* response class varies with the product of BI validity (the response class tried) and BI criteriality (the frequency with which it is tried). In all of these ways BI is an *operative rule*. And this equation refines what we commonsensically mean by "voluntary control."

Certainly not all behavior is intentional; some should follow, unintentionally, from prior habit:

$$H + 1 \longrightarrow R + 1$$
$$0 \qquad\qquad\quad 0$$
$$-1 \qquad\qquad\quad -1 \quad (4a)$$

And with BI at some constant value (Fig. 1), we can write

$$R + 1 = H + 1$$
$$0 \qquad\qquad 0$$
$$-1 \qquad\qquad -1 \quad (4b)$$

Written in this general form, the equation covers a set of relationships parallel to those described by Equation 3b. Thus Habit is a second operative rule, as we shall see more clearly by its origin in the first operative rule (Equation 11 below). This equation also refines one of the things ordinarily meant by "involuntary control."

HYPOTHESES OF REPORT VALIDITY. As can be seen in Figure 1, we hypothesize that RHs, RHd, RSv, BH, MC and BI—but *not* H—will be reflected in their corresponding reports. And as for any hypothetical relation, we specify its conditions: response classes no more finely differentiated than the subject's vocabulary, a usual amount of responsiveness to experimental instructions, and the assessment procedures to be described. Under these conditions the relation should be probabilistic but strong.[4]

ACQUISITION: EFFECTS OF MANIPULATIONS. For each of the hypothetical state variables there should generally be numerous, partially unrelated antecedents—and hence numerous sources of error in any single relationship of a stimulus variable to a state variable. But manipulations may have other roles than as terms in the central equations of a theory. They may serve to spread subjects more widely over the values those terms take, and those terms and equations may serve to formulate a question of the *locus of effect* of any of numerous manipulations. We achieve some order when we can categorize some of the infinitely possible manipulations by their common locus of effect.

[4] By virtue of the scaling of these reports, the hypotheses of report validity formally amount to a set of linear equations when making quantitative predictions: 5a-f.

And once this locus is determined, of course, the theory yields a set of predictions for that manipulation. For now I would only try to mention and categorize a few for which the evidence indicates relatively strong effects.

Certainly hypotheses of the distributions of reinforcement should in some degree be influenced by distributions of reinforcement:

$$\text{Rd} + 1 \longrightarrow \text{RHd} + 1$$
$$0 \qquad\qquad 0$$
$$-1 \qquad\qquad -1 \;(6a)$$

where Rd expresses the product of two basic reinforcement parameters, its "validity" and its "criteriality." Reinforcement may be contingent upon a response class having any degree of validity, from a correct response class, through a random response class, to a perfectly incorrect response class. And for response classes of any validity, presence and absence of reinforcement may have any order of association with presence and absence of response to (or with) the attribute marking the response class. Once we bother to put the matter this way, we can array distributions of consequences on the same variable we array rules and obtain a number for any reinforcement schedule we can construct over trials.

Since the distributions of reinforcers have validities and criterialities, "subjects" and "predicates," we should be able to say with instructions what we can say with reinforcers. Thus we expect describing a distribution to have some degree of influence on what a subject believes a distribution to be:

$$\text{RId} + 1 \longrightarrow \text{RHd} + 1$$
$$0 \qquad\qquad 0$$
$$-1 \qquad\qquad -1 \;(6b)$$

where RId is instruction about the distribution of a reinforcer.

Reinforcers also have "significance"

(Rs), which I would specify by judgments that we as experimenters may make: they signify that what they follow is what one is supposed to do, neither supposed to do or not, or not supposed to do. Granting a degree of organismic similarity, we can expect that our subjects will, in some degree, judge accordingly:

$$\text{Rs} + 1 \longrightarrow \text{RHs} + 1$$
$$0 \qquad\qquad 0$$
$$-1 \qquad\qquad -1 \;(7a)$$

Of course, too, we might instruct the subject that occurrence, or nonoccurrence, of some consequence means that what they have just done is what they are supposed to do (RIs), and expect the subjects' hypotheses to vary accordingly:

$$\text{RIs} + 1 \longrightarrow \text{RHs} + 1$$
$$0 \qquad\qquad 0$$
$$-1 \qquad\qquad -1 \;(7b)$$

We may also evaluate consequences, perhaps from very pleasant through neutral to very unpleasant, and expect some parallel influence on the evaluations made by our subjects:

$$\text{Rv} + 1 \longrightarrow \text{RSv} + 1$$
$$0 \qquad\qquad 0$$
$$-1 \qquad\qquad -1 \;(8)$$

Most directly, we might instruct subjects that they are to use or avoid using any response class in any degree and expect that to have some influence on what they think they are supposed to do:

$$\text{BehI} + 1 \longrightarrow \text{BH} + 1$$
$$0 \qquad\qquad 0$$
$$-1 \qquad\qquad -1 \;(9)$$

where BehI is a behavioral instruction.

And with various compliance instructions and implied inducements we should be able to influence a subject's motivation to comply,

Compliance Instructions $+1$ ⟶
$$0$$
$$-1$$
$$Mc +1$$
$$0$$
$$-1 \qquad (10)$$

ACQUISITION: PROCESS RELATIONS. Although in this paper I can describe only experiments bearing on the preceding portions of the theory, I should briefly describe two process relations, lest it be implied that the preceding portions must cover inappropriate domains.

On common sense, we should expect a voluntary response to habituate, to become automatic and involuntary, as some function of number of voluntary executions of that response:

$$(BI +1 \rightarrow R +1) \rightarrow H +1$$
$$0 \qquad 0 \qquad 0$$
$$-1 \qquad -1 \qquad -1 \quad (11)$$

In this way conscious rules should become nonconscious rules.[5] With the scales used, this expression covers the same kinds of relationships covered by Equation 3b. Most worth noticing, perhaps, is that other response classes than those named in the intention are said to habituate in the degree that they are correlated with the intentional response class. Not every response class now habituated would need to have once been before the footlights of consciousness—only those correlated enough to have gotten the habituated responses to occur repeatedly. Whatever rules we might use to systematize habituated behavior should be related to, but not necessarily identical with, the controlling rules for a subject.

Finally, how does the subject move to an RHd of nonzero value over trials? Under selective reinforcement, RHd is the cardinal rule that must combine with ascriptors to yield the operative rule, BI, if response selection is to occur. First imagine a subject with

[5] Within the University's controlled environment, subjects practiced four responses

perfect capacity for processing the information in instances and outcomes —for scanning, attention, inference, and memory. On every trial our perfect subject would infallibly predicate the exact frequency of consequences for presence and absence of every attribute and attribute relation exemplified in the instances encountered. And on every trial he should select a pool of those RHd's still relevant to his aim, those predicating the most extreme frequencies over any attribute values— then sample one. For the mortal, highly fallible, and highly variable processors of information we can still do the following: (1) We specify the *consequences* of imperfect processing of information on every trial by an array of RHd's, classified by relevance and stated by the subject. (2) We specify a sampling pool—those RHd's with predicates of most extreme $+$ and $-$ values. (3) We specify a rule of random sampling.[6] For any set of n trials and n' relevant hypotheses on trial n, the mean RHd on trials $n + 1$ should be given by

---

with a lever, position to color, on 20, 160, or 300 trials, receiving 10 seconds of cool, neutral, or hot air for each response. (Dulany, Schwartz, and Walker, 1965b). Habituation was tested in negative transfer under speeded conditions, a 1.2-second trial. After instructions presenting a new set of rules for position responses to colors, the ratio of intrusions of the practiced response to total errors varied with number of prior voluntary executions rather than reinforcement value. Compared to voluntary effects, however, the effects of habituation are very weak under these conditions.

[6] This hypothesis has been investigated by Schwartz (1966b) for simple, conjunctive, and disjunctive concepts and four methods of presentation. Within the University of Illinois' Plato system, subjects were able to express each of their multiple hypotheses by pressing a typewriter key. The array of relevant hypotheses predicted the controlling RHd by the sampling rule with an average r of .72. The constitution of this reported sampling pool predicted the start of a criterion series with an r of .90.

$$\frac{\overset{n-1}{\underset{0}{\sum}} \text{RHd} + 1, \text{trial } n + 1 = -1}{n-1}$$

$$\frac{\overset{n-1}{\underset{0}{\sum}} \overset{n'}{\underset{-1}{\sum}} \text{Relevant RHd's} + 1, \text{trial } n}{(n-1)\,n'} \qquad (12)$$

(4) Applying these processing and sampling rules, we can obtain a number on each trial for an ideal array of relevant RHd's. If subjects do arrive at an array of RHd's by approximating any such strategies of information processing, however imperfectly or sporadically, we should expect a discrepancy between the ideal and obtained arrays to vary with whatever varies the subjects' capabilities for scanning, attention, inference, and memory. This is where those variables should have their locus of effect.

Experiments

Where there is entrenched theory we cannot expect one or two experimental observations to give strong support to a newer competitor. Rarely, if ever, can we expect single critical experimental observations. Theorists are too adept at finding saving assumptions that will reconcile virtually any experimental observation with a prevailing theory. But a network of theoretical propositions can generate a network of experimental hypotheses. And multiple observations can follow gracefully from one theory, which in the aggregate are irreconcilable with the entrenched theory on any available set of reasonable assumptions.

In the present case, we must have multiple response measures and manipulations that help to spread the subjects over the extreme values those response terms may take. For a newer theory to be competitive it should also generate strong laws, tight relationships, not merely the novel or interesting relationships that are surprising because they are too weak to have been noticed before. We must expect the core propositions of this network to generate strong experimental relationships under refined experimental conditions. The two experiments I shall describe are not early experiments, but later ones in a series with progressively refined experimental procedures that have followed refinements in the theory. Still later do we ask whether we can derive other relationships, perhaps weaker ones, that will answer this, that or the other interesting question that is put to the theory. And where coordinations take the status of hypotheses, the scope of the theory is a matter of discovery rather than prior announcement.

Experiment I

We took the experiments to the University's Physical Environment Unit, where we could isolate the subject in a 12×7 chamber kept at a constant temperature of 110° and a relative humidity of 35 per cent.[7] In this setting, we were able to vary the affective value of a contingent stream of air—cool, neutral, or hot—orthogonally to instructions about its significance;—it signified "correct," "neither correct nor incorrect," or "incorrect." Our subjects were 138 female undergraduates, dressed for the occasion in gym clothes. Thus, the basic design was a 3×3 factorial with 12 subjects per cell; an additional 10 random reinforcement controls were run with each of the three

[7] This facility has been more fully described by Paul, Eriksen, and Humphreys (1962).

reinforcement values. (Dulany, 1964.)

After the subject was told that she would perform a verbal task under simulated climatic conditions, she entered the chamber and was seated with her head kept stationary in a head rest, so that the contingent stream of air could always arrive at the side of the face. Otherwise—as we had learned —even our hottest contingent stream of air at 150° would feel pleasantly cool as it evaporated perspiration.

Over an intercom, the experimenter read, "This is a study of verbal behavior. On each of these cards, there are two sentences. When you see the red light, you are to pick a card, look at both of the sentences, then select one and read it aloud. Speak loudly and clearly and read the sentence exactly as it appears on the card. Then place the card on the bottom of the deck. Is this clear?" The red light flashed every 20 seconds for 100 trials.

After a first block of 20 trials, a 10-second stream of air followed every sentence with "a" before "slippery" or "slick" for experimental subjects or an equal number of randomly selected responses for controls. The air was heated or cooled outside the chamber, forced by blowers through a heavily insulated pipe, and emerged two inches from the subject's cheek. In the positive reinforcement condition, the air arrived *at the face* (as measured) at 70°, in the neutral condition at 100°, and in the negative condition at 150°. These values were chosen for two reasons: they are neatly identical with, or symmetrical about, the chamber temperature; and they are values that over half of 20 pilot subjects rated as very pleasant, neutral, and very unpleasant respectively. With those adjectives as anchors for an 11-point scale running from $+ 1$ to $- 1$, the mean values were .81, $-$ .02, and $-$ .84.

Reinforcement instructions, too, were given after the first block of nonreinforced trials. In the positive condition we said, "Fine, now listen carefully. From now on a stream of air will sometimes blow across your face. The stream of air means that you have just said what you are supposed to say. I want you to understand and remember this." In the neutral condition, the third sentence was replaced by, "The stream of air has nothing to do with whether you have just said what you are supposed to say or what you are not supposed to say. We are merely readjusting the temperature of the chamber." And for the negative condition, the critical sentence was, "The stream of air means that you have just said what you are *not* supposed to say." The critical sentences were repeated for emphasis.

Immediately after the 100 trials the subject left the chamber and was given a set of questions directed at her awareness over the last 20 trials (Appendix).

Before she began, the experimenter carefully and seriously read these instructions: "I want you to read these questions one at a time. Read each question aloud and then write your answer in the space provided. Take your time: There is no need to hurry, and it is *important* that you answer each question as accurately as possible. Be sure to read the question and all alternatives aloud before you answer." If reports are to behave in lawful manner, we have learned, questioning must be presented as a serious and central part of the experiment. Lawfulness cannot be expected if the experimenter conveys, however unintentionally, that the real business of science is over and he merely wants to ask a few incidental questions. As each question was read and answered, the experimenter stood silently behind the subject and out of view.

Notice that to obtain reports of RHd,

RHs, BH, and BI, we use a pair of questions for each, a multiple-choice access question followed by a core question *only* when the subject checks one of the last two alternatives indicating she has information to report. Otherwise that report was scored zero. Access questions allow us to maintain the advantages of entirely objective scoring while reducing the likelihood of suggestion or guessing. The attribute words named give us the rule validities, the frequencies, their predicated criterialities. The subject values of the ascriptors—Rhs, RSv, and MC—are set at $+ 1$ by the *form* of the question once answered: they ask about the *occurrence* of the consequence or about *whatever one is supposed to do*. For RSv and MC the predicate values are given by the scale value checked from $+ 1$ to $- 1$; and for RHs they are $+ 1$ for "means correct" and $- 1$ for "means incorrect."

The form of these questions reflects a series of revisions in response to running hundreds of subjects over several years—and further refinements are still being made. Within each cell of the basic design, questions, sequences, and position in order were arranged within a replicated, nonsystematic 6×6 Latin Square.

POSSIBLE SOURCES OF ERROR. What do we find? First, what of some possible sources of *error*? As a check on experimenter bias I used two assistants, one my graduate assistant, the other an undergraduate in political science who was entirely unacquainted with any of our hypotheses. E_1 vs. E_2 was unassociated with any variable in the study. As a check on changing climatic conditions—since we ran the study from early winter to late spring—we numbered the subjects consecutively and correlated this variable with every other variable. Position in order of running was unassociated with any other variable, including our manipulations, an additional check on our randomization. Did *asking* a *sequence* of questions, as is so often thought, provide the subjects with more and more informational cues? A question's position in the order was unrelated to the level of report, as was its interaction with experimental conditions. Neither was there an effect of the six sequences of questions on level of report (F's about 1). Operant level was also unassociated with any variable in the study.

MAIN EFFECTS AND INTERACTIONS. As can be seen in Table 6, reinforcement instructions powerfully affected the report of RHs, as they should, and their effect falls off as we move across to BH, then to BI, and then to final perfor-

Table 6

EFFECT OF REINFORCEMENT INSTRUCTIONS AND REINFORCEMENT VALUE ON FINAL LEVEL OF PERFORMANCE

	RHd		RSv		RHs		BH		MC		BI		Final R	
	F	*r*	*F*	*r*	*F*	*r*	*F*	*r*	*F*	*r*	*F*	*r*	*F*	*r*
Reinforcement Value	2.2	.11	24.5	.58	2.4	.06	3.2	.18	.26	.07	4.6	.23	5.6	.26
Instructions	5.9	.18	.41	.05	82.5	.77	38.8	.64	6.5	−.21	31.9	.60	24.8	.55
Interaction	.3		1.2		.65		1.4		.61		.9		1.5	

r at .05 about .19   *F* at .05 about 3.10 for 2 and 99 d.f.   All interactions nonsignificant.
r at .01 about .27   *F* at .01 about 4.85 for 2 and 99 d.f.

mance. We should expect this if RHs, BH, and BI are sequential processes whose manner of association is controlled by parameters—RHd and MC—whose values vary over subjects. Reinforcement value affected RSv, as it should, and its effect on BI and final performance was significant but not large. Reinforcement value did not affect RHd or BH. What is most striking here is that reinforcement instruction was clearly a more effective control of behavior than was reinforcement value—even with about as extreme a manipulation as we could manage in the laboratory. None of the interactions was significant.

intentions with the two products (RHd × RSv) and (BH × MC). We found that "R" to be .88. As one can see from the beta weights and r's in Table 7, what the subject believes he is supposed to do and his motivation to comply are much the stronger correlate of reported intentions. Under these conditions, in fact, there is virtually no independent contribution to BI from hypotheses of the distribution of reinforcement and its subjective evaluation. With the use of standard multiple regression analysis, the multiple "R", although still strong, is probably attenuated by the use of beta weights that are estimates of "average" weights

Table 7

MULTIPLE " R " ANALYSIS WITH BI AS CRITERION
AND (RHd × RSv) AND (BH × MC) AS PREDICTORS

Multiple " R "	.88
r, BI and (BH × MC)	.86
r, BI and (RHd × RSv)	.40
r, (BH × MC) and (RHd × RSv)	.26
Dependent variable intercept	.16
Standardized regression coefficients	
(BH × MC)	.81
(RHd × RSv)	.19
Unstandardized regression coefficients	
(BH × MC)	1.03
(RHd × RSv)	.24

CENTRAL EQUATIONS. On Equation 1b, and hypotheses of report validity, we expect a correlation of BH and the product of RHd and RHs; we found it to be .87. For only 8 of 108 subjects was the prediction other than perfect. This is strong support for the theoretical sentence summarizing a set of inferences from what is believed about a reinforcer's distribution and its significance to what a subject believes he is supposed to do.

On Equation 2c, and hypotheses of report validity, we should expect a multiple correlation of behavioral

for the group. And so probably is the contribution of (RHd × RSv). Where (RHd × RSv) and (BH × MC) are not in agreement, subjects varied, with most matching their BI to the second component but some matching BI to the first component. If we could obtain satisfactory estimates of the individual weights for these components, the linearity of the subjects' behavior should be even more striking.

On Equation 3b, and a hypothesis of report validity, we should expect a strong correlation of level of reports of behavioral intentions to number of correct responses over the last 20 trials. We found an r of .94 for that relationship (Table 8).

Table 8

CORRELATION OF NUMBER OF CORRECT RESPONSES IN FINAL BLOCK OF TRIALS WITH EACH REPORT OF RULE OR ASCRIPTOR

Ascriptors			Rules		
RSv	RHs	MC	RHd	BH	BI
.31	.68	.09	.00	.78	.94

Since the mean level of MC is high and positive, BH is also highly correlated with final level of performance. RHd is uncorrelated with response selection *over all subjects*, as it should be where the parameters of that relationship take positive and negative values that are well balanced over subjects.

But recall that Equation 2d gives a pivotal role to RHd, the subject's awareness of the distribution of reinforcement: BI = RHd [(RSv) w_2 + (RHs × MC) w_3.] On this equation, and others specifying the consequence of BI and the antecedents of those ascriptors, we expect RHd to enter into an intricate pattern of relationships. RHd should be a critical parameter of a number of relationships, and the set of ascriptors should be a critical parameter of the relationships RHd enters into.

For the 55 subjects who report some positive value of RHd, we should expect a strong positive relation of behavioral intentions to the specified combination of subjective evaluation of a reinforcer, hypotheses of significance of the reinforcer, and motivation to comply. Taking BI as criterion and RSv and (RHs × MC) as predictors, we obtained a multiple "R" of .95. Furthermore, we expected, and found, that this relationship dropped to nonsignificance for the 51 subjects whose RHd reports were 0 (that "R" was .14 and not

significant). For ascriptors to be controlling in this circumstance, subjects apparently must know a correct or correlated distribution of the reinforcer.

Conversely, we should expect the relation of RHd to BI to vary with the value of our conjoint expression of RSv, RHs, and MC. We can obtain +, 0, and − estimates for that expression by using the linear regression of RSv and (RHs × MC) on BI to obtain *expected values* of BI for each subject. For subjects whose expected values were +, 0, and − respectively, the correlations of RHd and BI were very much as they should be: + .98 for $n = 40$, .00 for $n = 7$, and − .75 for $n = 61$.

Since the entire right side of Equation 2d goes to zero when RHd = 0, we should expect the performance of those subjects to show no effect of the reinforcer's distribution, the reinforcer's value, or reinforcement instructions. The effect of those variables should be exclusively through the terms that are at zero. This is the theoretical reason we expect no learning without awareness in either of the two important senses: an association of either Rd or Rv to performance for subjects at RHd zero. The 51 subjects reporting at RHd zero did not differ in slope from random reinforcement controls (F about 1), and neither did reinforcement value correlate with number of correct responses over the last 20 trials ($r = .13$). For that matter, the strong effect of instructions on final performance also dropped to nonsignificance for those 51 subjects ($r = .04$).

As you can see in the network (Figure 1), all of the variables of concern in this experiment are held to have their effect on the subject's response through his behavioral intentions. If true, then partialling out BI, we should expect the correlations of final performance with any manipulation or report to go to, or remain at, nonsignificance. Those partial r's varied from $-$ .06 to .14, all nonsignificant. Where habitual—or instinctive—variables are constant or irrelevant, all roads to response selection should lead through the subject's volition.

Finally, it seems worth noticing that reports of RHd and RHs combined multiplicatively to account for as much as 77 per cent of the variance in reports of behavioral hypotheses. With subjective value of the reinforcer combined multiplicatively with RHd, and BH combined multiplicatively with MC, the two aggregates accounted for 77 per cent of the variance in behavioral intentions. BI in turn accounted for 88 per cent of the variance in final performance. On the other hand, the affective value of reinforcement, about as extreme as we could manipulate, controlled 6 per cent of the total variance in performance; and reinforcement together with reinforcement instructions controlled only 36 per cent of the variance in performance. Neither manipulation controlled significant variance in final performance when the critical "R" terms, RHd and BI, were at zero or partialed out. When subjects are allowed to say what is on their minds—under reasonably refined conditions—we find the stronger relationships to be R-R, not S-R.

Experiment II

For Experiment II (Dulany, Schwartz, and Walker, 1965a) we went back to the heat tank with a number of questions that had come out of the theory and Experiment I. It seemed that behavioral hypotheses and motivation to comply had so strongly controlled behavioral intentions that hypotheses of the distribution of reinforcement and subjective evaluation of reinforcement had had only a negligible effect. We wanted to re-examine that effect, freed of social rules and

compliance, by fixing subjects at BH zero with instructions. Under these conditions the second component would drop from Equation 2c, and we should expect BI = (RHd) (RSv) to generate a stronger relationship among those reports. We also wanted to spread RHd over the full range of its scale by varying Rd, the reinforcer's distribution. What had been so critical as a free variant we wanted to vary further with manipulations—in order to see its role still more clearly. With only minor revisions in the task, questions, and general procedures, the reinforcer's distribution was now varied orthogonally to reinforcement value—the values used in Experiment I. Reinforcement was contingent either on "vanished" (now $+ 1$), "slippery" ($+.4$), "slick" ($-.4$), or "disappeared" (now $- 1$). With this design, and reports of rules and ascriptors, we could ask the general question: "Why do the distributional and value parameters of a reinforcer interact?"

The critical change in instructions came after trial 20: "Fine. Now ignore the red light for a moment and listen carefully. From now on a stream of air will sometimes blow across your face. There are three things I want you to know so that you can repeat them back to me and remember them throughout the entire experiment. (Pause) ONE: Remember that the stream of air has nothing to do with whether you have said something you are supposed to say or *not* supposed to say—nothing to do with something we want you to say or not say. (Pause) Two: There is *nothing* you are either supposed to say or not supposed to say—nothing that we want you to say or not say. (Pause) THREE: If you should discover anything that the stream of air always or usually follows, you may try to make the air come on, or to make it stay off. *Whether you do either, or not, is entirely up to you.* We neither want you to get the stream of air nor to avoid it. (Pause) Is that clear? Now would you repeat back to me the three things I have told you."

Every part of the instructions that was not correctly given back by the subject was repeated until the subject showed that she had learned all three components of the instruction. Even so it was necessary to run 169 subjects in order to obtain 120—10 per cell—who reported at BH zero and satisfied the conditions of the design. The correlational analysis of data from all subjects together gave results very closely comparable to those from the preceding experiment.

Now on Equation 2c, with BH at 0, and the coordinations of RHd, RSv, and BI to Rd, Rv, and final response, we should expect the interaction, (Rd) (Rv) → R. Part I of Table 9 shows that interaction to be strong,

Table 9

INTERACTION OF DISTRIBUTION OF REINFORCER (Rd) AND AFFECTIVE VALUE OF REINFORCER (Rv) ON FREQUENCY OF CORRECT RESPONSES WITHIN THE LAST 20 TRIALS (R)

I. Summary
 A. $(Rd+1)(Rv+1)$ on R, $F(6,108)=7.4, p<.001$
        0   0
       −1   −1
 B. $r[(Rd+1)(Rv+1)], "R"=.45$
        0   0
       −1   −1

II. Magnitude and direction of "simple effects" expressed in Pearson r's
 A. Subjects at Each Distributional Value of the Reinforcer
   at Rd +1.0$(n=30)$, $r_{RV,R}=.54$
   at Rd + .4$(n=30)$, $r_{RV,R}=.49$
   at Rd − .4$(n=30)$, $r_{RV,R}=-.56$
   at Rd −1.0$(n=30)$, $r_{RV,R}=-.40$
 B. For Subjects at Each Affective Value of the Reinforcer
   at Rv +1$(n=40)$, $r_{Rd,R}=.54$
   at Rv 0$(n=40)$, $r_{Rd,R}=-.46$
   at Rv −1$(n=40)$, $r_{Rd,R}=-.59$

and with Rv and Rd scaled from $+1$ to -1, we can express the magnitude of the linear interaction by an r of .45 for final performance and the product of Rd and Rv. With these scales, the expected interaction can be simply summarized in this way: the sign of the relation of either predictor to the criterion is given by the sign of the subjects' position on the other predictor. Consequently, we expect the strongly directional simple effects shown in Part II of Table 9. Only the $-.46$ correlation of Rd and "R" for the 40 subjects at Rv zero is momentarily puzzling; but this is derivable from the theory since the mean *subjective* value, the mean RSv, was slightly negative for those 40 subjects.

Table 10

RELATION OF REPORTED HYPOTHESES OF REINFORCER'S DISTRIBUTION (RHd) TO REINFORCER'S DISTRIBUTION (Rd); OF SUBJECTIVE VALVE OF REINFORCER (RSv) TO VALUE OF REINFORCER; OF BEHAVIORAL INTENTIONS (BI) TO FREQUENCY OF RESPONSE IN THE LAST 20 TRIALS

A. Rd and RHd: Main effect, $F(3,108)=70.8$
   $r_{Rd,RHd}=.79$ (Neither Rv nor Rd × Rv was significant on RHd; F's about 1)
B. Rv and RSv: Main effect, $F(2,108)=55.9$
   $r_{Rv,RSv}=.67$ (Neither Rd nor Rd × Rv was significant on RSv; F's<1)
C. $r_{BI,R}=.90$

Table 10 establishes that the reinforcer's distribution and value did strongly influence reports of RHd and RSv. And again we find a strong .90 correlation of reported behavioral intentions and response selection over the last 20 trials.

On the hypotheses mentioned, and the hypotheses of report validity, we expect a parallel "interaction" of RHd and RSv on BI. Part I of Table 11 shows this relationship to be a relatively

Table 11

" INTERACTION " OF HYPOTHESES OF REIN-FORCER'S DISTRIBUTION (RHd) AND SUB-JECTIVE VALUE OF REINFORCER (RSv) ON BEHAVIORAL INTENTIONS (BI)

I. Summary
$r[(RHd_{+1}) (RSv_{+1})], BI_{+1} = .72$

| 0 | 0 | 0 |
| −1 | −1 | −1 |

II. Magnitude and Direction of " Simple Effect " expressed in Pearson r's
   A. For Subjects at Each Value (or Range of Values) of Reported Hypotheses of Reinforcer's Distribution (RHd)
   at RHd + (n = 44), $r_{BI, RSv} = .73$
   at RHd 0 (n = 34), $r_{BI, RSv} = .01$
   at RHd − (n = 42), $r_{BI, RSv} = -.70$
   B. For Subjects at Each Value (or Range of Values) or Reported Affective Value of Reinforcer (RSv)
   at RSv + (n = 44), $r_{BI, RHd} = .64$
   at RSv 0 (n = 16), $r_{BI, RHd} = .38$ (ns)
   at RSv − (n = 60), $r_{BI, RHd} = -.80$

Table 12

INTERACTION OF THE DISTRIBUTION OF REINFORCER (Rd) AND VALUE OF REIN-FORCER (Rv) ON FREQUENCY OF RESPONSE IN LAST 20 TRIALS, AT ZERO VALUE OF EACH OF THE VARIABLES THEORIZED TO MEDIATE THAT INTERACTION BY THEIR PARA-LLEL " INTERACTION "

I. For Ss who report no correlated Hypothesis of the Reinforcer's Distribution (RHd$_0$), (n = 34)
   $r_{R, }[(Rd) (Rv)] = .02$
II. For Ss who report zero Value of the Rein-forcer (RSv$_0$), (n = 16)
   $r_{R, }[(Rd) (Rv)] = .16$ (ns)
III. For Ss who report no correlated Behavioral Intention (BI$_0$), (n = 33)
   $r_{R, }[(Rd) (Rv)] = .06$

strong .72 when subjects are set at BH zero. Part II shows the strongly directional "simple effects" to be about as expected.

Finally, why *do* the value and distributional parameters of reinforcement interact? According to the theory, this interaction is mediated by a parallel "interaction" of RHd and RSv on BI. If so, we should expect the results reported and three others: the strong interaction of Rd and Rv on performance should drop to nonsignificance for subjects who report at zero values of either of the critical mediating variables: RHd, RSv, or BI. As can be seen in Table 12, there is no encouragement for thinking otherwise. And although the *n*'s for subgroups are small, those results are consistent with those of Experiment I for Rd and Rv taken alone.

Again the stronger relationships were R-R rather than S-R. Even with the stronger component, (BH × MC),

at zero, reports of (RHd × RSv) still accounted for 51% of the variance in reported behavioral intentions. And BI accounted for 81% of the variance in final response selection. With the affective value and distribution of the reinforcer manipulated over extreme values, those manipulations together controlled only 18% of the variance in final performance—and no significant variance when values of the critical "R" terms were at zero.[8]

[8] These are only two experiments, but they are "core experiments" in the sense of providing multiple and interlocking observations in support of the "core" h. potheses of the theory. Other experiments have closely replicated the results of Experiment I but with a more common verbal conditioning task (Dulany and McHale, 1966) and with monetary reinforcement and noncollege populations (Smith, 1966). Additional evidence consistent with these findings has been reported and reviewed by Dulany (1961, 1962) and Spielberger (1962, 1965). Critiques of studies reporting learning without awareness can be found in these sources and in Adams (1957), Eriksen (1960), and Farber (1963). In the first report of Experiment I (Dulany, 1964) some of the r and F values differed slightly due to the use of a less finely differentiated scoring system.

Discussion

When a well-received theory is confronted by anomalous findings, its defenders have a number of historically honored lines of retreat and defense. Sometimes the theory is even said not to exist or really to be something else—until the danger is passed. Or "They do not . . . treat anomalies as counterinstances, though in the vocabulary of the philosophy of science that is what they are . . . for its defenders will do what we have already seen scientists do when confronted by anomaly. They will devise numerous articulations and *ad hoc* modifications of their theory in order to eliminate any apparent conflict." (Kuhn, 1962, pages 77–78). Or sometimes the scope of the theory is restricted to a more defensible domain. And since "All crises begin with the blurring of a paradigm and the consequent loosening of the rules of normal research" (Kuhn p. 84), we can expect the protests that the anomalous findings violate the rules of research strategy and methodology that we all learned and all tough-minded scientists must observe. Let us see.

The question of theory

As Kendler announces at the outset, ". . . I feel compelled to state bluntly that the concept of general S-R theory is neither valid nor appropriate." But for the moment please consider the following propositions:

(1) As a positive reinforcement follows an operant response, in the presence of some set of stimuli S, the probability of occurrence of that response in the presence of those stimuli increases. (2) As a negative reinforcement follows an operant response, in the presence of some set of stimuli S, the probability of occurrence of that response in the presence of those stimuli decreases. (3) An unconditioned stimulus will elicit an unconditioned response. (4) As a conditioned stimulus is temporally and spatially associated with an unconditioned stimulus, the probability increases that the conditioned stimulus will produce a conditioned response. Call this UCS a "reinforcement," too. (5) As stimuli are physically dissimilar to the set of stimuli S (or a CS), the probability of an operant response (or a CR) to those stimuli moves toward a chance level. (6) As an operant (or a CR) occurs in the presence of stimuli S (or a CS), in the absence of reinforcement, the probability of the operant response (or CR) to those stimuli moves toward a chance level.

From these basic propositions, and specification of frepuency parameters, we can derive an account of discrimination learning and any convergent or divergent stimulus-response hierarchy. Add the proposition that responses have stimulus properties and we logically entail an S-R mediation theory without saying anything more.

First of all, I would submit that this set of propositions does comprise a theory. It has predictive, explanatory, and systematizing power as we look for and find physical energies and pieces of behavior that go together in the ways those sentences assert. Historically, of course, sentences very like these were offered as a description of what happened in two simple experimental paradigms—and those paradigms comprise the pretheoretical model on which this theory was constructed. But the propositions themselves remain a model only in the too common sense of a theory we would rather not take full responsibility for. Furthermore, the terms "stimulus," "response," "reinforcement," etc., as a technical language, are in no sense independent of those theoretical sentences, and controversy over their "definition" could have been avoided if this had been more widely recognized. For the theory in use, "stimulus," "response," and "reinforcement" have been whatever experimental variables behaved in the way the theory uses those terms. Of course, too, anyone who has thumbed through a textbook on learning knows that there are a variety of S-R theories. The theory I outline is an abstraction upon them, omitting those postulated mechanisms not derivable from these propositions. (An account of r_g is derivable.) The abstraction could have been stated a little differently with a little different vocabulary. But it is an abstraction that I believe (a) is very close to the S-R theories *in use* in the area of verbal behavior and thinking (for example, Maltzman, 1955; Kendler and Kendler, 1962; Staats, 1961, 1964; Goss, 1961; Osgood, 1957; Dollard and Miller, 1950; and Skinner, 1953), and (b) covers what is critical to the confrontation I shall discuss. If we should be asked, "What is this theory called?" I think most would answer "S-R behavior theory."

Critical to the confrontation I see is the exclusion from this general theory and its variants of any propositions according a causal or instrumental role to conscious, volitional processes in mediating the effects of positive and negative reinforcers on response selection. In common usage, it is this very exclusion that defines "the automatic action of reinforcement," whatever the particular mechanism of reinforcement the variant of S-R theory offers. Of one variant, Miller (1962, pp. 195–6) writes, "The cornerstone of Hull's theory was the following idea: Whenever a response to some stimulus has the effect of reducing a biological drive, the strength of the stimulus-response association

will be increased . . . the daring featuring of this hypothesis is that, true to the behaviorist tradition, nothing is assumed about *understanding* the connection between the response and the satisfactions that follow . . . the habit of responding R to situation S will be *automatically* reinforced." (Italics his) And Dollard and Miller (1950, pp. 33–34) emphasize that "The assumption that reinforcement has a direct, unconscious effect is essential to the logic of this book . . . . An experiment by Greenspoon . . . clearly demonstrates that the effects of reinforcement can be entirely unconscious and automatic. A great deal of human learning seems to be of this direct, unconscious kind."

Now confronted with experiments in which subjects are asked to report their awareness, the S-R theorist then has a number of contingent options:

1. PREDICTION OF RANDOM ASSOCIATION OF REPORTS AND RESPONSE SELECTION. Unqualified by auxiliary assumptions or new elaborations of the theory, S-R behavior theory must predict learning unassociated with reports of awareness. Within that expected disassociation is the prediction of *learning without awareness*. This was the first option taken. Verplank (1956, p. 97), for example, in extending this language to the human level, writes that "This is the identification of responses and reinforcing stimuli, and the verification and eduction of laws relating them to one another in human behavior under conditions where the subject is acting as naturally as possible, and where in so far as possible, he is *not* 'aware' of what is going on."

In Experiments I and II (a) very strong relationships of response selection to several reports of awareness were found (as strong as $r = .94$), and (b) neither the distribution or value for reinforcement was related to response selection for subjects who did not report a correlated awareness of the distribution of reinforcement. Given the magnitude of the expected relationships and the extreme manipulation of these reinforcement parameters, these results seem as strong as any of this general nature thus far presented.

2. ASSIMILATION TO S-R BEHAVIOR THEORY. When private reports do show some systematic relationship with response selection, we might first attempt to degrade the theory that predicted them to S-R behavior theory. One theory "degrades" to another, in a nonpejorative sense, if we can hold that the theories say the same thing— as has been said, for example, of expectancy theory and r_g theory. Only their vocabularies are said to differ, not their syntaxes. At a glance the two sets of theoretical sentences I outlined do not look at all the same; and if they are not, they should certainly make different predictions.

On S-R behavior theory, we might hold that the reports, or the underlying awarenesses, are themselves conditioned. Their behavior should be predictable from some combination of the propositions I outlined, or their variants. We might hold either that the conditioning of reports and terminal responses was entirely independent, or that at some stage, the conditioned reports of awareness came to function as discriminative stimuli for those terminal responses. Once reports (and instructions) have become systematic experimental variables, the question simply becomes, "which theory offers a better account of their behavior?"

Under the heading "Some S-R Relations of Awareness" Maltzman reports that ". . . studies conducted within my laboratory indicate that 'awareness' varies according to the usual principles of behavior." And under the heading

"The Case for Concurrent Learning" Kanfer writes, "The behavioristically oriented group has taken the position that verbal reports and task responses are functions of the same experimental variables and that concurrent interdependent learning occurs as a consequence of such factors as the characteristics of the experimenter, the subject, the task, and of the interaction of these three." It is a common view: "The basic hypothesis is that reported awareness is a verbal operant behavior influenced by the same variables as any other responsivity to the verbal operant conditioning" (Krasner and Ullman, 1963, p. 197); ". . . A differential reinforcement administered for overt responses will at the same time selectively reinforce the correct mediating response" (Postman and Sassenrath, 1961, p. 132); "Our first guess was that the verbal statements of 'rules' would prove to be simple operant behaviors, conditionable as are other operants" (Verplank, 1962, p. 134).

This is a plausible enough interpretation of simpler experiments showing that a single reported awareness of the reinforcer's contingency accompanies conditioning. It is just as plausible as the interpretation that reinforcement produces awareness, awareness produces conditioning, and awareness produces reports. But that cognitive theory has only three propositions and two predictions. It is too impoverished to be competitively supported because any number of other theories will account for the correlation of reports and conditioning, including the theory that the reports were also conditioned.

In Experiments I and II of the present paper, however, we find a network of relationships among manipulations, response selection, and multiple reports of several awarenesses—generated by a network of theoretical propositions. Reports of six qualitatively different awarenesses and response selection appear in a number of fairly intricate and precisely specifiable relationships. That pattern is not predicted in any evident way from conditioning propositions. We should need additional assumptions, for example, to predict that a reinforcer simultaneously conditions *positive* report of RHd and an *increase* in response selection, *only* when it conditions a *positive* report of RSV, on the one hand, or positive reports of RHS, BH, and MC on the other hand. And conversely, we should have to explain the conditioning of a positive RHd and *negative* response selection when we condition the other report parameters with negative values.

In the present research it is even difficult to extend the conditioning theory to *one* rule, by virtue of the manner of scaling. For the subject who made 20 correct out of 20 responses, we must predict conditioning him to say that he tried to use sentences with "a" on all 20 trials. And for the subject who made about 16 of 20 correct responses, we must find an assumption that will predict conditioning him to say that he tried to use sentences with "along" on all 20 trials. In fact, the theory that rules are simple operants, conditionable as other operants, implies an intuitive absurdity that is clearly contrary to our data. On that theory, if response selection varies with reinforcement value—as it does—then so should a statement of a rule for the distribution of reinforcement. If positively reinforced, it should become more available. But with negative reinforcers, the rule of reinforcement should become highly unavailable; we punish it. In neither experiment was the cardinal rule statement, RHd, associated with positive, neutral, and negative reinforcement values.

No theory of the conditioning of propositional reports has yet been elaborated in such a way as to approach an account of the intricate pattern of relationships that we find among response selection and several propositional reports. And the logic of the problem is exactly the same for any attempt to explain these several kinds of awareness as classically conditioned. This is not to say that a conditioning theory could never be elaborated in that way. When that elaboration is provided, we can evaluate the theory that results. At present, the array of observations follows fairly naturally from a theory of propositional control, including the hypotheses that subjects validly reported their conscious, controlling processes.

The theory does not, of course, hold that propositional processes are unrelated to reinforcement, but that different reinforcement parameters have separable effects on different propositional processes and that these then combine by rules of inference and quasi-inference to yield intentions and final responses. This means that propositional processes should behave unlike simple responses in a number of significant ways. And when we meet the conditions for report validity, so should their reports. The usual line of retreat for S-R mediation theories—explain the mediator in the same way—may not be completely open.[9]

[9] (a) A similar problem is presented by explanatory references to instructions and verbal rules as "discriminative stimuli" for terminal responses (for example, Skinner, 1963, p. 514; Bijou and Baer, 1966, p. 775). In the first place, "discriminative stimulus" is a term defined by a history in which a stimulus *gains* control of a response by selective reinforcement of that response in its presence—not by any demonstration of stimulus control. When that history is absent, the term suggests a hypothesis but does not provide a behavior theoretic explanation. Furthermore, one can easily demonstrate that a subject will respond selectively to an instruction he has never heard before, much less been selectively reinforced for

responding to. And that is almost certainly the case for instructions in Experiments I and II. An appeal to "generalization" provides an unsatisfactory answer in the absence of a successful S-R analysis of response to novel utterances. In the absence of that history, however, terms for instructions take on explanatory value as we successfully predict from the *formal* properties of those instructional *propositions*, and the theory in which they appear. Instructions should influence responses when the information they convey combines with other propositions by logical and quasi-logical inference. They should enter into relationships not predicted by behavior theoretic assertions about "discriminative stimuli." For example, the effect of instruction was strongly positive for subjects at RHd +, and nonsignificant for subjects at RHd 0.

(*b*) For most theories and experiments on the trial by trial movement of a controlling hypothesis (Restle, 1962; Levine, 1963; Bower and Trabasso, 1964), I fully agree with Bourne that "It is an easy step from mediation to hypothesis. Whether there is any useful distinction is doubtful. Mediational and hypothesis testing theories seem to differ mainly in technical language." They "degrade" to S-R mediation theory because they adopt the reinforcement and extinction postulates—the ". . . assumption that reinforcement or feedback affects the selection and maintenance of internalized hypotheses . . ." (Bourne), and then quantitatively refine them with one or another assumption about sampling after nonpositive outcomes and hypothesis selection after positive reinforcement outcomes. A viably different alternative might come in two ways: (1) specification of the *inferences* that follow hypothesis selection (to BH and BI, for example) and (2) specification of the effect of outcomes and instances on *inferences* that constitute the sampling pool, rather than directly on the hypothesis sampled. The latter is close to Bourne's (1965) current work.

(*c*) The argument for concurrent learning is sometimes made on the essentially irrelevant findings that experimental variables influence (1) reports of awareness, and (2) the relationship of those reports to conditioning scores. No such interpretation can be drawn in the absence of the critically relevant parameters and tests, and where they are available the results have been negative for the concurrent learning hypothesis. In both Experiments I and II, experimental manipu-

3. AUGMENTING ASSUMPTIONS. If reports do show systematic relationships with conditioning—even to the extent of no residual error for learning without awareness—we might still try to reconcile the finding with S-R theory by going outside the theory for auxiliary assumptions which would explain that relationship. When I first began writing about these matters (Dulany, 1961, 1962a, 1963), I described several such auxiliary assumptions: suggestion, rationalization, and emergence (as well as common conditioning). On this reasoning, the reinforcer automatically conditions responses; but the questions asked suggest the reports of awareness. A subject rationalizes his performance by saying he was aware, or the awareness that is reported somehow emerged after the conditioning occurred.

We should first remember that these *are* auxiliary assumptions and not a part of S-R behavior theory. We should also remember that each of these assumptions requires additional *linking* assumptions, (*a*) for each report of awareness that enters into different relationships with a response selection, and (*b*) for the interrelationships among the reports themselves.

lations "controlled" reports of RHs, RSv, BH, BI, and response selection. That the manipulations did not control reports and response selection independently of reported awareness is shown by two, among other, findings: The effects of those manipulations were nonsignificant on response selection when the theoretically critical RHd or BI reports were at zero or partialled out. And the relation of RHd to BI (and response selection) varied from strongly positive through nonsignificant to strongly negative with the reports of parameters of that relationship—RSv and (RHs × MC). It is impossible to make a clear interpretation of the many studies in the literature that do not assess critical parameters and make relevant tests.

Again all these mechanisms seem plausible enough when an experiment shows that conditioning is associated with a single report of awareness. The additional linking assumptions readily come to mind: the questions suggested that the response conditioned was the response reinforced. The subject rationalized that he must have been reinforced for making the response he noticed was being conditioned. An awareness emerged after conditioning as the subject began to notice that he was oddly making the reinforced response more and more often.

But once a theory generates a network of experimental interrelationships, the necessary linking assumptions become less available. On what additional assumptions, for example, do we predict that a subject rationalizes that he tried to use "along" if 16 of his last 20 responses are correct, and "quickly" if only two? Or why should a subject show positive conditioning only if a question suggests a correlated distribution of the reinforcer, and other questions *also* happen to suggest either that the reinforcer was pleasant or that the reinforcer meant that he was correct and that he was motivated to comply? Or how do we predict that a subject will look back and notice that the reinforcer followed "*a,*" even sometimes when he *doesn't* condition—but only when the controlling parameters RSv or (RHs × MC) have both been suggested or rationalized or emergent at zero value? The present pattern of relations, I believe, is not derivable from S-R behavior theory, even as augmented by assumptions of rationalization, suggestion, or emergence—and any known set of further augmenting assumptions for those mechanisms. And I would add again that when such assumptions are found, we can evaluate the theory they comprise. At present a pattern of

strong relationships follows rather naturally from the theory of propositional control, including the hypotheses of report validity.[10]

[10] Salzinger (1965) and Kanfer and many others argue that awareness accompanies conditioning scores in some experiments (Dulany, 1962; Spielberger, 1962) where response classes and contingencies are figural and that reinforcement should act directly on response selection if the subjects' hypothesis testing and awareness were limited in some way, perhaps by interference. In the absence of a successful S-R reinforcement interpretation of findings where interference is *not* specifically introduced, this must become a restriction of the scope of the theory—to a point where it could not carry its expected explanatory load. Nevertheless the argument from those experiments is obviously specious because it has already been examined there with negative results: For from 30 to 100 percent of those subjects awareness was so limited in some way that they did not report simple contingencies over figural response classes after 80 to 100 trials, yet they showed no conditioning.

Both Kanfer and Maltzman (1966) go on to emphasize the study of Dixon and Oakes (1965) reporting that RH, BH, and BI reports were unassociated with conditioning with color naming between trials, and that RH, RH only, was associated with conditioning without color naming. But attributing this result to interference is rather strongly disconfirmed by Dixon and Oakes' own finding that color naming was unassociated with any of their reports. And the strength of the finding is questionable for other reasons: failure to replicate interrelations among reports and conditioning in the absence of color naming (already multiply replicated, Dulany, 1962), no report of instructions prior to assessment, nonsignificant *r*'s with *n*'s of 25, and unreported variance. With more adequate *n*'s and procedures, Dulany, Schwartz, and Schneider (1966) again found (*a*) no effect of naming of the same colors on final reports (or trial by trial statements of hypotheses in a second experiment), and (*b*) the previously found strong interrelations among reports and response selection. Using a concept attainment task for intertrial interference, Lubitz (1966) achieved strong interference effects on reports of awareness and found no conditioning for subjects at RHd zero.

The question of research strategy

S-R theories imply S-R laws. Still more common is the belief that R-R laws are somehow second-class laws, especially so if some of the "R" terms happen to be the subject's private reports. In the theory and experiments I have outlined, manipulations appear, but it is they that have a secondary status. They serve to spread subjects over, or fix subjects at, certain values of theoretical terms whose primary coordinations are to reporting responses. In the experiments, stimulus variables entered into some interpretations, but others rested primarily on R-R relations. I believe that the common objections to R-R relations as goals and supports for theory are essentially mistaken and that there are distinct advantages to an R-R strategy in the domain we are discussing.

Arguments against R-R strategy

1. Most fundamental, I think, is the common view that inference from R-R relations to hypothetical controlling processes is somehow weaker than from S-R relations. In fact, it is sometimes said that no such inferences can be defended unless the hypothetical process is "anchored" in some way on the stimulus side. Under the ingratiating heading "A studied intolerance," Underwood (1957, p. 215) writes, "A postulated process not tied to stimulus variables can be assigned all the properties required to explain anything, but the validity of these assigned properties can never be assayed experimentally. The soundness of an explanatory idea cannot be evaluated unless the idea is related to at least one stimulus variable." And Kanfer writes that

"Bechtoldt (1959) has pointed out that a response defined variable approach encounters difficulties because a given behavior can arise from many different combinations of experimental conditions. Therefore, any one of numerous sets of explanatory constructs can be postulated and be 'correct' in terms of agreement between prediction and observation." The clincher for Bechtoldt (p. 627) is an example taken from Johnson (1954, p. 723) and the ages: "If 'Old Dog Tray' was run through a large and powerful sausage-grinder, he is dead; he is dead, therefore, he was sausaged." The Bechtoldt-Johnson reconstruction of theory and evidence takes the logical from: $P \rightarrow Q$; and every beginning student of logic knows that assertion of Q does not imply P.

In the first place, I would insist that the logical problem of inductive inference from single experimental observation to one or two theoretical propositions mentioning a hypothetical process is exactly the same for S-R observations and R-R observations. If our theory is either $S \xrightarrow{a} H \xrightarrow{b} R$ or $R \xrightarrow{a} H \xrightarrow{b} R$, there are (a) an infinity of H's that will "explain" both the S-R and R-R relations, and, in fact, (b) an infinity of complementary pairs of functions that will assert the relations a and b. Weakness of inference from either relationship reflects the impoverishment of the observations and the impoverishment of the theories that led to them, not the S-R or R-R forms of the relationships.

But this simple logical model is plainly an erroneous construal of well-formed theory and experimental inquiry. A well-formed theory is not one or two propositions but may be a richly articulated network of propositions, and a network of propositions may generate a comparably rich network of experimental observations—not merely a single S-R or R-R relation. Where we have a fairly rich network of observations, the set of available constructs and relations—theories—that will explain those findings is finite, and usually small. The rule is fairly simple: the richer the array of observations, the narrower the range of available theoretical interpretations. On this logic the question resolves to a familiar one: From which of the competing theories does the array of observations follow most naturally, without unreasonable augmenting assumptions? The logic brings us to a familiar standard that draws no distinction between the strength of inferences from an array of S-R relations and an array of R-R relations. They are equally constraining upon the properties we assign unobservables in writing a theory.

The answer to this more fundamental objection provides the more fundamental answer to other objections.

2. But R-R relations, it will be said, simply cannot be used to support causal, or instrumental, hypotheses. How can we support a theory that awareness is causal, with relations among reports and responses? "Merely correlational" is the usual epithet. Let us agree that if we vary S_1 and observe R_1, we can, under certain conditions, say that S_1 caused, or influenced, R_1—and more readily than we can observe a correlation between R_1 and R_2 and say that R_1 influenced R_2. Correlation, as we say, is not necessarily causality. But for reasons given, we must recognize that R-R relations and S-R relations have the same logical status and equal weight in supporting *theoretical* statements about the *causal influences* of *unobservables*. The usual objection rests on a simple confusion between what we can say about R-R relations and what we can say about the theoretical propositions they support. The inference from R-R relations to hypothetical causes is as good as the competitive

support for the theory in which they appear.

3. The objection to R-R relations as supports for hypothetical controls becomes particularly insistent when a temporal order of measurement is reversed, and especially when the assessment of *awareness* follows the response this awareness is said to control. According to Kanfer and others, "The crux of the behavioristic criticisms of the cognitive position, however, lies in the fact that such information cannot be inferred to mediate learning when it is obtained in post-learning reports." Certainly there is no *logical* impediment to such inferences; if there were, significant portions of astronomy would have to be put aside. The question is entirely a matter for experimental control and the competitive examination of theories; it is not answered by a behavioristic dictum. We have already considered the question of which theory at present provides a better account of the available evidence—one assigning an instrumental role to several reported awarenesses, or one holding that a pattern of reports was suggested, rationalized, emergent, or conditioned independently of any instrumental role of awareness. From that exercise, it should be clear that the logic of competitive support of theories is insensitive to temporal differences between assessments and the assessed. When we ask which theory better accounts for the evidence, conventionalized behavioristic postures are a little less useful than the ordinary rules for examination of evidence and theories.[11]

[11] Multiple reports are obtained immediately after a critical block of responses so that *multiple* reports may be obtained and multiple relationships examined. Where trial-by-trial statements of a *single* rule are obtained (Dulany and O'Connell, 1963; O'Connell, 1965; O'Connell and Wagner, 1967; Schwartz, 1966a), rule validities and frequencies predict the following response

4. Also rather common is the odd belief that when subject's responses determine the values, they take on certain variables, the design or the prediction thereby becomes in some sense *post hoc*. Objecting to spreading or separating subjects on the basis of their reports (Dulany, 1962), Kanfer says, ". . .the *post hoc* nature of the design has

---

without significant error. The findings from the two procedures are mutually supporting. In both cases, however, support for a theory of control for the *processes* reported follows the same rules for inference from the competitive evaluation of theories. The same must hold for the experiments of Spielberger and DeNike (1966). Short of prescience, all observational reports are retrospective. The question is whether we can control for retrospective error and evaluate our degree of success.

Spielberger and DeNike (1966, pp. 315–316) take what superficially appears to be a different approach to this question: "In order to evaluate the temporal relationship between performance gains and awareness, the conditioning data for the aware subjects were examined as a function of the word block on which each first recorded a correct contingency in her notes." In their experiments, subjects recorded their "thoughts about the experiment" after each block of 25 responses. They found that the first significant performance gains came in the word block *after which* each subject first recorded a correct contingency in her notes. The temporal relation of reports of awareness to the critical performance measure is exactly what it is in previous studies and those reported here. The reports *follow* the critical measure of response selection, in their experiments a prior block of 25 responses, in ours a prior block of 20 responses. Their observations have another value: they show a strong *correlation over subjects* of the trial block number on which performance gains first occurred and after which reports of awareness first occurred. In this way the observations take a position in a network of observations jointly supporting the view that awareness is instrumental in response selection. Any interpretation that awareness was instrumental in the Spielberger and DeNike experiments must rely on that broader logic of the competitive examination of theories. It is inescapably a theoretical question.

often led investigators to make analyses and comparisons arising from initial findings. While such data may aid the researcher to plan his further strategy, their *post hoc* origin demands caution in interpretation." And in recognition that subjects do vary, he adds, "But the situation is not remedied by *post hoc* group splitting." The objection rests on a simple confusion of the time at which theoretical predictions and designs are formulated and the time at which subjects take values within the prediction equations. It should not require saying that antecedent predictions and designs are in no sense rendered *post hoc* by the responses of experimental subjects.

5. There is also a common feeling that use of R-R relations in support of theory leaves a number of unresolved problems of independence of measures and independence of constructs. Kanfer worries that, "Dulany's proposed network raises the practical question of how to measure BH, RH, and BI independently," and independently of final response; then he cites Bechtoldt's concern for the independence of constructs within a nomological network. The answer is only in part the practical matter of devising questions that are answered with reports of different propositions, propositions that make different assertions. As for the other experimental problems discussed, the more basic answer is given by the use of a network logic that allows us to evaluate our solution of the experimental problem.

Once we go beyond the simplest relationship, the usual logic is of no use: Variables are "dependent" if they are correlated and "independent" if they are not. Where a theory specifies interactions, pairs of variables may have positive, zero, or negative correlations depending upon the values taken by other parameters within the theory.

We must show measures to be independent by showing that they take different positions—as ours do—in a network of experimental relationships. And we show that the report measures do not behave in any degree contrary to this rule, by showing that level of report is insensitive to position in order of assessment and hence to other assessments. Constructs are inductively shown to have independence by specifying different positions for them within a network of theoretical sentences and then experimentally supporting the theory in competition with alternative explanations. And since measures of terminal reponse take a position in the network of experimental relationships that is different from that of reports of awareness, the logic generates an experimental answer to the concern that, "The possible contamination of the verbal report by the preceding learning experience may pose an unsolvable dilemma." It becomes incorrect to say that "The cognitivists' rebuttal of these criticisms is tantamount to arguing independence of two operationally interdependent responses."

6. One more objection to R-R laws rests, I believe, on a narrowly parochial and indefensible conception of experimental control: "When groups must be divided on the basis of postexperimental (sic) questionnaires to test uncontrolled or uncontrollable variance, it is apparent that the experimental manipulations were not sufficiently sharply defined, nor powerful enough to affect the behavior of all *S*'s without recourse to supplementary response inferred variables." But it is simply the fact that human adults come to experiments with widely varying genetic and learning histories. We can expect them to vary widely in their capacity to discern a distribution of reinforcement, to judge the significance and value of

consequences, to be compliant, and to respond. And it is the fact in our experiments that R-R relations account for 51 to 94 per cent of the variance, while reinforcement parameters manipulated over extreme values accounted for 6 to 18 per cent of the variance and no more than 36 per cent when combined with instructions. Not all experimental laws are causal laws, not even some of our favorite textbook examples (Nagel, 1961, p. 75–78). And on a broader, less parochial conception of "control," we ordinarily mean those experimental refinements that allow the strongest relationships to be revealed, be they S-R or R-R. What is error variance in S-R relations may become nonerror variance in R-R relations. As has so often happened before, we may examine the error in an expected relation, identify it with new variables, and learn that it is not "random" error, but systematic variance in other and possibly more powerful laws.

Arguments for R-R strategy

But what reasons might we have for seeing more promise in the pursuit of R-R laws than S-R laws in this domain?

1. It is undeniable that human subjects come to our experiments with highly variable learning and genetic histories. It is also perfectly clear that subjects in our experiments are highly variable in their reports of awareness and responses under common experimental conditions. Either we attribute this individual variance to caprice, or we recognize a problem of *historical residues*. Whatever the nature of these residues they apparently combine in ways reflected by individually varying awareness and reports. Given these histories we seek a strategy on more comfortable terms with the inevitable.

2. Within theory we may specify a

number of orders of awareness and their manner of combination just antecedent to response selection. Our measures of success are the inductive support for the theory in competition with alternatives and the degree of variance in response accounted for by the measure of those processes. Where measures of BI, for example, correlate .94 with response selection, or trial by trial statements of BI predict the succeeding trial response without significant error (Dulany and O'Connell, 1963; O'Connell, 1965; O'Connell and Wagner, 1967; Schwartz, 1966a), there is a relatively small margin of variance for neglected variables operating just antecedent to that response. Where theorized antecedents may be inductively said to explain 77 per cent of the variance in BI, we are encouraged to work with what we have and narrow the margin with further experimental refinements. To the degree we are successful, then, any historical variable, experimental manipulation, or stable residue called a trait, should have an appreciable effect on response selection in this paradigm only through the response indexed processes specified by the theory.[12] Experiments I and II support this expectation for powerful instructions and widely varying reinforcement parameters, Ronald Smith (1967) for a dimension of diagnosed pathology, and Blaufarb and Dulany (1964) for the question of "any trait." No significant variance over tasks was associated with subjects reporting at RHd zero.

3. If the awareness of subjects does vary in response to historical residues, in some degree independently of experimental manipulations, we should in principle be able to achieve greater "response validity" than "manipulation

validity" for our experimental coordinations of that awareness. Evidence that this is possible, with refined procedures, comes from both Experiments I and II. In all cases, reports showed appreciably stronger relationships with response selection than did the manipulations that varied those reports.

4. The central equations of the theory of propositional control specify a number of "interactions:" (RHd)(RHs) on BH, (RHd)(RSv) on BI, and (BH)(MC) on BI; and the experiments supported those theorized interrelationships. If we examine the relation of response selection to any manipulation varying one member of an interacting pair but leaving the second as a free variant, we still more seriously sacrifice experimental precision. The free variant is a slope parameter that can determine any relationship from perfect positive to perfect negative. In Experiment I, for example, instructions control RHs, and as the value of the parameter RHd goes from plus to zero, the correlation of instructions with performance goes from .72 to .04. To manipulate one or two variables, without assessment of the individually varying parameters, is to conduct a relatively insensitive experiment. Where those parameters vary in unknown ways over experiments, we should expect weak and inconsistent effects.

The rather general problem I raise has been recognized by Skinner (1963):

> These disturbances in simple causal linkages between environment and behavior can be formulated and studied experimentally as interactions among variables, but the possibility has not been fully exploited, and the effects still provide a formidable stronghold for mentalistic theories designed to bridge the gap between dependent and independent variables (p. 956).

Independent variables change the behaving organism, often in ways which persist for many years, and such

---

[12] The necessary qualification is that specified for Equation 3b: "where habit is at some constant value over response alternatives."

changes affect subsequent behavior. The subject may be able to describe some of these intervening states in useful ways, either before or after they have affected his behavior. On the other hand, behavior may be extensively modified by variables of which, and of the effect of which, the subject is never aware (p. 957).

For the latter contention he cites no evidence, and it is contrary to the evidence presented here and elsewhere (Dulany, 1961, 1962; Spielberger, 1962, 1965). For the former contention there remains a serious problem for the program at the level of human adults. If appreciable variance in awareness is in fact controlled by those historical residues, we should still be able to achieve greater report validity than manipulation validity—for the processes whose manipulations are the experimental variables participating in those interactions. And we should still expect stronger R-R than S-R laws as a result. In Experiment II, for example, the parallel "interaction" of subjective evaluation (RSv) and hypotheses of the distribution (RHd) accounted for more than twice as much variance in response selection as did the corresponding interaction of the reinforcer's value and distribution. Perhaps in principle these effects can be formulated as interactions of antecedent variables. But for human subjects the historical stimulus and genetic controls are in large part long ago or far away—and irrecoverable as experimental manipulations. This should be especially so for motivation to comply and subjective evaluations of outcomes—our three ascriptors—as well as for the processes of searching, inference, and memory that lead to awareness of what follows what. For these reasons, a program of functional S-R analysis at the level of human adults may be less productive of strong laws than an analysis of R-R relations—short of much

greater control of our subjects' genetic and environmental histories. And that may be too much to ask even of a species of behaviorism with an adjunct program of social engineering.

5. Finally, by strength of a law we ordinarily mean not only strength of relation, but deployability of that relation over significantly varying conditions. The form of the equation should remain constant while its basic terms and parameters are sensitive to and vary widely over conditions—for us, stimulus and trait conditions. It is precisely the converse *in*constancy of S-R relations over subjects—and extratheoretical experimental variables—that we recognize in human conditioning and concept attainment paradigms. (Skinner, 1963; Kanfer, Maltzman, and Bourne, this volume.) For reasons intrinsic to recognition and assessment of conscious, controlling process, I believe, that kind of deployability might be achieved with R-R laws. In Experiment I, for example, experimental manipulations widely varied the values taken by terms of our central equations and their report coordinations, but the form and strength of the relations they described remained relatively constant. Error of prediction from the central Equations 2b, 3c, and 4b—an expected-observed "d" score—was not significantly influenced by those experimental manipulations. And the finding was essentially the same when Smith (1967) asked the same question of those manipulations and a trait variable in addition— diagnosed schizophrenia. If we can successfully (*a*) specify the significant conscious controls just antecedent to response selection, and (*b*) achieve greater report validity than manipulation validity, this kind of deployability of R-R laws may be within reach.

On a strategy of seeking R-R laws, stimulus manipulations are by no means ignored, but they take on a different status. They may become "boundary conditions" by which we fix subjects at some particular parameter value—as by instructions in Experiment II. Or they serve to spread subjects more widely over values of response-indexed terms in the central equations of the theory—as in both experiments. Or we bring a degree of order to the infinite array of stimulus (and trait) variables by establishing a common "locus of effect" among the response-indexed terms of the theory. And once that locus is established we may use the theory to yield a prediction for that stimulus (or trait) variable. But research strategies, of course, are evaluated ultimately by time and results. It would be enough now if the strategy seems reasonable enough to give a thorough try.[13]

---

[13] (a) It is the argument that an R-R strategy may be the *better* strategy for the domain discussed, not that utility of the theory must be restricted to that strategy. Once we establish the loci of effect of manipulations on the several processes of the theory, where conditions of report validity may be met, the theory becomes useful in predicting S-R relations where those conditions cannot be met or are questionable—or we have an engineering aim.

(b) On the analysis presented, and our repeated findings of great intersubject variability in the subjective evaluation of reinforcement parameters, a common consideration of experimental design must now be viewed quite differently: "Proper experimental design would require independent verification of the effectiveness of the reinforcer and its motivational and informational properties prior to its utilization in an experiment" (Kanfer). Temporal order *per se* is logically irrelevant to the strength of inferences drawn, and the use of assessments by other subjects could only introduce error. What is conventionally called "proper experimental design" in this case merely reduces to the prescription for a relatively insensitive experiment.

(c) In fairness, an alternative answer to the problem of human variability in this domain has been proposed: "To preserve a closer analogy with animal conditioning, it would be more appropriate to conduct verbal

The methodological question

In one sense the methodological question seems the more fundamental one. Historically I believe rather basic methodological positions have been a source and protective support for the S-R theories and S-R strategies—early logical positivism and one or another species of operationism and behaviorism. If minds and mental states must be rejected, we look to Watson's program of specifying the stimulus for a physical response and the response for a physical stimulus. If what we intuitively experience as awareness is a "fictional cause," we look to a functional cause among the manipulable antecedents of operants. And if our subject's private reports are hopelessly untrustworthy anyway, we should have little temptation to look elsewhere. Besides, if our observational terms must be physicalistic, and all others defined by their operational definiens, how could we do otherwise? Either the defined term refers exclusively to those operations or it has "surplus meaning" that is a puzzle, impossible to validate rigorously and somehow to be got rid of. Pressed finally to recognize the obvious, we say that "man thinking is man behaving," then represent the thought as a movement, an utterance—or even a vaguely "cognitive" mediator—but always hold that the thought is describable by the behavior theory that describes the

---

conditioning procedures only after variability has been reduced, and S has shown relatively stable behaviors in an environment which he has had time to evaluate, scrutinize and test out" (Kanfer). This excellently illustrates the older behavioristic strategy of looking the other way until anything suspiciously mentalistic has passed. But where alternative strategies are available at the human level, we may be able to achieve more by trying more.

behavior of stimuli and responses. It is far from a universal history, of course, and it is a little unfairly characterized; but not, I think, by very much.

Confronted with the problem at hand—the question of conscious, volitional control—what are our methodological alternatives? For the philosopher of science these are logical construals evaluated by their coherence and adequacy as reconstructions of successful scientific practice. For the investigator, they are logics in use or potential use, methodologies evaluated even more significantly by their utility, first in the sense of their adequacy to meet the problems presented, and ultimately, of course, by their productivity.

METHODOLOGICAL BEHAVIORISM. In clarifying the usage of "S-R theory," Maltzman says that "It may be interpreted, on the one hand, as equivalent to methodological behaviorism, a prescription for the introduction and usage of concepts in psychology." As Bergman (1951, 1957) presents it, this methodology most closely reflects the early positivist's and operationist's strictures. The undefined observation terms are physicalistic in the sense that they are rather naturally taken to refer to objects and events "out there" and observed by the investigator. All other terms are explicitly defined by this primitive vocabulary. And the verification criterion of meaningfulness for psychological terms is preserved intact.

All very familiar—but it is the precise structure of that explicit definition as an operational definition that is so critical when we raise the question of conscious, volitional, *unobservable controls*. It would take the form of $Tx \longleftrightarrow (Cx \rightarrow Rx)$ and can be read an event x has, by definition, the property termed T if and only if an operational test condition C yields an operational result R. By virtue of the placement of that "if and only if," the

operations are completely and uniquely defining, and the defined term is therefore eliminable. This is true whether we assert the definition as is or interpose a transformation and define that misnomer as an "intervening" variable. "For methodological behaviorism," Maltzman insists, " 'awareness' must be a defined concept." And it is perfectly clear on that definitional form why Bergman (1951, p. 102) must "conclude, then, that there is no specific sense in which any defined concept refers to an 'entity' whose 'existence' we 'hypothesize.' "

Why the verification principle and the explicit definitional form have for twenty or so years been rejected as adequate construals of more advanced scientific practice can now be found in almost any basic work in the philosophy of science (Nagel, 1961; Pap, 1962; Kaplan, 1964; Sheffler, 1963; Hempel, 1952, 1966, etc.)[14] I want only to assert here that this form of methodological behaviorism, in principle, provides no response to the problem at hand—the question of a causal role for awareness of our subjects, a question that has been raised by behaviorists and nonbehaviorists alike. But within this logic the question can neither be asked nor given a negative or affirmative answer. In answer to *that* question, "awareness" refers to an unobservable whether preceded by "with" or "without." We are accustomed to a peculiar satisfaction in the discovery that a question is meaningless. But the methodology settles for too little, I think, if another methodology can be shown to

[14] Feigl (1959) presents a useful review of the positivist counterreformation. Blanshard (1965, p. 4) sums up one of its sidelights: "This curious 'physicalism' of the early positivists has now been abandoned by the positivists themselves; Ayer, Feigl, Hempel, Carnap have all renounced it. Behaviorists apparently still cling to it. They still think it demanded by science . . . ."

provide a meaningful question with a possible answer.

REDUCTIVE BEHAVIORISM. What both Maltzman and Kanfer apparently want is another species of operational behaviorism that might be called "reductive" behaviorism—after the reduction sentence form the operational definition must take. As Kanfer puts it, for "mediators, in general, the behavioristic group, once reduced to use the term 'awareness,' has attempted to stay close to operational definitions, mainly by content of a verbal report." And both lace their papers with repeated references to unobservables and multiple operations. Although reduction sentences were originally proposed by Carnap (1936, 1937) in answer to another question, the logical problem of counterfactual conditionals, it is their structure that permits them to have these other two properties. We may read the form $Cx \rightarrow (Tx \longleftrightarrow Rx)$ this way: If we apply an operational test condition C to an object x, then x has the property termed T if and only if there is the operational result R. When "if and only if" takes this position, the operational definition is no longer complete and univocal—there is no longer a logical impediment to multiple operational definitions or reference to unobservables. Since the set of possible operations is open, the reduction at any point in an investigation is partial. A term like "awareness" could be held to have "surplus meaning" (MacCorquodale and Meehl, 1948), reference to unobservable properties still unmanifest in operations still unperformed.

The same basic works in the philosophy of science provide the reasons this mechanism has been rejected as an adequate construal of the use of theoretical terms in other domains (see Pap, 1962, and especially Carnap, 1956). For the problem at hand, this form of operational definition provides an inadequate response for two fundamental and related reasons: (1) Any interpretive statement assigning a controlling—or noncontrolling—role to a hypothetical unobservable process obligates the investigator to validate the hypotheses linking his operational manipulations or assessments to that process. Operational reductions provide no logic for that validation. Nor is there an answer, of course, in the temporary retreat to a logic of explicit definitions: "But that's the way I *operationally defined* it." (2) In the same way we have no justification for saying that a number of operational reductions are linked to the same hypothetical process. The underlying reason is the one we have already seen: When we say so little, we may postulate innumerable controlling processes. Once we go beyond the simplest cases there is little help in the usual justifications of multiple operations.[15] We cannot say, for example, that an instruction and a report are linked to the same hypothetical intention if they are correlated, and not if they are not. In our experiments, instruction and report of intention may have any degree of correlation from perfect positive to perfect negative depending upon the values taken by other terms—parameters of that relationship. Nor can we say that discrimination is the fundamental operation and that operations define different constructs if we dis-

[15] These standards for linking operations were offered (Spiker and McCandless, 1954; Stevens, 1939) to justify the *practical* requirement for relaxing the *logical* requirement of univocality of operational definitions, in the form of explicit definitions. For explicit definitions, the question is whether the formalization gives an accurate *construal* of what we must do. For reduction sentences, the question is whether the formalization provides an *adequate response* to the consequences of what we must do.

criminate between them and one construct if we do not. We can discriminate between an instruction and report, or not, depending upon our criterion, and the criterion is unspecified by the logic. While the previous logic settles for too little, this one demands more than it can provide. We might, of course, go outside this methodology for those standards of justification. But then the question would become: Are we still operationally defining in any more than a liturgical sense? Is this logic still an adequate construal of what we are doing? Or does another methodology provide a more adequate response to the problem at hand?

DESCRIPTIVE BEHAVIORISM. Raise the question of conscious, volitional controls, and the position of Skinner's descriptive behaviorism is even harder to comment on briefly than other forms of behaviorism. Descriptive behaviorism is not so much a formal methodology in the epistemological sense. It is a deep suspicion of conscious controls supported by subtly shifting arguments that belong more to metaphysics, the logic of explanation, and an informal epistemology based on Skinner's (1945, 1957, 1963) theory of learning to describe private events.

As Skinner (1965, p. 7) puts it, "Behaviorism begins with the assumption that the world is made of only one kind of stuff—a stuff dealt with most successfully by physics but well enough known for most purposes by common sense. Organisms are part of that world, and their processes are therefore physical processes." Sometimes, however, "The experimenter has not been able to relate the behavior to the contingencies, and he is forced to conclude that the organism has done so mentally. Supposed cognitive processes of this sort may be disregarded. Others, however, may be a sort of internalized version of precurrent behavior. . . . It is

usually studied in overt form though it may eventually drop to the covert level. In either case it is defined as behavior which effects behavior rather than as mental activity" (Skinner, 1966, p. 216).

Where metaphysical positions still influence other views in science, as they apparently do, one thing needs to be resaid forcefully: Metaphysical materialism—as well as its mentalistic alternatives—are irrelevant to the problem raised in the exact sense that no such assumption is either necessary for, or supportable by, scientific inquiry as we know it. We need assume nothing about the ultimate ontological nature of awareness to recognize its indisputable fact and construct a theory of its function. And support for that theory— or one that omits terms for awareness— could tell us no more about its ultimate nature.

But on the other hand, "The objection is not that they (wishes, cognitions, motives, and so on) are mental but that they offer no real explanation and stand in the way of a more effective analysis" (Skinner, 1963, p. 951). Sometimes the matter is settled by a behavioristic dictum: "Professor Blanshard correctly paraphrases the behavioristic principle that ideas, motives, and feelings have no part in determining conduct and therefore no part in explaining it. . . " (Skinner, 1965, p. 7). Sometimes the matter is argued on implied canons of science: "Thus, where a scientific analysis relates behavior to the physical environment, the mentalist may insist that the mind observes only a none-to-reliable copy of the environment called subjective experience. Where a scientific analysis shows that we react in a given way because similar actions in our past have had particular consequences, the mentalist may insist that we act because we have stored memories of past actions and of their consequences, which we now scan in order to reach certain expectations leading to an act of will which initiates behavior" (Skinner, 1964, p. 482). And sometimes the matter is argued on a logic of explanation: "We may object, first, to the predilection for unfinished causal sequences. . . . An action is not explained by attributing it to expectations until the expectations have in turn been accounted for" (Skinner, 1963, p. 956).

But need it be said again? Certainly no canon of science proscribes the postulation of controlling processes or specifies required end points for causal explanation. Many successful theories postulate such processes, and all causal sequences they specify are "unfinished." Postulated processes take a useful place in explanation if they are part of a rich enough theory to provide satisfying explanation and predictive utility. The question simply resolves again to the familiar one of the competitive examination of theories and all that implies. There is even the hint that behavioristic dicta are irrelevant in Skinner's (1963, p. 958) concluding concession that "No entity or process which has any useful explanatory force is to be rejected on the ground that it is subjective or mental."[16]

Furthermore, Skinner (1963, p. 953) writes

It is particularly important that a science of behavior face the problem of privacy. It may do so without abandoning the basic position of behaviorism. Science often talks about things it cannot see or measure . . . . For one thing, a scientific analysis of behavior has yielded a sort of empirical

epistemology . . . . So far as we know, the same processes of differential reinforcement is required if a child is to distinguish among events occurring within his own skin . . . . Privacy thus causes trouble first for the verbal community. The individual suffers in turn. Because the community cannot reinforce self-descriptive responses consistently, a person cannot describe or otherwise 'know' events occurring within his own skin as subtly and precisely as he knows events in the world at large.

This epistemology amounts to a theory of the learning of language and knowing which implies limits on the usefulness of private reports. Twenty years after its first presentation (Skinner, 1945), however, the theory lacks support from developmental studies—and would present serious psycholinguistic problems (Chomsky, 1959). Nor are we told how "An adequate science of behavior must consider events taking place within the skin of the organism. . .but as part of behavior itself. . . without assuming that they have any special nature or must be known in any special way" (Skinner, 1963, p. 953). At present, however, we may specify experimental conditions in which (*a*) private reports show strong and intricate relations among themselves and to other experimental variables, (*b*) in ways that follow fairly naturally from a theory that those

---

[16] Skinner (1965, p. 7) recently writes that "No major behaviorist has ever argued that science must limit itself to public events." But for the science of psychology, Skinner (1938, p. 7) once held, with some influence,

that "The sole criterion for rejection of a popular term is the implication of a system or a formulation extending beyond immediate observation." For a critique of Skinner's earlier attempts (especially 1953) to press the epistemological reduction of mentalistic terms to behavior at least as far as possible, see Scriven (1956). The current effort of some descriptive behaviorists to define the "natural science approach" by an exclusive concern for observables is puzzling at best—as adjudged either by Skinner's recent views, or, or course, by common practice in what we ordinarily call the "natural sciences."

reports reflect conscious, controlling processes, and not from alternatives proposed thus far. This is only a start, of course, but a start that may provide a promising alternative to what seems so very like a circumvention of the experimental analysis of the mind. There is a logic that allows us to say when we are within the limits of report validity, whatever they may be.[17]

A NOTE ON PRIVATE REPORTS. With many, Kanfer worries that, "When *S*'s verbal or written reports are treated as indices or correlates of hypothesized internal processes, the full range of problems associated with introspectionism again beclouds the issue." It need not at all. Classical introspection was unproductive because it combined (*a*) a phenomenological observation

language, (*b*) an attempt to inventory the ultimate constituents of a generalized human mind, by observers with variable histories, and (*c*) refined analysis of conscious contents that exceeded the observer's capacities for linguistic description, memory, and veracity. With the resulting random error in single observer's reports, and systematic variance over observers' reports, the method could not provide what we require of an observation language. If we are to believe what is said to have happened, we must have strong lawfulness of observers' reports over specifiable stimulus conditions—the stimulus that is the experiment presented to the observer. This is the stronger requirement for the stronger belief in *data*.[18]

We should reject this alternative, but it is important to reject it for the right reason, lest we reject too much. It cannot be because the observations are private and thereby violate a publicity standard for science—which would rule out other private observational reports. All scientific *observations* are private: my observation of a bar-press as much as my observation of blue. But we accept private observational reports in a physicalistic language, without sharing another's observation, if our own or other's observational reports show the required strong lawfulness over those stimulus conditions we call experiments. This is simply not feasible where the genetic and environmental histories of our subject produce significant variance in their observations and reports over common experimental conditions.

---

[17] Of a "Skinnerian view of self-reports," Kanfer writes that "Self-reports cannot be given special status as indices of *other* events, any more than acquisition response or any other observed behavior. Therefore, their validity is not questioned." It would be more accurate to say that the validity of self-reports was rarely questioned so long as relatively crude experimental procedures resulted in findings of "conditioning without awareness." Once more refined procedures resulted in systematic interrelations among reports and conditioning, the validity of those reports was obviously questioned by attempts to attribute them to suggestion, rationalization, emergence, or concurrent conditioning. Despite methodological criticism (Eriksen, 1960; Dulany, 1962; Spielberger, 1962), it is still possible to publish reports of conditioning without awareness, without reporting assessment procedures for awareness, or even that any systematic assessment was made (for example, Keehn, *et al.*, 1965). For the question of conditioning without awareness, these studies have the weight of one reporting assessment procedures and results in detail but neglecting to mention the conditioning procedures or even that conditioning procedures were attempted. Furthermore, the principle Kanfer enunciates is an incorrect representation of Skinner's own view, as quoted here. It is merely a principle that has been applied in the literature as theoretically convenient.

[18] Zener (1958) and Zener and Gaffron (1963) suggest that this criterion might be met by a phenomenological observation language in certain areas of perceptual research. Whether or not, my concern in the present paper is for a confrontation with the right rather than the left.

If we are to judge whether the subject's *reports* show objectionable *error* variance, or whether their private *observations* show acceptable *systematic* variance, we must move those observations from the observation language to the theory language. We then evaluate the validity of their reports of private observations by competitively evaluating the theory in which they appear. It is the procedure by which we may evaluate the success of experimental controls for contaminants of language, memory, and deception. Of course, "The validity of the verbal report can. . .never be established in the sense of its 'truth'. . . ."(Kanfer)— if that is taken to mean meeting the stronger requirement for belief in observations as data. But as for co-ordinations of experimental variables to any hypothetical state—even a conscious state—our confidence in the *inductive* "truth" of what the theory says about it is as good as the competitive support for the theory. We are brought again to a familiar logic of evaluation.

A LOGIC OF THEORETICAL NETWORKS. There is a second sense in which a methodological matter is fundamental to the analysis presented in this paper. It is what might be called a "logic of theoretical networks" that has provided the methodology for the present investigation of conscious, volitional processes—in developing the theory, experiments, and research strategy. It is by no means a novel or monolithic position; and for the problem at hand, I have abstracted what seemed most useful from many sources—Hempel, (1952, 1958, 1965); Carnap (1956); Feigl (1959); Cronbach and Meehl (1956); Sellars (1956), and Nagel (1961), Since the logic has been used throughout this paper, its central principles can be briefly summarized at this point:

1. Theoretical terms are introduced by a network of theoretical sentences interlinking them among themselves and to observational terms. For the investigator, these sentences may have their origin in common sense, experimental implications, hunches, or other theory. Once formalized, ". . .the concepts of science are knots in a network of systematic interrelationships in which laws and theoretical principles form the threads" (Hempel, 1966, p. 96). Propositional constructs such as BI, BH, and RHs take their meaning from the set of sentences in which they appear. A strong view of the matter is that "In scientific inquiry, concept formation and theory formation must go hand in hand" (Hempel, 1966, p. 97).

2. The meaning of a theoretical term is empirical by virtue of interpretive sentences connecting those terms with experimental variables. In the present case, these are the hypotheses linking propositional constructs to reports, response selection, and manipulations. Since these interpretive sentences are hypotheses functioning within the theory, it would only be misleading to call them operational definitions.

3. A theoretical network is in principle open to new constructs and new interpretive sentences. A theory gains scope when we can link a term to a new experimental variable taking the same position as another in the network of experimental relationships. It may be coordinated to a reported intention to use a sentence, or a reported intention in the sexual arena (Fishbein, 1966), if both take the same position in a network of observations. A theory may be enriched by connections through other constructs to experimental variables taking a different position in the network—for example, the linking of an intention to instructions. And a theory may be enriched by new constructs and coordinations if predictive utility and elegance warrant. A multiple linear

regression equation such as Equation 2c is in principle open—to, for example, a personal rule of conduct and the value attached to it.

4. At any stage of the investigative process we specify the meaning of a theoretical term partially. Coordinations are probabilistic. New coordinations may be established. And as the theory is enriched and competitively supported, we converge upon the meaning of those theoretical terms.

5. Our confidence that the theory specifies the behavior of a hypothetical process—of a conscious, volitional process—depends upon the degree of confirmation of the theory in competition with alternatives. This is not a logic of critical experiments but of multiple observations that are critical in degree. Confirmation confers probable truth, not certainty. And the strength of confirmation increases with richness of the array of observations the theory generates. What is so critical is that a richly articulated network of theoretical relationships is required to predict a rich network of experimental relationships. A degree of complexity is required but redeemable by utility and simplifying principles that may run throughout. In the present case, for example, there is some comforting simplicity in the discovery that a single combination rule will hold for combining propositional subjects and predicates, whether rules or ascriptors, as well as for combining rules and ascriptors:

$$a + 1 = (b + 1)(c + 1).$$
$$0 \qquad\quad 0 \qquad\quad 0$$
$$-1 \qquad\quad -1 \qquad\quad -1$$

Once this much of the logic is followed, the rules for inference from experiments to hypothetical processes reduce to the familiar rules for comparative evaluation of theories.

But does so self-conscious a usage of this methodology really matter? Is this a tiresome recital of what many already know? Of course, to the second; and I definitely think so, to the first. Attempts to investigate, or avoid investigating, conscious volitional processes have too significant a history, and there is by no means agreement on the methodological issues those attempts raise. At this point I can again summarize:

1. A network methodology does provide a way of investigating and speaking of awareness with emprirical meaning. And the view expressed by Skinner is not all unique to Skinner and descriptive behaviorists: "If psychology is a science of mental life—of the mind, of conscious experience—then it must develop and defend a special methodology, which it has not yet done successfully" (Skinner, 1963, p. 951). Such a methodology does exist and is not so special in other domains, but might be more successfully examined here if we are as clear as possible about what we are doing.

2. The methodology provides the difficult question of the status of private reports with an answer that has theoretical significance and experimental utility. The relation of what is said to what is experienced becomes a hypothesis within a theory inductively supportable in competition with alternative explanations. If we are to venture those inferences, we must have a logic for evaluating them. It is this part of a logic of networks that we know as the logic of construct validity (Cronback and Meehl, 1956).

3. Both the richness of a theory and its scope depend critically upon multiple coordinations to experimental variables. Those hypothetical linkages are evaluated by observation of the positions those coordinations take in a network of experimental relationships. And if we must have a logic for evaluating one linkage, we must have a logic for evaluating multiple linkages.

4. Strong inference to hypothetical states logically requires a fairly complex network of experimental observations that are derivable from a fairly complex network of theoretical propositions—and not from available alternatives. The need for that richness is unusually great where there is such strong impetus from other theories, strategies, and methodologies to find those alternatives. Strong support for hypotheses of conscious control will not come from a few observations and scraps of cognitive conjecture.[19]

As a logic, something like this set of principles has been offered as a construal scientific practice that is working well in other domains of science. It is not evaluated by the discovery that it does or does not accord with early principles of positivism, operationism, or behaviorism. As a logic in use in this domain, it becomes a methodology to be evaluated, first by its response to the problem at hand and eventually, of course, by its productivity—as we evaluate the resulting theories, research strategies, and experiments in all the usual ways. It is an alternative to try.

Appendix

(1)

Did you come to think that the stream of air did follow, or would follow, anything in particular that you said, either every time, or more often than not?

—I did not think that the stream of air did follow or would follow anything in particular that I said.

—I thought that the stream of air *may* have followed something in particular

[19] According to Koch (1964), two major reactions to the Age of Theory have been greater resistance to (*a*) *formal theory*, and less resistance to (*b*) *hypotheses of cognitive control*, which had been proscribed by earlier principles of operationism, positivism, and behaviorism. The irony is that (*a*) is required for strong support of (*b*).

that I said, but if it did, I didn't know what it was.

—I thought that the stream of air did follow or would follow something in particular that I said, but I didn't know what it was.

—I thought that the stream of air did follow or would follow something in particular that I said, and I *thought* I knew what it was.

—I thought that the stream of air did follow or would follow something in particular that I said, and I *definitely* knew what it was.

(1a)

What word did you think the stream of air did follow or would follow? (Write that word below.)

_____

On how many of the last 20 trials did you think that?

(2)

Did you think that the stream of air in this experiment meant that you had just said either what you were supposed to say or not supposed to say?

—No, I did not think that the stream of air meant either of these things.

—The stream of air may or may not have meant one of these things, but if it did, I didn't know which it was.

—Yes, I thought the stream of air meant one of these things, but I didn't know which it was.

—Yes, I thought the stream of air meant one of these things, and I *thought* I knew which it was.

—Yes, I thought the stream of air meant one of these things, and I *definitely* knew which it was.

(2a)

What did you think the stream of air meant?

—I thought that the stream of air meant that I had just said what I was supposed to say.

—I thought the stream of air meant that I had just said what I was *not* supposed to say.

(3)

Over the last 20 trials, did you think that

there was anything that you were supposed to say, or not say, on each trial, at least more often than not? Was there something the experimenter wanted you to say or not say?

—No, I did not think that there was anything that I was supposed to say or not say.

—There may or may not have been something that I was supposed to say or not say, but if there were, I didn't know what it was.

—Yes, I did think that there was something that I was supposed to say or not say, but I didn't know what it was.

—Yes, I did think that there was something that I was supposed to say or not say, and I *thought* I knew what it was.

—Yes, I did think that there was something that I was supposed to say or not say, and I definitely knew what it was.

(3a)

Read both of the following questions and then answer the one that you can answer most confidently:

What word did you most think you were supposed to *say* over the last 20 trials?

_____

On how many of the last 20 trials did you think that?——————

OR

What word did you most think you were supposed to *avoid saying* over the last 20 trials?

_____

On how many of the last 20 trials did you think that?——————

(4)

Would you say that you *did* or *did not* try to say or avoid saying anything in particular over the last 20 trials?

—Yes, I did.

—No, I did not.

(4a)

Read both of the following pairs of questions and then answer the pair that you can answer most confidently:

What word did you most try to *say* over the last 20 trials?

On how many of the last 20 trials did you try to say that word?

_____

OR

What word did you most try to avoid saying over the last 20 trials?

_____

On how many of the last 20 trials did you try to *avoid* saying that word?——————

(5a)

How did the stream of air feel to you? (Place a check on one of the points.)

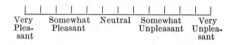

| Very Pleasant | Somewhat Pleasant | Neutral | Somewhat Unpleasant | Very Unpleasant |

(6a)

During the course of this experiment, how much did you want to say whatever you may have thought you were supposed to say? Or how much did you want to *avoid* saying whatever you may have thought you were not supposed to say? (Place a check on one of the points.)

| Very Much | Somewhat | Didn't Care | Somewhat Did Not | Very Much Did Not |

References

Adams, J. K., "Laboratory Studies of Behavior without Awareness," *Psychological Bulletin*, **54** (1957), 383–405.

Azuma, H. and L. Cronbach, "Cue-Response Correlation in the Attainment of a Scalar Concept," *American Journal of Psychology*, **70** (1966), 38–48.

Bechtoldt, H., "Construct Validity: A Critique," *American Psychologist*, **14** (1959), 619–629.

Bergmann, G., "The Logic of Psychological Concepts," *Philosophy of Science*, **18** (1951), 93–110.

——, *The Metaphysics of Logical Positivism*. New York: Longmans, Green and Co., 1954.

——, *Philosophy of Science*. Madison: University of Wisconsin Press, 1957.

Bijou, S. and D. Baer, "Operant Methods in Child Behavior and Development," in *Operant Behavior: Areas of Research and Application,* ed. W. Honig. New York: Appleton-Century-Crofts, 1966.

Blanshard, B. "The Problem of Consciousness: A Debate," American Psychological Association meetings, 1965.

Blaufarb, M. and D. E. Dulany, "Is There Consistency of Verbal Conditioning across Tasks?" Unpublished manuscript, 1964.

Bourne, L. E., "Informational Variables in Concept Formation," *Behavioral Research Laboratory, Report No. 62,* Institute of Behavioral Science, University of Colorado, March, 1965.

———, "Concept Attainment," Ch. 10 of this volume.

Bower, G., and T. Trabasso, "Concept Identification," in *Studies in Mathematical Psychology,* ed. R. C. Atkinson. Stanford: Stanford University Press, 1964.

Bruner, J. S., J. J. Goodnow, and G. A. Austin, *A Study of Thinking.* New York: John Wiley and Sons, Inc., 1956.

Brunswik, E., "Representative Design and Probabilistic Theory in a Functional Psychology," *Psychological Review,* 62 (1955), 193–217.

Carnap, R., "Testability and Meaning," *Philosophy of Science,* 3 (1936), 420–468.

———, "Testability and Meaning," *Philosophy of Science,* 4 (1937), 1–40.

———, "The Methodological Character of Theoretical Concepts," in *Minnesota Studies in the Philosophy of Science,* Vol. 1, eds. H. Feigl and M. Scriven. Minneapolis: University of Minnesota Press, 1956, 38–76.

Chomsky, N., "Review of *Verbal Behavior* by B. F. Skinner," *Language,* 35 (1959), 26–58.

Cronbach, L. and P. Meehl, "Construct Validity in Psychological Tests," in *Minnesota Studies in the Philosophy of Science,* Vol. 1, eds. H. Feigl, and M. Scriven. Minneapolis: University of Minnesota Press, 1956.

Dixon, P. W., and S. F. Oakes, "Effect of Intertrial Activity on the Relationship between Awareness and Verbal Operant Conditioning," *Journal of Experimental Psychology,* 69 (1965), 152–157.

Dollard, J., and N. Miller, *Personality and Psychotherapy.* New York: McGraw-Hill Book Company, 1950.

Dulany, D. E., "Hypotheses and Habits in Verbal 'Operant Conditioning,'" *Journal of Abnormal and Social Psychology* 63 (1961), 251–263.

———, "The Place of Hypotheses and Intentions: An Analysis of Verbal Control in Verbal Conditioning," in *Behavior and Awareness,* ed. C. Eriksen. Durham: Duke University Press, 1962a.

———, "Awareness, Consequence, and Mediation in Verbal Conditioning," *Technical Report, US PH MH Grant No. M3002,* Department of Psychology, University of Illinois, 1962b.

———, "How Can We Speak of Awareness and Volition as Instrumental?" Paper read at Southeastern Psychological Association meetings, 1963.

———, "The Separable Effects of the Information and Affect Conveyed by a Reinforcer," Paper read at the Psychonomic Society meetings, 1964.

———, and T. McHale, "The Information and Affect Conveyed by a Reinforcer," Unpublished manuscript, 1966.

———, and D. C. O'Connell, "Does Partial Reinforcement Dissociate Verbal Rules and the Behavior They Might Be Presumed to Control?" *Journal of Verbal Learning and Verbal Behavior,* 2 (1963), 361–372.

———, S. Schwartz, and C. Walker, "Why the Informational and Distributional Parameters of Reinforcement Interact," Paper read at Psychonomic Society meetings, 1965a.

———, ———, and ———, "Habit: Reinforcement Value or Number of Voluntary Executions?" Unpublished data, 1965b.

———, ———, and R. Schneider, "Propositional Control and Intertrial Activity," Unpublished manuscript, 1966.

Eriksen, C. W., "Discrimination and Learning without Awareness: A Methodological Survey and Evaluation," *Psychological Review*, 67 (1960), 279–300.

Farber, I. E., "The Things People Say to Themselves," *American Psychologist*, 18 (1963), 185–197.

Feigl, H., "Some Major Issues and Developments in the Philosophy of Science of Logical Empiricism," in *Minnesota Studies in the Philosophy of Science*, Vol. 1, eds. H. Feigl and M. Scriven. Minneapolis: University of Minnesota Press, 1951.

———, "Philosophical Embarrassments of Psychology," *American Psychologist*, 14 (1959), 115–128.

Flavell, J., *The Developmental Psychology of Jean Piaget*. New York: D. Van Nostrand Co., Inc., 1963.

Garner, W., "To Perceive Is to Know," *American Psychologist*, 21 (1966), 11–19.

Goss, Albert E., "Verbal Mediating Responses and Concept Formation," *Psychological Review*, 68 (1961), 248–274.

Hempel, C. G., *Fundamentals of Concept Formation in Empirical Science*. Chicago: University of Chicago Press, 1952.

———, "The Theoretician's Dilemma: A Study in the Logic of Theory Construction," in *Minnesota Studies in the Philosophy of Science*, Vol. 2, eds. H. Feigl, M. Scriven, and G. Maxwell. Minneapolis: University of Minnesota Press, 1958.

———, *Aspects of Scientific Explanation*. New York: The Free Press of Glencoe, Inc., 1965.

———, *Philosophy of Natural Science*. Englewood Cliffs, N. J.: Prentice-Hall, Inc., 1966.

Hursch, C., K. Hammond, and J. Hursch, "Some Methodological Considerations in Multiple-Cue Probability Studies," *Psychological Review*, 71 (1964), 42–60.

James, William. *Principles of Psychology*. New York: Henry Holt and Co., 1890.

Johnson, H. M., "On Verifying Hypoth-

eses by Verifying Their Implicates," *American Journal of Psychology*, 67 (1954), 723–727.

Kanfer, F. H., "Verbal Conditioning: A Review of Its Current Status," Ch. 11 of this volume.

Kaplan, A., *The Conduct of Inquiry*. San Francisco: Chandler, 1964.

Keehn, J., K. Lloyd, M. Hibbs, and D. Johnson, "Operant Eyeblink Conditioning without Awareness: A Preliminary Report," *Psychonomic Science*, 2 (1965), 357–358.

Kendler, H. "Some Specific Reactions to General S-R Theory," Ch. 14 of this volume.

———, and T. Kendler, "Vertical and Horizontal Processes in Problem-Solving," *Psychological Review*, 69 (1962), 1–16.

Koch, Sigmund, "Psychology and Emerging Conceptions of Knowledge as Unitary," in *Behaviorism and Phenomenology*, ed. T. W. Wann. Chicago: University of Chicago Press, 1964, 1–46.

Krasner, L., "Studies of the Conditioning of Verbal Behavior," *Psychological Bulletin*, 55 (1958), 148–170.

———, and L. P. Ullmann, "Variables Affecting Report of Awareness in Verbal Conditioning," *Journal of Psychology*, 56 (1963), 193–202.

Kuhn, T. S., *The Structure of Scientific Revolutions*. Chicago: University of Chicago Press, 1963.

Levine, M., "Mediating Processes in Humans at the Outset of Discrimination Learning," *Psychological Review*, 70 (1963), 254–276.

———, "Hypothesis Behavior by Humans during Discrimination Learning," *Journal of Experimental Psychology*, 71 (1966), 331–338.

Lubitz, R., "Propositional Control and Intertrial Interference," Unpublished master's thesis, University of Illinois, 1967.

MacCorquodale, K., and P. E. Meehl, "On a Distinction between Hypothetical Constructs and Intervening Variables," *Psychological Review*, **55** (1948), 95–107.

McHale, T., "How Conscious Is Transfer of a Particular Rule?" Unpublished doctoral thesis, University of Illinois, 1965.

Maltzman, I., "Thinking: From a Behavioristic Point of View," *Psychological Review*, **62** (1955), 275–76.

———, "Theoretical Conceptions of Semantic Conditioning and Generalization," Ch. 12 of this volume.

———, "Awareness: Cognitive Psychology vs. Behaviorism," *Journal of Experimental Research in Personality*, **1** (1966), 161–165.

Miller, G. A., E. Galanter, and K. H. Pribram, *Plans and the Structure of Behavior*, New York: Holt, Rinehart and Winston, Inc., 1960.

Miller, G., *Psychology: The Science of Mental Life*. New York: Harper and Row, Publishers, 1962.

Nagel, E., *The Structure of Science*. New York: Harcourt, Brace and World, Inc., 1961.

O'Connell, D., "Concept Learning and Verbal Control under Partial Reinforcement and Subsequent Reversal or Nonreversal Shifts," *Journal of Experimental Psychology*, **69** (1965), 144–151.

———, and M. Wagner, "Extinction after Partial Reinforcement and Minimal Learning as a Test of Both Verbal Control and PRE in Concept Learning," *Journal of Experimental Psychology*, **73** (1967), 151–153.

O'Neal, W., "Basic Issues in Perceptual Theory," *Psychological Review*, **65** (1958), 348–361.

Osgood, C. E., "A Behavioristic Analysis of Perception and Language as Cognitive Phenomena," in *Contemporary Approaches to Cognition*. Cambridge: Harvard University Press, 1957, 75–118.

———, "Toward a Wedding of Insufficiencies," Ch. 19 of this volume.

Pap, A., *An Introduction to the Philosophy of Science*, New York: The Free Press of Glencoe, Inc., 1962.

Postman, L., and J. Sassenrath, "The Automatic Action of Verbal Rewards and Punishments," *Journal of General Psychology*, **65** (1961), 109–136.

Paul, G. L., C. W. Eriksen, and L. G. Humphreys, "Use of Temperature Stress with Cool Air Reinforcement for Human Operant Conditioning," *Journal of Experimental Psychology*, **64** (1962), 329–336.

Restle, F., "The Selection of Strategies in Cue Learning," *Psychological Review*, **69** (1962), 329–343.

Rozeboom, W., "Analysis and the Language of Behavior Theory," in *Current Issues in the Philosophy of Science*, eds. H. Feigl and G. Maxwell. New York: Holt, Rinehart and Winston Inc., 1961.

Salzinger, K., "The Problem of Response Class in Verbal Behavior," Paper presented at the Verbal Behavior Conference, New York City, September 1965.

Schwartz, S., "Trial-by-Trial Analysis of Processes in Simple and Disjunctive Concept Attainment Tasks," *Journal of Experimental Psychology*, **72** (1966a), 456–465.

———, "A Paradigm for the Investigation of Antecedent Processes in Concept Attainment," Unpublished doctoral thesis, University of Illinois, 1966b.

Scriven, M., "A Study of Radical Behaviorism," in *Minnesota Studies in the Philosophy of Science*, Vol. 1, eds. H. Feigl and M. Scriven. Minneapolis: University of Minnesota Press, 1956.

Sellars, W., "Empiricism and the Philosophy of Mind," in *Minnesota Studies in the Philosophy of Science*, Vol. 1, eds. H. Feigl and M. Scriven. Minneapolis: University of Minnesota Press, 1956.

Sheffler, I., *The Anatomy of Inquiry*. New York: Alfred A. Knopf, Inc., 1963.

Skinner, B. F., *The Behavior of Organisms*. New York: Appleton-Century-Crofts, 1938.

———, "The Operational Analysis of Psychological Terms," *Psychological Review*, **52** (1945), 270–278.

————, *Science and Human Behavior.* New York: The Macmillan Company, 1953.

————, *Verbal Behavior.* New York: Appleton-Century-Crofts, 1957.

————, "Behaviorism at Fifty," *Science,* **140** (1963), 951–958.

————, " 'Man,' from 'Psychology: A Behavioral Reinterpretation,' " *Proceedings of the American Philosophical Society,* **108** (1964), 482–485.

————, "The Problem of Consciousness: A Debate," American Psychological Association meetings, 1965.

————, "What is the Experimental Analysis of Behavior?" *Journal of the Experimental Analysis of Behavior,* **9** (1966), 213–218.

Smedslund, J., *Multiple Probability Learning.* Oslo, Norway: Academisk Forlag, 1955.

Smith, Ronald., "Propositional Control and Schizophrenia," Unpublished master's thesis, University of Illinois, 1966.

Spielberger, C. D., "Theoretical and Epistemological Issues in Verbal Conditioning," in *Directions in Psycholinguistics,* ed. S. Rosenberg. New York: The Macmillan Company, 1965.

————, and L. D. DeNike, "Descriptive Behaviorism versus Cognitive Theory in Verbal Operant Conditioning," *Psychological Review,* **73** (1966), 306–327.

Spiker, C. C., and B. R. McCandless, "The Concept of Intelligence and the Philosophy of Science," *Psychological Review,* **61** (1954), 255–266.

Staats, A. W., "Verbal Habit Families, Concepts, and the Operant Conditioning of Word Classes," *Psychological Review,* **68** (1961), 190–204.

————, and C. K. Staats, *Complex Human Behavior.* New York: Holt, Rinehart and Winston, Inc., 1964.

Stevens, S. S., "Psychology and the Science of Science," *Psychological Bulletin,* **36** (1939), 221–263.

Tolman, E. C., "Principles of Purposive Behavior," in *Psychology: A Study of Science,* Vol. 2, ed. S. Koch. New York: McGraw-Hill Book Company, 1959.

Underwood, B., *Psychological Research.* New York: Appleton-Century-Crofts, 1957.

Verplanck, W. S., "The Operant Conditioning of Human Motor Behavior," *Psychological Bulletin,* **53** (1956), 70–82.

————, "Unaware of Where's Awareness," in *Behavior and Awareness,* ed. C. E. Eriksen. Durham: Duke University Press, 1962.

Zener, K., "The Significance of Experience of the Individual for the Science of Psychology," in *Minnesota Studies in the Philosophy of Science,* Vol. II, eds. H. Feigl, M. Scriven and G. Maxwell. Minneapolis: University of Minnesota Press, 1958.

————, and M. Gaffron, "Perceptual Experience, External Worlds, and Organismic Processes," in *Psychology: A Study of a Science,* Vol. 4, ed. S. Koch. New York: McGraw-Hill Book Company, 1963.

Some Specific
Reactions to
General S-R Theory[1]

14 HOWARD H. KENDLER

An evaluation of the three papers offered in the area of *Related Processes* demands some frame of reference. Presumably considerations of *truth, logic,* and *significance* should be sufficient, but they are not. And the reasons that they are not are twofold. First, the question posed by this conference is not as clear as it first appears. Second, and more important, personal subjective considerations must enter into any analysis that attempts to probe the fundamental issues of the psychology of verbal behavior. I will attempt to justify these two conclusions and, by so doing, erect a framework that will serve to guide my reactions to the individual contributions of Bourne, Kanfer, and Maltzman as well as to some of the general issues that pervade this conference.

I have strong reservations about both the meaningfulness and fruitfulness of one of the key concepts— *general S-R theory*—around which this conference has been organized. Although

this concept is often applied to characterize certain portions of the contemporary psychological landscape, its usage is both misleading and confusing because it implies some unitary conception with a set of clearcut assumptions that have determinate empirical consequences. Anyone who believes in this unitary conception of general S-R theory accepts a myth.

In my own analysis of S-R associationism (Kendler, 1965) I concluded that in order to make sense out of this concept it is necessary to distinguish among four major, relatively independent components. These are: (1) a technical language, (2) a methodological orientation, (3) a pretheoretical model, and (4) a group of theories.

The least controversial, and perhaps most useful, interpretation of S-R associationism is to view it as a technical language system analogous to notations used to represent moves in a chess game. The essence of stimulus-response language is represented by the widely publicized S-R paradigm which analyzes psychological events into three major categories: stimuli, responses, and the associations between them.

Two important points about S-R language must be noted. First, stimulus-

[1] The preparation of this paper was assisted by grants from the National Science Foundation (GB-1447) and the Office of Naval Research (Nonr-4222[04]). Appreciation is expressed to Dr. Tracy S. Kendler for helpful suggestions offered during the preparation of this paper.

response language is noncommital about empirical relationships in psychology and physiology. It can be used to represent empirical relationships, but it does not imply any. Second, an S-R linguistic analysis of psychological events does not insist that all behavior can be characterized in terms of only stimuli, responses, and the associations between them. The use of S-R language does not preclude the inclusion of other constructs in conceptualizing behavior (e.g., drive).

If we choose to equate the conception of *general S-R theory* with S-R language, then our task will be to determine not whether verbal behavior conforms to general S-R theory, but instead whether S-R language can be used to characterize the facts of verbal behavior. This is not a trivial question, but unfortunately it is at present an impossible one to answer. The language one uses influences the kinds of empirical questions one asks as well as the nature of the theoretical answers offered. But the truth-character of S-R language cannot be determined; only its pragmatic value can be ascertained.

Stimulus-response associationsim can also be conceived as a methodological orientation with an intellectual ancestry that includes Watsonian behaviorism, Machian positivism, and logical positivism. This orientation does not have a set of clearcut methodological prescriptions although it does contain a set of common orienting attitudes. These orienting attitudes can be succinctly characterized as physicalistic, operational, and experimental (Estes, 1959).

Stimulus-response psychologists have a preference for carrying over the goals and accepting the methods of the natural sciences. They aspire to clearcut operational definitions of the concepts they use. And finally they demand experimental evidence to prove their points—or disprove somebody else's point. Evidence from natural observation, clinical experience, and personal experience is neither convincing nor conclusive and is often viewed with suspicion and distrust (Kendler, 1965, p. 12).

Stimulus-response psychology can be conceived as a pretheoretical model in addition to being considered as a technical language and a methodological orientation. This orientation has occurred in the field of conceptual behavior in which numerous investigators have considered concept formation and attainment as analogous to discrimination behavior of the sort that S-R psychologists have investigated and theorized about.

The final conception of S-R associationism directly contradicts the implication that a general S-R theory exists. S-R associationism can be considered as representing a group of competing theories. Even a passing knowledge of the psychology of learning leads to the awareness that S-R theorists disagree about a wide variety of issues varying from the definition of the stimulus and response to the principles that govern associative formation and strengthening. I would maintain that it is impossible to formulate any set of theoretical assumptions acceptable to all psychologists who use S-R language.

I have attempted to describe S-R associationism as it really is, not as some would like to think it is. I recall how a former professor of mine in graduate school dismissed S-R associationism with a simple story. "A man has a letter in his coat pocket. He sees a postal box, approaches it, withdraws his letter, and inserts it into the box. One block later he sees another postal box. According to S-R associationism he should respond to the stimulus compound of the postal box in the same way as he did a block previously. Since he usually doesn't, S-R associationism must be wrong." This analysis is superficial, to say the least, since it ignores important stimulus, memory, and motivational factors as well as theoretical differences among S-R psychologists.

Similar sorts of criticisms involving neurological facts have been directed at S-R associationism. It has been argued that S-R associationism must be invalid because complex behavior is not mediated by organized patterns of stereotyped reflexes, or because a neural impulse that travels through the axon of one neuron that has synaptic junctions with over a hundred other neurons can follow a different route on successive transmissions, or because one small part of the motor cortex can deal with many different movements, while any one movement can be represented in several locations in the motor cortex. Such arguments are based upon a gratuitous grafting of a theory of neural transmission and organization onto S-R associationism. The study of the history of S-R associationism clearly reveals that it is not a closed conceptual system either in regard to psychology or physiology.

If my fourfold analysis of S-R associationism is accepted, then quite obviously simple overall conclusions about the relationship between verbal behavior and S-R associationism cannot be drawn. If our discussion and conclusions are to be productive, they must distinguish among these four components of S-R associationism.

The analysis of S-R associationism into four fundamental categories represents only the beginning of my attempt to complicate the issues of this conference. Now I am forced to bring up matters that eliminate any hope of offering simple answers to the questions that concern us. I would like to reassure you that my major aim is not to complicate matters but instead to characterize our problems as they really are rather than the way we might like them to be. The points I am going to offer now are not generated by deep convictions but more from puzzlements and disturbances resulting from my effort to achieve a clear picture about the contemporary scene in psychology. To some extent my present intellectual discomfort has been exacerbated by Thomas Kuhn's *The Structure of Scientific Revolutions* (1962), a book that has not received proper recognition among psychologists.

Dr. James Conant, while President of Harvard University, was interested in having a history of science taught to undergraduates who were not majoring in a science. Thomas Kuhn, then a graduate student working on his doctoral thesis in the field of theoretical physics, was persuaded to accept the responsibility for this course. When preparing his course, Kuhn was surprised to discover that scientific development and practices were radically different from what he was led to expect from his long standing avocational interest in the philosophy of science. Instead of scientific progress being based on the accumulation of individual discoveries and conceptual insights, Kuhn observed that the evolution of science is an outgrowth of two markedly different enterprises: *normal science* and *revolution*. *Normal science* refers to the accumulation of knowledge within a widely adopted combined methodological-theoretical framework, labeled by Kuhn as a *paradigm*. A paradigm possesses two major characteristics. First, it attracts to its fold a group of adherents; second, it provides them with a number of unanswered questions that keep them busy experimenting and publishing. The paradigm provides an intellectual structure that integrates "important" facts but at the same time generates numerous research opportunities. Therefore Kuhn describes normal science as a "mopping-up" activity.

The second kind of historical development in science is the *revolution*, an event in which a prevailing paradigm is overthrown by a new one. Revolutions are not achieved in a simple, objective fashion. A prevailing paradigm does not collapse in the face of embarrassing data, thereby paving the way for the adoption of a new, more adequate paradigm. What actually happens in a revolution is that facts embarrassing to an existing paradigm are discovered. The area of the anomaly is then extensively investigated, and modifications in the paradigm are suggested in hopes of preserving its validity. Typically these modifications are not successful, but nevertheless the existing, but inadequate, paradigm survives. The adherents of the existing paradigm learn to live with, or perhaps more properly speaking, to ignore, the inconsistent results. However, the anomalous results do inspire some young investigators, whose emotional attachments to the prevailing paradigm are neither deep nor enduring, to formulate a competing paradigm that can absorb the anomalous data. The struggle between the old and new paradigm requires many years to resolve, and its final resolution is more a result of the mortality of man than of any set of compelling data or logical analyses. The older paradigm typically is not relinquished by those who were trained and who worked within it. They refuse to understand the new paradigm, while arguing against its validity. The younger people recognize the superiority of the new paradigm, adopt its standards and conceptions, and investigate the unanswered questions it generates. With time the control

of the science passes from the hands of the older investigators with their outmoded paradigm to the younger scientists with their superior one. A stage of normal science results and prevails until a new set of anomalous data is discovered. Then the era of revolution begins once again.

A reader who is critical of S-R associationism no doubt resonates to Kuhn's analysis because it confirms his opinion about why the S-R paradigm is not rejected in favor of the one he prefers. However, a close reading of Kuhn does not necessarily support the idea that the alternating historical sequence of normal science and revolution is applicable to psychology. This historical model emerged primarily from Kuhn's analysis of the development of physics from the time of Copernicus. Physics was at one time at a preparadigmatic stage in which numerous interpretations about the fundamental methods and conceptions competed for collective acceptance. Psychology now seems to be in such a stage. Controversy exists because no single paradigm has yet achieved collective agreement about the nature of legitimate and significant scientific problems and methods.

This preparadigmatic characterization of contemporary psychology is appropriate even at this conference where we represent a relatively homogeneous segment of psychologists. Perhaps, if one really desires to be pessimistic, consensus will never be achieved in psychology because of the intrinsically different kinds of phenomena that interest those who identify themselves as psychologists. Although we aspire someday to integrate the facts of behavior, phenomenal experience, and physiology, no *a priori* reason exists to insure our success. For the present our attention should be focused on the lack of any clearcut frame of reference to judge the issues which confront us. Personal judgments, or what some would prefer to describe as a volitional decision—used in a broader sense than was suggested initially by Reichenbach (1938)—enter into the collection, selection, and interpretation of data.

The crucial epistemological question, as I see it, concerns the point in the scientific enterprise at which personal, subjective judgments enter. Most of us have been brought up in a philosophy of science in which we were taught that in the epistemological transition from *data* to *concepts* to *theory* the human element enters when the *data* are transformed into *concepts*. The data themselves, we were led to believe, are neutral and uninfluenced by preconceptions of the observer. It is at this point that some modern philosophers of science take exception, asserting that personal judgments influence the kind of data we observe. There is no denying the fact that the *choice* of the kind of data to collect is determined by our preconceptions. But the position I have just described goes one step further in that it assumes that the data themselves are *perceived* in light of these preconceptions. I find it difficult to believe that contradictory perceptions of the same experimental data cannot be eliminated from science, regardless of what paradigmatic orientation exists. But I can nevertheless understand how the very same experimental situation can generate entirely different observations because different investigators, with different preconceptions, can attend to entirely different events.

My intent here is not to be nihilistic but realistic. Personal judgments do shape scientific efforts over the entire range of scientific activities from observing data to constructing theories. Understanding the origins of these personal judgments and their future implications provides a more useful enterprise than offering definitive evaluations that are more a result of intuitive judgments than of compelling logical analyses.

Concept Attainment and Utilization

Bourne approaches the area of concept attainment with tolerant consideration and caution. I sympathize with this general attitude, because whenever I can become sufficiently detached from my own research efforts I become overwhelmed by the complexity and profound implications of conceptual behavior. Certainly concepts are crucial ingredients of the highest levels of intellectual achievements. If we understand how concepts are formed and utilized, we will be well on our way to understanding such important intellectual activities as creative thinking, verbal behavior, abstract reasoning, and so on.

Evaluating our current achievements against such potential goals forces us to conclude that we still have much to do. In a certain sense, our concern up to now has been to prepare opening wedges that will allow us to investigate conceptual behavior in a significant experimental fashion.

The state of our present knowledge is to some extent revealed by the uncertainty in which we define conceptual behavior. For a long time the definition of conceptual behavior was committed to a phenomenal characterization rather than a theoretical interpretation. No doubt this was a result of the early behaviorists' understandably greater interest in demonstrating how complicated forms of behavior could be investigated than in constructing broad theories of conceptual behavior. The generally used definition that a *concept is a common response to dissimilar stimuli* reflects this primary concern with experimental procedures to study conceptual behavior. The definition is highly inclusive since, strictly speaking, it ranges from cases of stimulus generalization with lower animals to abstract concepts of man such as *love, honor,* and *truth.*

Now that experimental procedures are established that allow us to investigate conceptual behavior in an intuitively acceptable way, we are no longer obsessed with problems of a "correct" definition. Our attention is turning away from the problem of defining conceptual behavior as a dependent variable to the more important task of characterizing its theoretical mechanisms. Even though a definition of conceptual behavior as *a common response to dissimilar stimuli* seems to offer an apt description, we question the implication that this wide-ranging definition reflects a common theoretical process.

To some extent this distinction between conceptual behavior as a dependent variable and as a theoretical mechanism weaves its way throughout Bourne's analysis of concept attainment. When he notes that "Words and concepts are often inextricably tied," he is, by implication, separating to some extent the conceptual behavior of lower animals and some forms of conceptual behavior of man. How this separation is to be characterized is, of course, one of the most significant questions in the fields of conceptual behavior. To base the distinction on the presence or absence of words is an invitingly simple solution. We should not be seduced into accepting the verbal foundation of conceptual behavior too rapidly.

Before accepting this alternative we must consider the possibility that our capacity to form and use abstract concepts does not result directly from our language ability but instead in some way emerges from a more fundamental capacity that permits us to learn and to use language. Admittedly, this distinction is a very subtle one and one that is perhaps for the time being removed from experimental attack. In any case this suggestion highlights the point that verbal processes are not necessarily the only processes that fail to be externalized in current experimental procedures used to investigate conceptual behavior.

My own preference in this matter would be to characterize the difference between the concepts of animals and men in a more open-ended fashion. The crucial difference, as I see it, is that the events that are grouped together by animals are directly associated with a common response while in the higher level conceptual behavior of humans the instances of a conceptual grouping are in some manner transformed into a representational response that serves as the primary cue for conceptual behavior. This open-ended conception provides a framework that can guide research in the identification of the processes involved in the conceptual behavior of man.

The distinction that Bourne makes between relevant stimulus attributes of concepts and the rules of their interrelationships is intuitively appealing and apparently significant. It illustrates how an important factor can be ignored by the uncritical adoption of conventional experimental procedures. Concept learning studies have depended on procedures designed to study the sensory capacities of animals. In such studies only one simple rule is used; the stimulus attributes are partitioned into two classes, each possessing one attribute and each being reinforced or nonreinforced. As a result, with this basic procedure, attention is paid only to problems associated with physical stimulus attributes while questions of rules are ignored.

The logical distinction between stimulus attributes and rules does not necessarily reflect a psychological difference. This point goes well beyond present considerations. With the enthusiastic adoption of many logical models to analyze behavior (e.g., information theory, mathematical models, computer simulation) a tendency has developed to assume an *a priori* isomorphism between the characteristics of a logical model and the behavior to which it is applied. Such an assumption need not be true. Only research can demonstrate whether the logical distinction has theoretical value.

It will not surprise me if we discover somewhat different psychological processes involved in learning the physical attributes and the rules of a concept. I would, however, warn against the too rapid adoption of this position. Verbal processes are deeply involved in both kinds of learning and may operate in a common fashion in both cases.

Bourne's review of the current research efforts in the field of conceptual behavior is fair and accurate. I cannot disagree with any of his major points, but I can comment about some. Distinguishing between theories of concept identification in which the subject is a *passive* recipient of information as contrasted with the view that he is an *active* participant in processing the information does lead to possible misinterpretations. By characterizing the subject as a *passive* recipient one gets the impression that the condition of the subject is unimportant when he processes information. Consider for a moment Spence's theory of discrimination learning (1936) which might be judged as the epitome of a single-unit *passive* conception of discrimination. But even in such a conception the organism operates on the stimulus and reinforcement contingencies of its environment. For example, his learning of a black-white discrimination will be influenced by whether or not he starts his training with a strong position preference. Now perhaps the term "position preference" does not have the same connotations as the term "hypothesis," but the fact of the matter is that both of these concepts imply that the information the environment supplies will be acted on in terms of the prevailing psychological condition of the organism. Although the passive-active distinction is open to misunderstanding and misinterpretation, it does probably possess some descriptive significance. As I see it, it refers to some dimension that emphasizes the importance of factors that have been typically subsumed under the inclusive term of "set."

The problems posed by mathematical models of conceptual behavior are no different, in my estimation, from those raised by mathematical models in other fields. If one accepts the possibility of a wide range of reasonable approaches in science, then it is obviously impossible to offer any definitive or final evaluation of mathematical models. Failure to endorse or reject, however, does not eliminate the alternative of judging. I believe that Bourne, more by implication, does raise issues that should not be hidden by the virtues of mathematical models, no matter how elegant and precise they may be. The kind of behavior that mathematical models are applied to, as well as the intuitive absurdity of some of their assumptions, are steep prices to pay for their apparent virtues. Assumptions such as randomly selecting a hypothesis from a pool of hypotheses, sampling with replacement, restricting hypotheses to the attributes of the stimulus cards, go counter to what can be learned without difficulty when testing college students in a simple concept learning task. One can argue, with justification, that it may be strategic to adopt the simplest assumptions initially in order to develop more complex ones. But such a strategy has not always been put into practice. Too frequently an experimental situation is developed which molds the subject to fit the oversimplified model. The model, instead of the behavior, becomes an end in itself. Dr. Bourne's conclusion that " . . . the boundary conditions of these models may be fairly narrow" is, I feel, a gross understatement.

My harsh comments do not reflect an aversion to mathematical models of conceptual behavior, but disappointment. The inadequate mathematical foundations of Hullian psychology served as a challenge and impetus to the development of mathematical models. Initially, as I read the history of psychology, the mathematical models were planned to cope with the same breadth of phenomena as did prevailing formulations but to do it in a more precise and elegant fashion. We have witnessed, however, the turning away from general models with significant empirical breadth. Today the attraction for the most part is toward models with excessively narrow application. As a result, some formulations of mathematical models appear to be exercises in ritualism instead of empiricism. The solution, I believe, is to formulate mathematical models that are more in tune with available evidence and more directed toward gaining insights into psychological processes. It may be that the real problem behind the psychological superficiality of mathematical models results more from too little mathematical training of our mathematical psychologists than from too much. Perhaps simple mathematical assumptions are made because most

present-day psychologists are not sufficiently powerful mathematicians to formulate the kind of models that are demanded by the reality of psychological complexity.

Verbal Operant Conditioning

No simple transition can be made from Bourne's paper to Kanfer's, unless one wants to assume the bold, and fairly defensible, position that conceptual behavior is a fundamental process in verbal conditioning. But I would be very reluctant to get involved in the controversies that surround *verbal operant conditioning*. Their complexities and subtleties, as well as their emotional overtones, remind me of the *latent learning* controversy, and frankly I have no desire to return to that sort of psychological engagement.

The verbal operant conditioning controversy illustrates a conflict between competing paradigms. If the resolution of this conflict could be achieved by experimental test alone, the controversy would never have developed to the proportion that it has. But within this controversy are components of basic epistemological issues, such as the mind-body problem and the difference between private and public experience. In addition, the controversy is imbedded within problems associated with the long enduring engagement between cognitive and S-R conceptions of behavior, historical and ahistorical explanations of behavior, and learning and perceptual theoretical models. It is not possible to resolve these issues, but it is possible to pinpoint some of the real differences.

Some of the methodological positions that Kanfer has accepted have added unnecessary problems to an already overburdened debate. Operant conditioning spawned the facts of verbal conditioning, but it is not necessary or advisable to analyze and interpret them within a highly restrictive methodological orientation that is usually identified with Skinner. Kanfer at times seems to try to escape from the confines of the radical positivistic approach that Skinner enjoys espousing, but his efforts are not sufficiently vigorous to be successful. A case in point is his statement, "The behavioristic position of writers in verbal conditioning is characterized by the general assumption that the determinants of performance can be isolated experimentally without recourse to complex theoretical constructs." This statement represents a more tolerant methodological position than a completely atheoretical approach. But this tolerance does more harm than good, because it removes the issues in dispute from any meaningful analysis. Characterizing some arbitrary limit of simplicity, beyond which theoretical constructs cannot go, is in my estimation a hopeless task.

Perhaps I am misreading Kanfer, but I get the impression, although he never states it as a strict methodological prescription, that behaviorism can best reject intervening variables, especially when they refer to processes that our ordinary language would identify as mentalistic. This was essentially the viewpoint of Watson, and it is the exact position against which Tolman reacted. Tolman's early efforts were concerned with objectivizing mentalistic processes. He was a behaviorist, in the sense of trying to achieve collective understanding about behavior within an operational and experimental framework. It might be added that his theoretical contributions were far more significant than the rather feeble efforts of Watson.

It would be unfortunate to restrict the entire behavioristic orientation to the parochial views of Watson and Skinner about mentalistic events and concepts. Phenomenal experience should not be banned automatically from consideration. Instead we must continuously try to improve our judgments about their relevance and usefulness in understanding behavior. A case in point is the concept of awareness.

The debate that surrounds the concept of *awareness* in verbal operant conditioning studies reflects theoretical preconceptions and methodological prejudgments that operate to prevent the resolution of the empirical issues. On one hand, the problem of awareness should not be ignored simply because it has mentalistic connotations. On the other hand, it should not be allowed to serve as an explanatory catch-all. It represents a kind of behavior that demands experimental and theoretical analyses, which should not be hampered by any unnecessary prejudgments. Is it necessary, as Kanfer implies, that awareness must be considered just another form of behavior, no more significant than other forms of behavior? He writes, "Self-reports cannot be given special status as indices of other *events*, any more than acquisition response or any other observed behavior." I understand this statement to mean that one form of behavior cannot be considered to be theoretically more important or, in everyday discourse, more causal than other forms of behavior. Cannot we attribute to intelligence a special status when attempting to explain the academic achievements of children? Do not the motivational conditions and past training of a rat have greater "causal" effects upon its behavior in a T-maze than its sleeping pattern in its home cage?

If self-reports can be shown to have some special predictive power over some other kinds of behavior, then it would seem sensible to analyze self-reports. It should be understood that the need for such introspective analysis cannot be justified by any prejudgments that assign to phenomenal experience the special status of being the royal road to the understanding of psychological events. Instead, its special status emerges only from specific experimental results. In my own research with children a discrepancy has been noted between the verbal reports of some children and their concept-attainment behavior (Kendler and Kendler, 1962). In this case certain other lines of investigation seem more promising than the analysis of introspective reports. Recently, however, I have completed a lengthy phase of a research project designed to discover whether concepts can be classically conditioned by contiguously presenting stimulus instances from a set of related cues from one behavioral chain with discriminative responses from a different chain. The evidence that we have obtained so far is that this "conditioning" occurs only when the subject is aware of the relationships between the stimuli and responses. In this case it seems sensible to investigate the processes associated with subjects' awareness of the stimuli, responses, and their relationships.

The key methodological issue in treating phenomenal experience within a behavioristic methodological orientation is to recognize that the subject's phenomenal field, unlike that of the experimenter's, is inferred and not directly observed. Since it is inferred, and not directly observed, its epistemological status is that of a theoretical construct instead of raw data. As long as theoretical constructs are permissible, the pragmatic value of phenomenal experience in different experimental situations can be evaluated within a behavioristic methodological orientation.

My methodological differences with Kanfer should not hide our basic areas of agreement. It is easier, and perhaps more fun, to disagree than to agree. I find Kanfer's analysis of the historical development of research in verbal conditioning into four stages interesting and relevant to other experimental techniques as well. I also am impressed with the possibilities of the verbal conditioning technique in helping to isolate functional verbal response units. Presumably fundamental verbal units should be more easily conditioned than artificial ones. Developmental studies along these lines should tell us much about the acquisition and utilization of language. Finally, I must reaffirm Kanfer's conviction of the importance of studies designed to study self-regulation. Problems of self-regulation are fundamental to any analysis of cognitive behavior.

Semantic Conditioning and Generalization

Maltzman's challenging paper on semantic conditioning and generalization ranges from analyses of experimental detail to discussion of broad methodological and theoretical issues. Without minimizing the importance of the empirical issues raised, my comments will be limited to several methodological-theoretical problems that bear upon the entire conference. Before beginning I would like to remind you of some of my earlier remarks about the history of science and suggest that perhaps Maltzman is in the midst of an *internal* revolution in which he is striving to acquire a new paradigm without relinquishing the one on which he was initially imprinted. His difficulty stems largely from problems associated with separating methodological from empirical issues.

Maltzman assumes a strong posture in denying the empirical validity of current S-R theories of semantic conditioning and generalization. Their failings, he believes, result from the inadequate conceptions of simple conditioning upon which current S-R formulations are based. And this, in turn, is to some extent a function of the peripheralistic bias that has dominated S-R thinking. His analysis is forcefully stated in the following way: "Current S-R theories are largely formulated as though the college sophomore is an empty shell."

My reading of the history of psychology and the observations of the current scene do not lead to the same conclusions. In my opinion we are now sufficiently past the inception of the behavioristic revolution to judge it in its proper historical perspective. The emphasis on peripheralism by S-R behaviorists is better understood as a reaction to the subjectivism of the structualists in an attempt to achieve collective agreement about the meaning of concepts and the reliability of facts than as an empirical assertion minimizing the importance of central processes in behavior. This interpretation is not offered to encourage a search of the literature for convincing quotations. I am more interested in understanding what was really going on in the history of psychology than to discover what some thought was happening. My conclusion is that peripheralism vs. centralism was never a significant issue; it was a confused by-product of the revolutionary emergence of methodological behaviorism.

According to behaviorism, all formulations must be methodologically peripheralistic in the sense that the dependent variable is some observable component of behavior. In this sense

cognitive theory, the orienting reflex formulation, S-R conceptions are all equally peripheralistic.

If one shifts from methodological issues to the problem of the relationship between a behavioral theory and physiology, then several options are available within the centralism-peripheralism frame of reference. One of these options, and a particularly strategic one, is to be physiologically noncommittal. This is the assumption I accept in my own work on mediational S-R theory. Basic to it is the premise that S-R language, by itself, is physiologically neutral.

The real problem raised by Maltzman is how we are to handle the input side of behavior, particularly within an S-R formulation. This has been, and still is, one of the fundamental questions facing psychology. There is no doubt that with their great interest in problems of associative formation and strengthening, S-R psychologists have tended to ignore problems of perception. But the S-R pretheoretical model of behavior is not so restrictive as to exclude dealing with the problem of how external stimulation is transformed into an effective stimulus pattern.

As I see it, there are two primary methods of coping with this problem. One is to postulate an observing-response mechanism. This refers to the orienting behavior of an organism which directs its receptors to certain portions of the environment. The second mechanism can be referred to as *attention*. Attention determines how a particular *pattern* of stimuli striking the receptors will be organized into an effective stimulus compound. The observing response mechanism fits easily into an S-R model since it can be tied to both stimulus and response experimental variables. On the other hand, the attention mechanism provides a more challenging, but not an impossible, problem. One can relate attention to the physical characteristics of the stimulus pattern, as Gestalt psychologists have attempted, and also to the motivation and prior learning of an organism. Attention can be defined in terms of some response characteristics independent of the behavior that is being experimentally analyzed. In recent years several physiological techniques of measurement have attempted to do this (e.g., Hernández-Péon, Scherrer, and Jouvet, 1956; Hess, 1965) by identifying physiological changes correlated to overt behavior. It seems to me that the orienting reflex conception of the Soviet psychologists is similar to these physiologically correlated conceptions of attention.

I cannot see how the orienting reflex approach is *methodologically* superior or even distinct from other attempts that have been formulated to cope with the problem of perception in general and attention in particular. Although, at present, it may be considered to have some special advantages in providing objective measures of attentive behavior, it seems to be especially weak in characterizing properties of the environment in terms of the attention-getting potential (e.g., figure-ground conception of the Gestalt psychologist) —a problem that will still be with us no matter how sophisticated our knowledge of physiological processes becomes. One can assume that the orienting reflex is not stimulus-specific, but it is difficult for me to accept the position that no relationship exists between attention and physical characteristics of the environment.

The value of the orienting reflex conception is not that it represents any methodological breakthrough, but instead its potential as an empirical technique and theoretical model. We should certainly be receptive to new ideas, but at the same time we should

be aware that the orienting reflex conception has not as yet been subject to the more stringent experimental design and statistical requirements demanded by American, as compared to Soviet, psychologists.

Concluding Remarks

An integrated overview of my discussion is difficult to formulate simply because the three topics for which I am responsible do not form a unified whole. If these topics were really integrated, I am sure that a more descriptive title than *Related Processes* would have been used. "Related" in this context proved to be more of a wish than an actuality.

It is not surprising that conceptual behavior, verbal operant conditioning, and semantic conditioning are not more highly related. These topics have emerged from entirely different backgrounds. First, conceptual behavior has a significant place in our ordinary language and everyday living, whereas verbal operant conditioning and semantic conditioning are purely laboratory phenomena. Second, the experimental foundations of each area differ. Conceptual behavior rests heavily on results obtained with discrimination learning techniques, while verbal conditioning is an outgrowth of operant conditioning, and semantic conditioning stems from classical conditioning. Although discrimination learning, operant conditioning, and classical conditioning are all widely used techniques to investigate learning, the models of behavior they usually generate are quite different (e.g., examine the conceptions of behavior proposed by Tolman, Skinner, and Hull). At present the data from each of these areas, especially those of verbal operant conditioning and semantic conditioning, fail to provide a nice, neat package of consistent information. One possibility, of course, is that everything will become clearer with additional research and clever theoretical notions. But that may not necessarily occur. We must entertain the possibility, without accepting it, that conditioning procedures, and other experimental techniques as well, may not be particularly effective in investigating verbal behavior in the sense of producing integrated bodies of knowledge and significant sets of ideas.

Although my primary task was to evaluate the papers of the three participants in the area of *Related Processes*, and I have tried to accomplish this within the limits of available space, I have for the most part skirted three questions that the editors directed at each discussant. I will terminate my remarks by responding to them.

QUESTION 1: Is there a systematic account of verbal behavior, or would it be possible to formulate one, that would encompass the major facts and principles involved in the three specific areas covered by the Area Discussant?

ANSWER: There is no systematic account of verbal behavior that integrates, at the present time, the facts of conceptual behavior, verbal operant conditioning, and semantic conditioning and generalization. One reason for this state of affairs has already been alluded to. These empirical areas of study have emerged from different experimental methodologies and, to a somewhat lesser degree, from different theoretical viewpoints.

Instead of these problem areas drawing closer together with time, the opposite trend has occurred. Research and theorizing have generated area-specific problems that have tended to encapsulate these three research fields. In principle, however, there is no reason why an account of verbal behavior imbedded in a general behavior theory

cannot ultimately integrate the facts of conceptual behavior, verbal operant conditioning, and semantic conditioning and generalization.

QUESTION 2: Taken collectively, does existing theory in these three areas conform to *general S-R theory* (both verbal and nonverbal) or alternative theoretical systems?

ANSWER: Allow me the privilege of expanding the scope of this question so that it focuses our attention on one of the dominant problems confronting this conference—the potentialities of any S-R conception to explain all kinds of verbal behavior. A difference of opinion exists about the meaning of *general S-R theory*. There are those who believe it is a rigid and dogmatic system that generates empirical assertions that are obviously inconsistent with known facts. Such a view emerges from a simple-minded notion of S-R associationism that has little contact with the history and current status of stimulus-response psychology. I have tried to show that the concept of general S-R theory can be more reasonably analyzed if it is broken down into four fundamental components (technical language, methodological orientation, pretheoretical models, and group of theories). Admittedly my analysis makes the task of judging the potentialities of S-R associationism to cope with verbal behavior more difficult than if we treat general S-R theory in an oversimplified global fashion. Distortion of reality, however, is a steep price to pay for simplicity.

It may be argued that by offering a fourfold interpretation of S-R associationism I have protected it from criticism. Such an appraisal is neither fair nor accurate. It is certainly possible to test—and this has repeatedly been done—the implications of a variety of S-R formulations. However, when it comes to the merits of S-R associationism as a language, or as a methodological orientation, or as a pretheoretical model, one is required to make his judgments in terms of pragmatic considerations instead of those of validity. For example, in judging the assets and liabilities of S-R language one can point to the historical fact that S-R language has forced psychologists to think in terms of manipulable environmental variables and objective behavior measures. In this way it has served as an impetus to research. Many problems which at first glance seemed removed from experimental analysis have been transformed into empirical questions following an S-R linguistic analysis. At the same time, the use of S-R language has stressed the importance of certain psychological processes while simultaneously deemphasizing others. S-R language, combined with socio-cultural factors that encouraged the study of learning, tended to interest psychologists in problems involving the association between stimulus and response elements while at the same time suppressing concern with questions of the organization of stimulus and response elements. Is S-R language incapable of coping with perceptual and response organization? I think not. Osgood (1953) long ago recognized some of these basic problems and offered solutions for them. As long as it is recognized that S-R language can be supplemented by new concepts and has potential for both vertical and horizontal integrations (Kendler and Kendler, 1962), it seems inappropriate to burden it with any intrinsic limitation.

Another reservation expressed about S-R language is that the linear-type relationship assumed to exist between a stimulus and response, usually indicated by the horizontal dash, is too restrictive to represent the various kinds of relationships that can exist between environmental events and behavior. Although the meaning of "various

kinds of relationships" is not entirely clear, it may be useful to note that if we examine the historical meaning of S-R linearity, we find that basically it represents a functional relationship that can, and has been, interpreted in a variety of ways ranging from neurological processes to probability statements.

To analyze completely the relationship between *general S-R theory* and *verbal behavior*, attention must be paid not only to the concept of *S-R associationism* but also to that of *verbal behavior*. The field of verbal behavior represents neither a single phenomenon nor an integrated research area. Experimental psychologists who operate within an S-R framework have for the most part been interested in how linguistic variables influence certain forms of behavior such as memory, concept learning, problem solving, etc. Psycholinguists, with a transformational orientation, on the other hand, are more interested in the acquisition and performance of natural language. It is not surprising to discover that different conceptions of verbal behavior have emerged from the investigation of different empirical problems.

In evaluating any particular conception of verbal behavior, two general questions can be asked. How adequately does this conception handle the data it was designed to explain? What potential does this formulation have for extrapolation to other areas of verbal behavior? If one is simply interested in scoring a debater's point, then he would be wiser, when attacking any formulation, to direct at it the second question instead of the first. However, if one is trying to achieve a fair and accurate view of the current scene in verbal behavior, then both questions are necessary.

Although I vigorously argue against placing any upper limits on the potential explanatory power of a S-R type theory, I am ready to admit that no existing S-R formulation covers adequately the broad spectrum of verbal behavior. But it must also be noted that the transformational view of language acquisition and performance has practically nothing to say about the facts of a large number of phenomena, such as concept attainment, verbal conditioning, semantic conditioning, retroactive inhibition, and others that have interested experimental psychologists for many years. It can be argued, with justification, that each empirical area is not necessarily of equal importance. The history of science has repeatedly shown that certain empirical problems have revealed general theoretical principles more readily than others. But typically, theoretical fruitfulness was demonstrated instead of heralded. Evidence is more persuasive than exhortation.

I can agree with the position that understanding the acquisition and performance of natural language will yield broad theoretical principles. I can also accept the idea that these phenomena will not prove, upon examination, to be simple cases of either classical or operant conditioning. Further, I believe that developmental factors play a crucial role in natural language behavior. But I would maintain that not one of these admissions is incompatible with an S-R approach to verbal behavior.

Of paramount importance in mining the resources of natural language behavior is to realize that the empirical evidence at present is embarrassingly thin. Information, of higher quality and greater quantity than exists now, is needed to resolve current disputes about language acquisition as well as to provide the empirical information upon which meaningful theoretical structures can be erected.

It would be unfortunate if in the heat of controversy the transformational view assumes an extreme, sterile position in an effort to set itself dramatically apart from S-R formulations that emphasize the learning process. One can recall the crippling effect that the hereditary vs. environmental debate had upon the development of theories of intelligence, a disabling effect that still shows its marks. I fear that we are now witnessing a similar debate, equally naive, about the acquisition of natural language. The acquisition of natural language is dependent on genetic and experiential factors. Neither can be ruled out. Their individual influences must be understood, not at the expense of one another, but in relationship to each other. The nature-nurture controversy about the foundations of intelligence has been likened to an argument about whether the base or the altitude is more important in determining the area of a rectangle. A similar analogy can be applied to any debate that asks the question whether language acquisition is due to innate *or* learning factors.

It is particularly important when analyzing the reciprocal influence between hereditary and environmental variables to realize that the influence of experience is not limited to the effects produced by the practice of a specific response as typically occurs in conditioning studies. The experimental analysis of instinctive forms of behavior shows that certain experiences, not of the specific response-training variety, can exert profound influence on later behavior. For example, Eibl-Eibesfeldt (1955, 1956) reports that female rats who failed to develop an attachment to any particular place in their cage did not build nests during pregnancy, even though nest-building material was available to them. If one operates within the assumption that the influence of experience is mediated only by response-specific practice, then one can easily be led into the error of attributing an innate causality to a particular response that has no clearcut history of being practiced. When looking upon what appears to be a relatively rapid acquisition of language competence by the human child, researchers should be particularly sensitive to the possible influence of experiences other than specific language training.

QUESTION 3: Do developments within these three areas forecast any significant changes in the orientation or structure of general behavior theory?

ANSWER: In my estimation they do. If one is addicted to S-R formulations, then the evidence suggests to me that an S-R mediational formulation has the greatest promise. The major task for this kind of formulation is to develop theoretical mechanisms capable of explaining the kinds of phenomena that have been characterized as linguistic rules of usage, information processing, and attention.

I will now step off the witness stand.

References

Eibl-Eibesfeldt, I., "Angeborenes und Erworbenes im Nestbauverhalten der Wanderatte," *Naturwissenschaften*, **42** (1955), 633–634.

———, "Fortschritte der vergleichenden Verhaltensforschung," *Naturwissenschaften*, **86–90** (1956), 136–142.

Estes, W. K., "The Statistical Approach to Learning Theory," in S. Koch, ed. *Psychology: A Study of a Science*. Vol. 2. New York: McGraw-Hill Book Company, 1959. pp. 380–491.

Hernández-Péon, R., H. Scherrer, and M. Jouvet, "Modification of Electric Activity in Cochlear Nucleus during 'Attention' in Unanesthetized Cats," *Science*, **123** (1956), 331–332.

Hess, E. H., "Attitude and Pupil Size," *Scientific American*, Vol. 212, No. 4, (1965), 46–54.

Kendler, H. H., "Motivation and Behavior," in D. Levine, ed., *Nebraska Symposium on Motivation*, 1965. Lincoln: Univ. of Nebraska Press, 1965.

———, and T. S. Kendler, "Vertical and Horizontal Processes in Problem Solving," *Psychological Review*, **69** (1962), 1–16.

Kuhn, T. S., *The Structure of Scientific Revolution*. Chicago: University of Chicago Press, 1962.

Osgood, C. E., *Method and Theory in Experimental Psychology*. New York: Oxford University Press, 1953.

Reichenbach, H., *Experience and Prediction*. Chicago: University of Chicago Press, 1938.

Spence, K. W., "The Nature of Discrimination Learning in Animals," *Psychological Review*, **43** (1936), 427–449.

Psycholinguistics

PART IV

On Theories
of Language
Acquisition[1]

15 DAVID MCNEILL

Those interested in linguistic development use the phrase "language acquisition" freely. Conferences are so named, lectures on the subject are given, and the present paper uses it as a title. However, the term "language acquisition" is without definite meaning. There is no sense in which one may speak of acquiring "language," as if it were an object apparent to perception. The locution omits a crucial step in our theoretical efforts. The missing part is the necessity of first understanding what is meant by "language." Only after having defined this term is it possible to ask how language so defined might be acquired. This requirement is inescapable: theories of linguistic development that make no explicit reference to an analysis of language are illusory. Actually they do assume some theory of language, but they do so implicitly, suffering thereby the dis-

advantage of not knowing precisely what it is they are to explain. A major requirement, then, for any theory of language acquisition is that it explain a known phenomenon, which means that theories of development must be related to particular grammatical analyses, to particular theories about language itself.

A suggestion sometimes made is that studies of child language can be used to decide questions in linguistics. Braine (1965), for example, writes: "If there is a possibility that the simpler of two possible grammatical solutions might require the more complex acquisition theory, then the domain over which simplicity is taken cannot be restricted to grammar alone and must include acquisition theory—otherwise the grammarian merely purchases simplicity at the psychologist's expense" (p. 491).

Braine was writing in response to the remark of Bever, Fodor, and Weksel (1965a, 1965b) that theories of acquisition must somehow account for the ability of children to develop abstract linguistic structures; that is, structures (such as the base form of sentences) that are never made manifest in speech. He then suggests the following gram-

[1] Preparation of this paper was supported in part by a grant from the National Institute of Child Health and Human Development (No. 1P01 HD01368–01) to the project on language development, the University of Michigan, and in part by a contract between the U.S. Office of Education (No. OE-5-14-036) and the Center for Research on Language and Language Behavior, the University of Michigan.

matical reform: " . . . surely the gain in simplicity accruing to an acquisition theory for taking the underlying structure as overt in simple sentences would likely to be so great that it would more than compensate for an increase in grammatical complexity involved in writing the grammar so that the underlying structure was overt" (1965, p. 491).

Braine's proposal, in other words, is to construct a new grammatical system, taking into primary consideration such factors as available theories of learning. This view, which is by no means limited to Braine, is mistaken, and mistaken because it confuses two distinct questions—the nature of linguistic competence and the nature of the device that acquires linguistic competence. It therefore violates the basic requirement stated above. A descriptively adequate grammar, to use Chomsky's (1965) term, accurately and explicitly states the linguistic knowledge of fluent speakers. Difficulties often confront the evaluation of a grammar, of course, but the lack of a psychological theory is no reason to reject a proposed grammatical solution. That is rather like not believing in the calculus because one does not have a theory of how mathematicians understand it. The problem, instead, is to formulate a psychological theory that is adequate to explain the acquisition of grammar. Thus, there are two alternatives open in the study of language acquisition. Either one does a novel kind of linguistics, attempting to discover the kind of linguistic competence that could be explained by current psychological theory, or one attempts to see how a particular characterization of competence (say, transformational grammar) could be acquired. Braine advocates the former course, whereas the latter will be advocated here.

The Problem of Language Acquisition

Superficial acquaintance with young children reveals one of the problems that a theory of language acquisition must face. At 18 months or so, children begin to form simple two- and three-word sentences. By the age of four, they are able to produce sentences of almost every conceivable syntactic type. In approximately 30 months, therefore, language is acquired, at least that part of it having to do with syntax—an achievement that any theory of linguistic development must consider.

We must also specify what it is that children acquire so rapidly. On this there can be little doubt: It is a transformational grammar. For arguments and evidence in support of transformational grammar, see Chomsky (1964, 1965), Chomsky and Halle (1965), Katz (1966), Katz and Postal (1964), Postal (1964), and the many papers referred to therein. The problem of language acquisition thus can be stated clearly. We aspire toward a theory of linguistic development that will explain the emergence of a transformational grammar by age four years, with the period of active acquisition covering a span of approximately 30 months. Once the problem is seen in this way, proposals for explaining language acquisition that can be derived from traditional psychological theories turn out to be simply inappropriate.

The next section passes two such proposals in review. The goal of the review is to meet the need for analysis by discovering the kind of grammatical system that a mechanism derived from S-R principles could acquire. This system, whatever it is, represents an assumption about the grammar of English. In both the cases to be reviewed, it is something less than a transformational grammar. In one case, it is less even than a phrase-structural grammar; in the other, although it is a phrase-structural grammar, it is one emasculated in precisely those features that justify phrase-structural grammars in the first place. The two proposals, of course, are merely representatives of a genre, but it will be argued later that their particular shortcomings are inherent to any application of S-R theory.

Two Traditional Accounts of Language Acquisition

An explanation based on mediated S-R connections

Jenkins and Palermo (1964) have made an initial effort to develop a mediational account of linguistic behavior. They conceive of a sentence as "a correct assembly of classes appropriately modulated" (p. 164) and therefore concern themselves with the formation of such fundamental categories of grammar as nouns, verbs, and adjectives. Their hope is that by understanding this process, as well as by understanding the process of organizing categories into sequences, they will understand a good deal about the acquisition of the structure of English sentences.

According to Jenkins and Palermo's hypothesis, mediation paradigms occur naturally in the speech a child hears from his parents. Random encounters with *John is pleasant* and *John is jolly*, for example, would lead a child to place *pleasant* and *jolly* in the same class. In general, words belong to a class because associations are established

among them when they occur in the same (or equivalent) contexts. In this example, the paradigm is the so-called "response-equivalence" paradigm because two terms (*pleasant* and *jolly*) both appear after a third term (*John is*). In other cases, the so-called "stimulus-equivalence" paradigm applies: for example, *John is jolly* and *Christmas is jolly* provide the conditions for establishing *John* and *Christmas* as a class. Other, more complex cases correspond to other, more complex paradigms, and it is not necessary for words to occupy identical environments in order to be classified together. Since grammatical classes derive from sequential associations, the organization of classes into sentences can be attributed to these same ancestral associations—thus, *Christmas is pleasant* arises from the sequential association between the two classes established in the examples above, even though *Christmas* and *pleasant* are not actually paired in any of the sentences presented.

It seems clear that the network of associations acquired in mediation paradigms comprises what Chomsky (1957) called a *finite-state grammar*. Such grammars are made up of a finite number of states, some of which are connected by transitions, with words produced on transition from one state to another. In the present case, the states are grammatical classes, the transitions are the associations among grammatical classes, and a single word from the preceding grammatical class is produced on each transition.

The difficulties with finite-state grammars are simple and arithmetical. In order to acquire grammar through mediation paradigms, a child must learn all the transitions among grammatical classes that are allowable in English. The number of these, however, is astronomical. Take, for example, the sentence *The people who called and wanted to rent your house when you go away next year are from California* (Miller and Chomsky, 1963). There is a dependency between the second word (*people*) and the seventeenth word (*are*). If this intuition was learned through mediation, then each of us has learned a unique set of transitions covering a sequence of 15 grammatical categories. Assuming (conservatively) that an average of four grammatical categories might occur at any point in the development of an English sentence, detection of the dependency between *people* and *are* signifies that we have learned at least $4^{15} = 10^9$ different transitions, which means, as Miller and Chomsky point out, that we learned " ... the values of 10^9 parameters in a childhood lasting only 10^8 seconds" (p. 430). Evidently, mediation paradigms yield the wrong kind of structure. At the very least, we need a theory which avoids assuming that sentences consist of nothing more than simple left-to-right transitions. The theory to be reviewed next thus represents an advance, since it meets this minimal (but still insufficient) requirement.

An explanation based on contextual generalization

Braine (1965) discusses two processes in the development of linguistic competence. One is "contextual generalization," the other a type of restricted association among various function words and other grammatical classes. With these two processes, Braine argues, children develop the fundamentals of grammar. Only the first will be considered here, since the second leads to another finite-state grammar.

The theory goes as follows. As a child hears sentences from his parents, he notices from time to time the position that particular words or phrases occupy

in them. For example, when hearing *Adam's bike is hitting the lamp*, a child may notice that *Adam's bike* occurs in the first half of the sentence. It is relative position that a child observes. The process of *contextual generalization* then carries *Adam's bike* into homologous, first-half positions in other sentences. Contextual generalization is regarded as being not different in principle from ordinary stimulus- or response-generalization, being a special case of these more general processes in which the property that mediates generalization is temporal location in an utterance. With respect to the linguistic problem, the merit of contextual generalization is that it provides a basis for productivity, the capacity to produce or comprehend novel but grammatical utterances.

A child learns not only the position of phrases within sentences through this process, but also the position of words within phrases. The result is to install the hierarchical structure of sentences as a part of children's competence; it is here that the advantage of contextual generalization over mediation theory resides. Let us return to the example. The phrase *Adam's bike* is in the first half of the sentence *Adam's bike is hitting the lamp*, and the word *bike* is in the last half of that phrase. If a child notices the relative positions of first the word and then the phrase, he could learn how to construct a type of *NP*. The position of the word is defined in terms of the phrase, and the position of the phrase, in turn, is defined in terms of the sentence. Contextual generalization carries this dual discovery to analogous contexts, thereby insuring productivity. A similar process leads to the *VP*. The phrase *is hitting the lamp* is in the last half of the sentence *Adam's bike is hitting the lamp*, and *is hitting* is in the first half of the phrase. Again, the smaller unit is defined in terms of the larger, and contextual generalization carries this inclusion relation to analogous contexts.

Contextual generalization thus yields the kind of structure that is conventionally represented by a phrase-structural grammar. However, it is a phrase-structural grammar that makes transformations, as they are understood in linguistic theory, quite impossible (Bever, *et al.*, 1965a, 1965b). Moreover, even as an account of phrase-structural grammar, the structures learned through contextual generalization lack the property that provides major justification of phrase-structural grammars over finite-state grammars—the property of recursion (Chomsky, 1957). Contextual generalization is therefore doubly limited. It denies the possibility of transformations on the one hand, and it reduces the power of phrase-structural grammar to the level of finite-state grammar on the other. These limitations, which seem fatal, will be discussed in turn.

The logic of a transformation involves a distinction between the base (or covert) and the surface (or manifest) structure of sentences. The former is connected with meaning and the latter with pronunciation. The two are related by transformations that operate on base structures to convert them into surface structures. Thus, to take an oversimplified example, the surface structure, ((*the psychologist*) ((*was berated*) (*by the linguist*)), is related to the base structure, ((*the linguist*) (*berated* (*the psychologist*) (*Passive*)), by the passive transformation.

Because of the existence of transformations, surface structures necessarily differ in various ways from base structures. This is true of the example above; it is also true of the simplest declarative sentences (Chomsky, 1957). Indeed, the entire justification of trans-

formational grammar rests on the distinction between base and surface structure in the sense that transformations would be unnecessary if the distinction were disallowed. But this is precisely what contextual generalization demands, because the process cannot apply to structures that a child never hears. Accordingly, in order to invoke contextual generalization, one is forced to assume that English has less than a transformational grammar; in fact, one is forced to assume that English has a phrase-structural grammar without abstract terms of any kind. Braine's reformulation of the grammar of English (see 1965, p. 2) is a manifestation of this assumption.

The difficulties with phrase-structural grammars are made clear throughout the writings on transformational grammar. The difficulties in the case of contextual generalization are discussed at considerable length by Bever, *et al.* (1965a), particularly in connection with Braine's new definition of a transformation (1963, 1965). According to this definition, some sentence types are transformed into other types via various "sublanguages." A sublanguage operates on the *surface structure* of one sentence to yield the *surface structure* of another sentence. The sentences transformed are always simple declaratives; the sentences produced by the transformation are such forms as questions, negatives, and passives. The whole forms a "transformational" grammar without base structures. The difficulty with this kind of grammar, as Bever, *et al.* point out, is that one needs a separate sublanguage for each variant of the declarative sentence. For example, with five tenses and two numbers (singular and plural), 10 different rules are necessary to produce passives alone, and this leaves out of account the further rules to form passive-questions (of several types), passive-negatives, etc. Add to this ascending total the need for still more sublanguages to form questions, negatives, embeddings, etc., all of which may appear in combination with any other, and the number can be seen to increase geometrically. Rather than achieving the economy of a true transformational grammar, contextual generalization achieves the theoretical maximum of inefficiency.

One difficulty with contextual generalization, then, is that it makes impossible the formulation of transformations. Transformations are defined in terms of base structures, whereas contextual generalization yields surface structures. The limitation is inherent to the conditions under which contextual generalization applies, namely, the surface features of the speech presented to a child. This, in itself, is sufficient reason to reject the theory, as Bever, *et al.* conclude.

However, there is yet another difficulty. Selection of contextual generalization as the process of acquisition is a self-defeating choice, for it eliminates the very effect it is supposed to explain.

A phrase structural-grammar is favored over a finite-state grammar because it allows recursion, a property essential to account for grammatical dependencies that extend across constituents (Chomsky, 1957). Take, for example, the sentence *The man whom the dentist drilled likes sweets*. There is a dependency between *the man* and *likes sweets*, which extends across the embedded portion, *whom the dentist drilled*. The two parts of the sentence are themselves independent. The embedded portion can be changed without affecting the connection between *man* and *likes;* and changing *man* to *men* requires changing *likes* to *like* but does not affect the embedded portion. A phrase-structural grammar with recur-

sion can easily express relations of this kind. One without recursion cannot.

The discussion will be facilitated by resorting to an artificial example. Let us take a series of "sentences" that includes the following:

ab
aabb
aaabbb
aaaabbbb
.
.
.
.

In this language, each *a* is paired with a *b*. Moreover, initial *a*'s always go with terminal *b*'s, no matter how long the sentence is. Sentences in this language therefore have the same embedded structure as the English sentence given above. One can give a simple phrase-structural rule that will generate all these sentences plus indefinitely more, but the rule requires the presence of an abstract term that is used recursively. With parentheses to indicate that an element is optional, the rule is:

$$X \longrightarrow a(X)b$$

The recursive element, X, is necessarily abstract and never included in the final form of any sentence. The sentence aXb, for example, would be ungrammatical.

Consider, now, the result of applying contextual generalization to "sentences" of this form. As Table 1 shows, each additional sentence introduces a separate node, k, $k + 1$, $k + 2$, $k + 3$, so evidently the result of applying contextual generalization to recursively produced sentences is to eliminate recursion. Each new node, and there are indefinitely many of them, must be learned separately. Contextual generalization therefore makes a grammar with recursion impossible to acquire, but it is in its property of recursion

Table 1

THE RESULT OF APPLYING CONTEXTUAL
GENERALIZATION TO SENTENCES
PRODUCED RECURSIVELY

Presented Sentence	Structure Learned
ab	a is first in k and b is second in k, or $(ab)_k$
aabb	a is first, k is middle, and b is last in $k+1$, or $(a\,(ab)_k\,b)_{k+1}$
aaabbb	a is first, $k+1$ is middle, and b is last in $k+2$, or $(a\,(a\,(ab)_k\,b)_{k+1}\,b)_{k+2}$
aaaabbbb	a is first, $k+2$ is middle, and b is last in $k+3$, or $(a\,(a\,(a\,(ab)_k\,b)_{k+1}\,b)_{k+2}\,b)_{k+3}$

that a phrase-structural grammar is justified. The grammatical system produced by contextual generalization can be called phrase-structural only in the misleading sense that a man not reclining can be called upright.[2]

The general inapplicability of S-R theory

We have reviewed two theories based on S-R principles, neither of which is able to account for the development of a transformational grammar. Indeed, one of them cannot account even for a phrase-structural grammar, and the other cannot account for a phrase-structural grammar of the type needed for language. This outcome is not accidental. Other S-R theories would not perform better, nor would Jenkins and Palermo's or Braine's theories be improved by the addition of (still undeveloped) concepts. The limitations are inherent to S-R theories in general.

The impasse arises because linguistic

[2] Braines' (1965) suggestion to use discontinuous constituents does not remove the difficulty here. A separate constituent is still needed for each additional embedding, thus making a grammar with recursion impossible to acquire.

knowledge includes information never present in the overt form of a sentence. In contrast, S-R theories apply only to the acquisition of overt S-R connections (Chomsky, 1959). Mediated S-R theories (e.g., Osgood, Suci, and Tannenbaum, 1957) are limited in the same way, since the mechanisms they provide serve to change overt S-R connections to covert ones and therefore can apply only to stimuli and responses that at first appear overtly. Indeed, Fodor (1965) has argued that mediation and nonmediation theories are logically identical and so suffer the same infirmities.

Because S-R theory is so limited, the problem of language acquisition simply falls beyond its domain. This in itself is not a serious matter. Not all psychological theories need account for language acquisition. More serious, however, is the fact that the application of S-R principles causes theorists to redefine language in such a way as to make the phenomenon fit the theory. There is perhaps some irony in this outcome of modern empiricism.

A Nativist Account of Language Acquisition

The advantage of the theory to be considered next is that it takes into explicit account the abstract structure of language and therefore applies where an S-R theory does not. However, it cannot be said to explain the acquisition of language in a definite or comprehensive way. At best, it states *what* in language is acquired and so offers a reasonably clear formulation of the problem of language learning. At the same time, however, it omits many details and ignores certain larger issues, the mechanism of acquisition perhaps being the most conspicuous among the latter.

The point of view to be taken is that children are endowed with a biologically based capacity for language. Stated so simply, this is not a particularly interesting hypothesis. For to assert that children have a capacity for language merely rephrases the observation that man is the only articulate creature, a status that derives most plausibly from some unique turn of events in his evolutionary history. To make the hypothesis more interesting, it is necessary to show what the specific features of this capacity might be; on this, some definite suggestions can be made.

Let us consider, not children for the moment, but the abstract Language Acquisition Device (LAD) described by Chomsky (1965). Doing so will help clarify the account of language acquisition to be given later. LAD receives a *corpus* of speech, a set of utterances, some grammatical and some not. The corpus is large, but it is not unlimited in size. It contains, let us say, the number of utterances usually overheard by a two-year-old child. Upon receiving the corpus, LAD formulates a *grammatical system*, which, in turn, may be regarded as LAD's theory about the regularities that appear in the corpus. LAD's theory concerns itself with the detection of essential aspects of utterances, with the structure of sentences, with the prediction of future sentences, etc. In short, LAD's theory comprises its linguistic competence, its knowledge of the grammar underlying the sentences of the corpus.

LAD formulates a grammar by passing the evidence of the corpus through some kind of *internal structure*. The sequence can be diagramed as follows:

Corpus ⟶ | **LAD** | ⟶ Grammatical System

If we knew LAD's internal structure, we would know how LAD formulates a grammar. It is this structure that processes the corpus and extracts grammatically relevant information. The structure is not well understood, but we can at least distinguish two components in it. One consists of various procedures of analysis; the other, of various kinds of preliminary linguistic information. Virtually nothing is known of the former, although Fodor (1966) has offered some speculations, but something can be said about the latter.

One clue about the nonprocedural part of LAD's structure arises from the fact that it must be able to acquire any language. LAD must not find Bantu, say, easier than English, Japanese, Russian, or Aztec. If LAD contains preliminary information, therefore, the information must be applicable to all languages; which is to say that LAD may contain information relating to features that are linguistically universal, but it must contain no information relating to features that are linguistically unique.

An hypothesis about LAD, then, is that part of its internal structure can be described by the *theory of grammar* (Chomsky, 1965; Katz, 1966). This theory is about the general form of human language, containing statements that hold true of natural languages everywhere, regardless of physical or cultural setting. If LAD were equipped with the information described in universal linguistic theory, it could then restrict its attention to acquiring those features that are *not* universal.

Conceiving of LAD in this manner will help clarify the acquisition of language by real children as well as by abstract ones, for the two pose exactly the same problem. Like LAD, children are exposed to a corpus of speech, and like LAD, they develop grammatical competence on the basis of this corpus. Moreover, in the case of both LAD and children, some kind of internal structure converts the corpus of speech into grammatical competence. Since the same corpus is input and the same grammatical system is output, LAD and children presumably have the same internal structure. In short, LAD's internal structure corresponds to children's capacity for language; and the theory of grammar, being a hypothesis about LAD, is also a hypothesis about children's inborn capacity.

The connection between the theory of grammar and children's capacity for language can be stated quite simply: languages possess the universal properties contained in the theory of grammar just because all languages are acquired. The renewed formulation of grammar by each generation of children automatically imposes features corresponding to children's capacity for language. As a result, they appear universally, and the theory of grammar is possible.

Although the theory of grammar is thus logically sufficient to describe children's capacity for language, the theory is not completely formulated. It is, however, far enough advanced to reveal that most universal features of language are situated in the base structure (Chomsky, 1965). The general form of a transformation is universal, and all languages have transformational grammars, but the particular transformations that appear in each language are unique. English, for example, includes a transformation for developing the auxiliary verb that involves permuting the order of verbs and affixes. This particular grammatical device probably occurs only in English, even though permutation occurs at some point in all languages. These facts lead to a useful conclusion.

If linguistic theory described a capacity for language, so that the process of acquisition is restricted to learning features that are linguistically unique, then the features that children must acquire are the particular transformations of their language. If this view is correct, we have an account of how abstract linguistic structures develop. They are the structures represented in the theory of grammar, and they are *made* abstract through the acquisition of transformations. The problem now is to present evidence in behalf of this hypothesis.

The basic grammatical relations

The basic grammatical relations are the concepts of the *subject* and *predicate* of a sentence, the *main verb* and *object* of a verb phrase, and the *modifier* and *head* of a noun phrase. They are defined in linguistic theory and are applied to the base structures of sentences. The fact that the definitions are included in linguistic theory means (on the present hypothesis) that they reflect some aspect of children's capacity for language. The fact that the definitions hold for the base but not the surface structure of sentences means that there is no way for a child to infer them from presented parental speech. Transformed sentences require inconsistent definitions of the basic grammatical relations. It is impossible, for example, to define subject and object in such a way as to cover both *the ball was hit* and *the ball was red*. However, the base structures of these sentences differ in just the way they must for the definitions of subject and object to apply in a consistent manner. The definitions have been discussed in several places, in particular, by Chomsky (1965) and by Katz and Postal (1964).

If the basic grammatical relations reflect an aspect of children's capacity for language, they should appear in children's earliest efforts to produce patterned speech. Base structures must be present before children can formulate transformations. Thus, even primitive two- and three-word combinations should be constructed so as to manifest one or more of these relations. To judge from the speech of two children exposed to two radically different languages, this is precisely what happens.

Evidence from English

Let us first consider evidence from a child exposed to English—a little boy studied by Brown and Bellugi (1964), whom they call Adam.

If an adult looks at Adam's speech, he is strongly impressed with the presence of the basic grammatical relations. Among Adam's sentences, for example, are such things as *hear tractor*, *two boot*, *Adam make tower*, all of which appear to include one or another basic grammatical relation. Although these impressions are vivid, they might also be wrong. Ascribing the basic grammatical relations to Adam depends on understanding what the child was trying to say, and we cannot judge this from a written record of his speech. Some other technique is needed.

At the time his speech was first recorded, at 20 months, Adam had three grammatical classes—verbs, nouns, and a so-called pivot class. The grounds for distinguishing these classes were distributional, which is to say that words in English that would be classified as verbs had privileges of occurrence different from words that would be classified as nouns. The pivot class had a third privilege of occurrence, but it was grammatically heterogeneous from the point of view of adult English.

With three grammatical classes, there are $(3)^2 = 9$ possible sentences two words long, and $(3)^3 = 27$ possible sentences three words long. However, not all these nine and 27 different combinations are direct (untransformed) manifestations of the basic grammatical relations. Only four of the nine two-word combinations manifest in one way or another the basic grammatical relations. The other five are inadmissible from this point of view. An admissible combination would be $N + V$ (*Adam run*), corresponding to the subject-predicate relations, whereas an inadmissible combination would be $P + P$ (*my that*). Of the three-word combinations, only eight are direct manifestations of the basic grammatical relations. The remaining 19 are inadmissible. An admissible combination would be $V + N + N$ (*change Adam diaper*), corresponding to the verb-object and modifier-head relations, whereas an inadmissible combination would be $V + V + N$ (*come eat food*).

The findings are as follows. The first three samples of Adam's speech, comprising some 400 sentences, included examples of every admissible combination but no examples of inadmissible ones. Thus, the entire corpus corresponded to the basic grammatical relations; although *change Adam diaper* might have occurred, *come eat food* did not. See McNeill (1966) for details.

This outcome is puzzling from any point of view that excludes consideration of the base structure of sentences. The surface structures of adult sentences include many examples of inadmissible combinations of Adam's grammatical classes. *Come and eat this food*, for example, represents a common sentence type. To judge from some of Braine's (1963a) experiments, adults find it difficult to avoid learning patterns to which they are exposed, even when told that the patterns are not examples of what they are to acquire. If young children are equally sensitive to linguistic input (and presumably young children are more sensitive than adults), then something must have prevented Adam from saying *come eat food* after hearing examples like *come and eat this food* in parental speech. On the present hypothesis, the explanation is that Adam had limited knowledge of the transformations of English. He therefore could express the basic grammatical relations as they are defined in the base structure, but he had to exclude all those combinations of grammatical classes that violate the definitions in the surface structure.

If these observations are correct, then the order of development for Adam was, first, some kind of universal base structure; then English surface structure, as would be the case if acquisition proceeds through the addition of particular transformations to a foundation given by an inborn capacity for language. A similar conclusion is reached from an examination of the early speech of a child acquiring Japanese.

Evidence from Japanese[3]

I have recently begun collecting samples of speech from two children who live in Tokyo. Each child is visited twice a month in her home, where everything she says and everything said to her is tape-recorded. Altogether, four hours of speech are recorded each month from each child. The findings to be described below are based on the speech of one of these children, the older of the two, and was collected when she was 27 months old. In the interests of maintaining Brown's tradition of naming subjects in these studies, I call her Izanami, after the goddess in Japanese mythology who helped create the world.

Unlike English, Japanese is a postpositional language. Very roughly, postpositions correspond to prepositions, although not all postpositions can be translated as prepositions, and *vice versa*. Among the postpositions without an English equivalent are two that follow the surface-subject of sentences. They are *wa* and *ga*, and their presence

is obligatory. These postpositions never co-occur in sentences, but they do have nearly identical distributions, which is to say that whenever the surface-subject of a sentence is followed by *wa*, one may replace *wa* with *ga* and the sentence remains grammatical. The actual sentence contexts of *wa* and *ga* are therefore the same in adult speech, so distributional evidence cannot distinguish the two postpositions for a child.

However, two other characteristics distinguish *wa* from *ga*, and they lead to opposite predictions concerning Izanami's speech. One is the frequency of use in adult speech. It so happened that Izanami's mother used *wa* twice as often as *ga*, which ought to favor acquisition of *wa*. On the other hand, only *ga* is introduced by a transformation that operates on the configuration in the base structure that defines the subject of a sentence (Kuroda, 1965). *Wa* is introduced by another transformation that operates on a completely different aspect of the base structure. Thus, we have a natural experiment: What does the child produce, *wa* or *ga*? *Wa* would suggest that Izanami had acquired the most frequent element in parental speech and that the mechanism of acquisition is one that scans and learns adult surface features. *Ga*, in contrast, would suggest that Izanami is trying to express the basic grammatical relation of subject and that the mechanism of acquisition is one that selects elements from the surface structure only when they can be related to aspects of the base structure.

The facts are as follows. In the first eight hours of Izanami's recorded speech, she used *ga* 75 times and *wa* six times.[4] *Ga* was never used incor-

[3] I am indebted to Nobuko B. McNeill for her willingness to provide counsel on the intuitions of a native speaker, without which the following results would not have been obtained.

[4] There is a second sense of *ga*, signifying subjective certainty, which Izanami used 25 times. These occurrences have been omitted from the present count.

rectly and was rarely omitted when called for. *Wa*, on the other hand, was used at all times (save one) with the same word, and there were many contexts calling for *wa* into which Izanami placed no postposition at all. It thus seems clear that Izanami knows how to use *ga* and does not know how to use *wa*. We can conclude that she has available the basic grammatical relation of subject, as did Adam at roughly the same age.

But how could Izanami tell that *ga* and not *wa* was the postposition introduced from the basic grammatical relation of subject? The very facts that make this natural experiment possible —the superior frequency of *wa* and its distributional identity with *ga*—should have posed a problem for the child, leading her erroneously to select *wa* as the postposition deriving from the underlying subject of a sentence. Izanami did not face this problem, however, for a reason that is important to explore. The postpositions encode very different concepts, and children's inborn abilities evidently are sensitive only to the one represented by *ga*.

Wa is used whenever the predicate of a sentence *attributes* something to the surface-subject. Thus, the subjects of sentences that state general truths, subjects that function like the logical premises of judgments, words like *this* and *that* when they appear in definitions, as well as subjects that have attributes given to them, all take *wa*. Often this usage can be translated into English with the expression *as for*, as in the following examples:

As for that man, he is standing on the corner.
As for man, he is mortal.
As for cats, they eat fish.
As for this, it is a digital computer.
As for Mt. Everest, it is there.

In each case, an attribute—standing on

the corner, mortality, fish-eating, machinehood, or presence—is judged applicable to the subject of the sentence. Thus, they receive *wa*. *Ga* differs at just this point.

In the case of *ga*, the predicate of the sentence is not regarded as an inherent part of the subject. Instead, the two are merely linked together, in a connection usually conceived as momentary and accidental. *Ga* therefore is the postposition for description and covers any situation that does not involve attribution.

There is no standard translation of *ga* into English, but the Japanese equivalents of the following sentences would all take *ga*:

Some man-*ga* is standing on the corner.
The cat-*ga* is eating the fish.
Izanami-*ga* is making too much noise.
It-*ga* is on Mt. Everest this morning.

These sentences do not claim that it is an attribute of the man to stand on the corner, or of the cat to eat the fish, or of Izanami to make too much noise. In fact, they deny attribution and assert instead a momentary connection. Hence they receive *ga*.

It may appear from these examples that sentences with *ga* take *-ing* in English. The English progressive does often capture the significance of *ga*, but the two are not identical. One of the *wa* examples above is correctly translated into the progressive, and the sentence *The pencil is on the table* is a correct translation of a Japanese sentence with *ga*. English is ambiguous with respect to the distinction between attribution and nonattribution, whereas Japanese is not.[5]

The fact that Izanami acquired *ga*

---

[5] Negro dialect of American English apparently is not ambiguous in this way. One can say *he busy*, which signifies description and corresponds to *ga*, or *he be busy*, which signifies attribution and corresponds to *wa*.

and failed to acquire *wa* indicates that she is sensitive to the circumstances of nonattributive description but not to those of attribution proper. Only those adult sentences used under the first set of conditions were accepted as manifesting the basic grammatical relation of subject. It was on this basis that Izanami was led to select the correct postposition, even though it was relatively infrequent and distributionally indistinguishable from *wa*.

Presumably children exposed to English are selective in the same way, but this fact is obscured by the ambiguity of the language. It is the case, nonetheless, that *-ing* is the first verb inflection to be acquired by English-speaking children (Bellugi, 1964).

Reference and the development of grammar

There is a theory of grammatical development that runs something like the following: Children begin to learn the names of objects, events, qualities, etc., at around one year of age. They continue in this way for some six to eight months, adding new words all the time but never uttering two at once. Eventually, however, they learn the names of two or more objects, events, or qualities that appear together in certain stable physical relations. Then, two or three old names are combined into a single new name for the stable relation, and sentences like *doggie bite*, *baby sleep*, and *Adam change diaper* result.

If this is what children do, then Izanami's postposition would have been *wa* and not *ga*. Japanese syntax requires all such stable relations to receive *wa* in parental speech. Thus, Izanami does the opposite from what would be predicted on the theory that grammar arises from names. Indeed, since Izanami (like all children) does name things and events a great deal, thus showing that

she is capable of forming attributive connections, one must conclude from the absence of *wa* and the presence of *ga* that the development of reference and the development of grammar are quite separate in children.

Conclusion

Japanese and English are radically different languages, but children exposed to them do the same things. To Izanami and Adam can be added a third child whose native language was Russian. Here, too, the basic grammatical relations were honored in earliest speech (Slobin, 1966). Even more significant than the fact of such similarity in the face of diversity is the further fact that these children resemble each other in possessing abstract linguistic features, ones not present in the speech received from adults. Children do the same things where they do not have linguistic input. The conclusion therefore seems clear: English-, Russian-, and Japanese-speaking children resemble each other because of abilities possessed by all, and they are abilities, moreover, that are correctly described by statements in the theory of grammar.[6]

[6] One suggestion occasionally made is that these abilities are not uniquely linguistic. The hypothesis has profound implications, though for reasons usually overlooked by those who urge it. If it is the case that children possess general cognitive but not unique linguistic abilities, then cognition generally must have the universal forms described by the theory of grammar. The general case cannot lack universal features possessed by the special case. If this hypothesis has any merit, it means that linguistics, which is carried on under the relatively ideal conditions of ample and clear data, offers perhaps the best available means for gaining insight into intellectual development, thought, and the rational life in general. This is not to say, of course, that language and cognition are one and the same; the two may have the same universal form and yet differ in many details, just as languages have universal and idiosyncratic features.

All children go on to acquire the particular transformations of their native language—English, Russian, or Japanese, as it may be. Izanami had just begun this process at the stage described above, and Adam began shortly thereafter (Bellugi, 1964). Eventually, children acquire transformations which enable them to produce surface structures that do not consistently define the basic grammatical relations. An embedding transformation will have this effect, as will conjunction, deletion, and a host of other grammatical forms commonly employed in all languages. It is in this way that children develop a grammar with abstract features. For with these transformations the basic grammatical relations cease to be marked, although they continue to be honored, in the superficial forms of children's as well as of adults' speech.

References

Bellugi, Ursula, "The Emergence of Inflections and Negation Systems in the Speech of Two Children," paper read at New England Psychological Association, 1964.

Bever, T. G., J. A. Fodor, and W. Weksel, "On the Acquisition of Syntax: A Critique of 'Contextual Generalization,'" *Psychological Review*, **72** (1965), 467–482.

———, ———, and ———, "Is Linguistics Empirical?" *Psychological Review*, **72** (1965), 493–500.

Braine, M. D. S., "On Learning the grammatical Order of Words," *Psychological Review*, **70** (1963), 323–348.

———, "The Ontogeny of English Phrase Structure: The First Phase," *Language*, **39** (1963), 1–13.

———, "On the Basis of Phrase Structure: A Reply to Bever, Fodor, and Weksel," *Psychological Review*, **72** (1965), 483–492.

Brown, R., and Ursula Bellugi, "Three Processes in the Child's Acquisition of Syntax," *Harvard Educational Review*, **34** (1964), 133–151.

Chomsky, N., *Syntactic Structures*. The Hague: Mouton, 1957.

———, "A Review of B. F. Skinner's 'Verbal Behavior,'" *Language*, **35** (1959), 26–58.

———, "Current Issues in Linguistic Theory," in J. A. Fodor and J. J. Katz, eds., *The Structure of Language*. Englewood Cliffs, N. J.: Prentice-Hall, 1964, pp. 50–118.

———, *Aspects of the Theory of Syntax*. Cambridge, Mass.: M.I.T. Press, 1965.

———, and M. Halle, "Some Controversial Questions in Phonological Theory," *Journal of Linguistics*, **1** (1965), 97–138.

Fodor, J. A., "Could Meaning Be An r_m?" *Journal of Verbal Learning and Verbal Behavior*, **4** (1965), 73–81.

———, "How to Learn to Talk: Some Simple Ways," in F. Smith and G. A. Miller, eds., *The Genesis of Language: A Psycholinguistic Approach*. Cambridge, Mass.: M.I.T. Press, 1966.

Jenkins, J. J., and D. S. Palermo, "Mediation Processes and the Acquisition of Linguistic Structure," in Ursula Bellugi and R. Brown, eds., *The Acquisition of Language, Monographs of Social Research and Child Development*, **29**, No. 1 (1964), 141–169.

Katz, J. J., *Philosophy of Language*. New York: Harper & Row, Publishers, 1966.

———, and P. Postal, *An Integrated Theory of Linguistic Descriptions*. Cambridge, Mass.: M.I.T. Press, 1964.

Kuroda, S. Y., "Generative Grammatical Studies in Japanese," unpublished doctoral dissertation, M.I.T., 1965.

McNeill, D., "Developmental Psycholinguistics," in F. Smith and G. A. Miller, eds., *The Genesis of Language: A Psycholinguistic Approach*. Cambridge, Mass.: M.I.T. Press, 1966.

Miller, G. A., and N. Chomsky, "Finitary Models of Language Users," in R. D. Luce, R. R. Bush, and E. Galanter, eds., *Handbook of Mathematical Psychology*, Vol. 2. New York: John Wiley, & Sons, Inc., 1963.

Osgood, C. E., G. J. Suci, and P. H. Tannenbaum, *The Measurement of*

Meaning. Urbana, Ill.: University of Illinois Press, 1957.

Postal, P., "Constituent Structure: A Study of Contemporary Models of Syntactic Description," *International Journal of American Linguistics*, Vol. 30, No. 1. (1964).

Slobin, D. I., "The Acquisition of Russian as a Native Language," in F. Smith and G. A. Miller, eds., *The Genesis of Language: A Psycholinguistic Approach.* Cambridge, Mass.: M.I.T. Press, 1966.

Sequential
Verbal Behavior

16   NEAL F. JOHNSON

One of the interesting developments during the past two decades in the area of verbal learning and verbal behavior has been an increasing concern with "what a subject is doing" as he is acquiring and executing verbal associations. This changing concern, along with an increasing sophistication in both our substantiative knowledge regarding the processes involved and the research techniques being used, is evident in our current research endeavors in a number of different ways.

One of the most obvious differences between today's work and that of three decades ago is the increasing recognition and appreciation of the analytic advantage of paired-associate tasks over serial-learning techniques. A correlated event is the increasing tendency to view learning as a multiple-stage process (e.g., see Battig). A second line of change is the increasing use of inferred events as explanatory devices. While, to a degree, the verbal learning work, both today and in the 1930's, has been concerned with defining the functional relationships between independent and dependent variables, there seems to be a greater tendency today to use the manipulations of the independent variable as an indirect estimate of variations or changes in some implicit

process. A related event is the tendency to approach learning with a somewhat less mechanistic view (e.g., the work on stimulus selection). Finally, there has been a change from verbal learning as a rather parochial endeavor to an increasing recognition of its contribution to our understanding of basic learning processes and behavior theory in general. The recognition is evident both in the nature of recent conferences (e.g., Melton, 1964, and the current conference) and the research on such phenomena as short-term memory, verbal conditioning, the effect of verbal responses on discrimination learning and classical conditioning.

In some very real respects the current work on the sequential characteristics of verbal behavior represents a manifestation of all these developments. Certainly, the attempts to account for verbal sequencing in terms of processes characteristic of all learning situations reflects a concern with behavioral sequencing in general (e.g., Deese, 1961). The work on Yngve's (1960) depth hypothesis (Martin, 1965) and the utilization of structure during learning and recall (e.g., Johnson, 1965a) clearly supposes implicit events during learning and response generation. Finally, much of the research on verbal sequencing has resulted directly from an attempt to study the response-integration stage of learning.

These considerations would suggest that much of the current work in psycholinguistics falls within the same tradition as does the current work in verbal learning, and furthermore, many of the issues under examination by verbal learners are the same problems that are being attacked in the current psycholinguistic research. Indeed, many of the individuals doing work with complex language behavior are doing so because that form of behavior seems uniquely suited to answering specific questions that originally arose in their own verbal learning research.

It would appear that the unique contribution to our evolving conception of the learning process that is being made by the verbal sequencing research is in the area of response integration. More specifically, the work has tended

becomes conditioned to the response-produced stimuli. The response is learned or integrated when an associative assembly like the following has been established. Each response element produces the stimulus which elicits the next element.

By and large, that conception of response learning, based on the direct association between elements, seems to have been based on a serial-anticipation learning model. As such, there were few apparent difficulties with the model. That view of response learning also received support in the late 1940's and 1950's from the conceptual advances made by information theory. Indeed, the research on the facilitating effects of contextual constraints on response production, perception, and learning seemed quite in accord with that model, with the exception that it was necessary to include the stimulus consequences of several preceding re-

to center on the nature of the associative assembly that is established when a response becomes integrated and the way that assembly is used to produce the response at the time of recall.

Hull (1930) presented an account of the process of response integration which assumed that, initially, the response elements in a sequence are elicited by external stimuli, and the order of the elements is determined by the order of external stimuli. However, as each response element is produced it has afferent consequences which have the properties of stimuli. These response-produced stimuli are then part of the stimulus complex which exists at the time the next element is produced, and, consequently, the element

sponses as the eliciting stimulus for each element (e.g., Gonzalez and Cofer, 1959). In addition, the model had great intuitive appeal because of both its simplicity and the fact that it seems as if we take our preceding behavior into account as we are producing a sequence.

The first serious attack on that chaining model was presented by Lashley (1951) in his consideration of language behavior. He suggested that language responses, like many other forms of serial behavior, occur at such a high rate that it is not plausible to assume that successive elements are dependent upon the stimulus consequences of their predecessors. The time between elements is too brief. In addition, he pointed out that an essential characteristic of most serially ordered behavior is that it conforms to a kind of "schema of action." In language, if we simply generated sequences according to the associative bonds between words, most of our utterances would look quite peculiar and meaningless. Because of that, Lashley suggested that in an account of serial ordering we must include some kind of central determining event which not only selects the response elements that will occur but, at least in part, will determine the order in which the elements will occur within the response sequence. For structured and meaningful language sequences, then, Lashley presented a good case against a rigidly behavioristic account of response generation which assumes that response elements are elicited by specific response-to-response associations.

Generally, the complex situations that Lashley used to argue against the associative-chain model were not those the model was initially designed to explain (e.g., serial-anticipation learning of nonsense syllables and maze learning). In addition, it would seem that one could explain away Lashley's objections for these two cases. However, recent research on serial-anticipation learning would suggest that even in that case such response-to-response associations may not be used spontaneously, although it does appear that *S*s can use them in some situations (Postman and Stark, 1967).

These considerations would suggest that a model of serial response integration based on simple response-to-response associations will have to be elaborated, if not rejected. While the ideas expressed by Lashley (1951) offered some suggestions as to the general format an alternative account should take, he provided few specific conceptual tools. Therefore, if one

examines the work on this problem during the 1950's, it is quite apparent that there was an absence of theoretical explanations, and the accounts given were data-oriented descriptions.

Approximations to English

One of the ways in which we have attempted to explore serial order in language is to use what most basically are transfer tasks in order to sample the nature of the associative system that speakers establish as a result of their previous language experience. If, as Lashley (1951) suggested, we do not learn and produce language in terms of word-to-word associations, then the problem is to identify what has been learned. The transfer studies were designed to explore that question.

In English, as in most languages, not all words follow all other words with equal probability. If a matrix were to be constructed whose dimensions were all-the-words-in-English by all-the-words-in-English, and the cell entries were observed transitional probabilities, the probabilities would vary from zero on up. The language would be redundant to the extent that there was variation in the probabilities. If another matrix were to be constructed with the rows being all possible two-word combinations and the columns being all the words in the language, again there would be variation in the magnitude of the cell entries, but there would be a greater tendency for these values to cluster at the lower and upper ends of the probability distribution, with fewer values in the middle. Other matrices could be constructed in the same manner, but with the number of determining words in each row margin increasing from matrix to matrix. One of the major effects of increasing the contextual determination of each row would be an increasing tendency for the probabilities to cluster around the upper and lower values of the probability distribution. In addition, if these matrices were used to construct language sequences with high transitional probabilities, the matrices with the greatest number of determining words in each row margin would produce the most "English-like" sequences.

While such a set of matrices could be constructed, and the sequences generated by using them would approximate English in proportion to the number of determining words in the row entries, there are a number of arguments against supposing that the matrices would represent a description of what had been learned when someone acquired the language. In addition to Lashley's points, Miller, Galanter, and Pribram (1960) pointed out that the number of entries in such a matrix would probably exceed the number of seconds in the average childhood. In addition, speakers generate novel responses quite frequently; therefore, at the very minimum, the model would have to be elaborated to include some generalization mechanism. (For a more detailed account of these problems see Chomsky, 1957; Miller, Galanter, and Pribram, 1960; Lees, 1964.) It is important to note, then, that while the matrices could be used to produce English-like sequences, they could not be used to explain how speakers produce those sequences.

One of the first attempts to define the nature of the influence of language habits on learning was a study by Miller and Selfridge (1950). They were concerned with whether Ss could use the increasing approximations to English that would be produced by the above matrices to facilitate learning. They attempted to approximate sequences that would be produced by the matrices by giving Ss sequences of varying lengths as determining context and asking them to construct a sentence containing the sequence. The first word of the context was then removed and the word the S used after the last word of the context was placed at the end; the resulting sequence was then used as a context for the next S, etc. The order of the approximation to English thereby produced was equal to one plus the number of words in the determining context. A zero-order approximation represented words chosen at random, and a first-order approximation was constructed by selecting words according to their relative probability of occurrence in the language.

The materials used by Miller and Selfridge were sequences of 10, 20, 30, and 50 words which varied in approximation to English from zero-order to seventh-order, plus some passages from texts. The sequences were recorded, and after each one was played to the Ss, they wrote down as many words as they could recall from the sequences. The Ss' responses were scored for the total number of correct words, without regard to the order in which they were written.

The results of the study indicated that as statistical approximation to English increased, the number of words recalled also increased. In addition, Miller and Selfridge reported that the facilitating effect from the constraint seemed to increase as the length of the sequence increased. Finally, the shape of the function relating approximation-to-English to degree-of-learning was negatively accelerated, with most of the effect occurring at the lower end of the scale of approximation and little change from the fifth-order approximation to text. Richardson and Voss (1960) have replicated these results.

A conservative interpretation of the results would suggest that because Ss did learn the English-like sequences more rapidly, they probably transferred a set of associations to the task which they had established in their previous use of language. The issue, however, concerns the nature of the associations that the *S*s transferred. Miller and Selfridge (1950) appeared to suggest that two factors might have been operating. First, they interpreted the results as suggesting that the sequences increased in meaningfulness as the degree of approximation increased. Furthermore, they argued that their curves suggested that meaningfulness was not a dichotomous variable, because there was a gradual increase in degree of learning from the zero-order approximation to the fifth-order approximation and no discontinuity between text and nontext material. Sharp (1958) and Richardson and Voss (1960) also obtained that effect. The second point made was that the materials would tend to preserve the short-range associations that the *S*s had established in their use of language as the degree of approximation increased. It is not entirely clear whether Miller and Selfridge saw these two points as just different ways of saying the same thing or whether they conceived of them as independent sources of transfer. Regardless of their position, however, it is possible to view these sources as making independent contributions to learning.

In addition to the above points, there are a number of other issues that must be examined if one is to detail the nature of the specific transfer effect that was demonstrated in the Miller and Selfridge experiment. For example, as approximation to English increases, there does appear to be an increase in the relative meaningfulness of the materials. However, it is also clear that there is an increase in the degree to which the materials approximate the grammar of the language.

The contribution to learning made by increasing grammaticality may not be the same as that from increasing meaningfulness. Finally, there might be interitem associations within the sequences that increase in strength as the degree of approximation increases, and it may be that these changes are independent of the increasing strength of the grammatical habits the *S*s are able to sample (Rosenberg, 1966). The critical issue to note seems to be that the function representing the relationship between learning ease and approximation-to-English may not reflect just a change in the strength of the associations that the *S*s are sampling, but also may reflect a change in the nature of the associations that the *S*s are transferring. That is, what the *S*s are transferring when learning the high-order approximations may not be the same as what they are transferring when learning the middle or low-order approximations.

There are now data available demonstrating the possibility that all the above mentioned sources of transfer may have an effect on learning. Marks and Miller (1964) had four groups of *S*s learn language sequences. For two of the groups the sequences were words from meaningful sentences, but one of the groups learned the words in a correct grammatical order while the other group learned the words in a scrambled order. The other two groups were similar, except the basic sentences they learned were meaningless. The grammatical and meaningful sentences were learned the most rapidly, and the scrambled meaningless sentences were learned the least rapidly. The interesting result, however, was that the meaningless but grammatical sequences and the meaningful but ungrammatical sequences were learned at about the same rate and their learning curves fell about halfway between the other two curves. It appears from these results that grammar and meaning may make approximately equal but independent contributions to learning.

An experiment was performed at the Ohio State laboratory (Johnson, 1965b) in an effort to examine the possibility that Ss might use short-range associations when learning word sequences. Two sets of eight paired-associate responses were constructed, each response consisting of a string of seven words. For the responses in the experimental list the first word was a Kent-Rosanoff (Russell and Jenkins, 1954) stimulus and the second was its primary response. The third word was another unrelated stimulus, the fourth word was its primary response, and the fifth word was the primary response to the fourth. The sixth word was unrelated to the fifth, but the seventh word was the primary response to the sixth. Therefore, strings like *lion tiger justice peace war salt pepper* were constructed in which two word-to-word transitions had very low associations spanning them and five transitions had high associations. The control set of seven-word responses was constructed using stimulus and response words from the Kent-Rosanoff list, but care was taken to insure that none of the words in a response sequence had any of the other words in the same response sequence as a strong association. Therefore, there were low associations spanning all of the transitions within these sequences. Digits were used as stimuli, and the Ss learned the task to a criterion of 14 trials.

As expected, the experimental list was learned more rapidly than the control list, suggesting that the Ss were able to use the associations that were provided. In order to get an index of the rate at which succeeding word pairs within the high-association sequences were integrated, the condi-

tional probability was computed that each word was wrong, given the preceding word was right. Therefore, the greater the probability, the slower the transition was integrated. If the Ss used the specific associations that were provided, then the probabilities should have been higher for the low-association transitions than for the high-association transitions. That result was obtained. As a matter of fact, the effect was so great that every S had a higher probability of a transitional error on the low-association transitions. It seemed clear from these results that Ss can use specific word-to-word associations as they attempt to integrate response chains, and the effect seems to be quite localized.

These studies demonstrate that not only are the Miller and Selfridge results highly reliable, but the explanation of the effect may not be as simple as initially assumed. There are a number of different transfer effects that separately, or in combination, may account for the data. Therefore, if we are to use a transfer situation to study the process of sequential integration of a response, it seems necessary to unravel the gross effect into its separate components.

Sequential Constraint

At this time the critical conceptual problem regarding response integration seems to be not with our understanding of the way in which S acquires the pool of items that make up the response, but rather with how to characterize the system of associations that results in the S's ability to generate the pool of items in the correct order. Put in other terms, we have a very limited understanding (both empirically and conceptually) of what we mean by the term *sequential constraint*. Therefore, if we are to use the approximation-to-

English technique, it is important to determine the extent to which the effect can be attributed to sequential associations or constraints.

As a first step it seems worthwhile to examine the rather surprising effect obtained by Miller and Selfridge that there was no increase in recall scores from the fifth-order approximation to the material taken from texts. In part, that could have been the result of the scoring method they used. As sequences become more like English, they should increase in both meaningfulness and grammaticality. Not taking into consideration the order in which the words were recalled, the scores probably reflected the increasing semantic determination or relatedness of the items within the sequences but not the increasing determination of word order that might have been provided by the increasing approximation to the grammar of the language. It could easily be the case that semantic determination or meaningfulness reaches a maximum by around a fifth-order approximation, but it seems clear that the determination of order by grammar should increase up to the text material.

Marks and Jack (1952) examined the issue using an experiment similar to that of Miller and Selfridge. They reported that scores based on words recalled in the correct order clearly showed advantages for text material over the higher-order approximations. While these data suggested that sequential constraints may have been an important variable, Miller (1956b) pointed out that the difference may have resulted from a difference in the nature of the text material used in the two studies.

Deese and Kaufman (1957), also using a free-recall procedure, were concerned about the order of recall of items from sequences that varied in degree of approximation. If Ss do use sequential constraints, there should be a shift from the usual recency effect obtained when using an unrelated set of words to a primacy effect for lists that represent high orders of approximation or text. They used the Miller and Selfridge 50-word lists and asked the Ss to free recall after a single presentation. When the response protocols were scored for the percentage of correct responses that came from the first half of the list, there was a clear and significant shift from a marked recency effect for the zero-order approximation to an equally marked primacy effect for the material taken from texts. Such a primacy effect appears when Ss learn short sentences as paired-associate responses as well (Johnson, 1965a). Deese and Kaufman (1957) also presented Ss with ten statements in a connected passage and asked them to free recall after a single presentation. The mean order of recall was perfectly correlated with the order of presentation, and the probability of recall showed a primacy effect.

Deese and Kaufman suggested that their recall curves for the various approximations to English gradually approached a standard serial-position curve as the sequences became more English-like. However, the results of Mandler and Mandler (1964) and the work at the Ohio State laboratory indicate that the shape of the serial-position curve for a sentence may be more a function of the grammatical structure of the sentence, and the function that the various words serve within the sentence, than the serial-position of the words (see also Simpson, 1965). In addition, the curves reported by Deese and Kaufman were somewhat more irregular than those usually obtained from the serial learning of unstructured lists.

Postman and Adams (1960) have also provided evidence supporting the possibility that there may be an increasing effect of sequential constraints as approximation to English increases. They capitalized on the fact that intentional learners are better than incidental learners in the recall of serial order (Postman, Adams, and Bohm, 1956). If increasing approximations to English result in an increase in usable sequential constraints, then there should be an increasing advantage for intentional learning as approximation to English increases. That result was obtained.

Another point made by Deese and Kaufman was that the shape of the curve relating recall to degree of approximation may, in part, have been influenced by what their data suggested was a change in recall strategy as approximation increased. Waugh (1961) has reported data which indicated that the shape of the learning curve for lists of words was different under conditions of free recall than under conditions of serial recall. When she scored for total number of words correctly recalled, regardless of order of recall, there was a linear relationship between trials and recall for the Ss instructed to recall in the correct order, but the typical negatively accelerated curve was obtained for free recall. Her data appeared to indicate that for the first few trials the free-recall group was superior to the serial-recall group, with a reversal occurring after the fourth trial. If there is an increasing tendency for Ss to recall in serial order as degree of approximation increases, as the curves reported by Deese and Kaufman would suggest, then part of the failure to get an increase in transfer beyond the fifth-order approximation may have been the result of a change in the recall strategy.

Colman (1963) looked at the relation between sequential constraint and recall behavior in somewhat more detail. He

argued that one problem some of the other studies might have had is that there were differences in the difficulty of the items or words in the various approximations to English. In particular, the text passages appeared to be difficult. He made an attempt to control both the cultural frequency of the words used and their mean length in number of syllables. When he did that he found significant differences in free recall between fifth-order approximations and text material. In addition to scoring for the correct recall of single words, he scored for the number of two-word sequences recalled; the number of three-word sequences; etc., up to the number of seventeen-word sequences recalled. When scoring for number of single words recalled, the function relating recall and degree of approximation was negatively accelerated and looked similar to that reported by Miller and Selfridge and Richardson and Voss (except for the significant advantage for the text material). However, as the size of the scored sequence increased from one word to seventeen words, the shape of the function showed a gradual and regular shift from negative acceleration to positive acceleration. These results would suggest, then, that the failure of Miller and Selfridge to obtain a difference between text and fifth-order approximations may have been a function of both the nature of the material they used and the fact that their scoring method did not take sequential constraints into consideration.

In the Colman study, as the length of the scorable sequence increased, there was also an increase in the degree to which the scores reflected the use of sequential constraints. That being the case, it is interesting to note that as the length of the scorable sequence increased there was a shift towards the higher approximations in the point at which the curve had its greatest rate of acceleration. That is, it appeared that length of the sequential dependency within a sequence was correlated with its degree of approximation to English. That point received added support from an experiment by Tulving and Patkau (1962). They also used a free-recall procedure and scored their Ss for both the number of sequences of responses (or chunks) that occurred in the order of presentation (regardless of the number of items within each recall sequence) and for the average number of items within the sequences recalled. They report that there was little variation in the number of sequences or chunks recalled related to degree of approximation, but there was a marked relation between mean size of the recalled sequence or chunk and order of approximation. Again, the span of constraint seemed to increase with degree of approximation.

The fact that Colman obtained a change in the shape of the function as the scores reflected the influence of sequential constraints to a greater degree argues that the influence of these constraints on recall may have been rather small when Ss were learning the sequences representing the lower-degrees of approximation to English. If that was the case, then it is apparent that some other variable or variables affected the recall of the sequences in the Miller and Selfridge experiment.

Deese (1961) suggested that the change in performance from zero-order approximations to first-order approximations may reflect an increase in the accuracy of the Ss' guessing behavior, and Cofer (1961) has suggested that there may be some associative factor operating as well. When Deese corrected recall performance for both the zero-order and first-order approximations, on the basis of an empirically deter-mined chance level, there was very little difference between the corrected means for the two types of sequence.

It is also quite possible that the advantage for the items from the middle approximations (i.e., second-order to fifth-order) may have stemmed from nonsequential interitem associations. It seems entirely reasonable to suppose that such associations should increase in strength as the item sampling more closely approximates that which occurs in the spontaneous use of language. The fact that such apparent semantically determined and nonse-quential associations exert an influence on recall is well demonstrated (Bousfield, 1953; Jenkins and Russell, 1952). In addition, the degree of such clustering in recall is related to performance (Tulving, 1962). Finally, the data reported by Colman (1963) would indicate that as the scoring procedure differentially favored sequential versus nonsequential clustering, there was a relatively greater reduction in recall for the middle degrees of approximation.

These considerations would suggest that the variation in performance related to the scale of approximation-to-English may not reflect variation in a unitary process, but at least three different processes that exert their influence at different points along the scale. For present purposes the primary concern is with the transfer of sequential constraints, and the data appear to indicate that the major influence of such constraints tends to be in the higher orders of approximation and text.

Assuming that the other two variables are word frequency and nonsequential interitem associations, the results of an experiment by Tulving and Patkau (1962) can be taken as approximating the function relating sequential constraint and recall. In addition, the data illustrate the way that function is related to the degree of approximation to English. The orders of approximation they used were first, third, fifth, and seventh, plus text material. They controlled for word frequency by having one list at all approximations consist of only Thorndike-Lorge (1944) 100 per million words, and another list at each approximation contained only words occurring four times per million (except for function words). A second aspect of their procedure curtailed differences between approximations in the strength of nonsequential associations. They made up lists of the words from the two frequencies and then selected one at random from the appropriate list. The Ss were then given the determining context and asked if they could make up a sentence within which the randomly selected item would occur as the word following the last word in the context. If they could, the item was placed at the end of the context, with the first word in the context being removed. Then that sequence, along with another randomly selected word, was presented to a new S, etc. In that the words were selected in that manner, it would appear that the nonsequential interitem associations should have been somewhat more equal across approximations than was the case for the previous studies.

For the sequences made up of high-frequency words the expected positively accelerated function was obtained, with the greatest effect being from the fifth-order approximation to text. The curve, then, was just the reverse of the one reported by Miller and Selfridge and, as expected, the greatest discrepancy between the curves from the two experiments was for the middle-degrees of approximation. It is also interesting to note the function obtained for the low-frequency lists. In that the words were relatively rare, sequential associa-

tions between the words would have been extremely low or nonexistent. While there was a significant increase in recall across approximations for these lists, the rate of increase was significantly less than for the high-frequency words, and there was no increase in recall from the fifth-order approximation to text.

The Effect of Grammaticality on Learning

The effect on learning of increasing the degree of grammaticality is much the same as increasing the degree of approximation to English (Frankart, 1964). The similarity of the effect probably results from the fact that the two scales are highly correlated. For example, Colman (1963) had a group of linguists rank, in terms of grammaticality, a set of sequences representing various degrees of approximation to English. His results showed a gradual increase in mean rank from zero-order approximations to fifth-order approximations, with some irregularity in the form of the function from the fifth-order approximation to text.

The concept of *degree of grammaticality* has been questioned on the grounds that it does not represent a real dimension for native speakers (Hill, 1961). For example, when Frankart (1964) collected the rating data for the sequences used in the above study, the Ss were asked to indicate whether they thought there were degrees of grammaticality or whether an utterance was either grammatical or not grammatical, with nothing in between those values. Exactly half of the Ss indicated they thought the variable was dichotomous and half thought it was continuous. It is hard to know what the data mean, however, because there were no differences in either the means or standard deviations of the ratings for the two groups. Rating data were not collected from the Ss who learned the sequences, but their performance indicated a systematic relationship between rated degree of grammaticality and learning ease. In addition, the data reported by Maclay and Sleator (1960) would indicate that Ss' judgments as to the grammaticality of sequences are independent of their judgments regarding the meaningfulness and ordinariness of the sequences.

In this regard a recent experiment by Colman (1965) is of interest. He attempted to operationalize the concept of degree of grammaticality. As he pointed out, the immediate-constituent (IC) structure of a sentence can be conceived as consisting of several levels of units. For example, at the highest level there is only one unit— the whole sentence. At the lowest level each word or morpheme is a separate unit. The levels in between these two points might be viewed as consisting of phrases of various sizes (e.g., *noun phrase* plus *verb phrase*, or *article* plus *modified noun* plus *verb* plus *noun phrase*, etc.). The words used to make up the sequences were selected at random with the exception that the rules of grammar must allow them to occur within the units for which they were being selected (e.g., a verb could not be selected for a noun phrase). Furthermore, the order of words within units was random, with only the order of the units being determined. For example, at the highest level, the sentence, only words that could occur within that unit were selected (in that case, any English word), but the order of the words within the sentence unit was random and the sequences looked like first-order approximations to English. If, at another level in the IC analysis, the sentence was characterized as a

noun phrase plus *verb phrase*, the sequence representing that level consisted of a random ordering of words that could occur in a noun phrase, followed by a random ordering of words that could occur within a verb phrase, etc.

In his first experiment Ss were given a set of sequences generated in the above manner and were asked to rank them in terms of their degree of grammaticality. The result was a significant agreement between the mean rank order of the sequences and the operation used to generate them. In a second experiment, Ss learned the sequences, and Colman reported that trials to criterion decreased significantly as grammaticality increased.

It is reasonably clear from these experiments that the behavioral effects of variation along a scale of grammaticality is very similar to the effects of variation along a scale of approximation to English. In addition, the sequences representing the various points along the two scales look very similar to one another. That being the case, there may be a question regarding the extent to which one can infer, from behavior, that there is variation in some unitary psychological process correlated with variation along the grammaticality scale.

Word-to-Word Associations

The next problem is to explain the apparent discontinuity that occurs at the fifth-order approximation. That is, as mentioned above, on intuitive grounds one would expect the obtained positively accelerated function. The sequences below the seventh-order approximation do not look like grammatical English sequences, whereas the seventh-order and text material do, although the results of Colman

(1963) might suggest otherwise. That intuition is supported, to a degree, by the fact that Tulving and Patkau (1962) reported that the curve relating mean size of the sequential chunks in recall to degree of approximation was very nearly the same as that relating total number of items recalled and degree of approximation.

In part, these considerations raise a question as to whether the sequential constraints reflect item-to-item associations. If that were what the functions reflected, one would expect a more nearly linear relationship between approximation and both total number of items recalled and size of the recall chunks.

Johnson (1966a) has also reported data that question the degree to which Ss use and form word-to-word associations when they learn grammatical materials. In that experiment the Ss formed an association between word pairs in a paired-associate task. After original learning they were presented with another PA task in which they were to learn sentences as responses to digit stimuli. The sentences contained, as adjacent words, the word pairs from the original learning list.

The results of the experiment indicated that the rate at which the word pairs were integrated, when they occurred within sentences, was not very closely related to the degree of original learning. Furthermore, whether there was any transfer at all appeared to be more dependent upon the structural characteristics of the word pairs within the sentences, than on degree of original learning, (e.g., there was significant transfer from original learning to sentence learning for adjective-noun pairs, but no such effect for noun-verb pairs). In addition, Johnson (1965) reported that the rate at which a word pair within a sentence was integrated (as measured in terms of the probability of their co-occurrence during learning) was not related to the rate the same word pair was learned in a simple PA task (also see Martin, Davidson, and Williams, 1965).

In that the earlier work indicated that word-to-word associations consistently have a sizable and localized effect when Ss learn sequences of words that do not closely approximate English, Frankart (1964) had Ss learn word sequences that varied in grammaticalness. The sequences sampled four points along a scale of rated degree of grammaticality, and the sequences that any S learned were homogeneous with respect to that variable. The sequences were learned as paired-associate responses. The lowest degree of grammaticality consisted of random sequences of words, and the list representing the highest degree of grammaticality contained only perfectly grammatical sentences. Half of the Ss in each group first learned a PA task which formed an association between a pair of words that later occurred adjacently in the sequences they learned. The rate at which the critical word pairs were integrated during the learning of the sequences was measured by determining the conditional probability that the first word of the pair would occur when the second member did not. That probability should be negatively correlated with rate of integration.

As expected, there was an overall facilitating effect on the critical word pairs from the prior word-to-word association. In addition, the rate at which the word pairs were integrated increased with increasing degrees of grammaticality. The interesting result, however, was the significant interaction between degree of grammaticality and strength of prior association. As degree of grammaticalness increased there was a marked decrease in the facilitation from the prior association. For the two lowest degrees of grammaticalness there was a sizable facilitating effect, but there was little or no effect for the two highest degrees of grammaticalness.

The results of these experiments would appear to question the extent to which the influence of increasing sequential constraints can be explained in terms of increasing word-to-word associations. In general, *S*s' ability to transfer such specific associations to a sentence learning task is very limited.

The Use of Grammar in Learning

The Frankart (1964) data, combined with the earlier discussion, results in a rather paradoxical situation. While the data appear to suggest that the effect of sequential constraints is limited to the high degrees of approximation, the Frankart study indicated that the influence of word-to-word associations was limited to the lower degrees of approximation. The paradox would be eliminated if it could be assumed that sequential constraints do not result from specific interitem associations but from some nonassociative "schema" which restricts the order of recall (as suggested by Lashley, 1951). That is, structure or grammar *per se* may both facilitate learning and determine the order of recall.

There have been several studies that have demonstrated that *S*s can use rules to facilitate learning even when the *S*s' knowledge of these rules cannot be characterized in terms of specific item-to-item associations (Aborn and Rubenstein, 1952; Rubenstein and Aborn, 1954; Miller, 1958). For example, in the Rubenstein and Aborn experiment *S*s learned sequences of nonsense syllables. Before learning the sequences the *S*s learned that the nonsense syllables were organized into

classes and, within the sequences, there were certain constraints as to which classes could follow which other classes. Their results indicated that the learning rates for the sequences were positively correlated with the degree of constraint. Miller had *S*s learn sequences of letters that were either randomly generated or generated from a set of rules. The specific letters that occurred within the two kinds of sequence were the same, with the redundancy being in their order of occurrence. The Miller experiment differed from that of Rubenstein and Aborn in that the *S*s had no prior knowledge regarding what elements could occur within the sequences, and they were not informed of the nature of the redundancy. Even under these conditions, however, there was a marked superiority for the redundant list, and the effect was apparent on the first trial.

In addition to the above studies, there have been several experiments which have attempted to use English grammar and controlled interitem associations by using semantically anomalous sentences. For example, Marks and Miller (1964) had one group of *S*s learn sentences like *Pink accidents cause sleeping storms* as opposed to *Accidents pink storms sleeping cause*. The grammatical sequences were learned more rapidly than the random sequences. Similarly, we had three groups of *S*s learning sentences as paired-associate responses. One group learned sentences like *The house across the street burned down* while another group learned a grammatically similar but semantically anomalous sentence like *The falsity calling flat sleep sang white*. The third group learned a random ordering of the anomalous sentence (e.g., *The sang white falsity sleep calling flat*). As expected, the learning rates for the three groups were all significantly different from one another. In addition, when

*S*s learn sentences as PA responses, the conditional probability that each word in the sentence will be wrong, given the preceding word was right, is highly correlated with the grammatical characteristics of the word-to-word transition in question (Johnson, 1965). When those conditional probabilities were computed for the grammatical but semantically anomalous sentences, the result was a pattern of conditional probabilities that looked about the same as those obtained for the meaningful sentences (e.g., they correlated .89) but very different from those obtained from the ungrammatical and anomalous sequences. These data would suggest, then, that there may be some residual effect on learning behavior from grammar when meaningfulness and word-to-word associations are severely reduced. It should be pointed out, however, that while reliable differences are consistently obtained between grammatical and ungrammatical material, the absolute differences are relatively small when compared to the differences between anomalous and meaningful sequences when both are grammatically correct.

In an effort to reduce the influence of meaning and prior associations to an even greater degree, several investigators have used nonsense words that are tagged with English inflections so as to produce sequences that appear to be grammatically correct. One of the first studies was an experiment by Swanson (reported by Osgood, 1957). His *S*s learned sequences like *The maff velms oothly um the glox nerfs* as opposed to *Maff velm ooth um glox nerf*. He reported that even though the grammatical sequences contained more items, they were learned more rapidly.

Epstein (1961, 1962, 1963) has reported similar results. He also used inflected sequences of nonsense words to form the grammatical sentences. His procedure was to present a sequence to a *S* for a very brief exposure, and then the *S* was to try to recall as much of the sequence as possible. The exposures for a single sentence continued until the *S* was able to recall the sentence perfectly. As was the case in the Swanson experiment, the grammatical sequences were learned more rapidly than the uninflected sequences of nonsense words. Epstein (1962) later replicated that result. James Martin (personal communication) has also obtained that effect and he reports that learning rate appears to be a function of the cultural frequency of the structure.

While these results indicate that grammar can have an influence on learning, the facilitating effect is rather small. In addition, the effect has not always been obtained when using nonsense materials. For example, Rosenberg (1964) reported that when he used short sequences (i.e., four nonsense words plus an English function word) and controlled for interitem formal similarity (no letter was used more than once in a sequence), he was unable to obtain any facilitating effect from grammar. Moran (1965), in an honors thesis at Pennsylvania State University, used Epstein's (1961) method of presentation and had sequences that were either four or seven words in length. Her procedure, then, was the same as that used by Epstein, except, like Rosenberg (1964), she used only CVCs as the word roots and controlled for intrasequence formal similarity. Her results showed no difference in learning rate between the sequences of CVCs and the sequences of CVCs that were inflected to make them look like grammatical sentences. In addition, there was no reliable tendency for the difference between the two types of sequence to increase as the number of words in the sequences increased. The only real difference between the Moran and

Rosenberg experiments and those reported by Epstein and Swanson was in the form of the nonsense-word roots they used. The two earlier experiments used more "word-like" nonsense forms, while both Rosenberg and Moran used CVCs and controlled for intrasequence formal similarity. Although these two experiments do not contradict the earlier work, they suggest that not only is the facilitating effect of grammar quite small, but it may be quite delicate as well (see Epstein, 1962).

Response Units

In addition to the facilitating effect that grammar may have on learning, it might also affect behavior by defining usable response units. Miller (1956a, 1956b) has pointed out an interesting distinction between the way in which Ss handle a discrimination task and the way in which they handle a memory task. Where the accuracy of judgment in a discrimination task appears to be dependent upon the number of alternative stimuli that can occur (for a review of the data, see Miller, 1956a), the accuracy of recall in a memory task seems to be relatively less dependent upon the size of the universe from which the items were drawn. For memory, the length of the sequence seems to be the important variable. For example, Miller (1956c) describes an experiment in which Ss were requested to learn sequences of symbols that varied in length from 10 items to 50 items. In addition, the sequences varied in terms of the number of different symbols that could occur within them, (i.e., 2, 8, or 32). He reports that while there were great differences in learning rate correlated with the number of items in the sequences, there was no difference in learning rate between the sequences constructed using only eight different symbols and those constructed using 32 different symbols. On the basis of these data he argues that performance in a memory task is more a function of the number of units to be retained than the uncertainty or information load of the individual items.

Miller (1956a) has suggested, then, that while absolute discrimination is a function of the number of bits of information conveyed by the stimulus, memory is limited by the number of chunks of information, and the amount of information carried by each chunk can vary over a considerable range. In order to account for the variation in information load of memory chunks, Miller (1956a) has proposed a process he calls recoding. Most simply, recoding involves integrating a set of responses into a single unit. If the S is asked to retain the set of response elements, he does so by retaining a single symbol representing the entire set. At recall the S simply recalls the symbol and then applies a set of previously learned translation rules to produce or generate the specific elements.

Miller (1956a) illustrated the recoding process with an experiment in which Ss learned to rename short sequences of binary digits with a single label (e.g., $00 = 0$, $01 = 1$, $10 = 2$, and $11 = 3$). Their memory span for the binary digits was then tested and was found to be greater than it was before they had learned the recoding scheme. In addition, the increase in span appeared to be a function of the degree to which the recoding scheme had been learned.

Miller (1956b) proposed that when Ss are faced with a learning task which exceeds their memory span, they attempt to reorganize or recode the material into chunks whose number does not exceed the span. He labeled this recoding process during learning *unitization* and suggested that the chunks may be unitized into higher-order chunks as well. When learning is complete, the S has learned a hierarchy of recoded response units and is able to produce the sequence by recalling a few information-rich units at the top of the hierarchy. Basically, he appears to suggest that recall is a reconstructive process in which Ss use rules formed during learning to translate or decode mnemonic devices into specific responses.

Tulving (1962) examined the Miller conception using a free-recall task. In that situation the S is maximally free to impose whatever recoding structure he chooses. If the list to be learned is presented in a different order on each trial, then recoding should be apparent in the sequential dependencies in the Ss' recall behavior. That is, even though there is variation in the order of presentation, there should be an increasing consistency in the order of the Ss' recall as trials progress. As a measure of the subjective organization (SO) imposed by an S, he uses a formula based on Miller and Frick's (1949) index of behavioral stereotypy, which is essentially a measure of sequential redundancy in the S's recall. Tulving's results indicate that there was an increase in both performance and sequential organization as trials progressed; across trials, the two behavioral measures correlated .96. In a related study, Tulving and Patkau (1962) demonstrated that in the free recall of various orders of approximation to English there was very little change across approximations in the number of chunks recalled (defined in terms of sequences of two or more words recalled in the order of presentation) but there was an increase in the mean size of the chunks recalled. That result conforms to Miller's (1956b) assumption that memory is limited by the number of information chunks that can be recalled, and the effect of ex-

perience is that of increasing the amount of information recoverable by recalling each of a limited number of chunks.

In a more recent study, Lachman and Tuttle (1965) were concerned about the extent to which the advantage for structured material in a learning situation should be attributed to:

1. increased accuracy of perception during learning;
2. increased efficiency in the method of storing the material during retention; or
3. the fact that Ss can use the structure to construct the material at the time of recall.

In order to manipulate the possibility of construction at the time of recall, one group was allowed to free recall while other groups were given individual items in a random order and were asked to indicate whether the word did or did not occur on the original list. The items were presented to the latter groups at a rate of one every 2.5 seconds so as to preclude construction or reconstruction of the OL list. Under both conditions a passage taken from the text material was recalled better than a first-order approximation consisting of the same words. However, there was no interaction between method of testing and order of approximation, indicating that a constraint on their freedom to construct at recall had little effect on their performance.

In order to manipulate accuracy of perception, Lachman and Tuttle had one group of Ss read them aloud during OL while the other group did not read them out loud. Again, the test material was recalled better than the first-order approximation, but the verbalization during OL had no effect on performance. Finally, in an attempt to manipulate the effect of construction during recall, one group was instructed to try to construct the material they could not recall, while the other group was simply asked to recall. The instruction to construct had no effect on performance for the Ss recalling the first-order approximation, but there was a significant increase in recall for the text material.

Lachman and Tuttle conclude from their data that the major influence of the structure is that of facilitating or increasing the efficiency of storage rather than facilitating perception or retrieval. However, their data also indicate that it is possible to use the structure to construct the material at recall, even though the Ss may not do so spontaneously.

These data provide at least some inductive support for Miller's (1956b) assumption that Ss attempt to organize a learning task into recall units. The Tulving and Patkau (1962) data indicate that the effectiveness of such units increases during learning, and the Lachman and Tuttle (1965) data suggest that the facilitation may come from an increased effectiveness in the method of storing the material during retention.

✓ *Grammar as a Recoding Scheme*

Returning to the influence of grammar on learning, it may be that the facilitating effect results from the fact that grammar provides Ss with a ready-made and reliable recoding scheme. It would seem entirely possible that if Ss are presented with completely unstructured material, part of the learning time during the first few trials may be devoted to trying to identify a usable method of recoding. If grammar provided the scheme, one would expect the rather small facilitating effect that seems to occur.

In the previous studies a free-recall procedure was used. If sequential chunking does occur with grammatical material, the effect might be somewhat more apparent if the Ss are required to recall in the order of presentation. Furthermore, if grammar is used as a recoding scheme, then the nature of the recall chunks should be predictable from the grammatical structure of the material being learned. That hypothesis was explored in an experiment in which Ss learned sentences as paired-associate responses to digit stimuli (Johnson, 1965). It was assumed that Ss would learn the sentences in terms of phrase-size chunks or recall units, and the unit effect should be apparent in that the elements or words from the same recall unit should be somewhat more dependent upon one another as recall events than are words from different units. In terms of the scoring procedure, if the Ss' response protocols are scored for the conditional probability that, during learning, each word in a sentence was wrong given the preceding word was right, then the unit boundaries should be apparent in the relatively high probability of a transitional error (TEP) at that point. In a sense, then, the TEP at each transition is a measure of the extent to which the words on either side of the transition are independent of one another as recall events, and the nature of the units that Ss use should be apparent from the pattern of TEPs for a sentence.

One group of Ss learned eight sentences whose structure is illustrated by *The tall boy saved the dying woman.* Another group of Ss learned sentences like *The house across the street burned down.* In that the sentences that an S learned were structurally identical, the TEPs were computed across all eight sentences and across 14 learning trials.

If Ss do learn sentences using phrase-size recoding units, then, for the first sentence above, there should be a higher TEP on the third transition (i.e., *boy-saved*) than on the others. Similarly, for the second sentence, the

and the magnitude of the TEP. The correlation between predicted and obtained rank order was .64 for the Figure 1 data and .75 for the Figure 2

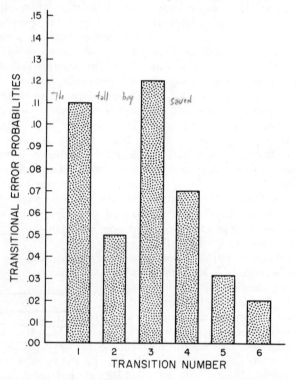

Figure 1. TEPs for sentences like *The tall boy saved the dying woman.*

TEPs on the second and fifth transitions should be higher than for the others. The results of the experiment are presented in Figures 1 and 2. As can be seen, the between-phrase transitions had a higher TEP than the within-phrase transitions.

The one unexpected result was that the within-phrase transitions were not equal. However, the pattern of within-phrase TEPs, for both sentence structures, appeared to be correlated with the within-phrase structure. The transitions within the sentences were ranked in terms of both the level in an IC analysis that each transition first represented a constituent transition,

data. The TEPs, then, reflected the entire phrase structure of the sentences.

A further illustration of the unit structure of a sequence having an effect on learning, independent of the effects of sequential habits, is an experiment in which *S*s learned phrase and non-phrase sentence segments as PA responses. It seems reasonable to assume that sentences like *The child hit the small ball* and *The ball hit the small child* are equally probable in English. Therefore, the segments *hit the small ball* and *ball hit the small* should be equally probable, and the within-sequence associations should be about

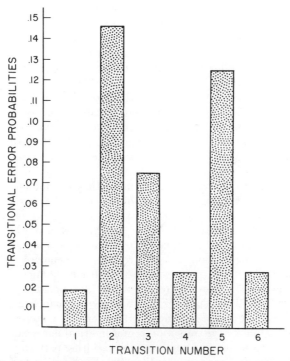

Figure 2. TEPs for sentences like *The house across the street burned down.*

the same. However, if the unit structure of a sequence makes a contribution to learning the segment *hit the small ball* should be learned more rapidly than *ball hit the small*. A third group of *S*s learned scrambled sequences like *the hit ball small*. Finally, three more groups like the above learned sequences based on three-word prepositional phrases (e.g., *of my father* vs. *father of my* vs. *my of father*). For both the three-word and four-word sequences the three word-orders were learned at significantly different rates. In addition, for both sizes of sequence, the grammatically acceptable but nonphrase sequences (i.e., *ball hit the small* and *father of my*) fell about two-thirds of the distance between the other two groups. Suci (1964) reported a similar study in which samples were taken of *S*s' spontaneous verbal behavior. Then

they learned, as responses, word sequences that occurred between hesitations in their spontaneous speech, or control sequences that had been interrupted by a hesitation. The latter sequences were learned more slowly than the former.

In order to explore this phenomenon further, Penny Odom had two groups of 17-year-old *S*s learn the sentence segments. One group was deaf, and the other group had normal hearing. Deaf children of that age have a reasonable command of English words and are able to read rather well. However, their spontaneous speech and writing indicates they have little usable knowledge of grammar and, to a degree, their spontaneous utterances appear like a "word salad." The results showed the same differences in learning rate between the three word-orders for the nondeaf students as was obtained in the previous study, but the three deaf groups did not differ in learning rate, and the three curves fell at about the same points as the curve for the grammatical but nonphrase sequences learned by the hearing Ss.

We have also looked at the TEP data in somewhat more detail. For example, in the discussion above it is clear that the prediction regarding the TEP pattern was based on the assumption that Ss will terminate their response attempt at a unit transition. This assumption has two implications. First, if the predictions are estimates of the probability that an S will terminate responding at a particular point, then only the probability of a transition from a correct response to an incorrect response (i.e., the TEP) should be related to the structure of the sentence. That is, the probability of a transition from an incorrect to a correct response (i.e., reverse TEP) may be independent of both the structure of the sequence and the TEPs. The results of several studies have now been analysed for both TEPs and reverse TEPs, and the latter consistently have a very low correlation with the pattern predicted by the structure. Furthermore, the correlation between the two kinds of TEP usually falls at about zero.

A second implication of the above assumption is that TEPs based on errors of omission, where no further words in the sentence are even attempted (i.e., the S terminated his response attempt), should be more closely related to the pattern predicted by the structure than are TEPs based on other kinds of errors (i.e., intruded words or deletions). That implication has also been supported by the data.

Finally, there are data (Mathews, 1965) illustrating the developmental emergence of the TEP pattern. The data on children's functional knowledge

of parts of speech seem to indicate a rapid increase in knowledge from age six to age nine, with the behavior of nine-year-olds being similar to that of adults (Brown and Berko, 1960; Ervin, 1961). The Mathews study examined the extent to which the same negatively accelerated function would relate the correlation between children's and adults' TEP pattern to age. The correlations for six-, seven-, eight-, and nine-year-olds were .71, .77, .91, and .94 indicating a function similar to that obtained for the acquisition of speech categories.

On the basis of these data the hypothesis that Ss use grammar as a recoding scheme seems quite tenable. In addition, it appears that the effect is not dependent upon the meaningfulness or semantic constraint (Osgood, 1963) of the material. When Ss learn grammatical but meaningless sentences, the resulting pattern of TEPs correlates with that predicted from the structure about as well as patterns obtained using meaningful sentences. Neither does the effect appear to be dependent upon the strength of pre-existing habits. When word pairs from the sentences are learned as simple paired associates, the learning rates are not related to the magnitude of the TEPs on the transitions between the words when they occur within the sentences. Finally, the effect appears to be sensitive to rather subtle structural distinctions (Johnson, 1966b).

Several alternative hypotheses have been offered as explanations for the nature of the TEP pattern (Johnson, 1964), but the one most consistent with the data assumes that Ss use the structure when they produce the sentence in a manner similar to that described by Yngve (1960, 1961). Figure 3 can be taken as an illustration of the process. A stimulus elicits some recoding device that represents the entire sentence

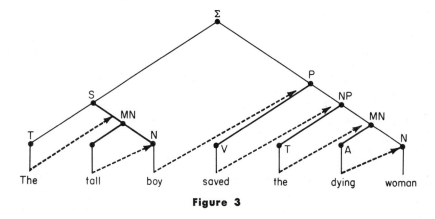

Figure 3

(i.e., Σ). The *S* then applies a decoding rule which translates Σ into *S* plus *P*. The speaker stores *P* in his short-term memory while he further decodes *S* into *T* plus *MN*. He stores *MN* in his short-term memory while he decodes *T* into *The*. He then retrieves the most recently stored item (i.e., *MN*) and decodes it in the same manner. The idea is very similar to the model proposed by Yngve (1960) and is quite consistent with Miller's (1956b) conception of response production.

A basis for predicting the TEP data can be obtained by adding the further assumption that *S*s attempt to produce only those response units that they are confident they can complete perfectly. For example, if a predicate unit like *saved the dying woman* is to be recalled, but the *S* is uncertain of the final noun (i.e., *woman*), there should be a marked tendency for the *S* to say nothing even though he is completely confident of his knowledge regarding the other three words. That phenomenon is apparent in standard paired-associate learning to the extent that most errors are omissions. There is a tendency for response compounds to occur in an all-or-none manner (Crothers, 1962).

It also seems reasonable to expect that the all-or-none occurrence of a

response unit should be some function of its size. Therefore, within a sentence, the probability that an *S* will terminate his response attempt at some particular point should be a function of the size of the constituent unit which begins with the word which follows the point of termination. Predictions based on that hypothesis match the TEP data remarkably well for a wide variety of sentence structures (Johnson, 1964).

Several experiments have been conducted which have attempted to examine: (1) the extent to which the above model represents the way in which *S*s produce sentences at recall and (2) the degree to which the diagram can be assumed to represent the associative structure that is established when *S*s learn a sentence. For example, one experiment (Johnson, 1966) studied the hypothesis that the associative assembly between words within a sentence varies depending upon the structural characteristics of the transition they represent. As can be seen in Figure 3, the model assumes that when an *S* produces *tall* the next step is to recover *N* from his short-term memory and decode it into *boy*. Therefore, it would be assumed that there should be some sort of direct association between *tall* and *boy*. However, after the *S*

produces *boy* the next step is to recover
P from his short-term memory (dotted
line) and decode it into *V* plus *NP*.
Only then does he decode *V* into *saved*.
Therefore, there should be no direct
association established between *boy*
and *saved* when *S*s learn the sentence.

To explore that possibility, *S*s learned
eight sentences as PA responses that
conformed to the Figure 3 structure.
Before learning the sentences, the *S*s
learned a PA task which established an
association between either the adjective
and noun or the noun and verb. On the
basis of the model it was expected that
the *S*s would be able to transfer the
prior adjective-noun association to the
sentence learning task and thereby
reduce the TEP on that transition.
However, such transfer effects should
not be apparent on the noun-verb
transition because the model supposes
that such a direct association is not
used to integrate that transition. The
results supported the hypothesis, with
no significant transfer effect for the
noun-verb transition but a marked
effect for the adjective-noun transition.

There have been a number of suggestions that there should be a relation
between pauses and hesitations in
speech and encoding processes (e.g.,
Lounsbury, 1954; Maclay and Osgood,
1959; Boomer, 1965). Unfortunately,
that area of research has not as yet
provided as much information as was
initially hoped because not only are
there many different kinds of disturbances in speech (e.g., Mahl, 1956) but
also there appear to be many non-
grammatical sources of disturbance
(Goldman-Eisler, 1958a, 1958b, 1961a,
1961b, 1961d; Maclay and Osgood,
1959; Tannenbaum, Williams, and
Hillier, 1965). For example, there
appears to be a relationship between
word predictability and hesitation
(Goldman-Eisler, 1958a, 1958b), but,
given a low degree of certainty for a
word, it is difficult to predict the conditions under which hesitations will
occur (Tannenbaum, Williams, and
Hillier, 1965).

One recent study has attempted to
examine the relationship between grammatical encoding and hesitations
(Boomer, 1965). The *S*s were asked to
speak extemporaneously for about
three minutes on any topic they wished.
Their speech was recorded and segmented into phonemic clauses (Trager
and Smith, 1957). The effect examined
by Boomer (1965) was the extent to
which the hesitations would tend to
occur at the beginning of the units.
His results indicated that there was
such a tendency and the probability of
a hesitation decreased from the beginning to the end of the segment. Assuming the segments were hierarchically
structured, the decrease is generally in
accord with the model discussed above.

Another experiment (Johnson, 1966b)
examined the degree to which latencies at various points in a sentence
might be related to the number of
operations that the model supposes
occur at that point. Take, for example,
the following two sentences: (A) *The
person who jumped near you is good;*
and (B) *The person near you who jumped
is good.* The IC structure of the type *A*
sentence would suggest that as the *S*s
attempt to produce it they should first
decode *sentence* into *subject* and *predicate*
(two decoding operations). Then they
would decode *subject* into *noun phrase*
and *relative clause* (two operations),
and, finally, *noun phrase* should be
decoded into *article* and *noun* (two
operations). Therefore, six decoding
steps should intervene between the
stimulus presentation and *S* vocalizing
"The." The type *B* sentence, however,
should require eight operations or steps:
two steps to produce *subject* and
predicate; two steps to separate the
relative clause (*who jumped*) from the
rest of the *subject;* two steps to separate
the *prepositional phrase* (*near you*) from

the *noun phrase;* and two steps to decode *noun phrase* into *article* and *noun.* Therefore, the latency between the stimulus and when the S says "The" should be greater for the type B sentence than for the type A sentence.

The Ss learned two sentences of each type as PA responses, and learning continued to a criterion of two perfect trials. The Ss then received 20 overlearning trials, during which the latency between the stimulus and the first word of each response was measured. As anticipated, the mean latency for the type A sentence was significantly shorter than the latency for the type B sentence.

A second aspect of the model which has been discussed by Yngve (1960) is the fact that sentences differ in terms of the load they place on short-term memory. He has developed a depth metric by which values can be assigned to each word in a sentence. Basically, the metric represents the number of items the S is holding in short-term storage as he produces each word. Yngve argues that the difficulty of recalling a sentence should be related to its depth. He discusses several language mechanisms that tend to reduce the depth of sentences we produce.

In part, the experiment just discussed supports Yngve's hypothesis. In that more decoding operations were needed to start producing the type B sentences, there were more items in short-term storage at that time, and the original learning data indicated that the type B sentences were learned more slowly. Similarly, Martin (1965) and Martin and Roberts (1966) had. Ss learn sentences that varied in both mean depth and transformational complexity. All the sentences were seven words in length, and there were an equal number of sentences at each of six levels of transformational complexity representing two levels of depth. Each S learned

six sentences, which were presented to him as a free-recall task for six trials. The results indicated little difference in recall attributed to transformations when sentence length and depth were controlled, but there were rather sizable differences as a function of depth. Martin (1965) also reports the same effect occurs in the short-term recall of single sentences and when Ss are asked to rate the ease with which they think they can recall sentences (Martin and Roberts, 1966a). A related finding is the fact that learning is related to degree of self-embedding (Miller and Isard, 1964).

In many different ways these data support the supposition that Ss tend to capitalize on the organization of language by using it as a recoding device. Furthermore, it also seems to be the case that Ss make several response decisions before attempting to produce overtly any of the responses within an encoding unit. Not only does it seem necessary to make that assumption to account for the TEP data, but the hesitation and latency data also are in accord with that assumption. These considerations support both Miller's (1956b) conception of response learning as a unitization process, and Lashley's (1951) argument that in any account of the way behavior is ordered we must include some mechanism that allows for the activation and ordering of response elements prior to their overt occurrence.

One final problem is the degree to which these considerations will generalize to nonlinguistic behavior. That is, if a response sequence consists of a random series of elements, will the same sequential unitization effects occur during learning as occur for grammatical sentences? In one experiment (Johnson, 1965b) Ss learned two seven-letter sequences as paired-associate responses. The sequences were constructed using the Underwood and Schulz (1960) tables such that succeeding letters within the sequences had very low associative connections. In order to "suggest" a possible unitizing scheme to the Ss during learning, when the materials were presented to them there were blank spaces left between certain letters in the sequence. One group of Ss learned sequences like $SB\ JFX\ LZ$, while a second group learned $SBJ\ FXLZ$. The TEPs for the six letter-to-letter transitions were then computed, and they were significantly greater for the transitions where there had been a blank during learning than for the nonblank transitions. In addition, the nonblank transitions were not significantly different from one another. The Ss did appear to use the blanks to define units during learning.

To determine the degree to which the same kind of unitization might occur spontaneously, another group of Ss learned the same sequences but with no blanks left between any of the letters. Again, the TEPs were computed for the letter-to-letter transitions. The results indicated that the Ss did break the sequences into subunits during learning. For 23 of the 24 Ss in the experiment, there were one or more transitions which had very high TEPs, with the rest of the transitions being very low. The distinction between what was a high TEP and what was a low TEP for an S was quite clear, because the range of the high TEPs and the range of the low TEPs were very small, but the difference between the lowest of the high TEPs and the highest of the low TEPs was several times the range of either. The analysis of exploratory experiments of this sort is usually very messy, but fortunately these results were sufficiently clear-cut to indicate that the study which used blanks between some letters was not a completely contrived situation, and the results approximated the spontaneous behavior of Ss.

In that the TEP data suggest that the use of units in the learning and recall of letter sequences is similar to that obtained using grammatical sentences, the next step was to examine the extent to which the model of sentence generation described above also accounted for the way the letter sequences were produced at recall. Suppose, during learning, Ss were to recall a sequence like $NBJ\ FQZ\ LT$, and, as the data suggest, they used the blanks to define functional response subunits. When the stimulus appears, the model assumes the S would first decode some encoding device representing the entire sequence into devices representing the three subunits (e.g., 1, 2, and 3). The S would then store 2 and 3 in his short-term memory while he decodes 1 into N, B, and J. Then he would produce N overtly. If, to that conception, is added the assumption that Ss attempt to produce only units they are confident they can complete perfectly (which is supported by the sentence-learning data), several predictions can be made. First, as the size of a subunit within a sequence increases:

1. the TEP on the transition to that unit should increase;
2. the tendency to emit the unit in an all-or-none manner should result in no variation in TEP within the unit as it increases in size; and
3. variation in the size of one subunit should have no effect on the TEPs within other subunits.

Four groups of Ss learned sequences like: (1) $NB\ J$; (2) $NB\ JF$; (3) $NB\ JFQ$; and (4) $NB\ JFQZ$. The procedure was the same as for the other letter learning studies (Johnson, 1965b). As predicted, as the size of the second subunit increased there was a marked and linear increase in TEP for the B–J transition but no significant variation on the N–B or the J–F transitions.

A second set of predictions also can be made from the assumption that the TEP at a transition is a function of the decoding decisions that an S makes at the transition. The unconditional probability of an error on the first letter of a sequence is the TEP for the transition from the stimulus to the first letter. If an S decodes a sequence into its major subunits and then decodes the first subunit into its response elements before he attempts to produce the first element or letter of the first subunit, then the TEP from the stimulus to the first letter should be a function of the number of subunits into which the sequence is divided plus the number of letters in the first subunit. However, since the model assumes that the other subunits are not decoded until after the first subunit is decoded, the probability of an error on the first letter of the sequence (or the TEP to that letter) should not be a function of the number of elements in the other subunits. To examine that implication of the model, six groups of 40 Ss learned sequences like: (1) *NBJ FQZ LT;* (2) *NBJ FQZLT;* (3) *NBJ FQZL;* (4) *NBJ FQZ;* (5) *NBJ FQ;* and (6) *NBJ.* Each S in each of the six groups learned two structurally identical sequences as PA responses to digits. For all six groups, the number of letters in the first subunit was the same, and, consequently the probability of an error on the first letter (e.g., N) should have been a function only of the number of other subunits. Therefore, the probability of an error on N should drop from Group 1 to Group 2, because the number of subunits following the first drops from two to one, even though the total number of letters or elements following the first subunit remains unchanged. From Group 2 to Group 5 there should be no significant variation in the probability of error on N even though the number of letters following the first subunit decreases from five to two. Finally,

there should be a significant drop in the probability of an error on N from Group 5 to Group 6 because the number of units following the first drops from one to zero. The unconditional probability of an error on the first letter of the sequences for each of the six groups was respectively: (1) .20; (2) .09; (3) .12; (4) .09; (5) .13; and (6) .003. As predicted from the model, there was a significant drop from Group 1 to Group 2; Groups 2, 3, 4, and 5 were not significantly different from one another; and, again, there was a drop from Group 5 to Group 6. In addition, there was a significant increase in TEP on the J–F transition from Group 5 to Group 2, supporting the result obtained in the previous study.

A final experiment was designed to determine whether the probability of an error on the first letter of a sequence would be a function of the size of the first subunit. The manipulation was similar to that in the previous study with the size of the second subunit remaining at three letters while the size of the first subunit decreased from five letters to two letters across groups. Again, as predicted, there was a significant drop in the probability of an error on the first letter of the sequence as the size of the first subunit decreased. The results of this study along with those of the preceding two studies offer rather striking support for the hypothesis that response production at the time of recall occurs in a manner similar to that described by the above model.

Conclusions

This discussion was initiated with a consideration of the Hullian (1930) conception of response integration. Basically, his model assumes the formation of item-to-item associations with each item being elicited by the stimulus consequences of the preceding item. Lashley (1951), however, attacked that position on several grounds and suggested that we must include some conception of a mechanism which both elicits and orders the elements prior to emission.

The present discussion has dealt primarily with two issues. The first question concerned the nature of the associative system established when an *S* learns a response sequence, and the second involved the temporal location of the response decisions. Regarding the first question, the data appear to cast doubt on the assumption that integration involves the establishment of simple item-to-item associations, at least in the case of structured responses. While it is reasonably clear that specific associations can exert specific facilitating effects on random sequences (Frankart, 1964; Johnson, 1965b), the transfer of such associations to the learning of structured sequences appears to be more a function of the structural characteristics of the transition within the sequence than the strength of the prior association. A possible interpretation of the data from random sequences is that the *S*s used the associative connection between items to define the nature of the recall chunks they used during learning.

The data on the loci of response decisions offers support for Lashley's (1951) argument that some arousal and ordering of response elements must occur before the *S* attempts to generate a response sequence. If the learning and production of a response sequence involves nothing more than the execution of sequential associations, it would be difficult to explain how varying the size of the sequence could have effects at points other than the place where the item is added. Even if it were supposed that the increase in size of a sequence slowed down the integration of all the elements and made all the elements more difficult to recall, there would still be the problem of explaining why: (1) the effect is confined to the transitions between units, with little within-unit variation attributable to size of the unit; and (2) there can be behavioral effects correlated with the number of units that are independent of the size of the units. The data, then, appear to offer a rather convincing argument that *S*s may plan out a response before attempting to emit it overtly.

One of the problems still remaining is how to characterize the associative relations that are formed and used between the elements from the same unit and between the units. While Jenkins and Palermo (1964) have offered a mediational account of the effect, it may be that some kind of position learning occurs (Braine, 1963; Smith, 1965).

References

Aborn, M., and H. Rubenstein, "Information Theory and Immediate Recall," *Journal of Experimental Psychology*, **44** (1952), 260–266.

Boomer, D., "Hesitation and Grammatical Encoding," *Language and Speech*, **8** (1965), 148–158.

Bousfield, W., "The Occurrence of Clustering in the Recall of Randomly Arranged Associates," *Journal of General Psychology*, **49** (1953), 229–240.

Braine, M., "On Learning the Grammatical Order of Words," *Psychological Review*, **70** (1963), 323–348.

Brown, R., and J. Berko, "Word Association and the Acquisition of Grammar," *Child Development*, **31** (1960), 1–14.

Chomsky, N., *Syntactic Structures*. The Hague: Mouton, 1957.

Cofer, C., "Comments on Professor Deese's Paper," in C. Cofer, ed., *Verbal Learning and Verbal Behavior*. New York: McGraw-Hill Book Company, 1961, pp. 31–38.

Colman, E., "Approximations to English: Some Comments on the Method," *American Journal of Psychology*, **76** (1963), 239–247.

———, "Responses to a Scale of Grammaticalness," *Journal of Verbal Learning and Verbal Behavior*, **4** (1965), 521–527.

Crothers, E., "Paired-Associate Learning with Compound Responses," *Journal of Verbal Learning and Verbal Behavior*, **1** (1962), 66–70.

Deese, J., "From the Isolated Verbal Unit to Connected Discourse," in C. Cofer, ed., *Verbal Learning and Verbal Behavior*. New York: McGraw-Hill Book Company, 1961, pp. 11–31.

———, and R. Kaufman, "Serial Effects in the Recall of Unorganized and Sequentially Organized Verbal Material," *Journal of Experimental Psychology*, **54** (1957), 180–187.

Epstein, W., "The Influence of Syntactical Structure on Learning," *American Journal of Psychology*, **74** (1961), 80–85.

———, "A Further Study of the Influence of Syntactical Structure on Learning," *American Journal of Psychology*, **75** (1962), 121–126.

———, "Temporal Schemata in Syntactically Structured Material," *Journal of General Psychology*, **68** (1963), 157–164.

Ervin, S., "Changes with Age in the Verbal Determinants of Word-Association," *American Journal of Psychology*, **74** (1961), 361–372.

Frankart, J., "The Relationship between Grammaticalness and Utilization of Short-Range Associations," Unpublished doctoral dissertation, Ohio State University, 1964.

Goldman-Eisler, F., "The Predictability of Words in Context and the Length of Pauses in Speech," *Language and Speech*, **1** (1958), 226–231.

———, "Speech Production and the Predictability of Words in Context," *Quarterly Journal of Experimental Psychology*, **10** (1958), 96–106.

———, "Hesitation and Information in Speech," in C. Cherry, ed., *Information Theory*. London: Butterworth, 1961, pp. 162–174.

———, "A Comparative Study of Two Hesitation Phenomena," *Language and Speech*, **4** (1961), 18–26.

———, "The Significance of Changes in the Rate of Articulation," *Language and Speech*, **4** (1961), 171–174.

———, "Continuity of Speech Utterance: Its Determinants and Its Significance," *Language and Speech*, **4** (1961), 220–231.

Gonzales, R., and C. Cofer, "Exploratory Studies of Verbal Context by Means of Clustering in Free Recall," *Journal of General Psychology*, **95** (1959), 293–320.

Hill, A., "Grammaticality," *Word*, **17** (1961), 1–10.

Hull, C., "Knowledge and Purpose as Habit Mechanisms," *Psychological Review*, **37** (1930), 511–525.

Jenkins, J., and D. Palermo, "Mediation Processes in the Acquisition of Linguistic Structure," in U. Bellugi and R. Brown, eds., *The Acquisition of Language. Monographs of Social Research and Child Development*, **29** (1964), 121–149.

———, and W. Russell, "Associative Clustering during Recall," *Journal of Abnormal and Social Psychology*, **47** (1952), 818–821.

Johnson, N., "A Model of Sentence Generation," Paper read at American Psychological Association, Los Angeles; Sept., 1964.

———, "The Psychological Reality of Phrase-Structure Rules," *Journal of Verbal Learning and Verbal Behavior*, **4** (1965), 469–475.

———, "Linguistic Models and Functional Units of Language Behavior," in S. Rosenberg, ed., *Directions in Psycholinguistics*. New York: The Macmillan Company, 1965, pp. 29–65.

———, "The Influence of Associations between Elements of Structured Verbal Responses," *Journal of Verbal Learning and Verbal Behavior*, **5** (1966), 369–394.

———, "On the Relationship between Sentence Structure and the Latency in Generating the Sentence," *Journal of*

Verbal Learning and Verbal Behavior, **5** (1966), 375–380.

Lachman, R., and A. Tuttle, "Approximations to English and Short-Term Memory: Construction or Storage," *Journal of Experimental Psychology,* **70** (1965), 386–393.

Lashley, K., "The Problem of Serial Order in Behavior," in L. Jeffress, ed., *Cerebral Mechanisms in Behavior.* New York: John Wiley and Sons, Inc., 1951, pp. 112–136.

Lees, R., "Models for a Language User's Knowledge of Grammatical Form," *Journal of Communications,* **14** (1964), 74–85.

Lounsbury, F., "Transitional Probability, Linguistic Structure and Systems of Habit-Family Hierarchies," in C. Osgood and T. Seboek, eds., *Psycholinguistics: A Survey of Theory and Research Problems.* Bloomington, Ind.: University of Indiana Press, 1954, pp. 93–100.

Maclay, H., and C. Osgood, "Hesitation Phenomena in Spontaneous English Speech," *Word,* **15** (1959), 19–44.

——, and M. Sleator, "Responses to Language: Judgments of Grammaticalness," *International Journal of American Linguistics,* **26** (1960), 275–282.

Mahl, G., "Disturbances and Silences in the Patient's Speech in Psychotherapy," *Journal of Abnormal and Social Psychology,* **53** (1956), 1–15.

Mandler, G., and J. Mandler, "Serial Position Effects in Sentences," *Journal of Verbal Learning and Verbal Behavior,* **3** (1964), 195–202.

Marks, M., and O. Jack, "Verbal Context and Memory Span for Meaningful Material," *American Journal of Psychology,* **65** (1952), 298–300.

Marks, L., and G. Miller, "The Role of Semantic and Syntactic Constraints in the Memorization of English Sentences," *Journal of Verbal Learning and Behavior,* **3** (1964), 1–5.

Martin, E., "An Explanation of Grammatical Factors in Sentence Retention: Amount vs. Kind of Structure," Paper read at Midwest Psychological Association, Chicago, 1965.

——, and K. Roberts, "Grammatical Factors in Sentence Rentention," *Journal of Verbal Learning and Verbal Behavior,* **5** (1966), 211–218.

Martin, J., J. Davidson, and M. Williams, "Grammatical Agreement and Set in Learning at Two Age Levels," *Journal of Experimental Psychology,* **70** (1965), 570–574.

Mathews, E., "Developmental Changes in the Functional Knowledge of Phrase-Structure Rules," Master's thesis, Ohio State University, 1965.

Melton, A., *Categories of Human Learning.* New York: Academic Press, 1964.

Miller, G., "The Magical Number Seven, Plus or Minus Two: Some Limits on Our Capacity for Processing Information," *Psychological Review,* **63** (1956), 81–97.

——, "Human Memory and the Storage of Information," *IRE Transactions on Information Theory.,* **IT-2** (1956), 129–137.

——, "Information and Memory," *Scientific American,* **195** (1956), 42–46.

——, "Free Recall of Redundant Strings of Letters," *Journal of Experimental Psychology,* **56** (1958), 484–491.

——, and F. Frick, "Statistical Behavioristics and Sequences of Responses," *Psychological Review,* **56** (1949), 311–324.

——, E. Galanter, and K. Pribram, *Plans and the Structure of Behavior.* New York: Holt, Rinehart & Winston, Inc., 1960.

——, and S. Isard, "Free Recall of Self-Embedded English Sentences," *Information and Control,* **7** (1964), 292–303.

——, and J. Selfridge, "Verbal Context and the Recall of Meaningful Material," *American Journal of Psychology,* **63** (1950), 176–185.

Moran, M., "The Effect of Syntactic Structure on the Learning of Verbal Material," Senior honor thesis, Pennsylvania State University, 1965.

Osgood, C., "On Understanding and Creating Sentences," *American Psychologist*, **18** (1963), 735–751.

——, "A Behavioristic Analysis of Perception and Language as Cognitive Phenomena," in *Contemporary Approaches to Cognition*. Cambridge, Mass.: Harvard University Press, 1957, pp. 75–118.

Postman, L., and P. Adams, "Studies in Incidental Learning: VIII. The Effects of Contextual Determination," *Journal of Experimental Psychology*, **59** (1960), 153–164.

——, ——, and A. Bohm, "Studies in Incidental Learning: V. Recall for Order and Associative Clustering," *Journal of Experimental Psychology*, **51** (1956), 334–342.

——, and K. Stark, "Learning to Learn: IV. Transfer from Serial to Paired-Associate Learning," *Journal of Verbal Learning and Verbal Behavior*, (1967), in press.

Richardson, P., and J. Voss, "Replication Report: Verbal Context and the Recall of Meaningful Material," *Journal of Experimental Psychology*, **60** (1960), 417–418.

Rosenberg, S., "Recall of Nonsense Sentences as a Function of Grammatical Cues," Paper read at Psychonomic Society, Niagara Falls, Canada, October, 1964.

——, "Associative Factors in the Recall of Connected Discourse," *Psychonomic Science*, **4** (1966), 53–54.

Rubenstein, H., and M. Aborn, "Immediate Recall as a Function of Degree of Organization and Length of Study Period," *Journal of Experimental Psychology*, **48** (1954), 146–152.

Russell, W., and J. Jenkins, "The Complete Minnesota Norms for Responses to 100 Words from the Kent-Rosanoff Word Association Test, *Technique Report No. 11, Contract N8-ONR-66216*, Office of Naval Research and the University of Minnesota, 1954.

Sharp, H., "The Effect of Contextual Constraint upon Recall of Verbal Passages," *American Journal of Psychology*, **71** (1958), 568–572.

Simpson, W., "Effects of Approximation to Sentence Word Order and Grammatical Class upon the Serial Learning of Word Lists," *Journal of Verbal Learning and Verbal Behavior*, **4** (1965), 510–514.

Smith, K., "Recall of Paired Verbal Units under Various Conditions of Organization," Unpublished doctoral dissertation, University of Minnesota, 1963.

——, "Mediation and Position Learning in the Recall of Structured Letter Pairs," *Psychonomic Science*, **2** (1965), 293–294.

Suci, G., "The Validity of Pause as an Index of Units in Language," in H. Levin, ed., *Project Literacy Reports No. 2* Ithaca, N.Y.: Cornell University Press, 1964, pp. 50–51.

Tannenbaum, P., F. Williams, and C. Hillier, "Word Predictability in the Environments of Hesitation," *Journal of Verbal Learning and Verbal Behavior*, **4** (1965), 134–140.

Thorndike, E., and I. Lorge, *The Teachers Word Book of 30,000 Words*. New York: Bureau of Publication, Teachers College, Columbia University, 1944.

Trager, G., and H. Smith, *An Outline of English Structure*. Washington: American Council of Learned Societies, 1957.

Tulving, E., "Subjective Organization in Free Recall of 'Unrelated' Words," *Psychological Review*, **69** (1962), 344–354.

——, and J. Patkau, "Concurrent Effects of Contextual Constraint and Word Frequency on Immediate Recall and Learning of Verbal Material," *Canadian Journal of Psychology*, **16** (1962), 83–95.

Underwood B., and R. Schulz, *Meaningfulness and Verbal Learning*. Philadelphia: J. B. Lippincott Co., 1960.

Waugh, N., "Free versus Serial Recall," *Journal of Experimental Psychology*, **62** (1961), 496–502.

Yngve, V., "A Model and an Hypothesis for Language Structure," *Proceedings of the American Philosophical Society*, **104** (1960), 444–466.

— —, "The Depth Hypothesis," in R.

Jakobson, ed., *Structure of Language in its Mathematical Aspects*. Providence, R. I.: American Mathematical Society, 1961, pp. 130–138.

————, "Implications of Mechanical Translation ·Research," *Proceedings of the American Philosophical* Society, **108** (1964), 275–281.

Psychological Theories and Linguistic Constructs

17

M. GARRETT AND J. FODOR

Psycholinguistics, a field recently characterized as amorphous (Saporta, 1961), has produced at least one issue on which the dialogue between psychology and linguistics has achieved more than an exchange of terminology. Osgood (1963, p. 735) put the matter in the form of a question: "Can our psychological theories incorporate and render comprehensible the way human beings understand and create sentences?" The salience of this question as a focal point for psycholinguistic investigation has been increased by renewed appreciation of the difficulty of applying usual psychological mechanisms to natural language behavior (cf. Bever, Fodor, and Weksel, 1965; Chomsky, 1959; Fodor, 1965; Miller, Galanter, and Pribram, 1960; Osgood, 1963).

Linguists attempt to formalize in grammar the inherent structure of natural languages. They contend that the grammatical description of a natural language represents a characterization of the verbal capacities a speaker of that language possesses. The nature of the relationship between the formal description of language and the implementation of the capacities it represents in the performance of the speaker is a matter only recently considered.

Although the information has been presented in several other places (see Chomsky, 1964; Katz and Postal, 1964; *et al.*), an outline of current assumptions about linguistic competence will be given here since much of the psycholinguistic research is incomprehensible without an appreciation of certain minimal assumptions about linguistic theory. We can best present this by starting with the analysis problem the linguist sets for himself.

It is necessary to specify with some precision what is meant by the proposition, "a speaker understands sentence S in language L." Roughly, we assume that speakers of a language are able to provide interpretations of sentences on the basis of their knowledge of the meanings of the words that comprise the sentence together with their knowledge of the syntactic character of the sentence. Formally it is assumed that understanding a sentence entails pairing it with an appropriate semantic interpretation and that the interpretation is uniquely determined by relevant lexical and syntactic data.

The sentences of a language comprise an indefinitely large set; the fluent speaker is, in principle, able to provide an interpretation for any member of the set. It is, therefore, necessary to assume that the speaker is equipped with a set of rules which project the infinite set of sentences and semantic interpretations from some finite set of elements.

The ability to provide interpretations for sentences is resolved into the abilities to provide *structural descriptions* and *semantic readings* for sentences. These areas of competence may be elaborated in analogous ways. In both cases, speakers of a language are able to provide judgments of well-formedness, ambiguity, and intersentential relationship. That is, on the one hand, grammatical competences include the abilities

1. to distinguish structurally well-formed utterances
2. to note when and in what ways an utterance is susceptible to more than one structural interpretation
3. to relate sentences to each other by virtue of their structural similarity or difference.

Semantic competences, on the other hand, include the abilities

1. to detect semantic anomaly
2. to note when and in what ways an utterance may be semantically ambiguous
3. to note paraphrase and synonymy relations among sentences.

The preferred linguistic description should provide a basis for the explanation of these and similar judgments by marking those features of sentence structure upon whose recognition they are contingent. The linguistic description outlined below is the only sort that has attempted to do so in a general way.

The Form of Linguistic Descriptions

Linguistic descriptions have three components: a syntactic component which serves as the source of structural descriptions of sentences in the language; a semantic component which provides a semantic interpretation of each sentence; a phonological component which phonetically interprets strings of formatives. The syntactic component is viewed as the central device in the sense that the semantic and phonological systems operate on its output but not conversely. The linguistic description "...as a whole can thus be regarded, ultimately, as a device for pairing phonetically represented signals with semantic interpretations, this pairing being mediated through a system of abstract structures generated by the syntactic component" (Chomsky, 1964, p. 52). Figure 1 provides a schematic representation of a linguistic description and of the relations presumed to hold between its components.

The syntactic component is considered to be a generative system of the sort originally proposed by Noam Chomsky: a postulational system in which each sentence is regarded as analogous to a theorem (Chomsky, 1957, 1961, 1964). Such a grammar consists of two subcomponents (see Figure 1), a *phrase structure* subcomponent and a *transformational* subcomponent.

The phrase structure subcomponent contains rules which operate on fixed strings of symbols by rewriting a single symbol as a new string. The successive application of such rules produces a derivation representable by a tree diagram where each node represents the application of a rewriting rule. Such a labeled tree diagram is called a *P-marker*. Here and subsequently, those P-markers whose derivation involves only phrase structure rules will be referred to as *underlying P-markers*.

The transformational subcomponent consists of rules which operate on the P-markers produced by the phrase structure. The new P-markers, produced by the operation of these rules, will be

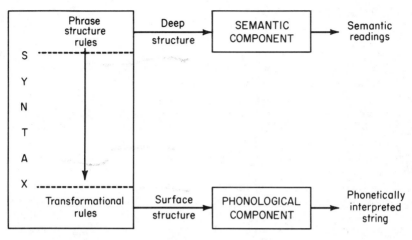

Figure 1. The components of a linguistic description

referred to as *derived P-markers*. It is important to recognize that transformational rules are of a distinctly different character than phrase structure rules. Transformational rules take account of the derivational history of the elements on which they operate. Such rules apply in terms of the labeled tree diagrams (P-markers) used to represent the successive application of phrase structure rules; they operate to change the form of P-markers. The types of operations performed by transformations (namely, elementary transformations) are substitution, deletion, addition, and permutation.

A significant distinction here is that between the output of the phrase structure subcomponent and the output of the whole syntactic system. The reference to underlying and derived P-markers given above reflects this distinction. Subsequently, this difference will be referred to as the difference between surface structure and deep structure (respectively, the final derived P-marker and the underlying P-markers). Consider, for example, sentences (1) and (2) below.

(1) ((the) (theorem)) ((was) (proved) (by) (induction))

(2) ((the) (theorem)) ((was) (proved) (by) (John))

Each of these sentences may be organized into the same hierarchically ordered set of constituents. But although the two sentences have the same surface structure—are segmented in the same way at various levels—it is clear that they are not structurally equivalent. For instance, we are willing to say that (1) may be paraphrased as

$$\text{the theorem was proved} \left\{ \begin{array}{l} \text{with} \\ \text{using} \\ \text{through} \end{array} \right\} \begin{array}{l} \text{inductively} \\ \text{induction} \end{array}$$

but none of these changes produces a satisfactory paraphrase of (2). Similarly, we will accept *John proved the theorem* as a paraphrase of (2), but a parallel form of (1) is not acceptable.

All of this is to say that speakers are aware of relationships among the elements of these sentences which are not plausibly representable by the bracketing. These relationships are, however, revealed in the deep structure of the sentences. In particular, the deep structure will reveal that John is the subject of the verb in (2), while in (1) the subject is not stated. The form of

(1) as it is expressed by the underlying structure (the output of the phrase structure subcomponent) is [someone proved the theorem by induction passive][1]. This form is changed by the transformational subcomponent to [the theorem was proved by induction by someone] and then to *the theorem was proved by induction*. The underlying form of (2) is the same as that for (1) except, of course, *someone* is specified as *John* and there is no manner adverbial. The underlying form [John proved the theorem passive] is transformed to *the theorem was proved by John*. There are many examples of this and other kinds of differences between surface and deep structures, and it is clear that an adequate grammar must account for differences such as those between (1) and (2). In the system described here, such differences are expressed by the relationship between underlying and derived P-markers.

The Psycholinguistic Problem and S-R Theory

Understanding a sentence has been defined as the association of some semantic interpretation with its struc-

---

[1] Strings in brackets are underlying forms. These forms are only partially rendered here and should not be construed to imply more than the example explicitly states. It should perhaps be emphasized that these underlying forms are not themselves sentences. It is a not uncommon misapprehension that in a transformational grammar sentences are derived from other sentences. This is not the case. In this example, for instance, the passive sentences are not being derived from their active counterparts. Rather, the underlying forms for passive and active are very similar. The resemblance of these underlying forms to actual sentences is due to the examples' simplified form; the simplification leaves out much of the structure and many elements which must be present in a proper

tural description. Summarized above is a conception of a linguistic theory for which the following claim is made: The underlying structures which well-motivated grammars assign to the sentences they enumerate preserve all the syntactic distinctions required for semantic interpretation. While this is an extremely strong empirical claim, it is not also claimed that the linguistic description is a model of the speaker or hearer. Rather, it characterizes the knowledge about the language a speaker or hearer must be presumed to have in order to produce or understand a sentence. Given such competence, the problem for psycholinguistic theory is to explain how the speaker utilizes his competence in his linguistic performance. That is, if we assume that the grammar formulates the information with which the speaker or hearer must be equipped, our problem is to determine how that knowledge is employed in sentence production or understanding.

Throughout this paper we shall assume that the model of linguistic competence just sketched is accurate at least in its essential properties. We shall not, however, attempt to determine the nature of the performance model this analysis of competence requires. Rather we raise the less ambitious question: To what extent could the present account of competence be integrated with a model of performance that preserves essential features of classical S-R theories?

The following features of S-R accounts of behavior seem to us central. The S-R theorist views the organism as possessing a finite repertoire of be-

---

representation. Such elements are omitted here (and elsewhere; cf. many of the references cited earlier for linguistic discussions) since they are not relevant to the point of the examples.

haviors, any one of which may, on occasion, be selected by specified stimulus parameters. The probability of such a selection is presumably determined, at least in part, by the organism's history of reinforcement and may be represented by some such construct as habit strength or associative connection.

S-R psychology thus seeks to provide an extremely parsimonious answer to the question of how an organism possessing finite performance capacity can respond appropriately to any of indefinitely many possible inputs; namely, by supposing that all the inputs to which the organism provides similar responses are characterized by correspondingly similar stimulus parameters. The appeal to principles of generalization in S-R theories should not obscure their essentially finite character. Insofar as the S-R theorist visualizes the organism as responding appropriately to "novel" stimulus situations, he also visualizes such situations as exhibiting some stimulus parameter to which the organism possesses a previously trained response. The set of such responses at the organism's disposal is thus inherently finite, although it may provide for appropriate behavior in indefinitely many input situations so long as these situations are similar in relevant respects. In short, the S-R theorist is committed to saying that the organism has at its disposal a finite repertoire of distinct responses, any one of which may be selected with indefinite frequency (by stimuli relevantly similar to those to which the response has been associated).

We assume, then, that the S-R model, if it makes any claims at all, must at least require (a) that the behavioral repertoire of an organism is finite, and (b) that the stimulus parameters that select behaviors are characterizable by reference to some finite set of parameters common to all stimuli capable of eliciting the same response.

We wish to argue that, if the linguistic competence model discussed above is correct, no performance model having these essential characteristics of S-R theories could be adequate for verbal behavior.

In the first place, it is essential to the competence model that the organism's behavioral repertoire be inherently infinite. That is to say that the finite set of linguistic rules a speaker internalizes are, in principle, sufficient to provide him with a repertoire of infinitely many distinct linguistic responses. This analysis of competence thus requires a performance model which explains how, in the characteristic case, the organism computes the novel response sequence appropriate to a novel input. Such a model contrasts in every respect with one which pictures the current input as selecting from a pre-existent response repertoire on the basis of some previous established association. If the "new" psycholinguistics is properly described as "mentalistic," that is because the information processing involved in such computations appears to be both abstract and extensive. The rejection of S-R performance models by psycholinguists who adhere to generative competence models is required by the fact that the former proposes a view of the organism as consisting of no more than a response library and a look-up; and such a model is incapable, in principle, of accounting for indefinitely diversified response repertoires.

The incompatibility of S-R performance models with generative analyses of the linguistic repertoire is in a certain sense logical. The competence model requires computing machinery that S-R performance models simply fail to make available. A somewhat similar point can be made about the S-R analysis of the stimuli governing verbalization.

We have seen that if the mathematical character of the organism is to be expressed by a finite set of pairings of input and output states (by a finite set of associations between stimuli and responses), an impoverished view of the organism's behavioral repertoire is entailed; in particular, the characterization of that repertoire contains no rules that enumerate infinite sets; the organism can be master of at most a finite number of distinct responses. Similarly, the view that behavior is to be explained by reference to a list of associative connections between stimuli and responses requires an impoverished view of the organism's perceptual capacities. The S-R account of perception is, in effect, posed with a dilemma: On the one hand, it is obvious that the organism is continuously confronted with novel stimulus configurations, to indefinitely many of which it may respond appropriately. On the other, it is assumed that the organism could not have learned more than a finite number of S-R connections. But how can an organism with a finite perceptual repertoire successfully analyze indefinitely many novel inputs?

It must be emphasized that it is not some religious aversion to S-R terminology that prompts the rejection of the abstractionist account of perceptual analysis. Rather, experimental questions are implicated in this analysis, and in the case of language comprehension, the experimental results have not usually been favorable. The question whether or not recurrent criterial attributes can be identified in the case of typical linguistic percepts has been the object of many experimental inquiries, some of which we shall presently discuss. Insofar as these results have been negative, they suggest

that the speaker's perceptual repertoire, like his response repertoire, includes the capacity to analyze indefinitely many distinct linguistic objects. Hence, an adequate account of perceptual performance requires a more complicated model than S-R theories can in principle provide, just as a model for behavioral performance does.

These remarks on the relation between S-R performance models and current accounts of linguistic competence are not materially affected by recent reformulations of associationism which accomodate mediation paradigms. The mediation approach recognizes two major goals: First, to do full justice to the importance of central processes in the etiology of behavior and therefore to encourage formulation of relatively enriched perceptual theories. Second, there is a commitment on the part of mediation theorists to canons of general S-R theory. That is, their attempt is properly characterized as an effort to use constructs defined in terms of overt behavior in accounts of the internal processes of the organism. These two goals have, however, proved mutually incompatible. For, when the putative mediating events are assumed to be related by the same principles of association as the S's and R's in terms of which classical learning theories are formulated, the postulation of such events does not materially aid in avoiding the problems discussed above. On the other hand, if the mediating events are assumed to be of unknown character and complexity and to interact in essentially unknown ways, no theory has in fact been offered.

Indeed, the theory of linguistic competence discussed earlier might be said to make explicit at least part of what the mediation theorist is inevitably forced to assume. A serious account of the information processing underlying speech perception would presumably require "mediating" constructs like NP, VP, S, etc., and "mediating" operations like transformation, etc. There is, however, no reason to suppose that mediating processes of this degree of abstractness and complexity could be described by any system which simultaneously sought to preserve the general character of associationistic models. On the contrary, attempts to employ paradigms of mediation learning to explain the assimilation of grammatical competence have at most supposed (Braine, 1963; Osgood, 1963; Jenkins and Polermo, 1964; Carroll, 1964) that such competence is expressible by simple class-and-sequence grammars. This is no accident; associationistic principles afford no basis for understanding the assimilation or deployment of more profound grammatical relationships.

With the above as preface, we now consider some experimental results relevant to an analysis of linguistic performance. Our discussion begins with the perceptual analysis problem at the phonological level and proceeds to consider data relating to analysis at the derived constituent structure level (surface structure) and then to analysis relating to underlying or deep structure of utterances.

The Acoustic Stimulus

It is characteristic of S-R attempts to cope with language that they initiate their discussion at the level of words or morphemes. This practice probably stems from the belief that the step from the acoustic signal to the lexical level can be rather straightforwardly accounted for in terms of subjects' discriminative responses to physical attributes of the signal. That is, it is often assumed that an analysis into phonemes, morphemes, or words can be arrived at by some sort of stimulus filter over certain physical parameters of the speech signal. Before examining the research relevant to an account of syntactic behavior, this assumption needs to be called into serious question.

We set aside for the moment concern with the problems of semantic and syntactic variables in the process of speech perception and look only at the translation of the acoustic stimulus into some discrete coding *capable of* being interpreted syntactically and semantically. The central problem, of course, is simply to specify those aspects of the acoustic stimulus which are significant in accounting for differential responses. Alternatively, what properties of the acoustic representation of a sentence are necessary and usable for sentence understanding?

Licklider and Miller in their 1951 review of research on speech perception conclude:

> Apparently no single dimension of speech is critical. Speech power can be varied over a range of a billion to one. Conversations are intelligible with only the upper half of the speech spectrum, but there is nothing unique about this half because we can throw it all away and get along equally well with only the lower half. The wave form can be distorted to a series of square waves or turned off half the time without severe effects. . . . Changes in the intensity, the fundamental frequency, the wave form, the envelope of the wave, or the spectrum do not affect intelligibility until the change is so great the spectrographic pattern is markedly altered (Licklider and Miller, 1951).

With only portions of a mutilated signal, subjects are able to perform near normal levels for connected speech.

This research was widely interpreted by S-R psychologists as evidence of the high redundancy of connected speech—

i.e., the assumption was that the signal contains *so many* cues that even a degraded version is sufficient for recognition. But the extent and variety of these distortions surely also provides indication of the tremendous reconstructive powers which the perceiver brings to bear on his task. The evidence is just as compelling an indication of the enormous contribution of the organism to the perceptual process as of the existence of a rich stimulus array.

These facts aside, a great deal of careful research (starting largely with the invention of the sound spectrograph) has been carried out using both natural and synthetic speech and aimed at determining just those aspects of the speech signal required for discrimination of phonemes or phoneme sequences. This research has been extensively reviewed elsewhere (see Lane, 1965; Liberman, 1957), and we will consider only some examples here.

There are two striking and complementary results which will interest us: (1) the same physical event, the same acoustic stimulus, gives rise to systematically different percepts; (2) different physical events, diverse acoustic stimuli, give rise to the same percept.

One can begin to illustrate the nature of these facts with the following observation (from Cooper, Borst, and Liberman, 1952). The same burst of energy at a particular point in the spectrum is identified as a different sound, depending on the vowel it is adjacent to. For example, a 1440-cps. burst is identified as /p/ when adjacent to /i/, but as /k/ when adjacent to /ɔ/.

There are other examples of the same effect. For a given starting point on the frequency scale one can, by varying the "following" vowel (i.e., the formant frequencies of the steady-state level of the vowel), produce the three stops /b/, /d/, and /g/ (Delattre, Liberman and Cooper, 1955). The transition from the common locus is affected by the change

of vowel and a change in the percept results. On the other hand, if the *same* steady-state frequencies for the vowel are maintained and only the nature of the transition is varied, the same result can be obtained. In a study by Liberman, Harris, Hoffman, and Griffith (1957) a series (14) of artificial speech stimuli (produced on the pattern playback device at Haskins Laboratory) were prepared by systematic variation in the transition of the second formant of a vowel sound with f_1 (first formant) at 360 cps. and f_2 (second formant) at 2160 cps. F_1 was invariant—only the "onset tail" of f_2 varied. These 14 syllables were identified in regular progression, as /b/ (with a rising onset to f_2), as /d/ (level onset to f_2), and as /g/ (falling onset to f_2). The labeling functions showed sharp cutoffs (i.e., there was a narrow range of signals between identifications as /b/ and identifications as /d/, or between /d/ and /g/).

Just the same sort of result has been obtained for various other systematic slight alterations in the spectra of vowels not associated with any energy burst normally accompanying production of consonants. Liberman, Harris, Kinney, and Lane (1961) demonstrated a progression from identification of signals as /do/ to identification as /to/ by simply changing the point of onset of f_1 relative to onset of f_2. As the onset of f_1 relative to f_2 is delayed, identifications as /do/ decrease and identifications as /to/ increase. Here again, the cutoff point was sharp—a relatively small range of cutback steps was required to produce full transition from /do/ to /to/ (10 ms. increased delay produces a shift from 75 per cent responses as /do/ to 75 per cent responses as /to/). Similar results (/b/:/p/ contrast) have been shown for variation in the silent interval between vocalic bursts (Liberman, Harris, Eimas, Lisker, and Bastian, 1961).

One can, in short, produce changes

in the perception of consonants without changing the segments of the signal which seem temporally associated with production of the consonant. A segmentation of the signal at the phoneme level by reference to parameters of the acoustic stimulus is not possible without reference to acoustic context at least at the syllabic level.

The second complementary result—different physical stimuli giving rise to the same response—is striking for /k/ and /g/ among consonants. The Liberman *et al.* (1957) study noted above showed a marked effect on the perception of /b/, /d/ and /g/ of the transition of the second formant. However, it was also found (Liberman, Delattre, Cooper, and Gerstman, 1954) that there are large changes in the transition for f_2 during the production of /g/, /k/ and /d/ when they are associated with different vowels. That is, quite different f_2 transitions are found for identifications as /g/ when associated with /i/ than when it is associated with /æ/. Changes sufficient to vary identification from /d/ to /g/ when the vowel is held constant are no longer effective when the following vowel changes.

The vowels themselves provide illustration of the wide variation permitted in the acoustic signal consonant with preserving a constant perceptual response. Though it is approximately the case for a particular speaker that a vowel is characterized by some unique combination of formant frequencies, this is not true across speakers—most strikingly in the variation between men, women, and children. Even among speakers of the same sex, approximate age, and dialect, and using vowels that are highly identifiable, formant frequencies (including f_3) are not sufficient to categorize responses unambiguously (Peterson and Barney, 1952). Further, it appears that no simple relational notion will account for this invariance. Fairbanks and Grubb (1961), for in-

stance, showed that a constant ratio relation between f_1 and f_2 will not discriminate vowels, even when the selection of vowel sounds is highly restricted (in terms of acceptability and identifiability). The identification of vowels in terms of some relatively constant set of physical parameters is feasible only under certain very restricted circumstances—circumstances which are not met when the speaker of a language listens with equal ease to his three-year-old son, his wife, and his boss.

The complexity of translation from acoustic to discrete phonetic objects might not be expected to be reflected in the prosodic features of utterances, with their apparently simple physical correlates. But close examination reveals that here too the step from stimulus to percept is neither simple nor direct.

Trained phoneticians are able to hear four levels of stress in English. And indeed, reliability in assigning stress patterns is high both across linguists similarly trained and across time for particular liguists. But despite this reliability, the obvious aspects of the physical signal have failed to show clear correspondence with stress patterns. It is clear that if stress can be accounted for in terms of variation of physical properties of the signal, it will be as an acoustic complex—i.e., though variation in fundamental frequency has been shown most closely related to stress (Lieberman, 1960), duration and amplitude are implicated as well. Most experimental results on stress refer to a special case—that is, "a sequential comparison involving two items only" (Morton and Jassem, 1965). Complex stress patterns are clearly an order of magnitude more difficult to account for. If the problems of two syllable sequences are considered in isolation from any other linguistic context, judgments of stress are significantly related to vowel quality, fundamental frequency (most effective variable), slope of frequency change, intensity, and duration. Whether the changes occur on the first or second of the syllables also has a significant effect (Morton and Jassem, 1965). When longer sequences are considered, however, *none* of these variables satisfactorily accounts for stress assignment; disjuncture must be added (Bolinger and Gerstman, 1957).

Recent linguistic analysis of stress patterns (see Halle and Chomsky, forthcoming) has revealed them to be not only complex but inextricably related to the syntax. What seems apparent is that linguists in assigning stress patterns to phrase-length utterances have *not* been responding primarily to some physical cue in the signal, which covaries with stress levels, but rather have "heard" the stress pattern in terms of their knowledge of the language and thus imposed the structure of the stress pattern on the stimulus.

Intonation contour has been traditionally considered primarily related to variations in fundamental frequency (i.e., f_0), four levels of which are usually recorded for English. Studies by Hadding-Koch and Studdert-Kennedy (1964) reveal, however, much the same sort of complexity that obtains in the case of stress.

Versions of a two-word utterance (*For Jane*) which could be viewed either as a question or as a statement, were prepared. All contours started at the same level and then rose to one of two high turning points, fell to one of three low turning points, and finally rose to one of seven end points. The utterance was such as to be acceptable to both English and Swedish speakers. Swedish and American *S*s were required to judge whether a presented item would be better classed as a question or as a statement and in another session to

judge only whether there was a terminal rise or fall at the end of the utterance.

The same terminal pitch levels give rise to both question responses and statement responses depending on preceding levels of f_0. There is not, in short, some value of the pitch level which invariably yields one categorization—for some contours terminal *falls* were classed as questions and terminal *rises* as statements. The psychophysical judgments of terminal glide were affected by the relation of the glide to the rest of the contour—*S*'s accuracy was not comparable to abilities for pure tone discriminations. Further, the language system affected the perception of what was an upward terminal glide and what was a downward terminal glide; on some contours what was judged a downward glide by American English speakers was judged an upward glide by Swedish speakers.

We do not imply by the foregoing that there are not some sorts of cues in the acoustic signal sufficient to render identification of sound sequences possible. That would be absurd. What is not absurd, however, is the observation that an acoustic characterization of these cues is both unclear and awkward as a scheme for classifying the perceptual responses to speech. There appears to be no clear structure in the acoustic signal which can be the basis for defining perceptual response to particular constructs. Rather, the basis for discrimination must be sought again in a structure which the perceiver *imposes* on the acoustic signal. There is reason to suppose that for phoneme recognition, this perceptual framework consists in some representation of the articulatory configurations which eventuate in the various speech signals (see Liberman, 1957; Liberman, Cooper, Harris, MacNeilage, and Studdert-Kennedy, 1964). The significant point for S-R accounts of language performance, however, is in the difficulty of establishing the mechanism for stimulus control of the organism. The relevant perceptual analysis is not to be found in the stimulus, but in the perceiver.

To bring this issue into clearer focus, it needs to be stressed that one of the most telling difficulties for an S-R account of language was long obscured by the approach taken to experimental investigation. That is, until quite recently a great deal of investigation of speech recognition proceeded through the testing of isolated sound units or at best of words, without any self-conscious effort to relate the results to recognition of continuous speech. The whole problem of segmentation of the continuous acoustic signal—at phonetic, syllabic, word, or phrase levels—was thereby avoided. A psychological explanation of language behavior which begins with a word analysis has already taken a most convenient and considerable "leg-up" on the problem's solution. The results referred to in the preceding section make it evident that the step from the continuous wave form in the acoustic signal to discrete phonological entities capable of interpretation in syntactic and semantic terms is not a trivial one. The question of how one defines the relevant relationship between stimulus parameters and perceptual response is perhaps insoluble in any plausible way if one is restrained from characterizing the stimulus by reference to the structural system which the perceiver brings to the analysis problem.

Surface Structure

In an earlier portion of this paper we discussed the character of the linguistic formalism which describes a speaker's competence. It was pointed out that in this formulation semantic interpretation is dependent on the deep structure

—i.e., the structure which reveals the grammatical relations (as subject, object, modifier) of the sentence elements. The implication is that the underlying structure is of paramount psychological significance. We will return to this point again. It might well have been emphasized, however, that surface structure—the bracketing relations among the sentence elements—also appears psychologically indispensable, because surface structure may provide a clue for the recovery of deep structure and because certain features of the phonetic shape of the utterance depend on its surface structure.

The psychological relevance of some sort of phrase-like units in perception and production of sentences has for some time been evident. For example, studies of hesitation phenomena in spontaneous speech (see Maclay and Osgood, 1959; Goldman-Eisler, 1958) show that certain discontinuities occur primarily at phrase boundaries and that repetitions characteristically involve minimal phrase units. A recent study by Boomer (1965) is especially interesting because of the relationship he found between hesitation phenomena and a phrase unit defined by reference to stress patterns. Boomer's unit of analysis was the "phonemic clause," i.e., a segment marked by only one primary stress and ending in one of the terminal junctures. When Boomer segmented his corpus in terms of such units, he found a significant regularity in the distribution of pauses; only in the position following the first word of a phrase unit did the frequency of hesitations depart significantly from a chance distribution. The disparity between frequencies of pause at this position and at other positions was great (a ratio of 2.46 to the category with next greatest frequency).

We have already remarked on the intimate relationship between syntax (surface structure) and stress patterns. Thus, Boomer's findings reinforce the earlier indications of a dependency between hesitations and phrase units in the surface structure. An observation by Boomer concerning juncture pauses (used to determine the ends of his units) is especially apposite to our earlier remarks. He points out that juncture pauses, which are linguistically determined, are *not* reported by observers as hesitation pauses in spite of the fact (Boomer, 1965, p. 155) that such pauses are of significantly *greater* duration than pauses reported as hesitations. In fact, such juncture pauses were long thought to be very much shorter than hesitation pauses. As we noted earlier, it seems clear that in their assignment of complex stress patterns, judgments of intonation contour, juncture, etc., linguists are responding to their knowledge of the structure of the language, not primarily to the character of the acoustic signal.

One of the claims made in the introductory pages of this paper was that people are able to make judgments of structural similarity or difference among sentences and that an adequate grammar should reflect that capacity. A rather simple demonstration of that point (for surface structure) is provided in an experiment by Kent (1963). In this experiment Ss were exposed to three sets of superficially very similar sentences. The three types of sentences can, in fact, be distinguished only in terms of their bracketing and labeling as: (1) (they ((are discussing) (books)) is distinguished from (2) (they) ((are) (falling leaves)) and (3) (they ((are) (parking meters)) by the bracketing relationships, and (2) can be distinguished from (3) by the labeling on the last constituent. After being exposed to a (written) set of one of the three types of sentences, Ss were given the sentence frame: they are _____ cups,

and three choices for the blank: (a) washing, (b) leaking, (c) drinking. Ss were instructed to provide the "best completion." Of Ss given a set of type (1) sentences, 96% chose (a); 83% given type (2) chose (b); 79% given type (3) chose (c). While this may be experimental demonstration of the obvious, it is worth paying attention to because of the lack of the kinds of differences among the sentences that are most often appealed to in neobehaviorist attempts to cope with structural judgments—especially "grammatical tags" (prefixes, suffixes, function words, etc.). The sentences are *all* of the form (they are _____ing _____s).

Two experiments demonstrate an effect of surface structure on learning and immediate recall. Johnson (reported in Osgood, 1963) recorded errors Ss made while learning sentences of different grammatical types. Errors proved most frequent at major phrase boundaries—i.e., the sentences were apparently learned in terms of phrase groups. When part of a phrase was learned, the rest of it tended also to be learned, and this was independent of the content of other phrase groups. An obviously related finding is one by Miller (1963). When Ss are required to copy text and are constrained to do so with minimal reference to the text, they tend to select phrase groups as units to be copied—i.e., Ss write to a phrase boundary and then consult the text again.

These findings reveal the relevance of constituent structure segmentations in learning and recall. But it is more difficult to demonstrate the salience of such segmentation for processes of production and perception of sentences. It is at least possible that strategems employed in a learning or recall task are not relevant to an account of actual processing, either in encoding or decoding.

Huggins (1964), using continuous speech alternated from one ear to another, varied its rate of presentation. Early experimentation (Broadbent, 1958) with alternation of a continuous message had shown that *S*s performed repetition of messages well, except in a restricted range of alternation rates. Huggins demonstrated that the critical alternation rate was directly related to speed of presentation of the message. This entails that the performance decrement caused by the alternation cannot be attributed to some constant switching difficulty—i.e., to a processing mechanism whose operation is unaffected by the character of its input. Rather, it is plausible to argue that *where* the message is interrupted is critical and that the difficulty is determined by the ease of integration of the segments created by the interruption of the signal. Huggins showed that the segment size at the critical switching rate remains approximately constant if expressed in average syllable length but changes when expressed in seconds per segment. Huggins' measure of average syllable length is somewhat longer than usual measures. Bever has pointed out that the duration more closely corresponds to measures of average constituent length[2]. That is, the suggestion is that the critical analysis of the sentence here is in terms of its immediate constituents rather than its syllables. The evidence from Huggins' experiment may thus very well reveal a real perceptual effect of the surface structure, though measures of average syllable length or average constituent length are admittedly awkward devices at best.

Several studies using a related technique demonstrate the salience of surface structures in the perceptual analysis of sentences. In these experiments the behavior of a nonlinguistic dependent variable is determined by the percep-

[2] Personal communication, T. G. Bever, 1965.

tual consequences of syntactic structures.

The experimental technique employed exploits the difficulty (first reported by Ladefoged and Broadbent, 1960) individuals encounter in locating short bursts of noise superimposed on recordings of continuous speech material. Ladefoged and Broadbent recorded several groups of test strings (sentences and randomly ordered digits) with superimposed sounds ("clicks") and presented them to various groups of listeners. Of interest here are their findings that errors were smaller with superposition of clicks on randomly ordered series of digits than with sentences and that for different types of sentences, different distributions of errors were obtained. In general, it was very often the case that *S*s displaced the click beyond the boundaries of the word in which it was located. Ladefoged and Broadbent regarded their results as evidence that perceptual units in speech were larger than a single sound unit (as, indeed, the evidence on perception of phonemes reviewed in the previous section indicates). They concluded that one could be no more explicit than this on the basis of their data since the size of the errors was variable.

The interpretation of these results as related to the size of perceptual units in speech is, of course, dependent on assumptions similar to those made by Huggins in the interpretation of results for perception of speech alternated between the two ears. In this case it is assumed that the switch from processing verbal material to processing nonverbal material is controlled, in part, by the segmentation of the speech—i.e., switching takes place at the boundaries of perceptual units. Assuming that in the assignment of structure to a string, each major phrase group constitutes a "subroutine," computing space would be available during the hiatus between such subroutines. At such points the click could be admitted to the perceptual channel. An examination of the Ladefoged and Broadbent data for which frequency distributions were reported does reveal that clicks may tend to shift toward major phrase boundaries. This possibility would account exactly for the variable error found by Ladefoged and Broadbent— structurally different sentences should produce different sorts of errors.

An investigation designed to reveal the effect of constituent structure segmentations on click location was carried out by Fodor and Bever (1965). The response conditions required Ss to

1. listen to the sentence
2. write it down
3. indicate by a slash (/) mark their judgment of the point of occurrence of the click.

The stimuli were presented to Ss dichotically. In dichotic presentation of the stimuli, subjects receive the sentence in one ear and the click in the other. This mode of presentation requires an integrative task of Ss similar to that in the Huggins experiment. Here, of course, the speech signal is continuous, but some segment of it must be temporally associated with a nonspeech event.

Fodor and Bever constructed 25 sentences with one major constituent break and five with two major breaks. We can define the notions of *constituent break* and *strength of constituent break* as follows. The boundary between any adjacent pair of words not a member of the same constituent is a constituent break. For example, in the sentence *the[1] men[2] who[3] whistled[4] were[5] happy*, 2 and 4 are constituent breaks. Strength of a constituent break is defined as being directly related to the number of constituents whose boundaries coincide

at the break. In the example sentence, boundary number 4 is the strongest since it is a boundary for five constituents: *whistled, who whistled, the men who whistled, were*, and *were happy*. Boundary number 2 has four constituents coterminous; no other constituent boundary is coterminous for more than two constituents.

Fodor and Bever made nine copies of each of the 30 sentences and placed clicks in nine different positions for each member of the set. The objective locations of the clicks were balanced around the major constituent breaks in the sentence. For example (where Δ indicates a click position):

(That he was happy) (was evident from
$\Delta \quad \Delta \quad \Delta \quad \Delta \quad \Delta \quad \Delta \quad \Delta \quad \Delta \quad \Delta$
the way he smiled)

That is, for every sentence, one copy had a click placed at the strongest constituent break, and on the remaining eight copies four clicks were placed at progressively farther distances on either side of the major break.

Their measure of the effect of the break was the number of responses shifted from the objective position in the direction of the break. Of all responses (36 Ss) Fodor and Bever found 80 per cent to be errors. For 25 of the sentences (those with only one major break) the error responses were in the predicted direction 78 per cent of the time. For the remaining five sentences (those with two breaks) 71 per cent of errors were in the predicted directions. Both these percentages are significant ($p < .01$).

The hypothesis that errors in the location of clicks in the Fodor-Bever experiment can be accounted for by structural descriptions of the sentences is susceptible to two interpretations. It may be argued that displacement of clicks is responsive to some acoustic correlate(s) of the phrase structure rather than to the active processing of the signal into its constituents during the decoding of the sentence. That this is a potential explanation of the effect is suggested by the finding (Garrett, 1965) that the imposition of structure on digit strings by introduction of relatively long pauses results in a displacement of clicks to such pause breaks. It is clear that the displacement of clicks placed in sentences cannot be fully accounted for by pauses since the hypothesized syntactic effect was found even in instances where no acoustic pause accompanied the position of the deep syntactic break (Fodor and Bever, 1965). It is not, however, possible to rule out the effect of other acoustic correlates since there is no way to determine the effect of intonation and its interaction with pause in the previous experiment. This issue is of crucial importance in the interpretation of *S*'s displaced location of clicks in sentential material. If acoustic variables such as pause, stress, and intonation contour can be uniformly correlated with syntactic juncture, an S-R account of the perception of surface syntactic structure as a discriminated response to such acoustic variables would at least be possible in principle.

An experiment which controlled for acoustic features which might mark the boundaries of constituents was performed by Garrett, Bever, and Fodor (1966). Identical acoustic materials were provided with alternate structures by varying the linguistic context.

Six pairs of sentences were constructed for which a substring of lexical items was common to each member of a pair. For example:

(a) (In her *hope of marrying*) (*Anna was surely impractical*)
(b) (Your *hope of marrying Anna*) (*was surely impractical*)

The pairs of sentences were tape-recorded, and copies of each pair were made. The common portions of each pair were made acoustically identical by tape splicing. For the above pair, for instance, the portion . . . *hope of marrying Anna was surely impractical* taken from the recording of (a) was spliced to the portion *Your* . . . taken from (b). When this spliced version of (b) is paired with the original recording of (a), there are two sentences with acoustically identical latter portions but in which the constituent boundaries are different. Clicks were placed in the middle of words around which the constituent boundaries were manipulated. Response conditions were as described for the Fodor and Bever experiment.

The primary objective of this experiment was the determination of whether the Fodor-Bever results were properly interpreted as reflections of the assignment of structure during the processing of sentences or were instead accounted for by correlated variables (as pause and intonation). The results clearly demonstrated that no physical property of the signal can fully account for the location of the clicks. Exactly the same acoustic signal was responded to differently in every case, and the differences were as predicted by the variation in the constituent boundaries (eleven of twelve changes were in the predicted direction; $p < .03$ for this pattern).

Since in both these studies of click location *S*s were obliged to write down the sentence as a part of their response, it is possible that the subjective shift of click location does not take place during processing but some time after—i.e., that the effect is not perceptual. Subsequent research with the same stimulus materials as used in Garrett, *et al.* (1966), showed an effect of structural manipulation under conditions in which *S*s were not required to reproduce the sentence —i.e., Ss were required to provide an interpretation for the sentence with only the auditory signal as input and responded immediately with the click judgment (Garrett, 1965). The same sort of results as the above were obtained by Kirk, Lackner, and Bever (1965) using a mild electric shock instead of an auditory click. In this study Ss verbally indicated their judgments of the shock location immediately following presentation of a sentence. Bever, Kirk, and Squire (1965) have obtained similar results using a flash of light instead of a click.

The experiments reviewed here, like those of the previous section, demonstrate that the perception of sentences is an active process in which the listener provides a structural analysis rather than responding passively to some acoustic cues which "program" his responses. Although these experiments do not allow us to distinguish clearly between the effects of deep and surface structures, the presence of differences in surface structure is the minimal claim that will account for the data.

Deep Structure

We come finally to those studies which purport to demonstrate the psychological relevance of certain aspects of deep structure—in particular, the transformational relationship between certain surface structures and their underlying forms. Several of these studies of aspects of the relation between surface and deep structures are similar both in the consistency of their results and in the nature of the sentence types investigated.

It was at one time supposed that one particular sentence form (the simple, active, affirmative, declarative-SAAD) was of pre-eminent psychological sig-

nificance. This was because the SAAD was considered to serve as the transformational source or basis for the production of all other sentence types. This assumption was due, in part, to a misunderstanding about the nature of the grammatical formalism and in part to a linguistic account which has since been discarded as mistaken.

In the earlier formulation of the grammar (Chomsky, 1957) the output of the phrase structure component was modified by a transformational component, as indicated in the introductory section of this paper, but the nature of the two components was quite different. Complexities of sentence structure which were introduced by transformational rules in the early formulation are currently introduced in the phrase structure. Notably, questions (Q) negatives (N) and passives (P) were produced by optional transformation of a common base form. These three forms are now differentiated in their generation by phrase structure rules and are no longer supposed to "intersect" in their base structures.

It was this "intersection" at a common base form which provided the linguistic basis for the assumption of a psychological centrality for one form of sentence. And it was confusion about this same point which engendered the misunderstanding about relationships among these sentences referred to earlier. Since this common base form shared by Q, N and P was also the base form for the simple active affirmative declarative (SAAD)—i.e., the result of the operation of the rest of the grammar on this base form, in the event that *no* optional transformations were applied, was a SAAD—it was very easy to assume that as the grammar was then formulated, Q, N and P sentences were derived from their SAAD counterparts. This confusion is mentioned only because it has often lead to misinterpretations of the work on the psychological relevance of transformational relationships among sentence forms.

The first experiment aimed at revealing the psychological relevance of transformational operations was performed by Miller, McKean, and Slobin (Miller, 1962). The attempt was to demonstrate that the relative difficulty of producing certain systematic changes in the surface character of sentences could be predicted as a function of the relative transformational complexity of the sentences.

*S*s were given two columns of sentences and required to match the members of one with their counterparts (systematically altered) in the other. The sentences in the two columns were assumed to differ by one or two transformational operations and were, of course, randomly distributed between the columns. For example, a sentence in one column might have been *Jane liked the old woman* (SAAD), while its counterpart in the other column was *The old woman was liked by Jane.* Before beginning the task, *S*s were instructed which operations were to be performed in a particular pair of columns (as Active←→Passive, or Affirmative←→Negative, etc.). Each pair of columns tested an operation or a pair of operations (as in the case of Affirmative Active←→Passive Negative). Base search time was determined by having *S*s locate untransformed versions of sentences in a scrambled list (as SAAD ←→SAAD, or P←→P).

The assumption was that differences in the time taken to perform these matches would reflect differences in the time taken to perform the various transformational operations (or their inverses). Given a sentence, the *S*s, in order to find its match, must perform the required transformation and then look for a new sentence which matches the result of the transformation.

Of the relationships among the types of sentences studied by Miller *et al.*,

two were considered to require two operations, and four, only one operation. Where a P sentence was required, for instance, and an N sentence given, it was assumed that one "undid" the work of the negative transformation and then applied the passive. But for the same initial condition (given an N sentence) where a PN sentence was required, *S*s were assumed to apply the passive while not being required to "undo" the result of the negative transformation. On this view, it would be predicted that the results of the experiment should find SAAD←→(N or P) and PN←→(N or P) comparable while SAAD←→PN and N←→P should both be more difficult (although comparable to each other). In fact, the order in the results was just that. The view that complexity of processing these sentences can be indexed by looking at the steps in its derivational history seemed supported. Further, there was the suggestion that these operations produced a linearly additive complication (sentences involving both negative and passive transformations required a time approximately equal to the sum of the average time required for negative and passives applied separately).

Table 1

"AVERAGE TRANSFORMATION TIMES"*

Sentence Change	Seconds More Than Base Search Time
SAAD←→N	1.13
SAAD←→P	1.43
P←→PN	1.66
N←→PN	1.87
SAAD←→PN	2.74
N←→P	3.50

* From Miller & McKean, 1964, p. 300.

Because of some dissatisfaction with the pencil and paper method used above, Miller and McKean carried out a refined version of this same experiment (1964). In the later version a sentence was presented tachistoscopically, and when S had performed the required transformation of the sentence, he pressed a button which presented a search list (and stopped a timer which had been started on presentation of the sentence). In this technique the search time is separated from the presumed processing time—the search simply provides a check on the accuracy of the task performance. In this way an independent measure (S's subjective estimation) of the transformation time is obtained, and variance introduced by the search is eliminated. The results obtained here were comparable to those with the pencil and paper method, but although the equivalence sets were ordered as before, there was some rearrangement among their members. That is, those sentences requiring two operations remained more complicated than those requiring one operation, but the rank order within these classes was altered. In the Miller and McKean results, applying the negative transformation to a passive sentence is easier than applying the passive to SAAD (i.e., P$\leftrightarrow$PN is easier than SAAD$\leftrightarrow$P). This makes the Miller and McKean results more uniform than Miller *et al.* Since the negative now appears as everywhere easier than the passive, and of each of the two applications of these two transformations the one involving transform from SAAD is the easier of the pair (i.e., SAAD$\leftrightarrow$N is easier than P$\leftrightarrow$PN, SAAD$\leftrightarrow$P is easier than N$\leftrightarrow$PN and SAAD$\leftrightarrow$PN is easier than N$\leftrightarrow$P). In short, negative transforms are easier than passive transforms, and SAAD forms are easier to handle than any other.

In fact, the two preceding studies cannot be supposed to show anything about the relationship of surface and deep structure, as these notions are characterized by the grammar, nor do they yield any very direct information about the relative difficulty of the various transformations *as they are formalized in the grammar*. For, in order to maintain the predictions confirmed by the results, one has to assume that Ss were operating with some *ad hoc* set of rules which do *not* apply to the structures specified as domains for these particular grammatical transformations. The relationship between what Ss are doing in the experimental situation and the operations defined by grammar is thus quite unclear.

Consider the sequence of operations which would have to occur if Ss were using the transformations as they are (or were) formulated in the 1957 version of the grammar. First, S is required to recover the underlying ("kernel") structure of the sentence he is presented with. Having recovered this deep structure, he can then perform the transformations necessary to produce one or another derived sentence form. He has to recover deep structure in order to apply the transformations, for it is only for deep structure domains that these transformations are defined. But, having recovered the deep structure, S has then to generate the required derived structure. This will include carrying out any transformational operations he may have "undone" in recovering the deep structure whenever that operation is required to produce the surface structure of the search sentence. For example, in the Miller and McKean formulation N$\leftrightarrow$P is more complex than N$\leftrightarrow$NP—presumably because it was supposed that one must undo the effect of the negative transformation in one case but not in the other. But in recovery of the deep structure in either case, one would have to perform the inverse negative transform (or some version of such an operation). Hence:

Neg sentence _____ UP$_{neg}$ delete neg UP _add pass_ UP$_{pass}$

UP$_{pass}$ _do pass_ Passive sentence

AND:

Neg sentence _____ UP$_{neg}$ _add pass_ ____ UP$_{pass-neg}$

UP$_{pass-neg}$ _do pass, do neg_ Negative-Passive Sentence

This would make it appear that N↔NP is *more* complicated than N↔P. This assumes that recovery of deep structure is equivalent in both cases, however. If we assume that N↔P has an extra operation required—i.e., that UP for negative sentences will have a negative marker which has to be deleted (as in current formulations of the grammar), the number of operations required is the *same* for both changes.

(1) adding *had*, (2) adding some form of *be*, or (3) adding both *had* and *be*. The predictions here were analogous to those for the transformations—difficulty was expected to increase with complexity of the verb phrase. The results were that there were no significant differences as a function of the changes introduced, with the exception that addition of *had* was very much easier than any other operation (.19

Neg sentence ____recovery of deep structure_____ UP

UP ___generation of___ apply passive transform_____Passive Sentence
          surface structure

AND:

UP ___generation of___ apply passive and _____Negative-Passive Sentence
          surface structure   negative transforms

This way of counting operations is required if one is going to make any claim about the relation of deep structure to surface structure or about the relative difficulty of the various transformational operations *as they are formulated by the grammar*. What is needed, of course, is some theoretically motivated way of saying which of the grammatically defined operations are psychologically relevant—i.e., which ones should be counted in predictions about complexity of perception, production, or recall.

Another result of Miller and McKean is relevant in light of the preceding. They carried out tests of sentences that differed in the expansion of the verb auxiliary. Sentences differed as follows: *Joe warned the boy; Joe had warned the boy; Joe was warning the boy; Joe had been warning the boy.* These differ by

seconds added compared with from .54 to .63 seconds added for the other operations). If one assumes the construct validity of Miller and McKean's procedures, this result suggests that *S*s may have been working with *ad hoc* rules devised to fit the experimental task rather than carrying out the operations specified for different expansions of auxiliaries in the grammar. An alternative conclusion, of course, is that the operations in the grammar which are related to the Q, N and P changes are somehow psychologically more relevant than are variations in the expansion .of auxiliaries. This situation is typical of the difficulty of interpreting negative results in the area of psychological reality of linguistic constructs. It is difficult to know whether to blame the experimental procedures, the grammatical theory, or the experimental assumptions about how grammatical and psychological constructs ought to interact.

Another experiment (McMahon, 1963) with negative and passive sentence types provides information of a different kind. McMahon's test of these sentence types required Ss to judge whether a presented sentence was true or false (by depressing a labeled key which stopped a timer activated when the sentence was presented). His sentences were of the form *5 precedes 13* or *3 is preceded by 7*, etc.

McMahon found that it required longer to judge the truth of negative sentences than of passives or active affirmatives. The order of difficulty from easiest to most difficult was:

Active Affirmative
          —small difference
Passive Affirmative
          —large difference
Active Negative
          —small difference
Passive Negative

These results are interesting when compared to those of Miller and McKean. The transformation easiest to perform is apparently the one whose truth value is most difficult to determine. It is not obvious how to interpret the difference between the Miller-McKean results and those of McMahon unless it is assumed that semantic considerations play a central role when questions of truth value are raised in the experimental situation. On that assumption, one can account for the observed proximity of synonymous forms (actives and passives) and for the reordering of sentence types.

An extensive study of the effects on recall of the differences between SAAD, Q, P, and N sentences was carried out by Mehler (1964). The addition of Q sentences yielded eight sentence types (SAAD, Q, P, N, PQ, NQ, and PQN).

Mehler used eight lists of eight sentences each; each list contained one of the eight syntactic types; each sentence on a given list was derived from semantically disparate SAAD's. S was presented with eight sentences one after another. After he had heard all eight, S attempted to recall the sentences in the set. Then the sentences were presented again and S was again tested for his recall—and so on, for five presentations. Ten Ss were run for each of the eight lists.

Scored for ease of acquisition (length in words did *not* predict ease of learning) SAAD is much easier to learn than any of the other types. This conforms to the results of both the Miller-McKean studies and the McMahon study.

Mehler assumed that sentences were recalled by Ss using a strategy in which the underlying form of the sentence was recalled independently of appended transformational "notes" which determine its derived syntactic form. That is, the sentence is assumed to be represented in memory, not by its surface form, but by some information minimally necessary to specify semantic content and by a set of specifications for deriving the surface structure. The minimal information required for semantic content is, as the linguistic description specifies, the deep structure. Since SAAD forms are those with a minimal number of syntactic "footnotes" (they most closely resemble their underlying form), they should be most easily and accurately remembered.

In these results, the sentences were ordered roughly as they were in the Miller and McKean study; the order for correct recall was similar to that for ease of transformation. SAAD was much the best for accurate recall; those cases with only one transformation were next, followed by those with multiple transformations. This indicates that for these types of sentences, length of derivation is related to ease of recall.

The nature of the errors made in recall supports the "coding hypothesis" (memory form = UP + transformations). There was a strong tendency for errors to be "in the direction of" the simplest form which preserved semantic information—400 errors were in this direction vs. 248 in the opposite (more complex) direction. Recall of the SAAD form was strikingly better than any other type.

Mehler also tested the effect of expansion of auxiliaries on recall. More complicated expansions (involving modals) were used than those of Miller and McKean (*The boy hit the ball; the boy has hit the ball; . . . could hit . . .; . . . was hitting . . .; . . . could have hit . . .; . . . could be hitting . . .; . . . has been hitting . . .; . . . could have been hitting . . .*). The same conditions (eight lists, eight syntactic types, eight semantic types) as for the first experiment were present here.

Subjects did not show any significant tendency to learn sentences with simpler auxiliary expansions more readily than those with complex expansions. Further, there was no tendency for response errors to be simplifications of the presented sentence; 155 errors were simplifications, and 157 errors involved complications of the auxiliaries.

This result corresponds to that obtained by Miller and McKean in their study of auxiliary expansion. The failure to find an effect of auxiliary expansion on ease of transformation or on recall indicates that a simple explanation in terms of length of derivation will not account for the facts of production or perception of sentences. Certain of the grammatical operations in the derivation are more relevant to explanations of linguistic performance than are others. This is just what was suggested by the disparity between counting the formal operations in

transforming sentences and counting surface changes. Further, the failure to get results with auxiliary expansion suggests that it is not just the semantic aspects of the changes produced by the transformational operations investigated by Miller and McKean, by McMahon, and by Mehler that accounts for their findings, since semantic changes were produced by the different expansions of auxiliaries. The reason for the special character of Q, N, and P is a matter yet to be clearly explained.

There are three more types of studies which represent particularly relevant approaches to performance variables. The first of these is by Savin and Perchonock (1965). It represents an attempt to relate the storage requirements of the various sentence types to aspects of their structural descriptions. The assumption is that the greater the complexity of a sentence's description, as indexed by the number of rules required for its production, the greater will be the demands on storage. Savin and Perchonock sought to determine this difference by requiring Ss to recall both a sentence and a set of unrelated words as follows. Ss were presented with a sentence followed by a string of eight unrelated words. S had to repeat the sentence and then as many of the eight words as he could recall. The number of words successfully recalled was the measure of storage requirements for that particular sentence type (always assuming that the sentence was correctly recalled, of course). Savin used the same sentences as did Mehler plus emphatic (E—heightened stress on auxiliary) and Wh forms. Hence, Savin and Perchonock investigated SAAD, Q, P, N, E, Wh and the combinations of any two transformations.

The ordering of sentence types from the results of this experiment was as follows in Table 2 (ordering is presumably from least storage requirement to greatest):

Table 2

MEAN NUMBER OF WORDS RECALLED FOR EACH SENTENCE TYPE

Sentence Type	Words Recalled	
SAAD	5.27	⎫
Wh	4.78	⎪
Q	4.67	⎪
P	4.55	⎬ (Presumably one
N	4.44	⎪ transformation)
Q_{neg}	4.39	⎪
E	4.30	⎭
PQ_{neg}	4.02	⎫
PQ	3.85	⎬ (Presumably two
EP	3.74	⎪ transformations)
NP	3.48	⎭

Note that in every case those sentences with one transformational operation required less storage (interfered less with recall of word strings) than those with two operations and that SAAD was least interfering of all.

More strikingly, Savin and Perchonock found a constant effect of given transformations. That is, a particular transformational operation apparently took the same storage space whatever other transformations it was associated with (Q added the same difficulty for P to PQ as for SAAD to Q, etc.). In this experiment (as for Mehler, etc.) length of the sentence in words will not account for the results.

The results of the Savin, Perchonock and Mehler studies are most persuasive as an argument for the relation of aspects of the derivational history provided by the grammar to processes of sentence production and perception. The objections raised to such an interpretation of the Miller-McKean results do not apply here since the ordering of sentence types depends only on the number of operations required for deriving the sentences and not upon questionable assumptions about the operations required to change one sentence type to another.

However, the suggestion implicit in the above results, that there is some simple relation between grammatical complexity and performance difficulty, is open to serious *caveats*. We have seen that complication of auxiliaries fails to introduce the same performance difficulties as complication effected by Q, P, N, etc. Moreover, recent preliminary results owing to Bever, Fodor, Garrett, and Mehler, suggest that increase in performance complexity is not uniformly associated with increase in transformational complexity in cases where synonymy and morpheme length are fully controlled. In pilot experiments, we have used a task analogous to that employed by Savin and Perchonok, except that S was required to identify one of a series of four tones heard prior to a sentence. Under this condition, no performance differences could be reliably associated with transformational differences like the one between *John phoned up the girl* and *John phoned the girl up* or like the one between *The bus driver was fired after the wreck* and *The bus driver was nervous after the wreck*. Further investigations in this area are currently being undertaken.

All the above studies have been occupied with the question of the performance significance of the segmentation of utterances or of particular operations (transformations) in their derivation. A recent study by Mehler and Carey (1966) attempts a direct demonstration of the effect of deep structure on perception. Two sets of sentences were constructed which differed only in their deep structure—as, *They are reluctant to consent* vs. *They are troublesome to employ*. (Note that corresponding to the latter, one says *To employ them is troublesome*, but corresponding to the former, one says *They are reluctant about consenting; they* is object of the verb in one sentence type and the subject in the other). Two sets of sentences differing in their surface structure also were constructed —as, *They are recurring mistakes* vs. *they are describing events*. (Notice that this is the same surface difference investigated by Kent.) The strategy employed by Mehler and Carey was as follows. *S*s were required to recognize sentences presented under noise. A particular sentence received a recognition score when it followed a homogeneous set of similar sentence types. That is, the effect of *S*'s expectation of a particular deep or superficial structure on the perception of a sentence congruous with that expectation was compared with its effect on perception of a sentence which was incongruous with that expectation.

The results showed higher recognition scores for sentences whose structure was congruent with the set they followed. The difference was significant ($p < .05$) for one of the comparisons of deep structure but not for the other, although the change in recognition score was in the expected direction. For the two sentences of different surface structure, the difference between test and control was significant ($p < .05$) in both cases. A supplementary source of information was the sort of error *S*s made in their recording of the sentences. An analysis of these errors showed that *S*s very frequently selected substitute words compatible with the syntactic set rather than making phonetically similar substitutions.

Although it is difficult to draw conclusions from only the two cases for each type, it appears that the effects of surface structure are more pronounced than the effect of deep structure. Unfortunately for the comparison, however, the sentences which differ in their surface structure also differ in their deep structure. Moreover, one of

the two types of sentences used for testing the effects of surface structure (*they are describing events*) is much more similar to its underlying form than is the other. The effect obtained for the surface structure comparisons could thus be confounded with an effect of differences in the relation between surface and deep structure.

Research now in progress using the techniques employed by Mehler and Carey seems to confirm the finding that deep structure influences perception[3]. In this instance, the sentence types being used put physical similarity and underlying structural similarity into conflict. Preliminary data indicates, for instance, that a set of short passive sentences (*John was surprised*) is facilitating for recognition of full passives (*John was seen by Bill*) but not for the physically more similar predicate adjective construction (*John was angry*).

An assumption of earlier studies (Mehler, Savin and Perchonock) is that sentences are remembered or perceived in terms of their underlying structure plus some specification of the operations required for generation of surface forms. In Mehler and Carey there is an effort to demonstrate a perceptual consequence of the structural expectations of *S*s where those expectations concern aspects of deep structure. Two experiments (Blumenthal, 1965; Blumenthal and Boakes, 1965) with prompted recall of sentences exploit the following property of deep structure (see p. 454): The sentence description given by deep structure specifies the information required for semantic interpretation. In particular, the grammatical relations of the lexical formatives are specified in terms of deep structure configurations. Blumenthal took sets of sentences for which the surface structure was similar but for

[3] Mehler and Fodor, personal communication.

which the deep structure was different. Ss learned the sentences and were then required to produce each one when a word taken from it was presented as a prompting cue. The sentences were of the type used in an earlier example (p. 453). In these sentences, the last nouns bear different relationships to the rest of the sentence; in one case the noun is logical subject (*The theorem was proved by John*) and in the other, the noun is part of an adverbial modifier (*The theorem was proved by induction*). Blumenthal found a significant interaction between the prompt words and the sentence type. When the final noun relates to the rest of the sentence in the deep structure as subject, recall was improved; i.e., when the prompt word implicated the whole sentence structure, recall was better than when it implicated only part of the structure.

A subsequent study (Blumenthal and Boakes, 1965) used sentences of different types and provided for more complete mastery of grammatical relations by Ss. The sentences were of the sort: (1) *John is easy to please* vs. (2) *John is eager to please*. In these sentences the noun is related either as subject of the sentence or as object in the verb phrase; the adjective is related as modifier either of the noun, as *John is eager*, or of a whole structure, as *For someone to please John is easy*. Using the first noun as prompt, better recall would be predicted for sentences of type (2); using the adjective as prompt, better recall would be predicted for sentences of type (1). Just these results were obtained by Blumenthal and Boakes. The effect of the verb as a prompt in these sentence types was also tested. Since the verbs in these two sentence types do not differ greatly in their relationship to the rest of the sentence, it was expected that no significant difference in recall of sentences would be found using verbs as the prompt. The data supports this prediction.

This demonstration of the effect on recall of deep structure relationships among sentence elements is compatible with the result of earlier studies showing a tendency toward recall of underlying forms (Mehler, 1964). While the Blumenthal and Boakes work is a rather clear demonstration of the effect of deep structural relationships on recall, it needs to be emphasized that aspects of structure relevant to accounts of learning or recall need not be relevant in the same respects to accounts of production or perception of sentences. The study by Mehler and Carey suggests that deep structures are in fact perceptually relevant, but the questions of what aspects of deep structure are significant and how they are related to surface structures is still unclear.

Conclusion

So long as fairly primitive competence models were widely endorsed by linguists, the prospects for a psycholinguistics that preserved the essential properties of associationism seemed good. Many psychologists have, for example, been enthusiastic about the possibility that correct grammars can be derived from a corpus by classifying together items that share environments in the corpus. It was natural to interpret the linguistic notion of sharing the same environment in terms of the psychological notion of contiguity with the same element. Since association by contiguity is held to be locally transitive, elements contiguous with a common element presumably become associated with one another. Thus, there seemed to be a natural psychological interpretation for the notion of belonging to a common grammatical class; namely, being in the associative set for the environment that defines that class. The linguist thought of *boy* and *girl* as elements to be classified together because of their common distribution (e.g., preceding plural *s*). The psychologist thought of them as elements related by an associative bond, the formation of which is mediated by their common association-through-contiguity with plural *s*: clearly these theories are compatible, hence the air of interdisciplinary celebration that marked the psychological discussion of language in the late '40s and early '50s.

Even the development of more powerful competence models was not in itself a basis for rejecting associationistic accounts of language processes. It was possible to claim (what many psychologists appear to believe) that such models are best understood as uninterpreted formalisms; that is, as mathematical systematizations of linguistic relations having no direct or obvious psychological pertinence, hence having no tendency to determine the character of an adequate performance model.

The research reviewed above, however, would appear to preclude such an interpretation. What this research appears to show is that relations marked by grammars whose formal power transcends that of class and sequence models are, in fact, employed in the decoding and encoding of speech. That is, the behavior of subjects in experimental situations can be made responsive to the recognition of syntactic interrelations of kinds that cannot be marked by the simpler grammatical systems.

The problem for general S-R theory is thus clear. Either it must be demonstrated how an appeal to the sorts of learning mechanisms S-R theory allows can account for the assimilation and application of the kinds of linguistic information that is incorporated in the more powerful competence models, or associationistic accounts of language learning and of speech must be abandoned.

Reference

Bever, T., J. Fodor, and W. Weksel, "Is Linguistics Empirical," *Psychological Review*, **72** (1965), 467–482.

——, R. Kirk, and R. Squire, "The Effect of Syntax on Judgments of Occurrence of Light Flashes during Auditory Presentation of Sentences," unpublished research, MIT, Cambridge, Mass., 1965.

Blumenthal, A., "Prompted Recall of Sentences," *Technical Report, Harvard Center for Cognitive Studies*, 1965.

——, and R. Boakes, "Prompted Recall of Sentences: A Further Study." *Technical Report, Harvard Center for Cognitive Studies*, 1965.

Bolinger, D., and L. Gerstman, "Disjuncture as a Cue to Constructs," *Word*, **13** (1957), 246–255.

Boomer, D., "Hesitation and Grammatical Encoding," *Language and Speech*, **8** (1965).

Braine, M., "On Learning the Grammatical Order of Words," *Psychological Review*, **70** (1963), 323–348.

Broadbent, D., *Perception and Communication*. New York: Pergamon Press, 1958.

Carroll, J. B., *Language and Thought*. Englewood Cliffs, N.J.: Prentice-Hall, Inc., 1964.

Chomsky, N., *Syntactic Structures*. The Hague, Netherlands: Mouton and Co., 1957.

——, "Review of *Verbal Behavior*," *Language*, **35** (1959), 26–58.

——, "On the Notion 'Rule of Grammar,'" *Proceedings of Symposia in Applied Mathematics*, XII, American Mathematical Society, 1961.

——, "Current Issues in Linguistic Theory," in *The Structure of Language*, eds., Fodor and Katz. Englewood Cliffs, N.J.: Prentice Hall, Inc., 1964.

——, *Aspects of the Theory of Syntax*. Cambridge, Mass.: MIT Press, 1965.

Cooper, F., J. Borst, and A. Liberman, "The Interconversion of Audible and Visible Patterns as a Basis for Research in the Perception of Speech," *Proceed-*

ings of the National Academy of Sciences, **87** (1951), 318–325.

DeLattre, P., A. Liberman, and F. Cooper, "Acoustic Loci and Transitional Cues for Consonants," *Journal of the Acoustical Society of America*, **27** (1955), 769–773.

Fairbanks, G., and P. Grubb, "A Psychophysical Investigation of Vowel Formants," *Journal of Speech and Hearing Research*, **4** (1961), 203–220.

Fodor, J., "Could Meaning Be an r_m?" *Journal of Verbal Learning and Verbal Behavior*, **4** (1965), 73–81.

———, and T. Bever, "The Psychological Reality of Linguistic Segments," *Journal of Verbal Learning and Verbal Behavior*, **4** (1965), 414–420.

Garrett, M., "Syntactic Structures and Judgments of Auditory Events," unpublished doctoral dissertation, University of Illinois, 1965.

———, T. Bever, and J. Fodor, "The Active Use of Grammar in Speech Perception," *Perception and Psychophysics*, **1** (1966), 30–32.

Goldman-Eisler, F., "Speech Analysis and Mental Processes," *Language and Speech*, **1** (1958), 59–75.

Hadding-Koch, K., and M. Studdert-Kennedy, "An Experimental Study of Some Intonation Contours," *Phonetica*, **11** (1964), 175–185.

Halle, M., and N. Chomsky, *The Sound Structure of English*. New York: Harper and Row, in press.

Huggins, A., "Distortion of the Temporal Pattern of Speech: Interruption and Alternation," *Journal of the Acoustical Society of America*, **36** (1964), 1055–1064.

Jenkins, J., and D. Polermo, "Mediation Processes and the Acquisition of Linguistic Structure," in *The Acquisition of Language*, eds., Bellugi and Brown. Chicago: University of Chicago Press, 1964.

Katz, J., and P. Postal, *An Integrated Theory of Linguistic Descriptions*. Cambridge, Mass.: MIT Press, 1964.

Kent, G., "The Influence of Syntactic Context on Interpretation of Discourse," unpublished paper, Institute of Communications Research, University of Illinois, 1963.

Kirk, R., J. Lackner, and T. Bever, "An Experiment in the Effect of Syntactic Structures in Speech Perception," unpublished paper, MIT, Cambridge, Mass., 1965.

Ladefoged, P., and D. Broadbent, "Perception of Sequence in Auditory Events," *Quantity Journal Experimental Psychology*, **12** (1960), 162–170.

Lane, H., "The Motor Theory of Speech Perception: A Critical Review," *Psychological Review*, **72** (1965), 275–309.

Liberman, A., "Some Results of Research on Speech Perception," *Journal of the Acoustical Society of America*, **29** (1957), 117–123.

———, P. Delattre, F. Cooper, and L. Gerstman, "The Role of Consonant-Vowel Transitions in the Perception of Stop and Nasal Consonants," *Psychological Monographs*, **68** (1954), 1–13.

———, F. Cooper, K. Harris, P. MacNeilage, and M. Studdart-Kennedy, "Some Observations on a Model for Speech Perception," paper given at the AFCRL Symposium on Models for the Perception of Speech in Visible Forms. Boston, Mass., November, 1964.

———, K. Harris, P. Eimas, L. Lisker, and J. Bastian, "An Effect of Learning on Speech Perception: The Discrimination of Durations of Silence with and without Phonemic Significance," *Language and Speech*, **4** (1961), 175–195.

———, ———, H. Hoffman, and B. Griffith, "The Discrimination of Speech Sounds within and across Phoneme Boundaries," *Journal of Experimental Psychology*, **54** (1957), 358–368.

———, ———, J. Kinney, and H. Lane, "The Discrimination of Relative Onset-time of the Components of Certain Speech and Nonspeech Patterns," *Journal of Experimental Psychology*, **61** (1961), 379–388.

Licklider, J., and G. Miller, "The Perception of Speech," in *Handbook of Experimental Psychology*, ed., Stevens. New York: John Wiley & Sons, Inc., 1951.

Lieberman, P., "Some Acoustic Correlates

of Word Stress in American English," *Journal of the Acoustical Society of America,* **32** (1960), 451.

Maclay, H., and C. Osgood, "Hesitation Phenomena in Spontaneous English Speech," *Word,* **15** (1959), 19–42.

McMahon, L., "Grammatical Analysis as Part of Understanding a Sentence," unpublished doctoral dissertation, Harvard University, 1963.

Mehler, J., "How Some Sentences are Remembered," unpublished doctoral dissertation, Harvard University, 1964,

———, and P. Carey, "The Role of Surface and Base Structure in the Perception of Sentences," *Journal of Verbal Learning and Verbal Behavior,* (1967), in press.

Miller, G., "Psychological Implications ...of Constituent Structure," *Third Annual Report,* Center for Cognitive Studies, Harvard University, 1963.

———, E. Galanter, and K. Pribram, *Plans and the Structure of Behavior.* New York: Holt-Dryden, 1960.

———, and K. McKean, "A Chronometric Study of Some Relations between Sentences," *Quantity Journal of Experimental Psychology,* **16** (1964), 297–308.

———, ———, and D. Slobin, "The Exploration of Transformations by Sentence Matching," in G. Miller, "Some Psychological Studies of Grammar," *American Psychologist,* **17** (1962), 748–762.

Morton, J., and W. Jassem, "Acoustic Correlates of Stress," *Language and Speech,* **8** (1965), 159–181.

Osgood, C., "Motivational Dynamics of Language Behavior," in *Nebraska Symposium on Motivation,* ed., Jones. Lincoln, Neb.: University of Nebraska Press, 1957.

———, "On Understanding and Creating Sentences," *American Psychologist,* **18** (1963), 735–751.

Peterson, G., and H. Barney, "Control Methods Used in a Study of the Vowels," *Journal of the Acoustical Society of America,* **24** (1952), 175–184.

Saporta, S., ed., *Psycholinguistics: A Book of Readings.* New York: Holt, Rinehart, and Winston, 1961.

Savin, H., and E. Perchonock, "Grammatical Structures and the Immediate Recall of English Sentences," *Journal of Verbal Learning and Verbal Behavior,* **4** (1965), 348–353.

Associations to Stimulus-Response Theories of Language[1]

18

THOMAS G. BEVER

I will emphasize four points in the course of this discussion. First, "Linguistic Theory" is a psychological theory: it accounts for a set of regular psychological intuitions about sentences. Second, stimulus-response associationism cannot account for the structure of language or language behavior: various attempts to offer S-R models as theories for *part* of language structure are not only pointless in principle but have been fruitless in fact. Third, we cannot hope to learn to understand verbal behavior by studying experimental manipulation of words: sentences are not special cases of word sequences; on the contrary, words are special cases of sentences. Finally, the reviews of recent psycholinguistic investigations demonstrate how little we understand the principles of the interaction between language structures and behavior.

What is a Linguist?

Today's papers have drawn clearly the distinction between the formal analysis of language and the psychological reflection of that analysis in actual speech behavior. I am reluctant to add even more smoke to an already congested problem, but some discussion is necessary to understand the different aspects of language study.

I would like to show you that there is no methodological conflict between linguistics and psychology since *both* approaches to language utilize two distinct types of facts: the structure which underlies behavior and the actual implementation of that structure. Certainly psychologists must include such structural notions as *word, sentence,* and *ambiguity* in their descriptions. On the other hand, it has often seemed as though linguists ignore all psychological facts in favor of so-called "linguistic facts" about language and that linguists are therefore concerned only with "structure" and not with "behavior." But linguistic facts *are* psychological since they are themselves behavioral intuitions. Consider five different "levels" of language which linguistic theories have described separately: sounds, words, phrases, sentences, and meanings. Each of these linguistic levels is differentiated intuitively from the others and has a particular kind of intuitively discovered

[1] The author is a Junior Fellow at Harvard University and a Lecturer at M.I.T. This work was supported by NASA Grant NsG–496 and Air Force Contract No. AF 916(628)–5705 and the Harvard Society of Fellows.

unit. For example, we "know" that *cats, stack, cast, task, tacks, scat* all make use of the same *sounds*, independent of their differences in meaning and word-class. We "know" that *look out* and *outlook* use the same words, that *the nice boy likes the nice girl* and *the nice girl likes the nice boy* use the same phrases; that *the boy, who is nice, likes the girl* and *the boy is nice and likes the girl* are made up of the same sentences; that *the man is a bachelor* and *the man has never been married* share the same semantic interpretation. Each of these different kinds of "linguistic facts" have been distinct in linguistic theories (although not all theories attempt to find a grammatical explanation for every level). What I wish to emphasize here is that linguists have fragmented language into different kinds of descriptive problems and that each problem is differentiated *intuitively* from the others.

It is not just the descriptive levels which are intuitively differentiated. Recent advances in linguistic analysis have depended on an intuitive limitation of the kinds of facts at each level which are to be explained by a theory of language. Linguists intuitively separate those facts which are pertinent to the grammatical theory of language ("langue," "competence") from those pertinent to the use of language ("parole," "performance") by actual speakers[2]. In this way they mercifully protect themselves from many of the caprices imposed on language structure by human performance.

The basic intuitive distinction formally represented in modern linguistic research is the separation of sequences into sentences and "nonsentences", an

adequate grammar of a language is *by definition* the grammar which produces the sentences of that language and does not produce any nonsentences. Linguistic theory must claim that the sentences of the natural language and those produced by the linguistic grammar are identical. *By assumption* the natural domain of linguistic theory is the set of all *intuitively* well-formed sentences: any systematic facts about speech which are outside that domain are *by assumption* part of the "performance" of the language.

The natural domain of linguistic theory might have been defined to include only more restricted kinds of facts. For instance, the natural unit to be explained by linguistic theory might be defined as the *phrase*. In this case any systematic analysis outside the phrase would not be included within the theory itself. The natural domain of linguistic theory has sometimes been even more restricted. Indeed, de Saussure, the first modern proponent of the distinction between the structure of language and the use of language, held that the essential linguistic unit is the *word* and that the formation of phrases and sentences is outside of the theory of the language.

There is, of course, no formal way of deciding which decision is most appropriate. In general, as we discover new types of theories for the formal analysis of language, our goals for the theory can expand. Thus one could view the "langue" theory of the *Cours*[3] as an explication of the phonological and semantic nature of words and the precise character of similarities and differences among words. One could further view the structuralist taxonomic phrase-structure approach of recent American theory (see Bloomfield, 1933) as a way of explaining the nature of

---

[2] For discussion of this distinction in the study of syntax and semantics see de Saussure (1916); Chomsky (1957, 1965); Fodor and Katz (1962); Bever, Fodor, and Weksel (1965).

[3] de Saussure (1916)

word-types and relations among them in phrases, as well as offering a precise characterization of similarities and differences among phrases. Similarly, the recent transformational developments can be viewed as a way of explaining the nature of phrases and relations among them in sentences. as well as formally explicating the characteristics of the similarities and differences among sentences themselves.

I have given you this brief review of the course of the domain of linguistic description to illustrate that there is no clear point where linguistic theory stops and psychological theory begins. There are, however, many arbitrary lines which have been drawn by linguists in order to partition off the kinds of facts about language which they felt prepared to describe. In each case there has been nothing formal *or* mysterious about the division of facts about language; the transformational grammarian appeals to an intuition shared by most of us about our language when he claims that he will consider only facts which pertain to complete sentences. We all agree roughly on what a sentence is, and no doubt we could define psychological tests which will distill most sentences most of the time. However, the fact that there are no generally used experimental procedures for isolating sentences does not mean that the distinction between sentences and nonsentences is psychologically irrelevant or invalid. On the contrary, in many cases the agreement on what is (or is not) a sentence is larger than for most behavioral distinctions. Even if the agreement were much weaker than it is, the point would remain the same—the linguist uses an introspective behavioral criterion to choose among his intuitions about the language he is studying.

Before discussing further the nature of this criterion, consider some of the intuitions which modern grammarians use to decide what data about sentences are relevant for description. The most important is *sentencehood* itself. Any sequence which meets the intuitive criterion of sentencehood must be included in the linguistic description. For example, the linguist assumes that (a) is a sentence which he must describe and that (b) is not:

(a) George is a nice boy.
(b) Boy is a nice George.

Another intuition is that of multiple interpretation (grammatical ambiguity). A grammar must give the sentences in (c) alternate grammatical structures.

(c) (1) The patient will inherit everything.
　　(2) They gave her dog candies.
　　(3) The duck is ready to eat.

Finally, the several levels of structural relations among words in sentences must be described. For instance, at the surface phrase structure level in (d) "dog" is more closely bound to "candies" than in (e).

(d) They gave him dog candies.
(e) They gave his dog candies.

Similarly at the deep phrase structure level the relation between "duck" and "eat" is quite different in (f) and (g).

(f) The duck is anxious to eat.
(g) The duck is tasty to eat.

I have gone through these familiar kinds of examples because I want to re-emphasize that there is nothing formal in the decisions which linguists make about their data. In fact, from a formal point of view the whole process is tremendously tenuous and fortuitous. The linguist must make various assumptions about the way in which his own intuitions reflect the knowledge of his language: his intuitions must be dependable, and they must be qualitatively invariant over different kinds of sentences. These assumptions are simple and certainly appear to be well founded, but they should not be considered inviolate. It is quite conceivable that the psychological reflection of grammar is inconsistent with respect to the sentencehood of individual sequences.

Such an inconsistency has been found in the case of sentences with center-embedded clauses. *Insecticides exterminators professors recommend manufacture fumigate apartments* is phenomenologically absurd as an example of English. General linguistic constraints require, however, that a grammar generate it (i.e., in order to be able to generate sentences with *one* embedding, e.g., *Insecticides exterminators manufacture fumigate apartments*, the grammar must allow *any* number of center-embeddings). Thus the linguist claims that sentences with two embeddings may *seem* ungrammatical, but only as a psychological illusion; it is a case for which the usual intuitions about sentencehood cannot be trusted. Ultimately, the linguist is making a very strong psychological claim: the phenomenological unacceptability of two-center-embeddings is not related to the structure of the language while the unacceptability of sentences like (b) is dependent on the language structure.[4]

---

[4] Another example of this occurs with verb-particle separation. Surely we can say (1) *He called the girl up*, but what about (2) *He called the not very nice or attractive young girl whom you like anyway up?* There seems to be some kind of length restriction on the object noun-phrase which can occur between the verb and particle. At the moment there is no satisfactory structural explanation for this; that is, in order to be able to generate acceptable sequences like (1), the theory must also generate sequences like (2).

Often the linguist uses extremely subtle criteria in his decisions about intuitions which he himself cannot make explicit. Who can say that (h) is grammatical but (i) is not?

(h) Personally, I don't disagree with a word he didn't ask you not to say.
(i) The whole group are here.

or which of the sentences (j)—(m) is ambiguous and which is not?

(j) John will make a wonderful story-teller.
(k) John will make a wonderful statue.
(l) John will make a wonderful rug.
(m) John will make a wonderful microscope.

or whether *the troops* phrase is more closely related to the preceding verb in (n) than in (o)?

(n) The general defied *the troops* to fight.
(o) The general desired *the troops* to fight.

In each of these cases it is possible to make fairly consistent decisions, and this is what linguists in fact do. I do not doubt the self-consistency that a person can achieve in these decisions, but I doubt very much that he can tell me what he's doing.

In brief, a linguist utilizes the strategy diagramed below—he assumes that a speaker has a knowledge of his grammar and that some of the structural distinctions in the grammar are *consistently* reflected in his intuition about sentencehood, structural relations, ambiguities, and so on. He uses these consistent reflections in behavior to decide what data about the language he must describe (Diagram 1).

The data are themselves enumerated by a *grammar* which meets the general requirements of all grammars.

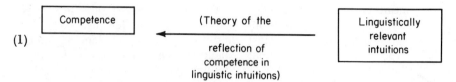

(1)

In contrast a "psycholinguist" who is concerned with generative grammar is the complement of the corresponding linguist. The linguist assumes that the psychological reflection of structure is stable and investigates the formal structure. The psycholinguist assumes

The psychologist takes this analysis in conjunction with a particular behavioral theory to predict new data. In combination the entire scientific process has the form of Diagram 3.

I perform this exercise in taxonomy not because it is explanatory but be-

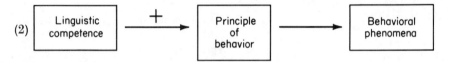

(2)

that the formal structure is correct, and he studies its psychological ramifications by combining the grammar of a language with some general principle of behavior to predict new facts about language behavior (Diagram 2).

This strategy uses the same assump-

cause it is instructive. In both linguistics and psychology we can observe that the most uncertain link is the particular psychological theory of how structure is implemented in actual behavior. There are many psychological concepts which we would like to integrate with

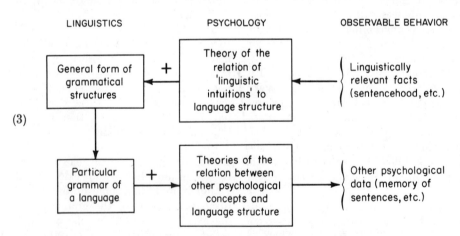

(3)

tions about the relation between grammar and psychology as the linguist, but in the reverse direction. The linguist assumes that his intuitions are consistent with respect to the grammar, and he combines them with his assumptions about the general form of grammars to produce a particular analysis.

grammatical structure: long-term memory, short-term memory, forgetting, attention, perceptual constancy, recognition, comprehension, the learning of structure, the neurological reflection of structure. The problem is that our general psychological theories of how structure is implemented in behavior are miserable. We do not even really understand the psychological nature of the procedures that linguists use to isolate facts relevant for linguistic description. Thus I hardly think that we are in any position to do crucial experimentation on the psychological "reality of transformational grammar" any more than the "physical reality of the parallelogram of forces" could be tested without an understanding of how to avoid (or compensate for) friction effects. In fact, the grammar itself seems to be the most secure element in our research strategy since it does account for a large set of consistent intuitions. This implies that psycholinguistic experimentation should tell us at least as much about general rules for implementing structure in behavior as it does about the structure of languages itself.

I should emphasize that despite the difficulties with certain data, the transformational theory of language is supported just by the clear psychological data which the theory does account for. Intuitions about sentencehood, ambiguity, and structural relations are psychological data of the most diverse kind. A theory which accounts for them is thus a *psychological theory* of the first order.

This bipartite strategy is common in the theoretical treatment of natural phenomena. To quote an example we have given before[5]:

> It is not at all surprising that the analysis of speech behavior should proceed from two empirical and theoretical sources. Indeed, distinguishing among the different kinds of data that constitute superficially homogeneous phenomena is absolutely universal in scientific explanations; it occurs whenever considerations of simplicity and explanatory power require that the observations be represented as inter-

[5] See Bever, Fodor, and Weksel (1965).

action effects. Consider, for example, the analysis of a block sliding down an inclined plane. There are two kinds of variables that interact to determine the block's behavior—first, the forces acting downward on the body and determining the acceleration for an ideal system; second, the reactive forces (e.g., friction) due to the character of the particular body and plane under study. The observed behavior is susceptible of systematic explanation only on the view that it is the product of interactions between these distinct systems.

I think that it is a universal scientific strategy to approach scientific description in this manner. The value in it is quite obvious—it allows us to describe natural behavior in terms of structure which exists as a constant component of many superficially distinct behaviors. What else is scientific study for, except to extract general constant principles from heterogeneous phenomena?

In the above example the points of contact between the theory (parallelogram of forces) and regular phenomena is sufficiently rich to make unreasonable a rejection of the theory. We can use the same essential concepts for the description of bodies on inclined planes, falling bodies, ballistic paths, strain, and so on. In each case the essential concepts are systematically reflected in slightly differing ways but always remain intact. Unfortunately, the number of different points of contact between modern linguistic theory and natural speech phenomena has not been much richer than the basic intuitions of linguists which I reviewed above. This is largely because we have no general theory of how any structural theory of behavior should interact with psychological phenomena. Later in this paper I shall summarize the different empirical loci of interactions between transformational grammar (TG) and natural phenomena. I shall try to convince you that there is a sufficient number of them to recommend acceptance of TG and to expand our understanding of how behavior in general reflects its own structure.

S-R Theory and This Strategy

It is clear that the usual formulations of S-R theory cannot possibly interact with the bipartite strategy of research which I have outlined. The reason for this is quite simple: S-R theory would attempt to account for both components of language behavior without distinguishing them. With or without mediating concepts (as Fodor has shown), S-R models appear to cover the whole of language behavior. They are proposed simultaneously as accounts of the structure of language and the reflection of that structure in actual behavior (notably in learning). The various reasons why this global approach cannot work are summarized in McNeill's paper and elsewhere, and I do not wish to repeat them here.

We can ask next if S-R theory is compatible with either the structure of grammatical competence or the psychological theory of performance. It takes only a moment to see that S-R principles cannot adequately enumerate the structure of sentences. This issue has also been discussed in detail, and I shall restrict myself to a recent attempt at this conference and elsewhere to resuscitate S-R models.

In summarizing our interchange with Braine, McNeill correctly analyzes Braine's work as an attempt to integrate the theory of linguistic competence with associationistic principles, by ignoring all aspects of linguistic theory that associationism cannot handle. Braine and McNeill agree that simple associationism cannot handle the learning of transformations; Braine concludes that there is something wrong with transformations, while we and McNeill conclude that there is something wrong with simple associationism. Braine, however, disagrees with our claim that associationism cannot even account for the structure of simple context-free grammar (CFG). In addition, Osgood has recently proposed a similar way of viewing the structure of language so that associationistic principles can allegedly account for it. The goal of these enterprises seems to be to save at least some part of linguistic theory for S-R explanation. Even if transformational grammar as a whole cannot be accomodated by S-R approaches, the implication of these efforts is that something will be gained if part of it can be.

The claim that associationistic theory can account for the structure of CFG appears important since, if true, it would offer a stronghold for the S-R treatment of limited parts of language behavior. Braine, for example, is perfectly happy to restrict his theory to an account of the learning of a nontransformational grammar in young children and let others explain the learning of transformations. The essential mechanism is that of "word class and substitution"; by learning position classes for individual words and type of allowable orders of classes, a child can develop a small "phrase structure" system which could provide the basis for his later language development.

The problem with this idea is that the only kind of CFG that could be learned in this way is one with a finite number of allowable class orders, that is, a grammar *entirely without recursion* and therefore inadequate to natural language. A general CFG is one in which there are ordered phrase structure expansion rules of the type:

(1) Sentence $\longrightarrow$ noun phrase, verb phrase

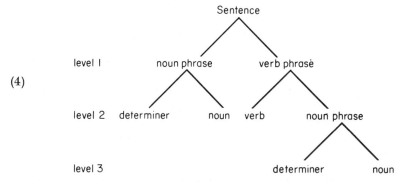

(4)

(2) Verb phrase ⟶ verb, noun phrase
(3) Noun phrase ⟶ determiner, noun

which enumerate tree structures with definite levels (Diagram 4).

A phrase structure grammar with recursion is one in which a given constituent (e.g., "sentence") can dominate itself in the tree and the rules do not apply in any particular order, e.g., a grammar like the above with this additional rule:

(4) Noun phrase ⟶ sentence

This grammar (rules 1–4) enumerates phrase structure trees like:

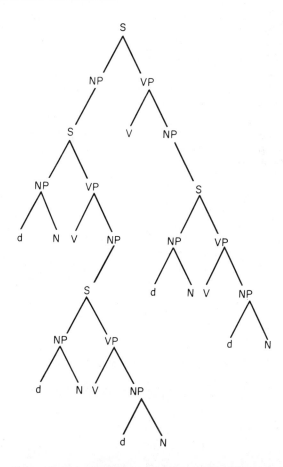

It is inherent to recursive CFG that the sentences it produces are of arbitrary length. Yet it is just this that Braine cannot allow, since substitution and word-class grammars require an upper bound on the allowable word-class sequences.

In a related attempt to integrate CFG and the descriptive principle of transitional probability, Osgood has proposed that we can measure not only the transitional probabilities between words but also those between constituents and that this complex of hierarchical probabilities can represent the structure of sentences. Thus in the first tree above we can determine at level 1 the probability that "nounphrase" precedes "verbphrase" in a corpus of sentences. In this way behavioral effects due to the sequences of groupings of words can be treated in the same way as the effects of individual word sequences. Again recursion in phrase structure is incompatible with this proposal. If the grammar generates structures like those in the second tree above, coherent phrase structure levels are not available. Regular statements about the sequential probabilities of tree structure nodes *presuppose a way of deciding whether or not any pair of nodes are at the same phrase structure level*. In phrase structure without recursion, levels are specifiable, and at a particular level "K" a node, "N_1", is followed by a restricted number of nodes "$N_{2....n}$" each with a particular probability.

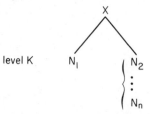

level K

In this system a grammar consists in a hierarchically ordered set of Markov sources, each set at a particular level.[6] Suppose now that the phrase structure system were recursive. It is impossible to define a concept of phrase structure level which relates to the grammar: there is an arbitrary number of levels, and *any* sequence can now appear at any level (see Chomsky, 1957, p. 35ff). Of course, many arbitrary relations between pairs of nodes can be defined, and then the probability of any particular pair satisfying that relation can be calculated. This might in some cases be an interesting set of statistical statements about a particular corpus. But in no case could it be used as a basis for a system which could *generate* tree structures. Such a system could generate all the existing tree structures only if the notion of phrase structure level is characterizable and there is a finite number of them.

Of course, the fact that Braine's and Osgood's formulations are not integrated with transformations and the kinds of facts which transformations describe is sufficient for their rejection as viable theories of language structure. But these formulations are not even able to represent the weak phrase structure system that could account for a language with an arbitrary number of dependent clauses in a sentence (e.g., I like the girl who hit the man who left the store . . .). In any case, it has been shown that S-R theory and related associationistic descriptive techniques are inadequate to account for the structure of language or of transformational grammar as a whole. I think that the redoubt of trying to show that it can account for

[6] I am not sure that anybody knows what the formal properties of this system would be, but I am trying to capture the systematic nature of Osgood's proposals. For a discussion of the incompatibility of associationism and recursion see Bever, Fodor, and Garrett in this volume.

part of the grammar is extremely uninteresting. The grammatical theory itself is not divisible; transformations are defined to operate on particular trees, and phrase structure rules are formulated to provide just the necessary tree structures for transformations: the form of one depends on the form of the other. Any isolated component of transformational grammar cannot account for the structure of natural language, and any theory of language structure which proposes to account for one component as though the others did not exist is futile.

S-R theory is severely limited as a basis for a linguistic theory. We now can ask whether it could represent a possible account for the performance or "psychology" of the structure of language.

There are two ways of answering this question. In the first place (as Fodor and Garrett emphasize), S-R principles cannot account for the "linguistic" structure of language as expressed in the formalisms of transformational grammar. I have already argued that linguistic analysis is itself an explanation for *psychological* data, so S-R theories fail on psychological grounds if they fail on linguistic grounds.

The second answer is that S-R theories have no bearing on most psychological research into the manipulation of *sentences*. I can see no form of legerdemain that reconciles the findings of Miller and his students with the principles of associationism. Perhaps a connection can be made for particular experiments. S-R theories are primarily learning theories, yet they cannot even account for the learning of language (as McNeill reviews); I see little point in arguments on their behalf for other kinds of language behavior.

What Is the Role of Probability in Language Behavior?

I have reviewed the facts which show that S-R theory is neither a general theory of language behavior nor a general theory of language structure nor a general theory of the performance of that structure. Clearly the past few days have demonstrated phenomena dependent on contextual probability of occurrence. What then is the theoretical status of the many phenomena correlated with probability of occurrence in the behavioral manipulation of words and sentences?

In brief, probability effects in language behavior are due to constraints inherent to the performances of language structure. Thus probability is an effect, not a cause: if a speaker follows certain statistical regularities, we cannot infer that those statistics directly reflect the structure of his language *or* the structure of his performance of the language. Suppose it is the case that nouns occur with a probability of k and verbs of n in natural discourse. Can we infer that it is a rule of language or speech behavior to produce these probabilities? No. Can we assume that this is a part of the story? No. Language structure is not an array of nouns and verbs, and certainly the principles for the performance of that structure are not expressed in terms of nouns and verbs. According to the strategy for language study which I have outlined, every probabilistic fact is an empirical fact, not an answer or explanation.

Suppose passive sentences are said more frequently than active sentences. No doubt this may reflect the relative psychological complexity of performing the passive rules.[7] We take this as a *problem* in need of an explanation, not a theoretical claim about the language. For example, we might suggest that the basis for this fact is that the grammatical derivation of passive sentences involves more transformations than for active sentences. In effect, experimental and natural probabilities are the only measures of psychological work on units which we can observe. I do not see this as a scientific virtue, and I find wholly irrational the assumption that since that's all we can see directly, that's all there is.

Yet it is true that words in sentences seem to constrain each other. In (p) the word "hill" fills in the blank more often than the word "water."

(p) John will run up the _____ .

We might then postulate that certain features which affect sequential probabilities in sentences are the left-right probabilities of adjacent words. Johnson has effectively argued that it is the left-right probabilities of constituents. I think, however, that if these constraints are part of the story at all, they are needlessly superficial. Consider the constraint between "duck" and "eat" in the two sentences below:

the duck is tasty to eat
the duck is eager to eat

[7] Of course, the way in which psychological complexity is reflected in frequency of occurrence is itself a general phenomenon. In experimental studies the usual technique has been to assume that the probability of experimental success with a particular stimulus (e.g., on a long-term memory task) is inversely related to the number of psychological units which the stimulus evokes (the so-called null-hypothesis). Indeed the demonstration that a random interaction of hypothetical units is matched by the actual probability of experimental success is often taken as support for the psychological reality of those units (see Mehler, 1963).

Clearly the probability of occurrence of *duck* is dependent on the logical relation which it bears to *eat* (and vice versa). These relations are, of course, specified in TG in the base structure of sentences. Thus statements about the probability of any two words appearing in the same sentence are simplified by reference to the deep structure. Consider the associative probability of *John* and *hill* in the sentence above; I think it is the same as in these sentences:

It is up the hill that John will run.
The hill will be run up by John.
John will be the one to run up the hill.

There are, in fact, an enormous variety of sentences, all stemming from the same deep structure and, I believe, all with the same basic associative probability between *John* and *run*. With this kind of example in mind, I propose the following principle: *the associative probability of words in actual sentences is a direct function of the associative probability in their underlying structures.*

This principle is not surprising if one remembers that underlying structures are related to the meanings of sentences by a simple function, while the structure of the actual form of sentences is much more removed from the sentence meaning. Johnson's point in his paper that word sequences of more than 5th order probability are treated psychologically like real language supports this principle. If the relevant unit of associative probability were actually the surface structure constituent (as Johnson seems to believe), then sequences with 3rd order probability should be language-like since they contain many well-formed phrases. Fifth-order approximations to English may contain a number of whole clauses and sentences, that is, units which are coherently related to real sentences with associated deep structures.

I do not think that anyone should be startled by the proposal that associative probabilities are more easily related to deep structures. I mention it because these structures are themselves abstract. If we count probabilistic statements in terms of them, then we must reject any claim that the probability effects in language behavior are *directly* observable in the properties of actual language sequences. Since S-R approaches are *in principle* dependent on the observable sequences, S-R theory is even incompatible with the language phenomenon it ought to handle best— associative probabilities of words.

Psycholinguistics in the Child and Adult

Language learning and the psycholinguistic structure of the child

McNeill has pointed out how amazing it is that the child masters his language by the age of four and yet has not mastered many other cognitive functions. In fact, it is so amazing that I do not believe it, in its simplest form (just consider the well-known fact that the child shifts from syntagmatic to paradigmatic word associations much later, at age 6 or 7). It is one thing to say that a child's competence is characterized by a transformational grammar; it is quite another to assume that *ipso facto* the child has the same psychological implementation of transformational grammar as the adult. Obviously the child must be endowed with the capacity to develop deep and surface sentence structure, but how he does it and in what order are open questions.

I have no direct counterevidence to the assumption that the child has the *full* adult psychological structure underlying language by the time he goes to school. But there are indications in the ways children use language that they initially are more sensitive to the superficial structure. For example, if we examine the progression of how children play with language and the jokes they understand, we can see that at first the child uses a superficial level. At the age of five, the child is delighted with the riddle, "Why can't you starve on the desert?" (because of the sandwiches there) and at the age of ten, with the riddle, "Why can you jump higher than the Empire State Building?" (because it can't jump). Thus, as the child grows older, his language reveals increasing sensitivity to deep structure.

Superficially the child appears to deal with the world as adults do, but it can be shown that his cognitive approach is actually quite different. It seems reasonable that he could also appear to talk like an adult and actually have quite a different psychological basis for the same grammar. This suggestion bears *not* on the child's eventual competence (which I assume to be TG) but on the structure of his performance, and therefore the suggestion is quite testable. If I am right, a child of four appears to have mastered his language but will react differently from adults in certain experimental situations. Experiments with comprehension and memory for transformations in children have been inconclusive because the transformations used also lead to increased surface structure complexity or increased length. However, other experiments may bring out differential effects and show that the child is psychologically dealing with surface structure in situations where adults use deep structure. I have in mind a series of experiments which I have run with Donald MacKay and Jacques Mehler on the way various different types of ambiguous sentences are treated by adults. In certain tasks lexical ambiguities (The sailors like the port) and surface structure ambiguities (They fed her dog biscuits) are more difficult than deep structure ambiguities (The duck is ready to eat); in other tasks they are easier. With Mehler I plan to use children in some of the same experiments. If I am right, the behavioral ordering of these different kinds of ambiguities should yield different results in children than in adults.

Modern psycholinguistics in the adult

For the past six to seven years, psychologists have made various kinds of attempts to integrate the developments in linguistic theory with other kinds of behavior. The problem with most of these experiments is that they were in large part devoted to the confirmation of the "psychological reality of TG." This, of course, was due to the force of the original artificial distinction between "competence" and "performance," in which it was an issue to "prove" that the grammar is "real." Our problem now is somewhat different —to determine by what mechanisms sentences are understood, remembered, recognized, and so on.

When we look at the problem in this way, we discover that we don't know anything at all. It is easy to show that phonological, surface, and deep structures of sentences have psychological reality (other than that inherent to the linguistic intuitions themselves). But the problem of exactly how these structures interact in actual psychological processes such as perception, short-term memory, and so on, is bewildering. Let me now review some of the relevant findings discussed today

and from our own research. In each case I have inklings of some general principles that are operating; but even if they are true, they are depressingly far from the correct story.

PHONOLOGY. Issues in the perceptual segmentation of the speech signal have paralleled recent theoretical linguistic controversies. Within the linguistic analysis of phonology it has been shown that the relation between the abstract and phonetic speech segments do not maintain the behaviorist principles that a distinction of the abstract level is *directly* reflected phonetically in the same segment (see Chomsky, 1966). For instance, in the words "medal, mettle" the only phonetic difference is in the length of the vowel for many speakers, although the "t" and "d" are kept distinct at the abstract level. Garrett and Fodor point out that in phonetic perception itself it now appears that the principle of linearity between psychological levels is also not maintained between the phonetic interpretation of a segment of sound and the actual *acoustic* properties of that segment. For example, the acoustic structure of the "t" in "stew" is identical with that of the "k" in "ski," yet they are perceived as phonetically distinct. This kind of finding (largely due to Haskins Laboratory) is particularly important since the phonetic-acoustic level appeared to be the last reasonable hope for the application of behaviorist principles to the structure of language.

SURFACE STRUCTURE. Within linguistic theory certain syntactic and phonological rules must apply recursively; that is, they reoperate on the output of their own previous operations.[8] Each time the rules reapply, it is to a larger constituent in the phrase structure of sentences. Several

---

[8] See Chomsky and Halle, forthcoming.

psychological phenomena reflect this linguistic cycle. In his experiments on transitional error probability with prelearning of isolated sequences, Johnson found that the more deeply embedded a word pair is, the more it profits from pretraining. This is to be expected if the memory unit is the linguistically defined constituent and the memory process is defined recursively over successively larger constituents—the more deeply embedded the constituent, the more times the memory process applies to it. Recently Jacques Mehler, Peter Carey, and I have found a striking example of this psychological cycle in the eye-movements of subjects reading sentences. More deeply embedded structures received more eye fixations. Garrett and Fodor review other effects of this sort in the perception of pauses and the placement of clicks in sentences; the more deeply embedded a structure is, the more perceptual coherence it has.

From these data I suggest that there is a general *psychological cycle* defined over surface phrase structures; in linguistic analyses these cycles acquire rules peculiar to a given language; in other psychological phenomena the kind of rules depends on the kind of behavior. But the principle is the same —the psychological rules reapply to themselves at each successively larger constituent.

DEEP STRUCTURE AND TRANSFORMATIONS. Garrett and Fodor review the recent work of Miller, *et al.*, which shows that for certain transformations (Passive, Negative, Question) the number of transformations correlates with experimentally derived measures of psychological complexity. These results are important because they indicate that there may be a direct mapping of TG onto more kinds of behavior than producing linguistic intuitions: that is, for memory we would

like to be able to claim "one linguistic operation equals one psychological operation in memory." It is understandable therefore that Garrett and Fodor then lament the lack of a simple correlation of the number of grammatical rules with difficulty in the perception and memory of sentences for all types of transformations. After all, they reason, if grammar is reflected in behavior, why not assume that more rules always mean more complexity? Their claim that the matter is all very confused is easily supported by many experiments, some of which seem very confused. However, some of the experiments are artifactual, and some are misunderstood. I agree with them that if all the rules and their application to word sequences are undifferentiated, then no coherent relation between the grammar and behavior appears. But if the different formal characteristics of the rules are taken into account, the simple relation between the grammar and psychological complexity can be maintained for the cases which have been studied. In particular, their strongest "negative" fact is that sentences with auxiliaries, like "John *will have been going* to town," are no more difficult to remember and understand than simple sentences, like "John goes to town" (found by both Mehler and Savin). Yet sentences with auxiliaries ought to be more complex if TG interacts straightforwardly with memory and perception, since auxiliary sentences involve more rules.

In fact, in this case there may be no dilemma at all. These sentences are "kernels" (sentences with no optional markers in the deep structure and no optional transformations in the derivation). The only transformation which applies to them is the affix-movement transformation. This transformation *also* applies to the very simplest declarative sentences. Thus in transformational terms, these sentences are just like simple declarative sentences and should be no more complex (assuming that within sentence lengths from two to seven words, memory is not differentially affected).

COMPLEXITY AND KERNELIZATION. The search for a *general* theory of psychological complexity is quite frustrating, and in many other cases the relation between rules and behaviors is obscure. For example, differences in experimental paradigm can greatly affect the way the grammar is reflected in orderings among types of sentences. Mehler and I have recently found that in a short-term memory paradigm, sentences with adverbs and particles are recalled with distortions which do *not* relate to their deep syntactic structure. These errors characteristically include placing the adverb at the beginning and the particle at the end of the sentence. (For example, if subjects hear the sentence "The salesman carelessly sent over a large check," they repeat it as "Carelessly *the salesman sent a large check* over." Errors in the reverse direction rarely occur.) On the other hand, in a long-term memory paradigm the results follow predictions based on the deep structure of the sentence. This latter result supports the "coding" hypothesis found for the original optionals, which claims that sentences are remembered in their deep structure form with indications as to what transformations will apply.

These results show that in different psychological tasks behavior can be related to the grammar in different ways. In short-term memory the psychologically less complex form is the one with *more* transformations. In long-term memory it is the one with fewer transformations. I interpret these results as the consequence of a general "kernelization" routine in the psychological manipulation of sentences. As a

strategy it is stated: *Reduce sentential material to simple declarative sentences.* This routine applies to the surface structure of the sentences *or* to the deep structure, depending on the psychological task. In short-term memory this routine applies to the surface phrase structure of the sentence and tends to reduce the structure to a *simple sentence* (italicized in the example above) preceded by an adverb and followed by a preposition. In long-term memory this routine applies to the deep structure and causes errors in which the transformations are forgotten, but the deep structure kernel remains.

Kernelization appears as a perceptual phenomenon in our research on the location of clicks, shocks, and flashes presented during the course of speech. Using materials in which the fine phrase structure was carefully controlled, we have found that the *only* phrase structure break which has an effect on the location of the extraneous stimulus is the boundary between clauses. That is, it is *not* the case that the "constituent" is the unit of speech perception (as we have claimed). Rather the ongoing perceptual processing of the speech signal segments it into sentence groups. Thus even as we hear sentences, we attempt to kernelize their surface structure.[9]

The Lowly Word

During the previous days of this conference, we have considered various behavioral effects which pertain to words and their mutual associations. I should like to submit now that these papers implicitly (some explicitly) distinguish "verbal behavior" from "lan-

[9] See T. Bever, J. Fodor, and M. Garrett (1966); T. Bever, R. Kirk, J. Lackner, and L. Squire (1967); and T. Bever and J. Mehler (1967).

guage behavior." During this conference I have come to realize the comfort of the study of words if they are stripped of their relevance to language. But I am concerned with the difficulty of integrating the results from these experiments with the study of language behavior in general. There are both theoretical and empirical demonstrations that a sentence is greater than the sum of its words.

In linguistic analysis the syntactic and phonological role that a word can play in sentences determines its internal structure: the internal analysis of words depends on a prior general analysis of sentences. Consequently, study of individual words or groups of words can be understood only as a special case of the study of sentences. Various results support the related psychological fact that randomized sequences of words are manipulated in entirely different ways from words organized into sentences.

First, Johnson's analysis of the literature has highlighted the behavioral discontinuity of graduated increases in approximations to English. Roughly, a sequence is either treated as language or it is not. In a series of recent experiments, Mehler and I have found that the apparent duration of sentences follows a power function lower than that for randomized sequences. This is also true of the actual durations of sentences and random word sequences read aloud by subjects who think they are reading at a constant speed. In a finding which may be related I have discovered that the subjective centrality of speech presented alternately to the two ears is significantly closer to a step function for speech than for random word sequences.

Several experiments indicate a physiological difference in the processing of these two kinds of material. In the click experiments, in which subjects locate clicks presented during sen-

tences, loud clicks in th
perceived as occurring la
presented in the left ea
metry does not appear
sented during random word sequences. Second, in a short-term memory paradigm I have found that more order mistakes are made in the left ear than in the right for sentences, but this also does not appear in random word sequences.

These experiments only provide some more empirical support for the obvious. Insofar as an experiment with words is concerned with them as part of language behavior, it is concerned with them as units determined by their role in sentences. Insofar as these properties are ignored, the relevance of the research for language behavior is diminished.

Conclusion

I have reviewed these confusing results because I want everyone to be aware that we do not think we have the answers. For reasons that have appeared in the discussions, we are convinced that sequential probability statements cannot account for the structure of the performance of intuitions about language. Nor can probability statements account for the interaction of linguistic structures with many other kinds of behavioral phenomena. So we are sure that that is *not* the answer. We think we see some of the questions. Our problem is that we need a whole new set of theories and facts to start answering those questions. Obviously, we need help.

References

Bever, T., J. Fodor, and W. Weksel, "Is Linguistics Empirical?" *Psychological Review,* **72** (1965), 493–500.

——, and J. Mehler, "Kernelization of Speech in Short and Long Term Memory," 1967, in press.

——, J. Fodor, and M. Garrett, "Speech Perception: Some Experimental Results for Sentences," paper presented to the International Congress of Psychology, Moscow, 1967.

——, ——, and ——, "The Perceptual Kernelization of Speech," 1967, in press.

Bloomfield, L., *Language*. New York: Holt, Rinehart & Winston, Inc., 1933.

Braine, M., "On the Basis of Phrase Structure: A Reply to Bever, Fodor, and Weksel," *Psychological Review*, **72** (1965), 483–492.

Chomsky, N., *Problems in Linguistic Theory*. The Hague, Netherlands: Mouton and Co., 1957.

——, *Syntactic Structures*. The Hague, Netherlands: Mouton and Co., 1957.

——, *Aspects of the Theory of Syntax*. Cambridge, Mass.: M.I.T. Press, 1965.

——, and M. Halle, *Sound Patterns of English*. New York: Harper and Row, Inc., in press.

De Saussure, F., *Cours de Linguistique Generale*. Paris: Payot, 1916.

Fodor, J., "Could Meaning Be an r_m?" *Journal of Verbal Learning and Verbal Behavior*, **4** (1965), 73–81.

——, and J. Katz, "What's Wrong with the Philosophy of Language?" *Inquiry*, **5** (1962).

MacKay, D., and T. Bever, "In Search of Ambiguity," *Perception and Psychophysics*, **2** (1967), 193–200.

Mehler, J., "Some Effects of Grammatical Transformations on the Recall of English Sentences," *Journal of Verbal Learning and Verbal Behavior*, **2** (1963), 346–351.

——, T. Bever, and P. Carey, "What We Look at When We Read," *Perception and Psychophysics*, **2** (1967), 213–218.

Osgood, C., "On Understanding and Creating Sentences," *American Psychologist*, **18** (1963), 735–751.

Toward a Wedding of Insufficiencies

19

CHARLES E. OSGOOD

The thrust of my commentary on the papers of Garrett and Fodor, McNeill, and Johnson will be that neither the models of the language *user* proposed by contemporary behavior theory nor, by inference, from contemporary linguistic theory are sufficient. Each needs supplementation from the other. Although these papers differ in substance, they are similar in other respects which concern me as a psycholinguist. First, they provide evidence for the psychological relevance of transformational grammars (i.e., such grammars are not mere logical exercises, as some psychologists would like to believe); second, they stress the "competence" of native speakers as the primary criterion toward which psycholinguistic explanations must aspire ("competence" remaining a concept to be conjured with); and third, McNeill and Garrett and Fodor, at least, repeatedly state that S-R theory (as they call it) is incapable of incorporating the phenomena described by a transformational grammar—*in principle*.

I agree completely with the concluding remarks of Garrett and Fodor: "The problem for general S-R theory is thus clear. Either it must be demonstrated how an appeal to the sorts of learning mechanisms S-R theory allows can account for the assimilation and application of the kinds of linguistic information incorporated in the more powerful competence models, or associationistic accounts of language learning and of speech must be abandoned." But this particular shoe fits on their feet as well as mine. The implication given in the Garrett-Fodor paper, as well as in the McNeill paper, is that any kind of S-R theory has *already* been ruled out of the running, as far as incorporating language behavior is concerned. It is their responsibility to demonstrate, rigorously and conclusively, that this is the case. I will try to show that this has not been done and, further, that a sophisticated behavior theory, utilizing S and R constructs along with principles of association, is becoming increasingly compatible with theories of linguistic competence, as both mature. Since I want my comments on theory to apply to my discussion of experiments, I shall take up theory first and experiments second.

On The Psycholinguistic Status Of Contemporary Behavior Theory

Varieties of behavior theory

None of the papers under discussion makes a clear distinction among the

495

varieties of behavior theory, so I must do so. In the first and simplest case, there is single-stage S-R theory; it has two versions, (Pavlovian) conditioning and (Skinnerian) operant learning. Second, there is the type of nonrepresentational mediation theory, represented by Bousfield, Jenkins, and others, and somewhat more complexly by Braine. Third, there are several varieties of representational mediation theory, represented by Mowrer and myself among many others. Finally, there is a three-stage behavior theory, utilizing S and R constructs but including S-S and R-R association as well as S-R association (both single and two-staged), which—as far as I know—is uniquely my own. These varieties have been described in the literature in considerable detail. I shall refer to their totality as "behavior theory," but obviously I shall rely primarily upon my three-stage version, since it includes the major assumptions of the others.

It would seem to me that, just as psychologists interested in language have an obligation to master as best they can the intricacies of generative grammars, linguists interested in models of the language-user have an obligation to master as best they can the parallel intricacies of behavior theory—particularly if they are going to make statements about its inadequacy. What pains me, frankly, is not that Garrett and Fodor believe my version of behavior theory to be inadequate, but rather that they fail to support this conclusion by references to my own papers. They list, for example, both my Nebraska Symposium paper of 1957 and my APA address of 1963 among their references yet never refer to my notions of sensory and motor integration or of semantic and grammatic coding—even to refute them.

To make the distinction between nonrepresentational (e.g., Jenkins *et*

al. and Braine) and representational (e.g., Mowrer and Osgood) mediation theories is crucial for my evaluation of Fodor's (1965) recent critique of mediation theory of the Mowrer-Osgood type. It can be illustrated by one of Jenkins' several mediation paradigms: originally learn A–B and C–B; then train A–D; finally, test for the association C–D. This is an operational statement of mediated or semantic generalization, for which there are probably a thousand experimental demonstrations. Let A equal the word JOY, B equal the word HAPPY, C equal the word GLEE, and D equal the novel response (in this hypothetical experimental situation) of raising the finger to avoid shock. The nonrepresentational mediation theory assumes that, in the original learning phases, both JOY (A) and GLEE (C) have become associated with a common response, say HAPPY (B), and that, in the experimental training phase, mediating response B (HAPPY) is also being connected with the novel finger response (D)—since JOY (A) has originally been associated with HAPPY (B); thus it follows that, when in the test phase GLEE (C) is presented, the novel finger response (D) will occur—since GLEE (C), but not the physically more similar word BOY (X), for example, has previously been associated with the common mediator.

Note carefully that this kind of mediation theory *requires* no symbolic processes; it is, indeed, merely an extension or complication of the Skinnerian single-stage model. But note also that it could quite easily *become* a representational mediation theory by changing the nature of element B— from an implicit linguistic response (which is required by the fact that nothing overt occurs between C and D in the test situation above) to an implicit nonlinguistic response, r_m. Herein lies the fundamental difference between representational and non-representational mediation theories. Figure 1 describes the basic paradigm for representational mediation theory.

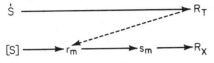

Figure 1. Basic Paradigm for Representational Mediation Theory

The solid arrows represent learned (or sometimes reflexive in the case of $\dot{S}$—R_T) *eliciting* relations, whereas the dashed arrows represent dependency relations that are not acquired by experience—thus the $r_m \longrightarrow s_m$ dependency is a consequence of automatic motor-sensory feedback, and the $R_T \longrightarrow r_m$ dependency is a consequence of the $\dot{S}$-with-$[S]$ pairing, but neither are eliciting relations. Capitalized symbols refer to overt observables, lower-case to unobservables. In this paradigm, $\dot{S}$ represents "significate," R_T represents total behavior to significate, $[S]$ represents "sign," and R_X represents the mediated response to the sign, which may be either linguistic or non-linguistic—all of which are explicit physical events, presumably observable.

What do r_m and s_m represent? In the first place, one might ask why I use the more restrictive symbols r and s rather than the looser symbol x. This reflects my assumption that r_m's and s_m's retain their response-like (in decoding) and stimulus-like (in encoding) *functional properties*. On the one hand, this allows all of the conceptual baggage of single-stage learning theory (like habit-formation, generalization, inhibition, and so forth) to be brought to bear on both decoding ($[S] \longrightarrow r_m$) and encoding ($s_m \longrightarrow R_X$) stages of mediation; on the other hand, this creates a restriction on the freedom of this theory to interpret data. *If* the constructs and the associated principles of learning theory are postulated, the total data of be-

havior (including language behavior) must be consistent with them. Note, however, that nothing is presupposed in this theory as to the physical nature of the mediators; they might consist of minimal but nonobservable (except by subtle means) reactions of the peripheral system, along with feedback; or they might, as I think is the case, consist of purely central (cortical) representations of what were originally peripheral events. A decision on this matter is not a prerequisite for use of such mediators in behavior theory.

Now let me return to the contrast between nonrepresentational and representational mediation theories. It comes down, as I indicated earlier, to the nature of element B or r_m in the respective paradigms. For nonrepresentational mediation theory (as represented most clearly by Skinner but also by Bousfield in our debate at the first conference on verbal learning and verbal behavior, in 1961), this critical mediating response is a nonobservable replica of some R_x in my diagram—e.g., a subvocal representation of the response of saying "happy." For representational mediation theory, on the other hand, this critical mediating response is a nonobservable, proper part (but *not* replica) of some R_T in my diagram. Thus, by virtue of being highly similar in their patterns of usage, both JOY and GLEE will occur in situations producing highly similar R_T's; it therefore must follow, in theory, that their r_m's will be componentially similar and hence also their automatic s_m's; and finally, applying the principle of generalization across similar stimuli, a novel reaction associated with the one (JOY) will tend to transfer to the other (GLEE)—the similarity in this case being purely semantic, based on similar s_m's.

To the distinctions already made, I must add the fact that my own variety of behavior theory is not, strictly speaking, an S-R theory. In order to account for symbolic processes (within which I will include both semantic and grammatic features) I utilize a two-stage, mediational S-R theory. But it has been obvious to me from my first contact with linguistics (see *psycholinguistics: A Survey of Theory and Research Problems*, 1954, particularly section 3.1.1.2) that even an extended S-R theory is insufficient—*in principle*. In order to incorporate the essential characteristics of gestalt theories of perceptual organization (which are obviously involved in the development of linguistic perceptual units) and the essential characteristics of motor skill, as so well described by Lashley in 1951 (which are obviously involved in the development of linguistic response units, like the syllable), I found it necessary to add what I call *an integration level* (or stage) to both decoding and encoding processes.

The integration level includes both S-S and R-R learning, based upon frequency, redundancy, and contiguity principles, but not reinforcement (sheer exposure is assumed to be sufficient). The underlying principle is this: the greater the frequency (redundancy and contiguity) with which sensory signals at the termini of sensory projection systems, or motor signals at the initiation of motor projection systems, are simultaneously active, the grater will be the tendency for their more central (integrative) correlates to activate each other. This may be a simple assumption, but it has rather broad implications. As well as being an attempt within associationistic theory to incorporate the well-documented gestalt data on perception—including the basic notions of closure, good figure, "thing"-perception and the like—it provides a natural basis for the stable relation between frequency-of-usage of word-form units and their perceptual thresholds, both visual and auditory.

It also provides psycholinguistics with what I believe is a crucial distinction—between words as meaningless forms (sensory and motor integrations) and words as psychological units of meaning (by virtue of their semantic and grammatic coding). Evidence for integration mechanisms in language is presented in both the 1957 and 1963 papers of mine which Garrett and Fodor cite.

The focal issue

In Chomsky's recent work, *Aspects of the Theory of Syntax* (1965), a very signification distinction between the "deep structure" and the "surface structure" of sentences is stressed. The deep structure represents, as I understand it, the basic grammatical categories and their relations, along with special coding as to certain transformations (e.g., passive), which are now considered obligatory. These basic grammatical categories are the concepts of subject and predicate, main verb and object of a verb phrase, and modifier and head of a phrase. It is at the level of deep structure that one expects to find language universals and hence general linguistic theory as contrasted with specific linguistic theories; that is, grammars of particular languages. It is also in the deep structure, according to McNeill, that one may expect to find the innate propensies, or predispositions, which will direct the child's acquisition of language and explain the speed of such acquisition. However, the relations between deep structure and the surface structures of particular languages will differ, and this is part of what a child must learn in order to become a fluent speaker of his own language.

Chomsky has repeatedly stated that an adequate grammar of language merely characterizes the linguistic competence which its users must have without in any obvious way characterizing how they utilize this competence. In a paper titled *On the Notion "Rule of Grammar"* (1961) he says, "The attempt to develop a reasonable account of the speaker has, I believe, been hampered by the prevalent and utterly mistaken view that a generative grammar in itself provides or is related in some obvious way to a model for the speaker." I judge from the contents of the psycholinguists' papers at this conference, and from discussions with Fodor, Garrett, and particularly Bever during the conference, that a transformational grammar is now being considered as a possible model for language performance. This raises many important issues.

Psycholinguists seem pretty well agreed on some differences that must be expected between models of the speaker and models of the language:

1. *The model of the speaker will certainly be a finite device, whereas a grammar is not.* Thus a grammar can generate an infinitely self-imbedding sentence, whereas a speaker with his limited storage capacities cannot.
2. *The model of the speaker will certainly be a time-dependent device, whereas a grammar is time-independent.* Thus the structural description of sentence gives no indication of the ordering of expansions, whereas the speaker necessarily talks and listens through time—or from left-to-right, to use the standard visual metaphor.
3. *The model of the speaker will certainly be a context-dependent device, whereas a grammar is relatively context-free.* By "context" here I refer to linguistic context beyond the boundaries of single sentences as well as to nonlinguistic context (e.g., situational and motivational factors). The distinction in syntactical theory between context-sensitive and context-free grammatical rules is not the issue here.
4. *The model of the speaker will be one in which (in encoding, at least) the*

syntactic component operates output from the semantic compon~~ent~~, rather than the reverse, as may be true for grammars.

If I read Chomsky's recent book correctly, then he is moving in precisely this direction, as seems to be apparent in both the distinction between deep and surface structures and in the introduction of subcategorizing and selection rules. I shall have more to say about this later.

The focal issue raised by the Garrett-Fodor and the McNeill papers is this: *any behavior theory which utilizes S and R constructs and associationistic laws is inadequate in principle as a model of the speaker.* This is a much stronger assertion than the claim that existing behavior-theory conceptions are inadequate in detail or in elaboration; indeed, it is an assertion which, if invalid and yet accepted by the younger generation of psycholinguists, can serve to damp effectively further attempts to improve theories of this type. Throughout these papers runs the implication that experimental demonstration of the behavioral validity of distinctions made in a transformational grammar in itself constitutes evidence against any S-R theory. This is not the case; it has to be demonstrated that such theories are, in principle, incapable of incorporating such phenomena. This demonstration has not been provided in these papers.

Both papers make numerous assertions about the inadequacy of S-R theories in principle—having lumped them together rather indiscriminately—but these assertions can be shown to be either false or highly debatable. For example, Garrett and Fodor state that "the S-R theorist views the organism as possessing a finite repertoire of behaviors, any one of which may, on occasion, be selected by specified stimulus parameters," and later that this same benighted S-R theorist supposes "that all the inputs to which the organism provides similar responses are characterized by correspondingly similar stimulus parameters." Certainly the organism operates with a finite number of alternative response *components*—in exactly the same sense that any language operates with a finite number of phonemes—but the laws by which these components can be combined into larger units (e.g., words) and these in turn into larger units (e.g., phrases and sentences) are such that the number and variety of compound responses is potentially infinite. Apart from the fact that in mediated generalization the external stimuli need not be similar in any physical respect (e.g., compare *joy* and *glee* vs. *joy* and *boy*), it is also an obvious fact of learning theory that two or more arbitrarily different physical stimuli can be associated with the same response by simple replicative conditioning. Thus the second assertion is demonstrably false.

Evaluation of the Adequacy of Various Behavior Theories

Single-stage S-R theories

It is my opinion, expressed in many places, that single-stage learning theory models are indeed insufficient in principle, although not erroneous—and on strictly psychological grounds. We can identify two major types of single-stage theory: (a) Pavlovian respondent conditioning, whose basic postulate states that reactions to significates ($\dot{S}$ in my Figure 1) simply become transferred to signs ([S]) via conditioning, the strengthening operation being mere contiguous occurrence of the significate (or unconditioned stimulus); (b) Skinnerian operant conditioning,

whose basic postulate states that the mere emission of a response, followed by reinforcement, serves to strengthen the dependency of this response upon any and all antecedent conditions (stimuli?).

The critical insufficiency of both these versions of single-stage theory is that they make no provision for symbolic processes, including meaning—in principle. In terms of my mediation model (Figure 1), the Pavlovian substitution theory requires that the response to the sign *be the same as* the response to the significate (i.e., that R_X equal R_T): This is patently false; responses to signs typically have little to do, in any obvious way, with responses to the things signified. The Skinnerian operant theory, on the other hand, requires that if signs produce something other than the overt R_x, then this something must be an r_x (i.e., an unobservable subvocal replica of the overt verbal response), and hence "meanings" of words become their subvocal forms (i.e., that "r_m" equals R_x). This approach leads to conclusions that are patently nonsensical intuitively—e.g., we must subvocally mimic a speaker in order to understand him.

Nonrepresentational mediation theories

I have already indicated what I believe to be the essential difference between nonrepresentational mediation theories of the Bousfield, Jenkins, *et al.*, and Braine type and representation mediation theories of the Mowrer and Osgood type. It comes down to the nature of the mediating process itself and its derivation: nonrepresentational mediation models require no symbolic process, since r_x is derived from R_x (e.g., some linguistic response functioning as element *B* in the mediation paradigm cited earlier); representational mediation models do postulate a symbolic process, by virtue of deriving r_m from R_T, the latter being the overt behavior characteristically made to significates. Thus [S] *means* $\dot{S}$ by virtue of producing part of the same behavior originally elicited by $\dot{S}$. The fundamental insufficiency, then, in nonrepresentational mediation models is also the failure to provide any account of symbolic processes. Thus they can explain mediated transfers in verbal learning among words having certain (specifiable) associative histories, yet they say nothing about the meanings of these words themselves. How children can develop meanings for perceptual signs well ahead of language learning—as they obviously do—is also not at all clear here.

Representational mediation theory

It is obvious that nonrepresentational mediation theory can easily be reduced to single-stage theory of the Skinnerian operant variety and thus become subject to all of the criticisms of this single-stage model. It is not as obvious that representational mediation theory can be so reduced. Both of the papers under review assume that this has already been successfully demonstrated, but they refer solely to a paper titled "Could Meaning be an r_m?" by Fodor (1965). I have recently written a reply to this article, (Osgood, 1966) and I will simply paraphrase the most pertinent sections of this paper for brief statement here.

Before developing his critique of mediation theory, Fodor correctly notes the following: (a) *that r_m is functionally characterized in two-stage theory;* (b) *that r_m is not the same thing as R_T* (total behavior to the significate, $\dot{S}$), *but rather* r_m *is proper part of* R_T. His

major criticism is that mediation theory can be shown to differ from single-stage theory in only one respect—r_m *differs from* R_T *only in terms of observability*—and hence is subject to the same limitations. His argument proceeds as follows: Beyond stating that r_m is a proper part of R_T, mediation theory requires an additional postulate, namely, that each r_m which unambiguously mediates the meaning of a sign must bear a one-to-one unique relation to its R_T. The consequence of rejecting this postulate (i.e., of assuming that one and the same r_m could be part of many R_T produced by many different $\dot{S}$) would be that signs would necessarily refer ambiguously to many different significates.

With this I entirely agree. Both in 1957 (in Osgood, Suci, and Tannenbaum), with the argument restricted to three gross affective factors, and in 1963, the argument here being more generalized, I have proposed that r_m is not a single reaction but rather a multicomponential affair. Whereas within a given component reaction system (factor, feature) only one alternative can occur to a presented sign (e.g., r_m cannot be simultaneously $+$ and $-$ in the same component reaction system any more than one can simultaneously clench and open his hand), the possibilities for combination across N independent components of r_m increase with at least 2^N (discrete, all-or-nothing alternatives) or some larger value (e.g., 7^N if one assumes seven discriminable alternatives within each component).

But at this point Fodor moves in with what he feels is the *coup de grace*. If one accepts the necessity of a one-to-one relation between r_m and R_T—which I do, with the proviso that it is still a part-to-whole relation—then, he claims, the formal difference between single-stage and mediation theories disappears and we are left with the trivial difference of observability. Thus, we have

$$[S] \longrightarrow (\longrightarrow r_m \dashrightarrow s_m \longrightarrow) \longrightarrow R_X$$

instead of

$$[S] \longrightarrow R_T \dashrightarrow S_T \longrightarrow R_X$$

and are subject to all of the criticisms of single-stage theory. "To put it still differently, once we grant a one-to-one relation between r's and R's, we insure that the former lack the 'surplus meaning' characteristic of terms designating *bona fide* theoretical entities (Fodor, 1965, p. 81)." As should now be clear, I must accept the one-to-one relation between r_m and R_T, but not that between r_m and R_X.

Let me point out first that this difference in observability is by no means trivial. In the well-documented experiments on semantic generalization it is obvious that the basis of the transfer is semantic similarity. But it is equally obvious that nothing remotely like R_T (total overt behavior originally occurring in *glee* and *joy* using situations) occurs between *glee* and the novel finger-lifting response; indeed, no particular mediating responses of an overt nature typically occur. Psychological theory in general, and psycholinguistic theory in particular, must be able to incorporate such phenomena.

Let me point out, second, that Fodor apparently misses the primary difference between two-stage and single-stage theories—*the functional separation of decoding and encoding phases* (S-r and s-R). It is the lack of such functional separation that forces Skinner (1957) into such intuitively unsatisfying assumptions as that we must subvocally mimic a speaker in order to comprehend what he says or that having learned to name objects (tacting) we will not therefore be able to ask for them (manding), since they are independent single-stage operants. In sum, it is the functional separation of decoding and encoding stages—yet both utilizing the full machinery of single-stage theory—that provides the greater flexibility and explanatory power of the mediation model, including its capacity to incorporate symbolic processes. The real danger, as I see it, is that by proliferating unobservables (albeit of the same *kind* as overt S's and R's), mediation theory may be able to "explain" too much and hence become untestable.

And, third, let me stress again that the notion of r_m as a simultaneous bundle of events in a limited number of component reaction systems possesses combinatorial properties which should render distinctive representation compatible with biological economy. The total momentary pattern of components of r_m can be thought of as a kind of code, which represents for the organism those differences among R_T's which make a difference with respect to responding appropriately to S's or things signified. To maintain this capacity, there is neither the requirement that each r_m be unique from all others in all respects (a single feature difference would be sufficient) nor the requirement that all ways in which R_T's differ from each other be represented in their r_m's (only those ways which make a difference in meaning are required).

On The Psycholinguistic Status Of Contemporary Linguistic Theory

Despite the strictures of Chomsky, Miller, and others—that an adequate model for the language is not necessarily an adequate model for the user—there has been a tendency in the recent writings of many psycholinguists to treat models of the language as if they were indeed models of the users. In its most extreme form, sentence understanding and creating is "explained" by reference to the number of nodes in a tree diagram, to the number of steps in a transformation, or to entries in a dictionary. In the more moderate form characterized by the three papers under consideration, the constructs and operations of a transformational grammar are hypothesized as a theory of the speaker which can be tested like any other theory. Given both the presumed demolishing of behavior theory and the lack of any alternative psychological theory, this step is entirely natural. But if a transformational grammar is to be proposed and tested like any other theory of the language-user, then it too must be shown to be sufficient. One cannot set the goal (as McNeill does in his paper, for example) as being *merely* to explain how the user achieves the competences characterized by a transformational grammar; there is much more involved in full-blown language behavior than what is presently described by any grammar.

Particular languages are learned

It is true that psycholinguists like myself, coming out of learning theory, have paid too little attention to innate factors in language development; but I think it is also true that psycholinguists like Lenneberg and McNeill, in their zeal for finding new sources of insight, have pushed the pendulum too far the other way. In any case, there is much about any particular language which is arbitrary and must be learned. Certainly this applies to meaning. The elaborate rules of reference (the class of events correlated with the usage of a particular term), of signification (the features which define membership in reference classes and hence project to

new instances), and of implication (the nondefining but correlated features) must be learned; to put it crudely, there is nothing innately horsey about the word *horse*. The same thing applies to syntax. Although there are undoubtedly innately determined universals in language, particularly with regard to deep structure, languages differ markedly in the ways in which deep structure is related to surface structure, and these rules must be learned if the child is going to understand and create well-formed sentences in his particular language. The point here is this: Transformational grammars *per se* have nothing to say about learning; when they are treated as models for the language-user, they will be necessarily to that degree insufficient.

Language performance includes Markov-type transitional dependencies

It is one thing to claim that (learned) transitional dependencies provide an insufficient characterization of language performance; it is another thing to deny that they exist or have any psycholinguistic significance. Neal Johnson does a remarkably fine job in summarizing and making sense out of an extraordinarily complicated and confusing literature on sequential processes in language behavior—on approximations to English and their effects upon recall, on other evidences for sequential constraints, and so on. Although he concludes that such processes are not sufficient to explain the effects of grammatical structure upon learning and other performance, I doubt if he would assert them to be erroneous or irrelevant. The point here is that any complete theory of the user must deal with transitional dependencies — between sentences and between phrases, as well as between words, and operating on semantic and associational as well as grammatical levels. There is nothing in the performance models adopted from transformational grammars that accounts for such phenomena in any obvious way.

Performance models require selection among alternatives

This applies to understanding sentences as well as creating them, but the issue is particularly clear in the latter process. Given the presentation of a string of forms, a grammar can assign them a structure and test their sentence-hood, but it cannot initiate particular sentences, as Chomsky has noted in several places. The underlying reason for this is that in a grammar there is no inherent limitation on the number of rewrite rules which may contain the same left-hand element. Thus NP *may* be rewritten as T + N (*the boy*), or it *may* be rewritten as T + A + N (*the tall boy*), or it *may* be rewritten as N + Poss. + V + ing + T + N (*John's proving the theorem*), and so on through a large number of possible expansions. There is nothing in the grammar *per se* which serves to select one as against any other alternative. What I have termed "dictionary rules" provide the extreme example of this; there is nothing in the grammar that says N should in a specific instance be rewritten as *man* as against *sincerity* as against *idea* as against *milk* and so forth. The subcategorizing and selection rules that Chomsky discusses in his latest published work (1965) do place some restrictions upon such dictionary rewriting, but they still leave large classes of forms undifferentiated. I, at least, would claim that they are really semantic rules. Nor does a context-sensitive grammar, as I understand the notion, solve this problem, since within exactly the same XAY

context, A still may be rewritten by a variety of expansion rules. In the model of the speaker there obviously are determinants operating here, since we rarely talk grammatical gibberish—which leads directly to the next point.

In performance models of the speaker the semantic component will be central and the syntactic component will operate on its output. It is perfectly obvious to me as a native speaker that I decide roughly *what* I am going to talk about before I decide *how* I am going to say it. To assume that I generate an empty grammatical sentence structure and *then* decide what to say with it is intuitively absurd. Yet this is precisely what a transformational grammar, posed as a model of the speaker, would have us believe. To quote Garrett and Fodor, "The syntactic component is viewed as the central device in the sense that the semantic and phonological systems operate on its output but not conversely." Here they are referring explicitly to transformational grammar as a model of the language, but it becomes clear that this is also part of their implicit theory about the speaker.

Neal Johnson makes this assumption entirely explicit when he discusses his conception of how people recall sentences: "As can be seen . . ., the model assumes that when an S produces *tall* the next step is to recover N from his short-term memory and decode it into *boy*. . . . However, after S produces *boy* the next step is to recover P from his short-term memory. . .and decode it into V plus NP. Only then does he decode V into *saved*." If we are to believe that this is a model of how people create sentences, then we must ask such questions as these: Why does the syntactic component in this instance expand S (subject phrase) into T + A + N rather than T + N or something else? Why is A + N "decoded" as *tall boy* rather than *slimy fish* or what have you? Somehow, this syntactic device is being guided by prior decisions in a semantic device.

Actually, in all of these papers and elsewhere there is ample evidence for the primacy of meaning as far as the behavior of ordinary language users is concerned, along with a rather blissful unconcern with syntactics; this applies to decoding as well as encoding sentences. In the Garrett-Fodor paper, for example, we find that negative transforms consistently require less time than passive transforms—as long as sentences are abstracted from any relation to the real world. As soon as the truth value of sentences is introduced, however, we find negative transforms taking longer than passives; the former involve a change in meaning. In McNeill's paper we find ample evidence that the earliest sentences of Adams and Eves are telegraphically semantic. In Johnson's paper we find this: "It should be pointed out, however, that while reliable differences are consistently obtained between grammatical and ungrammatical material, the absolute differences are relatively small when compared to the differences between anomalous and meaningful sequences when both are grammatically correct."

Now, it is not possible to dodge these insufficiencies in transformational grammars by stating that they are merely theories of "competence." They lose this immunity to behavioral evidence just as soon as they are presumed to be models or theories of performance. Indeed, we seem to be developing something of a mystique about concepts like "competence" and "rules." In David McNeill's paper we find that "competence . . . is the linguistic knowledge possessed by speakers of a language" and later that "children search for linguistic features that can be expressed by rule." George Miller, in a paper titled "The Psycholinguists,"

(1964) has the following to say: "It is necessary. . . to distinguish between a description of the language in terms of the rules that a person *knows* and uses and a description of that person's *performance* as a user of the rules. The distinction is sometimes criticized as 'psycholatry' by strict adherents of behaviorism; 'knowing' is considered too mentalistic and subjective, therefore unscientific. The objection cannot be taken seriously." Well, I do take it seriously. It is one thing to use notions like "competence," "knowledge" and "rules" as heuristic devices, as sources of hypotheses about performance; it is quite another thing to use them as *explanations* of performance—unless, of course, one is ready to give up his behavioristic moorings entirely in exchange for a frankly dualistic mentalism.

I still believe it will prove possible to find what corresponds to "knowing the rules" (i.e., "competence") within the principles of behavior and their dynamic interaction. The clearest statement about the nature of "rules" I have found is that given by Dan Slobin in the University of Michigan's Language Development Programs Report # 8 (1965, pp. 144–146). He says that "the productivity of language . . . impels one to characterize linguistic competence in terms of rules, whereby the individual can project a limited amount of experience with a limited number of sentences to the capacity to produce and understand an unlimited number of sentences." Fair enough. He then asks what are the operational criteria for the existence of rules and concludes as follows; "We can be fairly sure that a child has some rule system if his production is regular, if he extends these regularities to new instances, and if he can detect deviations from reguliaty in his own speech and the speech of others."

Precisely *why* are any of these criteria inconsistent in principle with behavior theory? Regularity is not incompatible with the notion of habit (as ugly and old-fashioned as that word may be!); extension to new instances is not incompatible with the principle of generalization (particularly if one escapes the restriction to physical similarity among external stimuli by invoking mediated generalization); and detection of deviations from regularity in self and others is not incompatible either, if one assumes that the regularities themselves lead to *predictions* which will conflict with the input being decoded. I might point out in passing that the three-stage (or level) behavioral model I described earlier provides for predictive mechanisms, both at integrative and representational levels.

Toward A Wedding of Insufficiencies

I conclude from the first section of this paper that contemporary behavior theory has *not* been proven inadequate in principle as a model for the language user. I myself would also conclude from the second section that contemporary lingistic theory has *not* been proven inadequate in principle. But I think it is obvious that neither has yet been shown sufficient in detail—and I doubt if anyone would contend otherwise. The papers upon which I have based this discussion all provide convincing evidence for the psycholinguistic relevance of syntactical structures, and I have not yet shown—or even attempted to show—how such phenomena might be incorporated within my own variety of behavior theory. On the other hand, neither in these papers, nor anywhere else that I am aware of, has there been any attempt to demonstrate how a transformational grammar might

handle sign learning, transitional dependencies, and the other phenomena taken up in my second section.

What I think is likely to happen is that, as each approach to a theory of performance attempts to overcome its own insufficiencies, it will take over more of the characteristics of the other, yet retaining the conceptual flavor of its origin. At some point it will begin to become clear that both are utilizing much the same principles functionally and that the one can be rather easily translated into the terms of the other. I know that this has been happening in my own thinking, and, if I read Chomsky's *Aspects of the Theory of Syntax* correctly, this has also been happening in his thinking, particularly when he tries to deal with problems of linguistic performance. Of course, I may be wrong about this. Behavior theory, with its S's and R's and its associationistic principles, may be shown to be insufficient in principle to handle syntactic phenomena; but then, linguistics-based models of the user could prove incompatible in principle with the primacy of semantics in language behavior. Although I am well aware that a "wedding" is premature at this time—and I refuse to extend the analogy to "courtship"!—nevertheless I should like to take some steps in that direction. They will necessarily be very tentative in nature.

First, I must report very briefly on some research begun by Kenneth Forster and myself a couple of years ago on what might be called *semantic feature analysis;* more recently we have had the assistance and intellectual stimulation of Agnes Niyakawa and Danny Steinberg at Hawaii and Marilyn Wilkins at Illinois.

We began with the assumption that, in a manner analogous to Jakobson's conception of a phoneme, the meaning of a word-form can be conceived as a simultaneous bundle of distinctive semantic features. This bundle can be represented by a strip-code—of plusses, zeroes, and minuses, if we make the simplifying assumption of a discrete model. In decoding, the meaning of any higher-order constituent (phrase or sentence) would be represented as the *fusion* of the strip-codes of the word elements involved, to the degree that syntactic structure forces these words into semantic interaction. In encoding, the breakdown and exhaustion of the compound strip-codes for higher-order constituents into the component strip-codes of the word elements as they are generated—again according to syntactic rules—would represent a *diffusion* process.

We also assumed that words could be combined in phrases (in ordinary language usage, at least) according to an ordered set of rules: (1) If the codings of the word elements in any combination display opposed signs on any shared feature, then the combination will be *semantically anomalous* (e.g., *green thought*, *it shouts*). This is the condition for experienced incongruity, which I have described in earlier papers as being based on the simultaneous tendency toward antagonistic reactions within the same component response systems (see Osgood, Suci, and Tannenbaum, 1957, Ch. 5). (2) If rule 1 does not apply (there are no opposed signs), but the codings of the word elements display the same sign on any shared feature, then the combination will be *semantically apposite* or fitting (e.g., *hopeful sign*, *plead humbly*). This is the condition for intensification of meaning, or congruity. (3) If neither rule 1 nor rule 2 apply (there are neither opposed nor shared signs in the fused strip-codes), then the combination will be semantically permissible (e.g., *sad face*, *walk swiftly*). This is the usual condition for "modifying" meaning.

All this might be fine, but ho to determine in a reasonably way what the features for a given semantic domain are? We have been trying to systematize what I hope was a felicitous insight from Gilbert Ryle—namely, that the bundles of semantic features of word elements can be inferred from their rules of usage in combinations. In practice, we make an intersection of two form-classes which are linked syntactically (e.g., 30 interpersonal verbs with 30 adverbs, 40 nouns for emotion states with 30 adjectives), we generate all of the possible combinations within the intersection (e.g., *sudden surprise, hopeful disgust, hot complacency, sincere pity*, etc.), and then we submit them for judgments of anomaly, appositeness, or permissability to samples of native speakers, usually starting with ourselves as the basis for an *a priori* analysis. We have applied factor analysis, which assumes a continuous model, as well as new computer programs designed to be appropriate to the discrete model I have described here; we are still struggling with the discrete method, but results are at least encouraging. Table 1 on page 508 gives a small illustration of the kinds of features we are finding.

Note that *corrupt hopefully* and particularly *plead with desperately* should be intensifying combinations, the latter sharing activity, ego-oriented, subordination, and future-orientation features. One should not be able to *corrupt sincerely* (morality feature) or *corrupt desperately* (deliberateness feature). Adding *sincerely* to *plead with* should modify it by simply making it a more moral endeavor. You will note that heads of phrases (here verbs) tend to be more richly coded than the modifiers; this is typical of our data.

The kinds of features we derive from such intersections as these appear to be clearly "semantic" in nature. But

Table 1

	A +moral / −immor	B pot / impot	C act / pass	D assoc / disoc	E init / react	F ego / alter	G supra / sub	H fut / past	I term / interm	J delib / impuls
V corrupt	−	o	−	o	+	o	+	+	−	+
AV hopefully	o	o	o	o	o	o	o	+	−	o
AV sincerely	+	o	o	o	o	o	o	o	o	o
AV desperately	o	o	+	o	o	+	−	+	o	−
V plead with	o	o	+	o	+	+	−	+	o	o

note that we have selected rather narrow classes of words, and many features which might be interpreted as "syntactic" are, in effect, held constant. All interpersonal verbs, for example, must be transitive and must be coded for human subject and human object. Early in this exploration, we took a wide sample of verbs (the first verbs appearing on each of the second hundred pages of Michener's *Hawaii!*) and intersected them with pronouns, prepositions, and nouns; in this case, the features that appeared by the same operations looked very much like what Chomsky (1965) describes in terms of subcategorization and selection rules, e.g., verb codings for such things as humanness (*shouts* vs. *shrieks*), transitivity, concreteness, animateness, and so on. I am being led to the conclusion that there is really a continuum between what can clearly be called semantic features and what can clearly be called syntactic features, with no essential difference in principle between them. Chomsky appears to be moving the same way when he says (1965, pp. 153–4): "One might propose, therefore, that selectional rules be dropped from the syntax and that their function be taken over by the semantic component. ....The syntactic component of the grammar would not, in other words, impose a hierarchy of degrees of grammaticalness at these lower levels of deviation. This task would now have to be taken over by the semantic component." And, one might add, this would also greatly increase the simplicity and elegance of the syntax of a language—leaving most of the messy little distinctions to semantics, where they have traditionally been and probably belong.

In this sketchy description of our recent research into semantic features I have deliberately avoided reference to little r_m's. I did not want to cloud the main issue with irrelevant controversy.

But I think it is fair to say at this point that there is nothing inconsistent with the notion of a bundle of distinctive semantic features, representable as a strip-code, and the notion of multicomponential r_m as presented earlier in this paper. In fact, it was out of the notion of multicomponential r_m, and the reciprocal antagonism of opposed reactions within the same components it implies, that the work on semantic features came. Nevertheless, I would certainly agree that the semantic features model, even if it were to some degree valid, does not require any r_m substratum; many other models could be compatible. We are now doing some experiments to test certain hypotheses that do derive from mediation theory; for example, we are trying to see if a specific feature can be satiated by exposure to acceptable and anomalous phrases that pivot on that feature, even though the same words are not repeated.

Now let me attempt to put semantics back in the driver's seat, as far as sentence creating is concerned, via some speculations which, although rather loose at this point, do not appear inconsistent with the notion of deep vs. surface structure. Let us suppose that the deep structure behind the initiation of any complex act of sentence creating can be characterized essentially as three substantive sets of multiple codings, corresponding to SP (subject-phrase), VP (verb-phrase) and OP (object-phrase)[1], and one set of strictly syntactic operating codings (essentially codings for extraction ordering and transformations). We might imagine each of these sets as a long bank of rollers, as in an old-fashioned desk calculator, each of which can be set (for simplicity sake) for only $+$, 0, or $-$. Within the SP, VP, and OP banks, codings might be ordered from left to right in terms of the obligatoriness and generality of the features they represent, i.e., from what would be classified as subcategorizing features through selection features to more finely differentiated semantic features like *supra-ordinate/subordinate*.

Now, we can spin the dials in these banks to a particular pattern or strip-code by means of input on the decoding side, either via linguistic signs or perceptual signs. We might, for example, present the picture of a hairy dog chasing a black cat; coding appropriate to *a hairy dog* is stored temporarily in the SP bank (the dog being perceived as actor), coding appropriate to *a black cat* sets the dials in the OP bank, and coding for *chasing* appears in the VP bank. Note that any one of these banks may have all zeroes (e.g., OP, given a picture of only a hairy dog running); note also that the operating bank may be driven into certain settings by the input (e.g., to $T_{passive}$ by recognition of the fact that the cat belongs to ego).

Any theory of the speaker will face the problem of postulating something more than an obvious analogy, such as my banks of dials, in explaining how he generates acceptable surface structure, as well as nonanomalous dictionary selections, from this deep structure. From the work of McNeill and others, it would appear that LAD (Language Acquisition Device) is *constructed*, through evolution of the species, to organize input and output in terms of some such basic and universal deep structure. But it would also appear that LAD must *learn*, through individual experience, how perceptual and then linguistic signs are coded, what are acceptable orderings of extraction of information from his deep structure

[1] I am aware, of course, that this is more like the tripartite organization of sentence types suggested by Greenberg (1963) in his discussion of universals of grammar than like Chomsky's description of the base components, but the same notions could be applied to the latter.

(which we might call his global "intentions"), and how various transformations must be applied in order to get from the deep structure to admissable and cogent surface structures in his particular language.

I assume that, in the process of such learning, transitional dependencies are built up both within and between these "banks" in the deep structure. Thus the syntactic component will develop certain sequences in which it extracts information from SP and OP (*five red brick houses* but not *brick red five houses*) or from VP (*might have been coming* but not *coming been might have*); thus codings in SP will operate selectively upon possible codings in VP (− human and + plural codings in SP, for example, will respectively eliminate, or render anomalous, codings in VP which could generate *shout* or *breaks*); thus a coding of VP that could generate selection of *pleads with* will serve to eliminate any remaining coding in VP that could generate *tolerantly* as a modifier.

In just what sense does this kind of model give primacy to the semantic component in encoding? Let us assume that, when given the set for talking, the total set of codings (or s_m or "intention") creates a drive for their own elimination — in other words, the purpose of sentence creating is to roll all of the dials in all of the banks in the deep structure back to zero. The syntax of a given language describes the rules by which this is to be done, but it is literally driven by the semantic content of the deep structure. If the coding of SP is such that a single word form will eliminate it, then NP will be re-written as N, N as that particular word form, and the speaker says *boys*. Note carefully that (a) it must be coded for plural in this case (or else two steps, *a boy*, for example, will be required) and (b) it is the semantic coding which can

only be exhausted by *boys* in English which determines this dictionary selection rather than *Wednesdays, milk*, or what have you. But what if there is no single word-form in the English of our particular speaker which will exhaust the semantic codings in SP? As far as I know, there is no single term in English that is synonymous with *the tall boy* (to go back to one of Neal Johnson's sentences). If there were a form like *tallster*, we might expect our speaker to opt for this expression, but if there is not—and he is faced with differentiating between two boys on the beach—then he will expand NP$_s$ into T + A + N and come out with *the tall boy* (*saved the dying woman*). In our Institute, James Martin is designing his doctoral dissertation as a systematic test of these notions.

We can see the same semantic driving-force operating upon the development of grammar in children, I think. If we assume that decoding regularly precedes encoding in the course of development—and this appears to be the case—then it must follow that the child will find "things on its mind" (coding patterns in the deep structure) for which it as yet has neither the output vocabulary nor the syntax to express. For example, Adam at some point will be decoding *big dog* vs. *little dog* correctly (as evidenced by his nonverbal behavior); this means that SP and OP "banks" will be registering this discriminative feature; but there is no single, unexpanded NP in his English for encoding the code-strip representing *BIG DOG*, so Adam has a problem. If he says "doggie run" when there are big and little dogs present and only the big one is running, then there will be something left over as an irritant in his SP code-strip. What is left over, of course, is precisely the strip-coding associated with "big," and one might expect to hear something like "doggie run ...

big!" at some stage in Adam's development. When Adam happens to come out with "big doggie," the auditory feedback will match what he had already learned to expect in his prior decoding learning. This, presumably, is the basis for strengthening the particular syntactic rules in English for expanding NP into A + N *when the semantic component demands it.*

I consider McNiell's summary of Bellugi's analysis of the acquisition of the negative transformation to be reasonably consistent with this picture. (1) "In the earliest phase of development, negative sentences are formed simply by affixing *no* or *not* to an otherwise affirmative sentence. A child will say *no drop mitten* or *not fit.*" At this stage the child has acquired the affirmative/negative semantic feature *in decoding*, but it does not yet have the requisite encoding skills; the most frequent, single-word negatives (*no* and *not*) are simply attached to the other expressions of SP, OP, or VP codings but typically *pre*-fixed because of the contrastive psychological emphasis in negation. (Even in adults, intense motivation to negate may produce reiterative encoding, as when the young lad confronted by a policeman says, "I ain't never done nothing to nobody nohow!) (2) "Somewhat later, he uses *don't* and *can't* apparently as independent vocabulary items, as in *I don't sit on Gromer coffee* or *he can't do that . . . do* and *can* not yet occurring alone in the child's speech." If these were, in fact, independent vocabulary items, one would expect them to appear elsewhere as well as antecedent to main verbs, e.g., *don't cookie* as well as *don't go*; I suspect this is, rather, a provisional method for extracting VP coding based upon the reinforcing analogy with the child's existing decoding model. (3) "Finally . . . *do* and *can* appear in affirmative sentences . . . as well as in

negatives, and the child appears to have developed a transformational system." The affirmative/negative feature and the do/0, can/0 and other VP-modifying features have now become extractable according to acceptable (syntactical) sequences—again, presumably, developed by the reinforcement provided by matching familiar decoding models.

Although the conception I have sketchily illustrated in this section is very crude, I nevertheless think it has some merits, in principle if not in detail. For one thing, it makes full use of the apparent fact that decoding skills antedate encoding skills at all levels of language development, the former providing both a model and a differential strengthening mechanism for the latter. For another thing, it represents a blending or fusion of notions derived from learning theory with notions derived from linguistic theory. And finally, it does suggest a way in which meaning—or the semantic component—can participate in the initiation of sentence-creation and literally drive decisions among alternative syntactic rules, both in the performance of the mature speaker and in the course of development of the language learner.

Some Comments on The Papers Under Discussion

At long last I am in a position to make certain specific comments about the McNeill, Johnson, Garrett, and Fodor papers. I particularly want to take note of the most exciting research reported in each of the papers.

McNeill

I find McNeill's emphasis upon what he calls "Nativist Theories" of language development a healthy corrective to what has characterized this area in the past. The identification of what is innate as being in part predispositions toward organizing language input and output according to what linguists today are talking about as "deep structure"—presumed to be part of the universals of human language—is also an intriguing notion. It suggests, for example, that child languages should be more similar cross-culturally than adult languages in structure; it also suggests that one good measure of the complexity of a language would be the deviation from its child language (and perhaps the time required for mastery by the child). Particularly impressive to me was the way McNeill was able to show what types of constructions would be predicted from the deep structure and then, given the grammatical classes being used by Adam when first recorded, show that *all 400* of Adam's sentences were of the admissible type— no exceptions.

However, I do wish McNeill had included Joe Greenberg's paper on Universals of Grammar (1963) among his references and in his thinking, because it contains many relevant ideas. I also think that the basic proposition here could be put much less mysteriously. Rather than saying that "the acquisition of language can be regarded as the guided (principled) choice of a grammar, made on the basis of a child's innate capacity . . . ," I would prefer a statement which indicates the nature of the innate propensities but also makes room for the facts of learning. Not only may many of the universals of language be based upon common learning, given certain nonlinguistic innate capacities, but it just simply *is* obvious that children do not "mature" to speak a particular language.

As a matter of fact, for an old behaviorist like myself, there is much in McNeill's way of putting things that is anthropomorphic (if one can apply that term to human children!). We read, for example, that "a child hopes to become such a speaker, so he too must reconstruct the competence of fluent speakers," that "the explanation that suggests itself is that Adam was attempting to use only those sentence patterns that express the basic grammatical relations" and that "this would seem to be very strong evidence of a child's imposition of conceptual restraints onto the speech he produces." Would one say that when an infant happens to emit "papa" he knows his relationship to his biological male parent? I do not think McNeill actually wishes to confer adult cognitive processes upon a two-year-old LAD, but rather this is part of the fervor that goes with the exposition of fresh ideas. I myself find it very difficult to conceive of a two-year-old deliberately testing an abstract theory of language against the inputs he receives from adults. But, as I say, this seems to be mainly a way of talking about something.

Another point raised by McNeill's paper relates to the notion of "rules." McNeill asserts that the speed of acquisition of language depends upon the child's predisposition toward the most abstract (which are also, incidentally, the most primitive in a sense) features of language, those characterizing deep structure. (I am not sure why this follows, but that is not my main concern.) He claims that the speed of acquisition, as well as its manner, requires the notion of rules rather than the principle of generalization. For example, "children search for linguistic features that can be expressed by rule. When a rule is formulated, it is applied generally, contrary past experience not withstanding." Thus children say (correctly) *did, came,* and *ran* before they make the false overgeneralizations to these strong verbs, producing *doed, comed,* and *runned;* yet these false overgeneralizations occur earlier than the correct regular forms, "...as if the children were overgeneralizing before there was anything to overgeneralize from." Along similar lines, in discussing language development in Russian children, Slobin (1965) says "One is struck by the rapidity with which a principle is suddenly applied to an entire domain—and to the correct domain. . . . For example, gender agreement appeared simultaneously both in regard to adjective-noun agreement and noun-past tense of verb agreement (p. 97)."

If indeed, such acquisitions over an entire and proper domain did appear simultaneously, this would be convincing evidence for "formulating a rule" rather than "generalizing a habit." But note, first, that the notion of "simultaneity" is inherently untestable, for the simple reason that Adam cannot say two things at once. Generalization is also rapid, indeed immediate, given sufficient habit strength and the presentation of similar contexts. Note, second, that if we agree that decoding precedes encoding, then semantic features (e.g., for past/present tense, for masculine/feminine gender, and so forth) will already be coded in SP, OP, and VP "banks," as appropriate, as part of the information to be encoded as developing syntactic mechanisms make this possible. It does not, therefore, seem surprising that agreements both within and between such constituents, e.g., in gender, should appear "simultaneously."

As to overgeneralization to strong verbs which were earlier produced correctly, let us note that, although specific strong verbs are more frequent in usage than specific regular verbs, the over-all frequency of the regulars far exceeds that of any set of strong verbs sharing the same past-tense inflection. Now, if decoding antedates encoding, one would expect a child to learn the regular distinction as the basis for correct decoding and then to predict it for his own encoding operation; but his most available verbs (whose past forms were earlier learned as independent words) are the high-frequency strong verbs; hence the initial overgeneralization to *doed, comed,* and *runned.* Developmental psycholinguists should pay more attention to the relations between decoding and encoding (I note that Bellugi, 1965, does this, and she reports that *wh* questions are correctly decoded before they are correctly encoded, for example).

Johnson

As I said earlier, Neal Johnson has done our field a real service by integrating the diverse and often confusing literature on sequential verbal behavior. What he is searching for, and that most persistently, is an explanation of exactly *how* grammatical structure facilitates learning. He quickly disposes of the early Hullian (really, pre-Hullian) notion of simple response chaining $(S \longrightarrow R_1 \longrightarrow S_1 \longrightarrow R_2 \longrightarrow S_2,$ etc.) by contrasting it with Lashley's (1951) insistence on the need for central programing of response sequences into skills or "schema of action." He does not, however, dispose of the notion of r-r integrative mechanisms (Osgood, 1957, 1963) which, interestingly enough, I proposed as a necessary extension of S-R learning theory for exactly the same reasons that Johnson gives. It provides for both evocative (motor skill units) and predictive (transitional dependencies) central programing based upon output redundancies. I also suggested (1954 and elsewhere) that such predictive integrations might contribute to the facilitative effect of grammar upon sentence production and learning.

While I would agree that neither such integrative mechanisms nor the transitional dependencies at many levels which Johnson documents in the early part of his paper provide a *sufficient* explanation of the effect of grammar upon sentencing, I would insist that these characteristics of the performer are part of the total phenomenon to be explained. For example, in the series of studies using meaningful vs. nonsense stems, with or without syntactic structure, beginning with Louis Carroll's "Twas brillig...," continuing with experiments by Swanson and Epstein (reported in Johnson's paper), it has been shown that if one allows free recall of the sequence but imposes a two-second interval between word items during exposure, all evidence for SYNFAX (effect of syntax upon recall) disappears. Yet, when one *instructs* the subjects to look for grammatical cues for sentences under the same conditions, as in one of Forster's experiments, SYNFAX appears significantly. A straightforward prediction is this: If one were to progressively reduce the time interval in serial presentation of such nonsense (but syntactically correct) sentences, uninstructed subjects would gradually approach the performance of instructed subjects, because the normal predictive mechanisms (r-r integrations) of people in ordinary decoding and encoding are much shorter than the two-second interval imposed by the use of the memory drum. In other words, this is like the effects of delayed feedback upon speech monitoring.

But Johnson's own experiments are making it clear that word-to-word transitional dependencies interact with syntactical structure. Paired-associate pretraining of A-N pairs later to be sequential parts of sentences clearly facilitates subsequent sentence learning, but equivalent pretraining of N-V pairs does not. Similarly, a related experiment by Frankart shows that prior paired-associated learning of word pairs has decreasing effect as the degree of grammaticality of the terminal sentences to be learned increases. All this seems to be adding up to the conclusion that *neither* transitional dependencies *nor* syntactical structure in themselves provide sufficient explanations of ease of sentence learning. In keeping with the notions of deep versus surface structure, and my own notions of semantic and syntactic coding of word forms, let me suggest that prior paired-associate learning of the word units which will eventually be assigned to the same "bank" (in the deep structure) will be facilitative, whereas the same prior treatment of items to be later assigned to different base categories will necessarily be less so.

But the question remains: How does grammatical structure facilitate learning? Here Johnson introduces his ingenious TEP measure (transitional error probability). This is the probability that, given correct recall of an antecedent word item, the immediately subsequent item will be wrong or blanked. In one study, he reports that the pattern of negative conditional probabilities for grammatical but semantically anomalous sentences approximates that obtained for grammatical and meaningful sentences. This indicates that, beyond transitional prediction based on a long history of form-class to form-class sequencing, grammatical structure also imposes the kind of "chunking" (into phrases) suggested by George Miller some time ago. But as the final sections of Johnson's paper make clear, more than "chunking" is involved—a kind of "recoding" of subsets of verbal material, already carved out in the "chunking" operation of syntax.

TEP proves to be a sensitive index of structure. "The TEP at each transition is a measure of the extent to which the words on either side of the transition are independent of one another as recall events, and the nature of the units that Ss use should be apparent from the pattern of TEPs for a sentence." If this is true—and I believe it is—then we must add that "structure" as Johnson uses the term (operationally defined by TEPs) includes left-to-right predictive mechanisms and the "chunking" effects of grammar, along with the possibility of recoding. Note, for one thing, that within phrases there is typically a progressive reduction in TEP from left to right; note, for another thing (which Johnson does not discuss), that the TEP between *house* and *across* in the sentence *the house across the street burned down* is actually larger than the major SP/VP break (syntactically) between *street* and *burned*.

Now, Johnson' theory, as I have already indicated, explicitly puts the syntactic cart before the semantic horse—"a stimulus elicits some recoding device that represents the entire sentence (i.e., Σ)... the S then applies a decoding rule which translates Σ into S plus P," and so on—but let us note that Johnson is not dealing with ordinary sentence creating, but rather with a very special case of multiple sentence learning. Both decoding (during exposure) and encoding (during attempted recall) are involved. May I suggest that, during decoding, the subjects are learning to make certain semantic and grammatical assignments to SP, OP, VP, and O (operator) "banks" as representational reactions to the digit stimuli which (during recall) are to elicit the recall of the sentences. Much like LAD, they first get the deep structure (e.g., stimulus #7 early elicits the codings corresponding to "some male associated with some female") and only later do they get the finer detailed coding, e.g., #7 $\longrightarrow$ /specific male young tall/saved (past)/female mature dying/). If subjects edit their own anticipatory encoding attempts—which they probably do—then, as Johnson says, they will tend to inhibit completely segments they recognize as incomplete. An experimental procedure which would get around this difficulty, and also segregate decoding from encoding operations, would be to substitute *recognition* for recall. After only a few presentations of a list of sentences, given multiple sets of alternatives (e.g., *the boy helped the lovely woman, the tall man chased the girl swimmer*, etc.), I would guess that the dispersion of false recognitions would indicate just what representational codings the subject has and has not associated with #7; and, of course, a progressive narrowing toward the correct sentence would be expected.

In his pursuit of the nature of recoding, Johnson has most recently applied his procedures and the TEP measure to sequences of material (letters) which are structured by spacing but which in no sense represent English grammar. Here, I think, lies his most significant contribution to date. He has shown that essentially the same "rules" that apply in structuring grammatical sentences also seem to apply here as well. On the one hand, this suggests that the principles that characterize "deep structure" and guide the child in his learning of a language also characterize nonlinguistic behavior; on the other hand, this suggests that the innate propensities which enable man to be a talking animal are not inherently linguistic but are part of what enables man to be man. I interpret Tulving's evidence for the subjective organization people impose upon free recall of random, unrelated words as pointing in the same direction.

Garrett and Fodor

After some general statements about contemporary linguistic and behavior theory, Garrett and Fodor organize the substantive portions of their paper in terms of three levels of research and its implications: the acoustic stimulus, surface structure, and deep structure. I shall follow the same organization in my specific comments.

THE ACOUSTIC STIMULUS. From two "striking and complementary results" —that "the same physical event, the same acoustic stimulus, gives rise to systematically different percepts" and that "different physical events, diverse acoustic stimuli, give rise to the same percept"—Garrett and Fodor conclude that "the problem of establishing a perceptual analysis of the acoustic input is not plausibly solved in terms of discriminative responses to some set of acoustic parameters." I agree with this conclusion but object to the use to which it is put—to deny the plausibility of all behavior theories employing S's and R's as constructs. In both of my papers which Garrett and Fodor cite (Osgood, 1957, 1963) I have tried to demonstrate that the mechanism of sensory integration—which, to be sure, is S-S learning and not S-R learning—is consistent with exactly the same kinds of evidence they report.

First, all of the data that Garrett and Fodor cite in support of the same physical event participating in different percepts are cases of temporal patterning. For example, "the same burst of energy at a particular point in the spectrum is identified as a different sound, depending on the vowel it is adjacent to." The sensory integration process explicitly includes the effects of *convergent context*; sensory signal *a* will contribute to closure X in the presence of *b* and *c* (perhaps filling in missing *d*) and to

closure Y in the presence of *f* and *g* (perhaps filling in missing *h*). The evidence supporting different physical events participating in the same percept actually follows from the same principle, *given the added assumption that they do not make a* difference in meaning (i.e., are not phonemic). Thus if elements *a*, *b*, and *c* are constant, but element *d* is varied (e.g., basic pitch level for men, women, and children, $d_1, d_2 \ldots d_n$), and this is nondistinctive, the same integration will occur—in effect, overriding variations in *d*. I interpret the findings of House, Stevens, *et al.* (1962) as consistent with this conception; they generated synthetic speech ensembles varying through four levels of approximation to English and found that, although English nonsense syllables were learned most easily, the *closer* the non-English materials came to English the more difficult they were to learn. The dominant closure tendencies "washed out" the slight variations from expected English integrations.

Just what is the role of meaning in determining phonemic sensory integrations? I think a well-documented psychological process underlies it—*the acquired distinctiveness of cues*. For the rat, stimulus differences (e.g., black vs. white walls) which make a difference in outcome (that is, are consistently relevant to reward or punishment) come to be "selectively attended" as compared with equally present and prominent cues which are not consistently relevant (e.g., sandy vs. smooth floors); this is shown by the fact that the animals will subsequently transfer to novel problems more easily if these relevant cues are again employed, even when their significance is reversed. At the time when children begin developing phonemic systems (as contrasted with earlier sound systems)—*when they begin contrasting word units* (the definition of a phoneme is a sound difference that makes a difference in meaning)—they already have their familiar world well organized in terms of perceptual signs, and these signs have meaning. When, in the helter-skelter of language input, the child is exposed to many contrasting forms with different meanings and is corrected by adults and then by himself for errors in interpretation, it seems reasonable to assume that he comes increasingly to pay selective attention to those aspects of the acoustic signal which repeatedly make a difference and to disregard those aspects which repeatedly do not make a difference. The data of Liberman *et al.* (1957), demonstrating sharper discriminations of speech (but not nonspeech) physical sounds across phoneme boundaries than within phoneme boundaries seem consistent with this analysis.

SURFACE STRUCTURE. The "click" studies of Fodor and Bever, Garrett and others cited in the paper under discussion, provide most convincing evidence for the psycholinguistic reality of syntactic structure, and I am happy to have had a small part in encouraging this line of research when both Fodor and Garrett were at Illinois. However, the results to date are not uncomplicated (as the present paper indicates), and it is not even clear that it is surface rather than deep structure that is being reflected. Garrett's experiment, in which tapes of exactly the same sentence segments (including their intonation patterns and pauses) were spliced into whole sentences having different syntactical structure, seems to rule out any peripheral explanation as being sufficient. The fact that "external pauses" (e.g., as introduced in the taping of a series of digits) attract clicks suggests the possibility that "internal pauses" (e.g., occurring when the listener must shift from SP to VP, from VP to OP "banks") would also be periods for processing clicks. It would seem that

deep structure is thus more involved than surface structures.

DEEP STRUCTURE. Most of the experiments reported as demonstrating the psycholinguistic reality of deep structure involve measuring the effort (time, errors, etc.) required to make various types of transformation. Whereas I feel that the "click" experiments probably relate primarily to deep structure, I feel that most of the experiments reported in this section relate to surface structure—or, rather, the process of moving from surface to deep structure (decoding) or the reverse (encoding). As I understand it, unraveling or raveling the transformations characteristic of a particular language is one of the major modes of transition between these two levels. In any case, these experiments, certainly, are full of complications upon which I can only touch here.

First, we must distinguish between sentencing behavior which is abstracted from any relation to the nonlinguistic environment (obviously more of an intellectural exercise than a part of ordinary language usage) and sentencing behavior that is interactive with the nonlinguistic environment. There are some rather consistent and, I think, very significant shifts in the relative difficulties of various transformations under these two conditions, and they underscore the primary role of meaning in ordinary language usage. For example, the passive transformation is more effortful than the negative in dealing with abstracted sentences (which it should be, in terms of the complexity of the operations involved), but the reverse holds true for sentences being related to their extralinguistic truth value. The negative transform involves a shift in meaning; the passive transform does not—or, at least, not to the same degree. I conclude from evidence such as this that the semantic component is involved in transformations under ordinary conditions of listening and speaking. Garrett and Fodor reach the same conclusion but do little further about it.

Second, as our authors admit in several places, just how the latency data for various transformations are to be related to the notions of surface and deep structure is by no means obvious. They state: "What is needed, of course, is some theoretically motivated way of saying which of the grammatically defined operations are psychologically relevant—i.e., which ones should we count in making predictions about complexity of perception, production, or recall." I certainly agree, and I suggest that the answers will not be found in any transformational grammar *per se*. Witness, for example, what happens when sentences differing in the syntactic complexity of expanding VP are studied: *There are essentially no differences in psycholinguistic difficulty!* Why? Let me suggest that the "rules" for depositing (decoding) or extracting (encoding) information from the same constituent in the deep structure are quite different from those involving interactions between constituents. Thus, whereas passive transformations involve interactions between SP, VP, and OP information, VP expansions do not. The latter are essentially alternative modes of *semantically* coding forms, analogous to the differences between future-oriented *promise* and past-oriented *apologize*.

Third, there is a tiny matter about intuitive sense vs. nonsense which is highlighted by Mehler's interpretation (and George Miller's) of his experiment on ease of learning sentences of various syntactic types (kernels, Q, P, N, PQ, PN, NQ, and PQN). "Mehler assumed that sentences were recalled by *S*s using a strategy in which the underlying form of the sentence was recalled inde-

pendently of appended transformational 'notes' which determine its derived syntactic form. That is, the sentence is assumed to be represented in memory, not by its surface form, but by some information minimally necessary to specify semantic content and by a set of specifications for deriving the surface structure." I find it intuitively unrealistic to assume that in remembering *Jane is not here*, I really recall *Jane is here* and then append a "note" to make it come out negative. The issue is again meaning; the decoding meaning of *Jane is not here* (in my theory, at least) is the simultaneous pattern of s_m produced by the multiple reactions (coding) to the word forms, including the negation coding of *not*. Now when I am asked to *recall* this sentence, to be sure, I must encode from the stripcodes, which, if I do recall will include the negative marker in VP. Note also that in the second portion of the Mehler study, when various expansions of the auxiliary in VP were studied by the same methods, again no significant differences were obtained. I interpret this result as also consistent with my analysis of the difference between within vs. between deep constituent operations.

However, the most recent studies reported by Garrett and Fodor do directly pivot on differences in deep structure (e.g., that between *John is easy to please* and *John is eager to please*), and the results are clearly consistent with predictions. Sentences whose surface structures correspond more closely to the deep structure assumed in contemporary linguistic theory do, in fact, prove easier to handle. But let me say it again: the demonstration of psycholinguistic relevance of syntactic structure is not in itself a refutation of behavior theories. It poses problems for any theory of the language-user, those deriving from transformational grammars as well as those deriving from S-R constructs and associationistic principles. None of us is very close to an understanding of how people create and understand sentences. We will be wise to learn what we can from each other.

References

Bellugi, U., "The Development of Interrogative Structures in Children's Speech," *Report No. 8, Center for Human Growth and Development,* The University of Michigan, 1965.

——, *Report No. 8, Language Development Programs,* University of Michigan, 1965.

Bousfield, W. A., "The Problem of Meaning in Verbal Learning," in C. N. Cofer, ed., *Verbal Learning and Verbal Behavior.* New York: McGraw-Hill Book Company, 1961.

Chomsky, N., "On the Notion 'Rule of Grammar,'" in *Proceedings of Symposia in Applied Mathematics, American Mathematics Society,* 12 (1961), 6–24.

——, *Aspects of the Theory of Syntax.* Cambridge, Mass.: M.I.T. Press, 1965.

Fodor, J. A., "Could Meaning be an r_m?" *Journal of Verbal Learning and Verbal Behavior,* 4 (1965), 73–81.

Greenberg, J. H., "Some Universals of Grammar with Particular Reference to the Order of Meaningful Elements," in J. H. Greenberg, ed., *Universals of Language.* Cambridge, Mass.: M.I.T. Press, 1963.

House, A. S., K. N. Stevens, T. T. Sandel, and J. B. Arnold, "On the Learning of Speech-Like Vocabularies," *Journal of Verbal Learning and Verbal Behavior,* 1 (1962), 133–143.

Lashley, K. S., "The Problem of Serial Order in Behavior," In L. A. Jeffress, ed., *Cerebral Mechanisms in Behavior.* The Hixon Symposium: New York: Wiley and Sons, 1951.

Liberman, A. M., K. S. Harris, H. S. Hoffman, and B.C. Griffith, "Discrimination of Speech Sounds within and across Phoneme Boundaries," *Journal of Experimental Psychology,* 54 (1957), 358–368.

Miller, G. A., "The Psycholinguists," *Encounter,* 23 (1964), 29–37.

Osgood, C. E., "Motivational Dynamics of Language Behavior," in *The Nebraska Symposium on Motivation.* Lincoln, Neb.: University of Nebraska Press, 1957.

——, "On Understanding and Creating Sentences," *American Psychologist,* 18 (1963), 735–751.

——, and T. A. Sebeok, eds., "Psycholinguistics: A Survey of Theory and Research Problems," Suppl. to *Journal of Abnormal and Social Psychology,* 49 (1954), 203ff.

——, G. J. Suci, and P. H. Tannenbaum, *The Measurement of Meaning.* Urbana, Ill.: University of Illinois Press, 1957.

——, "Meaning Cannot Be an r_m?" *Journal of Verbal Learning and Verbal Behavior,* 5 (1966), 402–407.

Slobin, D., *Report No. 8. Language Development Programs,* University of Michigan, 1965.

——, "Grammatical Development in Russian-Speaking Children," *Report No. 8, Center for Human Growth and Development,* The University of Michigan, 1965, 144–146.

General
Discussants

PART V

Problems, Issues, and Implications

20

It has seemed to me, as I read the papers prepared for this conference and listened to both the formal and informal discussions, that there is a great variety in the interests and problem areas which have been brought together here. The variety of problems is greater than that considered, at least formally, in many conferences of the past, but I think it was intentional on the part of the instigators of this enterprise that it be so. The statement of the theme as involving verbal behavior theory in relation to general S-R theory suggests that many of the problems in the verbal area should be examined with respect to the congruence or dissonance of their phenomena with the precepts, whatever they are, of general S-R theory, whatever that is.

It is desirable first to identify the major problems in the verbal area which have been treated here, to view them in at least brief historical perspective, and to attempt some kind of characterization of "general S-R

theory," especially as it has been employed by students of these problems. It will be worth mentioning that S-R theory (or associationism, more generally) has often been attacked in the past, and it may be instructive to ask what the consequences of these attacks have been and why S-R or association theory has apparently remained viable, despite these attacks. Throughout this discussion I shall make some reference to specific papers and discussions presented at this conference.

Some Major Problems in Verbal Behavior in Historical Perspective

In some ways, it is odd to find, in the same meeting, discussions of such diverse topics as, for example, "Paired Associate Learning" and "Sequential Verbal Behavior." On the other hand, at a superficial level, it may seem appropriate to find the first of these topics in the same conference as the topic "Acquisition of Language." It is not clear to me that this second conjunction is any more congruous than the first.

Gough and Jenkins (1963) have

---

[1] During the preparation of this paper copies were available of the papers of only four of the area discussants—Deese, Kendler, Mandler, and Osgood. Remarks made about the papers by other discussants are based on memory and on notes made during the conference.

distinguished sharply between the area of verbal learning on the one hand and psycholinguistics on the other while indicating that the two fields share an interest in the verbal behavior of individuals. This is a distinction which I think is a sound one, especially insofar as problems of concern and of study are the foci of interest (some of the methods and variables are common to the two fields). Verbal learning as an area has its problems, and they are largely different from those of psycholinguistics.

Epitome! + Implications

Verbal learning

The beginning of the experimental study of verbal learning is easy to identify. It is the work of Hermann Ebbinghaus, whose monograph *On Memory* is clearly the book of Genesis for this field. Ebbinghaus identified his problem with some clarity. There are, he said, states of mind which have been lost from consciousness but which continue to exist, as several kinds of effects demonstrate. Such effects include the recall of lost states by "an exertion of the will," the spontaneous reappearance of mental states which we recognize as having been experienced previously, and the facilitative influence on the course of similar states and processes which lost states have, even when the original experiences cannot be made to enter consciousness. Ebbinghaus described some of the conditions which influence retention, emphasizing differences among individuals and among materials, the attention and interest devoted to the mental states in the first place, and number of repetitions, but he spoke also of the deficiency in knowledge of the details of processes such as these. It was for this reason that he went ahead with the experiments which are reported in his monograph.

Perhaps enough has been said to indicate that, for Ebbinghaus, the problem area whose investigation he initiated was *retention* (and it is pertinent here to mention that four of the five chapters in which he presented major results contained the word "retention" in their titles). He developed methods and materials which he thought would enable him to control the learning he accomplished, but he did so primarily in the interest of making conclusions about retention (or remembering). It has occurred to me, from time to time, that perhaps Ebbinghaus might have studied the problem which concerned him by means of a nonverbal task, such as the retention of a simple movement, rather than with a verbal task. Naturally, however, he recognized the verbal character of much of human memory, so for that reason it was foreordained that he would use verbal materials. But my point is that it was retention or memory which engaged Ebbinghaus' interest in his monograph, not language as such.

Irion (1959, pp. 541–542), seconded by Deese (1961, p. 14), has asserted that Ebbinghaus' work was "a fairly exact application of the doctrine of associationism to laboratory experimentation," seeing a parallel between the nonsense syllables used by Ebbinghaus and the "ideas" postulated by the associationists and indicating that the methods employed by Ebbinghaus could be used to study the laws of association. Further, Irion points out, Ebbinghaus was an empiricist, staying close to his data and indulging in little speculation. This last characteristic has been referred to by a number of writers as the "functionalist" approach of students of verbal learning, by which is meant, I think, that such investigators seek and are largely satisfied with finding functional relations between the variables they manipulate experimentally and the dependent variables which they assess.

Interest in the conditions for the formation, retention, and transfer effects of associations, with special emphasis on retention and transfer effects, has, I think, dominated work in verbal learning throughout its history. Most ~~of the principles, hypotheses, or~~ theoretical integrations in this field, as reflected in summaries of the literature like those by McGeoch (1942) and McGeoch and Irion (1952), ~~pertain to retention and transfer~~. This is to say, then, that the study of language has been but a minor or secondary aspect of the work of students of verbal learning in the Ebbinghaus tradition. The papers on serial learning, paired-associate learning, and retroaction and proaction in this conference represent the methods and many of the topics of this tradition. And I think it is fair to say that retention and transfer are important problems, whose investigation is well worthwhile.

Psycholinguistics

Gough and Jenkins (1963, p. 463) follow Osgood and Sebeok (1954) in identifying psycholinguistics as a discipline which represents the convergence of three fields: linguistics, information measurement, and, from psychology, learning theory (see also Osgood, 1963a, pp. 246–249). They refer to it as a hybrid and indicate the kinds of problems those influenced by each of the source disciplines have been concerned with. I believe that information measurement is perhaps less influential than it once was; and, of course, linguistics has recently become more influential, especially on the question of what knowing a language means for the psychology of the user of a language. (Jenkins' discussion develops this point more explicitly and

fully than will be done here.) Gough and Jenkins identify three aspects of learning theory which have had impact on psycholinguistics: Osgood's theory of meaning, couched in terms of mediational processes (and supplemented more recently by an analysis of sentences—Osgood, 1963b, and his paper in this conference); Skinner's analysis of verbal behavior (Skinner, 1957); and verbal association, " . . . a set of informal theoretical assumptions about verbal habits, elaborated and developed by individual psycholinguists into distinct theoretical conceptions . . . , but shared as the common property of a number of investigators" (Gough and Jenkins, 1963, p. 467). In general, Gough and Jenkins indicate, this last position is largely a working hypothesis which leads to many experiments in which measured associations, conceived as habits, are examined for their effect in a number of other situations—free recall, for example (see Tulving's paper), recognition of briefly presented words, concept attainment (see Bourne's paper) and the like (see Pollio's and Kjeldergaard's papers).

The verbal associationists have been largely concerned, I think, with finding low-order empirical relationships between measured associations and the performance of verbal units in other situations. Theoretical analysis has not proceeded very far, although Deese's paper and his book (1965) represent attempts to go beyond measurement to a conception of the structures which underlie the measurements made and the correlations discovered. There has been and is a controversy about meaning—not, interestingly enough, about the mediational interpretation of meaning but rather over the nature of the mediator (see Maltzman's paper; Bousfield, 1961; Osgood, 1961; Jenkins, 1963, pp. 211–212). Aside from Osgood's recent attempts to cope with the problem of "sentencehood," the incorporation of structural linguistic variables in much recent research, and perhaps Skinner's (1957) apparent attempt to deal generally with language (but see Skinner, 1966, p. 217), there has been relatively little effort on the part of learning theorists to deal with language *as a system*. Some efforts were reported in the psycholinguistics monograph (Osgood and Sebeok, 1954) involving learning theory and Markov processes. Investigators like Brown (Brown and Fraser, 1963) and Ervin-Tripp (Miller and Ervin, 1964) in their studies of the development of language have been much influenced by linguistics and see their findings as making difficulties for current learning theory. Braine (1963) and Jenkins and Palermo (1964) have made applications of concepts from learning theory to the matter of early language development.

The Major Issues of this Conference

What I have said in the foregoing section is an attempt to identify the general problems with which, from a psychological point of view, psycholinguists and students of verbal learning have been concerned, at least until recently. In the present conference I perceive three major points of conflict (leaving aside disagreements on many specific issues of fact and interpretation). They are related but can be described separately.

1. Verbal learning experiments conducted within the framework of S-R associationism and the Ebbinghaus tradition have led us to ignore the complexity of such procedures as paired-associate learning and to ignore important processes involved in all such human learning. Battig's attack in his paper on S-R interpretations of paired-associate learning is the best example of what I have in mind here, although Tulving's emphasis on the organization of free recall in terms of subjective rather than experimenter arrangements and Mandler's question to Postman (in the general discussion) as to how it can be that associations are altered by instructions are also pertinent.

2. The attack (by Fodor, Garrett, McNeill, and Bever in their papers) on S-R theory (including its mediational supplements) as in principle inadequate to account for the facts of the development and the functioning of language as it is conceived and investigated from a generative and transformational grammatical viewpoint.

3. An impatience with the snail's pace. of progress in reaching an understanding of human learning and of language development and functioning based on principles arising from conditioning studies and the verbal learning laboratory.

I will comment on these issues in the second following section in the context of the problems already raised in the first section, the nature of S-R theory and method, and the problem of finding or formulating alternatives to it.

Associationism and S-R Theory

Associationism is an analytic approach to the problems of behavior, and S-R theory is its modern counterpart, from a theoretical standpoint. The functionalist tradition is also compatible with associationism and an S-R approach, because it too is analytical. However, I do not see, nor have other writers such as Gough and Jenkins (1963), Underwood, Deese and Wickens (in Cofer and Musgrave, 1963, pp. 72, 375) seen that the functionalists in the field of verbal learning, who are also referred to as S-R theorists, have made many theoretical assertions or been closely bound to descriptions of behavior in terms of only stimuli and responses.

Perhaps it is worth a little space to expand this point by commenting on it, again historically. As most of us know, psychology had two "revolutions" around the turn of the century. One of them was the functionalist revolt which redefined the goals of psychology so that rather than being concerned primarily with the analytic description of the contents of the mind, such as sensations, images, feelings, and their attributes, it turned its interest to the adaptive functions of consciousness and the mind and of behavior. The second revolt was methodological and was the behavioristic development (Bergmann, 1956). But, as Maltzman and Kendler point out in their papers and as has been said many times by others as well, neither the functionalist nor the behaviorist revolt carried any necessary theoretical commitments. Nor did it necessarily carry the implication that observable events constituted the only acceptable items in an account of behavior. Hull's theory (1943, 1952a) is replete with intervening constructs, although he says in his autobiography (Hull, 1952b, p. 154) that rather than converting him to Gestalt Psychology, Koffka at Wisconsin provided the basis for " . . . a belated conversion to a kind of neobehaviorism—a behaviorism mainly concerned with the determination of the quantitative laws of behavior and their deductive systematization." Perhaps it is pertinent to mention that Hunter, who postulated intervening symbolic processes to account for the data he observed in the delayed reaction (1913) and temporal maze (1920) situations, found no reason to discard these processes when (1922) he

chose behaviorism to be his point of view, nor as a continuing behaviorist did he find reason to deny the concept of instinct (Hunter, 1947) when the data seemed to him to call for it.

What I am trying to suggest here is that an objective, functionalist, or even S-R viewpoint carries no necessary theoretical commitments and no necessary aversion to postulating intervening processes. It is perhaps those who follow the highly positivistic approach of Skinner who should be attacked because of emphasis on stimulus control and on reinforcement contingencies and because of an unwillingness to consider intervening states and processes. Yet even Skinner (1957) in his account of verbal behavior seems to some writers (see Jakobovits, 1966) to employ mediational processes, and in at least one place (p. 336) he speaks of "autoclitic 'frames' (which) combine with responses appropriate to a specific situation." Thus, the speaker, having acquired expressions "such as *the boy's gun, the boy's shoe,* and *the boy's hat,* we may suppose that the partial frame *the boy's* ——— is available for recombination with other responses." This autoclitic frame, whatever its merits, seems to fall outside the range of observable responses and stimuli.

Having made these points, that functionalist (S-R) associationism involves neither a necessary commitment to particular theoretical ideas nor a necessary aversion to the postulation of unobservables, it is necessary to say two additional things before discussing the three issues mentioned above. One is that, in fact, students of verbal learning and the psychological psycholinguists have shown an attachment to principles of conditioning. The other is that their theoretical analyses have been low-order ones and restricted to small-scale statements.

Principles of conditioning

It is, I think, generally true that psychologists interested in verbal behavior have had a penchant for *borrowing* theoretical principles. In doing so, perhaps they have been influenced by Hull's (1935a) solution to the problem of the "conflicting psychologies of learning." At any rate, notions like generalization, differentiation or discrimination, extinction, reinforcement, and spontaneous recovery have been borrowed from classical and instrumental conditioning. There are probably several reasons for this borrowing, two of which appear to me to be paramount. One is that theoretical elegance, insofar as it was ever achieved in psychology up to about 1950 or 1955, was greatest in the accounts of the phenomena of conditioning and in their extensions to selective learning and to matters of verbal process. The monograph on rote learning by Hull, *et al.* (1940) and the theoretical derivations and experiments in the verbal learning area by students at Yale such as Eleanor Gibson, Carl Hovland, and Charles Osgood, to name some of the most influential ones, have seldom been equaled and perhaps never excelled as systematic integrations of fairly rigorously stated theory and sophisticated experimental work. Yet the theoretical formulations, from Hull to Osgood, were rooted in the principles of conditioning. Even the mediation process, mentioned in several of the conference papers, is found in Hull's writings and in Shipley's reports on conditioning from the Yale laboratories.

The other reason for the appeal of conditioning principles to students of verbal processes may lie in a sense of identity between the basic problem in conditioning and the basic problem in verbal learning. In both, this problem may be defined, as I have already said, as determining the conditions and parameter values of which the formation of an association and its retention are a function. As I have said, this was Ebbinghaus' problem, and it is not perhaps too farfetched to say that this was Pavlov's problem, too, though he placed more emphasis on acquisition.

It is important too, I think, to mention that these borrowings of conditioning principles were not without success when applications were made to verbal learning. It must have been a period of high excitement at Yale when, on the basis of the analysis of remote associations formed during serial anticipation learning as delayed conditioned responses, deductions were made of the short-term (Ward-Hovland) reminiscence effects, shifts in the serial position curve as a function of distribution of practice and length of list, and differences with respect to serial as opposed to paired-associate learning. Hull gave a colloquium at Brown University in 1936–37, and the next year the story was told that Hull had reported making the deductions with respect to reminiscence, had not believed that they could be verified, and then said, "I sent Mr. Hovland into the laboratory" to find out whether they were so or not. Hovland, of course, verified the deductions, and this "nonobvious" result, i.e., a rise in the retention curve, lent great credibility to analysis of serial learning in terms of conditioning principles.

Of course, we know now that reminiscence is a "sometime" effect, that remote associations may not really exist, that the serial position curve is relatively invariant when calculated in terms of relative errors rather than in terms of absolute errors. But Gibson's theory stimulated much work, some of it, at least, supportive of her analyses, and the unlearning of associations and their recovery in time are still facts, of significance to the understanding of at least some forgetting, whatever their relations to extinction or spontaneous recovery. And mediation theory continues to prosper, though it has had its share of attacks and of difficulties.

The borrowings from conditioning were made, I think, for adequate if not good reasons, and their applications have stimulated investigation and have been maintained, where indeed they continue to be used, because they show some relationships to the data.

Restricted and low-order theoretical statements

I have already said that students of verbal learning have concentrated their efforts on retention and transfer, that the psychological psycholinguists have emphasized meaning and associative processes (and, from information theory, sequential aspects of language), and that the over-all system, which a language is, has not been given much consideration. It may also be said that human learning and retention, in some over-all or broadly gauged perspective, has not been given attention either. Rather, investigators of almost all these problems have set themselves the task of studying retention, transfer, meaning and association in the context provided by particular situations. Illustrative are the major verbal learning situations (serial list learning, paired associate list learning, verbal discrimination, and free-recall learning), the retroaction and proaction paradigms, short-term memory, the mediational paradigms, word recognition, concept attainment, and the like. These situations have provided for the manipulation of many variables and have revealed themselves as complex

enough to occupy the time of the investigators who have tried to understand them. Substantial information has been achieved with respect to these topics, but no one yet feels that any of them is fully understood. Theoretical conceptions and problems, when they have not been borrowed from other areas, have been relatively specific: the selector mechanism, list discrimination, generalized response competition, the interference paradox, the associative probability hypothesis, the two-stage notion of learning, response competition, reproductive inhibition, etc. Many of the relationships found have been essentially correlational (see Pollio's paper)—low order, it is true, but entirely satisfactory, at least as steps on the way to fuller understanding, to many investigators.

The theoretical levels of aspiration of this group of investigators, then, have not been high, having been limited, I think, to the hope of developing accounts (miniature theories, as they have been called) of the data amassed in relatively specific situations. And the theoretical conceptions do not depart far from the data themselves or the circumstances under which they were obtained.

The Three Issues

1. Complexities of usual learning tasks and important processes in human learning.

I have lumped several subproblems and subissues together here. One is exemplified by Battig's attack on S-R conceptions of paired-associate learning, in the course of which he identifies a number of processes that go on in this situation and of which an S-R account makes no mention. A curious feature of this list of processes is that many of them were identified or discussed, in the first instance, by Underwood or Postman. Among these are list differentiation, classification of items as stimuli and as responses, and the limitation of responses to those actually present in the list. I know of no one who has explored more thoroughly than Underwood and his associates the matter of interstimulus and interresponse similarity; this exploration implies a concern for discrimination among members of these classes. Response learning, though it did not originate as a concept at Northwestern or at Berkeley, has certainly been a central notion at both places, and one cannot discuss stimulus selection and reverse associations without citations to significant papers on these topics authored or co-authored by Underwood. Mediational processes are also mentioned in papers from Northwestern. Postman's (1963) analysis of factors involved in the difficulty that interference theory has in predicting too much forgetting (see Keppel's paper) makes use of several processes like those mentioned by Battig. I come neither to honor nor to defend Underwood and Postman but only to indicate that, as workers usually identified as exemplifying the S-R tradition, they have originated or accepted at least seven of the processes which Battig offers as evidence for the complexity of paired-associate learning. In addition, it was Postman (1954) who studied learned *principles* of organization and memory, and it was Underwood and Keppel (1963) who began the systematic study of *coding rules* in rote learning.

In the general discussion, Battig indicated that he follows Underwood in many of the proposals his paper makes. I presume that he is, then, attacking the Skinnerians or perhaps certain writers who have proposed

simple mathematical models of paired-associate learning. But neither of these groups is really identified with the long-standing Ebbinghaus tradition.

It may be said, however (as Battig does), that the information on which his processes are predicated represents recent developments. The question that can be raised is: Why did it take so long (70 years) for students of verbal learning to recognize the complexity of the tasks they employ? There are probably several answers to this query. There have been, until recently, relatively few workers in verbal learning (Irion, 1959), and they have been mostly interested in retention and transfer, where perhaps the issues Battig raises, which concern acquisition, do not appear so prominently. Another answer that some would give is that the S-R or the associationist orientation has blinded these workers to such processes. The testimony I have just adduced, in the cases of Underwood and Postman, does not fit well with this interpretation.

Conferences of this kind have heard, for several years now, the refrain that hypotheses and strategies, notions which perhaps encompass Battig's processes, must be taken into consideration in accounts of human learning. I have little doubt that such processes exist and occur. It is recognized in the parallels that have been made between PA learning and concept attainment and can be made in treatments of verbal learning as forms of problem-solving or selective learning. Yet, as Battig recognizes, hypotheses and strategies appear to be inextricably tied up with individual differences, and it is noteworthy that general trait or ability predictors have not had much use or success in relation to verbal learning. We find these same terms in Bourne's paper, in Young's, and in Kanfer's, and Kanfer's discussion certainly highlights the difficulties and the hazards involved in attempting to bring hypotheses and strategies under experimental scrutiny (see, however, Dulany's paper).

One of the difficulties in identifying and studying hypotheses and strategies in verbal learning has arisen from the tasks we use. In PA and serial learning, for example, the only data typically available are the responses made to the stimuli presented, and these responses convey remarkably little direct information indicative of other processes that may go on. This leads the investigator to have to rely heavily on inference if he is to speculate about hypotheses and strategies. Even if there were strong correlations between predictors like ability tests or measures of personality traits and learning scores, the identification of hypotheses and strategies would be an indirect process with presently available predictors, so far as I can see.

We need methods for externalizing what the subject does as he learns. A number of beginnings have been made along these lines, with varying degrees of closeness to what we may mean by hypotheses and strategies. In verbal learning, they include modified free recall in all of its versions, attempts to discover the functional stimulus and the properties of nominal stimuli which make them more or less functional, comparisons of intentional and incidental learners, reports of how associations were made during learning, and the like. But these are not very direct, and verbal learning experiments may have to be contrived along lines suggested in studies of concept attainment such as those of Bruner, or of Osler, or in studies of verbal conditioning as outlined by Kanfer and Dulany. Greatest progress in verbal learning along these lines has perhaps been made with free recall and free recall learning. Tulving's measure of subjec-

tive organization, Mandler's emphasis on concepts and categories identified in the first instances by Ss themselves, Marshall's Recognition Association Test, and Seibel's study sheet and study board techniques are illustrative. But the identification of hypotheses and strategies, shared by Ss or unique, carries with it the problem of what to do with them. Do we end up with a collection of "case histories," as Goss (Cofer and Musgrave, 1963, p. 75) once asked? Or is there more to it than a conclusion which would amount to a revelation of uniqueness and the richness of human experience?

Obviously, I do not know the answers to questions such as these, but I am convinced that the use of a variety of tasks and of materials which vary along denotable and measurable dimensions will help to define and characterize the processes involved in hypotheses and strategies. I was impressed by Marshall's finding (Cofer, 1965) that if experimenter-defined interitem associational or conceptual relations are strong and salient, they will be used in the organization of materials in a free recall task, and more individualized bases for organization are not employed. These findings have been confirmed by Seibel (personal communication) in independent investigations employing very different procedures. Does it not make sense to find experimenter-defined materials which provide the S with his "hypotheses" or his "strategy" and then systematically to observe how behavior changes as we manipulate materials in such a way as to deprive them of compellingness and salience? Would not a theory of how the S functions with compelling experimenter-defined materials, if successful, have a great deal of carry-over to the processes involved in the case of materials where the S has to find relationships (hypotheses? strategies?) on the basis of which he can accomplish his task? It is difficult at the moment for me to see how the procedures of PA and serial-anticipation learning can be modified to permit the observation of hypotheses and strategies, but it should be possible. The comparison of instructed and uninstructed Ss in the serial learning-PA learning transfer studies, as reviewed by Young, is certainly worthy of much further inquiry. I agree with Mandler that a conceptualization of the effects of the instructional variable is necessary.

It is, of course, possible that those who object to the traditional study of verbal learning, whatever the willingness of its investigators to talk of concepts not easily interpretable in S-R terms, do so because they can see little or no correspondence between the standard verbal learning and retention situations and the problems of learning and memory as they occur outside the laboratory. Or they may see the techniques, especially serial and paired-associate list learning, as being intrinsically incapable of being informative with respect to significant issues. Mandler's question (in discussion) as to what list-learning tells us about the formation of a single association and Deese's apparent insistence that emphasis on contiguity is not necessary for the formation of associations (as is implied in paired-associate methods) or that associative structures will not be revealed in the manifest organization of free recall are illustrative.

Admittedly, verbal learning experiments provide little direct information with respect to nonlaboratory learning situations. We know so little, in even a taxonomic sense, about such learning situations that it is difficult to know, in fact, how well or how poorly verbal learning concepts apply. I would agree that a considerable expansion of the range of situations studied would be desirable. I think the same thing must be said with respect to Deese's insistences. It is from studies of free association combined with factor analysis and linguistic analysis that he has rejected contiguity and postulated structures. Perhaps he should be the first to propose answers to the questions; Where do we go from here? What further do we need to know? How do we set up the experiments appropriate to answer the questions which remain?

2. Insufficiency in principle of S-R theory to account for the development and functioning of language.

There is much overlap between these issues and the previous one, because of the emphasis here on the language user as an employer of rules; rules are, no doubt, like strategies and hypotheses, or even plans. Throughout both of these issues run the themes that structure, not association, and thought, not habit, are characteristic of human functioning; the themes represent almost an alternative conception of man, rather than a theory.

These are not new ideas, though to say this is not to derogate them. Bartlett (1932) rejected the Ebbinghaus tradition many years ago and went on to speak of the organization of memory in terms of schemata rather than associations. I have always thought that free recall, when organization in it as reflected in clustering of related items is studied, has become popular because some investigators saw it as a way of investigating Bartlett's conceptions in a situation in which variables could be better controlled and manipulated than in the kinds of materials he used.

Even before Bartlett, of course, were the students of thought at Würzburg, who required more than association to cope with the results of their experiments. And there were and are the Gestalt psychologists. Referring to all these currents, Humphrey (1951, p. 28) concludes the first chapter of his book on thinking as follows: "It may be said that the history of the psychology of thinking consists largely of an unsuccessful revolt against the doctrine of association."

It is interesting to speculate as to why association and its modern counterparts are still viable, but it is difficult to be convincing about the exegesis of history. The Würzburgers came up with directional aspects of thinking but did little more than name a phenomenon. Bartlett is, I think, still read, and many of his ideas, in a general way, are accepted though not the source of much investigation (unless I am right about clustering in free recall). Gestalt psychology, according to Boring (1950, p. 600) has been successful.

> Its old enemies of the Wundt-Titchener line are gone. Introspection in the sense of analysis of consciousness into sensory elements is no longer practised. The movement has produced much new important research, but it is no longer profitable to label it as Gestalt psychology. Had Gestalt psychology resisted the inclusion of behavioral data in psychology, there might have been a long war over whether psychology is or is not principally the study of direct experience. As it was, Köhler's chimpanzees were admitted as data from the start. The result is that Gestalt psychology has already passed its peak and is now dying of its success by being absorbed into what is Psychology.

I am not sure that Boring is entirely correct in the assertion that Gestalt psychology has been absorbed into psychology as a whole. It is true that many of the Gestalt findings, from the laws of perceptual organization and the behavioral facts of insight to the problem of transposition on a relative basis, have entered into the majority of the introductory textbooks, either as facts or as phenomena about the explanation of which there has been and is controversy. But on three significant counts, I think Gestalt psychology has not been widely accepted. These counts are its nativistic orientation, its concern for the phenomenological approach to experience, and its emphasis on structure, rather than associations, as the fundamental processes underlying behavior. Ulric Neisser, in an unpublished paper which I have had the privilege of seeing, has drawn parallels between the propositions of modern linguists and those of Gestalt psychology, and Asch, in his paper here, has made similar comments. I think Asch welcomes the approach of these linguists as an aid to the revivification of the more philosophically and methodologically important features of Gestalt psychology.

Gestalt and other nativisms did not suit the temper of the radical environmentalism characteristic of many functionalists and behaviorists, though it is not theoretically incompatible, as I have said, with either viewpoint. But in its forms as proposed by the ethologists and the behavior geneticists, a good deal of acceptance of nativism may be found in the contemporary literature of animal psychology. Yet, as the positive reactions to Hebb's (1949) notion of "early learning" show, there has been a concern over the specification of the relative contributions of nature and nurture to the heredity-environment interaction and over the precise specification of the processes and variables by which the native contribution is made and of which it is a function. I think this means that investigators are wary of glib postulations of the role of nature (and they should also be wary of glib assertions about the effects of experience). Perhaps this means that when we analyze behaviors closely in relation to the situations in which they occur, grand sweeping generalizations seldom are supported by the evidence.

I can see no way of escaping the proposition that all statements about experience or structure (or about habits or associations, for that matter) must be inferences, based upon what can be seen in some aspect of behavior or performance, including verbally made statements, judgments, recognitions, preferences, and the like (see Brody and Oppenheim, 1966). Our success in gaining reliable information from verbal reports and introspections has not been great, as witness the disagreements over what happens in verbal operant conditioning. (Dulany's paper may point the way to some solutions here.) When we talk about rules, strategies, and hypotheses, we are making inferences, direct evidence of which in the sense of descriptions from our subjects is difficult to obtain or to rely on, and our inferences typically are based on features of performance. I think that many functionalist-behaviorist psychologists are cautious in this respect because (1) sometimes postulation of high-level processes seems to involve circularity or sometimes such processes can be extended because of their vagueness to explain almost anything and (2) they are aware that there are many conditions which govern behavioral phenomena. They have perhaps learned well the lesson implied by the titles of several of McGeoch's chapters which had the form, "Conditions of which X is a Function."

It is not without interest that the older literature contains instances in which formulations alternative to relational responding or to purpose and insight were presented and with some

success. Illustrations are Spence's (1936, 1937) analysis of transposition and Hull's (1930, 1935b) reformulations of purpose or of problem-solving. I do not assert that these alternative formulations were without difficulties or remain unmodified as solutions of the problems with which they were concerned. I wish only to indicate that, in the past, provocative and at least temporarily successful formulations were achieved for problems which, when originally proposed, seemed to sound the death knell for approaches which did not postulate processes like hypotheses, strategies, or rules.

In the case of language, as presented in the formulations of Chomsky and his associates, we certainly have a situation, as seen in this conference and in the recent literature, which bears similarities to some of the cases of the past. I believe that the key notion here is competence, with all that implies for language productivity, deep as opposed to surface structure, the detection of syntactic ambiguity, and rapid ontogenetic development. One difficulty for the functionalist is that the theory (if that is what it is) changes rapidly, so that today's experiment may be almost irrelevant to today's theoretical formulation. Another, of course, parallels the Gestaltist's *experimentum crucis* and is the *exemplum crucis*, as illustrated in the various sentences which despite identical surface structures are readily perceived to be different when suitable rearrangements of their words are provided. (There are, also, instances of the *experimentum crucis* in, for example, the paper by Garrett and Fodor.)

One of the difficulties with experiments and examples of this kind is that we do not know all that we should like to know about the circumstances that may be involved in their results. This is to say, perhaps, that few if any parametric studies have been undertaken, that systematic manipulation of linguistic, instructional, *and environmental* variables have seldom been reported, that we often do not know whether reactions in accordance with expectations from a structural viewpoint are immediate or take time to become manifest. If we are to believe the evidence of our eyes and ears that speech and writing are often ungrammatical and of our own experience that the grammaticality of our own statements, oral or written, is often difficult to determine, we are led to believe that competence may not be a unitary, constant thing, on the one hand, or that there are conditions of which the manifestations of competence are a function. I realize that I speak here of performance, but I can see no way in which competence can be inferred save from some set of performances, carried out under some set of conditions. The history of Titchenerian introspection, which insisted that the valid results could be obtained only from specially trained observers, should warn us of the pitfalls associated with taking only certain kinds of testimony as evidence for underlying content or structures.

When I read Garret and Fodor's paper and heard Bever's account of some of his experiments, I felt that experiments of this kind chart the course which must be followed (and extended parametrically) in order for us to understand the phenomena of language as a system. Psycholinguists ought to be concerned with these matters, and it may have taken the linguists' formulation of "what is learned" to provide the guidance for these inquiries. But I do not think we are ready to discard analytic experimentation in the course of such inquiry or that we should eschew our attempts to comprehend theoretically limited sets of data or restricted sets of phenomena. When we know more empirically, the less certainty we often have about the correctness or the adequacy of a grand viewpoint.

In this investigation of the problems which the linguists have set, our conceptual formulations may change. I doubt that this will bother anybody very much, in view of the theoretical "noncommitment" of many investigators, to which I have alluded already. I recently gave a colloquium at Toronto, in the course of which I included a brief presentation of a highly informal "model" of the processes of controlled association. Bennet Murdock pointed out later that the model was not formulated in S-R terms but rather sounded like an information-processing model. I could not care less. We obtain data on problems of interest and we attempt to make sense of the data, trying to remain moderately rigorous in its formulation in the sense that its terms are open to test by further observation and experiment.

As to the problem of whether associationistic, or S-R, or S-R mediational accounts are in principle incapable of handling certain phenomena, as McNeill, Garrett and Fodor, and Bever have averred, I can do perhaps no better than to remark that several years ago, from aerodynamic considerations, it was concluded that, *in principle*, bumblebees cannot fly. Admittedly, the present attack is in the reverse direction, i.e., from fact to theory rather than from theory to fact, but I believe that Osgood's comments in his paper and those made by Berlyne (1966) in his reply to Fodor (1965) say as well as anything I can say in this already extended discussion to indicate that the issue is hardly settled once and for all.

Before I leave this topic, I should like to place myself squarely with Osgood and, I think, with Deese, who stress the semantic and associative aspects of language as the features on which syntactical structures operate, rather than the reverse. "We think," Deese (1965, p. 167) says, "directly in associations, and it is not necessary for sentences to appear in the process." Osgood appears to believe that we know first what we wish to communicate before operating on this content by means of syntactic constraints. I often think that despite the possession, presumably, of linguistic competence, I have nothing to say. Our interest in communication arises in the first instance from a desire to say something, rather than from the pleasure that exercising syntactic structures may provide us.

I think it is worthwhile to consider why we have grammar at all. The answers, I suspect, lie in limitations on our capacity for serial processing of information and in the necessity that is present, in the absence of contextual and referential constraints, to make specific what it is we are talking about. The redundancy of language, provided at least in part by syntactic factors, helps to overcome limitations on our intake capacity; the serial position curve is perhaps a good example of such limitations. A careful study of the communication situation might illuminate why it is that we choose one transformation (e.g., the passive) rather than another, functionally speaking. The linguistic description of grammar has the highest value, but I think it cannot solve all the problems of language which functions in the main in communication, in thought, and in the control of behavior.

3. The slow pace of progress

One can have little success in disputing the proposition that our progress in understanding human learning, retention, and transfer, in all of their manifestations, and the development and functioning of language, despite the amount of past effort devoted to these problems, has been limited. It is understandable that objection can be taken to the manner of attack on and the conceptualization of these problems. Perhaps modern linguistic formulations hold the key to language; perhaps hypotheses, strategies, and rules are the true stuff of human learning, retention, and transfer; perhaps one of Kuhn's revolutions is now in progress and I am among the last to be aware of it.

One answer to the question of rate of progress was given by Spence (1956, pp. 21–24), some years ago, who speaks of the inability of psychology to give answers to practical and pressing problems but sees no alternative, in view of the complexity of behavioral problems, to their ultimate solution through the time-consuming device of basic research, which, he seems to believe, will be most productive if simpler processes are investigated before complex ones. Spence's attitude has recently found a similar expression, in essentials, by Skinner (1966, p. 217).

This answer is, I suppose, in the present context, one of "normal science." If so, the historical answer is clear: the new paradigm or way of looking at things and investigating them will prevail and solutions to the practical problems of learning and language will be forthcoming. I hope so, but I am not sanguine about it. Analytic experimentation is, I think, requisite if we are to have more than a pseudo-understanding; and an analytic experimentation, in my reading of psychology's history, leads to miniature theories of data gathered in relatively specific situations. Behavior is responsive to many variables, and quite a lot of these, in the real world, are neither predictable nor controllable.

References

Bartlett, F. C., *Remembering: A Study in Experimental and Social Psychology.* New York: Cambridge University Press, 1932.

Bergmann, G. "The Contribution of John B. Watson," *Psychological Review*, **63** (1956), 265–276.

Berlyne, D. E., "Mediating Responses: A Note on Fodor's Criticisms," *Journal of Verbal Learning and Verbal Behavior*, **5** (1966), 408–411.

Boring, E. G., *A History of Experimental Psychology*, (2nd ed.) New York: Appleton-Century-Crofts, 1950.

Bousfield, W. A., "The Problem of Meaning in Verbal Learning," in C. N. Cofer, ed., *Verbal Learning and Verbal Behavior.* New York: McGraw-Hill Book Company, 1961. pp. 81–91.

Braine, M. D. S., "On Learning the Grammatical Order of Words," *Psychological Review*, **70** (1963), 323–348.

Brody, N., and P. Oppenheim, "Tensions in Psychology between the Methods of Behaviorism and Phenomenology," *Psychological Review*, **73** (1966), 295–305.

Brown, R., and C. Fraser, "The Acquisition of Syntax," in C. N. Cofer and B. S. Musgrave, eds., *Verbal Behavior and Learning: Problems and Processes.* New York: McGraw-Hill Book Company, 1963. pp. 158–197.

Cofer, C. N., "On Some Factors in the Organizational Characteristics of Free Recall," *American Psychologist*, **20** (1965), 261–272.

———, and B. S. Musgrave, eds., *Verbal Behavior and Learning: Problems and Processes.* New York: McGraw-Hill Book Company, 1963.

Deese, J., "From the Isolated Verbal Unit to Connected Discourse," in C. N. Cofer, ed., *Verbal Learning and Verbal Behavior.* New York: McGraw-Hill Book Company, 1961. pp. 11–31.

———, *The Structure of Associations in Language and Thought.* Baltimore: Johns Hopkins University Press, 1965.

Ebbinghaus, H., *Über das Gedächtniss.* Leipzig: Duncker and Humblot, 1885; trans., H. Ruger and C. Bussenius, New York: Columbia University Press, 1913; reprinted, New York: Dover Publications, Inc., 1964.

Fodor, J. A., "Could Meaning Be an r_m?" *Journal of Verbal Learning and Verbal Behavior*, **4** (1965), 73–81.

Gough, P. B., and J. J. Jenkins, "Verbal Learning and Psycholinguistics," in M. H. Marx, ed., *Theories in Contemporary Psychology.* New York: The Macmillan Company, 1963, pp. 456–474.

Hebb, D. O., *The Organization of Behavior.* New York: John Wiley & Sons, Inc., 1949.

Hull, C. L., "Knowledge and Purpose as Habit Mechanisms," *Psychological Review*, **37** (1930), 511–525.

———, "The Conflicting Psychologies of Learning—A Way Out" *Psychological Review*, **42** (1935), 491–516.

———, "The Mechanism of the Assembly of Behavior Segments in Novel Combinations Suitable for Problem Solution," *Psychological Review*, **42** (1935), 219–245.

———, *Principles of Behavior.* New York: Appleton-Century, 1943.

———, *A Behavior System.* New Haven: Yale University Press, 1952.

———, "Clark L. Hull," in E. G. Boring, H. S. Langfeld, H. Werner, and R. M. Yerkes, eds., *A History of Psychology in Autobiography, Vol. 4.* Worcester, Massachusetts: Clark University Press, 1952. pp. 143–162.

———, *et al. Mathematico-Deductive Theory of Rote Learning.* New Haven: Yale University Press, 1940.

Humphrey, C., *Thinking: An Introduction to Its Experimental Psychology.* London: Methuen & Co., Ltd., 1951.

Hunter, W. S., "The Delayed Reaction in Animals and Children," *Behavior Monographs*, **2** (1913), 86.

————, "The Temporal Maze and Kinaesthetic Sensory Processes in the White Rat," *Psychobiology*, **2** (1920), 1–17.

————, "An Open Letter to the Anti-Behaviorists," *Journal of Philosophy*, **19** (1922), 307–308.

————, "Summary Comments on the Heredity-Environment Symposium," *Psychological Review*, **54** (1947), 348–352.

Irion, A. L., "Rote Learning," in S. Koch, ed., *Psychology: A Study of a Science*. Vol. 2, New York: McGraw-Hill Book Company, 1959.

Jakobovits, L. A., "Mediation Theory and the 'Single-Stage' S-R Model: Different?" *Psychological Review*, **73** (1966), 376–381.

Jenkins, J. J., "Mediated Associations: Paradigms and Situations," in C. N. Cofer and B. S. Musgrave, eds., *Verbal Behavior and Learning: Problems and Processes*. New York: McGraw-Hill Book Company, 1963. pp. 210–245.

————, and D. S. Palermo, "Mediation Processes and the Acquisition of Linguistic Structure," in U. Bellugi and R. Brown, eds., *The Acquisition of Language. Monographs of the Society for Research or Child Development*, **29** (1964), 141–169.

McGeoch, J. A., *The Psychology of Human Learning: An Introduction*. New York: Longmans, Green & Co., Inc., 1942.

————, and A. L. Irion, *The Psychology of Human Learning*, (2nd ed. rev.), New York: Longmans, Green & Co., Inc., 1952.

Miller, W., and S. Ervin, "The Development of Grammar in Child Language," in U. Bellugi and R. Brown, eds., *The Acquisition of Language. Monographs of the Society for Research on Child Development*, **29** (1964), 9–34.

Osgood, C. E., "Psycholinguistics," in S. Koch, ed., *Psychology: A Study of a Science*, Vol. 6. New York: McGraw-Hill Book Company, 1959. pp. 244–316.

————, "Comments on Professor Bousfield's Paper," in C. N. Cofer, ed., *Verbal Learning and Verbal Behavior*. New York: McGraw-Hill Book Company, 1961. pp. 91–106.

————, "On Understanding and Creating Sentences," *American Psychologist*, **18** (1963), 735–751.

————, and T. A. Sebeok, eds. *Psycholinguistics: A Survey of Theory and Research*. (Suppl. to *Journal of Abnormal and Social Psychology*, Vol. 49, No. 4, 1954.)

Postman, L., "Learned Principles of Organization and Memory," *Psychological Monographs*, **68** (1954), 1–24.

————, "Does Interference Theory Predict Too Much Forgetting?" *Journal of Verbal Learning and Verbal Behavior*, **2** (1963), 40–48.

Skinner, B. F., *Verbal Behavior*. New York: Appleton-Century-Crofts, 1957.

————, "What is the Experimental Analysis of Behavior?" *Journal of the Experimental Analysis of Behavior*, **9** (1966), 213–218.

Spence, K. W. "The Nature of Discrimination Learning in Animals," *Psychological Review*, **43** (1936), 427–449.

————, "The Differential Response in Animals to Stimuli Varying within a Single Dimension," *Psychological Review*, **44** (1937), 430–444.

————, *Behavior Theory and Conditioning*. New Haven: Yale University Press, 1956.

Underwood, B. J., and G. Keppel, "Coding Processes in Verbal Learning," *Journal of Verbal Learning and Verbal Behavior*, **1** (1963), 250–257.

The Challenge to Psychological Theorists[1]

21 JAMES J. JENKINS

It is difficult to present some concluding note that will capture for the reader the excitement and irritation of the mealtime and evening arguments among the participants, the interest and intensity of the discussions, the positions explained informally, the changes of opinion and the new understandings generated by this conference. Surely the record in this book, however, makes clear that clashes of opinion did occur and that both understandings and misunderstandings developed spirited debate.

From the very outset of the conference the challenge to established positions in psychology was obvious. Proponents of "the establishment" felt that their positions were distorted and caricatured. Opponents felt that "the establishment" was being evasive and blind. Both groups, while trying to avoid doing so, came dangerously near the treacherous tactic of telling the other THE CORRECT WAY to conduct science. Since I feel quite strongly about the issues involved and especially

strongly about telling someone else how to pursue his job, an appropriate focus for my remarks might be the recent histories of psychology and linguistics and the prescriptive tendencies of psychologists and linguists.

In the 1930's and '40's, psychology was shaken with furious debates about what was and what was not "scientific" in psychology. Advocates were outrageously prescriptive. It is easy to remember meetings at which distinguished psychologists, purple in the face, told other distinguished psychologists that what they were doing might be entertaining or clever but it was not and would never be scientific psychology. At many schools graduate students were given the "correct" view and carefully inoculated with the proper philosophical serum against the "incorrect" views. One must seriously question whether the cause of science was advanced by these battles.

During the same period the linguists were also impressed with a strong view about the philosophy of science, and Bloomfield firmly enjoined linguists not to have anything to do with mentalism and with psychologists.[2] As a result,

[1] Preparation of this paper was supported by grants to the Center for Research in Human Learning from the National Science Foundation, the National Institute of Child Health and Human Development, and from the Graduate School of the University of Minnesota.

[2] L. Bloomfield, *Language* (New York: Holt, Rinehart and Winston, 1933), pp. 37–38. "A linguistic observer therefore can de-

linguists remained psychologically innocent except for naive behaviorism, and at the same time the psychologists remained in ignorance of the concepts of linguistic structure. With few exceptions, psychologists at the beginning of this period treated language as a "word heap." Psychological theories of meaning were (and for the most part still are) theories about the reference relation—a kind of linkage between words and the world. With increasing sophistication, psychologists progressed toward models which considered language as consisting of strings of words (the "information theory" approach) or as composed of whole utterances which were relatively unanalyzed.

In the early 1950's the great meeting of the fields of linguistics and psychology took place under the gentle guidance of the Social Science Research Council (see Osgood and Sebeok, 1954). I remember quite well the fervor with which we were informed by some of the leading linguists of the day that linguistics was virtually a "closed book," "the most nearly complete of the social sciences," the "most objective of all behavioral disciplines." In a class on grammar one could hear the astonishing claim that in principle one could feed an appropriately programed computer the right phonetic transcription of a large corpus and the computer would produce the phonemics, morphemics, and syntax of the language. It was also explained that in practice "short cuts" (such as pair tests and knowledge of meanings) were used to achieve this result but that they could always be replaced by completely objective analysis that produced the correct set of concepts for the language. The psychologist, green with envy, confessed that he had not yet reached such a blessed state but felt that he was on the way. Surely we were encouraged by the obvious success of the simple, operational, positivistic approach of the linguist and determined to pursue the same tactics. The psychologist had a nice theory that made contiguity and succession the key ingredients, and the linguist had just the data to show that that was the right approach. All that remained was to bridge the gap between the linguists' putatively perfect analysis and the psychologists' entirely adequate theory. It turned out that bridging the gap was no great problem. Item-and-arrangement grammars and mediation theory were seen to be variations of the same line of thought. The linguist looks at distribution of an item in the corpus and if he finds another that has the

---

scribe the speech-habits of a community without resorting to statistics. Needless to say, he must work conscientiously and, in particular, he must record every form he can find and not try to excuse himself from this task by appealing to the reader's common sense or to the structure of some other language or to some psychological theory, and, above all, he must not select or distort the facts according to his views of what the speakers ought to be saying. Aside from its intrinsic value for the study of language, a relevant and unprejudiced description of this kind serves as a document of major importance for psychology. The danger here lies in mentalistic views of psychology, which may tempt the observer to appeal to purely spiritual standards instead of reporting the facts. To say, for instance, that combinations of words which are "felt to be" compounds have only a single high stress (e.g., blackbird as opposed to black bird), is to tell exactly nothing, since we have no way of determining what the speakers may "feel": the observer's task was to tell us, by some tangible criterion, or, if he found none, by a list, in which combinations of words are pronounced with a single high stress. A worker who accepts the materialistic hypothesis in psychology is under no such temptation; it may be stated as a principle that in all sciences like linguistics, which observe some specific type of human activity, the worker must proceed exactly as if he held the materialistic view. This practical effectiveness is one of the strongest considerations in favor of scientific materialism."

same distribution, he knows that it is the same item (or belongs to the same class of items). To the psychologist, items which follow the same kinds of items or precede the same kinds of items are equivalent responses and equivalent stimuli; if they are not at the outset, they become so via mediation (see Jenkins and Palermo, 1964, and Jenkins, 1965). The only sad note in this little story is that by the time the bridge was completed, someone (namely Chomsky) dynamited the structure at the linguistic end.

Though many of us read *Syntactic Structures* when it first appeared, I think most of us failed to appreciate what was in store. We felt that transformations were appealing devices that we would have to give some thought to as soon as we had worked out the basic problem of the item and arrangement grammar. We failed to realize that a fundamentally new approach to grammar had been presented and that a "generative grammar" was a quite different kind of object from the old "descriptive grammar," exemplifying a different approach to science and making radically different claims.

As the consequences of the linguistic revolution became clearer, the psychologist's position became more and more painful. Having worked hard to build his bridge to linguistics, it was difficult (to say the least) to hear that the discipline was no longer there and that no one had really ever said that it was there anyway. Accompanying this was the consequent charge that the psychologist had been wasting his time by trying to do what he felt he had just done. The words "trivial" and "uninteresting" (even though used in their logical sense) are scarcely palatable. As one tries to understand what has happened, it is not helpful to be beaten about the ears or to be told that the thing that one does not understand is "obvious." If, in addition, the linguist has just been battling with his colleagues, he is in no mood for quiet explication. What the linguist was saying was that the new object he was describing was a fundamentally different kind of thing from what one thought it was and that it required a fundamentally different kind of machinery than the old system implied. In short, he was saying, no amount of revision, patching, or adding *neo-* before the name was going to make it work.

Now, let us all agree that no one can tell another how to do his science. Philosophers of science in the main have quit trying to prescribe, and so, I think, must we. The job of the philosopher is to find out what it is that scientists do, especially when they are doing their science well or when the science is going wrong, and try to understand the process. One of the things that he should be able to do, however, is to answer questions about the formal properties of models that a science might employ. Essentially that is what happened here. We asked what a model, written in the surface language alone, might do, and when that question was answered, everyone said, "Don't tell me that! Tell me something different." I don't think that Fodor, Bever, Garrett, or McNeill care whether anyone says that they are being prescriptive or not. What I seem to hear them say is that if you want to know how they feel about a psychology of language and why they feel this is an answer. If you think you have a better way to handle language, you can try, but if you think you are going to use the old kind of machinery, you will be disappointed because there is a formal proof that this kind of machine won't do it.

You are free to try the rejoinder that Cofer has suggested. Lots of formal proofs seem wrong. Bumblebees *do* fly. But note that the "bumblebee proof" is telling you, not that bumblebees cannot fly, but rather that you cannot explain the flight of bumblebees. Bumblebees can *not* fly as other insects do. That is what the proof said. When one finds a new kind of stabilizer (vibrating rods with knobs on the end of them), one has in fact a different kind of machine. The assertion being made here is that if language depended on surface chains, it could not be the kind of language that it is. If flying depended only on gross body structure, weight, and wing shape, bumblebees could not fly.

The intuitive argument concerning the nature of language structure rests on a very simple set of notions having to do with many-to-one and one-to-many mappings. The purpose is to show in what way things that are said to be similar are similar and ways in which things that are different are said to be different. You have all seen such illustrations before; a typical complaint is that the same examples always come up over and over again. If the thing being illustrated is so important, why aren't there more examples of it? Or, as a distinguished psychologist recently said, "All the linguists go around with their little bags of sentences."

I think that psychologists need some coaching concerning the use of arguments by example and illustration. Each example is supposed to be an instance of a whole class of such behaviors. One is supposed to twist and turn and examine each such example until he is sure that he understands the implication. The same example may be used all the time because it serves as a familiar label for the distinction being made. I can say, "We are running a discrimination test on the 'growling of lions' versus 'raising of flowers' difference," and everybody who is in the club is supposed to know that means

we are testing sentences that differ in the base though there is no difference in the derived sentence structure. Notice that the verbal learning fraternity can say, "I ran an *A–B, B–C, A–C* paradigm against an *A–B, A–B'*." And within a very small club (a few Minnesotans) you can talk about "running paradigm I and III." But one does not conclude because of the labels that there is a single instance being examined. In fact, just the opposite is intended. Similarly, when I say that "The boy hit the ball" and "The ball was hit by the boy" are the same, implying that there is an abstract level at which the two sentences are represented in the same way, I also mean to imply that this relation holds for some indefinitely large number of pairs of sentences. The sentences are obviously different at the physical level, but the theory of the language must show the equivalence of active sentences to their appropriate passives at at least one abstract level.

In a different way the ambiguous sentence furnishes a compelling argument. The traditional references to "The shooting of the hunters was dreadful" or to "flying planes" or "cooking apples" serve to direct your attention to the fact that some sentences can be understood in more than one way. What does it mean to take a sentence in two ways? It presumably means that there are ways you can operate on that stimulus to see it as the outcome of two different derivations. The stimulus is *in some sense* two different things. Specifying exactly *in what sense* the stimulus is two different things demands levels of abstraction that can project overlapping or identical outcomes onto the surface level. How one recognizes this possibility when confronted with the surface level alone is indeed a formidable puzzle for the psychologist.

Another interesting variation is the case where, though the physical product is different, the sentences may be seen to be the same at a low level of abstraction. And, at still more abstract levels, they may be seen to be different again. Here the canonical examples are: "The growling of lions is unpleasant" and "The raising of flowers is difficult." Clearly the words are different and the messages are different. However, it is easy to see that the sequence of form classes is identical and at that level of abstraction the sentences are the same. Another and much deeper look, however, shows that the sentences must differ in some more fundamental sense. The illustration is intended to lead you to the conclusion that two vast sets of sentences differ in exactly the same way and that when you encountered the sentence "The shooting of the hunters was dreadful," you put first one of these derivations on it and then the other. The ambiguous case is the case where these two families of sentences fuse at the surface level.

Thus, sentence examples are used to indicate the unlimited numbers of cases where (1) the same structure of the obvious stimulus is mapped on different derivations, (2) different structures in the obvious stimuli map on to the same derivation, and (3) different structures in the obvious stimulus map on to the same abstract structure and then diverge again. The way to make clear what one is talking about is to specify exactly what is meant when one talks about these various abstract levels. And that, as Bever said more elegantly than I can, is a purpose of the grammar. When someone then asks about the nature of the stimulus, you can tell him at each level of representation what it is that you are talking about.

Now, surely, the psychologist working in his laboratory can choose one level and never move away from it. He need not concern himself with any other. And to some reasonable extent he can get away with it. But he must also, of course, be willing to be told that he is not studying all of language behavior. Language behavior is not at a particular level. It is the entire representation that is entailed at all levels of description. It can be *represented* at each of those levels but it cannot be identified with any one level.

Notice that the implications of this kind of thinking are far-reaching. This analysis implies that there are no simple ways to treat the surface level to make it yield up the deeper levels in some automatic fashion. If one takes the large corpus in a fine phonetic transcription and puts it in the computer for analysis, all one can expect to get now is confetti. If the psychologist picks one level and sticks to it, he will never see the rest of language behavior, and he is going to have to solve some very funny problems, like accounting for data that are the same when there is no reason to suppose that they should be the same and data that are different when there is no reason to suppose that they should be different. Such a decision puts one in the world of Alice's white knight in *Through the Looking Glass*, wandering about in a two-dimensional world and trying to explain the unfathomable events of the three-dimensional world that intersects his plane of observation. The notions of deep structure and abstract equivalence that the linguist is bringing to us are important notions for all psychologists, not just those interested in language. The ethologists are coming with the same message from a very different base. My feeling is that psychologists of this generation ought to give them very careful and attentive hearings.

Similarly, this conception of language has many important practical consequences. It helps explain, for example, why it is that we have failed to build a reading machine for the blind. As long as language is regarded as a collection of diverse, arbitrary sounds that have some simple invariance, it seems as if we should be able to get letters in a book to make distinctive sounds and we would have a bookreader that anyone could be trained to listen to. The newer conception of language suggests that the nature of language is different from that, and the research of the Haskins Laboratories shows that the notions of simple invariance have to be replaced with a variety of many-to-one and one-to-many mappings. The same set of reasons explain why it is that we do not yet have the voice typewriter that has so often been promised. And the prospect of high-quality, automatic machine translation of language has shifted from something that was to be achieved by next week to something that may well be impossible in our lifetimes.

One thing that psychologists also need to note is that the new viewpoint does not by any means "wipe out" or destroy the research that has been done. Clearly, what is known must be integrated with the more elaborate conception at the appropriate levels. We know that subjects can form point-to-point correspondences between colored figures and nonsense syllables. We know that such learning is tedious, slow, and difficult; but we also know that there are rules for manipulating these correspondences (e.g., giving a color syllable before a shape syllable) which subjects can learn with great speed. Learning new point-to-point correspondences is very hard; if we scramble the colors and names, we have a messy and difficult task; but if we change a manipulation rule (e.g., reverse the order of the color and form syllables), the new set of responses can be pro-

duced appropriately with amazing speed. This suggestion concerning the differences in the processes involved is very like the suggestions made by Lyle Bourne concerning the separation of rule learning from other learning in the concept formation domain. It does not imply that one kind of learning is better or worse or more important than another; it merely says that the task involves more than one kind of learning, that it has more than one level.

We psychologists have often shown our reluctance to study learning tasks that deviate from traditional procedures. We would like to have situations in which there is no question concerning the units that the subject is employing and the ways in which he employs them, but we also know that we have not been able to find such a case. Subjects seem to persist in trying to do more than we want them to do; and as a result we have to concern ourselves with response integration, stimulus differentiation, response differentiation, stimulus and response classes, selective fractionation of the stimulus, etc. If we present the subject with textual material, we face the problem that he may have perfect recall of the content but not of the form—i.e., he gives us a good paraphrase. Our inability to handle this kind of complexity drives us back to observations that we can call "more objective," but we must note that our retreat does not remove the importance or relevance of the original problem. It ought not act to redefine the field of acceptable problems. At this meeting, Dulany has shown us that one can use one's own knowledge of the meaning of a proposition to interpret the subject's verbal behavior and that this information can be used in objective fashion to describe the subject's other behaviors with great accuracy. In my eyes, this is a very important demonstration.

I believe that our experience in our own laboratories is pushing us in the directions that the linguist is arguing for. Tulving points out that subjects have units, that experimenters have units, and that they are not the same in the general case. Osgood pointed out long ago that subjects in one of Cofer's experiments could have been *generating* the lists they were supposed to be "learning" in the transfer stage of Cofer's experiment. In essence he was saying that the subject learned the first list one way and then learned to produce the second list in some other way. Surely something different was happening for the transfer lists. Just because it was not what the experimenter had in mind does not take it out of the domain of psychology or relieve us of the necessity of dealing with it. It does, however, argue against some kind of single principle, single process, single operation kind of psychology. Maltzman talks about an odd abstraction; a stimulus in which the critical property of a word is not what it is but whether it has been heard before in the experiment. This means, of course, that the first time the word appears in the experiment and the second time it appears, it is a dramatically different stimulus. Surely this is a different level from the raw stimulus of acoustic disturbance. All of us who have worked in verbal learning have dealt with the many phenomena of integration of sequences. One begins with a behavior which is best seen as a series of elements, but during the course of the experiment the string becomes something different. It becomes a unit and a member of a pool or collection that is new.

I used to ask myself the question that someone asked here in the last few days, "What is *the* unit of language behavior?" I have folders full of notes on that question that never seem to get anywhere. I now believe that the reason these discussions never go anywhere is that this is the wrong kind of question to ask about complexly organized behavior. If we were omniscient and knew all that there was to know about language behavior all the way from the semantic structures down through the syntactics, the phrase structures, the transformations, down into the terminal strings and the mapping into symbols and the symbols into motor commands going on through the articulators and the effects of those on the air flow and the acoustic effects impinging on someone else's ear, etc., it would not occur to us to ask what *the* unit of behavior was supposed to be. We would know, I presume, that the behavior could be represented at any level, and at that level we would know what kinds of units or structures were appropriate to that representation; and, importantly, we would know how these were constrained by adjacent levels.

An example of linguistic constraint is found in our own invention—the nonsense syllables. If one talks about the meaningfulness of patterns of consonant-vowel-consonant in English, it is difficult to make sense of the data without taking "the right kind" of constraints into consideration. Raw frequency of letters or sounds is of little use. For example, one must attend to syllable boundaries and the differing effects of initial and final position. In the interpretation of a graphic symbol one must ask what the context is (e.g., C before O is $/k/$ but C before E is $/s/$; however, C in final position is $/k/$ in both cases). If one permits onself to look both up and down the hierarchy, it is possible to make sense of the otherwise mystifying difference in C-V-C nonsense syllables.

Similarly, if we are interested in observing how a skilled reader reads a sentence, we find him responding to many cues that are not represented in any simple way in the material before him. We can *hear* parentheses or brackets or pauses in his sentences which he (and we) arrange to get in the right linguistic places, but we will not find much in the way of cues in the written material to explain this behavior. Similarly, he will be able to provide paraphrases and rereadings which must look for their explanation even further up the hierarchy of the sentence but are not present in any direct way in the surface structure or the symbols on the page. In these cases it is manifestly irrelevant to ask what is *the* unit of language.

If we grant that we must provide at least some levels of representation in language, it appears that we will find greatest agreement in making a division between syntax and semantics. It is the consensus of this group that the semantic problem is formidable. Indeed, all of psychology and linguistics must agree that this is a most important problem and one on which little progress has been made. The philosophers to whom we might turn for guidance seem to be in the same difficult position.

Deese and Osgood (and, long before them, Rogét) have a feeling that there ought to be some way to represent meaning by a set of distinctive features or dimensions. There is a persistent hope that we will be able to specify dimensions or domains which can systematically exhaust the varieties of meanings. Yet Deese, who has just completed such an effort, told us on the first day of the conference that he believes that it cannot be done in that fashion. At present, he can see no end to the number of dimensions one might have to employ; and that outcome is, of course, fatal to the approach. An infinite set of dimensions to describe meaning is no gain over no dimensions at all.

How, then, shall we consider this problem? Mandler proposes that we regard words as clustered in arrays and that we consider the arrays as being multi-dimensional; but he must wind up in the same situation. How many arrays do we need? How many relations between arrays will be required to specify all the interconnections? It seems to me that Mandler, too, fails to solve the problem; rather, his work suggests how great a problem we have.

Kjeldergaard offers help in the other direction. His work convinces him that the typical measures that we use in the laboratory (frequency, m, association value, semantic differential ratings, etc.) are all highly related. While one can find instances where the measures conflict (e.g., similar words that are associates *vs.* similar words that are not associates), by and large, there is a component of psychological importance that is common to all of these measures and may be characterizable in some simple way. Osgood's position is similar to this, I think. While he will concede that there may be something to the notion that the dimensions of meaning are inexhaustible, he believes that there is a large core of meaning that we *can* isolate and that we ought to do that and try to get ahead with the task. While I have some sympathy with this pragmatic point of view, I cannot believe that it is going to be very useful in the long run in advancing psychological theory. In part, the commonalities we observe and the intercorrelations we find between measures are the consequence of our crude manipulations and our weak tests of equivalence. If one even approaches the question of the degree to which subjects *can* discriminate between meanings of words under the most favorable conditions (i.e., if one asks about competency), it is clear that we have not begun to touch the problem.

I feel with Deese that the need is for a device which can generate the dimensions of meaning we want for given purposes and given situations. What such a device might look like, I cannot imagine, but it is easy for me to believe that human beings have such a capacity and that the counting of observed dimensions is a never-ending task which perhaps indexes human needs more than human capacities.

This leads me naturally into the issue of instructions with which Dr. Postman has already treated. I only want to echo his remarks as strongly as possible. The investigator must ask himself what it is that he wants to know. If he is interested in what the subject *will do*, that is one kind of problem. The questions are phrased, "What does S do under conditions X, Y, and Z?" But, if you want to know what the subject *can do*, it should be clear that this is a different kind of question. One is presumably trying to ask a question about the subject's capacity under the most favorable circumstances that can be provided.

In the research that we are trying to do in our laboratories at Minnesota, we are more interested in the second kind of question. We know that the subject brings all kinds of special instructions to the laboratory with him. If we want him to sort sentences into active and passive sentence types, we will have to wait for him to sort through all manner of semantic groupings (pleasant-unpleasant, animate-inanimate, happy-sad, common-uncommon, etc.) and obvious physical properties (order, length, position, etc.) before he arrives at grammatical sorts at all. However, if the experimenter keeps rejecting sorts that the subject makes he will, in over half the cases, eventually get to the one wanted—actives *vs.* passives. This kind of experiment is rich in information about

what the subject *does do*, but that is not what we wanted to know about. We want to know whether he *can* sort active and passive sentences. A very simple thing to do is to ask him; it is surprising how fast one can cover the ground in that way.

As an aside, it is of some interest to note that many of our psychological friends regard this kind of experimentation as unethical, immoral, or simply nonscientific. They seem to believe that one must make the subject guess what the experimenter wants or that one must show that the behavior is some kind of automatic consequence of a reinforcement program to have the experiment "count" as real psychology. I think this is a direct result of confusing the two types of experimentation. An error on the other side is to assume that if one does not get the desired behavior under verbal instruction, it is not part of the capacity of the subject. This view is equally naive, of course. Many subjects make fine discriminations for which they have no verbal labels or even incorrect labels. To expect them to respond to the experimenter's words appropriately is wildly optimistic. In informal conversation, Dr. Postman furnished an excellent example of appropriate procedure. He was running subjects in successive three-stage mediation problems. He explained the relation between the lists on the first day. Subjects said that they understood. On the second day he repeated the entire procedure, and this time the subjects said, "Now I *really* understand." The instructions which seem to be understood are more thoroughly and deeply understood once the subject has actual experience with the situation.

Particularly with problems concerning the linguistic system, where so much of the subjects skill and knowledge is unconscious, the questions of what constitute appropriate and adequate instruction are thorny ones. An instance is furnished here by a study that we have recently completed (see Jenkins, Foss, and Greenberg, 1966). Subjects were presented with a six-pair paired-associate list to learn. The list was systematically structured from a linguistic point of view. The stimuli were unvoiced stops (PA, KA, TA, etc.), and the responses were the appropriately matched voiced stops (BA, GA, DA, etc.). If subjects are merely instructed to learn this set of pairs in the usual fashion, the systematic arrangement of the pairs confers no advantage over a list that is non-systematically arranged. This shows that this variable *under these conditions* does not influence what a subject *does do*. If, however, we inject more information into the instructions by telling the subjects that there is a system in the arrangement, the learning is faster. If we also add that it has something to do with the way the syllables sound, however, there is no added advantage. If, on the other hand, we add, "Pay attention to what your mouth is doing" and omit reference to sound, subjects show markedly faster learning. Interestingly enough, though the instruction to "pay attention to your mouth" helps engage the appropriate system of regularities, many of the subjects report at the end that they were helped by the fact that the syllables "sounded alike." In this case it is clear that the capacity of the subject can be brought to bear on this problem by a specific instruction which at the end he may not even acknowledge that he used. In the various conditions of this experiment we have a series of lessons concerning the difference between can-do and does-do experiments and the tricky business of finding ways to instruct subjects which will, in fact, engage the capabilities that we believe

can be brought to bear on the task.

Finally, I would like to add a brief word to the discussion of the job of science and the relative importance of description, prediction, and control on the one hand and explanation and understanding on the other. I do not think that it is wise to try to legislate another person's interests in the pursuit of science, but I do feel that we can try to understand what the other person is saying. As I see it, much of the argument hinges on whether one wants to do a psychology which at some point has a box labeled "organism" or "human being" or whether one wants to go ahead and analyze that portion of the system too. Surely, if one wishes to develop a technology to shape or control a piece of behavior, it should be possible. I care very much about this problem when I think of applications of psychology and most especially when I think of my children in school. However, when I ask myself what I want to know when I go to work in the laboratory, I find that I am interested in what goes on inside the organism. I really do want to know what goes on "in the head." I would hate to have to support an argument to the effect that this will necessarily lead to better control or better prediction. I must insist that these are not my immediate aims and that I am not at all crestfallen if I fail to show someone how to teach Freshman English better than it is now taught. Understanding and explanation themselves are adequate goals for me at this time. And though I will bet that in the very long run they will make better prediction and control possible, I do not think that makes much difference right now.

A charming and intriguing example of the difference between understanding and description is found in the persistent puzzle of the great English monument, Stonehenge.[3] In the last three years renewed attention has been given to these "rude, enormous monoliths" of Salisbury Plain. Stonehenge poses a set of disturbing questions: Why was it built? What is it supposed to be? How was it to be used? What is its purpose? None of the questions are answered, of course, in the straightforward description of the site as a physical object.

If one has some hypotheses, however, he can distinguish between relevant and accidental features of the monument with respect to that hypothesis and perhaps seek confirmation or disconfirmation of his notions by relating these features to other phenomena. The recent excitement was generated by a set of hypotheses concerning the function of Stonehenge as an astronomical observatory and computer. Confirmation of the hypotheses required the aid of ancillary sciences for describing the monument as it must have been originally, for dating purposes, for ascertaining the positions of astronomical objects and celestial events that one might assume to have been important, etc. In short, an elaborate theoretical and constructual net had to be built up to provide the basis for identifying confirmatory evidence if it did exist. Then a computer was set to work to compare relationships at the site to maximum and minimum elevations of the sun and moon and to the dating of events such as eclipses which were assumed to be of import to astronomical observers.

These studies yielded overwhelming evidence that this enormous device could have been used as a precise calendar, quartering the year with great exactness and providing counting points sufficient to keep track of events of importance between the quarters and to provide sufficient information to predict eclipses of the moon. Indeed, the very location of the monument can then be seen as determined since it makes possible regularities of the physical design features which would not have been possible in another latitude if the same celestial events were to be observed.

It is also interesting to note that this speculation is not without independent corroboration. If one addresses his attention to other, presumably related, stone circles of the same historical period in England, Scotland, and continental Europe, one should now be able to predict in what respects these other structures would be different from Stonehenge because of differences in latitude, given that the astronomical hypotheses are correct. If this proves possible, one must believe that Stonehenge is now understood and explained in a different, more elegant, and more beautiful way than it was when it was described only as a collection of physical properties.

I hope the point of the analogy is clear. The identification of important and relevant aspects of behavior to include in our descriptions is likely to be in large part dependent on our deeper understanding of the roots and sources of the behavior itself. When we understand the deep structures of behavior, our understanding of the relevant aspects of the surface structures should be greatly enriched.

[3] For an account of the research and its related developments the reader is directed to *Stonehenge Decoded*, by Gerald S. Hawkins in collaboration with John B. White. The book provides not only an extensive account of the older and newer research but also reprints Hawkins' articles from *Nature* and *Science*.

References

Jenkins, J. J., "Mediation Theory and Grammatical Behavior," in S. Rosenberg, ed., *Directions in Psycholinguis-*

tics. New York: The Macmillan Company, 1965.

————, D. J. Foss, and J. H. Greenberg, "Phonological Distinctive Features as Cues in Learning," (manuscript) 1966.

————, and D. S. Palermo, "Mediation Processes and the Acquisition of Linguistic Structure," in U. Bellugi and R. W. Brown, eds., *The Acquisition of Language. Monographs of the Society for Research Child Development*, Vol. 29, No. 1, 1964. pp. 79–92.

Osgood, C. E., and T. A. Sebeok, "Psycholinguistics: A Survey of Theory and Research Problems," *Supplement to the Journal of Abnormal and Social Psychology*, 1954. pp. 203.

Association
and Performance
in the Analysis
of Verbal Learning[1]

22 LEO POSTMAN

An increasing number of basic issues in learning theory is being debated in the context of research on verbal processes. The question of whether associative learning is all-or-none, the relationship between perception, learning and memory, the properties of habit-family hierarchies, the generality of concepts derived from conditioning, the role of contiguity and frequency as opposed to perceptual and cognitive organization—all these have recently been considered in studies of verbal learning and ·memory. It may be an opportune time, therefore, to consider two related conceptual problems which historically have been a central focus of interest in behavior theory and which deserve equal consideration in the analysis of verbal learning, namely (a) the status of the concept of association and (b) the distinction between learning and performance. For better or for worse, the concept of association is at the roots of much of the research on verbal learning and continues to enjoy high frequency of usage in our theoretical and experimental vocabulary, although its definitions and the implications

attached to it vary widely. It will be useful to ask what some of its current definitions and connotations are and how differences in usage relate to theoretical disagreement. As for the distinction between learning and performance—more specifically, between the acquisition and utilization of associations—I shall try to show that it is implicit in much of what we do but that it deserves to be brought into sharper focus in the interest of clarifying the problems of method and of interpretation which it entails.

The Concept of Association

Definitions and usages

The pivotal importance of the concept of association derives from the fact that verbal behavior characteristically occurs in orderly sequences. Historically association has been invoked to account for sequential order in terms of linkages between successive verbal units. The denotation of sequential order has remained the descriptive core of definitions of association, but additional meanings and usages have progressively accrued to the concept which reflect

[1] The preparation of this paper was facilitated by grants from the National Science Foundation and the National Institutes of Health to the Institute of Human Learning.

assumptions about the conditions and characteristics of the learning process. It is possible to discern at least six different senses in which the concept of association is used, and most if not all of these are represented in the papers of this conference.

(1) DESCRIPTIVE USAGE: ASSOCIATION AS SEQUENTIAL PROBABILITY. As a purely descriptive term, association refers to the probability of a response R in a situation S: the stronger the association, the higher the probability. This is the working definition adopted by McGeoch (1942) to which Tulving refers in his paper, and he is quite correct in pointing out that association in this sense is a fact to be explained. This usage is theoretically neutral and entails no assumptions about the conditions of association. Recent experiments have made it clear that frequently the response becomes associated not to the nominal stimulus defined by the experimenter but rather to some component of that stimulus selected by the S (Underwood, 1963). The occurrence of stimulus selection must, however, be demonstrated by means of transfer procedures after the end of learning and does not enter into the empirical definition of association.

(2) ASSOCIATIVE MEDIATORS IN LEARNING AND RECALL. Since verbal units are part of, or related to, the linguistic repertoire which the S brings to the laboratory, it is apparent that the development of prescribed new associations will be heavily influenced by transfer from pre-experimental sources. The mode of operation of such transfer effects is usually described in terms of implicit associations elicited during acquisition, recall, or both. During the presentation of a series of words each item is assumed to elicit both representational and implicit associative responses, and both recall and recognition have been successfully

predicted on the basis of the similarity relations among these assumed responses (e.g., Underwood, 1965). Wide reliance is, of course, placed on the role of mediating associations in paired-associate learning. The large body of research on mediation has as its objective the determination of the conditions under which such associative links are established and used (see Jenkins, 1963a; Earhard and Mandler, 1965). There is evidence that even in the absence of pre-existing or experimentally produced associative links Ss develop mediators between stimulus and response terms (e.g., Bugelski, 1962; Dallett, 1964; Runquist and Farley, 1964).

Such events intervening between the stimuli and responses defined by the experimenter constitute what the Kendlers have called horizontal processes (1962). The concept of horizontal processes makes explicit the assumption that stimulus-response sequences "do not occur in isolation, but instead are linked together to form integrated continuous behavior" (1962, p. 3), and they point to the demonstrated importance of chaining mechanisms in establishing and maintaining complex sequences of behavior. Implicit associations, then, are horizontal processes which permit the development of chains of verbal responses. The widespread assumption that mediational chains play an essential part even in the simplest forms of paired-associate learning reflects a basic doubt about the efficacy of sheer contiguity as a condition of acquisition. It may be noted in passing that in the light of some recent experimental evidence (Birnbaum, 1966; Spear, Ekstrand and Underwood, 1964) the role of contiguity in verbal learning may perhaps have been depreciated unduly.

To continue with the classification scheme proposed by the Kendlers, implicit vertical as well as horizontal processes are frequently assumed to take place during the acquisition of verbal tasks. The term "vertical" refers to the simultaneous occurrence of different independent or interacting processes. The assumption that both response learning and associative learning are required for the mastery of a paired-associate task is a case in point. When one attempts to give an exhaustive account of all the changes produced by training, the structure of assumed vertical processes can become exceedingly complex. Consider, for example, the list of ten processes which Battig suggests are likely to unfold during the acquisition of a paired-associate list. Several, if not all of them, can be seen as requiring the development of differential associative responses to the stimulus and to the response terms. While Battig tends to leave open the question of the specific mechanisms represented by the various component processes of paired-associate learning, the reliance on a network of vertical associative processes is quite explicit in the models of McGuire (1961) and of Newman (1961) which he views as first steps toward the development of an adequately complex multiprocess theory. For purposes of the present discussion a characteristic feature of such a theoretical analysis should be noted. The number and the nature of the intervening processes are defined in terms of the apparent accomplishments of the learner: classification of items as stimulus and response terms, discrimination of stimulus and response terms, response learning or integration, stimulus selection or coding, S-R associations, etc. A separate process, and presumably a separate class of intervening events, is coordinated with each of these discernible consequences of practice. By contrast, one may in the construction of theoretical models

recognize the multiple consequences of training but attempt to hold down to a minimum the number of separate processes postulated to account for these effects. That is, to the extent that such consequences vary together, it is reasonable to conceive of them as different but complementary facets of a single process.

(3) PRE-EXPERIMENTAL ASSOCIATIVE HIERARCHIES. Once the role of pre-experimental language habits in acquisition and retention is recognized, it becomes essential to specify the associations which the S brings to the experimental situation. A sharp distinction has to be made between the conceptual status of pre-experimental habits and of implicit mediators which are assumed to function during acquisition. Pre-experimental habits have the status of independent variables whereas implicit mediators must be treated as dependent variables. That is, pre-experimental habits delimit the implicit events which may be expected to occur during acquisition; whether or not such mediators are in fact aroused in a given situation is an empirical question.

The conventional approach to the description of pre-experimental associative habits has been the specification of habit-family hierarchies. For purposes of predicting associations which are likely to be aroused during learning, associations elicited by verbal items are determined in independent test situations and ordered with respect to number, strength, and distributional characteristics. Among the procedures used for determining the hierarchies of verbal habits, the methods of continued and free association are by far the most widely used (for reviews of different methods of scaling verbal materials, see Noble, 1963; Underwood and Schulz, 1960). These methods yield information about the number and distribution of associations, respectively. There has been increasing recognition, however, that single-step habits constitute a very restricted sample of pre-experimental associative tendencies and that account must be taken of the networks of associations which characterize the relationships among verbal units. The shift from habit-family hierarchies to associative structure was brought to the fore in the work of Deese (1959, 1960, 1962) and is the focus of Pollio's discussion in the present symposium.

Normative associative hierarchies are invoked so widely as intervening constructs in the analysis of verbal learning that it has become easy to overlook some of the difficulties and limitations inherent in their use. The determination of the normative hierarchies is made under conditions which are drastically different from those which obtain in the learning situation. To the extent that the normative hierarchies are specific to the procedures by which they are obtained, the validity of norm-derived assumptions about intervening horizontal processes is reduced. There is, of course, evidence for effects of practice, set, and response biases in such normative test procedures as free association (e.g., Horton, Marlowe and Crowne, 1963; Jenkins, 1959; Kjeldergaard, 1962; Wynne, Gerjuoy and Schiffman, 1965).

Normative procedures characteristically order associative responses by rank or relative strength and do not permit an assessment of absolute habit strength. However, it may be absolute rather than relative strength which determines the influence of pre-existing associations on learning (see Postman, 1962; Turnage, 1963). Also, it is frequently assumed, explicitly or implicitly, that the presentation of a word arouses its total associative hierarchy; thus, the similarity among words is measured in terms of the degree of overlap among their associative hier-

archies (e.g., Bousfield, Whitmarsh and Danick, 1958). A more plausible assumption is, however, that associative arousal is selective. Again, when no account is taken of such selectivity, predictions based on norms lose some of their validity.

While I recognize the fallibility of predictions from normative responses to learning, I cannot agree with Tulving's conclusion concerning the relationship between associative processes observed in these different situations. Tulving states that whatever correlations are found require explanation but do not constitute one. This point is valid as far as the ultimate nature and origin of associations are concerned. However, if normative hierarchies do predict, although imperfectly, horizontal processes that occur in learning, they serve to specify some of the conditions of acquisition and in that sense do have explanatory status.

The definitions to which we turn next take us from interverbal associations to associations between nonverbal stimuli and verbal responses.

(4) CONTEXTUAL ASSOCIATIONS. It has long been recognized that verbal responses may become associated not only to specific verbal stimuli but also to nonspecific situational cues, both external and internal (e.g., Robinson, 1932). Such associations are designated as contextual. Contextual associations have largely had the status of inferred hypothetical processes, but they are clearly capable of direct manipulation. The explanatory value of contextual associations has come to the fore in several distinct types of experimental analyses. In the examination of the process of free recall the assumption of contextual associations has appeared to be all but indispensable for specifying the conditions initiating the recall sequence. Regardless of the degree to which the amount of free recall is a

function of interitem associations or subjective organization, at least one response must become attached to the experimental situation if the recall sequence is to unfold. These considerations appear to be reflected in Tulving's statement that "it is logically necessary that at least one, and psychologically plausible that a small but fixed number of items be initially associated with the context to make later recall of the list possible." In a two-stage conception of paired-associate learning a clear distinction is made between response recall and the establishment of specific associations. Response recall has typically been viewed as a function of contextual associations and assessed by free recall of the responses (Ekstrand, 1966; Underwood, Runquist and Schulz, 1959).

The explanatory power of the distinction between contextual and specific associations is brought out most fully in the analysis of the component processes of unlearning. This analysis was first developed by McGovern (1964) who presented strong support for the hypothesis that the successive acquisition of responses conforming to the *A–B, A–C* paradigm reduces the availability of contextual as well as specific associations. Different experimental paradigms permit the orthogonal manipulation of the conditions of transfer for contextual and specific associations. Thus, it has been possible to test the implications of theoretical position which assign differential roles to the extinction and recovery of contextual and specific associations as determinants of forgetting. An example is the hypothesis that distribution of practice facilitates retention to the extent that it provides an opportunity for successive cycles of extinction, recovery and re-extinction of competing contextual (but not specific) associations (Underwood, Keppel, and Schulz, 1962). The distinction between the two

classes of associations has also led to a progressive refinement in the methods of evaluating the amounts and characteristics of unlearning. The recent developments in this area reviewed by Keppel indicate that independent assessments of the components of unlearning are indeed possible, and that reduced availability of contextual associations contributes heavily to the overall losses measured on MMFR tests.

Studies directed at the identification of the components of negative transfer and interference also provide useful examples of the direct manipulation of the conditions of contextual association. The reference studies here are those of Bilodeau and Schlosberg (1951) and of Greenspoon and Ranyard (1957) which showed that retroactive inhibition varies with the similarity of the environmental context in which successive lists are practiced. It is worth emphasizing that while the concept of contextual association has frequently served a *post hoc* explanatory function, it is capable of being tied down operationally—by manipulation of the environmental conditions during acquisition and by the use of testing procedures which are differentially sensitive to contextual and to specific associations.

(5) Nonverbal Mediators. The contextual associations which have been postulated in analyses of verbal learning are between nonverbal environmental (or internal) cues and verbal responses. The complementary pattern has also received consideration, namely the evocation of nonverbal mediators by verbal stimuli. In his discussion Pollio assigns to such nonverbal mediators the function of placing verbal units along dimensions of meaning such as those derived from the semantic differential. He recognizes that there are considerations which suggest that dimensional relations may be reducible to interverbal ones (Bousfield, 1961)

but he tends to side with Osgood (1961) in concluding that the total range of experimental data does not justify such a reduction. Pending a resolution of this controversy it is fair to say, however, that evidence for systematic effects of nonverbal mediators on speed of acquisition has been accumulating slowly. It is true that speed of paired-associate learning appears to be a direct function of the level of polarization of both the stimulus and the response term; amount of mediated transfer has likewise been shown to increase with the degree of polarization of the mediator (Shanmugam and Miron, 1966). However, rate of learning does not appear to be influenced by the degree of similarity of nonverbal mediators, as inferred from ratings on the semantic differential (Higa, 1963; Wimer, 1963; Youssef and Saltz, 1964). Such results are to be contrasted with the large and orderly effects of similarity as defined by associative relationships (see Underwood, Ekstrand, and Keppel, 1966). This state of affairs reminds us that there can be no *a priori* assumption that functional relations which obtain for verbal units will be paralleled when nonverbal and verbal units enter into association. This caution was expressed earlier by Underwood (1961) in his discussion of the Gibson theory of verbal learning where much of the basic supporting evidence was obtained in experiments in which geometric designs served as stimuli and verbal units as responses.

(6) PHYSIOLOGICAL USAGE. We shall mention only briefly a potentially important additional definition of association,—the specification of underlying physiological mechanisms. This is not to say that there are no physiological models which have influenced research on verbal learning. The question of whether the principles governing the establishment of associa-

tions conform to the laws of perceptual organization continues to be debated (e.g., Asch, Ceraso, and Heimer, 1960; Kohler, 1941; Postman and Riley, 1957). While this is an important substantive question in its own right, the arguments typically include explicit or implicit assumptions about underlying trace mechanisms. Appeal has been made to the hierarchical neural structures postulated by Hebb (1949) as providing a possible mechanism of categorical clustering in recall (Bousfield and Cohen, 1953, 1955). It is also clear that the recent upsurge of work on short-term memory has revived interest in physiological and quasi-physiological models of the memory trace (e.g., Broadbent, 1958; Brown, 1958). Since physiological interpretations of association are not a concern of this discussion, it may be sufficient to say that at the present time physiological assumptions have failed to yield specific predictions which are systematically different from, or more precise than, those generated on the basis of purely behavioral constructs.

Association as a dispositional concept

Our survey of current usages and definitions may be summarized in terms of a set of contrasts. Conceptions of association refer to

1. relationships between verbal units or between nonverbal cues and verbal units;

2. observable conditional probabilities of responses or implicit processes intervening between nominal stimuli and overt responses;

3. pre-existing habits which have the status of independent variables or processes which develop during practice and which are treated as dependent variables in studies of learning and retention;

4. descriptions of the changes produced by practice in either behavioral or physiological terms.

In spite of their diversity these definitions and usages are consistent with each other in pointing to the conclusion that association must be viewed as a dispositional concept. Classification of the concept as dispositional gives explicit recognition to the fact that reference is being made to *potential* behavior sequences. To assert that there is an association between A and B does not imply that whenever A occurs B will follow; rather B will follow if the requisite conditions of performance are met. This view was expressed a long time ago by Robinson (1932) when he wrote about associations as psychical dispositions: "The vase upon the mantel has as one of its characteristics the fall it would take if touched by the lightest breeze. The breeze may not come for months, yet the capacity to fall five feet and break itself to bits remains. . . . What endures is a likelihood of certain acts appearing in certain orders and contexts. The Frenchman's actual possession is a capacity to say *Bonjour*! when he sees his friend. And there should be no objection to talking about such capacities or dispositions as if they were real" (pp. 33f.). Since that time reference to disposition terms has, of course, become commonplace in the analysis of psychological concepts (e.g., Mandler and Kessen, 1959, p. 115).

It is obvious, of course, that we are here calling attention to the generally recognized and well worn distinction between learning and performance: in any given situation the probability of a particular response will be a function not only of associative strength but also of the conditions of performance. One might ask, therefore, why it appears necessary to make this obvious point.

The answer is that while the distinction between learning and performance is in fact often used, explicitly or implicitly, in the formulation of experimental problems, there has been relatively little systematic concern with the determiners of performance as distinguished from the conditions of learning. The reason is perhaps that most conventional experiments on verbal learning are carried out under conditions where instructions, self-instructions and pre-experimental habits all combine to maximize performance of what has been learned. The dependence of behavior on motivational arousal, which has served to bring the distinction between learning and performance into clear focus in the animal laboratory, has rarely become salient in the analysis of verbal processes.

Nevertheless it is easy to show that the distinction between learning and performance provides the underlying rationale for many of our experimental designs, analytic procedures and theoretical interpretations. We shall now examine a number of experimental paradigms in which the distinction between learning and performance becomes important in the choice of operations and the theoretical interpretation of the findings. This analysis takes its point of departure from the assumption that a useful distinction can be made between general principles of association, i.e., sufficient if not necessary conditions of learning which hold under any experimental arrangement and for all Ss on the one hand, and principles of performance which are a function of the specific procedures used for training and testing. It will also be assumed that principles of performance regulate not only S's overt responses but implicit responses to the learning materials as well. Thus, one of the important domains of operation of principles of performance is that of implicit responses. The reason for pressing the distinction between principles of learning and of performance is the belief that there are laws of association which are trans-situational and that much of the variability among experimental arrangements and *S*s is due to the effects of performance factors.

Evaluation of Performance Variables

Interaction of habit and drive

The closest parallel in verbal learning to the conventional methods of behavior theory for assessing the role of performance variables is provided by the experiments of Spence and his associates on the effects of anxiety. These experiments were designed to show that the influence of drive level, as indexed by *S*s' emotionality, on rate of acquisition depends on the position in the associative hierarchy of the responses to be learned. When the correct responses are dominant, a high drive level should be beneficial, in accordance with the assumption that performance is a multiplicative function of habit strength and drive. As the amount of response competition increases, a high drive level should become more and more detrimental by maximizing the strength of the error tendencies. Several studies yielded evidence consistent with these expectations (Montague, 1953; Spence, Faber and McFann, 1956). This analysis assumes that the initial associative dispositions are the same for high-drive and low-drive *S*s and that the differences in speed of acquisition are produced by performance factors.

Intentional vs. incidental learning

Spence's analysis considers the effects of performance variables on the development of associations between nominal stimuli and responses. Such variables may be expected to determine the activation of implicit responses and mediators as well. Within this framework it becomes possible to view differences between intentional and incidental learning as reflecting the effects of instructions on the performance of implicit representational and associative responses during exposure to the test items. Given the assumed effects of instructions on the frequency and distribution of implicit responses, there is no evidence for systematic differences between the functional relations which obtain in intentional and incidental learning (Postman, 1964a). This conclusion receives direct support from Mechanic's (1964) demonstration that the usual difference between intentional and incidental *S*s is eliminated when experimental arrangements are used which serve to equalize the frequency of representational responses under the two conditions of practice.

It can be seen that both Spence's analysis and the present treatment of incidental learning reflect the assumption that the course of acquisition is determined by two conceptually distinct sets of factors: (a) the laws governing the establishment of associative dispositions which are assumed to be general principles which remain valid regardless of the specific conditions of practice, and (b) the conditions of performance which determine the activation of these dispositions during practice. Thus, in Spence's experiments the patterns of associative facilitation and competition are taken to be independent of Ss' drive level; the latter determines the effective differentials in response strength when these dispositions are activated. In intentional and incidental learning alike, the establishment of new associative dispositions is assumed to depend on the frequency and distribution of representational and mediating responses; the extent to which these implicit responses are in fact performed is significantly influenced by instructions.

Instructional effects in intentional learning

The range of effectiveness of instructional variables is, of course, not limited to the establishment of a set to learn. Given such a set, the method of practice, and presumably the performance of implicit responses, can be systematically influenced by instructions. The following experimental findings illustrate this point.

With the conditions of practice held constant, performance depends on the initial instructions given to Ss concerning the method by which they are to be tested (Postman and Jenkins, 1948). In general, full and correct information about the method of testing to be used maximizes performance. The results indicate that the instructions lead Ss to respond selectively to those features of the materials which are relevant to the requirements of the expected test.

When Ss are instructed to learn the serial order of a list of words, the accuracy of their recall for order is, as expected, higher than when the learning instructions make no reference to order. However, the increase in the retention for order is achieved at the expense of a substantial reduction in the number of items recalled (Postman, Adams, and Bohm, 1956). The amount that can be acquired during a given exposure period is limited (see Murdock, 1960,

1965), and instructions determine how this time is distributed in responding to different characteristics of the stimuli.

As Young has pointed out, instructions can significantly influence the course of serial learning. Specifically, instructional effects have been demonstrated under conditions deviating from the classical procedure in which the starting point of the series is held constant and successive presentations are separated by an intertrial interval. Advance information to Ss about the conditions of presentation reduces the difficulty produced by trial-to-trial variation of the starting position (Winnick and Dornbush, 1963). Instructions can be used to define anchor positions for S, e.g., the item which is to be responded to as the initial point of the series (Bowman and Thurlow, 1963; Glanzer and Dolinsky, 1965). Serial position effects develop with respect to such subjective reference points, i.e., objective and instruction-defined anchor points tend to have the same functional properties.

Instructions about a forthcoming test influence Ss' method of practice on a transfer task, just as they do in single-list learning. When successive lists conform to the $A = B, A = C$ paradigm, Ss informed just prior to the transfer task that they would later be tested for recall of the first list adopted the procedure of simultaneously rehearsing the two responses to a given stimulus (Postman and Stark, 1962). Consequently such instructions lead to a reduction in the amount of retroactive inhibition (see also A. H. Schwartz, 1963).

The evaluation of the effects of instructions becomes a critical issue in the interpretation of the studies of transfer from serial to paired-associate learning. Subjects informed about the relationship between the two tasks just prior to the test show substantially greater transfer than do uninformed *S*s (Postman and Stark, 1967). The results may be taken as evidence that habits established during serial learning can be utilized most effectively when *S* knows how he is to use the associations he has learned in the acquisition of the new task. Such a finding is consistent with the conception of association as a disposition which may be activated to varying degrees depending on the conditions of performance.

At this point some comments are in order on Young's discussion of the differential effects of instructions on transfer performance. He points out correctly that the instructed *S*'s ability to make effective use of the end products of serial learning in the acquisition of the transfer task does not permit any definitive conclusions about the manner in which the serial list was acquired. But he goes on to say, "For this reason, conclusions about the functional stimulus in serial learning when subjects have been instructed should be made with considerable caution." The apparent implication of this statement is that the conclusions are more uncertain and require greater caution when *S*s are instructed than when they are not. If such is indeed the intended implication, I must disagree. The point would have merit only if we conceived of associations as response tendencies which are elicited automatically whenever the appropriate stimulus is presented; such tendencies could presumably be assessed most directly in the uninstructed *S*, uncontaminated by the influence of instructions. However, once it is recognized that the concept of association refers to a disposition, it is clear that *S*'s behavior is always jointly determined by what he has learned and the conditions of performance. Thus, the behavior of the uninstructed *S* comes no

closer to yielding a "pure" measure of association than does the behavior of the instructed *S*. Rather they are tested under different conditions of performance. The empirical results show that there is better differentiation among the effects of prior training when the conditions of performance include instructions than when they do not.

Rules of encoding and decoding

The application of rules of encoding and decoding has effects on the selectivity of implicit responses which are continuous with those of instructions. In fact, as Mandler (1967) points out, one obvious method of getting a learner to apply such rules is to give him the appropriate instructions. In the absence of instructions the rules may be established more gradually and applied less consistently; however, there is no reason to expect systematic differences between the effects on acquisition of rules which are discovered and rules which are provided to *S*. When rules are verbalized by *S*, they become self-instructions. For purposes of the present discussion we shall mean by the application of a rule the restriction of implicit responses to a specified set. Typically such a restricted set is more effective than a less restricted one in mediating response recall and the establishment of new associations, e.g., by making the units more meaningful. An example is provided by the use of anagrams as learning materials such that each unit can be encoded as a word. There is evidence that *S*s can use such rules with positive effects on acquisition, although it should be emphasized that the demonstrated amounts of facilitation have been relatively small, and the effectiveness of rules of encoding is severely limited by *S*'s ability to carry out the necessary decoding operations at the time of recall, e.g., decoding words into the prescribed letter sequences of the anagrams (Underwood and Erlebacher, 1965).

Our present concern is with the conceptual status of rules of encoding and decoding. It has been suggested that, like instructions, rules govern the selective arousal of mediating responses to the learning materials and in this sense constitute a potentially important performance factor in acquisition. It does not follow, of course, that the application of rules of encoding is a necessary step in the establishment of new associative dispositions. Such an assumption is, however, implied in Mandler's (1967) explication of his information-processing model of verbal learning. According to this model, an operating program specifies the rules according to which stimulus input is coded for storage in long-term memory. In paired-associate learning this operating program is likely to include the search for mediational rules. In many cases, however, successful mediators must be made highly specific to individual pairs. Under these circumstances, Mandler suggests, "the subject applies very specific rules to very specific items, and these rules generate the correct response." Elsewhere, in discussing mnemonic devices such as idiosyncratic images, abbreviations, labels, and the like, he refers to them as "cues or rules that are specific to a particular output."

The question is whether it is useful to conceptualize highly specific or idiosyncratic cues and mnemonic devices as instances of rules, i.e., to abandon applicability to different instances as a defining characteristic of a rule. The issue here is not primarily one of semantics; rather the concern is with the criteria which are to be used in inferring the operations of rules. As

the studies of Underwood and Erlebacher (1965) show, it is possible to anchor the concept of encoding rule to manipulations of the learning materials on the one hand and such dependent variables as the error patterns in acquisition on the other. If the presence of an association (in the empirical sense) becomes the criterion for inferring the operation of a rule, the interpretation of associations as the product of rule-directed processing is in danger of becoming circular. For the time being it would appear preferable to view the application of rules of encoding and decoding as potential performance factors but not as a defining characteristic of the acquisition process.

Preference effects in acquisition

Selectivity in response to learning materials also becomes apparent in the preferences which Ss show for dealing with particular stimuli, to which Underwood (1964) has called attention. Direct evidence for such preferences comes from studies of paired-associate learning using compound stimulus terms. Under these conditions Ss can and usually do select one of the components as the functional stimulus (Musgrave and Cohen, 1966; Underwood, Ham, and Ekstrand, 1962). Components which favor ease of learning, e.g., those of greater meaningfulness or distinctiveness, are typically selected. In addition, Ss show biases in their selection which do not appear to be related to ease of learning. For example, colored frames are favored over words even though independent tests fail to show a difference in speed of learning with these two classes of stimuli (Underwood, Ham, and Ekstrand, 1962). We have recently obtained clear evidence for similar biases when Ss are given an opportunity to choose between alternative responses to each of the stimulus terms in a list of paired associates. Again the choices are not only related to ease of learning, as when high-frequency words are preferred to low-frequency ones, but also reflect systematic biases. Thus, Ss favor conceptually related responses over unrelated ones, although the conceptual similarity of responses is known not to influence speed of learning.

The other examples cited by Underwood point to the fact that preferences may come into play whenever a list contains distinctive subsets of items, i.e., when a mixed list is used. To determine whether variations in rate of acquisition reflect preferences or differences in ease of learning, it is necessary to compare the same classes of items when they appear in a mixed list and when each class is represented by an unmixed list. Differences which are the result of preferences will disappear when unmixed lists are used; those which are due to ease of learning will persist. By the use of these operations it was possible to show that the advantage of homogeneous pairs (in which stimulus and response are from the same class) over heterogeneous pairs (in which the two terms are from different classes) is entirely a matter of preference (Postman and Riley, 1957). This result brings out sharply the distinction between performance factors and associative factors as determinants of the rate of acquisition. It is useful at this point to reiterate Underwood's conclusion that "when task variables are manipulated, the mixed design may lead to erroneous conclusions about rates of learning when what in fact is being measured is preference for dealing initially with certain stimuli over others" (1964, p. 68). From the point of view of the present discussion, such erroneous conclusions would reflect the failure to distinguish between

performance factors and principles of association.

While recognizing the potential importance of preferences, we must guard against attributing preferences and related strategies to S when the data do not compel it. The following is a case in point. It has recently been suggested that preferences for dealing with selected responses may be a significant factor during both acquisition and test trials in free learning. Battig, Allen, and Jensen (1965) present data from three independent experiments showing that there is a clear tendency for newly learned items to be given earlier in recall than items which had been recalled correctly on previous trials. They suggest two possible but not mutually exclusive interpretations of these findings: (a) items not previously recalled receive special emphasis or attention; (b) Ss may attempt to reproduce newly learned items first, recognizing as it were that such items are liable to be forgotten more quickly than those which had been given correctly on earlier tests. The authors point out that the trend in recall priority "is diametrically opposed to that expected on the assumption that order of recall provides a direct index of item strength . . . and would seem to demonstrate conclusively the paramount importance in free-recall performance of factors other than response strength" (Battig, Allen, and Jensen, 1965, p. 178). Tulving likewise cites these results as contrary to the spew hypothesis according to which order of recall is a direct function of the strength of items.

There is a simpler explanation of this finding. As is well known, the serial position curve in the free recall of unrelated words shows a steep recency and a less pronounced primacy effect. Order of recall and probability of recall are highly correlated. When the order of presentation changes from trial to trial, the items occupying the favorable positions and having a high probability of being recalled and given early during recall will change likewise. (This will be necessarily the case when no item is allowed to occupy the same serial position more than once; since the number of favorable positions is small, it will also be true on the average when the assignment of items to positions is strictly random.) To the extent that the preponderance of newly given items comes from favorable serial positions, the recall-priority effect would follow. This alternative explanation was considered by Battig and his associates but discarded largely on the grounds that in one of the experiments under consideration the percent of newly recalled items presented in each serial position was found to be "relatively consistent across serial positions, except for a slightly greater frequency of such items in the initial and final positions" (Battig, Allen, and Jensen, 1965, p. 179). This test of the alternative explanation is, however, inadequate. The critical question is not how the newly recalled items were distributed over serial positions but whether they occupied more favorable positions than the previously recalled items. A forthcoming report by Postman and Keppel will present evidence that such is indeed clearly the case; for example, the percentages of newly recalled items in the three terminal positions, which account for the bulk of the recency effect, are about twice as high as those of previously given items.

Transfer: tests of what has been learned

The distinction between learning and performance becomes the explicit point of departure in the formulation of the experimental problem when tests of transfer are used to assess what has been learned as a result of practice under a given set of conditions. It is recognized that performance requirements imposed during practice limit the possibilities of determining what it is that S is learning; while he is meeting the criteria of the learning task, he may be acquiring other dispositions as well which cannot be reflected in his performance. By the same token, when he fails to meet the criteria of the current task there may be learning which can be brought out under changed conditions of performance. A few examples will be sufficient to illustrate these points.

The developments of backward associations during forward practice is demonstrated by tests of transfer, i.e., by means of a change in the response requirements. This example at once calls attention, however, to the problems of interpretation which may be expected to arise when tests of transfer are used to determine what has been learned. As is well known, the question has been raised of whether transfer tests provide valid measures of the strength of backward associations after a given period of practice. We are referring here to the arguments advanced by proponents of the hypothesis of associative symmetry (Asch and Ebenholtz, 1962; Horowitz, Norman, and Day, 1966) which have been reviewed by Battig. A few additional comments which bear on the implications of the controversy for the distinction between learning and performance may be in order. The basic contention in support of associative symmetry is that the apparent greater strength of forward than backward associations is an artifact of the lower availability of the stimulus terms as responses. Thus, asymmetry is said to reflect a performance bias. To eliminate this bias, various procedures such as prior familiarization have been used to equate availability. If the advantage of forward over backward associations is eliminated under these conditions, the results are taken as evidence for the principle of associative symmetry. This chain of reasoning runs into a serious difficulty which stems from the question of whether it is possible to make inferences about what happens under standard conditions of forward learning from results obtained by the special procedures designed to equalize availability of the stimulus and response terms. It is possible that associative strength is related to response-term availability; if that were the case, asymmetry in both these respects would be joint consequences of forward practice. The general point here is that any transfer test has characteristic response requirements of its own. If it is believed that these requirements reduce the sensitivity of the test, the solution must be to devise a more sensitive test and not to change the antecedent conditions. Since a test measuring sheer associative strength in the forward and backward direction, regardless of availability, has not been devised, there is no basis for the conclusion that the existing evidence for asymmetry is artifactual. These obstacles to definitive tests of the hypothesis of associative symmetry illustrate some of the inherent limitations of transfer tests as a means of answering the question of what has been learned. However, transfer tests have provided less equivocal answers to this question in other cases.

The hypothesis that sheer contiguity is a sufficient condition for the development of associations is of considerable theoretical interest but not readily testable because of the difficulty of isolating contiguity from other conditions of acquisition. Important evidence in favor of the hypothesis was obtained in a study by Spear, Ekstrand and Underwood (1964) which used a transfer test to assess the amount learned as a function of contiguity *per se*. The critical transfer effects were those from verbal discrimination learning to paired-associate learning. In the verbal discrimination procedure a list of paired words was presented and S had to learn which arbitrarily chosen member of each pair was correct. The requirements of this task call for neither response learning nor associative learning. Nevertheless there was substantial positive transfer when the correct and incorrect items were appropriately paired as the stimulus and response terms in paired-associate learning, and negative transfer when the pairings were inappropriate. These transfer effects may be reasonably interpreted as reflecting the effects of contiguity during verbal discrimination. It may be noted in passing that such intertask transfer is not in agreement with Mandler's conclusion that the various methods of verbal learning do not study the same basic processes. The evidence for significant nonspecific transfer (learning to learn) from one type of learning task to another, e.g., from serial to paired-associate learning or vice versa, is likewise at variance with this conclusion (Postman and Schwartz, 1964).

Tests of transfer may show that learning has occurred even when there was no evidence of improvement during acquisition. An excellent example is provided by the study of Taylor and Irion (1964) which was designed to test the all-or-none hypothesis of associative learning. This study showed that significant and orderly transfer effects are produced by prior practice on items which are themselves never given correctly during the acquisition trials. Essentially the same logic underlies the design of other studies of the all-or-none hypothesis (M. Schwartz, 1963; Underwood and Keppel, 1962). In fact, the learning-performance distinction is central in the formulation of experimental tests of the all-or-none hypothesis. The basic question at issue is whether any learning occurs on the trials preceding the first correct response. According to the all-or-none view, the answer is in the negative, whereas the incremental position holds that prior to the first correct response there are increments in associative strength which are not reflected in performance. A decision between these alternatives requires a test which permits such increments to become manifest in performance.

Transfer: identification of functional stimuli

Transfer measures of what has been learned have been used as a basis for drawing inferences about the nature of the functional stimuli in acquisition. Such second-order inferences are, however, beset with difficulties because S's ability to perform the transfer task may be consistent with more than one possible assumption about the functional stimuli in learning. As a first example, consider a recent study (Jenkins, 1963b) which was designed to determine the extent to which different single letters are selected as the functional stimuli in paired-associate learning when trigrams are the nominal stimuli with digits as responses. After acquisition of the list the individual letters were used as stimuli in a test of recall for the digit responses. Correct responses to letters from each of the three positions were above chance although the first and final positions were favored. It was concluded that all three letters had been selected, although with varying frequencies. Such a conclusion is not warranted, however, as long as it is not known how often

responses to a single letter were mediated by recall of either one or both of the remaining letters. That is, a failure of recall shows that a letter was not selected, but a correct recall may or may not indicate selection. Thus, there is an essential asymmetry of the amount of information yielded by correct and incorrect test responses. An unequivocal inference of single-letter selection requires the application of a dual criterion of performance: S must be unable to reproduce the remaining letters of the trigram at the time of recall *and* he must give the correct response. Application of this criterion in a subsequent study (Postman and Greenbloom, 1967) showed that selection is limited almost entirely to letters in the initial position. Clearly the conclusions about how learning occurred depend critically on the choice of transfer measures.

The obstacles to inferences about the functional stimulus in acquisition on the basis of transfer measures are well illustrated in the case of serial learning. After reviewing a number of studies directed at the identification of the functional stimulus in serial learning on the basis of transfer to paired-associate learning, Young concludes that "beyond the apparent continued demonstrations of the null hypothesis, the . . . research has given us little insight into what might be the stimulus in serial learning." We shall defer comment on Young's willingness to accept the null hypothesis and suggest first of all that transfer measures could not in principle be expected to yield conclusive information about the nature of the functional stimulus. It is true that a complete failure to find positive transfer is evidence against the chaining hypothesis. More important, however, positive transfer does not constitute compelling evidence for chaining because it is consistent with other hypotheses as well. For example, mediation by associations to serial position cannot be ruled out. Thus, even after obtaining evidence for positive transfer, Postman and Stark (1967) found it necessary to conclude that "it will be difficult to arrive at a definitive identification of the functional stimulus in serial learning on the basis of transfer effects in paired-associate learning." (It should be noted in passing that Young incorrectly attributes to Postman and Stark the view that their results constitute "strong evidence . . . supporting the chaining hypothesis of serial learning.")

The methodological point which deserves emphasis at this juncture is that while tests of transfer normally yield information about what has been learned, they will often provide only ambiguous evidence about how a task was acquired. Failure to find transfer may rule out certain classes of functional stimuli; the uncertainty of interpretations based on positive transfer increases with the number of different assumptions about the functional stimulus which are consistent with the observed transfer results.

Let us now return briefly to Young's assertion that the studies of transfer from serial to paired-associate learning have provided "continued demonstrations of the null hypothesis." Quite apart from the fact that null hypotheses cannot be demonstrated, I must disagree on the basis of the evidence. The issue must be faced squarely whether failure to find significant differences on trials to a criterion of one perfect recitation, frequently accompanied by evidence for positive effects on early trials, is to be accepted as evidence for absence of transfer. The reasons which make trials to criterion a highly insensitive measure of transfer have been discussed elsewhere (Postman and Stark, 1967) and are also referred to by Young. The basic point, which is directly relevant to our present concern with the evaluation of performance measures, is that there appears to be no justification for giving precedence to an insensitive measure when more sensitive ones are available and are known to give results at variance with the null hypothesis.

It is necessary to press this point because there are important implications beyond the experiments on transfer from serial to paired-associate learning. For example, if the logic used in the interpretation of these experiments were applied generally, it would be necessary to conclude that there is little evidence for either retroactive or proactive inhibition because such interferences tend to dissipate rapidly and often fail to produce significant differences in the number of trials required in relearning to criterion. In studies using the $A-B, A-B'$ paradigm, large amounts of positive transfer on the early trials are frequently followed by convergence of the experimental and control conditions, attributable to increasing difficulty of differentiation as mediators and mediated responses approach each other in strength (Postman, 1964b). Declining amounts of transfer as a function of trials have also been reported for verbal discrimination, and for related reasons (Underwood, Jesse, and Ekstrand, 1964, Figure 1). In such cases differences in trials to criterion are likely to yield a null result and lead to conclusions at variance with the substantial evidence to the contrary from the early trials. In sum, the sensitivity of the performance measure is of critical importance in the development of transfer tests of what has been learned, and on this basis the validity of Young's conclusion must be questioned.

Retention tests

The choice of specific transfer tests depends on the hypotheses one wishes to evaluate about the components of what has been learned. Thus, theoretical reasons may dictate the use of multiple tests of transfer, each directed at a different component. It is precisely this possibility of focusing separately on different dispositions established by practice which constitutes a major analytic advantage derived from the learning-performance distinction. The same considerations apply to the use of different tests of retention which in the context of the present discussion may be considered as a special class of transfer tests. Apart from the time variable, the essential characteristic which distinguishes tests of retention from other methods of measuring transfer is that the criteria of correct performance are based on the original task rather than a new one; as is always true in the determination of transfer, there may be varying degrees of similarity between the conditions of training and testing, with identity as the limiting case. Systematic manipulation of the performance requirements on the test of retention makes it possible to determine the degree to which the different dispositions established during practice have remained intact after a given interval of time. Reference has already been made to the proven usefulness of this approach in the identification of two distinct components of unlearning, viz., the reduction in the availability of contextual associations on the one hand, and of specific associations on the other.

It is probably fair to say that the significant methodological advances which have characterized recent developments in interference theory have come in large measure from the analysis of performance variables. The classical interference theory as formulated by McGeoch was essentially a theory of performance interference. McGeoch equated retroactive inhibition which he regarded as the major cause of forgetting with reproductive inhibition, i.e., interpolated learning was assumed

not to reduce the strength of prior habits but only to inhibit their performance (see Postman, 1961). This view became untenable when retroactive inhibition continued to be obtained under conditions which were assumed to minimize performance interference, i.e., on tests of MMFR. As a consequence there has been a pronounced shift of emphasis in analyses of the mechanisms of interference from such performance factors as competition and failure of differentiation to changes in associative strength, i.e., unlearning. The lessened emphasis on performance factors represents a blurring of the historical lines between interference theory and other interpretations of forgetting because the concept of interference has always carried a strong connotation of competition between available responses at the time of recall. A case in point is Keppel's speculation that nonspecific unlearning during the retention interval is the basic mechanism of forgetting. Such a view represents a version of interference theory because it relies on intervening activity rather than the sheer passage of time as the essential condition of forgetting. The critical departure is that the role of performance factors such as those implied by the concept of reproductive inhibition is minimized. It may, however, be too early to discount the significance of such factors. As Keppel points out, it is far from certain that procedures such as MMFR tests entirely eliminate the conditions making for reproductive inhibition. While the phenomenon of unlearning appears to be firmly established, the degree to which reduced availability and specific habit interference interact remains to be determined. The possible importance of such an interaction is suggested by the increasing indications that tests of MMFR yield evidence of proactive as well as retroactive inhibition. Proactive interference cannot be attributed to unlearning and has been assumed to be entirely a matter of reproductive inhibition. Either the validity of this assumption can be confirmed, or new concepts—inside or outside the existing framework of interference theory—must be developed to account for proactive interference. It should not be taken for granted that unpaced tests which eliminate the requirement of list differentiation are more representative of the total range of forgetting phenomena which an interference theory must encompass than are paced tests of recall. It is possible, therefore, that reproductive inhibition, and the performance factors responsible for it, play an essential part in many cases of extra-experimental forgetting. The continued systematic exploration of performance factors remains, therefore, a central task for interference theory.

Concluding Comment: On Terminological Preferences

In conclusion, let me return briefly to some questions of definition and usage. We have tried to show that the concept of association retains today both a clear descriptive meaning and a set of defining properties when it denotes an implicit process. There has, however, been in recent years a growing tendency on the part of some investigators to substitute for the language of association—as indeed for the conventional descriptive language of verbal learning in general—more or less equivalent terms derived from the vocabulary of information theory and computer programing. Thus, input is substituted for stimulus presentation, output for response, storage for memory, retrieval for recall, and so on. There is obviously no need to argue about preferences for

words, but it is useful to remind ourselves of the fact that a change in terminology neither alters any facts nor changes our theoretical understanding of them. More important, we must be wary of the introduction of theoretical presuppositions by means of terminological changes if the requirements of definition and explication of observable consequences are bypassed-in this fashion. Thus, if the term "retrieval" implies the assumption of search and scanning processes, it is important that this be made explicit and that the criteria for the inferences of such processes be specified. If such theoretical implications are not intended, then there is no reason to abandon the use of the theoretically neutral term "recall." The same cautions apply, of course, to the use of the language of association—which has, however, the historical advantage that many implicit connotations have been made explicit through years of criticism and self-examination.

A final comment on matters of terminology is prompted by Battig's objection to what he calls the "surreptitious" preservation of S-R concepts by treating them as theoretical constructs rather than as designations of observable phenomena. For example, extinction refers to an observable phenomenon in classical conditioning and as such requires explanation. In the analysis of paired-associate learning phenomena exactly analogous to the extinction of conditioned responses have not been demonstrated; nevertheless extinction and spontaneous recovery have continued to be used as hypothetical explanatory concepts in theoretical accounts of forgetting. Such practice, Battig argues, has "served primarily to obscure the need for and prevent the development of alternative theoretical interpretations adequate to the complexities of the paired-associate learning situation." The practice may not be as reprehensible as all that for several reasons.

There should be no objection to using a term which is used descriptively and refers to observables in the case of a "simple" process as a theoretical construct in the analysis of a more "complex" process. There is an advantage in doing so if the borrowed term has functional properties which are useful for purposes of generating testable predictions. Such changes in the status of concepts will inevitably occur when one discipline builds upon another. The fact that operations of extinction do not produce analogous results in paired-associate learning and in classical conditioning does not necessarily legislate against the use of extinction as a theoretical construct. The basic point at issue has been stated very clearly by the Kendlers: "We do not *find* behavior atomized into individual S-R associations: we *represent* it as consisting of such S-R associations. The concept of S-R association, therefore, must be judged not in terms of its ability to provide a clear image of behavior, but rather in its capacity to represent the facts of behavior." The same applies to concepts such as extinction. As for the prevention of the development of alternative theoretical interpretations, history suggests that a bad theory cannot for long keep out a better one.

References

Asch, S. E., and S. M. Ebenholtz, "The Principle of Associative Symmetry," *Proceedings of the American Philosophical Society*, **106** (1962), 135–163.

———, J. Ceraso, and W. Heimer, "Perceptual Conditions of Association," *Psychological Monographs*, Vol. 74, No. 3, 1960.

Battig, W. F., M. Allen, and A. R. Jensen, "Priority of Free Recall of Newly Learned Items," *Journal of Verbal Learning and Verbal Behavior*, **4** (1965), 175–179.

Bilodeau, I. McD., and H. Schlosberg, "Similarity in Stimulating Conditions as a Variable in Retroactive Inhibition," *Journal of Experimental Psychology*, **41** (1951), 199–204.

Birnbaum, I., "Incidental Learning with 'Omitted' Context Cues," *Psychonomic Science*, **4** (1966), 49–50.

Bousfield, W. A., "The Problem of Meaning in Verbal Learning," in C. N. Cofer, ed., *Verbal Learning and Verbal Behavior*. New York: McGraw-Hill Book Company, 1961.

———, and B. H. Cohen, "The Effects of Reinforcement on the Occurrence of Clustering in the Recall of Randomly Arranged Associates," *Journal of Psychology*, **36** (1953), 67–81.

———, ———, "The Occurrence of Clustering in the Recall of Randomly Arranged Words of Different Frequencies of Usage," *Journal of General Psychology*, **52** (1955), 83–95.

———, G. A. Whitmarsh, and J. J. Danick, "Partial Response Identities in Verbal Generalization," *Psychological Reports*, **4** (1958), 703–713.

Bowman, R. E., and W. R. Thurlow, "Determinants of the Effect of Position in Serial Learning," *American Journal of Psychology*, **76** (1963), 436–445.

Broadbent, D., *Perception and Communication*. London: Pergamon Press, 1958.

Brown, J., "Information, Redundancy and Decay of the Memory Trace," *Symposium on the Mechanization of Thought Processes*, National Physical Laboratory, H.M.S.O., 1958.

Bugelski, B. R., "Presentation Time, Total Time, and Mediation in Paired-Associate Learning," *Journal of Experimental Psychology*, **63** (1962), 409–412.

Dallett, K. M., "Implicit Mediators in Paired-Associate Learning," *Journal of Verbal Learning and Verbal Behavior*, **3** (1964), 209–214.

Deese, J., "The Influence of Inter-Item Associative Strength upon Immediate

Free-Recall," *Psychological Reports,* **5** (1959), 305–312.

———, "Frequency of Usage and Number of Words in Free Recall: The Role of Association," *Psychological Reports,* **7** (1960), 337–344.

———, "On the Structure of Associative Meaning," *Psychological Review,* **69** (1962), 131–175.

Earhard, B., and G. Mandler, "Mediated Associations: Paradigms, Controls and Mechanisms," *Canadian Journal of Psychology,* **19** (1965), 346–378.

Ekstrand, B. R., "A Note on Measuring Response Learning during Paired-Associate Learning," *Journal of Verbal Learning and Verbal Behavior,* **5** (1966), 344–347.

Glanzer, M., and R. Dolinsky, "The Anchor for the Serial Position Curve," *Journal of Verbal Learning and Verbal Behavior,* **4** (1965), 267–273.

Greenspoon, J., and R. Renyard, "Stimulus Conditions and Retroactive Inhibition," *Journal of Experimental Psychology,* **53** (1957), 55–59.

Hebb, D. O., *The Organization of Behavior.* New York: John Wiley & Sons, Inc., 1949.

Higa, M., "Interference Effects of Intralist Word Relationships in Verbal Learning," *Journal of Verbal Learning and Verbal Behavior,* **2** (1963), 170–175.

Horowitz, L. M., S. A. Norman, and R. S. Day, "Availability and Associative Symmetry," *Psychological Review,* **73** (1966), 1–15.

Horton, D. L., D. Marlowe, and D. P. Crowne, "The Effects of Instructional Set and Need for Social Approval on Commonality of Word Association Responses," *Journal of Abnormal and Social Psychology,* **66** (1963), 67–72.

Jenkins, J. J., "Effects on Word Association of the Set to Give Popular Responses," *Psychological Reports,* **5** (1959), 94.

———"Mediated Associations: Paradigms and Situations," in C. N. Cofer and B. S. Musgrave, eds., *Verbal Behavior and Learning.* New York: McGraw-Hill Book Company, 1963.

———, "Stimulus 'Fractionation' in Paired-Associate Learning," *Psychological Reports,* **13** (1963), 409–410.

Kendler, H. H., and T. S. Kendler, "Vertical and Horizontal Processes in Problem Solving," *Psychological Review,* **69** (1962), 1–16.

Kjeldergaard, P. M., "Commonality Scores under Instructions to Give Opposites," *Psychological Reports,* **11** (1962), 219–220.

Kohler, W., "On the Nature of Associations," *Proceedings of the American Philosophical Society,* **84** (1941), 489–502.

Mandler, G., "Verbal Learning," in *New Directions in Psychology III.* New York: Holt, Rinehart and Winston, Inc., 1967.

———, and Kessen, W., *The Language of Psychology.* New York: John Wiley & Sons, Inc., 1959.

McGeoch, J. A., *The Psychology of Human Learning.* New York: Longmans, Green & Co., Inc., 1942.

McGovern, J. B., "Extinction of Associations in Four Transfer Paradigms," *Psychological Monographs,* Vol. 78, No. 16, 1964.

McGuire, W. J., "A Multiprocess Model for Paired-Associate Learning," *Journal of Experimental Psychology,* **62** (1961), 335–347.

Mechanic, A., "The Responses Involved in the Rote Learning of Verbal Materials," *Journal of Verbal Learning and Verbal Behavior,* **3** (1964), 30–36.

Montague, E. K., "The Role of Anxiety in Serial Rote Learning," *Journal of Experimental Psychology,* **45** (1953), 91–98.

Murdock, B. B., Jr., "The Immediate Retention of Unrelated Words," *Journal of Experimental Psychology,* **64** (1960), 222–234.

———, "A Test of the 'Limited Capacity' Hypothesis," *Journal of Experimental Psychology,* **69** (1965), 237–240.

Musgrave, B. S., and J. C. Cohen, "Abstraction in Verbal Paired-Associate Learning," *Journal of Experimental Psychology,* **71** (1966), 1–8.

Newman, S. E., "A Mediation Model for Paired-Associate Learning," *Technical Report No. 1, Contract Nonr 486 (08)*. 1961. North Carolina State College.

————, Noble, C. E., "Meaningfulness and Familiarity," in C. N. Cofer and B. S. Musgrave, eds., *Verbal Behavior and Learning*. New York: McGraw-Hill Book Company, 1963.

Osgood, C. E., "Comments on Professor Bousfield's Paper," in C. N. Cofer, ed., *Verbal Learning and Verbal Behavior*. New York: McGraw-Hill Book Company, 1961.

Postman, L., "The Present Status of Interference Theory," in C. N. Cofer, ed., *Verbal Learning and Verbal Behavior*. New York: McGraw-Hill Book Company, 1961.

————, "The Effects of Language Habits on the Acquisition and Retention of Verbal Associations," *Journal of Experimental Psychology*, **64** (1962), 7–19.

————, "Short-Term Memory and Incidental Learning," in A. W. Melton, ed., *Categories of Human Learning*. New York: Academic Press, 1964.

————, "Studies of Learning to Learn: II. Changes in Transfer as a Function of Practice," *Journal of Verbal Learning and Verbal Behavior*, **3** (1964), 437–447.

————, and R. Greenbloom, "Conditions of Cue Selection in the Acquisition of Paired-Associate Lists," *Journal of Experimental Psychology*, **73** (1967), 91–100.

————, and W. O. Jenkins, "An Experimental Analysis of Set in Rote Learning: The Interaction of Learning Instruction and Retention Performance," *Journal of Experimental Psychology*, **38** (1948), 683–689.

————, and D. A. Riley, "A Critique of Kohler's Theory of Association," *Psychological Review*, **64** (1957), 61–72.

————, and M. Schwartz, "Studies of Learning to Learn: I. Transfer as a Function of Method of Practice and Class of Verbal Materials," *Journal of Verbal Learning and Verbal Behavior*, **3** (1964), 37–49.

————, and K. Stark, "Retroactive In-hibition as a Function of Set During the Interpolated Task," *Journal of Verbal Learning and Verbal Behavior*, **1** (1962), 304–311.

————, ————, "Studies of Learning to Learn: IV. Transfer from Serial to Paired-Associate Learning," *Journal of Verbal Learning and Verbal Behavior*, (1967), in press.

————, P. A. Adams, and A. M. Bohm, "Studies in Incidental Learning: V. Recall for Order and Associative Clustering," *Journal of Experimental Psychology*, **51** (1956), 334–342.

Robinson, E. S., *Association Theory Today*. New York: Appleton-Century, 1932.

Runquist, W. N., and F. H. Farley, "The Use of Mediators in the Learning of Verbal Paired Associates," *Journal of Verbal Learning and Verbal Behavior*, **3** (1964), 280–285.

Schwartz, A. H., "Influence of Instructional Set and Response Frequency on Retroactive Interference," *Journal of Expermiental Psychology*, **66** (1963), 127–132.

Schwartz, M., "Transfer from Failed Pairs as a Test of One-Trial vs. Incremental Learning," *American Journal of Psychology*, **76** (1963), 266–273.

Shanmugam, A. V., and M. S. Miron, "Semantic Effects in Mediated Transfer," *Journal of Verbal Learning and Verbal Behavior*, **5** (1966), 361–368.

Spear, N. E., B. R. Ekstrand, and B. J. Underwood, "Association by Contiguity," *Journal of Experimental Psychology*, **67** (1964), 151–161.

Spence, K. W., I. E. Farber, and H. H. McFann, "The Relation of Anxiety (Drive) Level to Performance in Competitional and Non-Competitional Paired-Associates Learning," *Journal of Experimental Psychology*, **52** (1956), 296–310.

Taylor, A. B., and A. L. Irion, "Continuity Hypothesis and Transfer of Training in Paired-Associate Learning," *Journal of Experimental Psychology*, **68** (1964), 573–577.

Turnage, T. W., "Pre-Experimental Associative Probability as a Determinant of Retention," *Journal of Verbal Learning and Verbal Behavior*, **2** (1963), 352–360.

Underwood, B. J., "An Evaluation of the Gibson Theory of Verbal Learning," in C. N. Cofer, ed., *Verbal Learning and Verbal Behavior*. New York: McGraw-Hill Book Company, 1961.

———, "Stimulus Selection in Verbal Learning," in C. N. Cofer and B. S. Musgrave, eds., *Verbal Behavior and Learning*. New York: McGraw-Hill Book Company, 1963.

———, "The Representativeness of Rote Verbal Learning," in A. W. Melton, ed., *Categories of Human Learning*. New York: Academic Press, 1964.

———, "False Recognition Produced by Implicit Verbal Responses," *Journal of Experimental Psychology*, **70** (1965), 122–129.

———, and A. H. Erlebacher, "Studies of Coding in Verbal Learning," *Psychological Monographs*, Vol. 79, No. 13, 1965.

———, and G. Keppel, "One-Trial Learning?" *Journal of Verbal Learning and Verbal Behavior*, **1** (1962), 1–13.

———, and R. W. Schulz, *Meaningfulness and Verbal Learning*. Philadelphia: J. B. Lippincott Co., 1960.

———, B. R. Ekstrand, and G. Keppel, "An Analysis of Intralist Similarity in Verbal Learning with Experiments on Conceptual Similarity," *Journal of Verbal Learning and Verbal Behavior*, **4** (1965), 447–462.

———, M. Ham, and B. Ekstrand, "Cue Selection in Paired-Associate Learning," *Journal of Experimental Psychology*, **64** (1962), 405–409.

———, F. Jesse, and B. R. Ekstrand, "Knowledge of Rights and Wrongs in Verbal-Discrimination Learning," *Journal of Verbal Learning and Verbal Behavior*, **3** (1964), 183–186.

———, G. Keppel, and R. W. Schulz, "Studies of Distributed Practice: XXII. Some Conditions Which Enhance Retention," *Journal of Experimental Psychology*, **64** (1962), 355–363.

———, W. N. Runquist, and R. W. Schulz, "Response Learning in Paired-Associate Lists as a Function of Intra-list Similarity," *Journal of Experimental Psychology*, **58** (1959), 70–78.

Wimer, C., "An Analysis of Semantic Stimulus Factors in Paired-Associate Learning," *Journal of Verbal Learning and Verbal Behavior*, **1** (1963), 397–407.

Winnick, W. A., and R. L. Dornbush, "Role of Positional Cues in Serial Rote Learning," *Journal of Experimental Psychology*, **66** (1963), 419–421.

Wynne, R. D., H. Gerjuoy, and H. Schiffman, "Association Test Antonym-Response Set," *Journal of Verbal Learning and Verbal Behavior*, **4** (1965), 354–359.

Youssef, Z. I., and E. Saltz, "The Semantic Differential as a Measure of Individual Differences in Mediated Generalization," *Journal of Verbal Learning and Verbal Behavior*, **3** (1964), 226–230.

Traditions, Trends, and Innovations[1]

23

DAVID L. HORTON AND
THEODORE R. DIXON

A number of conferences have been held in the past few years in which various aspects of theory and research in the area of verbal behavior have been elaborated (e.g., Cofer, 1961; Cofer and Musgrave, 1963). While such previous efforts have been highly productive systematic overviews of research and current substantive problems, they have indirectly provided support for two important assertions. First, there is a need for an over-all evaluation of the wealth of miniature theories available in verbal behavior, both in terms of integrating this important realm of behavioral phenomena into a more comprehensive system and in terms of more generally relating verbal behavior theory and general S-R theory. Second, there is an ever-widening gap between empirical findings and theory, with available theory too frequently inadequate to incorporate extant findings. The present conference was arranged to provide at least an initial effort toward the resolution of these problems.

At the outset, we were of the opinion that an integrated theory of verbal behavior had not been advanced previously because of diversified interests

and activities within the field, as well as the absence of an occasion between our colleagues to discuss theory explicitly. We assumed, of course, that the fundamental conceptions of "S-R theory" would serve as a common reference for almost everyone—with reasonable dissension and alternatives being provided by "non S-R" representatives. These beliefs were strengthened during the planning workshop which preceded the conference, although several problems received emphasis which potentially stood in the way of the desired integration.

The general conclusion voiced at the workshop clearly indicated that present theory had not kept pace with advances in experimentation. Research findings existed in virtually every area of verbal behavior that could not be readily integrated within current theoretical systems. While most of us interpreted this state of affairs as an indication of the need for a theoretically oriented conference, certain doubts remained. In the first place, S-R theory has largely been a development stemming from animal research, and we questioned the extent to which the concepts and principles derived in this fashion could be invoked to explain the unique verbal repertoires of the human organism.

[1] This paper was prepared especially for this volume.

Secondly, while the numerous miniature theories within verbal behavior bore superficial resemblance to an S-R structure, they seemed to lack any decidedly common set of concepts and principles. Nevertheless, we were hopeful that many of these difficulties could be resolved during the conference itself, and we proceeded with invitations to the participants.

As the precirculated papers began to come in, it became increasingly apparent that there would be considerable difficulty in arriving at a set of theoretical statements which would be acceptable even to a majority of the contributors. As the present volume attests, quite another thing happened. The clear majority of those we thought would be most committed to various aspects of "S-R theory" were, instead, registering significant objections concerning its restrictions and inadequacies. We began to doubt whether even the miniature theories—most of them employing S-R language—would admit to integration. Then came the psycholinguists with rather uncompromising claims that S-R theory cannot accommodate behavioral phenomena as complex as natural language or any very complex behavioral system. As the conference itself approached, it appeared that we had created the occasion for a large-scale debate concerning behavior theory in general, rather than the opportunity for initiating the integration of verbal behavior theory. Thus, while the conference began with an attempt to accomplish the objectives stated initially, the major emphasis kept drifting back to the question of the adequacy of S-R theory itself.

In part our apprehensions were justified; in part we were pleased by what followed. Indeed there were heated discussions, but also many shadows and myths were cleared away. By the conclusion of the meetings it was apparent that a number of very major issues had been brought to the fore. These issues, in our opinion, must be resolved before it will be possible to even consider the original goals of this conference.

The Conference

As Professor Cofer pointed out at the beginning of his paper, the variety of interests and the range of problems manifest in the conference papers and discussions is extremely great. While such diversity has proved to be very stimulating, it does present certain problems in any attempt to characterize the essential issues raised and the solutions recommended at this conference.

In what follows we shall begin by examining some of the specific theoretical issues raised by the conference participants, especially those relating to the problems noted above. This treatment will be brief, since the formal discussion papers have already covered much of this ground. Our major concern, however, will be an attempt to present and discuss the basic question repeatedly raised in the informal discussions: Can S-R theory or any theory grounded in the language, methodology, and pretheoretical assumptions of behavioristic psychology be considered adequate to the ultimate task of explaining human behavior?

Specific theoretical issues

Several writers have raised serious questions concerning the adequacy of miniature theories of verbal behavior for their respective areas. Professor Young, for example, has provided an excellent review of the research on serial learning and has concluded that *no* present theoretical effort can be considered adequate to the task of explaining serial learning. This may come as a surprise to many psychologists outside the verbal learning area since textbook accounts of serial learning have scarcely deviated in any major way from standard associative chaining theory for more than a quarter of a century. Nevertheless, Young has shown that while specific theoretical mechanisms cannot be ruled out entirely, no single process or set of processes found in current theory can provide a satisfactory account of extant findings. Young goes on to suggest that the serial learning task does not of itself constitute a good vehicle for the investigation of processes which are assumed to underlie verbal behavior and learning. More specifically he says, ". . . no advantage to the use of serial learning techniques can be seen other than when one is interested in studying those processes specifically involved in serial learning."

In the area of paired-associate learning, Professor Battig has similarly argued for the essential inadequacy of present theory. Battig's basic point is that the paired-associate task is considerably more complex than present theory indicates. As an alternative he argues for a multiprocess account of paired-associate learning with particular emphasis on the need to account for interpair relationships and on learning processes whereby subjects overcome intratask interference.

Professor Maltzman finds a similar situation to exist in the area of semantic conditioning and generalization. Maltzman argues that current theories, largely S-R associative theories of mediation, ". . . assume an antiquated S-R peripheralistic theory of learning and oversimplify the great complexity of classical conditioning." In addition, he suggests that such theories have generated surprisingly little research considering the assumed importance of the problem. While adopting what is essentially an S-R methodological position, Maltzman argues for an approach in which the recent views of classical conditioning emphasized in the Soviet literature—particularly the concern with orienting and defensive reflexes—are of paramount importance.

Other writers also have expressed concern with current theoretical formulations in their areas, but space does not permit us to enumerate all of the exceptions taken. Suffice it to say that, in addition to those writers mentioned above, significant objections to current theoretical conceptions were raised by Bourne, Johnson, and Tulving. Several of these objections received added emphasis in the formal discussion papers.

The import of the above remarks appears to be twofold. First, they serve to emphasize the gap between data and theory which currently characterizes the field of verbal behavior; secondly, they reflect substantial agreement among the writers concerning the need for greater theoretical complexity. It may be suggested that both of these factors are symptomatic of much *deeper* problems in psychology, but we will postpone comment on this possibility until later.

A second matter raised in the conference concerned the extent to which general S-R theory of the variety derived from classical and instrumental conditioning research and represented in the writings of Hull, Skinner, Spence, and others provides a useful framework for the study of verbal behavior. The majority of conference participants apparently believe it does not. Battig, for example, stated that the concepts provided by general S-R theory are oversimplified and grossly inadequate to the task of handling the complexities of the learning process. In fact, he concludes ". . . that research in PA learning is much richer in implications for general S-R behavior theory than the latter has been with respect to implications for theories of PA learning . . . ."

We have already seen that Maltzman rejects in large part the previous theories of classical conditioning as providing any foundation for the study of semantic conditioning and generalization. In addition, he argues for the inadequacy of existing theories of classical conditioning simply as theories of classical conditioning. Several other participants made similar remarks both formally and informally, but it is of particular interest to note Tulving's conclusion: "It looks as if conceptual analyses of free recall have been developed not just in isolation, but almost in defiance of the traditional S-R models of behavior."

Apart from the obvious fact that many participants see little common-alty between theory in verbal behavior and general S-R theory, the preceding remarks suggest that any attempt at integration is not likely to be successful. It may be suggested that one fundamental reason for the lack of commonality lies in the considerably greater complexity of the experimental tasks chosen for research in the verbal behavior area. That is, while paired-associate learning, for example, may represent a relatively simple experimental situation, it is considerably more complex than the typical classical or instrumental conditioning situation, and it is not very surprising to find that theory developed in a highly simplified behavioral situation fails to apply in a less simplified one. Of course, it is also quite possible that the investigation of those tasks typically employed in verbal behavior research may result in a very simplified theory—one that has little generality outside of the specific situation for which it was developed. This certainly seems

to be the import of Young's remarks concerning the study of serial learning.[2]

General theoretical issues

As we have seen in the preceding section, there is good reason to question the adequacy of S-R theory as it has been developed both within the field of verbal behavior and in the more traditional framework of classical and instrumental conditioning. Although the earlier papers have been concerned with specific formulations of S-R theory, a much deeper issue concerning the adequacy of the whole behavioristic approach was raised during the conference. Before examining this issue we will turn our attention to the question of what is meant by general S-R theory.

THE MEANING OF GENERAL S-R THEORY. Prior to any evaluation of a general theory, one must come to grips with the essential characteristics of that theory. As several participants have indicated—particularly Professors Cofer, Kendler, and Maltzman—the meaning of the term "general S-R theory" is far from being completely obvious. Kendler has suggested that it is necessary to distinguish four relatively independent components of S-R theory. Of the four, he says that perhaps only the view of S-R theory as a technical language is noncontroversial. He further states that this language, which analyzes events into stimuli, responses, and the associations between them, is noncommittal about empirical relationships in psychology and physiology and does not insist that all be-

[2] Note that the position stated here in no way constitutes a rejection of experimentation or of the need for control. What is being stated is that situations which greatly restrict the capacity of the subject may well be accounted for by theoretical systems of a considerably more simple nature than would otherwise be required.

havior can be so analyzed. While acknowledging reasonable agreement among psychologists concerning S-R theory as a methodological orientation —physicalistic, operational, and experimental—and perhaps as a pretheoretical model, Kendler argues that it is impossible to formulate any set of theoretical assumptions (e.g., particular definitions of the stimulus and response terms) that would be acceptable to all or even most psychologists who use the S-R language.

Maltzman's position is that "S-R theory" may be interpreted as being equivalent to "methodological behaviorism"—a prescription for the introduction of terms and concepts in psychology. Within this framework a concept, no matter how far it is removed from immediately observable events, must be relatable to observed antecedent stimulus conditions and consequent observable responses. According to Maltzman, this view asserts that the basic undefined terms of science refer to properties of physical objects and the relations between them and as a consequence such a prescription is neither true nor false but simply constitutes a volitional decision which influences the problems to be investigated and the methods employed in such investigations.

In a somewhat different although related vein, Cofer has indicated that the functionalist tradition in psychology—which has dominated the field of verbal learning—represents an analytical approach to psychological problems. As such it is compatible with both associationism and an S-R approach, for these also constitute analytic approaches to the problems of behavior. However, Cofer emphasizes that while compatible with S-R psychology, functionalism carries no necessary commitments or aversions to the postulation of intervening processes.

While the positions stated by Cofer, Kendler, and Maltzman differ in certain aspects of detail and emphasis, there appears to be considerable agreement in their views concerning the meaning of "general S-R theory." It is first a technical language, to use Professor Kendler's term, and second, it represents a decision to adopt methodological behaviorism as this concept is employed by Maltzman. Although Cofer states that such an orientation does not involve any necessary commitment to particular theoretical ideas or any necessary aversion to the postulation of unobservables, the adoption of the S-R position does influence the nature of the problems selected for investigation. Not everyone will agree with the foregoing characterization of the meaning of "general S-R theory," but we believe that it represents a reasonable and essentially correct view of the concept. It may also be added that this characterization is overwhelmingly consistent with the statements found in most introductory and advanced textbooks. (After all, what is psychological theory if it is not what we say it is in our textbooks?)

LIMITATIONS OF GENERAL S-R THEORY. The dominant theme of the informal discussion centered around the adequacy of general S-R theory as a model of human behavior. Although there were many facets of the discussion, some of which can be found in the papers by McNeill, Garrett and Fodor, Deese, Mandler, Asch, Jenkins, and Osgood, the most direct statement of the problem can be found in the Bever, Foder, and Garrett paper in the appendix to this volume.

The position stated by Bever, Fodor, and Garrett is, in essence, that association theory (or general S-R theory) is incapable, *in principle*, of explaining the complexity of the conceptual competences which characterize human behavior. That is, the claim is made that on purely formal (i.e., logical) grounds it is possible to show that such theory, given the type of principles with which it operates, cannot account for a significantly large proportion of behavior. While the writers acknowledge the fact that association theory can describe many behavioral repertoires, they emphasize the point that such theories cannot be considered as alternatives to more powerful theories —ones with fewer formal constraints— but rather that associative rules would be more appropriately regarded as special cases of the rules employed by more powerful theories.

Of course, there are many possible objections to the Bever, Fodor and Garrett argument. Perhaps the most obvious of these concerns the particular characterization of association theory —or general S-R theory—that these writers claim is insufficient. The statement of association theory employed in the Bever, *et al.* paper hinges on the restriction, "that the vocabulary chosen for the description of output states must also be the vocabulary over which the associative rules are defined." That is, the theory may not contain any elements abstractly related to the elements of behavior. Note that, according to this view, there is no objection to intervening states or to associations between overt behaviors and intervening states so long as the internal processes can be described in the same vocabulary that the theory uses to describe overt behavior. For example, in mediation theory the intervening states are drawn from the stimulus and response elements in which overt behavior is described.

The basic question, then, is whether or not Bever, Fodor, and Garrett have adequately characterized association theory or, more generally, S-R theory.

We have previously argued that the meaning of general S-R theory (apart from any particular theorist's formulation) is based upon the acceptance of the technical language—stimulus, response, and associations between them —and methodological behaviorism, where all concepts must be related to observable antecedent stimulus conditions and consequent observable responses. Certainly the technical language aspect of S-R theory is not in conflict with the characterization summarized above. Either the terms *stimulus* and *response* are used to describe physical events or they are left undefined. In either case, no conflict arises. However, it should be noted that the clearly dominant position in behavioristic psychology is to define these terms with respect to the observables.

The adoption of methodological behaviorism is also consistent with the characterization offered by Bever, Fodor, and Garrett. Now, it is certainly the case that psychologists have employed concepts which cannot be described in the same language that the theory uses to describe overt behavior —as in the concept of "set"—but such processes do not meet the constraints required by methodological behaviorism. Certainly the prevailing tendency in psychology—as any survey of psychological textbooks would indicate—is to write and talk as if one intends to stay within the constraints imposed by methodological behaviorism.

Before consideration of alternative objections, there is another aspect of what has been said above that requires elaboration. Although psychologists typically define the stimulus concept with reference to physical events (as is clearly shown in psychological textbooks), many of us are prone to use this term in an extremely vacuous manner —intending it at various times to refer to observable events, abstract relations, or almost anything else required for *post hoc* explanation of the occurrence of a response. Under this view of a stimulus, the solution to the mirror image problem, cited by Bever, *et al.* for illustrative purposes, can be obtained by referring to the stimulus as a concept. In addition, with this manner of defining the stimulus term, we would have to agree that the claim made by Bever, *et al.* is unjustified. However, to reach this state of affairs, we also must admit that our theory says nothing. After all, if we don't have any idea what a stimulus is, how can we possibly talk about associations being formed between stimuli and responses?

An alternative reply to the Bever, *et al.* position is to argue that if we stay close to the data and remain theoretically neutral, as most psychologists in the field of verbal behavior are wont to do, the truth or falsity of the claim has little bearing on psychology. This would undoubtedly be a reasonable position to take if it were fully justified; unfortunately, it is not. While few psychologists are committed to any specific set of theoretical propositions—as Kendler has pointed out—there is a commitment on the part of most contemporary psychologists to what Thomas Kuhn (1962) calls a paradigm. In this case it is the behavioristic paradigm. A paradigm, in the sense employed by Kuhn, can be thought of as a set of pretheoretical rules which govern the type of theory and research problems that will be considered acceptable by scientists. It is our contention that contemporary psychologists, whether they call themselves S-R theorists, associationists, or functionalists, overwhelmingly subscribe to the behavioristic paradigm. In other words, they adopt the technical language commonly associated with general S-R theory and, in essence, methodological

behaviorism. The result of this is that the research activities of most psychologists are likely to remain fixated on those problems and problem solutions that are seen as being acceptable within the behavioristic paradigm.

A difficulty related to the type of problem typically studied by psychologists concerns the distinction between what an organism "does do" and what it "can do." Jenkins has discussed this difference in orientation and its consequences, and there is little more that can be said here. However, we would like to suggest that whether or not a particular psychologist selects one or the other of these strategies depends to a great extent upon his conception of the complexity of the organism— that is, in a certain sense upon which paradigm the psychologist adopts. What is being suggested here is that all psychologists may typically study what the organism "can do." Where they differ, as the point of Jenkins' discussion suggests, is in what they *think* the organism "can do." That is, if you believe that behavior is composed of stimuli, responses, and the associations between them, then those are the things you will look at, since the only thing an organism "can do" is to associate stimulus and response events. On the other hand, if you believe that the organism is much more complicated than that and may require a great deal of internal apparatus to do the things it does (as McNeill, Garrett and Fodor, and others have argued), then your choice of what to look at will be very different. It appears that the behaviorist's view in these matters is primarily attributable to his belief in empiricism or environmentalism rather than nativism and the inclusion of this philosophy as the cornerstone of the behavioristic paradigm.

Perhaps this point can be further illustrated with a rather extreme example. Few, if any, of the psychologists present at this conference would claim that an adequate theory of human behavior could be obtained by investigating behavior in push boxes, mazes, runways, etc. We all believe human behavior to be more complicated than that. However, introductory textbooks and even some animal psychologists tell us that theories developed in just such situations provide an adequate explanation not only of animal behavior but of human behavior as well. It is inconceivable that hard-headed psychologists could come to such a conclusion for the rat, let alone the human, without having very restricted, *empirically unconfirmed* notions about what organisms are capable of learning and doing.

While the specific views presented by Bever, Fodor, Garrett, McNeill, and others are of a relatively recent origin, there is no great lack of evidence which can be offered in support of these views. Evidence of the type recently accumulated in the study of language has been adequately reported by McNeill, Garrett and Fodor, and Bever and will not be discussed further. However, a considerable amount of substantiating evidence has been available in perception—as Asch has indicated—for a long time. Most of this has come from Gestalt psychology and concerns phenomena such as perceptual constancy and the illusions. In addition, the characterization of animal behavior offered by the ethologists, particularly the emphasis on innate structures as in imprinting, supports similar conceptions about the nature of organisms. Further evidence comes from the relatively recent attempt at computer simulation of human cognitive functions. Positive programs of simulation do not look very much like S-R, and efforts to write S-R programs have generally failed. Consider also the problem of providing an adequate

explanation of the behavior of an IBM machine by looking only at the inputs and outputs. It probably cannot be done, and yet the task is strikingly similar to the behaviorist approach to human behavior. In any case, it should be clear that the limitations of S-R theory are supported by factual evidence and are not simply restricted to the language case.

In this discussion, we have placed primary emphasis on the papers offered in the psycholinguistics section, as these appeared to stimulate the greatest controversy and were more clearly directed toward the fundamental issues. However, a great deal in the way of supporting evidence and opinion can be found in other papers. We have already suggested that the gap between data and theory, emphasized by several writers, may reflect a basic difficulty with S-R theory. Deese has emphasized that a similar implication may follow from the extremely slow progress which has been made in the field and the fact that the fundamental assumptions concerning associative processes have remained essentially unchanged for more than a century. Deese has also noted that even the possibility of radically different views of the nature of associations has apparently never occurred to many students of verbal behavior. This latter claim appears to illustrate the influence of paradigm choice.

In a slightly different vein, Mandler has raised significant questions about instructional effects in learning and the difficulty that any association model would have in dealing with such factors. Bourne has indicated the importance of rules in concept formation while at the same time pointing out the paucity of research dealing with such phenomena. Dulany has emphasized the critical role of awareness and other cognitive activities in verbal conditioning in addition to providing a clear justification for cognitive theory. Other instances could easily be cited but we have probably said enough to convey the point that something more than we have previously known or theorized about is going to be needed if these important and diverse problems are to be solved.

We shall close this paper on an autobiographical note. When this conference was planned, we did not anticipate the way in which it would evolve. The conception of the conference was motivated by considerations similar to those which troubled many of our colleagues—namely, the widening gap between data and theory in the field and the multiplicity of miniature theories which appeared to lack any decidedly common structure. In short, we wondered whether or not any real progress would be made, even *eventually*. Nevertheless, we proceeded on the assumption that others could enlighten us as well as the numerous other psychologists who felt as we did. We leave it to the reader to judge for himself whether or not the undertaking provided the desired enlightenment. To us, it appears that a revolution is certainly in the making.

References

Cofer, C. N., ed., *Verbal Learning and Verbal Behavior*. New York: McGraw-Hill Book Company, 1961.

———, and B. S. Musgrave, eds., *Verbal Behavior and Learning*. New York: McGraw-Hill Book Company, 1963.

Kuhn, T. S., *The Structure of Scientific Revolution*. Chicago: University of Chicago Press, 1962.

Appendix

A Formal Limitation
of Associationism

24

T. G. BEVER, J. A. FODOR,
M. GARRETT

Classical associationism has attempted to elucidate principles whereby complex ideas are constructed out of simple ones. Similarly modern associationism has attempted to devise a body of learning principles which can explain how complex skills are constructed out of simple operants and reflexes. Given such a set of principles, one might validate them in either of two ways. In the first case, one might attempt to show that complex behaviors can be added to the repertoire of an organism by the formation of associations between appropriate rudimentary behaviors. That has been the course that associationists have typically chosen for testing their principles. They have tried to show that manipulation of the variables upon which associative strength depends permits the laboratory simulation of complex behaviors (such as the construction of "response chains" in maze learning) or of complex psychological phenomena (such as the production of "selective forgetting" by variation of stimulus order). For the cognitive psychologist in particular, the continuing interest of associationism rests on the assumption that conceptual behaviors can be approximated in the laboratory by techniques based on the putative laws of association.

There is, however, a second approach to the validation of associative principles. For, given any theoretical principles for psychological description, one may study the kinds of behavioral repertoires their operation can represent *in principle*. That is, assuming that the principles exhaustively characterize the learning mechanisms available to a hypothetical organism, one can determine the limits their operation imposes upon the organism's behavioral repertoire. A partial ordering can thus be imposed upon the set of behaviors so that learning principles capable of describing the assimilation of the more complex of them can describe the assimilation of the simpler ones, but not conversely. Thus, for associative principles in particular there is an upper bound on the richness of the repertoires they are capable of explaining, and we can ask of any particular behavioral ability whether it lies above or below that bound.

The important point for present purposes is that certain human abilities lie beyond the upper bound on *any* set of learning principles that could reasonably be called "associative." Certain kinds of conceptual competences fall outside the explanatory power of associationism, given the kinds of constraints on learning principles that have traditionally defined associationism. Moreover, it can be shown that there are infinitely many such counterexamples to the adequacy of associationistic accounts of learning.

We assume that the following meta-postulate is a necessary condition on any set of principles being called "associative": that is, by definition, no theory of learning counts as associative unless it satisfies this postulate.

The Terminal Meta-Postulate: Associative principles are rules defined over the "terminal" vocabulary of a theory, i.e., over the vocabulary in which behavior is described. Any description of an n-tuple of elements between which an association can hold must be a possible description of the actual behavior.

Notice, first, that the satisfaction of this meta-postulate is independent of the particular choice of a vocabulary for describing behavior. It does not matter whether psychological relations are taken to be relations of ideas, as in classical associations, or relations among stimuli and responses. The postulate requires only that the vocabulary chosen for psychological descriptions of output states must also be the vocabulary over which the associative rules are defined. That is, the psychological theory will not contain any element which is abstractly related to the elements of the behavior.

Second, the terminal meta-postulate does not preclude associations between 'overt behaviors' and 'intervening states' so long as the internal processes can be described in the same vocabulary (or isomorphic derivatives) the theory uses to describe overt behavior. In particular, the postulate is satisfied by "mediation" theories, since such theories suppose the intervening states in associative chains to be drawn from the stimulus and response elements in

which the behavior itself is described (see Fodor, 1965).

A corollary of the terminal postulate is that, since behavior is organized in time, every associative relation is a relation between left and right elements of a sequence. In a well-known article, Lashley (1951) showed that a special case of this corollary is unsatisfied for many sorts of behavior; namely, the case in which each right member of a behavior chain is associated with the immediately preceding left member. Lashley showed that, for a great variety of behaviors (of which typing mistakes may be considered paradigmatic), a left member of a chain is dependent upon a nonadjacent right member (as when we type *Lalshey* for Lashley).

Lashley's argument was, in effect, generalized in Chomsky's 1957 monograph, which showed that there are indefinitely many learnable behaviors not describable by principles which allow association (or any other form of dependency) only between left and right members of a behavior chain; in particular, by principles which satisfy the terminal postulate.

Consider what a subject does when he learns to recognize mirror-image symmetry in figures without explicitly marked contours. The infinite set of strings belonging to a mirror-image language is paradigmatic of such symmetrical figures, i.e., all sequences of a and b of the form $X\bar{X}$,

accept	reject
aa	ab
abba	aaab
aabbaa	baabba
abbbba	abbabb
etc.	etc.

Someone who learns this language has acquired the ability to accept as well formed in the language all and only strings consisting of a sequence of *a*'s and *b*'s followed immediately by the reverse of that sequence.

The question is whether or not an organism whose behavior is determined solely by associative principles can select just the set of sequences that satisfy this criterion. In fact, it is provable that the answer to this question is no. This is *not* simply because the set of strings consonant with the rule is infinite (it is easy to design an automaton with a finite memory but an infinite behavioral repertoire, e.g., the language containing any number of *a*'s followed by any number of *b*'s). It is rather because of the particular kind of relation holding between the left and right halves of strings in the mirror-image language. (The rules are unordered; "ϕ" stands for the null element in the diagram below.)

Notice that the *X* in these rules explicitly violates the terminal postulate of associationism. If it were to appear in a terminal string, the system would generate strings not in the mirror-image language (e.g., *aXa*). (Intuitively, the *X* in the rules above is a formal representation of the hypothetical "center" around which each element on the left is rotated to the right.) Thus, an organism that has learned the mirror-image language has learned a concept that cannot rest on the formation of associations between behavioral elements. In general, behav-

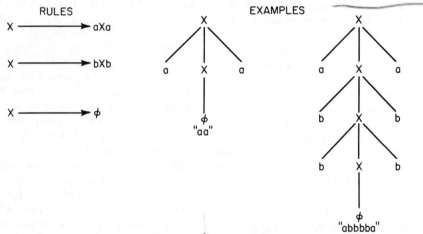

mirror-image language; namely, that dependencies are allowed to nest within dependencies (for further discussion, see Chomsky, 1957, 1963).

Interestingly, the weakest system of rules which allows for the construction of a mirror-image language is precisely one which violates the terminal postulate. That is, it is one which allows rules defined over elements that are precluded from appearing in the terminal vocabulary (e.g., rules defined over items other than *a*'s and *b*'s in the example just cited). Such rules yield a simple characterization of the

ioral abilities which involve recursion over abstract elements violate the terminal meta-postulate, since there are usually elements in the description which do not appear in the behavior. Such abilities include the distinguishing of sentences from non-sentences, verbs from nouns, and many other abilities related to natural language.

This argument appears to us to provide a conclusive proof of the inadequacy of associationism for these kinds of natural behaviors. It might be replied that there are indefinitely many behavioral repertoires which *can* be described by associationistic principles (e.g., all the finite state languages in the sense of Chomsky *op. cit.*). Hence, continued research on associationism could be justified by the illumination it might cast on such behaviors. However, this is to evade the point of our argument. We have considered associationism to require certain constraints upon the formulation of learning principles. Theories that are more powerful than associationism are at least theories that have weaker constraints. Hence, any behavior that can be characterized by associative principles can *ipso facto* be characterized by the more powerful models. Such models should not, therefore, be considered as alternatives to associative models; rather, associative rules are simply special cases of the rules employed by more powerful theories. If the rules are allowed, you are allowed the associative rules, but not conversely. As Sol Saporta has put it, anything you can do with one hand tied behind your back, you can do with both hands free.

References

Chomsky, N., *Syntactic Structures*. The Hague, Netherlands: Mouton and Co., 1957.

——, "Formal Properties of Grammars," in *Handbook of Mathematical Psychology*, Vol. II, R. Luce, R. Bush, and E. Galanter, eds. New York: Wiley & Sons, Inc., 1963.

Fodor, J. A., "Could Meaning Be an r_m?" *Journal of Verbal Learning and Verbal Behavior*, 4 (1965), 73–81.

Lashley, K. S., "The Problem of Serial Order in Behavior" in *Cerebral Mechanisms in Behavior*, L. A. Jeffress, ed. New York: John Wiley & Sons, Inc., 1951.

Index

A

Acoustics, acoustic stimuli, 457-61, 490, 516. *See also* Sounds

Acoustic traces. *See* Traces, acoustic

Acquisition. *See also* Learning and retention

  preference effects in, 560-62

  and propositional control, 351-54

  and recoding, 442

  transfer and mediation and, 75, 76, 82

Adjectives, 50, 56. *See also* Paired associates; Sentences; etc.

"Adopted chunks," 9-10

Adverbs, 49-50, 492

Aggressive behavior, 278

Alpha blocking, 316

American speech, 460

Anagrams, 559-60

Analogs. *See* Mediation

Animals, animal conditioning, 256, 261-66, 572, 579

  available reinforcers, 262-63

  habituation, 261-62

  interaction of S and E, 265

  response acquisition *vs.* response discrimination, 263-65

  task requirements, 265

Anticipation, 123, 127, 321ff., 422ff., 531

Antonyms, antonymy, 107. *See also* Paired associates; Structure; specific parts of speech

Anxiety, 557

Appendix, 581-85

Asch, Solomon E., 214-28

Ascriptors, 348-49

Association, associationism, 300ff., 523-528ff. *See also* Associative processes; Chaining; Semantic conditioning and generalization; S-R theories; etc.; specific writers

  and concept attainment, 234ff.

  concept of, 551-57

  contextual, 553-54

  as dispositional concept, 555-57

  doctrinal tyranny of, 214-28

  a formal limitation of, 581-85

  and performance in analysis of verbal learning, 550-71

    terminological preferences, 567-68

  physiological usage of term, 555

  pre-experimental hierarchies, 552-53

  as sequential probability, 551

Associative processes, 1-119. *See also* Association, associationism; Context; Paired associates; etc.

  associative structure, 37-66

  memory and association, 97-108

  organization and association, 109-19

  theoretical issues in free recall, 2-36

  transfer and mediation in verbal learning, 67-96. *See also* Transfer and mediation

Associative symmetry, 156-57, 219-21

"Attention," 319, 334, 398-99

Attributes:

  of concepts, 231ff.

  rules and, 346ff.

"Autoclitic" frame, 526